Internet GIZMOS™ For Windows

by Joel Diamond, Valda Hilley, and Howard Sobel

IDG BOOKS

IDG Books Worldwide, Inc.
An International Data Group Company

Foster City, CA ♦ Chicago, IL ♦ Indianapolis, IN ♦ Braintree, MA ♦ Dallas, TX

Internet GIZMOS™ For Windows®

Published by
IDG Books Worldwide, Inc.
An International Data Group Company
919 E. Hillsdale Blvd., Ste. 400
Foster City, CA 94404

Library of Congress Catalog Card No.: 94-72818

ISBN: 1-56884-451-4

Printed in the United States of America

10 9 8 7 6 5 4 3 2 1

1B/SV/QU/ZV

Distributed in the United States by IDG Books Worldwide, Inc.

Distributed by Macmillan Canada for Canada; by Computer and Technical Books for the Caribbean Basin; by Contemporanea de Ediciones for Venezuela; by Distribuidora Cuspide for Argentina; by CITEC for Brazil; by Ediciones ZETA S.C.R. Ltda. for Peru; by Editorial Limusa SA for Mexico; by Transworld Publishers Limited in the United Kingdom and Europe; by Al-Maiman Publishers & Distributors for Saudi Arabia; by Simron Pty. Ltd. for South Africa; by IDG Communications (HK) Ltd. for Hong Kong; by Toppan Company Ltd. for Japan; by Addison Wesley Publishing Company for Korea; by Longman Singapore Publishers Ltd. for Singapore, Malaysia, Thailand, and Indonesia; by Unalis Corporation for Taiwan; by WS Computer Publishing Company, Inc. for the Philippines; by WoodsLane Pty. Ltd. for Australia; by WoodsLane Enterprises Ltd. for New Zealand.

For general information on IDG Books in the U.S., including information on discounts and premiums, contact IDG Books at 800-434-3422 or 415-655-3000.

For information on where to purchase IDG Books outside the U.S., contact IDG Books International at 415-655-3021 or fax 415-655-3295.

For information on translations, contact Marc Jeffrey Mikulich, Director, Foreign & Subsidiary Rights, at IDG Books Worldwide, 415-655-3018 or fax 415-655-3295.

For sales inquiries and special prices for bulk quantities, write to the address above or call IDG Books Worldwide at 415-655-3000.

For information on using IDG Books in the classroom, or ordering examination copies, contact Jim Kelly at 800-434-2086.

For authorization to photocopy items for corporate, personal, or educational use, please contact Copyright Clearance Center, 222 Rosewood Drive, Danvers, MA 01923, or fax 508-750-4470.

Some of the screen shots in this book are based on Windows 95 made public by Microsoft as of January 1995. Because this information was made public before the final release of Windows 95, the final interface may be different than illustrated herein. We encourage you to visit your local bookstore after Windows 95 is released for updated books on Windows 95.

About the Authors

Joel Diamond serves as technical director of the Windows User Group Network, the official advocacy technical organization for Microsoft Windows. As the lead author for *Internet GIZMOS For Windows,* Joel was responsible for evaluation and selection of software included on the CD-ROM and covered in the book. In addition, Joel assisted in the development of the *Internet GIZMOS For Windows CD-ROM* with Larry Budnick.

Joel currently manages and directs the Windows Users Group Network family of Windows forums on the CompuServe Information Network, leading an on-line staff of over 60 professionals and on-line support to millions of Windows users around the world. Joel also writes the Windows Connectivity column for *Network World,* the newsweekly for enterprise computing. Joel serves as technical editor of the *Windows 95 Journal* for IDG Newsletters, formally the Windows Journal technical newsletter. You can reach Joel via e-mail at 76702.1023@compuserve.com or on CompuServe's WINUSER FORUM, where Joel is the WIZOP.

Valda Hilley is the Publisher and Editor-in-Chief of *Ohio Valley Computing,* a regional newspaper for computer users who have entered the information age.

Valda, a former engineer and systems designer, has been involved with computers since 1980. Ms. Hilley is a Microsoft Certified Professional and the author of several computer books including *Windows 3.1 Configuration SECRETS,* (IDG Books Worldwide). She writes a bimonthly newsletter titled *WinNotes,* filled with clips from her Certified Professional's notebook. Valda also serves as a contributing editor to various computing publications.

You can reach Valda on the Internet at valda@cpress.com or via CompuServe e-mail at 72520,1710. Or write to Valda at P.O. Box 40683, Cincinnati, Ohio 45243.

Howard Sobel has held the position of Executive Director of the Windows User Group Network, (WUGNET) since the organization was formally incorporated in 1990. For the past five years his responsibilities have included management of WUGNETs business operations including its print publications, CompuServe Forums, books, and software products. Howard has served as publisher and managing editor of one of the industry's oldest independent Windows newsletters WUGNET's *Windows Journal.* The first issue of the journal was published prior to the introduction of Windows 3.0.

Howard has been an active participant of the on-line community since the early 1980s when he first started BBSing to exchange information on desktop publishing with other publishing enthusiasts. It was one of these exchanges that introduced Howard Sobel to Joel Diamond, which led to the formation of WUGNET. Howard's is a sysop on WUGNETs forums on CompuServe.

Howard also serves on the advisory committee to the LibertyNet, a nonprofit organization whose mission is to bring public access to the Internet for residents of the Philadelphia metropolitan area.

Contributing Author **Larry Budnick** has been involved in programming, computers, and computer communication since 1976. He has been active in Windows and WinSock programming for many years, and has written a number of programs ranging from device drivers to application demonstrations. He has developed applications with Assembler, C, C++ and Visual Basic.

Mr. Budnick received his B.S. in Systems Engineering from Rensselaer Polytechnic Institute and an M.S. in Computer Engineering from Boston University. He has worked in a variety of computer and communications areas ranging from ISDN telephony to computer networking to wireless communications.

Contributing Author **Howard Gold** is a professional technical writer, which means he writes reference books showing business people how to use commercial software in order to make their jobs easier. Howard is also a contributing technology editor for *Ohio Valley Computing* and *Troika Magazine.* Using his creative side, Howard wrote *Late Arrival,* a one-act play which was produced in his youth (Oneonta, NY,1978). He also writes children's stories and other forms of fiction, and acts a literary agent for other writers of fiction. Howard can be reached on the 'Net at howardg@savvy.com.

Welcome to the world of IDG Books Worldwide.

IDG Books Worldwide, Inc., is a subsidiary of International Data Group, the world's largest publisher of computer-related information and the leading global provider of information services on information technology. IDG was founded more than 25 years ago and now employs more than 7,200 people worldwide. IDG publishes more than 233 computer publications in 65 countries (see listing below). More than sixty million people read one or more IDG publications each month.

Launched in 1990, IDG Books Worldwide is today the #1 publisher of best-selling computer books in the United States. We are proud to have received 3 awards from the Computer Press Association in recognition of editorial excellence, and our best-selling ...*For Dummies* series has more than 12 million copies in print with translations in 25 languages. IDG Books, through a recent joint venture with IDG's Hi-Tech Beijing, became the first U.S. publisher to publish a computer book in the People's Republic of China. In record time, IDG Books has become the first choice for millions of readers around the world who want to learn how to better manage their businesses.

Our mission is simple: Every IDG book is designed to bring extra value and skill-building instructions to the reader. Our books are written by experts who understand and care about our readers. The knowledge base of our editorial staff comes from years of experience in publishing, education, and journalism — experience which we use to produce books for the '90s. In short, we care about books, so we attract the best people. We devote special attention to details such as audience, interior design, use of icons, and illustrations. And because we use an efficient process of authoring, editing, and desktop publishing our books electronically, we can spend more time ensuring superior content and spend less time on the technicalities of making books.

You can count on our commitment to deliver high-quality books at competitive prices on topics consumers want to read about. At IDG, we value quality, and we have been delivering quality for more than 25 years. You'll find no better book on a subject than an IDG book.

John J. Kilcullen

John Kilcullen
President and CEO
IDG Books Worldwide, Inc.

IDG Books Worldwide, Inc., is a subsidiary of International Data Group, the world's largest publisher of computer-related information and the leading global provider of information services on information technology. International Data Group publishes over 220 computer publications in 65 countries. More than fifty million people read one or more International Data Group publications each month. The officers are Patrick J. McGovern, Founder and Board Chairman; Kelly Conlin, President; Jim Casella, Chief Operating Officer. International Data Group's publications include: **ARGENTINA'S** Computerworld Argentina, Infoworld Argentina; **AUSTRALIA'S** Computerworld Australia, Computer Living, Australian PC World, Australian Macworld, Network World, Mobile Business Australia, Publish!, Reseller, IDG Sources; **AUSTRIA'S** Computerwelt Oesterreich, PC Test; **BELGIUM'S** Data News (CW); **BOLIVIA'S** Computerworld; **BRAZIL'S** Computerworld, Connections, Game Power, Mundo Unix, PC World, Publish, Super Game; **BULGARIA'S** Computerworld Bulgaria, PC & Mac World Bulgaria, Network World Bulgaria; **CANADA'S** CIO Canada, Computerworld Canada, InfoCanada, Network World Canada, Reseller; **CHILE'S** Computerworld Chile, Informatica; **COLOMBIA'S** Computerworld Colombia, PC World; **COSTA RICA'S** PC World; **CZECH REPUBLIC'S** Computerworld, Elektronika, PC World; **DENMARK'S** Communications World, Computerworld Danmark, Computerworld Focus, Macintosh Produktkatalog, Macworld Danmark, PC World Danmark, PC Produktguide, Tech World, Windows World; **ECUADOR'S** PC World Ecuador; **EGYPT'S** Computerworld (CW) Middle East, PC World Middle East; **FINLAND'S** MikroPC, Tietoviikko, Tietoverkko; **FRANCE'S** Distributique, GOLDEN MAC, InfoPC, Le Guide du Monde Informatique, Le Monde Informatique, Telecoms & Reseaux; **GERMANY'S** Computerwoche, Computerwoche Focus, Computerwoche Extra, Electronic Entertainment, Gamepro, Information Management, Macwelt, Netzwelt, PC Welt, Publish, Publish & Multimedia World; **GREECE'S** Publish & Macworld; **HONG KONG'S** Computerworld Hong Kong, PC World Hong Kong; **HUNGARY'S** Computerworld SZT, PC World; **INDIA'S** Computers & Communications; **INDONESIA'S** Info Komputer; **IRELAND'S** ComputerScope; **ISRAEL'S** Beyond Windows, Computerworld Israel, Multimedia, PC World Israel; **ITALY'S** Computerworld Italia, Lotus Magazine, Macworld Italia, Networking Italia, PC Shopping Italy, PC World Italia; **JAPAN'S** Computerworld Today, Information Systems World, Macworld Japan, Nikkei Personal Computing, SunWorld Japan, Windows World; **KENYA'S** East African Computer News; **KOREA'S** Computerworld Korea, Macworld Korea, PC World Korea; **LATIN AMERICA'S** GamePro; **MALAYSIA'S** Computerworld Malaysia, PC World Malaysia; **MEXICO'S** Compu Edicion, Compu Manufactura, Computacion/Punto de Venta, Computerworld Mexico, MacWorld, Mundo Unix, PC World, Windows; **THE NETHERLANDS'** Computer! Totaal, Computable (CW), LAN Magazine, Lotus Magazine, MacWorld; **NEW ZEALAND'S** Computer Buyer, Computerworld New Zealand, Network World, New Zealand PC World; **NIGERIA'S** PC World Africa; **NORWAY'S** Computerworld Norge, Lotusworld Norge, Macworld Norge, Maxi Data, Networld, PC World Ekspress, PC World Nettverk, PC World Norge, PC World's Produktguide, Publish& Multimedia World, Student Data, Unix World, Windowsworld; **PAKISTAN'S** PC World Pakistan; **PANAMA'S** PC World Panama; **PERU'S** Computerworld Peru, PC World; **PEOPLE'S REPUBLIC OF CHINA'S** China Computerworld, China Infoworld, China PC Info Magazine, Computer Fan, PC World China, Electronics International, Electronics Today/Multimedia World, Electronic Product World, China Network World, Software World Magazine, Telecom Product World; **PHILIPPINES'** Computerworld Philippines, PC Digest (PCW); **POLAND'S** Computerworld Poland, Computerworld Special Report, Networld, PC World/Komputer, Sunworld; **PORTUGAL'S** Cerebro/PC World, Correio Informatico/Computerworld, MacIn; **ROMANIA'S** Computerworld, PC World, Telecom Romania; **RUSSIA'S** Computerworld-Moscow, Mir - PK (PCW), Sety (Networks); **SINGAPORE'S** Computerworld Southeast Asia, PC World Singapore; **SLOVENIA'S** Monitor Magazine; **SOUTH AFRICA'S** Computer Mail (CIO),Computing S.A.,Network World S.A., Software World; **SPAIN'S** Advanced Systems, Amiga World, Computerworld Espana, Communicaciones World, Macworld Espana, NeXTWORLD, Super Juegos Magazine (GamePro), PC World Espana, Publish; **SWEDEN'S** Attack, ComputerSweden, Corporate Computing, Macworld, Mikrodatorn, Natverk & Kommunikation, PC World, CAP & Design, Datalngenjoren, Maxi Data,Windows World; **SWITZERLAND'S** Computerworld Schweiz, Macworld Schweiz, PC Tip; **TAIWAN'S** Computerworld Taiwan, PC World Taiwan; **THAILAND'S** Thai Computerworld; **TURKEY'S** Computerworld Monitor, Macworld Turkiye, PC World Turkiye; **UKRAINE'S** Computerworld, Computers+Software Magazine; **UNITED KINGDOM'S** Computing /Computerworld, Connexion/Network World, Lotus Magazine, Macworld, Open Computing/Sunworld; **UNITED STATES'** Advanced Systems, AmigaWorld, Cable in the Classroom, CD Review, CIO, Computerworld, Computerworld Client/Server Journal, Digital Video, DOS World, Electronic Entertainment Magazine (E2), Federal Computer Week, Game Hits, GamePro, IDG Books, Infoworld, Laser Event, Macworld, Maximize, Multimedia World, Network World, PC Letter, PC World, Publish, SWATPro, Video Event; **URUGUAY'S** PC World Uruguay; **VENEZUELA'S** Computerworld Venezuela, PC World; **VIETNAM'S** PC World Vietnam.   04/07/95

nts

WUGNET HQ, who provided the incredible support from the day we
)M project to project finalization. Their behind-the-scenes activities
ions with IDG, authors, and vendors resulted in a few extra hours sleep for

ithors, and WinSock gurus who provided guidance.

make up the on-line sysop and technical associates on WUGNET's
ET Sysop Brian Moura whose advice and knowledge kept us up-to-
nternet software during the testing and evaluation stages. A special
echnical advice and troubleshooting from WUGNET on-line Windows
rs Steve Scoggins, David Wolfe, Peter Buckley, and David Yon for their
ifiguration and troubleshooting.

Waterside Productions, including Matt Wagner, who always knows
)portunity.

sser, Executive Director and Technical coordinator for the Philadel-
ject, who officially acted as the official Internet Provider for *Internet*
me WWW site for WUGNET's books.

lison Jenkins, and Greg Russell, for their support and assistance for
Beaverson and David Bezaire of CompuServe's Internet Group for
s to compuserve.com.

of *NetworkWorld;* Joe Pierce of IDG Newsletters; to Allistair Banks and
)n, whose support for the open API of WinSock 1.1 allowed program-
world to create a new category of software for the Windows user
o the desktop.

il of First Floor, Phil Schnyder of askSam Systems, Paul Earl of ETA,
Camm, Shelly Sofar, and Jack Bzoza of Delrina for their inclusion of
nd to all the members of alt.winsock newsgroup, especially Craig

ch loved wife Jill and daughter Allison Jennifer.

t to see him as often as they wanted during the writing of this book.
inda, Howard's parents Toba and Harry, Howard's grandmother
ry. To The WUGNET Staff for their assistance: Joe Kleponis, Howard
Logan.

no Guru.

IDG Books, for "staying the course;" to the coauthors for their
reeling in the loose ends.

special thanks to Patrick J. McGovern, without whom this book

---

COSTCO WHOLESALE
WAREHOUSE #55
6880 11 STREET SOUTH EAST
CALGARY, ALBERTA
T2H 2T9

WHOLESALE MEMBER #05300825000

37287 FRUIT GUMMIE	4.99 G
37287 FRUIT GUMMIE	4.99 G
101568 BL'INTER SEC	30.79 G
19736 SONYES/DT120	12.99 G
33821 PISTACHIOS	7.39 G
300 SCENTED RICE	9.49

**** 7% GST	4.44
TOTAL	77.60
Cash	80.00
CHANGE	2.40

TOTAL NUMBER OF ITEMS SOLD = 6
CASHIER:DEBBIE D   REG#12
12/28/95 17:16 0053 12 0298 65

G = GST
THANK YOU!
GST # 12147 8329RT

Credits

Contents at a Glance

Table of Contents

Part IX: Windows NT Internet Server Tools and Clients 727

Chapter 32: The Windows NT WAIS ToolKit 0.6 731

Chapter 33: HTTP Server Version 0.95 745

Introduction

It was a spring day in Media, PA, when Joel, Howard, and I began to ponder this project. Everyone in the office was buzzing about this thing called the Internet. By now you probably know the Internet is a collection of computer networks tied together through a single protocol or language. Knowing what the Internet is is only part of the excitement. The other part is making the Internet connection.

Until recently, the "Net" was a virtual place where a privileged few gathered, exchanged mail, traded files, and exercised remote control over one another's machines. The Internet world was comprised of government agencies, universities, large corporations, and seemingly a handful of individuals who had given their lives over to UNIX years ago.

Although WUGNET is certainly no stranger to "cyberspace," having its electronic home on CompuServe, the Internet held a certain mystique. As we began researching and planning this project, we discovered the mass appeal of the Internet. And that's why we put together this book — so that you can explore and enjoy this vast network of resources called the Internet.

We spent the better part of the year following software developments, looking at commercial and shareware products that would provide you with a wide range of features, flexibility, and power. We think we put together a powerhouse collection — everything from Web browsers to e-mail, to Gophers and Fingers, to tools to create your own World Wide Web pages. We even gathered together some unique communications programs to expand your electronic universe even further.

You'll find the CD-ROM packed full of commercial and shareware (commercial quality) programs and utilities to get you on the Net. Go forth and explore!

To Joel and Howard — for the way we were.

Valda Hilley
Cincinnati, Ohio
February 1995

Shareware, Freeware, Public Domain: What it Means

Free software cannot be purchased, because it has no purchase price. This does not mean that it is without cost. You spend time acquiring it, time installing it, time evaluating it, and time learning how it works. For every ten free programs you put through this ordeal, you may find only one that really meets a need, that you truly adore and use. Some of the software provided with this book is free. We've cut your acquisition costs and ensured that it is virus-free, but you still need to determine if it meets your needs. That has been simplified by the documentation provided in this book and on the CD-ROM.

This book also contains some commercial software samplers. We've provided these samplers so that you can try an earlier or limited version of software before you decide whether you want to buy the latest full version. The commercial software provided in this book/CD package is generally limited in some way, but enough usage and functionality is provided so that you can decide whether you would like to purchase the complete package.

Shareware is software that is free for trial use, but for which you must pay some fee for continued use. Shareware is normally distributed through bulletin board systems (BBSs), and shareware authors are normally individuals who program nights and weekends in their homes.

Shareware is a great idea. It enables you to try software before you buy it. Because the normal dealer channels are bypassed, there are no middlemen to raise the price of the product. And because marketing can be replaced by word-of-mouth recommendations, your purchase dollar goes to the programmer, not to marketing or administration.

But shareware isn't a completely perfect idea. Most shareware users have not paid for the shareware they use every day, and authoring shareware is not always financially rewarding. Just because a shareware program is included on the CD-ROM that accompanies this book, and just because you paid for the book, doesn't mean that you have paid for the shareware. Please try it out, decide if you want to use it, and send the program's author the required payment if you choose to use it.

Freeware is the name used by Andrew Flugelman for his concept of shareware. He pioneered the idea of shareware back in 1982 with his shareware communications program, PC-Talk. He has since died, and with it understanding of the word freeware. Freeware was never free but was distributed and priced as shareware is today. Andrew suggested a payment of $25 for his PC-Talk.

Public domain software is software whose ownership is no longer the author's. It is not copyrighted. No fee is expected for its use, and no support is available to users. It cannot be bought or sold. It may differ from free software (described previously) in that free software may be copyrighted by the author, and may come with some usage restrictions.

There are many ways to get shareware, free software, and public domain software besides buying more books like this. You can call BBSs. You can use CompuServe, Prodigy, or the Internet.

The Association of Shareware Professionals (ASP)

A *shareware professional* is someone who writes shareware. They are professionals because they sometimes get paid, and because they behave in a *professional* way. Many are members of a professional association, the *Association of Shareware Professionals*. Formed in 1987, the association certifies software to ensure that it conforms to normal standards, sponsors events at trade shows, and does other association stuff. You can find out more by writing the Executive Director, Association of Shareware Professionals, 545 Grover Road, Muskegon MI 49442-9427, or by sending mail to CompuServe account 72050,1433. If you have a problem with a shareware author, the ASP has a program to help — the ASP Ombudsman. The ASP Ombudsman *cannot* help you with technical questions but *can* help you settle or resolve any problems you may be having with a member author. You may write to the Ombudsman at POB 5786, Bellevue WA 98006, or through CompuServe at 70007,3536.

General License Agreement

Each of the shareware programs on the disks accompanying this book has its own license agreement and terms. Check the CD-ROM for this information. You should assume that any shareware program adheres to at least the following licensing terms suggested by the ASP, where *Program* is the specific shareware program and *Company* is the program's author or publisher:

"The program is supplied as is. The author disclaims all warranties, expressed or implied, including, without limitation, the warranties of merchantability and of fitness for any purpose. The author assumes no liability for damages, direct or consequential, which may result from the use of this program.

The Program is a 'shareware program,' and is provided at no charge to the user for evaluation. Feel free to share it with your friends but please do not give it away altered or as part of another system. The essence of 'user-supported' software is to provide personal computer users with quality software without high prices, and yet to provide incentives for programmers to continue to develop new products. If you find this program useful, and find that you continue to use the Program after a reasonable trial period, you must make a registration payment to the Company. The registration fee will license one copy for one use on any one computer at any one time. You must treat this software just like a copyrighted book. An example is that this software may be used by any number of people and may be freely moved from one computer location to another, as long as there is no possibility of it being used at one location while it's being used at another — just as a book cannot be read by two different persons at the same time.

Commercial users of the Program must register and pay for their copies of the Program within 30 days of first use or their license is withdrawn. Site-license arrangements may be made by contacting the Company.

Anyone distributing the Program for any kind of remuneration must first contact the Company at the address provided for authorization. This authorization will be automatically granted to distributors recognized by the ASP as adhering to its guidelines for shareware distributors, and such distributors may begin offering the Program immediately. (However, the Company must still be advised so that the distributor can be kept up-to-date with the latest version of the Program.)

You are encouraged to pass a copy of the Program along to your friends for evaluation. Please encourage them to register their copy, if they find that they can use it. All registered users will receive a copy of the latest version of the Program.

Each of the programs and documentation thereto is published and distributed with this book with the written permission of the authors of each. The programs herein are supplied as is. WUGNET Publications and IDG Books Worldwide Inc. individually and together disclaim all warranties, expressed or implied, including, without limitation, the warranties of merchantability and of fitness for any particular purpose; and assume no liability for damages, direct or consequential, which may result from the use of the programs or reliance on the documentation."

What the Icons Mean

Throughout the book, we've used *icons* in the left margin to call your attention to points that are particularly important.

Note icons highlight a special point of interest about the topic under discussion.

Tip icons point to useful hints that may save you time or trouble.

Caution icons alert you to potential problems.

The CD icon cross references other programs on the CD that you can use with the program under discussion.

Part I
Getting Started

What you need to use this book, the accompanyng CD-ROM, and the CD-ROM's software depends largely on what you are doing right now with TCP/IP and the Internet. If you already have a TCP/IP connection to the Internet, you can skip steps 1 and 2 of the upcoming instructions. Also, at any time, you can install the software from the CD-ROM that accesses the short program descriptions.

Although this book focuses on software that directly accesses the Internet, Part III covers programs that use other means to access Internet information. If you want to check out these programs, back up your PC and go to Part III. Also, Part X covers programs that have little directly to do with the Internet but are quite useful communications or information programs.

If you use Windows 95 or Windows NT, you can forget about having to buy a TCP/IP protocol stack and basic programs — these operating systems include them. You still need to find an Internet service provider, though. Additionally, Windows 95 includes software that connects you to Microsoft's own information service, code-named *Marvel*.

Backing up your PC

You are about to explore new software programs and test them to see which you like. Doing so is not without risks! Therefore, I must recommend *before you begin, completely back up your computer.*

I would be remiss if I did not recommend backing up your PC, or at least backing up anything crucial that you can't easily restore. Why let an unrecoverable system crash mar your exploration? If you back up your computer, you can recover from anything you or an errant program can do to your system. While you're at it, make copies of your Windows initialization (INI), AUTOEXEC.BAT, and SYSTEM.INI files, and print a list of what is in the Windows Main and System directories. Many of the programs add entries to your WIN.INI or SYSTEM.INI, add new files to your hard disk, or replace existing files with newer versions. Actually, the CD's installation program adds a few new files to your hard disk, too: some in a directory you specify and others in your Windows directory. Make copies of these key system files before you try any new piece of software so that you can always gracefully back out from testing a program.

If you are a Windows NT or Windows 95 user, note that this CD's programs put information in the old-fashioned INI files. Therefore, this information applies to you as well. The Windows NT programs on this disk may also make changes to your System Registry.

A complete system backup also protects your system from any computer viruses that may be hiding on software you decide to download from the Internet.

Step 1: Accessing the Internet

This book and CD are not designed for beginning Internet users. If you're brand new to the Internet, buy a book that will get you started, such as *The Internet For Dummies* (IDG Books Worldwide, Inc.) by John Levine and Carol Baroudi. If you've used the Internet before, you can probably jump right in.

If you are at a college or university, jumping in may be as simple as hooking into a network connection in your dorm room or lab. Check with your computer services organization. They will probably assign you an IP (Internet Protocol) address and give you other important information you need to make your Internet connection.

If you have a network connection at your workplace and use the TCP/IP protocol, you might have an Internet connection. Many companies, however, place special *firewall* routers between their local networks and the public Internet to secure their private internal network from hackers and villains. To get past a firewall router to the public Internet, you need special software for telnet and FTP, which this CD does not provide. World Wide Web clients can be configured to use special firewall routers called *Proxies;* ask your IS department about them.

If you're a home computer user, you probably have to connect to the Internet through a local commercial provider. Rates in the United States start at about $1 per hour of connect time for a dial-up modem connection, and increase from there depending on the type of service you're using. Use a high-speed modem — old 2400 baud modems are just not worth the frustration. If you plan to stay on-line for any length of time, a second phone line is a good idea. To find a local service provider, either check a book that specializes in getting you started on the 'Net, or ask around for a recommendation. If you have friends with access to the Internet, ask them to find a copy of the Pdial list for you. This list is a reasonably current list of Internet providers. This list changes constantly, so the information quickly becomes out of date. If you are a CompuServe user, ask for a recommendation on the WINCON forum (type **GO WINCON** at the ! prompt). After you've contacted an Internet provider, follow their directions for dialing into their network.

Modem specifications are really an alphabet soup of acronyms and standards. Just get the fastest modem you can. The fast 28,800 bits-per-second (bps) modems are only a little more expensive than the older 9,600 bps modems but clearly worth it. Modems vary not only by their raw speed, but by what kind of compression they use. The latest modem standard, V.34, controls line speed and compression type. If you access uncompressed data over the Internet, a V.34 modem can support transfer rates of over 28,800 bps. (Most World Wide Web text is not compressed, for example, although the images are.) The response speeds that you'll actually get from an Internet host depend on much more than your modem's speed, though. Sometimes, congestion on the Internet or on the host you are calling reduces the data transfer rate to well below your modem's speed.

V.FC modems (also known as V.fast) preceded V.34 modems. Don't buy a V.FC modem unless your Internet service provider can and will continue to support V.FC modems.

Step 2: Installing the TCP/IP access software

If you have a commercial program, just follow the directions that came with it to install the basic TCP/IP networking software. If you have Windows NT 3.5 or Windows 95, then the software you need is included on your installation disks. Otherwise, use the TCP/IP access solution in Part II of this book.

Your commercial service provider or computing support group will give you the information you need to configure the software. It includes

Your IP address — This is a number like 198.20.225.200. (This is the real address of one of the Internet information FTP servers.) Some Internet service providers don't tell you your IP address in advance. They assign an address to you each time you call.

Newbies (brand-new Internet users) note that address 127.0.0.1 is another name for your own computer! If anyone ever tells you that wealth and riches can be found at that address, don't be fooled.

Your DNS server's IP address — This is a computer that changes user-friendly names like ftp.cica.indiana.edu to their real number-based addresses like 129.79.26.27. A number address can change at any time, but the names hardly ever change.

You might also get addresses for:

Your mail server — Sometimes this is called a POP3 (Post Office Protocol 3) server.

A news server — This is a computer that is tied to the Internet Usenet network. Typical news servers have thousands of newsgroups in which you can read and maybe even write articles. News is one of the Internet's most popular aspects.

Your netmask — You have a *netmask* only when you are directly connected to a TCP/IP network. This number, which looks like an Internet address, tells your PC which IP addresses are on your local network, and which require going off your local network through a router. If you are a dial-up user, then you don't need to worry about a local network, and all addresses (other than your own) need to be sent to a router.

If you have a permanent network connection (you are not connected by phone line) and are using Microsoft's Windows for Workgroups 3.11, then you can use a free TCP/IP protocol stack from Microsoft. This software works *only* with Windows for Workgroups 3.11. You can get it from the Microsoft Software Library (MSL) on the following services:

- **CompuServe**
  GO MSL
  Search for WFWT32.EXE
  Display results and download

- **Microsoft Download Service (MSDL)**
  Dial (206) 936-6735 to connect to MSDL
  Download WFWT32.EXE

- **Internet (anonymous FTP)**
  ftp ftp.microsoft.com
  Change to the SOFTLIB\MSLFILES directory
  Get WFWT32.EXE

Step 3: Installing the CD viewer software (optional)

The CD contains three main parts: the software described in this book, a Microsoft Multimedia Viewer documentation file that contains short descriptions of each piece of software, and a directory of help files the Viewer documentation file accesses. To view the documentation file, run SETUP.EXE, which is in the CD's main directory. This installs the files needed to run the Multimedia Viewer on your hard disk.

After you've installed these files, you can browse all the descriptions, as well as perform a full text search of all the Multimedia Viewer documentation.

Step 4: Installing applications you want to test

Many TCP/IP packages come with applications. If you have such a package, use its applications until you learn what you like and don't like.

This book is about finding cool software that does what you like. Much of this book's software is shareware. If you like and use any of it, then *pay for it*. This is no joke. Shareware is *not free*. Using the software without paying for it is stealing. Your registration fee keeps these programmers and companies in business. You'll find handy registration forms throughout the book that you can photocopy and use to register your shareware.

 Check the last pages of this book for coupons that offer substantial discounts from some of the commercial vendors who contributed to this book.

Each part of this book contains a different category of software. The introduction to each part comments on the part's contents to help you find what you want. Here's a breakdown of the parts:

Part I: Getting Started

This is where you are reading now. The coolest thing to check out on the CD for this part is the Internet For Everybody demonstration program. It is a very impressive teaching and reference tool with tons of video clips built in. Be warned, though: This demonstration is not for those with wimpy PCs; you need at least 8 MB RAM.

Part II: WinSock Samplers

This section covers four packages, and three of them come with TCP/IP protocol stacks. This is the place to start if you don't already have a TCP/IP stack installed. After you have installed a TCP/IP stack and are connected to the Internet, come back here to install the applications you might have missed.

Part III: Non-WinSock Internet Solutions

You don't need direct Internet access if you want to only read news groups and use e-mail. These chapters cover programs that access the Internet indirectly and tell you how to access the Internet via CompuServe.

Part IV: Windows E-Mail GIZMOS

This part covers two programs that access the Internet e-mail systems directly (Eudora and Pegasus) and one that accesses non-Internet service providers (RFD Mail). The introduction has details on other mail programs you might want to check out, too. Wincode is also included in this section because it is a Windows 3.1 program that converts 7-bit ASCII (text) files to 8-bit binary (.EXE, .COM, .GIF, and so on) files and vice versa, which enables you to send and receive binary files over any ASCII-based communications system, such as electronic mail.

Part V: WinSock Client GIZMOS

This part discusses WinSock-compatible programs that are not part of a complete TCP/IP stack and applications package. These programs are worth checking out because they'll make your time spent on the Internet easier and more productive. You'll find two Gophers, a finger server, and an FTP program, a 3270 terminal emulator for mainframes, and XRay, a Windows Sockets tracing program.

Part VI: World Wide Web Tools and GIZMOS

World Wide Web browsers and tools are doubtlessly the next killer applications. This part of the book discusses several tools that help you access the Web and create information to put on the Web yourself! The CD contains one Web browser, SPRY's AIR Mosaic, which is a limited edition of the full product. This viewer is located and discussed in Part II, in Chapter 5. Information about other World Wide Web browsers is in the introduction to Part VI.

Part VII: Conferencing Applications GIZMOS

This part covers three applications that enhance user-to-user communications over the Internet: Face-to-Face Conferencing, Mr. Squiggle, and Sticky. You'll also find some information about other programs available on the Internet that you may want to check out.

Part VIII: Games

What book on the Internet would be complete without a section about entertainment? This part contains three Internet games: chess, Go, and backgammon.

Part IX: Windows NT Internet Server Tools and Clients

These server tools are for Internet power users who want their Windows NT system to be a WAIS, World Wide Web, or Gopher server.

Part X: Windows Internet Information GIZMOS and Tools

Although the programs covered in this section are not specifically Internet tools, you'll be glad to have these applications. After all, you won't spend all your time on the Internet. Delrina, for instance, put their WinFax LITE and WinComm LITE on the CD.

Step 5: Protecting yourself

When you connect to the Internet via a modem or network connection, you open a *two-way street*. Although security risks are typically low, remember that when you have an Internet connection, your computer is an Internet host and is subject to risk from hackers. Consider the following safety tips:

Do not install server applications unless you trust them completely. As soon as others are allowed to connect to your PC via a server application, you open a door to hackers. UNIX system administrators are always alert to Internet hackers — you must be, too.

Do not leave your PC connected to the Internet when you are not using the Internet. This advice may be obvious to the dial-up user who pays by the hour, but not so for those who have a direct network connection.

Check on what built-in services your protocol stack offers. Some of them offer standard Internet services that you may not want, such as FTP, finger, or RCP. Turn off anything you don't want to use.

Check downloaded software for viruses. When you gather software or other files from the Internet, scan the programs for viruses before installing and running the programs on your computer. Keep your eyes open for unusual system behavior after you've installed new software.

Never, never, *never* send credit card information over the Internet without taking special means to encrypt the information. Even then, understand that you are taking a risk. Particularly in campus environments, a villain can eavesdrop on your connection and steal your credit card information.

Be extremely cautious about establishing business relationships on the Internet. Plenty of dishonest computer users see the Internet as a great way to defraud people. The Internet has very few rules and virtually no oversight from law enforcement. Many people have already been defrauded via electronic mail. Don't become a victim.

Never make financial decisions or take risks based on who sent you the e-mail. The sender's name may be fake.

Always assume that communication from your PC can be traced back to you. Don't do something stupid that you may regrest just because you are doing it from the comfort of your home or school.

Passwords can be broken. If you log into personal accounts, change your password frequently. Assume that your password can be stolen from you. Passwords can be gleaned by LAN sniffers, shoulder surfers, or fake login screens. Choose a password that has no obvious connection to you. Don't use important dates or friends' names because passwords are easily cracked.

Step 6: Keep exploring

A printed page just can't keep up with all the new stuff that keeps rolling out of the Internet programming community. Also, because of legal restrictions (yes, even on shareware!), we couldn't include all the software on the CD that you may want to use for your Internet access. If you don't find exactly what you want on the CD, keep looking. Here are a couple of key spots to check for WinSock shareware and information:

- The CompuServe WINCON forum. You can find a good amount of software here, as well as get advice from others who have tried an application.

- Craig Larsen's WWW WinSock Application FAQ:
  http://www.lcs.com.faqhtml.html

  You'll read about Craig's consulting service every time you look up the FAQ, but it is a very complete list of WinSock applications with hyperlinks to a place you can find them.

- The FTP archives of CICA: ftp://ftp.cica.indiana.edu

  This is a very busy site, so you will probably connect to one of the mirror sites eventually. These sites are listed after your anonymous login is rejected because the site is too busy. The list of mirror sites changes frequently, so we didn't include it in this book/CD package.

- The alt.winsock Usenet newsgroup

  A great deal of valuable information is buried in the messages on this newsgroup. If you don't find what you want, just ask.

A note about how addresses are shown in this book: Many of the Internet addresses shown in this book use a format called Uniform Resource Locator (URL):

> http://www.mcs.com

In this form, the first part of the address (to the left of the colon) is the protocol needed to reach the site:

> http://www.mcs.com   = Protocol name

Common protocols are ftp, http, and telnet. *http* is the protocol most often used on the World Wide Web. To the right of the colon is the actual site address:

> http://www.mcs.com   = Host address

If you are using a World Wide Web client, type the address in this format exactly. If you are using a dedicated function client, like an FTP client, just type the host name.

Summary

Connecting to the Internet is neither trivial nor daunting. You can always get help from the authors of this book and many others on the CompuServe WINCON forum (GO WINCON) if you run into trouble. You also can reach WUGNET at 610-565-1861.

At the risk of sounding like a father (which I am), let me add a personal note: The Internet is cool. It contains more information, entertainment, and fun than one person can possibly absorb. But it is still a computer network and just electrons on a wire. Don't let the Internet substitute for live people, in-person art, live music, spoken conversation, and physical activities.

If you are a parent, limit the amount of time your children spend surfing the Internet, and always check up on what they are doing. Cyberspace has few rules. Some of the fun is for adults only.

Don't waste too much time in cyberspace. There are plenty of great things to do that have nothing at all to do with the Internet or computers. (Or so my wife says.)

Chapter 1

The Internet For Everybody: Accessing the Electronic Superhighway

The Internet is booming! Over 20,000,000 people all over the world use it to communicate, inform, research, and market. Nearly 1,000,000 new users are jumping on each month! If you're fascinated by this phenomenon but don't know how to get started, The Internet For Everybody is for you (see Figure 1-1). The Internet For Everybody is a lively and entertaining interactive CD on how to use the Internet successfully. It is targeted for people who have a need for on-line information and communicating capabilities in their work, home, personal enrichment, and recreational activities. The Internet For Everybody covers Internet services, tools, access options, and much more.

A demo version of this product is included on your *Internet GIZMOS for Windows* CD-ROM, which offers you a free sneak preview! Occasionally, you come to an endpoint in the demo version where no further material is included. If you like the demo and would like to order the full product, please refer to the back of the book for ordering information.

The Internet For Everybody contains over two hours of *how-to* video instruction as well as help screens, useful tables, an index, key products and services, a glossary, and interactive menus for exploring this material from several perspectives. The personal guided tours give you the benefit of firsthand experience in exploring the Internet. Dick Rubinstein, whose business is to make new technology accessible, leads you through the intricacies of the Internet in a congenial manner (see Figure 1-2).

Figure 1-1: The Internet For Everybody.

For the average computer user, getting started with the Internet is the hardest part. Many good books and magazines try to explain the Internet; and several programs are available from on-line services or on the Internet itself. But many "normal" people find these aids are not enough to give them the confidence they need to get started in a foreign environment. Seeing the actual steps involved in connecting and navigating through the Internet is invaluable to new users.

The Internet For Everybody demonstrates many of the on-line environments of the Internet. The guide, Dick Rubinstein, discusses various methods of connecting to the Internet — universities, commercial services, and companies — and shows how the computer screens look and act when on-line (both the front-end software and terminal emulators). He also shows you Internet services: e-mail, WAIS, Gopher, Lynx, WWW, and others. The Internet For Everybody shows you what to type and how each connection appears on the computer screen. The interactions are in real time.

In addition to the on-line and video segments, this CD-ROM contains help screens that you can refer to or print for later review. You can choose to approach the Internet from the viewpoint of a business person, teacher, retiree,

Figure 1-2: Dick Rubinstein leads the way.

or high school student; or view Dick on-line while he uses a particular search engine or looks for certain types of information; or move directly to the area of your greatest interests using the index. The innovative menus and index allow you to find the exact information needed.

Nothing else in the marketplace provides this kind of instruction and guidance. The combination of video presentation, in-depth information, help reference, and interactivity is the best arrangement for novice and intermediate users of the Internet.

Three Methods of Approaching the Internet

There are three major methods of examining information: *Tours,* the *Map,* and an *Index.*

Tours

In the *Tours* segment you can approach the Internet from the viewpoint of any of four different people:

- ■ Mark, a consultant living in Hong Kong, who finds that the Internet is indispensable in the operation of his business.

- ■ Frank, a retired chemist, who keeps connected to the outside world with the help of the Internet. He also gets gardening tips for his wife's greenhouse.

- ■ Carrie, a seventh grade science teacher, who uses the Internet with her students as a research tool and a source of inspiration, ideas, and academic stimulation.

- ■ Adam, a teenager entrepreneur, who explores the Internet to help with his budding bicycle repair business.

In addition, you can choose a subject area such as e-mail, newsgroups, Gopher, hints and tips, and many others. *Tours* is comparable to the table of contents in a book. (See Figure 1-3.)

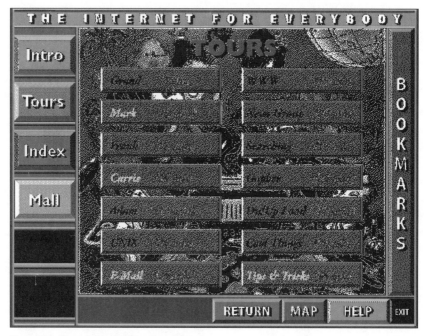

Figure 1-3: *Tours* is like a table of contents.

The Map

The *Map* is a navigational tool that provides a visual description of what information is contained in a particular segment. When you highlight a button in the program, the *Map* shows you where you will go. The *Map* allows you to navigate directly to a video clip and keeps track of where you have been. You can also bypass sections that you have already viewed. This method of examination is more detailed than *Tours* but less detailed than the *Index*. (See Figure 1-4.)

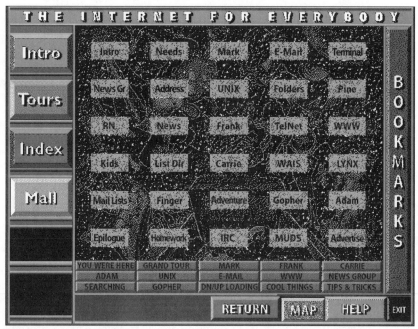

Figure 1-4: Navigating with the *Map*.

The Index

The *Index* is just like the index of a book. Any subject or concept that is covered in any part of the CD-ROM is noted and accessible with a click of the mouse. The *Index* is a complete list of topics, services, and products.

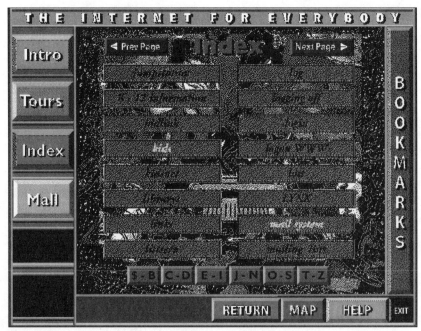

Figure 1-5: The *Index* lists topics, services, and products.

Special Features

The CD-ROM includes several special features. Throughout the program, *context-sensitive buttons* offer additional help screens, more information, or products that are related to the subject being considered. In the *Sweepstakes*, you can fax back (or mail) the built-in entry form for prizes which are awarded several times a year. It is a convenient way to receive more information on particular products or services mentioned in The Internet For Everybody, and it is fun as well.

The *Mall* is an "Electronic Store," providing a showcase for Internet-related products and services. (See Figure 1-6.) You can request additional information on any of the products and services contained in the *Mall*. Each store is different, and window-shopping in the *Mall* is interesting in itself. (This feature is not included in the demo version.)

Figure 1-6: The *Mall* is a great place to go window shopping.

Hardware and Operating Requirements _____

The Internet For Everybody (IFE) is targeted for MPC-compliant 486 machines, with 33 MHz, 8MB of RAM, Microsoft Windows 3.1 or higher, 256 color video card, sound card, and double-speed CD-ROM drive.

Installation

The runtime version of QuickTime 1.1.1 is required to run the video segments of IFE and is included in the IFE subdirectory on the CD-ROM. The video segments will run much more efficiently if a runtime version of QuickTime 1.1.1 is installed on your hard drive.

The IFE installation program will look for QuickTime on your system, and if it is not found, will offer you the option to place the QuickTime files on your hard drive. The default directory for the placement of QuickTime is C:\QTW\BIN.

The installation program also offers you the option to modify your AUTOEXEC.BAT file. The only change that is made is that C:\QTW is added to the path so that the QuickTime program can be located on your system. If you do not modify the AUTOEXEC.BAT, the program will not know where to find QuickTime.

De-installation

The IFE program affects your system very little. If you want to delete all files associated with IFE from your system, you will need to complete the following steps:

1. Delete C:\QTW from the PATH= line in the AUTOEXEC.BAT file. This step is not required since it will not affect anything if left there.

2. Delete QuickTime from your system using the File Manager. If you selected the default directory option during installation, the files are located in C:\QTW\BIN. Only delete if you do not need QuickTime for any other programs.

3. Delete the IFE Program Group icon from the Program Manager window by highlighting the icon and using the File\Delete option. The icon file itself is on the CD-ROM and is never placed on the system.

Operating instructions

To run The Internet For Everybody, simply select the menu item on the Microsoft Viewer menu. An automated installation program will offer to install a runtime version of QuickTime on your system if it does not already exist, and then the IFE program will initialize. The program is set up in a simple manner with *point and click* options. For more information or for technical support, please call ETA at (508) 879-0006. E-mail: tife@aol.com.

This interactive CD-ROM is created by Emerging Technology Applications (ETA), an electronic media and database marketing unit of the International Data Group. ETA works with publishers and other organizations to design, develop, market, and implement electronic products and services. E-mail address: tife@aol.com.

The video "The Internet For Everybody" is produced by Point. E-mail address: tmudge@delphi.com. Point Productions is a video production company that develops reference, education, and entertainment works in various electronic formats.

For ordering information, please refer to the coupon in the back of the book.

Part II
WinSock Samplers

This part includes all the software you need to connect to the Internet. All you need to do is find an Internet service provider. On the CD-ROM, the Internet service provider map from Frontier directs you to the nearest service provider. If you already have a connection to the Internet through work or school, then you don't need to worry about setting up a protocol stack. Just check out the applications on the CD.

This part also tells you why the Windows Sockets specification is important to you, as a TCP/IP and Internet user, and to application developers.

Some people think of the Internet as a giant, distant, unreachable, impenetrable cloud of unknowable content and incomprehensible information. After you get over the starting hurdles, though, you can be as much of an Internet expert as anyone. It will all seem simple. If you need help getting started, many books are available to help you. This book isn't one of them. If you're ready to jump right in, and know something already about computers and technology, then this book and CD-ROM give you the tools you need. This part helps you chart a course for successful connection to the Internet.

The Importance of WinSock

Windows Sockets are a critical element in the widespread use of the Internet among Windows PC users. The Windows Sockets specification creates a standard interface between the TCP/IP protocol — the heart of the Internet — and Windows applications. Other operating systems have a similar standard. Many UNIX-based systems support the Berkeley Sockets standard, on which the Windows Sockets standard is based. The Windows Sockets standard specifies how a Windows application can use the TCP/IP protocol, regardless of the protocol stack's implementation.

The WinSock specification is publicly available. It's even on the CD-ROM.

The heart of the WinSock implementation is a special Dynamic Link Library called WINSOCK.DLL. Every application written for WinSock can call functions in this library and get the same (well, at least similar) results, regardless of who created the library. Even though the WinSock interface is a standard, as are the library's calling procedures, the libraries themselves depend strictly on the protocol stack brand. Each of the three protocol stacks available on the CD-ROM contains its *own version* of WINSOCK.DLL — and they are not interchangeable.

Your interface to the network is probably one of two connections — either a LAN (local area network) card in your PC or a serial port connected to a modem.

 Other kinds of connections are available, such as ISDN and private lines, but they aren't used widely enough to warrant much discussion yet. Ask your Internet service provider if you think a higher-speed ISDN connection or a permanent connection is right for you.

LAN connections

With a LAN connection, the LAN carries packets (small chunks) of information from your PC to its destination on the network. If the other end of your network connection is a computer across the hall, then information sent between your computer and the other computer probably never leaves the local network. If the other end of your connection is farther away, however, packets from your computer are routed through a special purpose computer called, oddly enough, a *router*. A router decides which packets to send from one network to another. A router can be connected to almost any number of networks, and several routers can be connected to a single network. Most of the time, however, a local network has just one router.

Data lines connect thousands of routers all over the world. A packet that leaves your computer traverses at least your local router and the router in the distant computer's LAN. The packet also passes through any number of routers in between. This worldwide collection of interconnected routers and computers comprises the Internet.

What's a protocol stack?

A protocol stack is a program that provides TCP/IP services on your PC. It connects your interface to the network and WINSOCK.DLL. It is called a *stack* because it *builds* protocols modularly, like building blocks. A complete protocol logically stacks several of these blocks. This is true even though many TCP/IP brands are contained in a single executable or driver file. The WINSOCK.DLL adds a final block to the TCP/IP protocol stack.

Modem connection

If you are not connected to a LAN, then you have to use a modem and phone line to connect to the Internet.

Because a phone line is, by its nature, a point-to-point connection and TCP/IP is, by its nature, connectionless, special protocols connect your PC to a dial-up router. The two protocols used are SLIP (Serial Line Internet Protocol) and PPP (Point to Point Protocol). SLIP is an older, more widely used protocol, while PPP is a newer protocol and is not as widely used yet. Expect to see a broad PPP expansion in the next few years. SLIP and PPP are Internet standards, defined in part in Internet RFC numbers RFC-1055 and RFC-1661, respectively. RFCs are available via anonymous FTP from ftp://ds.internic.net. Your Internet service provider will tell you which of these two protocols is available and/or preferred. To maximize your usage of *Internet GIZMOS for Windows,* you'll probably want a SLIP or PPP connection.

Regardless of the protocol, when you connect your computer to your service provider's network, you are directly connected to the Internet. Every packet of information destined for the Internet is sent across the phone line to another modem at the service provider's location. From there, it is sent to a router that understands how to measure and bill your network use, and then out to the Internet.

 Most dial-up Internet providers charge for time used, because you tie up a modem regardless of how much or little data you send or receive. The hundreds of networks that are part of the Internet do not charge each other for the amount of information sent across their networks. This may change as the Internet becomes increasingly commercial, but not without stiff resistance from many in the Internet community. Wireless connections are a different story, however. The packet-based cellular services (such as CDPD) generally charge per kilo-packet or kilobyte of data transmitted or received. Any number of users can be active in a particular area at any one time, and the limited resource is the amount of information that can be transmitted over the AIR at any given instant in time.

The Future of Windows Sockets _____

If you have an application that uses Windows Sockets, you almost certainly use TCP/IP. In the future, however, Windows Sockets will include other transport protocols, perhaps including OSI protocols, Decnet, AppleTalk, IPX/SPX, and specialized wireless protocols. Version 2 of the Windows Sockets interface specification will name the protocols to be used. If you want to keep track of how the WinSock 2 specification is coming along, you can check out the following:

```
ftp://sunsite.unc.edu/pub/micro/pc-stuff/ms-windows/WinSock/
WinSock-2.0
```

You can find information here about mailing lists for WinSock 2, as well as a good selection of software that is compatible with the existing WinSock specification.

Finding an Internet Service Provider

Finding a service provider is no longer a mystery. For starters, check out the hypertext map of the U.S. and Canada available on the CD-ROM's Introduction topic. This map, provided by the Frontier Corporation, shows the service providers near you. The CD-ROM also includes some sample rates (as of November 1994) for these service providers. You can find service providers in and near many major U.S. and Canadian cities. If the map does not list your state, try a national service provider (which costs more). Also, be sure to check out the lists of service providers available at the following gopher site:

```
gopher://is.internic.net/11/infoguide/getting-connected/
```

If you can't access this server, ask for help on the CompuServe WINCON Forum. Check out the WinCIM software in Part III for information about CompuServe.

If all you want to do is read Usenet newsgroups or transfer a file occasionally, you might be well served by a commercial service provider's Internet gateway. Check out CompuServe, America Online, or Delphi. Expect to pay a lot more for those gateway services than you'll pay for a straight Internet connection, but expect a higher level of service and guidance.

What's in This Part?

This part consists of special versions of four software samplers. Look on the CD-ROM in the \FILES\PART2 directory. Each sampler comes with complete documentation, but the next few pages comment on them briefly.

Which do you pick?

You will probably choose a TCP/IP-solutions vendor based on which applications you like best, because most commercial vendors bundle their applications with their protocol stack. For starters, follow the guidelines. After you find your favorite applications and are ready to put money on the line for applications, go with whatever stack is cheapest and best meets your needs.

If you already have Windows 95 or Windows NT 3.5, then try the included SLIP/ PPP software. TCP/IP software vendors are now busy making sure that their applications work over the Microsoft TCP/IP stack because many people will use it just because it came in the box. Contact the vendors of these samplers in this part to see how much an applications package costs — you may find out that you get their protocol stack "free" as part of the package. Right now, Microsoft's TCP/IP stack is not very "tunable." For most people, this doesn't matter, since they wouldn't know what to tune anyway. If you're a real tinkerer, or are connecting to an unusual network, you may want a more flexible proto- col stack. Check the documentation to see if what you want is included.

Getting started

If you don't have Windows 95, and your service provider and modem are in Frontier's list, then use the Frontier stack while you test applications. It config- ures easily, and doesn't pester you with reminders about how to get the rest of their products every time you start it. If your service provider and/or modem is not in their list, then you'll have to tinker with the setup, just like the other two solutions. Of the other two, Trumpet is probably the more stable and straight- forward in its setup. Also, you can find a *lot* of peer help for Trumpet because Trumpet is widely used on the Internet.

If you find you love SPRY's sample programs (and their FTP front end — NFM — is *great*), then it may pay to buy their entire suite of programs, including the TCP/IP stack. You'll get top-to-bottom tech support with no finger pointing about who is responsible for a particular bug.

Frontier's SuperHighway Access Sampler

This Internet sampler consists of a Windows Dynamic Link Library-based TCP/IP protocol stack. This means that the protocol stack does not take up any of your precious real-mode memory, leaving room for your existing device drivers and programs that need to run under DOS only.

When Frontier's lists include your service provider and modem, this program is an easy point-and-click setup experience. You just select the service provider name and the modem type, and the setup program loads most of the needed information. You can set up the program to dial out only when you are trying to send information to the Internet, and then hang up after a period you specify.

This can save you money if you pay by the minute for Internet access. The sampler comes with two demonstration applications: an FTP client and a news reader. Most of their functions have been disabled. The sampler also includes an icon to connect to Frontier's FTP server to get more sample applications.

 The setup program contains the area codes and phone numbers for many Internet service providers. If you choose a local number, you don't need to dial the area code. To remove the area code, select the setup icon from the sampler's program group and delete the area code from the phone number.

During the installation of the software, your system may seem to lock up for up to a minute. Do not panic! Give the installation program a chance to work — get a cup of coffee or something before you give up and hit the big red Reset button.

 These sample programs let you connect only to Frontier's FTP server. You can, however, use the other WinSock programs available on the CD as clients with Frontier's protocol stack.

Frontier is on the Internet at

```
http://www.frontiertech.com.
```

Distinct's FTP and telnet

The Distinct TCP/IP solution for SLIP and PPP is based on an executable file that starts whenever a connection is needed. Unlike a DLL-based solution, you can quit Distinct's solution when you're not using it. It does, however, clutter up the screen with yet one more executing program icon.

This program is a bit nonintuitive to set up and may require a support call or two to get going. The configuration routines draw no distinction between SLIP and PPP setups. The two protocols require very different information, so ignore the fields that don't apply to the protocol you are using. Ask your service provider if you are not sure which fields to ignore. The sampler contains two fully functional WinSock-based programs, telnet, and an FTP client. The programs do require a serial number and key, which are installed during setup. The telnet program supports ANSI terminal emulations and has a fixed display size but does allow you to select fonts. See the online help for full coverage of telnet.

 You must edit the logon script to make it match your service provider's login sequence. This protocol stack occasionally locks up some systems. Be alert for this problem, and use another vendor's product if it does lock up.

These sample programs use a "helper" program called GHOST.EXE. Whenever one of the samples starts, an icon with the Distinct TCP/IP logo appears.

Distinct is on the Internet at

```
ftp://ftp.distinct.com
```

Trumpet WinSock Stack Sampler

The Trumpet WinSock protocol stack has no setup program. You have to follow the directions in the INSTALL.DOC or INSTALL.TXT file. The directions are fairly simple, and the login script needs only a few changes to make it work with your service provider. Of the three application suites in this part, only Trumpet asks that you pay for the basic protocol stack — $25 per copy. Trumpet, like Distinct, is an executable-based SLIP TCP/IP stack.

 You must edit the logon script to make it match your service provider's login sequence.

Trumpet is on the Internet at

```
ftp://ftp.trumpet.com.au
```

SPRY's Sampler

SPRY doesn't include a protocol stack with their sampler, but you already have three choices (four if you're running Windows NT 3.5 or Windows 95), so who cares? The two sample applications are really cool. First, you get a limited-edition version of SPRY's AIR Mosaic Express for roaming the World Wide Web. (See Part V for how to get other WWW browsers.) Second, you get the best FTP front end available. SPRY's FTP is called Network File Manager (NFM), and it runs side by side with your Windows File Manager. Transferring files is as simple as drag and drop. Plus, NFM understands different kinds of remote hosts and displays detailed information based on the remote host type.

 AIR Mosaic Express has its own installer, SETUP.EXE, located on the CD-ROM in /FILES/PART1/SPRY/AIRMOS. You must install the Network File Manager manually, following the instructions in the README.TXT file in /FILES/PART1/SPRY/NFM .

AIR Mosaic Express is limited to six URLs (Universal Resource Locators) — that is, pages — per activation. You can exit and then restart the program to keep exploring. Get the full copy on-line.

SPRY is on the Internet at http://www.spry.com

Chapter 2
Frontier SuperHighway Access Sampler

Welcome to SuperHighway Access Sampler. SuperHighway Access for Windows™ is a complete Internet access package containing a full set of information retrieval tools, as well as the award-winning applications from Frontier Technologies' SuperTCP/NFS for Windows. You can perform multiple concurrent search and retrieve operations using the popular World Wide Web, Gopher, CSO Phonebook, and telnet tools — plus enjoy the convenience of MIME compliant e-mail, VT100 terminal emulation, a network news reader, and FTP file-transfer capability. SuperHighway Access for Windows includes

- Gopher
- World Wide Web
- CSO Phonebook
- WAIS
- FTP Client
- VT100
- Network News Reader
- E-mail (SMTP, POP2 and POP3, MIME)
- Global Login

Standard features

- **Gopher** provides a hierarchical browser to allow information search and retrieval from any of the numerous Gopher servers on the Internet.

- **World Wide Web** offers another popular search-and-retrieval tool based on *hypertext* links to allow users to browse for information regardless of the order or location in which the information is stored.

- **CSO Phonebook** provides the means to retrieve information about individuals from any of the numerous CSO servers on the Internet.

■ **FTP Client** provides object-oriented file transfers using the intuitive file folder directory structure of Windows File Manager. The FTP module can be used independently or in conjunction with WinTapestry.

■ **VT100** terminal emulator offers multiple sessions, session printing and logging, keyboard mapping, font selection, color selection, scripting, and much more. Like the FTP module, VT100 can operate independently or in conjunction with WinTapestry.

■ **Electronic Mail** supports SMTP, POP2 and POP3, and MIME binary file attachments, allowing users to send and view mail messages with attached graphics, spreadsheets, sound, video, and more!

■ **NNTP Network News Reader** gives you access to the thousands of news and information databases available on the global Internet.

■ **Global Login** allows users to login globally to protected applications.

■ **Setup TCP** provides easy access to network configuration parameters.

Options

■ **ONC RPC/XDR API** allows you to develop Windows Sockets applications using Sun's ONC RPC/XDR specifications.

■ **Windows Sockets Toolkit** features sample Windows Sockets source code and C++ class libraries, providing an object-oriented interface for developing network applications compliant with the Windows Sockets API standard.

Pre-installation

In order to successfully install SuperHighway Access for Windows, you should carefully review the information provided in this section *prior to* installation.

System files

The installation process modifies your AUTOEXEC.BAT and Windows system files. When you're installing SuperHighway Access for Windows, the file AUTOEXEC.*NNN* is automatically created as a backup of your AUTOEXEC.BAT file, in which *NNN* is the number of the backup file. During installation, you are asked if you wish to modify your AUTOEXEC.BAT file; if you elect not to modify AUTOEXEC.BAT, the file SUPERTCP.BAT will contain the batch file commands required to start the network before Windows is started.

Before proceeding with installation, you may want to create backups of the following Windows system files:

■ C:\WINDOWS\WIN.INI — Windows configuration file

■ C:\WINDOWS\PROGMAN.INI — Windows configuration file

System requirements

SuperHighway Access for Windows is designed for the following operating environments:

■ IBM PS/2 MicroChannel Architecture computer or compatible.

■ EISA bus 80486.

■ ISA bus 80386.

■ IBM PC computer or compatible.

■ 4MB RAM is required, 8MB is recommended.

■ At least 10MB free hard disk space for program code. Data storage requires more disk space. (The amount of space needed varies according to the user's data storage requirements; 20MB total free disk space is recommended for user convenience.)

■ A previously installed copy of Microsoft Windows 3.1 or Windows for Workgroups 3.11.

■ A previously installed copy of PC-DOS or MS-DOS Version 3.3 or later.

■ A LAN or WAN network interface card.

Installation

Installation is done from the CD. The following sections describe installing SuperHighway Access for Windows over an existing SuperTCP for Windows; installing SuperTCP for Windows over an existing SuperHighway Access for Windows; and installing SuperHighway Access for Windows alone.

Installing SuperHighway Access for Windows over an existing SuperTCP for Windows installation

Use the following steps if you have a version of SuperTCP for Windows on your PC and you want to install SuperHighway Access for Windows on top of it:

1. Start Windows from the DOS prompt. Do *not* start Windows automatically or by rebooting using AUTOEXEC.BAT because this file may be modified.

2. Place the CD in your CD-ROM drive, and choose Run from the File menu of the Windows Program Manager or File Manager. Type path to SuperHighway Access:

   ```
   install
   ```

   You may be asked to restart Windows. (This step is necessary because Windows loads drivers which cannot be unloaded until you exit Windows — installation cannot proceed until these drivers are unloaded.) When Windows is restarted, SuperHighway Access for Windows shuts down (if it runs automatically when you start Windows).

3. You will be prompted for your SuperHighway Access for Windows serial number and authorization key (described later in this chapter). You receive a *different* serial number and authentication key for SuperHighway Access for Windows; that is, you cannot use the same serial number and authentication key you used to install SuperTCP for Windows.

4. The SuperHighway Access for Windows installation process can detect whether you have SuperTCP for Windows already installed on your system. If this is the case, installing SuperHighway Access for Windows replaces any SuperTCP for Windows modules it detects with new copies. At this point, you can continue or abort the installation. Click on the Install button to continue.

After the modules have been installed, a SuperTCP for Windows group box will appear displaying icons for the newly installed applications.

Should you experience difficulties during the installation procedure, you may need to uninstall SuperHighway Access for Windows. See the section on uninstalling later in this chapter.

If you need to install additional modules after you have completed the installation and setup procedure, simply run install on your desired modules. Do not attempt to install additional modules until you have completed installation and setup of previously selected modules.

Installing SuperTCP for Windows over an existing SuperHighway Access for Windows

If you have a version of SuperHighway Access for Windows installed on your PC and want to install SuperTCP for Windows on top of it, perform the following steps:

1. Start Windows. Do *NOT* start Windows automatically from boot up using AUTOEXEC.BAT because this file may be modified.

2. Choose Run from the File menu of the Windows Program Manager or File Manager. Type

   `ftcinst d:pathname`
   where "d" is the letter of the CD-ROM drive.

Please refer to your SuperTCP for Windows documentation for detailed installation instructions for that product.

Installing SuperHighway Access for Windows

To install SuperHighway Access for Windows for the first time, follow these steps:

1. Start Windows. Do *NOT* start Windows automatically from boot up using AUTOEXEC.BAT because this file will be modified.

2. Run the INSTALL.EXE file from the File menu of the Windows Program Manager or File Manager.

3. The Package Authentication dialog box (Figure 2-1) will appear, prompting you to enter Your Name, Company Name, Serial Number, and Authentication Key. Each SuperHighway Access for Windows package must have its own Serial Number and corresponding Authentication Key. Both are eight-digit numbers in the form *xxx-xxx-xx*. Installation of SuperHighway Access for Windows cannot proceed without proper authentication information. Please note that SuperHighway Access for Windows will not operate if a duplicate serial number is detected on the network.

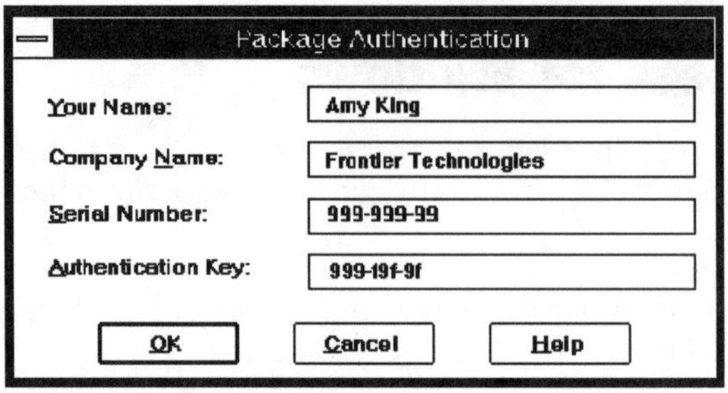

Package Authentication

Your Name:	Amy King
Company Name:	Frontier Technologies
Serial Number:	999-999-99
Authentication Key:	999-19f-9f

OK   Cancel   Help

Figure 2-1: Package Authentication dialog box.

4. Next, the Installation dialog box appears. You are prompted to select an Internet Services provider. Select a provider from the list supplied, or select Other if your provider is not on the list. Enter the user name and password assigned to you by your selected provider. If you selected Other, you must enter a description of the provider (usually, the provider's name) and its data (that is, modem) phone number. You must also enter a user name and password as noted above.

5. Now select the COM port on your computer to which your modem is connected. SuperHighway Access for Windows is capable of detecting whether your modem is already attached to your computer. If so, it will "auto-sense" the baud rate and COM port, and you will not receive this prompt.

6. Select a modem type from the list provided or select Other.

7. Now click OK and verify that all the information in the Installation dialog box is correct. If it is, click the OK Install button to proceed. If not, you can correct any faulty information then click OK Install, or you can abort the installation by clicking the Don't Install button.

After the files are installed, a SuperHighway Access for Windows Group Box will appear, displaying icons for the newly installed applications.

The WinTapestry application is now automatically launched. You can click on the Frontier Home Page for an introduction to WinTapestry's features. The kernel is activated, and dials your selected Internet service provider to ensure that all your setup parameters are correct. If, for some reason, the connection fails, you can check the kernel message log for hints as to what may have occurred. Common problems include needing (or not needing) a 9 in front of the telephone number, not needing an area code in the telephone number, and so on. See the on-line help for details on how to check kernel messages.

At this point you can optionally click on the SetupTCP icon in the group box and further configure SuperHighway Access for Windows and its associated applications. Of particular interest might be the Internet Provider icon in the setup column — you can click on this to make any changes to your provider selection, modem selection, and so on This configuration dialog is also where you edit the scripts that control your modem's behavior. Refer to the on-line help for a detailed discussion of modem script configuration.

Should you experience difficulties during the installation procedure, you may need to uninstall SuperHighway Access for Windows. If a module does not properly install, you can uninstall the module and then reinstall it.

Files and Directories Used by SuperHighway Access

This section describes the configuration files and paths used by SuperHighway Access for Windows.

In your AUTOEXEC.BAT file, the following lines and all lines contained between them:

```
REM Frontier Begin Modifications
...
REM Frontier End Modifications
```

In your WIN.INI file, located in your Windows directory, the entire section labelled:

```
[FRONTIER TECHNOLOGIES CORPORATION]
```

This section is located near the end of your WIN.INI file.

In the main Windows directory, C:\WINDOWS:

All *.FTC files.

All SUPERTCP.* files.

All FTC*.* files

All files in the C:\SUPERTCP directory (including its subdirectories and their files.

Setup Window

You can modify the services provider, modem, connection protocol, and user settings that you defined during installation by clicking on the SetupTCP icon in the SuperHighway Access group box. When the Setup dialog box appears, you are at the Internet Providers window. Table 2-1 describes the SuperHighway Access settings.

Table 2-1	Setup options
Options	*Description*
Select your Provider	Enter a new Internet Services Provider name in this field, or select one from the drop-down list provided. To add a new provider to the list, select Add a new provider and enter a text description and the data (that is, modem) phone number.
Modem Setup	Select a COM port from the drop-down list provided.
	Select a baud rate from the drop-down list provided.
	Check the flow control box to specify hardware flow control. Uncheck it to use no flow control. (XON/XOFF Flow Control cannot be used.)
Options	*Description*
Login Setup	Enter the user name assigned to you by the Internet Services Provider.
	Enter the password assigned to you by the Internet Services Provider. If a password is not assigned to you, you can ignore this field.
	Click the Advanced button to access the Advanced parameter setup dialog box, described in the following section.

Advanced SuperHighway Access Setup Window

Table 2-2 describes the options you can set through the advanced SuperHighway Access Setup Window.

Table 2-2	Advanced SuperHighway Access Setup Options.
Option	**Description**
Select your Provider	Enter a new Internet Services Provider name in this field, or select one from the drop-down list provided. To add a new provider to the list, select Add a new provider and enter a text description and the data (that is, modem) phone number.
Data Phone Number	This field displays the provider's actual modem phone number.
Modem Setup	Select a COM port from the drop-down list provided.
	Select a baud rate from the drop-down list provided.
	Check the Flow Control box to specify hardware flow control. Uncheck it to use no flow control.
Auto Redial	Check this box to enable your modem to auto-redial. Auto-redialing is the capability to keep dialing a remote modem automatically until connection is made (for example, in the event that connection is not made due to a busy signal).
Edit	Click this button to access the Script Selector dialog. From this screen you can create, edit, or delete modem scripts. For more information, see the on-line help.
Modem list	Select your modem from the list displayed. If your modem is not included in this list, select Other. The installation process then initializes the modem for you. Selecting Other still initializes your modem but does not take advantage of any special capabilities your modem may have.
Login Setup	Enter the user name assigned to you by the Internet Services Provider.
Password	Enter the password assigned to you by the Internet Services Provider. If a password is not assigned to you, you can ignore this field.
Prompt for Password	Check this box to be prompted for a password as soon as your modem receives a password prompt from the remote system. Otherwise, the value you have placed in the Password field in the Setup Provider dialog is used.
Protocol	Check the SLIP box if you are using the SLIP protocol.
	Check the CSLIP box if you are using the Compressed SLIP protocol.
	Check the PPP box if you are using the PPP protocol.
Setup	Click this button to access setup dialog boxes for the driver type you have selected. For the SLIP and CSLIP types, you can specify the packet size. Enter the packet size you wish to use, or click the Default button to use the default SLIP/CSLIP packet size (1006). For the PPP type, choose from the following:
LCP Options	LCP Configuration Options allow modifications to the standard characteristics of a point-to-point link to be negotiated. Click this button to modify.
Authentication	On some links, it may be desirable to require a peer to authenticate itself before allowing network-layer protocol packets to be exchanged.

(continued)

Table 2-2 *(continued)*

Option	*Description*
User ID	Specifies the PAP (PPP Authentication Protocol) user ID of the PPP user at the local end. This character string will be passed to the remote for authentication purposes.
User Password	Specifies the PAP password of the PPP user named above. This character string will be passed along with the User ID to the remote for authentication purposes.
Field Compression Settings	Check the Protocol Field box to enable negotiation of compressed Data Link Layer Protocol fields.
	Check the Address and Control Fields box to enable negotiation of compressed Data Link Layer Address and Control fields. Because these fields have constant values, they are easily compressed.
Maximum Receive Unit	This option provides a way to negotiate the Maximum Transfer Unit size on each end of the link. If the MRU of the remote side is less than the MTU on the local side, then the MTU will be equal to the MRU of the remote side. (Note that the Maximum Receive Unit covers only the Data Link Layer Information field; it does not include the header, padding, FCS, nor any transparency bits or bytes.)
Asynch Control Character Map	Provides a way to negotiate the use of control character mapping. By default, PPP maps all control characters into an appropriate two-character sequence. However, it is rarely necessary to map all control characters, and often unnecessary to map any characters. The Asynch Control Characters field is used to inform the peer which control characters must remain mapped. To enable mapping for a character, enter the hexadecimal equivalent of the character's ASCII value.
Counters and Timers	Click this button to configure the following:
	Maximum Retry Counts.
	Configure Request, which specifies the maximum number of consecutive Configure Requests sent to the peer without an appropriate reply. An error is returned when the specified number is reached. Configure Requests are used to open an LCP connection.
	Terminate Request, which specifies the maximum number of consecutive Terminate Requests sent to the peer without an appropriate reply. An error is returned when the specified number is reached. Terminate Requests are used to close an LCP connection.
	Configure NAK, which specifies the maximum number of consecutive Configure NAKs sent to the peer without an appropriate reply. An error is returned when this number is reached. Configure NAKs indicate that an LCP option is not acknowledged.

Table 2-2 *(continued)*	
Option	**Description**
Counters and Timers *(continued)*	Restart Timer (Msec), which specifies the time (in milliseconds) that a PPP line should be allowed to be blocked. The Restart Timer is used to time transmissions of Configure Request and Terminate Request packets. Expiration causes a timeout and retransmission of the corresponding packet. The Restart Timer should not be set lower than two times the round-trip time of the network (which is shown when a ping is performed between two systems).
Network Address settings	
DNS Name Server	The IP Address of the host used for address resolution using the Domain Name System Protocols. If you do not have a Domain Name Server or do not know its address, use 0.0.0.0.
Default Gateway	Your Gateway is the IP Address of the nearest Internet Route Gate. The Internet Route Gate is the host used to get to network addresses not on your local network — that is, all hosts that are not directly connected. This address is used by the Internet Protocol when the route of a packet is unknown.
Local IP	Click this radio button and enter the IP Address assigned to you by the Internet Services Provider. If an IP Address is not assigned to you, select BOOTP or Dynamic.
BOOTP	Click this radio button to implement the BOOTP protocol. BOOTP obtains the IP address, subnet mask, and a default gateway address from the Bootp server's boot files.
Dynamic	Click this radio button if the server you are connecting to will assign you an IP address *at connect time* (as opposed to being preassigned an IP address by your chosen Internet Services Provider).
IP Mask	The IP Address Mask is a four-part number, in the same format as the IP address. Retain the default value assigned by SetupTCP unless you need to define a SubNetwork Mask. If you have selected Bootp as the IP Address Type, the IP Address Mask supplied by the Bootp Server will take precedence.
Go Back	Click this button to return to the Internet Providers main dialog box.
Connection	Click this button to access the Connection Setup dialog. Here, you can configure *Dial On Demand* — Check this box to make the dial-up connection as soon as any application attempts to use the connection. If left unchecked, the dial-up connection is made as soon as Master Services or other applications start. *Inactivity Timeout* — This parameter specifies the number of minutes after which an inactive (that is, no transmitting or receiving) interface will be shut down. The parameter is active *only* if Dial on Demand has been checked. The value can range from 1 to 32,767 minutes; if you enter 0, the line will *not* be shut down.

WinTapestry

WinTapestry is a powerful package designed specifically for the personal dial-up Internet user. Derived from Frontier Technologies' award winning *SuperTCP/NFS for Windows* networking software, WinTapestry offers the popular World Wide Web (WWW) and Gopher Internet tools to assist the user in accessing the wealth of Internet information services. The World Wide Web is an information retrieval tool based on *hypertext* links. Hypertext is text that is linked in a "web" of associations. This web is nonsequentially oriented, thus allowing you to browse related information without regard to the order (or even location) in which the information is actually stored. Gopher is a hierarchical (similar to Windows File Manager) browser to access information from the numerous Gopher servers on the Internet (several Gopher server locations are included). Other search tools, such as Archie, Veronica, and Jughead, are available from Gopher servers to which you can connect. In addition, all these tools may be employed concurrently — *WinTapestry* supports up to 30 sessions at a time.

Getting started

Following are some specific examples based on the Internet Organizer file provided with WinTapestry. The examples, using real bookmarks, servers, Gopher items, and World Wide Web searches, are designed to demonstrate

- How to perform a World Wide Web search.
- How to connect to a server and read a text file.
- How to download an image file to your computer.
- How to launch a telnet session to connect directly to a remote host.

Unless you are an experienced Internet/Gopher user, we recommend you follow the examples step by step on your own computer.

Before you launch *WinTapestry*, there are a couple of important terms to review — specifically, bookmark and Gopher.

A *bookmark* is a description of how to retrieve a Gopher item. Bookmarks contain the features listed in Table 2-3.

Table 2-3	Tapestry Bookmark Feature
Feature	*Description*
Descriptor	A description of the bookmark.
Hostname	The host on which the item is stored.

Table 2-3 *(continued)*

Feature	Description
Port	The port needed by the network software. Usually, you can leave this blank because standard ports are used in the various search tools. If you are manually adding a site (bookmark), you may need to enter a nonstandard port number.
Selector	The selector or the protocol used to retrieve the item, that is, Gopher, WWW, and so on.
Type	Gopher item type. This may be a menu (directory), text file, image file, telnet session, and so on.
Gopher+ check box	Indicates whether the server understands Gopher+. This is a display item only.
ASK+ check box	Indicates whether the item is actually a Gopher+ ASK block. This is a display item only.

WinTapestry allows you to add, modify, delete, and categorize bookmarks.

In general, an *item* is an object to be retrieved or launched from a Gopher, CSO, or WWW window. This includes text files, image, audio and other binary files, indexed searches of remote databases, telnet sessions, and so on.

Examples

Double-click on the WinTapestry icon in the SuperTCP group box. The Internet Organizer tab control window now appears. The tabs along the top of this window list the bookmark categories contained in this bookmark file.

Performing a search via the World Wide Web

This example demonstrates how to connect to a World Wide Web (WWW) server to search for and retrieve information. Using a previously defined WWW bookmark, you will browse through information from the National Center for Supercomputing Applications WWW server regarding information resources for teachers. For this example, let us assume you are a science teacher doing a unit on earthquakes.

1. Open the Internet Organizer window as described in the preceding section.

2. Select the Home Pages (WWW Sites) tab and click the left mouse button.

3. Click twice on the NCSA item.

4. When the NCSA Home Page appears, page down until you see the NCSA General Information section and then click once on that icon (or the associated hypertext).

5. When the General Information window appears, page down and click once on the Education Program text.

6. When the Education Program window appears, page down and click once on the Internet Resources for the K-12 Classroom text.

7. When the Internet Resources window appears, you have a selection of topics available for browsing and downloading. Page down and click once on the Earthquakes text.

8. Similarly, next click once on the Earthquake Statistics text and The Ten Largest Earthquakes in the United States text. This file now downloads to your computer. At this point, you can click the Save As button in the button bar to save this file to disk.

9. Notice that the forward and backward arrow buttons have become active. As you have proceeded, you have been building a list of documents representing each window or actual file we have been viewing. The arrow buttons allow you to jump backward and forward in this document list. The advantage to this ability is that you can now back up (or jump ahead) to a point where you have several options to click on, and can thus start an entirely different search without needing to return to the top of the document list.

10. You can exit this WWW search by either repeatedly clicking the backward arrow button or clicking the Close Window button.

Accessing a Gopher server and reading a text file

In this example, the text file to be accessed is a description of the on-line services available to Internet users on the Library of Congress Information System (LOCIS).

1. Select the Interesting Places tab and click the left mouse button. Below the tabs, the window displays all the bookmarks associated with this category.

2. Select the Library of Congress (LC Marvel) bookmark from the bookmark list and double-click on it. A Gopher search window opens in front of the Internet Organizer window. WinTapestry now connects to the gopher server and expands the gopher tree; that is, displays *child nodes* analogous to subdirectory listings in Windows File Manager.

The Status Bar at the bottom of your window displays the status of WinTapestry's attempts to connect to the server defined in the bookmark you have selected. You will see a message similar to *[Server name]: Connecting to Server...* and *Awaiting response from Server*. If WinTapestry has difficulty resolving a host name, attempting to connect again usually resolves the problem. When a connection has been made, the status bar displays *Done!* You may also click the Abort button at any time to halt the connection attempt.

3. Double-click on the Library of Congress On-line Systems node. The Gopher tree expands again, this time displaying Gopher items on the right side of the window.

4. On the right side of the window, double-click on the Overview item. Note that the item is represented by the Text File bitmap. WinTapestry connects to the server again and retrieves the file to your window for reading. As it does so, the status bar displays a running total of the number of bytes retrieved. After the entire file has been retrieved, you can save the file to your own disk, search the file for a particular text string, and copy the file to the Windows Clipboard for pasting into another document. You can also print the file to your local printer.

Accessing a Gopher server and downloading an image file

In this example, the file to be downloaded is a satellite-generated weather image of the entire United States.

1. Open the Internet Organizer window as described in the beginning of this section in the paragraph following "Examples."

2. Click on the Weather & Time tab.

3. Double-click on the Weather Machine (from the University of Illinois) bookmark.

4. On the left side of the Internet Organizer Window, double-click on the Images node. The Gopher tree expands into several child nodes.

5. Double-click on the Satellite Images child node. The Gopher tree expands further.

6. Double-click on the Satellite USVIS child node. The right side of the Internet Organizer window now displays the individual Gopher items (in this case, represented by the Image file bitmap).

7. Double-click on the 00LATEST.GIF Gopher item to begin downloading the Image file. As the download progresses, the status bar displays a running total of how many bytes have been received. When the download is complete, you can view the file or save it to disk for later viewing.

Accessing a Gopher server and running a telnet session

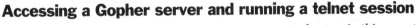

This example demonstrates how to connect to a remote host — in this case, the Library of Congress Information System (LOCIS). When you click on the telnet Gopher item bitmap (step 5 below), the telnet application is invoked.

1. Open the Internet Organizer window as described in the beginning of this section under "Examples."

2. Select the Interesting Places tab and click the left mouse button.

3. Select the Library of Congress (LC Marvel) bookmark from the bookmark list and double-click on it. A Gopher search window opens in front of the Internet Organizer window. WinTapestry now connects to the Gopher server and expands the Gopher tree, displaying child nodes analogous to subdirectory listings in Windows File Manager.

   The status bar at the bottom of your window displays the status of WinTapestry's attempts to connect to the server defined in the bookmark you have selected. You will see a message similar to *[Server name]: Connecting to Server...* and *Awaiting response from Server.* If WinTapestry has difficulty resolving a host name, attempting to connect again usually resolves the problem. When a connection has been made, the Status Bar displays *Done!* You may also click the Abort button at any time to halt the connection attempt.

4. Double-click on the Library of Congress On-line Systems node. The Gopher tree expands again, this time displaying Gopher items on the right side of the window.

5. On the right side of the Internet Organizer window, double-click on the Connect to LOCIS (Public Users - No Password Needed) Gopher item. Note that this Gopher item is represented by the telnet bitmap. WinTapestry now invokes the telnet application, connecting to and allowing you to log into the remote host LOCIS.

Master Services Messages

Master Services is used to control and monitor the activities of all the active network Protocol Servers through a single, efficient interface. Depending on the modules you choose to install, background services controlled by Master Services may include SMTP and POP. Master Services is installed automatically.

Master Services may log as many as 80 lines of information messages. These messages may come from Master Services or any of the active, upper-level Protocol Servers. Messages are of several distinct types and may be filtered and/or logged to a file for debugging or auditing purposes. The following list indicates what the various message numbers generally indicate:

0000-0999	Debugging Messages
1000-1999	Fatal Errors
2000-2999	Non-Fatal Errors
4000-4999	Warnings
5000-5999	General Information

For example, when Master Services is started, it logs a message similar to the following, to indicate initialization time:

```
MSRV5003: Master-Services start up at Mon June 7 15:35:00
1993.
```

For a complete description of Master Services Messages and suggested corrective actions, see the on-line help.

Login

SuperHighway Access for Windows Login allows a user to login and out globally from restricted applications, such as e-mail and the News Reader. Logging out or closing Login will log you out from all user name-associated applications that were started after you globally logged in. Except for these applications, login is not required.

Optional settings provide notification to the user who is currently logged in when new mail arrives. If mail arrives while the user is logged in, the Login program may be set to notify the user by beeping, by showing a mail carrier on the Login icon, or by pop-up notification. Login also allows users to change their passwords. The Change Password feature is described below. Note that the Login module is required.

If there is only one user (other than SYSADMIN), the system is considered single-user and you don't need to enter a user name. For validation purposes, you can add a password to the account.

For more information about the features and functions of Login, see the on-line help.

Change password

Passwords may consist of up to 32 uppercase or lowercase characters, including punctuation. Passwords *are* case sensitive. If you forget your password, contact your system administrator. This password is independent of the password that may have been supplied to you by your Internet Services provider. Figure 2-2 shows the Change Password dialog box.

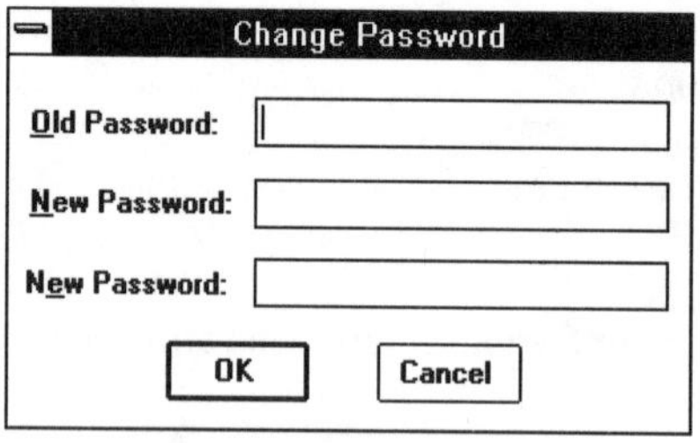

Figure 2-2: Change Password dialog box.

Old password

Enter the same password you entered when you logged in. This step is a precaution against unauthorized access.

New password

Enter the new password twice. The second field is used to verify that no typing errors were made in the first.

For a detailed discussion of user issues such as disk access, signature, and so on, refer to the on-line help.

File Transfer with FTP Client

The SuperHighway Access for Windows File Transfer module allows you to send and receive files between your machine and a remote host using the File Transfer Protocol (FTP). The File Transfer modules allow you to access the file management system of a remote host through convenient Windows interfaces. Further, you can run the FTP independently of the WinTapestry application or in conjunction with it.

The client File Transfer module allows you to send and receive files between your machine and a remote host using the File Transfer Protocol (FTP).

Connecting to a remote host

Use the following steps to connect to a remote host via FTP:

1. Double-click on the FTP icon. The FTP Connect dialog box will appear.

2. In the Hostname field of the Connect dialog box, enter the name of the remote host to which you wish to connect; then either click OK or proceed to specify a profile. If the name you enter is not valid, the error message *Unknown Host* will be displayed — click OK and enter a valid name. If the error message *Cannot Connect* is displayed, the name you have entered is valid but your FTP Client is unable to connect to the remote FTP server — the remote machine may be down or may have its FTP server disabled.

3. Select a profile from the listbox provided or accept the Default profile by clicking OK or by moving on to the Port specification. The Default profile contains factory default settings, and always takes effect if no other profile is selected. If the profile you select has a host name or port number associated with it that *differs* from the host name or port number you have manually entered, your choices are overridden by those of the profile. For more detailed information on profiles, see the on-line help.

4. Enter a port number (up to a maximum value of 65,535) or click OK to accept the default port number.

5. Next, the dialog box in Figure 2-3 will appear; you will be prompted to login by entering a user name and then a password for an account on the remote host. Your access to the remote file system may be limited depending on the account you have specified. If you enter an invalid user name or password, the error message *Login Failed* is displayed.

```
┌─────────────────────────────────────────────┐
│ ═         Connection Information             │
├─────────────────────────────────────────────┤
│                                              │
│   Hostname:    ┌──────────────────────────┐  │
│                │ bbs                      │  │
│                └──────────────────────────┘  │
│   Username:    ┌──────────────────────────┐  │
│                │ tim                      │  │
│                └──────────────────────────┘  │
│   Password:    ┌──────────────────────────┐  │
│                │ ·······                  │  │
│                └──────────────────────────┘  │
│   Startup      ┌──────────────────────────┐  │
│   Directory:   │ c:\system                │  │
│                └──────────────────────────┘  │
│                ☒ Always Prompt               │
│                                              │
│   ┌─────────┐  ┌─────────┐  ┌─────────┐      │
│   │   OK    │  │ Cancel  │  │  Help   │      │
│   └─────────┘  └─────────┘  └─────────┘      │
└─────────────────────────────────────────────┘
```

Figure 2-3: FTP Login to Remote Host dialog.

When you are logged in, the List View window opens (Figure 2-4), displaying local and remote file systems. The FTP title bar displays your account name on the remote host, identifying the FTP session in case of multiple sessions. If a named profile is in use, the title bar will display the profile name rather than the account name. To initiate another session, iconize the FTP application and repeat the preceding steps.

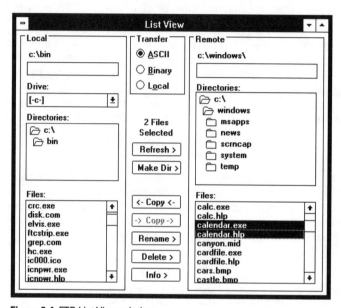

Figure 2-4: FTP List View window.

Copying files to the remote

To copy one or more files from your PC to the remote host, use the following steps:

1. In the remote Directory listbox, double-click on the directory to which you wish to copy the local file(s). The current remote directory will be the target directory for the file transfer.

2. In the local Files listbox, click on the local file(s) you wish to transfer. The Copy button will be enabled.

3. If you wish the selected file to have a new name on the remote, type the new name in the remote Edit field. If you specify a remote name, only one local

file may be selected for transfer. If no remote name is specified, the local name will be used by default.

4. Select the appropriate File Type for the file(s) you wish to transfer. You may select from ASCII, Binary, or Local file types.

5. Click the Copy button. The selected file(s) will be copied to the remote directory you have selected.

Copying files to your PC

To copy one or more files from the remote host to your PC, use the following steps:

1. In the local Directory listbox, double-click on the directory to which you wish to copy the remote file(s). The current local directory will be the target directory for the file transfer.

2. In the remote Files listbox, click on the remote file(s) you wish to transfer. The Copy button will be enabled.

3. If you wish to give the selected file a new name on your PC, type the new name in the local Edit field. If you specify a local name, only one remote file may be selected for transfer. Note that the local name must be a valid DOS filename. If no local name is specified, the remote name will be used by default.

4. Select the appropriate File Type for the file(s) you wish to transfer. You may select from ASCII, Binary, or Local file types.

5. Click the <- Copy <- button. The selected file(s) will be copied to the local directory you have selected.

Using drag and drop

You can use the drag and drop feature to select and copy single files or groups of files from one directory to another. Use the following steps:

1. Select a file or group of files in the local or remote files list.

2. Click on one of the selected files, and while holding the mouse button down, move the cursor to the target window. The cursor will change shape to indicate where the files may be dropped.

3. When the cursor is over the desired target, release the mouse button. Files may be dropped onto the files list (they will be copied to the current directory) or may be dropped into a specific directory in the directory list.

Terminal Emulation

SuperHighway Access for Windows offers terminal emulation capabilities for connecting your PC to remote hosts supporting the VT or tn3270 series of terminals, as well as "generic" TTY devices. Further, the Telnet Redirector module allows you to reconfigure your PC's COM ports to function with your favorite Windows-based communications program. You can remap your PC's keyboard to more closely match the VT and tn3270 keyboards, and you can select fonts, screen colors, and column widths. All three of the modules described below can be optionally installed using the Custom Installation procedure; if you select the Default Installation, all three modules are installed automatically.

VT100

SuperHighway Access for Windows VT100 allows you to logon to a remote host via the telnet protocol and process commands as if you were at a directly connected terminal. VT100 provides VT terminal emulation so that communication and presentation of data are made in an understandable manner (both for you and the remote host). VT100 provides emulation of VT100 (7-bit and 8-bit mode) terminals and standard TTY devices.

The VT100 button bar (toggled by Window⇨Show Button Bar) provides fast access to the most frequently used functions. The buttons are as follows:

Connect
Disconnect
Color Selection
Font Selection
FTC Font Selection
Auto Scale Fonts
Print
Continuous Print
Log
Continuous Log
Auto Scroll On
Auto Scroll Off
Exit VT100

Connecting to a remote host

Use the following steps to connect to a remote host via VT100:

1. Double-click on the VT100 icon. The Connect dialog box will appear. In the Hostname field of the Connect dialog box, enter the name of the remote host to which you wish to connect, then either click OK or proceed to specify a profile. If the name you enter is not valid, the error message *Unknown Host* will be displayed — click OK and enter a valid name. If the error message *Cannot Connect* is displayed, the name you have entered is valid but your FTP client is unable to connect to the remote FTP server — the remote machine may be down or may have its FTP server disabled.

2. Select a profile from the listbox provided or accept the Default profile by clicking OK or by moving on to the Port specification. The Default profile contains "factory settings," and always takes effect if no other profile is selected. If the profile you select has a host name or port number associated with it that differs from the hostname or port number you have manually entered, your choices will be overridden by those of the profile. For more detailed information on profiles, see the on-line help.

3. Enter a port number (up to a maximum value of 65,535) or click OK to accept the default port number.

4. When you have connected to a remote host, you will be prompted to login by entering a user name and then a password for an account on the remote host. Your access to the remote host may be limited depending on the account you have specified. If you enter an invalid user name or password, the error message *Login Failed* will be displayed.

5. Now that you have established a connection to the remote machine, you may enter commands as if you were sitting at a terminal directly connected to the remote. The VT100 title bar displays the name of the remote host in case of multiple sessions. Multiple sessions may be initiated and may use different emulations. To initiate another session, minimize the VT100 application and repeat steps 1 through 4 above.

Changing the emulation type

By default, VT100 uses VT100 (7-bit, non-DEC) terminal emulation. You may select another emulation type. To select a VT emulation type, use Terminal Params on the Preferences menu. You may also select an ID used to inform the remote host of the capabilities of your terminal. Available IDs are VT100, VT101, and VT102.

Using command-line parameters

If you frequently need to run VT100 with the same default parameters, you may create different profiles for various remote hosts, specifying different default parameters for each host. For details, see the on-line help.

Exiting VT100

Before exiting VT100, make sure you properly logoff the remote machine by issuing the appropriate logoff command for the remote. Exiting VT100 will only close the connection to the remote host — it will not log you off. Most remote systems will log you off when a connection is terminated, but this may not hold for all systems. Follow the correct logoff procedure before closing the connection using File⇨Exit. If you are still connected to the remote, you will be asked for confirmation. In addition, you will be prompted to save any configuration changes you may have made during the session to the loaded profile.

For more information about VT100's features and functions, see the on-line help.

Electronic Mail

SuperHighway Access for Windows Electronic Mail allows you to create, send, and read electronic mail messages. SuperHighway Access for Windows is the first Microsoft Windows SMTP mail application to support MIME (Multipurpose Internet Mail Extension) file attachments, which allow you to attach a variety of special files to your messages. Special files may include spreadsheet files, database files, and even digital audio and video files. The e-mail module can be optionally installed using the Custom Installation procedure; if you select the Default Installation, e-mail is installed automatically.

To start e-mail, double-click on its icon. If you have not already logged in using the Login program (described on the previous page), you will be prompted to enter your user name and password. The title bar of the main e-mail window displays the name of the currently logged-in user. The e-mail button bar provides fast access to the most frequently used functions:

Compose Message
New Mail
Open Inbox
Open Outbox
Open Mail Folder
Reply-To
Reply-To All
Forward
Move
Delete
Print Message
Exit E-mail

Creating and sending a mail message

Use the following steps to create and send a mail message:

1. Click the Compose Message button from the button bar or select New from the Message menu. A Compose window appears (Figure 2-5).

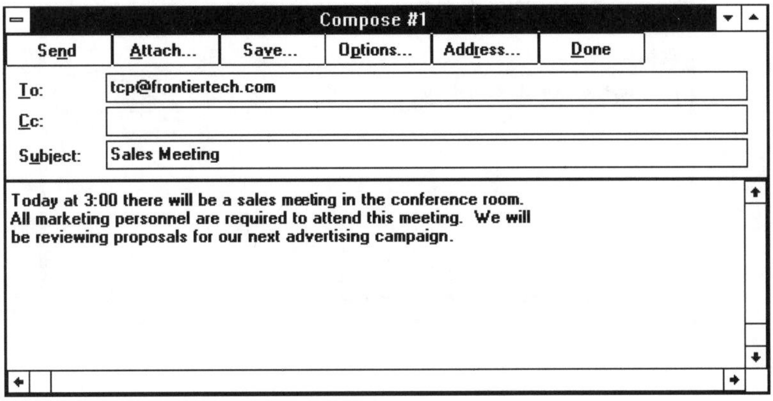

```
┌─────────────────────────────────────────────────────────────────┐
│ ─                        Compose #1                        ▼ ▲   │
├──────┬─────────┬───────┬──────────┬──────────┬─────────┬─────────┤
│ Send │ Attach… │ Save… │ Options… │ Address… │  Done   │         │
├──────┴─────────┴───────┴──────────┴──────────┴─────────┴─────────┤
│ To:     ┌──────────────────────────────────────────────────────┐│
│         │ tcp@frontiertech.com                                 ││
│ Cc:     ├──────────────────────────────────────────────────────┤│
│         │                                                      ││
│ Subject:├──────────────────────────────────────────────────────┤│
│         │ Sales Meeting                                        ││
│         └──────────────────────────────────────────────────────┘│
│ Today at 3:00 there will be a sales meeting in the conference room. │
│ All marketing personnel are required to attend this meeting. We will │
│ be reviewing proposals for our next advertising campaign.        │
│                                                                  │
└─────────────────────────────────────────────────────────────────┘
```

Figure 2-5: E-mail composition window.

2. To address a mail message, type an alias (an alias can be the name or the Internet address of the recipient if you do not want to create an alias for this recipient) into the To and/or CC fields. Use commas to separate multiple recipients. At least one alias must be entered in the To/CC fields in order to send a mail message. To avoid typing frequently used aliases, you can place an alias in an address book, or make an alias temporary and use it only for this message. To choose an existing alias from an address book, click the Address button. If you use the Internet address, remember that a valid Internet address is in the format *user-id@hostname*. For example:

Bill@Company.COM

3. In the Subject field of the Compose window, enter a brief description of the message you are sending.

4. In the Message area at the bottom of the Compose window, type the body of your message. You can also use the Windows Clipboard to copy and paste text created in another application.

5. If you wish to attach one or more files to your message, click the Attach button. A dialog box (Figure 2-6) will appear allowing you to specify a file by clicking the Add button. Note that the recipients of your message need to possess the program associated with the attached file in order to be able to access it. See the section later in this chapter on using MIME file attachments for more details.

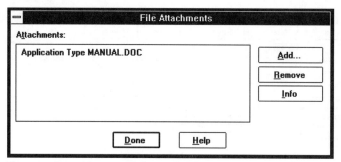

Figure 2-6: E- mail File Attachments dialog box for attaching files.

6. To specify message options such as additional addressing information, deferred delivery, or message expiration, click the Options button. The Message Options dialog box will appear.

7. To send your message to the address(es) specified in the Recipient List, click the Send button. You will be asked to verify that you want to send the message. If you used an unrecognized alias (that is, e-mail could not locate the alias in any existing address book), you will have the option at this time of adding the alias to your personal address book or creating a temporary alias with the QuickAlias feature. For more information on the QuickAlias feature, please see the on-line help.

The Outbox is used to store your outgoing mail messages until they are delivered, at which time the message will be placed in the Sent Mail folder.

Viewing mail messages

When someone sends you mail, the message is stored in your Inbox. If you are globally logged in, the Login program will notify you of the arrival of new mail sent to you by beeping and showing a new mail indication on the Login icon. If you receive new mail while the e-mail program is iconized on your desktop, the e-mail icon will flash. If you receive new mail while the e-mail program is open, the New Mail button on the button bar will become available and the status bar will flash the message *New Mail*. Clicking the New Mail button or selecting Folder⇨New Mail will display a window listing those folders containing new mail messages. Select a folder to open it and display the messages.

1. Open the mail folder in which the message is currently stored. To open a mail folder, click the Mail Folder button or select Folder⇨Open and choose the mail folder. The Inbox and Outbox may be opened using the Inbox and Outbox buttons or by selecting Folder⇨Inbox and Folder⇨Outbox.

2. From the list of messages, double click on any entry (or click the View button) to view that message. Multiple messages are selected for view by dragging the mouse then clicking the View button.

3. To view any files attached to the message, click the Attachments button. The File Attachments dialog box opens (Figure 2-7). To run an attached file, select the file from the Attachments listbox and click the Run button. Note that you need to possess the program associated with the attached file in order to be able to run it. For details on using MIME file attachments, see the next section.

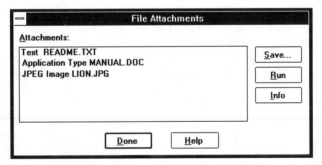

Figure 2-7: E-mail File Attachments dialog box for viewing received files.

MIME file attachments

SuperHighway Access for Windows is the first TCP/IP SMTP mail application to support MIME (Multipurpose Internet Mail Extension) file attachments. MIME support allows you to send and receive mail messages with attached files. Any type of files may be attached, including ASCII text files, PostScript files, spreadsheet files, database files, word processor files, graphic files, audio files, and digital video files.

When you are composing a mail message, you may click the Attach button in the Compose window to attach one or more files to the message.

The Attachments listbox displays all files currently selected to be attached to the message. To attach a file, click the Add button. You will be prompted to specify a file. You may provide your recipient(s) with a textual description of a specified attachment by clicking the Info button. The Description field can be used to identify the program necessary for your recipient to run the file. The Type Description is used only when it is necessary to override the default file type with a MIME-specific file type. Do not override the default type unless you are certain that the file is of a MIME-specific file type.

When you are reading a mail message with MIME file attachments, you may click the Attachments button in the Message window to view any of the attached files.

The Attachments listbox displays all files currently attached to the message. The filename will be preceded by a MIME-specific type and followed by any description provided by the sender.

You may save a specified file attachment by clicking the Save button. You will be prompted for the filename and location. To run a specified attachment, click the Run button. Attached files may be run directly, without closing the e-mail application (as shown in Figure 2-8); note that you need to possess the programs associated with the attached file in order to run it. To create a file association, use File⇨Associate in Windows File Manager. For information on the attached file's name, type, and so on, click the Info button to access the Attachment Info dialog.

For more information about e-mail features and functions, refer to the on-line help.

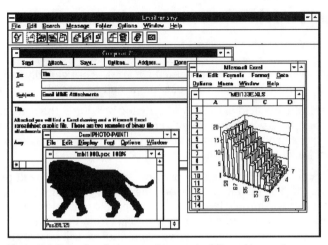

Figure 2-8: Example window running attached files with e-mail open.

Network News Reader

The Network News Reader provides the simplest and most efficient means of accessing the thousands of news and information databases available through the Internet News System. The Network News Reader is based on the NNTP (Network News Transport Protocol) and provides client access to NNTP Servers which are available from almost all universities and computer centers. The News Reader is the first product to allow users to access network news from the Windows desktop. You can connect to an NNTP server, subscribe to any newsgroups available on that server, and read, download, and post articles. The News Reader can be optionally installed using the Custom Installation procedure; if you select the Default Installation, the News Reader is installed automatically.

The Internet News System is a set of bulletins, discussion groups, program sources, and other items of information distributed around the world under the name *Usenet.* The information is commonly called *news* and is divided into *newsgroups.* Each newsgroup deals with a particular topic or set of topics. The topics for newsgroups range from discussions about versions of UNIX to movie reviews or comments on current social or political issues.

Connecting to an NNTP server

Use the following steps to connect to an NNTP Server:

1. Double-click on the News Reader icon. If you are not globally logged in, you will be prompted to enter your user name and password.

2. In the Hostname field of the Connect dialog box, enter the name of the NNTP Server to which you wish to connect; then either click OK or proceed to specify a profile. If the name you enter is not valid or if a connection cannot be made, an error message will be displayed.

3. Select a profile from the listbox provided or accept the Default profile by clicking OK. The Default profile contains "factory settings," and always takes effect if no other profile is selected. If the profile you select has a host name or port number associated with it that *differs* from the host name or port number you have manually entered, your choices will be overridden by those of the profile. For more detailed information on profiles, see the on-line help for this topic.

4. The News Reader now connects to the selected NNTP Server. During this Initialization phase, the News Reader creates a list of the available newsgroups on the selected NNTP Server. The status bar at the bottom of your screen will display the message *Updating Available Newsgroups:nnnn*, where *nnnn* is a running counter of available newsgroups. Because thousands of newsgroups may be available, it may take many minutes to create this list. Provided you subscribe to at least one newsgroup during your first connection to this server, subsequent sessions will initialize much more quickly. Faster connections to the NNTP Server are also facilitated by checking the Quick Start checkbox — the Server will forego displaying the number of articles in each newsgroup.

5. When initialization is complete, a Subscription List window will appear with the title bar displaying the Internet name/address of the NNTP Server. The Subscription List window lists the newsgroups to which you are currently subscribing. If you are running the News Reader for the first time or if you are not currently subscribing to any newsgroups, the Newsgroup Subscription dialog box opens, allowing you to select one or more newsgroups to which you wish to subscribe. See "Subscribing to newsgroups" on the next page for details.

Using the button bar

The News Reader button bar provides fast access to the most frequently used menu commands (shown below in parentheses).

Connect	(Connect⇨Connect)
Disconnect	(Connect⇨Abort)
Subscribe	(Groups⇨Subscribe)
Unsubscribe	(Groups⇨Unsubscribe)
Read Newsgroup	(Groups⇨Read)
View News Article	(Article⇨View)
Post News Article	(Article⇨Post)
Print News Article	(File⇨Print)
Exit the Application	(File⇨Exit)

Subscribing to newsgroups

In order to give users easy access to the information they want, the Internet news system groups articles by topic. A newsgroup contains a set of articles on a given topic. The first time you use the News Reader, you will need to subscribe to one or more newsgroups before you can view news articles. Use the following steps to subscribe to a newsgroup and gain access to its articles:

1. Select Groups⇨Subscribe or click the Subscribe button on the button bar. The Newsgroup Subscription dialog box (Figure 2-9) will appear, displaying a Root Group listbox and a Newsgroup listbox.

2. Click on any one of the root group names shown in the Root Groups listbox. The Newsgroups listbox will display the newsgroups found within the root group you selected. (The contents of some major root groups are shown in the following list.) Other groups are available on a by-request basis and may not be available from all locations. Users who are not familiar with Usenet are encouraged to subscribe to the news.newusers.questions group.

Name	*Content*
comp	Newsgroups related to computers and source code distribution
news	Newsgroups about Usenet itself
rec	Discussions of various recreational activities

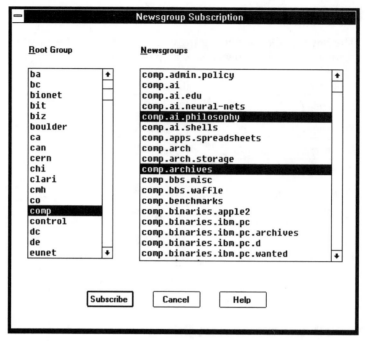

Figure 2-9: Newgroup Subscription dialog box.

sci	Scientific newsgroups
talk	Serious discussions on current social and political issues
soc	Newsgroups oriented toward social interaction
misc	Miscellaneous newsgroups
alt	Alternative culture groups (distributed by request only)

3. Select one or more of the newsgroups shown in the Newsgroups listbox and then click the Subscribe button. The newsgroups you have selected will appear in your Subscription List window (Figure 2-10). For convenience, this subscription information can be automatically retained for subsequent sessions by saving a profile of your configuration parameters (see the on-line help for information about profiles).

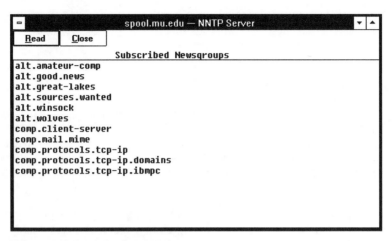

Figure 2-10: Subscription list window.

Unsubscribing from newsgroups

Use the following steps to unsubscribe from a newsgroup:

1. In your Subscription List window, select the newsgroup from which you wish to unsubscribe.

2. Select Unsubscribe from the Groups menu. Click the Unsubscribe button on the button bar. The newsgroup will be removed from your subscription list.

Viewing news articles

To view news articles contained within a newsgroup, follow these steps:

1. In your Subscription List window, double-click on any newsgroup shown. An Articles List window will appear displaying a list of news articles contained within the selected newsgroup. The name of the newsgroup is displayed in the title bar. List entries show the Article Number, Number of Lines, Subject, and Author. Previously read articles normally will not be listed in the Articles List window. To read these articles, select Groups, Read All.

2. To view any of the news articles listed, double click on the news article. A News Article window will appear displaying the text of the article. In the Articles List, a plus (+) sign will appear to the left of the article's list entry to indicate that the article has been viewed.

Note that when you are viewing news articles, the Network News Reader displays a maximum of 200 of the most recent articles in a newsgroup.

Posting your own news articles

Usenet recommends that new users subscribe to a newsgroup for six months prior to posting to that group. Before posting, consider whether your article would be more appropriate as an e-mail message. For example, articles that simply reply "Me too!" should be e-mailed to the originator of the idea rather than posted. Use the following steps to post your own news articles to a newsgroup:

1. Select Post from the Posting menu or click the Post button on the button bar. If you have a news article currently open, you may select Follow Up from the Posting menu to post a reply. A Post window will appear (See Figure 2-11).

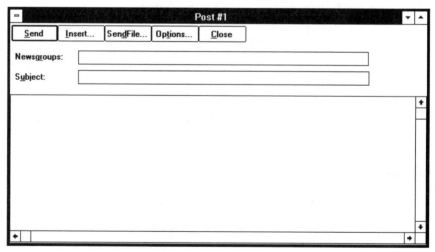

Figure 2-11: Newsgroup Post window.

2. In the Newsgroup field, enter the name of the newsgroup to which you wish to post. In the Subject field, enter a description of the subject of your article. If any newsgroup is currently open or selected, the Newsgroup field will be automatically filled with the name of that newsgroup. If you selected Follow Up on the Posting menu, the Newsgroup field and the Subject field will be automatically filled for your reply.

3. Click the Options button to specify a Distribution level and other header information. A Distribution level specifies the area within which your article will be received by available NNTP Servers. The default distribution is world, which is inappropriate for messages with only local interest.

4. Type the body of your message in the Message area at the bottom of the Post window. You may insert an existing text file into the Message area by clicking the Insert button. If you wish to use an existing text file as your message and do not need to modify the file, select Send File; then specify a file by using the Browse button or by entering its full pathname in the Filename field.

5. When you are ready to send your news article, click the Send button. Your article will be posted to the newsgroup.

You may optionally include your full name in the header of your article. Use SetupTCP to access the User Configuration module. For more information on the features and functions of the News Reader, see the on-line help.

Chapter 3
Distinct FTP

The process of file transfer means that files are copied from one machine to another. The Internet suite of protocols includes a File Transfer Protocol (commonly known as FTP) that enables users to log into remote systems, look at the contents of remote directories, copy files to and from the remote system, and carry out some basic management functions such as creating directories. Distinct FTP is a Windows application built on the FTP protocol, providing you with all the FTP functionality from a user-friendly drag-and-drop front end. Distinct FTP is unique in that it displays your remote system in a tree-like fashion, making it easy for you to navigate through notoriously complex systems. For instructions on using Distinct Telnet, please check the CD-ROM.

Starting Distinct FTP

You start Distinct FTP, as you start any other Windows program, by double-clicking its program icon or by selecting the FTP button in the Telnet Quick Menu. You also can start Distinct FTP by selecting the FTP Client button in the Distinct toolbar.

The Distinct FTP program screen is split into two main sections, with each section divided into two parts. The top section enables you to select any directory on your local system that you want to copy to or from, and the lower section enables you to log into any remote host that you have defined in the configuration program and to which you have authorized access. As with all FTP programs, at the start of a Distinct FTP session, you establish a connection to the FTP server by logging into the remote system. Once you have logged in, you may select one or more files or an entire directory that you want to transfer to or from your local system, and you must select the directory to which you want to transfer files.

Logging into the remote system

Logging into remote systems is done via the Host: drop-down list box located about halfway through your program window. To log into a remote host:

1. You must either enter the host name or its IP address in the Hosts pull-down text box or use the pull-down text box to select a previously accessed system. If you enter the machine name, make sure that you have defined it in your local host's table if you are not using Domain Name Service (DNS). With the Distinct TCP/IP protocol stack, you define the local host's table using the commands in the Hosts menu of the Network Configuration program.

   By default, up to ten names or addresses are saved in this list, which is also shared by other Distinct TCP/IP programs. You can increase this number by setting the Global Hosts parameter in the SOCKET.INI file. You can also create a list of machine names just for the FTP program by setting the UseGlobal parameter in the SOCKET.INI file. To create a separate database for each application, set UseGlobal=0; then set Global Hosts to a value between 3 and 50. To delete a host name, you need to select the Connect command from the Action menu. Then select the host name you want to remove and choose the Remove button.

2. Enter the user login name in the User: text box (see Figure 3-1). The name of the last user who logged into the selected system using Distinct FTP from the same PC appears in this field. If you want to log in with a different name, just change the name in this field.

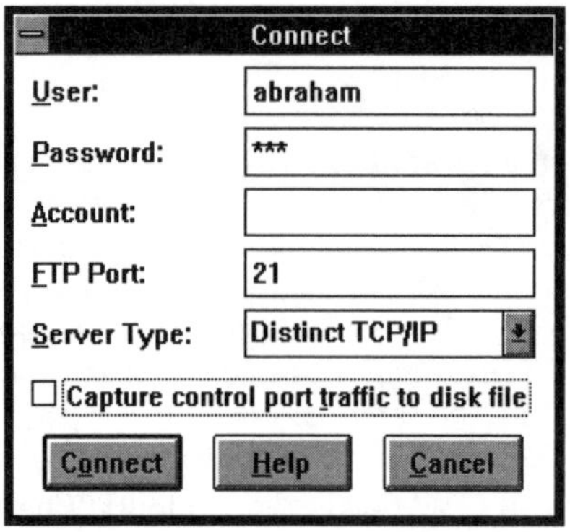

Figure 3-1: The Connect dialog box.

3. Enter your login password in the Password: text box.

4. If your company requires you to specify your account name before executing FTP commands, enter this name in the Account: text box; otherwise, leave this box blank.

5. Distinct FTP allows FTP connections to nonstandard systems that use a port number other than 21 for FTP. If you are trying to connect to one of these systems, you may change the port number in the FTP Port: text box. Most systems do not require modification of the port number.

6. Distinct FTP includes support for several remote types of TCP/IP systems. Use the Server type: pull-down list box to select the type of server you are about to connect to. Although FTP is a standard protocol, its implementation varies on different systems. In order for Distinct to display the remote tree structure correctly, it must know the file and directory structure that the remote FTP server is using. Most remote systems run some version of UNIX. If you want to connect to a VAX or an IBM mainframe, you need to find out which vendor's TCP/IP is running on that system. To choose a system other than UNIX to connect to, pull down the Server Type pull-down menu and select the appropriate system.

7. Select Connect.

 If you are already connected to a remote system with FTP and want to change your connection to a different system, all you have to do is to select the host from the Host: drop-down list box. A message pops up asking you whether you want to disconnect from the current host. Select Yes to connect to the next host.

Moving around

Distinct FTP has two types of menus: the traditional Windows menu bar and a Quick Menu. The Quick Menu is provided in the form of seven colorful buttons below the menu bar that include the name of the command each button executes (see Figure 3-2).

The command descriptions in this chapter assume that you do not disable the button menu by deselecting the Quick Menu option in the Options menu. If you do disable the buttons, the corresponding commands in the Action menu found in the menu bar may be used instead.

The FTP program screen has four main program windows. When you're executing a Rename, Delete, or Make Directory command, you must always make sure that the currently selected window is the one you want to execute the command on.

To move around the FTP program efficiently, we strongly suggest that you use a mouse for most operations. When you're using the keyboard, you can select the current window using the Tab key. You also access the Drive: and Host: drop-down list boxes using the Tab key. Press F4 to pull down the list box; use the up- and down-arrow keys to select the drive or remote host and then press F4 again.

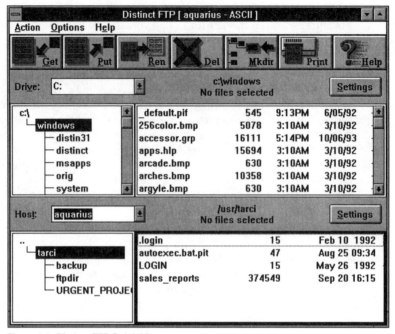

Figure 3-2: Distinct FTP Quick Menu.

You can view the filenames in a long or short format. To do so, check the appropriate option in the Settings dialog box.

To locate a particular file when the directory listing is the current window, all you have to do is type its first letter. Doing so scrolls the window to the first file in the list that starts with that letter.

Disconnecting from a remote system

While you are connected to an FTP server, the Connect command in the Action menu changes to Disconnect. Choosing this command with a single click disconnects FTP from the server. You may also disconnect by selecting the None entry in the Host: pull-down menu.

Using Distinct FTP

Once you have established a connection to your remote host, you can execute any of the commands that are available to you. The seven buttons at the top of the program screen provide you with immediate information on what commands are available. More precisely, you can get files from your remote host to a directory on the local system, put files that are on your local system into a directory on the remote host, put or get an entire directory, rename or delete files and directories on your local or remote system, and print text files to any connected printer. For details on how to use these commands, see the following sections.

Getting files or directories from the remote host

To copy files from a remote host to your local hard disk:

1. Select the local drive to which you want to copy the files from the Drive drop-down box. If you are using the keyboard, you need to select the drop-down box using the Tab key and then press the up- and down-arrow keys until you discover the required drive (see Figure 3-3).

Figure 3-3: Drive selection drop-down list box.

2. Move down the local directory tree until the directory name to which you want to transfer the files is highlighted. To change to a given directory without moving up and down the directory tree, position the mouse pointer in the directory area and click the right mouse button; then type the path.

3. If you have not already done so, establish a connection to the host from which you want to get files or directories. Follow the appropriate instructions in the next sections for the operation you want to execute. Before you start the file transfer operation, ensure that all the appropriate options are checked in the Options menu. For a description of each option, see the section "Setting Your Options."

> ⚠️ Before you transfer files, always stop to think whether these files need to be transferred in Binary or ASCII format.

Transferring an entire directory

To transfer all the files in a particular directory, click the directory name and, keeping the mouse button pressed, drag the folder-shaped cursor to the selected local directory.

Transferring files using wild cards

If you want to transfer all files that meet certain wild-card criteria from a given directory, highlight the directory name and then select the Settings button located toward the middle of your screen. Select Display Partial and enter the wild-card filter required (see Figure 3-4) in the "Wildcard(s) for partial display:" field. For example, your entry could read ***.txt *.marketing**. When you are done, click the directory name and, keeping the mouse button pressed, drag the folder-shaped cursor to the selected local directory.

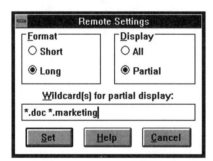

Figure 3-4: Remote Settings dialog box.

Transferring selected files only

To transfer only selected files from any given directory, select the directory and tag all the files that you want to transfer. When you are done, select the Get button. Alternatively, while you're tagging the last file that you want to transfer, keeping the mouse button pressed, move the document-shaped cursor up to the selected directory above and release the button.

Whichever transfer method you are using, a transfer rate information box containing two progress bars is displayed. This display shows the percentage of the current file being transferred in the top progress bar and the percentage of the entire transfer done in the one below (the extreme left of the bar is equal to 0 percent and the extreme right is 100 percent). The number of bytes completed on the bottom bar reflects the number of bytes of complete files transferred and does not include the file currently being transferred.

While the transfer is in progress, you may carry on with other tasks. You cannot minimize the program window; however, you can open other programs on top of it without disturbing the transmission.

Transferring remote files with long filenames

When you're transferring files having names that are longer than eight characters or extensions that are longer than three characters, Distinct FTP suggests a new filename that the DOS operating system can accept (see Figure 3-5). You may accept this filename or change it to a more meaningful name before proceeding with the transfer.

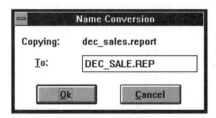

Figure 3-5: Name Conversion dialog box.

Copying local files to the remote system

The procedure for copying your local files to a remote host is very similar to that of copying from a remote host to the local system. Following is a detailed description of how to copy files:

1. If you have not already done so, establish a connection with the host to which you want to put your local files or directories. Then select the directory in which you intend to place the files from the directory tree at the bottom left of your screen.

2. Select the local drive from which you want to copy the files from the Drive: drop-down list box. Move down the local directory tree until the directory

name from which you want to transfer the files is highlighted. Then follow the appropriate instructions in the next sections for the operation you want to execute.

Before you transfer files, always stop to think whether these files need to be transferred in Binary or ASCII format.

Transferring an entire directory

To transfer all the files in a particular directory, click the directory name and, keeping the mouse button pressed, drag the folder-shaped cursor to the selected remote directory.

Transferring files using wild cards

If you want to transfer all files that meet certain wild-card criteria from a given directory, highlight the directory name; then select the Settings button located toward the top right-hand corner of your screen. Select Display Partial and enter the wild-card filter required. For example, your entry could read ***.txt *.c**. When you are done, click the directory name and, keeping the mouse button pressed, drag the folder-shaped cursor to the selected remote directory.

Transferring selected files only

To transfer only selected files from any given directory, select the directory. All the files contained in the directory are displayed to the right of the directory tree. Tag all the files that you want to transfer. When you are done, select the Put button from the button menu. Alternatively, while tagging the last file that you want to transfer, keeping the mouse button pressed, move the document-shaped cursor up to the selected directory and release the button.

Whichever transfer method you are using, a transfer rate information box containing two progress bars is displayed. This display shows the percentage of the current file being transferred in the top progress bar and the percentage of the entire transfer done in the one below (the extreme left of the bar is equal to 0 percent and the extreme right is 100 percent).

As you can do while getting files, while the transfer is in progress, you may carry on with other tasks. You cannot minimize the program window; however, you can open other programs on top of it without disturbing the transmission.

Renaming files or directories

You can rename the currently selected file or directory on your local or remote system. To rename a local or remote file or directory, all you have to do is

select it and then select the Ren button from the Quick Menu. A dialog box is
displayed showing the old file or directory name (see Figure 3-6).

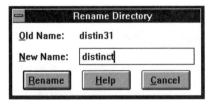

Figure 3-6: Rename Directory dialog box.

Type the new name in the New Name text box and select the Rename button.

If you get an *Unable to complete rename operation* error message, first check
that you have entered a valid alternative name; check also that you are the
authorized owner of the file or directory name that you are trying to change.

Deleting files or directories

You can delete one or more files from any local or remote directory. You can
also delete an empty directory. To delete files, all you have to do is tag them
and then select the Del button from the Quick Menu.

To delete an empty directory, you must first select it and then select the Del
button from the button menu, or drag it over the Del button and release the
mouse button.

It is advisable to have the Confirm Delete option always on, thus avoiding the
inadvertent deletion of files. You set the Confirm Delete option from the
Options menu in the menu bar at the top of the program window. When it is on,
a check mark is displayed to the left of the option name.

Creating directories

You can create new subdirectories on either the local or the remote system to
which you are connected. To create a subdirectory, click the directory that is to
contain the new directory to make it the current one. Select the Mkdir button
from the Quick Menu.

If the *Unable to create subdirectory* error message is displayed when you're trying to create a subdirectory on the remote system, you should check that you are the rightful owner of the directory under which you are trying to create a new directory.

Moving directly to a specified path

To switch to a specific path without using the directory tree:

1. Make sure that the local or remote directory tree is selected. Then press the spacebar or click the right mouse button on the appropriate directory tree.

2. Enter the complete path of the directory that you want to switch to and press Enter.

Printing remote or local text files

To print text files that are located on either your local or remote system, select the files; then choose the Print button from the Quick Menu or just drag and drop them on the Print button.

Setting Your Options

Distinct FTP enables you to set certain options before starting your file transfer. These options can be selected or deselected from the Options menu in the menu bar.

The Options menu

Figure 3-7 shows the commands in the Options menu. Options that are currently active display a check mark to the left of the option name. To select or deselect an option, just click it.

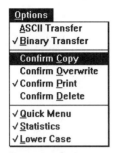

Figure 3-7: Options menu.

ASCII or Binary

You can specify whether you want the file transfer to take place in ASCII or
Binary format. You may need to reset this option each time you transfer files if
they are of different types. The default option (unless you modify it) is ASCII.
ASCII transfers text files and carries out format-character conversion automatically. When you put them to a remote system, it transforms all Carriage Return
+ Line Feed (CR LF) to LF only, and when you get files to the PC, it transforms all
LF into CR LF. You should use the Binary option for all files that are not pure
ASCII files. The Binary option transfers correctly all file types but does not carry
out format-character conversion on ASCII files. The currently selected transfer
type is displayed in the title bar of the FTP program when a connection is
active.

The Confirm options

You may choose to enable or disable any of the Confirm options. You can
decide whether you want to be asked to confirm the transfer of each file, to
confirm before overwriting a file on the destination directory that has the same
name as the one being transferred, or to confirm the deletion of each file. We
strongly suggest that you leave the last two options permanently selected.

You may also disable the Quick Menu and the Statistics option if you want to
have more room in the directory listing box.

Viewing directories in different ways

Both the local and remote host sections have a Settings button that is located
to the right of the screen. This button enables you to customize the way you
view the contents of your local or remote directories. In the following sections
are the options that you can set.

Format

The file format may be set to Short or Long. The Short format lists only filenames, whereas the Long format lists the file size, date and time of creation or last modification, and the file attributes (for local files) or authorization access rights (UNIX files).

Display

It is possible to display All the files in a given directory or to get a Partial view of the directory contents by displaying only those files that meet certain criteria. In this case, you need to enter the criteria in the Wildcard(s) for Partial Display text box.

For example, if you want to view only those files that start with the word "sales," you enter

```
sales*.*
```

When you use wild cards in this way, you are able to transfer all the files displayed by just dragging the directory name and dropping it over the destination directory.

Getting help

On-line help is available at any time if you select the Help button from the Quick Menu or select Help from the menu bar.

Support for the Distinct Sampler in Windows Internet Gizmos will be mailed through online means only on CompuServe's Windows Connectivity Forum (GO WINCON). WINCON is managed and operated by professional WinSock experts through the Windows Users Group Network organization (WUGNET). The online staff will assist in answering questions on installation, configuration, and general answers to the applets included in Distinct Sampler. Distinct Corporation will handle direct inquiries for upgrades and full version product and pricing information through sales at distinct.com.

Chapter 4
Trumpet WinSock Stack Sampler

Trumpet WinSock

By Peter R. Tattam, bugs@petros.psychol.utas.edu.au

Managed by Trumpet Software International, listproc@petros.psychol.utas.edu.au

Copyright 1993,1994 by Peter R. Tattam

Introduction

The Trumpet WinSock is a Windows Sockets 1.1-compatible TCP/IP stack that provides a standard networking layer for many Windows networking applications; it has been a major vehicle in achieving widespread use of WinSock 1.1.

The product is a shareware item. Evaluate it for a period of 30 days. If you are satisfied with it, fill out the provided registration form and send it to Trumpet Software International. Please send a registration fee so we can develop and support this software. We have made arrangements for site licenses; details are in a later section.

Instructions for installing Trumpet WinSock

The Trumpet WinSock runs on your PC in the following conditions:

- You must have either a packet driver available for use by network programs, or if you wish to use SLIP, a free COM port. You can also reliably use packet drivers, but preferably under enhanced mode using WINPKT. You can use standard mode, but take care to avoid system crashes.

- You can use NDIS and ODI via packet driver shims, but their use is not supported.

■ You can use PKTMUX (Version 1.2c or later) rather than WINPKT, but again, its use is not supported.

If you already have some kind of TCP/IP networking package installed, the Trumpet WinSock probably will not run; if it will not run, you'll have to massage your system configuration to install the Trumpet WinSock. You may possibly need to uninstall that networking package.

Alternatively, a WinSock may be available for your networking package, in which case the Trumpet WinSock is not required.

Installing Trumpet WinSock over a packet driver

A *packet driver* is a small piece of software that sits between your network card and your TCP program. This software provides a standard interface that many programs can use in a similar manner to BIOS calls using software interrupts.

Why is this software called a packet driver? Modern networks send information in groups — *packets* — rather than one byte or character at a time. For example, Ethernet sends information in packets up to 1,514 bytes long. The process compares to the way people read: most absorb sentences and paragraphs at a time, rarely stopping after each word or letter.

The Trumpet WinSock also uses a special virtual packet driver *wrapper*, enabling your packet driver to function correctly in Windows. Although the packet driver communicates effectively with your network card, it cannot work correctly from Windows without the wrapper. The program WINPKT was written by some clever people on the Internet to allow a packet driver to work correctly in Windows. WINPKT makes sure that packets get directed to the correct *virtual machine* under Windows enhanced mode. A virtual machine can be either the entire Windows session or any DOS session active within Windows.

You also need to have some understanding of IRQ vectors and I/O addresses that may be relevant to installing your network card. Check the Windows reference manual and your network card documentation for more details.

Where do you get packet drivers?

Packet drivers are usually provided with your network card. If not, a comprehensive collection of public domain packet drivers may be obtained from the Crynwr Packet Driver Collection. Information on where to get this packet driver collection is provided later in this chapter.

Actually installing the WinSock

Before you do anything, copy the essential files listed in Table 4-1 to a suitable directory, such as C:\TRUMPET.

Table 4-1	Essential Files for Using Trumpet WinSock
File	*Explanation*
WINSOCK.DLL	The guts of the TCP/IP driver.
TCPMAN.EXE	Interface program for managing the WinSock.
WINPKT.COM	Virtual packet driver interface for Windows.
hosts	List of host names and aliases.
services	List of Internet services.
protocol	List of Internet protocols.

Modify the path line in your AUTOEXEC.BAT to contain a reference to that directory (for example, path C:\DOS;C:\WINDOWS;C:\TRUMPET). Then make sure the path is active by rebooting or executing AUTOEXEC.BAT.

The most basic setup of packet driver and WINPKT looks something like this:

```
ne2000 0x60 2 0x300
WINPKT 0x60
```

The first line installs an NE2000 packet driver on vector 0x60 using IRQ 2 and I/O address 0x300. The second line installs the WINPKT virtual packet driver using the same vector where the NE2000 packet driver was installed.

Your mileage may vary. Some sample configurations are described later in this chapter. Choose the configuration that best suits your needs and modify it to your requirements.

Now you are ready to start Windows. Start it up!

From Windows, start up TCPMAN. From the File Manager, choose File⇨Run and then TCPMAN. If this procedure fails, check that the path is set up correctly. Later, you can add an icon to your desktop to use it directly.

Assuming that you are a first-time user, a setup screen appears, giving you a number of options to fill in. These options are described in Table 4-2. You need to fill in these details to enable the TCP package to function. (If you are unclear about any of the options, seek some help from qualified Internet support staff. Doing so will save you a lot of time.)

Table 4-2	Setup Options
Option	*Description*
IP address	Your IP (Internet Protocol) address — bootp or rarp. (Use lowercase, please. If you use BOOTP, be sure to have a BOOTP service on the network, or the WinSock will not load.)
Netmask	Your Internet network mask (for example, 255.255.0.0).
Default gateway	Your default Internet gateway (IP address).
Name server	Your name server IP (Internet Protocol) address for DNS searches. You may provide more than one address by separating the addresses with spaces. (IP addresses only.)
Timeserver	Unused. Future WinSock APIs may support this option. (IP addresses only.)
Domain suffix	A space-separated list of domain suffixes to be used when resolving names in the DNS system.
Packet vector	Either leave this as 00 to search for the packet driver or use the vector under which you installed the packet driver. The number is required in hexadecimal without the leading *0x*. In this example, you provide 60 (numeric).
MTU	Maximum Transmission Unit (numeric). For Ethernet, 1500 is the maximum and is recommended.
TCP RWIN	TCP Receive Window (numeric) — defaults to 4096 but can be larger.
TCP MSS	TCP Maximum Segment Size (numeric). Usually MTU — 40.

The rest of the details should appear grayed out, so don't try to fill them in. The Internal SLIP check box should not be checked. The first four parameters and the packet vector are required for successful functioning of the WinSock, whereas the rest can be tailored to suit your needs.

When you are done, click OK. If all goes well, the Trumpet WinSock is initialized. You are now ready to start using the WinSock.

What to do if something goes wrong

The Trumpet WinSock requires that you have the correct combination of TCPMAN.EXE, WINSOCK.DLL, and WINPKT.COM. When upgrading to a new release, replace each file to be sure that everything is up to date.

If you get the messages about not finding a packet driver or being unable to load TCP, make sure that

■ The packet driver loaded properly

■ WINPKT managed to find it

■ The correct vector was chosen from TCPMAN

At the moment, only Ethernet and SLIP packet driver types are supported. Token ring is available only via the ibmtoken packet driver; it should work but is untested by the author. ODI can be used via the ODIPKT shim, and NDIS via the DIS_PKT shim. Examples are provided later with examples of installations using NetWare. Possible causes for TCPMAN load errors specific to packet drivers are listed in Table 4-3.

Table 4-3	TCPMAN Load Error Descriptions
Error Message	*Problem*
Unable to bind protocol 0806	Another TCP stack is using the packet driver. Remove the other TCP stack.
WINPKT or pktdrv not found	Couldn't find the correct packet driver. Also check the vector number in TCPMAN.
Unable to allocate network buffers	Critical error. Try to free up some special driver memory by removing Windows device drivers.
Network buffers low	Not critical but inadvisable. Free up driver memory by removing Windows device drivers.

If WINPKT can't load (no packet driver found), check your packet driver vector number. Some drivers may choose a default vector that is not at 0x60 (for example, the ODIPKT default is 0x69).

If you are using ODIPKT and you can't get any response, you probably accessed the wrong protocol. If you have the ARP trace on, you may get *ARP timed out* messages as well. The first parameter of ODIPKT selects the correct protocol. Try adjusting this.

Installing Trumpet WinSock over internal SLIP

The Trumpet WinSock has facilities for managing a SLIP connection, as well as the ability to use dialing scripts for logging in and out of your SLIP server. Install Trumpet (as described in the previous section). Then click Internal SLIP. Some of the parameters will be grayed; others are listed in Table 4-4.

Table 4-4	Trumpet WinSock Internal SLIP Parameters
Parameter	*Meaning*
IP address	Your Internet IP address — bootp. Lowercase only. Use BOOTP only if you are not intending to use a dial-in script. If using a dialer script with the address extracted by the script, or BOOTP later, just leave it with the default value of 0.0.0.0. Also, be sure that your server supports using BOOTP; otherwise, the WinSock delays for about 15 seconds and the message *Unable to load TCP* comes up.
Name server	Your name server IP address for DNS searches. You may provide more than one address by separating the addresses with spaces. (IP addresses only.)
Timeserver	Unused — future WinSock APIs may support this. (IP addresses only.)
Domain suffix	A space-separated list of domain suffixes used when resolving names in the DNS system.
MTU	*M*aximum *T*ransmission *U*nit. Related to TCP MSS; usually TCP MSS + 40. (Numeric.)
TCP RWIN	TCP Receive window. It is recommended that this value be roughly three to four times the value of TCP MSS. (Numeric.)
TCP MSS	TCP Maximum Segment Size. It is recommended that this value be small when using SLIP — for example, 512 bytes for SLIP and lower for CSLIP. CSLIP can compress data more efficiently when it is less than 255. (Numeric.)
SLIP port	Your COM port number; 1=COM1, 2=COM2, and so on. (Numeric.)
baud rate	The speed at which your modem is running. (Numeric.)
hardware handshake	Recommended if your link supports it.
Van Jacobson CSLIP Compression	If your server supports it. You also may have to adjust MTU, MSS, and RWIN to be suitable.
Online Status Detection	If your modem supports it, select DCD or DSR on-line status detection.

The rest of the details should be grayed out, so don't try to fill them in. When you are done, click OK. If all goes well, the Trumpet WinSock is initialized for SLIP access. You are now ready to start using the WinSock.

Logging in to the server

You can use either the manual login or the automatic scripting to access your server. For the time being, choose manual and login to your server with the appropriate commands. Don't forget to press Esc to get out when you have finished dialing in. After logging in, you may need to set your IP address if it is allocated dynamically.

If you want to use another terminal program to dial in to the server, don't forget to issue AT&D0 or disable DTR dropping when exiting the program; otherwise, the connection will be severed when the application closes the COM port.

Try out pingw to a well-known host IP address to see whether all is well.

Problems

Check your baud rates! If using hardware handshaking with an external modem, make sure the cable is correctly wired. At the moment, all dialing must be done with 8 bits, no parity (8,1,N). If this doesn't work, you will need to use an external dialer. The next revision will have an extension to the dialer to allow this.

After you have determined your login sequence, you can set up a login script. A sample script is provided, along with a listing of a typical session.

Automatic dialing

Minimal scripting is supported. The script commands are described in Table 4-5. Table 4-6 describes string arguments.

Table 4-5	Script Commands
Command	*Meaning*
input *time-out string*	Wait for string received
output *string*	Send string
display *string*	Display string on display
wait *time-out* {DSR I CTS I RLSD I DCD}	Wait for DSR or CTS or RLSD (DCD)
trace (on I off)	Useful for debugging scripts
echo (on I off)	Default to on
password *prompt*	Message box for password
username *prompt*	Message box for username
address *time-out*	Parse IP address

(continued)

Table 4-5 *(continued)*

Command	Meaning
set (DTR | RTS) (on | off)	Set/reset the modem lines
sleep *seconds*	Pause for so many seconds
exec *string*	Program is started up concurrently using winexec()
online	Enter SLIP mode. Commands that depend on received characters do not work correctly after this command is issued because the WinSock then interprets data as SLIP frames. Useful before an exec command that uses the WinSock.
BOOTP	Inform the WinSock that a BOOTP is required after the script has finished.

 # indicates the beginning of a comment, except inside a string.

Table 4-6   String Arguments

Argument	Meaning
\l	Line feed
\r	Return
\n	cr/lf pair
\f	Form feed
\t	Tab
\b	Backspace
\nnn	ASCII value in decimal
\i	IP address
\p	Password
\u	Username
\c	COM port number (as you have configured it)

The following is a sample script for logging in to our Xylogics terminal server:

```
output atz\13
input 10 OK\n
#output atd242284\13
output atd241644\13
input 30 CONNECT
input 30 \n
wait 30 dsr
output \13
input 30 username:
output tattam\13
input 30 password:
password Enter your password
output \p\13
input 30 >
output who\13
input 30 >
output slip\13
input 30 Your address is
address 30
input 30 \n
display \n
display Connected. Your IP address is \i.\n
exec pingw 131.217.10.1
```

Here's a log of a typical session. Names have been blanked out for security.

```
Trumpet WinSock Version 1.00 Alpha #18
Copyright (c) 1993 by Peter R. Tattam
All Rights Reserved.
SLIP ENABLED
Internal SLIP driver COM3 Baud rate = 38400 Hardware hand-
shaking
My ip = 131.217.8.4 netmask = 255.255.0.0 gateway =
131.217.250.1
Executing script c:\dev\tcpip\WinSock\login.cmd
SLIP DISABLED
atz
OK
atd241644
CONNECT 38400
```

(continued)

(continued)

```
Annex Command Line Interpreter * Copyright 1991 Xylogics,
Inc.
Checking authorization, Please wait...
Annex username: xxxxxx
Annex password:
Permission granted
University of Tasmania
AARNet Terminal Server
SLIP users:
Use a maximum segment size (MSS) of 209
and a maximum transmission unit (MTU) of 255.
Async AppleTalk users:
Configure MacTCP to use the Computing Centre zone.
 *** Note change in procedures for starting async AppleTalk.
 *** After typing atalk you will be prompted for your password
 *** again.
AARNET TS5 >who
Port What User Location When Idle Address
 2 CLI xxxxxxxx — 8:01pm [local]
 +1 'telnet tasman.cc'
 3 CLI xxxxxxxx — 8:15pm [local]
 +1 'rlogin franklin.cc'
 4 SLIP modem4 — 8:19pm ants
 5 CLI xxxxxxxx — 8:34pm [local]
 6 CLI xxxxxxxx — 7:19pm [local]
 +1 'rlogin baudin.cc'
 17 SLIP modem18 — 6:39pm ants
AARNET TS5 >slip
Switching to SLIP.
Annex address is 131.217.250.10. Your address is
131.217.8.5.
Connected. Your IP address is 131.217.8.5.
Script completed
SLIP ENABLED
```

Sample configurations for packet driver

■ Plain ne2000 packet driver using WINPKT:

```
ne2000 0x60 2 0x300
WINPKT 0x60
```

■ ne2000 packet driver with Novell NetWare access using WINPKT:

```
ne2000 —n 0x60 2 0x300
WINPKT 0x60
pdipx
```

```
netx
path c:\dos;c:\network\win31
f:
login
```

Note the specification of the -n switch of the packet driver. Some packet drivers don't support this switch. In that case, you may be forced to use ODI instead. An example could be the Xircom Pocket Adapter.

■ Ne2000 packet driver with Novell NetWare access using PKTMUX:

```
ne2000 —n 0x60 2 0x300
pktmux 4
pktdrv
pktdrv
pktdrv
pktdrv
pdipx
netx
path c:\dos;c:\network\win31
f:
login
```

Notice that WINPKT is not required because PKTMUX does a similar job.

■ ODI setup with NetWare access. You will need ODIPKT. The latest known release is 2.4. It is important that ODIPKT reference the correct protocol for IP access. This can be specified as the first parameter to ODIPKT (0=1st, 1=2nd, and so forth).

Here's a sample of my network attach batch file:

```
@echo off
cd \
lh lsl
lh \odi\ne2000
cd \net
lh ipxodi
lh odipkt
lh WINPKT 0x69
lh netx
path c:\dos;c:\net\win31
f:
echo on
login
```

Also, your NET.CFG file must be suitably configured. Here are the relevant excerpts from my NET.CFG:

```
Link Support
 Buffers 8 1586
 MemPool 16384
Link Driver NE2000
 Port #1 300 20
 Int #1 2
 Frame Ethernet_II
 Frame Ethernet_802.3
 Protocol IPX 0 Ethernet_802.3
```

The ordering of the frame protocols is important for the default setup of ODIPKT. Also, users should be aware that there are two versions of ODIPKT: one released commercially and one in the public domain. This chapter refers to the public domain version.

Also note that two programs are named NE2000.COM. One is a packet driver, which I referred to in an earlier section. The one referred to in this section is actually an ODI driver and doesn't function as a packet driver.

Extra information

You may use environment variables or command-line options to override some of the network parameters. They have the same names as the saved parameters in TRMPWSK.INI. This file normally resides in the WINSOCK directory rather than the WINDOWS directory because this organization facilitates setting up the WinSock in a networked environment. IP addresses can be overridden by using the environment variables or the command line.

The following line is an example of the command line:

```
TCPMAN -ip=123.231.213.123 -netmask=255.255.255.0
```

The following lines are examples of environment variables:

```
set ip=123.231.213.123
set netmask=255.255.255.0
```

Table 4-7 provides a list of parameters.

Table 4-7	Environment Variable Parameters
ip/myip	Your IP address or 'bootp' or 'rarp' (lowercase only)
netmask	Your netmask (for example, 255.255.0.0)
gateway/mygateway	Your gateway (IP address)
dns	List of DNS IP addresses
time	List of timeserver IP addresses
domain	List of domain name suffixes
vector	Packet driver vector in hex
MTU	Maximum Transmission Unit
RWIN	TCP Receive Window
MSS	TCP Maximum Segment Size
slip-enabled	0 = off, 1 = on
slip-port	port number (1-9)
slip-baudrate	baud rate in decimal
slip-handshake	0 = off, 1 = on
slip-compressed	0 = off, 1 = on

The Crynwr packet driver collection

The Crynwr packet driver collection is available by mail, FTP, e-mail, UUCP, and modem. The drivers are distributed in three files, as follows:

- DRIVERS.ZIP contains executables and documentation.
- DRIVERS1.ZIP contains the first half of the ASM files.
- DRIVERS2.ZIP contains the second half of the ASM files.

Mail

Columbia University distributes packet drivers by mail. The formats are 9-track 1600 bpi tapes in ANSI, tar, OS SL format, or PC diskettes (360K 5.25 inch and 720K 3.5 inch). The exact terms and conditions have yet to be worked out. Please call (212) 854-3703 for ordering information or write to:

Kermit Distribution, Department PD
Columbia University Center for Computing Activities
612 West 115th Street
New York, NY 10025

or send e-mail to kermit@watsun.cc.columbia.edu (Internet) or KERMIT@CUVMA (BITNET/EARN).

FTP/e-mail

The packet driver collection has its own directory devoted to it: pd1:<msdos.pktdrvr>. The drivers are there, along with many free programs that use the packet drivers.

SIMTEL20 files are also available from mirror sites OAK.Oakland.Edu (141.210.10.117), wuarchive.wustl.edu (128.252.135.4), ftp.uu.net (192.48.96.9), nic.funet.fi (128.214.6.100), src.doc.ic.ac.uk (146.169.3.7) or rana.cc.deakin.oz.au (128.184.1.4), or by e-mail through the BITNET/EARN file servers.

Modem

If you cannot access the drivers via FTP or e-mail, most SIMTEL20 MSDOS files, including the PC-Blue collection, are also available for downloading from Detroit Download Central at (313) 885-3956. DDC, a subscription system with an average hourly cost of 17 cents, has multiple lines that support 300/1200/2400/9600/14400 bps (103/212/V22bis/HST/V32bis/V42bis/MNP). It is also accessible on Telenet via PC Pursuit and on Tymnet via StarLink outdial. New files uploaded to SIMTEL20 are usually available on DDC within 24 hours.

UUCP

The packet driver files are available from UUNET's 1-900-GOT-SRCS, in uunet!~/systems/msdos/simtel20/pktdrvr. See UUNET.DOC for details.

ODIPKT location

Trumpet believes that the originating site for ODIPKT is

Host hsdndev.harvard.edu
Location: /pub/odipkt
FILE —rwxr-xr-x 2915 Aug 21 20:01 odipkt.com

A copy of the NDIS shim is there also.

Trumpet general discussion group

The machine petros.psychol.utas.edu.au is now running a local news service with the newsgroups

trumpet.announce

trumpet.bugs

trumpet.feedback

trumpet.questions

If you do not have access directly to this service, these newsgroups are gatewayed to the following mailing list. You may join the new Trumpet mailing list by sending a message to listproc@petros.psychol.utas.edu.au with just one line in the body:

```
subscribe trumpet-user Your Full Name
```

where *Your Full Name* is your actual full name.

The list is called trumpet-user@petros.psychol.utas.edu.au and is running on a 486/50 FreeBSD system. With luck, it will cope. ;-)

You can ask questions or discuss any aspect of any Trumpet program on this group. Feedback is always welcome. There is also an anonymous FTP area with all the latest Trumpet programs and prereleases. If you do use a prerelease, be prepared for unexpected problems because such programs are in alpha/beta test.

Bugs or comments

Send to trumpet-bugs@petros.psychol.utas.edu.au.

For bug reports, please send a copy of CONFIG.SYS, AUTOEXEC.BAT, TRUMPWSK.INI, and any other relevant network configurations. In the case of ODI, also send NET.CFG. I will do my best to sort out your problem. Due to the high demand for the Trumpet WinSock, the mailbox is overloaded at times. Be patient. Someone will answer you.

TCPMAN — the Trumpet WinSock TCP Manager Menu options

Option	Purpose
File⇨Setup	Calls up the Setup dialog box for configuration.
IP address	Your IP address, bootp or rarp (lowercase). (BOOTP works only if a bootp service is on-line; rarp works only if you're using Ethernet and there is an rarp service on-line).
Netmask	Your network mask.

(continued)

(continued)

Option	Purpose
Default gateway	Your default Internet gateway or router.
Name server	Your Domain Name Server address.
Timeserver	Unused (leave empty).
Domain Suffix	A space-separated list of suffixes to be tried when looking up names via the name server.
Packet Vector	For accessing the packet driver in hex.
MTU	Maximum Transmission Unit.
TCP RWIN	TCP Receive Window.
TCP MSS	TCP Maximum Segment Size.
Demand Load Timeout	Number of seconds TCPMAN stays loaded after the application has finished with it.
Internal SLIP	Click this for internal SLIP support and dialer support.
SLIP port	Which COM port to use.
Baud Rate	Speed of the connection.
Hardware Handshaking	Turn on for RTS/CTS handshaking; may require the AT&K3 modem command to function properly.
Van Jacobson CSLIP compression	Turn on for CSLIP TCP header compression.
Online Status Detection	Needed for dialer autologin / autologout enabling.
None	No on-line status detection.
DCD (RLSD) check	May require AT&C1 modem command to function.
DSR check	May require AT&S1 modem command to function.
File⇨Register	Calls up the Registration dialog box.
File⇨Exit	Quits the TCP manager, forcing the WinSock to be unloaded.
Edit⇨Copy	Copies selected text on TCPMAN display to the Clipboard.
Edit⇨Clear	Clears the TCPMAN display.

Tracing options

Use tracing options with care because some applications may crash when the traces are active. Should a program crash with stack overflow, the WinSock may remain loaded in memory even though TCPMAN has exited. It is advisable to restart Windows if this happens; you may even need to reboot your machine.

Also, timing measurements of the WinSock throughput will be severely affected by the trace options.

Option	Meaning
Trace/TCP	Turn TCP trace on/off
Trace/UDP	Turn UDP trace on/off
Trace/IP	Turn IP tracing on/off
Trace/ARP	Turn ARP tracing on/off
Trace/RARP	Turn RARP tracing on/off
Trace/Ethernet	Add Ethernet headers to IP/ARP/RARP trace
Trace/Extra detail	Add some extra detail to TCP, UDP, and IP traces
Trace/Socket calls	Trace each WinSock call; most parameters are displayed as well
Trace/DNS	Trace Domain Name Server operations; use with care — stack overflows can be frequent
Trace/Messages	Trace Async Socket messages
Dialer/Login	Invoke the login.cmd dialer script
Dialer/Bye	Invoke the bye.cmd dialer script
Dialer/Other	Invoke other scripts; a File selection dialog box of *.CMD is displayed
Dialer/Options	Call up the Dialer options dialog box (Options are No automatic login, Automatic login on startup only, and Automatic login and logout on demand)
SLIP inactivity time-out (minutes)	Number of minutes to wait before exiting WinSock (when no application is using the WinSock). Automatic login and logout must be enabled for this option to close the SLIP connection. A value of 0 disables the time-out.
Dialer/Manual Login	Invoke the dialer manually; press Esc to exit from the manual dialer
Dialer/Edit Scripts	Invoke Notepad to edit any script
Help/About	Display the version number and copyright

Trumpet for Windows Version 1.0

By Peter R. Tattam

Disclaimer and copyright

This program is copyright ©1991,1992,1993 by Peter R. Tattam, all rights reserved. It is provided as shareware with the following limitations:

> This program is shareware and is not to be resold or distributed for sale with other programs which are for sale. There is no warranty or claim of fitness or reliability. The programs is distributed *as is*, and as such neither the author nor the University of Tasmania shall be held liable for any loss of data, down time, loss of revenue, or any other direct or indirect damage or claims caused by this program.

What is Trumpet for Windows?

Trumpet for Windows is a network news reader for Windows that uses the Network News Transfer Protocol (NNTP) to link into the Usenet news system. Usenet is a distributed computerized news system that is part of a network consisting of thousands of interconnected computer systems — *the Internet* — which reaches most countries in the world. Many services are available on Usenet, ranging from technical discussions of many aspects of computers, scientific topics such as physics or mathematics, and even recreational topics such as sports or literature. It is beyond the scope of this document to outline the full features of Usenet, but suffice it to say that there is more than enough material on Usenet created every year to tear down forest after forest were it printed.

Central to the Usenet system is the notion of newsgroups. A *newsgroup* is a grouping of articles with a related topic. Some examples of newsgroups are *sci.physics* and *rec.art*. The newsgroups are arranged in hierarchies so that related topics are grouped. Each of these newsgroups contains a list of articles usually transient in nature; therefore, topics generally don't stay on the news server for more than a week or so.

Usenet is growing at an incredible rate. Trumpet for Windows seeks to provide the user with a smooth and easy-to-use interface. It runs on the world's most popular graphical environment (Windows) and even on Windows NT.

Trumpet uses NNTP (Network News Transfer Protocol) to speak to a *news server,* normally a large computer system storing all the news articles.

Installing Trumpet

The installation program assumes that you have the basic skills to operate the Program Manager from Windows and that you are using Version 3.1 of Windows. The examples use a default directory of C:\WINTRUMP to install WinSock Trumpet. Trumpet is normally distributed in .ZIP file format, and four versions are distributed together. The versions are

- For WinSock: WT_WSK.EXE

- For Trumpet TCP: WT_ABI.EXE

- For Lan WorkPlace for DOS: WT_LWP.EXE

- For Packet Driver: WT_PKT.EXE

First, you must unpack the Windows Trumpet distribution. You will need a program such as PKUNZip to extract the Trumpet files. Place the distribution files in a suitable directory. From a DOS shell, you might follow these directions.

1. First, create the new directory to which you want to install Trumpet:

   ```
   md c:\wintrump
   cd c:\wintrump
   .....
   .....   move wntrmp10.zip to the current directory
   .....
   pkunzip wntrmp10.zipc
   ```

2. Now, create a Program Manager item by choosing File⇨New from the Program Manager. Choose Program Item and then the OK button.

3. Type a description in the Description box, for example, **Trumpet for Windows**, and then type the full pathname of the trumpet executable file in the command-line area (for example, C:\WINTRUMP\WT_WSK.EXE).

   Windows fills in the working directory automatically, so leave it blank.

4. Press OK and a new icon appears in the current program group. If so desired, you can drag the icon to another suitable group.

5. Now you are ready to start up Trumpet. Just double-click the icon, and if all goes well, you are presented with a copyright message dialog box. Click the OK box to continue.

If you are running Trumpet for the first time, the Setup dialog box should appear. After filling in the details outlined in the next section, you will be ready to use Trumpet.

The Setup dialog box

The Setup dialog box is available at any time by choosing File⊅Setup, and is presented automatically for first-time users. The Setup dialog box appears in Figure 4-1.

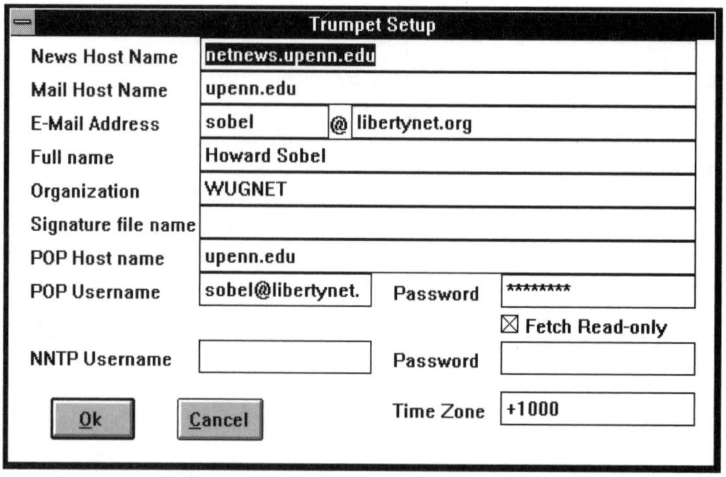

Figure 4-1: The Setup dialog box.

You must fill in most of these fields in order for Trumpet to operate correctly.

NNTP Host Name

This required field is the Internet name of the NNTP news server you will be using. Type either the full Internet domain name or a dotted IP address. This host name establishes the main news reading session.

SMTP Host Name

These two fields are required when posting articles or replying to e-mail. This field is the Internet name of the SMTP mail server to which you send any replies to articles. It is also used by the e-mail section of Trumpet when sending new e-mail messages or replies to e-mail messages. Type either the full Internet domain name or a dotted IP address.

Username @ Site Name

These two fields are required when posting articles or replying to e-mail. They comprise your e-mail address. The first field is the user name part of your full

Internet e-mail address. For example, if your e-mail address is *Mike@Imperial.Bolt.Makers.Com,* you type **Mike** into the first field and type **Imperial.Bolt.Makers.Com** into the second field. It should be noted that the user name part of an Internet address may be case sensitive, so make sure that the user name is correct in this respect, or your e-mail and/or postings may be rejected.

Organization

This optional field is a description of your organization.

Full name

This optional field is for your full name or any other descriptive information to be added to the e-mail address. Do not use the double quotation characters (" or ") because they delimit the descriptive information. Likewise, do not use the ", <, or > characters in this section because they will probably cause your address to be deciphered incorrectly on some systems and your messages will be rejected.

Signature file name

This optional field specifies the location of a signature file to be appended to every article that you transmit. You can place useful information such as your full name, telephone, address, and other relevant information. Some news servers will not accept articles that have signatures longer than three or four lines, so try to keep it short.

POP Host name

Required to fetch mail, this field is the Internet name of a POP3 mail server. This is the server that stores your mail, and is usually the same address as the SMTP host name.

POP Username and Password

These fields specify the user name and password required to login to the POP3 server when you want to fetch mail.

Fetch Read Only check box

If you want Trumpet to fetch e-mail for previewing but don't want the mail to be deleted at the server after fetching, check this optional field. This option can be useful if you normally use another POP mailer to read your e-mail, or your e-mail is managed by a central server and is not normally read from the POP server.

No other additional setup should be required.

After you have filled in all these details, click OK, and with the exception of the packet driver version, a news session is initiated.

If you are a first-time user, you will be subscribed to all the newsgroups. This may take some time, so be patient.

Additional notes for specific versions

For WinSock

No additional setup should be required apart from the timeserver.

For Trumpet ABI

No additional setup should be required apart from the timeserver.

For Novell's Lan WorkPlace for DOS

No additional setup should be required apart from the timeserver.

For Packet Driver

When the main setup dialog box has completed, you are asked to fill in the Network Setup dialog box.

The Network Setup Fields

IP Address

In this box, enter the IP address assigned to your workstation. You can get this address from your local network administrator. If your network supports the BOOTP protocol to assign IP addresses, you can type **bootp** here. You can leave the values for those fields that are sent by your BOOTP server blank.

If your network uses RARP protocol to assign IP addresses, you can enter **rarp** here. If you use RARP to assign IP addresses, you must enter values for the other fields.

Netmask

Enter the Subnet mask value in this box. Please use a correct value for your network. It can be obtained from your local network administrator.

Nameserver

Enter the IP address of the domain nameserver on your network. The domain nameserver translates common names, such as Imperial.Bolt.Makers.Com into IP addresses.

Default Gateway

Enter the IP address of your local network's gateway. Trumpet needs this value if the NNTP, SMTP, and POP3 servers you use are not within your local subnet.

Timeserver

Enter the IP address of the Network timeserver for your network. The timeserver is used by Trumpet to add a GMT date and time stamp to your posts during posting. If no timeserver is available on your network, leave this field blank (0.0.0.0), and Trumpet uses the PC clock to generate a local time stamp (not GMT) for posts.

Domain Name

Enter the name of the domain your computer is located within in this box. In the example used, Mike's computer, is within the domain Bolt.Makers.Com.

Packet Vector

Enter the software interrupt that the packet driver for your network interface is loaded on. If you are using a Crynwr driver, this is the first hexadecimal value, without the leading 0x. For example, if your packet driver is loaded as driver 0x65 5 0x300, the software interrupt to be entered in this box is 65.

However, Trumpet should not be loaded directly over the packet driver. For smooth operation in Windows when it is a background application, it is better that you load Prof. Joe Doupnik's double-ended packet driver shim WINPKT.COM over the hardware packet driver. Here is an example with WINPKT.COM:

```
driver 0x65 5 0x300 (actual hardware packet driver)
winpkt 0x60 0x65
```

DOS and Windows applications can use the virtual packet driver that Winpkt creates at 0x62. The value to enter in the packet vector configuration box is 60. WINPKT.COM can be found where Crynwr packet drivers are archived.

Trumpet also works well with the virtual packet drivers created by Graham Robinson's PKTMUX packet multiplexor. If you use PKTMUX, you must use Version 1.2c or later.

TCP RWIN and MSS

Use values that are recommended for use with your network for the Receive Window and Maximum Segment Size. These values can also be obtained from your network administrator. As a general rule, you can use an RWIN value that is 3–4 times the size of the MTU (depending on your CPU and amount of memory) and an MSS that is 40 bytes smaller than the MTU. When you are done, select OK.

Getting started with Trumpet

After you complete the Trumpet configuration process, Trumpet will try to connect. Assuming you have typed all the correct information, Trumpet will display a status box stating that it is attempting to connect. The connection time defaults to 30 seconds, excluding the time to look up the name of the server.

What if Trumpet won't connect?

Should a message come up saying that Trumpet doesn't know how to look up the name of your server, try changing the name of the NNTP server to that actual IP address of the server. Doing this bypasses the Name lookup, which can fail for a number of reasons. After you have changed the name to an IP address, choose File⇨Reconnect.

You can use this handy command at any time to force a new news session. Should there be any other problems with the setup, check it carefully, and try File⇨Reconnect. Should you need to change any parameters in the network setup, quit Trumpet and restart it again so the new network parameter can take effect.

Now you can start to use Trumpet. It's kind of like driving a car, a little strange at first, but once you've got the knack, there's nothing to it.

News Viewer window

After you have completed setting up Trumpet, you should see a screen similar to the one shown in Figure 4-2.

In this document, this screen is referred to as the *News Viewer window.* This name distinguishes it from the Mail Viewer window described in the next section. The following bullets describe each part of the News Viewer window.

- On the very top line, you have a standard Windows program *title bar.* It should say something like *Trumpet News Reader - (News).* It will also have some standard Windows controls such as a system menu control on the left side, and maximize and minimize controls on the right.

- The next line is the main Trumpet *menu bar* with some additional controls.

- The third line is called the *status bar.* Trumpet uses this line to display various pieces of information.

- Below the status bar is a listbox containing a list of your subscribed news groups. If there are more news groups than can fit on-screen, you can scroll the listbox using the horizontal scroll bar. You can select any particular newsgroup by clicking it. If you are a first-time user of Trumpet, this listbox may have thousands of newsgroups in it. You have to wade through the many items to select a group.

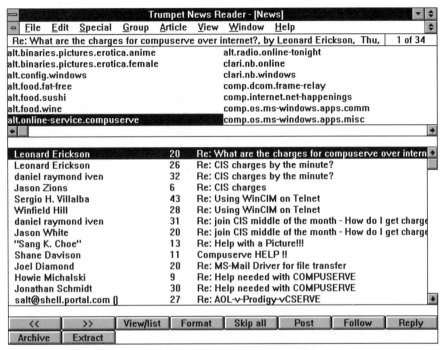

Figure 4-2: The News Viewer window.

Some news servers may contain many thousands of articles. Should the number of newsgroups exceed 3,000–4,000, it may not be possible for Trumpet to display them all. Under these circumstances, Trumpet may possibly have the display and its internal tables out of step, although measures have been taken to prevent this from happening. If there are too many newsgroups for you to handle, you should unsubscribe some newsgroups.

■ Below the listbox is an empty part of the screen. This area displays the headers of any articles available for viewing. In Figure 4-2, you see a long list of newsgroups and topics in this area.

■ Below the news group area is a *button bar*. The buttons help you negotiate through the articles and newsgroups. You can click any button with the mouse and most of the buttons also have keyboard equivalents. A short description of the buttons follows:

Button	Keyboard	Action
<<	F7	Scroll newgroups previous to the current one.
>>	F8	Scroll newsgroups after the current one.
View/List	F9	View the list of articles from the current article.
Format	F10	Change the format of the article list, or if you are reading an article, view that article in 12-point Courier type.
Skip All	Control-S	Skip all the articles in the current group and proceed. These articles will not be marked as read.
Post	Control-P	Post a new article to the current newsgroup.
Follow	Control-F	Post a follow-up article to the current newsgroup.
Reply	Control-R	Reply via e-mail to the author of the current article.
Archive		Save the current article in an archive folder.

The buttons are also described in detail in the WinHelp file distributed with Trumpet.

Mail Viewer window

When you the select the item Window⇨Mail from the menu bar, the Mail Viewer window appears. You should see a screen similar to the one shown in Figure 4-3.

Akin to the News Viewer window, there is a menu bar, followed by a status bar (which is blank), followed by an area that lists all your mail and news archive folders. If you have none, don't worry. Trumpet will automatically create at least the *Incoming Mail* folder the first time that you fetch your mail using Trumpet. As you archive news articles, other folders appear in this area. You can also use the menu item Special⇨Insert Folder to create new folders of your choice in this area.

Below the list area, in the bottom half of the Mail Viewer window, is a blank area that lists all the messages present in the selected folder. You can delete listed messages by pressing the Del key or using the Article⇨Delete Article command.

Below this area is a *button bar* (not enabled in Figure 4-3). You can click any button with the mouse (left button down). Table 4-8 gives a short description of the buttons.

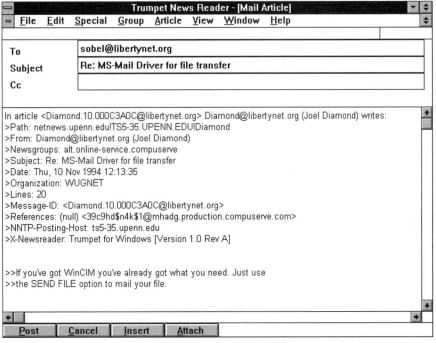

Figure 4-3: The Mail Viewer window.

Table 4-8		Mail Viewer Window Buttons
Button	**Keyboard**	**Action**
<<	F7	Read the message that immediately precedes the current one.
>>	F8	Read the message that immediately follows the current one.
View/List	F9	View the list of messages or the current article.
Format	F10	Change the format of the message you are currently reading to 12-point Courier type.
Fetch		Fetch your mail from the POP3 server.
Mail	Control-M	Mail a new message.
Reply	Control-R	Reply to the current message.

The Menu Bar

The Menu Bar, described here, is common to both the News Viewer and Mail Viewer windows.

File

The following commands appear on the File menu:

- *Setup, Network Setup,* and *Reconnect* have been already discussed as part of the setup procedure.

- *Save Settings* allows you to save changes in newsgroups to the NEWS.INI file while you are still working in Trumpet.

- *Print* prints the current article in the same font and size as displayed.

- *Printer Setup* allows you to change the printer options.

- *Exit* allows you to exit Trumpet. It also saves changes to the NEWS.INI file.

Edit

The following command appears on the Edit menu:

- *Copy* allows you to copy portions of an article or mail message to the Clipboard. You can select the portion that you want to copy using the mouse. Press the left mouse button at the point where you want to begin selecting text, and release it when the desired text has been selected. While you are in a composer window, you can paste information by using standard Windows commands (Control-V or Control-Ins).

Special

The following commands appear on the Special menu:

- *Font* allows you to choose the font, point size, and color for viewer windows.

- *Zap all Subscribed Groups* marks all groups as unsubscribed.

- *Discard Unsubscribed Groups* deletes unsubscribed groups from the NEWS.INI file.

- *Insert Folder* and *Delete Folder* allow you to manage your news/mail folders when you are in the mail window.

- *Registration* allows you to register your copy of Trumpet using the appropriate user name and password provided upon receipt of the shareware registration fee.

Group

The following commands appear on the Group menu:

- *Read All* marks all retrieved articles in the current group as read.

- *Unread All* marks all the articles in the current group as unread.

- *Unread 20* (Control-U) and *Unread 10* mark the last 20 or 10 articles in the current groups as unread.

- *Catch-Up* marks all the articles in the current group as read without retrieving them. This capability is particularly useful if you are reading news after a hiatus of a week or two and do not want to browse through hundreds of articles.

- *Subscribe* displays a list of all the newsgroups carried by your local NNTP server in a listbox. Be careful — this list often can include 4,000 or more groups. In low memory situations with a very large number of groups, not all the newsgroups carried by the NNTP server are displayed in the subscribe listbox.

- *Unsubscribe* marks the current group as unsubscribed, but it is still retained in NEWS.INI.

Article

The following commands appear on the Article menu:

- *Reply*, *Mail*, and *Forward* allow you to reply to the current article, mail the author of the current article, or forward the current article to someone else via e-mail.

- *Post*, *Follow,* and *Cancel* allow you to post an article to the current group, post a follow-up to someone else's article, or cancel an article. You may cancel only those articles that you have authored.

- *Toggle* (Control-T or F5) marks the current article as read or unread.

- *Skip* allows you to skip the current article.

- *Save to File* and *Append to File* permit you to save the current article to a new file or to append it to a preexisting file.

- *Delete Article* permits you to delete an existing article or mail message while you are browsing through your archive folders.

- *Move Article to folder* moves the current article to the archive folder for that newsgroup. If no archive folder for the group exists, one is created.

View

The following commands appear on the View menu:

- *View Headers* allows you to view the article headers. They usually contain detailed information about the poster's NNTP host, the path along which the article has been received, and similar information.
- *Word Wrap* turns on word wrap in the viewer and composer windows.
- *Rot 13* permits the decoding of Rot 13-encoded articles.

Window

The following commands appear on the Window menu:

- *Tile* and *Cascade* allow you to view the two main viewer Windows (News and Mail) in either tile or cascade mode.
- *News* and *Mail* activate that particular viewer window.

Help

The Help menu functions similarly as it does in other Windows applications. Help can also be invoked by the F1 key.

- *About...* brings up information about the version of Trumpet you are using.

Additional hints for NetWare users

Trumpet for Windows can be managed fairly easily in a NetWare environment. There are a few things to remember, though.

- If you are logged in, Trumpet first searches for its configuration files from your NetWare mail directory. Should a shared copy of the NEWS.PRM file be found in the program directory, this file overrides the existing parameters as a security feature. Any parameter defined in the global NEWS.PRM file overrides the same parameter in the user's local NEWS.PRM file. This feature enforces some form of security over e-mail and postings.
- Additionally, the *username* and *fullname* can be automatically filled in from the bindery by specifying an * as the parameter value.
- The NEWS.INI file (which holds the newsgroup information) is automatically loaded from the global directory if one exists there.
- If you are having difficulties using this arrangement, you can use the command-line option -disable_nw to disable any NetWare processing. Also the -maildir=.... option can specify that the configuration files be stored in a specific directory.

Registration information

Trumpet for Windows is currently distributed as shareware. You may use
Trumpet for Windows for 30 days to evaluate its usefulness. If, at the end of that
time, you are satisfied with Trumpet for Windows, you can register it. The basic
registration fee for a single-user version of Trumpet for Windows is U.S. $40. See
the following section "Site licenses" for details on multiuser site licenses. The
distribution site is ftp.utas.edu.au:/pc/trumpet/wintrump/*.

Australian users should contact the author regarding Australian pricing
information and availability. Checks or postal orders should be made out to
Trumpet Software International and sent to:

Trumpet Software International
GPO Box 1649
HOBART, TAS AUSTRALIA 7001

Please note that international mail can be rather slow, and it may take up to two
months to receive your registration.

Site licenses

Site licenses for Trumpet for Windows are available, the cost of which is determined
by the number of simultaneous users. Unless otherwise indicated, upgrade fees for
future versions of Trumpet for Windows will be 25 percent of the original fee.

Trumpet for Windows Version 1.00

Please note that these prices are subject to change at six-month intervals.
Contact Trumpet for correct pricing.

License Type	Users	Cost
Single-user license	1 user	$40 U.S.
Unlimited educational site license	1–24 users	$40 U.S. per user
Unlimited educational site license	25+ users	$1000 U.S.
Multiuser commercial site license	1–24 users	$40 U.S. per user
	25–99 users	$1000 U.S. + $20 U.S. per additional user over 25
	100–399 users	$2500 U.S. + $10 U.S. per additional user over 100
	400–999 users	$5500 U.S. + $5 U.S. per additional user over 400
	1000+ users	$8500 U.S. + $2 U.S. per additional user over 1000 (site restriction 10km radius—negotiable).

(continued)

(continued)

License Type	Users	Cost
Unlimited commercial site license		$10,000 U.S. for first year
		Subsequent years, 25% of current site license fee. This includes maintenance support and upgrades to future versions. Site restriction 100km radius (negotiable).

NEWS.PRM, command-line, and environment variable options

Option	Meaning
nntp-host	Domain name or IP address of the NNTP server.
smtp-host	Domain name or IP address of the SMTP server.
time-host	IP address of timeserver.
user	Your e-mail user name (* to fetch from bindery under NetWare).
site	Your e-mail site name.
fullname	Your full name (* to fetch from bindery under NetWare).
igname	Your signature filename.
organization	The name of your organization.
protect	Disallow users to change setup.
options	Your saved Trumpet options.
title-format	Your saved Trumpet title format.
timeout	Timeout in seconds for commands to time out. Leave large (> 600).
debug	Debug options (a=arp,e=ethernet,i=IP,r=RARP,t=TCP,u=UDP).
dbfile	Debug filename.
d	Equivalent to -debug=t.
maildir	Specification of the maildir location (command line or environment variable only).
disable_nw	Disable any NetWare features of Trumpet (command line or env. var. only).
nobatch	Disable batching of XHDR commands.
viewer-font	The font details for viewing and printing.
viewer-colour	Color of viewed article text.
pop-host	Host name of the POP server used for fetching e-mail.

Option	Meaning
pop-username	Saved POP user name.
pop-password	Saved POP password.
pop-readonly	Saved state of the pop-read only option.
win-posn	Saved position and zoomed state of the main window.
registered-name	Encoded registration name.
registered-password	Encoded registration password.

Packet driver specific options

Option	Meaning
myip	An IP address, rarp, or bootp (in lowercase).
netmask	Your IP local network mask.
mygateway	IP address of your gateway outside your local net.
mtu	Maximum transmission unit that the hardware can handle.
mss	Maximum segment size that TCP can send (default is 512).
rwin	The size of the TCP receive window.
dns-host	IP address of domain name server.
vector	Hex specification of the packet driver vector number.

Trumpet Registration Form

Name _____

Company _____

Address _____

City _____

State _____ Country _____

Zip _____ Phone _____

Remit to:

Trumpet Software Int'l.
GPO Box 1649
Hobart, TAS
AUSTRALIA 7001

Pricing

❏ Trumpet WinSock 2.0 $25 (U.S.) single user

❏ Trumpet for Windows 1.0 $40 (U.S.) single user

Please contact Trumpet for other licensing information.

Chapter 5

SPRY Internet Applications Sampler

This chapter covers documentation for SPRY's Network File Manager and AIR Mosaic Express, a World Wide Web browser. Part VI covers more World Wide Web tools and gizmos.

Network File Manager _____

The Network File Manager™ (NFM) was developed as an enhancement to traditional FTP-based file transfer programs. The term *FTP* (file transfer protocol) is a UNIX term referring to a protocol that is used to copy files to and from UNIX hosts. The Network File Manager can be used to transfer files between your PC and a local host (a host on your network) or to a remote FTP server on the Internet (a system containing publicly accessible files).

[handwritten margin note: fixed rules & agreement which govern the mean of talking & acting.]

The Network File Manager offers sophisticated file transfer between your PC and a remote host or between two remote hosts using an intuitive Windows interface that works side by side with your Microsoft Windows File Manager. Using NFM, you can drag and drop files directly from your host onto your Windows desktop, and vice versa.

The Network File Manager is enhanced to provide advanced file management functions (such as sorting, filtering files, and copying and moving directories), all using a familiar Windows interface, making host file manipulation quick and virtually painless. NFM menu items are similar to those in the Windows File Manager; NFM also provides buttons that help simplify repetitive tasks.

Note that while you're using NFM, it supports only procedures and file listings that are supported on the host you're connected to.

Network File Manager features

- Drag-and-drop file transfer between a host and the Windows File Manager or between two remote hosts

- Complete file management: move, copy, delete, and rename files and directories on a remote host; can be used as a stand-alone, full-windowed application

- Familiar Windows File Manager-style interface

- Multiple connections to multiple hosts

- Automatic reconnection to one or more hosts

- Set up a default login, password, or other information for a host

- Save window positions, fonts, or other settings

- Multiple file sorting methods

- Edit NFM host names, addresses and descriptions, and connection information: user name, password, account number, and host type

- Support for many host types, including NetWare, VMS, VM, and Windows NT, and enhanced Generic host driver

- Log FTP session activity to screen or printer; FTP open log provides connection troubleshooting

Network File Manager requirements

- Remote hosts must be set up as FTP servers (be running the FTP demon) to be accessed by Network File Manager.

- The Microsoft Windows 3.1 File Manager program is required to use the drag-and-drop file transfer capabilities of the Network File Manager.

Starting the Network File Manager

You start the Network File Manager (NFM) by clicking the NFM icon.

When you first start NFM, you see a Connect To dialog box asking you to log in to a host. A completed sample dialog box is shown in Figure 5-1.

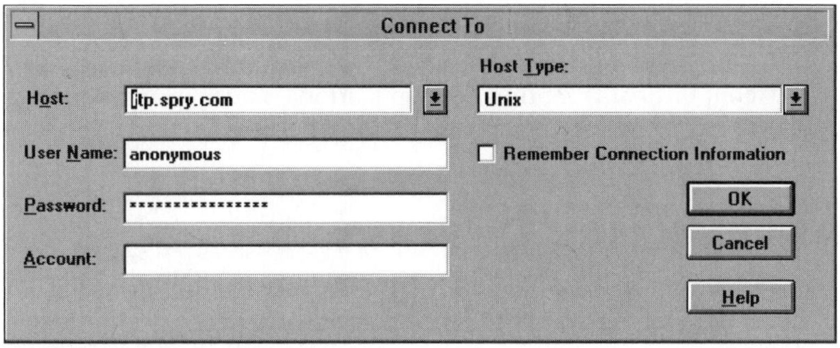

Figure 5-1: The Connect To dialog box.

This dialog box prompts you for a host name to connect to and asks for your login name, password, and other optional information.

After you have filled out the connection dialog box, you can have NFM remember the host, login name, password, account, and host type for this host for the next time you login. If you check Remember Host Login Info this host information is added to NFM's host database, and the host name is added to the drop-down Host list in this dialog. The next time you connect, you can choose the remembered host from the drop-down list and have your user name, password, and the host type for that host filled in automatically (you can change some of this information before you connect).

The Connect To dialog box fields are described in the following sections.

Host (required)

Type the name of a host in the Hosts field, or choose a host from the Hosts list by double-clicking its name.

You can also specify a host by its IP address, such as 165.121.100.1, or its Fully Qualified Domain Name (FQDN), such as circe.spry.com, by typing the IP address or FQDN in the Hosts field.

The drop-down Hosts list is made up of two kinds of hosts:

■ Hosts in your NFM hosts list.

You connect to these hosts with Remember login info already selected. You can maintain this list of hosts inside NFM using the Edit Hosts command; see "Editing the NFM Hosts List" for more information.

■ Hosts in your hosts file.

You can create this file on your system to store host names. This file can contain hosts for other AIR applications. You may or may not have a hosts file on your system, according to how you set up your AIR Series installation.

User name (required)

Specify your user name on the host you have specified. If you are connecting to an anonymous FTP site on the Internet, you usually are asked to specify a login name of *anonymous* with a password of your IP address (that is, john@spry.com).

Password (required)

For the Password field, specify your password on that host. You must specify a password; if none is required on the host you are connecting to, type in a few random characters.

Account (optional)

Some FTP sites require an account number. If this is the case, fill out the account number in this field; it is passed to the host.

Host type (optional)

To use NFM's advanced features, you should specify the type of host you are connecting to (more accurately, the file format of the host you are connecting to). Select a host name from the drop-down box (UNIX is the default host type). It is important to choose the correct host type so that NFM operations perform correctly. If you are unsure of the host type, choose Generic.

After you have typed in the host name or IP address, user name, and password (along with other optional information, if desired), click OK.

You can reconnect to one or more hosts automatically; see "NFM Startup Options" for information on reconnecting to a host without logging in.

The Network File Manager attempts to open a session to the specified host. You see *Connecting to <hostname>* in the status bar at the bottom of the NFM screen.

If a connection is made, the Network File Manager opens a directory window displaying the files on that host. You can immediately begin transferring files; see "NFM File Operations" for more information on file transfer.

Connecting to hosts

When you are connecting to FTP sites on the Internet, you may run into situations like the following:

■ FTP sites may sometimes be unavailable due to system downtime or technical problems.

■ Some hosts on the Internet do not permit anonymous FTP, or they require you to be an authorized user on their host.

■ Anonymous FTP sites often carry restrictions on the number of users that can connect during prime-time (that is, workday) hours.

In most cases, NFM alerts you to the particular problem by showing you an alert screen when you try to connect to the host. However, due to the number of different FTP host types on the Internet, NFM is not always able to filter these messages correctly. If you are unable to connect to an NFM host and do not get a message on your screen indicating the problem, you can check the NFM File Open Log, saved as FTPOPEN.LOG in your \AIR\BIN directory. See "Logging Your NFM Session" for more information on logging in NFM.

Exiting NFM

You can exit the Network File Manager by choosing Exit from the File menu or by double-clicking the Windows System menu in the upper left-hand corner of the NFM Console. Doing this closes all open NFM sessions.

The NFM Console

The first time you start the Network File Manager, the program starts, and the Microsoft Windows File Manager is also opened, as shown in Figure 5-2.

The Network File Manager screen lists all the files and directories in the current directory on the host. The file and directory display are described further in the "NFM Settings" section on the CD.

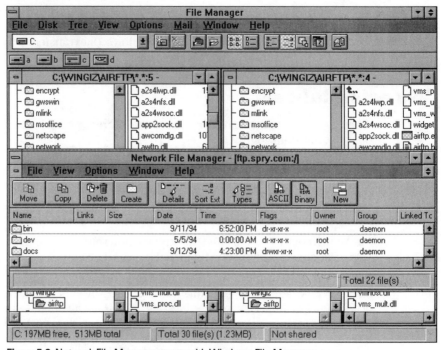

Figure 5-2: Network File Manager opens with Windows File Manager.

The toolbar at the top of the NFM Console has buttons displaying frequently used commands. You can see the meaning of a toolbar button by moving your mouse on top of it; the status bar displays the function of the button. The toolbar can be displayed with Picture only, Text only, or Both Picture and Text, by choosing Toolbar Style from the Options menu.

The status bar at the bottom of the NFM Console displays information on the current status of NFM operations, such as connecting to a host or copying a file.

You can hide both the toolbar and the status bar by unchecking Show Toolbar and Show Status Bar in the Options menu. The toolbar and status bar are displayed if checked.

Network File Manager buttons and menu items may be grayed out when a function cannot be performed.

NFM Startup Options

NFM has two dialog boxes that you can use to specify start-up options: the Connect Information dialog box and the Startup dialog box.

You can also specify whether connections automatically are restored when you start NFM and whether the Windows File Manager automatically starts when you start NFM using the Startup Options dialog box in the Options menu, shown in Figure 5-3.

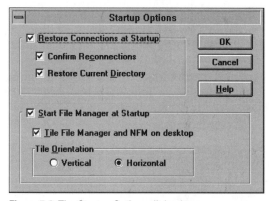

Figure 5-3: The Startup Options dialog box.

Restore Connections at Startup

If you check this option before you exit NFM, the next time you start NFM it tries to open all your current network connections.

By default, you are prompted with a connection screen for each connection that NFM tries to reopen. To reconnect to that session, click OK. You can choose Cancel to decline the reconnection.

You can choose to disable this login prompt so that NFM transparently reconnects to all the current network connections the next time you start NFM, without requiring you to log in to each session. You do so by unchecking Confirm Reconnections. If this option is unchecked, the connections are restored automatically. (You also can set this option using the Confirmation dialog box.) You can also check Restore Current Directory to automatically display the directory you have current when the session is restored (as opposed to the home directory on that host).

Start File Manager at Startup

If you check Start File Manager at Startup, the Windows File Manager automatically starts when you start NFM. If you uncheck this option, only NFM is started. If the File Manager is started with this option, it closes when you exit NFM. You can then check Tile File Manager and NFM at Startup to open Windows File Manager and NFM tiled. You can specify to tile them horizontally (Windows File Manager on top, NFM on bottom) by choosing Horizontal, or tile them vertically (Windows File Manager and NFM side by side) by choosing Vertical.

You can also switch between horizontal and vertical views at any time. Choose Tile FM and NFM Horizontally from the Window menu (or press F6) to tile the Windows File Manager and NFM horizontally, or choose Tile FM and NFM Vertically (or press Alt+F6) to tile the Windows File Manager and NFM vertically (on top of one another).

NFM Connect Information

You can use the Connect Information dialog box to specify a default user name, password, and host type to be used when connecting to hosts; this capability could be useful if you connect to many hosts using anonymous FTP, or if you have the same user name or password on many different hosts.

Choose Connect Information from the Options menu. Fill in the Connect Information dialog box fields with the user name, password, and host type you want to appear automatically in the Connect To dialog box when you connect to hosts. You can fill out some or all of this information.

After you have filled in these fields, click OK. This information is filled out automatically in the Connect To dialog box the next time you try to connect to a host with NFM.

The information you provide in this dialog box is also used by default when you add a new host using the Edit Hosts feature.

Opening Other NFM Sessions

You can open other NFM sessions, keeping your current sessions open, by choosing New Directory Window from the Window menu or clicking the New button on the toolbar. You see the Connect To dialog box and can log into another session.

If you have several NFM sessions open, you can change the way the session windows are displayed. The Cascade command in the Window menu cascades all open NFM windows (windows are stacked on top of one another), and the Tile command in the Window menu automatically tiles all open NFM windows (windows are displayed side by side).

You can also minimize NFM sessions by choosing Minimize from the Microsoft Windows System menu, and specify Arrange Icons to arrange any minimized NFM icons so that they are evenly spaced and do not overlap.

The next section describes settings in NFM that you can use to change the appearance of your screen.

Editing the NFM Hosts List

NFM now includes an Edit NFM Hosts feature that allows you to edit the name, address and port, and descriptions of each host you have connected to. This dialog box, shown in Figure 5-4, displays all the hosts that you have "remembered" using the Remember Login Info.

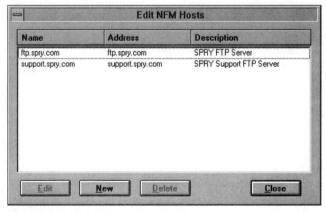

Figure 5-4: The Edit NFM Hosts dialog box.

Hosts from your hosts file (as opposed to the hosts list stored by NFM) do not appear in the Edit NFM Hosts dialog box. You must edit them directly in the hosts file using a text editor. See the TCP/IP Concepts in the Technical Reference section on the CD for more information on hosts files.

Adding or editing a host

To add a host, click the New button; or click Edit to edit an existing host. A dialog box appears; if you are adding a host, the fields in this dialog box are blank.

To add a host, fill in the host name, host address (either IP address or fully qualified domain name), and a description for the host (optional), and click OK. The host is added to your hosts list.

You can have the User Name, Password, and Host Type fields filled out with default information by using the Connect Information command in the Options menu.

To edit a host, change the appropriate fields and click OK. You see the changes you made the next time you start NFM.

Deleting a host

To delete a host, select that host with your mouse by clicking it to highlight the host's name; then click Delete. The host is removed from the hosts list and will not appear the next time you start NFM.

NFM Display Options

NFM enables you to set several options for displaying files on your screen, including the fonts, which file details to display, how to sort files, and the format for displaying files. These options are described in the following sections.

You can save general NFM settings (whether to open File Manager on start-up, displaying the toolbar, and so on), as well as display options, by checking Save Settings on Exit in the Options menu. The general settings will be preserved for use the next time you open an NFM session, whereas display options are preserved only for the session that you saved them in.

Setting the NFM font

You can change the font that is used in NFM by choosing Font from the Options menu. A Windows font dialog box appears. Select the font you want to use and click OK.

Changing the NFM file listing

When you display files and directories on a remote host, they are brought up in a directory window. The files are displayed as documents, and the directories as folders in a tree structure, similar to the Windows File Manager. A sample directory window is shown in Figure 5-5.

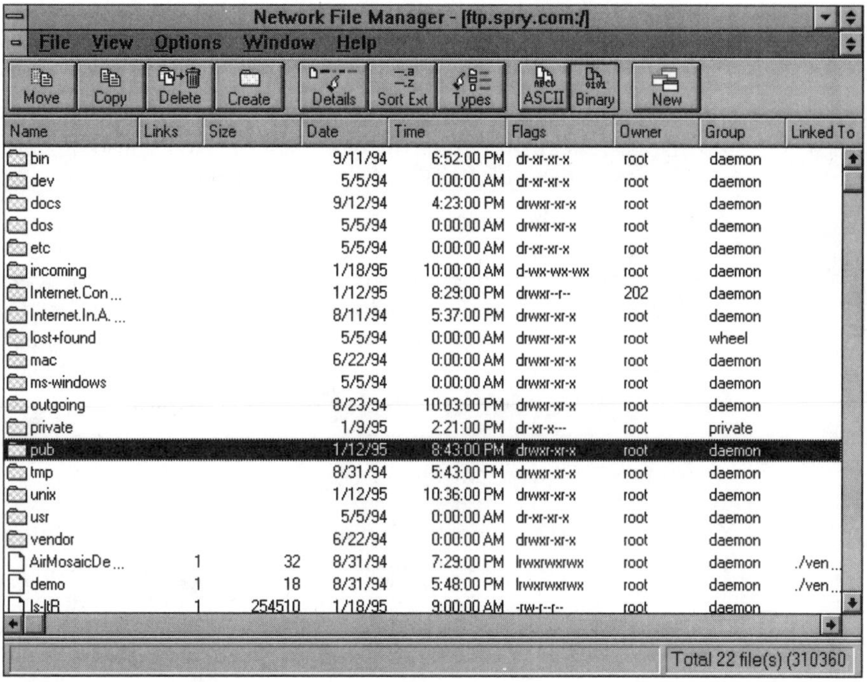

Figure 5-5: A directory window.

There are several ways to change how files are displayed in the Network File Manager. You can change the following:

- Which file details are listed

- The order in which files are listed

- Which files are listed

- The format that the file listing uses

The methods you use to change these settings are described in the following sections.

Setting which file details are listed

You can change which of the file details (such as Name, Date, Size, Owner, and so on) are listed by choosing All File Details or the Partial Details options from the NFM View menu.

- **All File Details**: Displays all available file details for files on the host you are connected to. These details vary according to the host.

- **Partial File Details**: Enables you to specify which file details you want to display. Check the details that you want to display and click OK. (You can also select this item by clicking the Details button on the toolbar.)

You can change the size of the Name field by moving your cursor to the separator to the right of the Name field until it turns into a double-headed arrow, holding down your mouse button, and moving it left or right to change the size of the field. This feature does not apply if you are in host directory list format or if you are using the Generic host driver to connect to hosts.

Setting the order in which files are listed

By clicking the detail header for a detail (as shown in Figure 5-6), you can change how NFM sorts the files in a listing.

You can also sort by choosing the Sort by... options from the Options menu. The sorting is done by the methods described in Table 5-1.

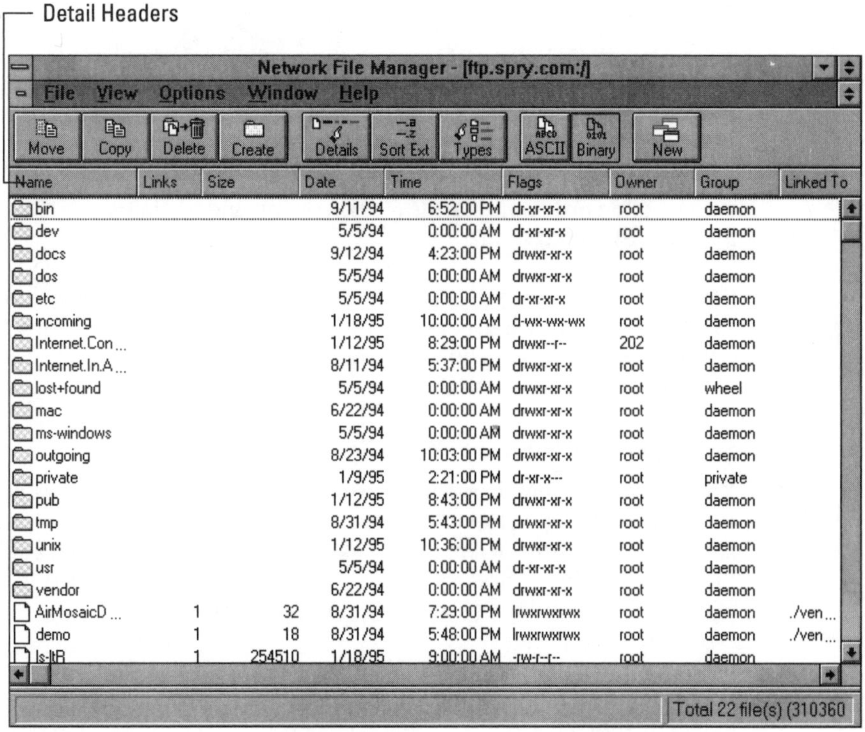

Detail Headers

Figure 5-6: Clicking on a detail header determines how NFM sorts remote files.

Table 5-1	NFM File Sorting
Sorting method	**How it lists files**
Sort by Name	List files in alphabetical order (this option is the default).
Sort by Type	List files in alphabetical order by their extensions (that is, LINK.DLL, TEST.DLL, AUTO.EXE, TIMER.EXE, STORY.TXT).
Sort by Size, Date, Owner, Group, and so on	Other sorting options appear in this menu based on the available file details of the host that you are connecting to. Sort by Size lists files from smallest to largest; Sort by Date, from oldest to newest.

Setting which files are listed

You can also select which files are listed using By File Type from the View menu.

The By File Type... screen enables you to specify whether directories, programs, documents, or other files (nondirectories, programs, and documents) are listed.

You can also list files with any given file specification by typing the specification using a wild-card combination (*, ?) in the provided dialog box. To select all files, leave this box blank.

If you use wild cards, you must use the wild-card conventions used on the file system you are viewing. For example, on a UNIX system, specifying ***.txt** lists only files with the extension TXT, and specifying **doc*** lists only files that begin with the first three letters DOC.

Setting the format that file details use

You can set the NFM directory window to display files as they are displayed on the host by choosing Host Directory List Format. For example, a UNIX host may list file details in this order: flags, links, owner, group, size, date, and name. Choosing Windows Directory List Format lists files in standard Windows order, with name first and then size, date, time, and so on.

If you have the file displayed in Windows directory list format, you can change the size of the Name field by dragging the right divider line of the Name field longer or shorter.

Displaying and Printing Remote Host Files

After you have connected to a host, you may be able to open or print files directly using Network File Manager. NFM recognizes files just the way the Windows File Manager does: by examining the file's extension and checking to see what application is associated with that type of file. For instance, the file HELLO.TXT has the extension TXT, which is associated by Network File Manager with the Windows Notepad application. Therefore, when you try to open or print this file in Network File Manager using the Open or Print commands, the file is automatically opened or printed using Windows Notepad.

Only files with file extensions can be opened by Network File Manager.

Using file associations

File associations in NFM work just the way they do in the Windows File Manager. You use an Associate command to tell NFM how to recognize and open associations, so you can open or print a file directly from NFM.

NFM automatically uses any associations that were set up in Windows File Manager; you can also examine and change those associations and add additional associations.

You can add a new association at any time. You may find it convenient to add associations when you are actually highlighting a filename that you want to associate. Choose Associate from the File menu. An Associate dialog box appears, showing a list of file associations. If you currently have a file highlighted, any association for that file appears.

You can create a new association or change an existing association by typing the extension you want to associate into the Files with Extension field (if you highlighted a file, it is already there). You can then choose the application to associate this extension with from the Associate With drop-down list. If the application is not in the list, you can use the Browse button to locate the application on your PC.

Because you are basically transferring the files (into your system memory) before you open or print them, you may need to specify the file transfer type for each file association. For text files, make sure that the association is set to ASCII to ensure that they open correctly; for any other files (including word processing documents), you probably want to specify Binary.

Click OK when you have finished making associations.

Opening a remote file

You can open a file on a remote host by selecting the file and pressing Enter, or choosing Open from the File menu. If there is an association set up for that file, NFM launches the program associated with that file and displays the file. (If there is no association for that file, NFM displays a message informing you that there is no association for that file.)

If the file does not have an extension that you can associate with an application, you have to transfer the file to your PC before you can open it.

You can check the Minimize on File Open command if you want to minimize the Network File Manager Console automatically when any NFM files are opened.

Printing a file

If you have an association set up for the file you want to print, you can print the file by choosing Print from the File menu. NFM launches the program associated with that file and prints the file.

If the file does not have an extension that you can associate with an application, you have to transfer the file to your PC before you can print it.

NFM File Operations

Once the Network File Manager is open and connected to a remote host, you can begin copying or moving files between your PC and that remote host, or between two remote hosts. You can also perform other file operations such as creating directories and renaming and deleting files or directories. The following sections explain basic file operations in NFM.

You can perform only file operations that you have rights to perform or that the FTP server you are connected to supports. Some systems do not allow you to move files or create directories, or may not display all available file attributes.

Operations in the Network File Manager are similar to operations in the Windows File Manager. You can view the files or directories inside a directory by double-clicking the directory folder. You can also choose Open from the File menu to open a directory folder.

To move up to the previous directory level, double-click the up arrow, as shown in Figure 5-7.

Some host systems do not support using a mouse to change directories. In these cases, you can use the Change Directory command in the File menu to specify the name of the directory you want to change to. This method is also a quick way to change directories if you know the full pathname of the directory you want. The next section explains how to specify remote host files and directories in this and other NFM dialogs.

Selecting files and directories

There are two ways to select files and directories for operations in NFM: you can specify them by filename, or you can select them using drag-and-drop techniques. These two methods are described in the following sections.

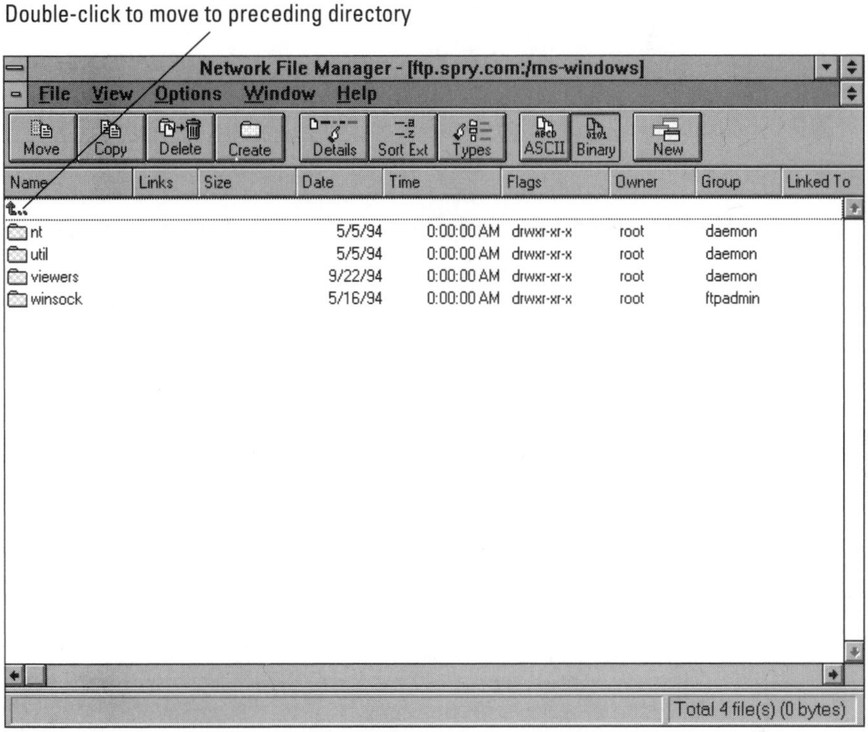

Double-click to move to preceding directory

Figure 5-7: Double-click the up arrow to change "up" to the preceding directory.

Specifying files and directories by filename

Specifying file and directory names for a remote host is similar to specifying file and directory names on your local PC.

Files and directories on a host are denoted in NFM by a host name, followed by a colon. They then use the pathname syntax of the host system. For example, a UNIX file from host bart.marge.com is displayed in an NFM dialog box as follows:

```
bart.marge.com:/home/files/myfile.txt
```

Notice that UNIX files use the forward slash (instead of the backslash used in DOS) to denote subdirectories.

A DOS file is specified in the dialog box with the standard DOS filename syntax:

```
c:\files\filename.ext
```

The host name you use is based on the name or address you provided when you started the NFM session.

It is important not to name any of your hosts with a one-character name (a–z) because it may also correspond to DOS drive letters and NFM cannot distinguish it from DOS drives.

Selecting files and directories with drag and drop

You can select a file or directory to operate on by clicking the file or directory name with your mouse. You can also select multiple files by clicking them with your mouse while holding down the Ctrl or Shift keys. Shift selects a series of adjacent files, and Ctrl enables you to select a number of nonadjacent files individually.

When the files and directories are selected, you can then use File menu operations on them, or drag and drop them onto a remote host or your local PC (via Windows File Manager).

When you're filling out the file operation dialog boxes, the Current Directory (the currently selected or highlighted directory in NFM) is shown at the top of the screen. If you do not specify a pathname for any files you are manipulating, their origins or destinations are assumed to be the currently selected directory. To simplify operations, select the file or directory you want to operate on before choosing an NFM command.

Renaming a file or directory

You can rename a file or directory by highlighting the file or directory you want to rename and clicking Rename from the File menu. You are then prompted for a new filename or directory name. Type the name and click OK.

You can also specify the original and new names for the file or directory in the dialog without highlighting them first.

Creating a directory

You can create a directory on an NFM host by selecting the location where you want the directory and choosing Create Directory from the File menu (or clicking the Create button on the toolbar). You can then specify the new directory name and click OK to create the directory.

Deleting files or directories

To delete files or directories, select those files or directories using the mouse and choose Delete from the File menu or press the Delete key on your keyboard. (You can also specify the file or directory names in this dialog box.) Click OK to delete the files or directories.

Confirming file operations

When you copy or move files, or delete or replace files on the host, you automatically are prompted to confirm that you want to perform those actions. You can enable or disable this confirmation step using the Confirmation dialog box in the Options menu, shown in Figure 5-8.

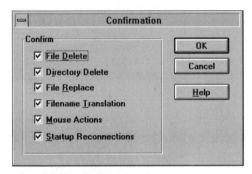

Figure 5-8: The Confirmation dialog box.

In this dialog box, you can also specify whether to confirm mouse actions (any drag-and-drop activity), whether to confirm automatic reconnection to a host, and whether to ask for confirmation when translating a long filename during file transfer.

Copying and Moving Files with NFM _____

The Network File Manager supports copying and moving files:

■ From your PC to an NFM host

■ From an NFM host to your PC

■ From one NFM host to another NFM host

You can copy and move files either by dragging and dropping them or by using the File menu's Copy or Move commands and specifying the filenames and locations.

NFM does not permit you to copy or move entire directories.

You may want to customize your file transfer method to the task at hand. Drag and drop is useful for moving many adjacent files or selecting files with nothing in common. It also permits you to move files without having to know the entire file pathname. The File menu technique is useful when you want to specify a group of files with similar names (using wild-card techniques), all the files in a large directory, or when you want to copy or move files that aren't currently displayed on your screen.

Setting file transfer options

Before you begin copying or moving files, you may want to change the file transfer options. Select File Transfer from the Options menu to set file transfer options. You can set two options using this dialog box, described in the following two sections.

Changing the file transfer method

When you're transferring files with NFM, you need to choose between ASCII (text) and Binary (nontext files, such as executable files or graphic and sound files) methods of file transfer. Basically, if a file contains special control codes, it should be transferred as Binary. Be sure to select the correct mode for the files you are transferring: if a file is transferred using the wrong transfer mode, ASCII files may not display properly, and Binary files may not execute properly. To avoid using the wrong transfer method, do one of the following:

■ Click the Binary or ASCII button on the toolbar before transferring files.

■ Specify Binary or ASCII as your default File Transfer method using the File Transfer command in the Options menu.

Because it is sometimes difficult to know what file transfer method to use *before* you transfer files, you may want to select Binary for most file transfers, and choose to examine text files using the Open command. See "Displaying and Printing Remote Host Files" earlier in this chapter for more information.

Setting the filename translation option

You can also specify whether files that are transferred are automatically renamed by NFM. Often, remote files have names longer than DOS allows (DOS allows up to eight characters with a three-character extension). A long filename (for example, TCP.IP.INTRO.TXT) is automatically translated by NFM into a legal DOS filename by using up to eight characters of the filename and adding an extension, if one was provided. (In the example, the file becomes TCPIPINT.TXT).

Selecting the Confirm Filename Translation option means that you are always prompted whether to change the filename using this conversion method. When this option is turned on, and you copy or move one or more files with long filenames, you see a Confirm Filename Translation dialog box.

This dialog box suggests a default filename for a file with a long filename. You can select Yes if you want to accept the provided filename, or you can change the filename to one you prefer before selecting Yes. If you are copying or moving several files, you can select Yes to All to accept the default filenames for all long files in your copy/move transaction. (If you are copying or moving several files, and you select Yes, you are prompted with this dialog box for each file with a long filename.) Select No if you do not want to copy or move the file at the current time. Selecting Cancel cancels the current file transfer or any file transfers in the batch.

Copying and moving files using drag and drop

You *drag* by clicking the filename (or group of filenames) you want to transfer and holding down the mouse button while you move the mouse, thereby dragging the file with you. You can drag/copy (drag a copy of the selected file(s)) by simply dragging the file(s). You can drag/move (removing the original file(s)) by holding down Ctrl as you drag the file(s); note that this procedure does not work when you're dragging files from the Windows File Manager.

You then *drop* the file(s) by releasing the mouse button at the place that you want to copy or move the file(s). The file or files are then copied or moved, as simple as that.

Dragging and dropping from your PC to an NFM host

You can copy files from your PC to an NFM host using the Windows File Manager. Select the file or files you want to copy in the Windows File Manager, drag them to an NFM directory window, and drop them onto the area where you want to move them. (You can copy files to an NFM host only if you have permission to do so on that host.) Moving files from the Windows File Manager to NFM using drag and drop is not supported (due to Windows File Manager operation).

Dragging and dropping from an NFM host to your PC or other NFM host

You can copy or move files from an NFM host to your PC or another NFM host by selecting the file(s) on your NFM Directory window, dragging the file(s) you selected (pressing Ctrl and dragging to move) to your Windows File Manager screen, and dropping them onto the area where you want to move them. (You can move files from an NFM host only if you have permission to do so on that host.)

Copying and moving files using the File menu

You can also copy or move files from an NFM host to your PC or another NFM host (or from your PC to an NFM host) by typing the file origin and destination using the NFM File menu, as described in the following steps. You follow the same procedure no matter where the source and destination files are located.

1. Select the files or directories you want to copy or move using the mouse (this step is optional; if you don't select any files, you can specify the file by pathname as described below).

2. Choose Copy or Move from the File menu (or press F8 for Copy or F7 for Move). A Copy or Move dialog box similar to the one in Figure 5-9 appears, asking you to specify the file origin and destination.

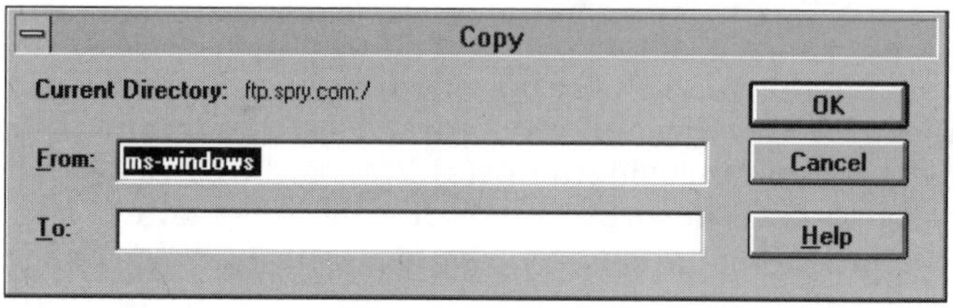

Figure 5-9: The Copy dialog box.

If you highlighted any files or directories before beginning the file transfer operation, NFM assumes that you want to work with those files and fills in the dialog box with those filenames.

If you provide no pathname in this dialog box, NFM assumes the files you are specifying are found in the current directory on the current host (the host directory window that is currently highlighted). The advantage to selecting your origin directory before beginning a file operation is that you eliminate having to type a long pathname.

3. Specify the names of the origin and destination file(s) in the appropriate format.

For a file on an NFM host, you use the following format:

```
host:/home/files/myfile.txt
```

where host is the name of the host you are connected to and /home/files/myfile.txt is the path and filename of the file in that host's format.

For a file on your PC, you use the typical DOS format:

```
c:\files\myfile.txt
```

You can use them in any order; from NFM host to NFM host, from NFM host to PC, or from PC to NFM host (even from PC to PC, if you really must!).

The Copy and Move Command dialog box supports the use of file wild cards (? and *), which enable you to substitute for characters that you do not know (or want to type). For example, you can copy files from sunhost:/home/files/data??? or from c:\files*.txt.

4. Click OK. The specified file or files are copied or moved.

Remember that you cannot copy or move files to an NFM host or move files from an NFM host unless you have permission on that host.

Copying and moving files on a single host

You can copy and move files on one NFM host using the techniques described in the preceding section; however, you do not have to specify the host name as you did there because the origin and target destination are on the same system.

Logging Your NFM Session

NFM provides a log of connection information whenever you connect to a host and has the capability to log all session activity to a file or printer. Logging your session activity may help you if you are having problems accessing directories or transferring files by showing you the messages the host sends to NFM.

Logging your connection information

Each time you connect to a host, NFM creates a file called FTPOPEN.LOG, which saves all the messages provided by the host when you first connect. This procedure is done automatically. Each time you connect to a host, it overwrites this file, so this file holds only your most current connection log.

NFM enables you to log your current NFM session to a file or to the screen. Keep in mind that logging your NFM session slows down your NFM session activity slightly.

Choose Logging from the Options menu. You see a dialog box like Figure 5-10.

Figure 5-10: The Logging Options dialog box.

You can log two types of activity in NFM: FTP Requests and FTP Replies. FTP Requests are basically your activity on the host: when you ask to change directories or copy files. FTP Replies are the acknowledgment of those requests, such as *File Copied*. The example in the next section shows sample FTP Requests and Replies.

Logging to a window

If you enable Log to Window (by checking FTP Requests or FTP Replies under Log to Window), a hidden window underneath NFM is used to log your session.

To display this window, move your cursor to the thin border between your NFM directory window and the NFM status bar (if you are not displaying your status bar, it is a border right on the bottom of your screen). Your cursor turns into a double-headed arrow, which you can push up to display the logging window. (If you need more space to view logging activity, maximize your NFM Console by clicking the Maximize arrow in the upper right-hand corner of the Console.) Adjust the logging window until you can view the session activity. Figure 5-11 is a sample logging window.

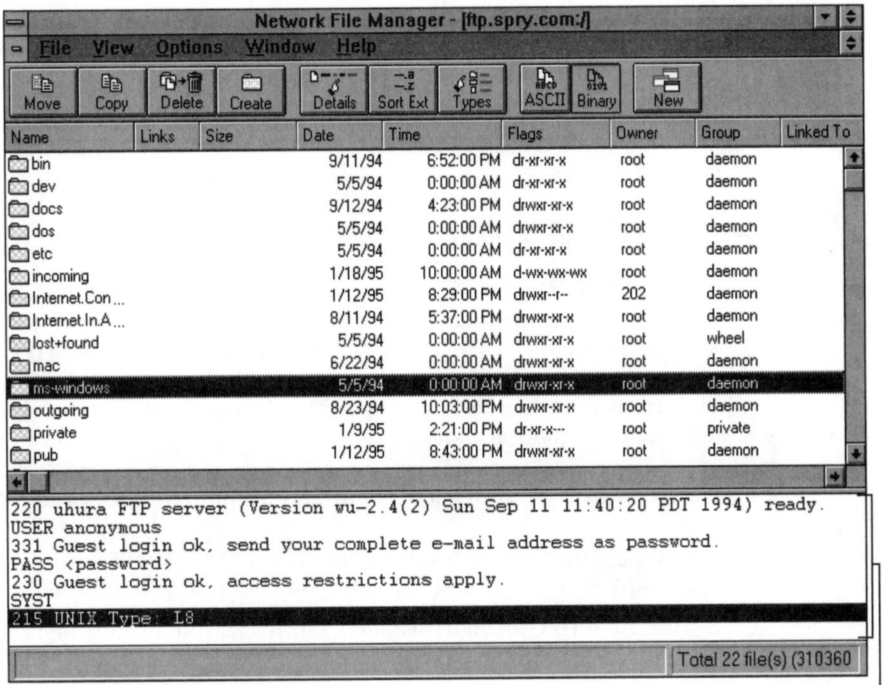

Figure 5-11: A sample logging window.

Logging windows ⎯

Session activity is logged to this window whether or not you view it; you can leave it closed and examine it at any time during the session. When you exit your session, the logging window is cleared; if you want to save session activity permanently, log to a file, as described in the following section.

The Clear Log command in the Window menu clears all logging window contents at any time.

Logging to a file

You may want to log all NFM activity to a file instead of the logging window. To do so, choose FTP Requests or FTP Replies under Log to File in the Logging Options dialog. You can either specify a filename for the log file by clicking the button next to the filename and choosing a file to be your log file (this file is overwritten), or you can use the default log file, FTP.LOG in your \AIR\BIN directory.

All your session activity is written to the file that you specify. This file, like the connection log, is overwritten each time you start a new session. If you want to save your last session log, change the name of the log file you are using; then exit and restart NFM.

Viewing Information about a File

NFM enables you to view file information from the host using the Properties and Quick Properties commands. The information that appears is virtually the same information you see if you are connecting to the host with the correct host driver and are displaying all the file details; therefore, this feature is really helpful only if you are currently using the Generic host driver or if you need additional information about a file.

Properties displays all available information about the file in a dialog box:

1. Highlight the filename and choose Properties from the File menu. A dialog box opens, displaying all available information from the host.

2. You can scroll through the dialog box to read all the information. Click OK to close the dialog box.

Quick Properties summarizes the information about the file in the NFM status bar:

1. Highlight the filename and choose Quick Properties from the File menu (or press Ctrl+Alt+Enter). The Quick Properties information appears in the status bar and stays there until you highlight another file.

Properties and Quick Properties work only for files; highlighting a directory name indicates that the highlighted item is a directory.

AIR Mosaic Express

AIR Mosaic Express™ is a graphical, sophisticated Internet Browser application, enabling you to access the Internet World Wide Web. World Wide Web (also referred to as WWW, W^3, or the Web) is a *hypermedia* environment on the Internet. You can browse World Wide Web information by merely pointing and clicking (similar to using a CD-ROM-based reference tool) — you can view pictures or movies, play sounds, read documents, and easily copy files to your PC.

AIR Mosaic Express is designed to be the optimal tool for browsing the World Wide Web. Developed from NCSA's original Mosaic tool, it has been updated to incorporate more Windows functionality and to be easy to configure and customize.

AIR Mosaic Express features Hotlists and advanced menu support, enabling you to incorporate your own Internet "finds" easily and quickly jump to the information you want to access. Fonts, colors, and performance are easily configured using one configuration screen.

Features

- Advanced *Hotlist* capability, enabling you to add WWW documents into Hotlists with folders and subfolders, and easily add multiple Hotlists to your AIR Mosaic Express menu for quick access. (Also enables you to import NCSA menus.)

- Configure Mosaic preferences (colors, fonts, default home page), viewers, and options via a straightforward Configuration dialog box. The Advanced Viewers dialog box enables you to configure viewers easily or add new ones.

- *Kiosk mode* enables you to hide the toolbar and other information. Ideal for presentations, it also enables you to set up AIR Mosaic Express for "unattended" use.

- Customizable caching feature; quickly access documents you've already browsed in the session.

- Easily connect to the last Web sites you accessed via a drop-down History list or pull-down Document Title/Document URL menus.

- Search for keywords in any document you are browsing.

- Support for proxy servers for http, WAIS, FTP, and Gopher.

- Print WWW document text and graphics.

- Save, edit, or copy HTML document source code.

Starting AIR Mosaic Express

Although there are thousands of Mosaic sites on the Internet that you can explore, you may not know where to start. AIR Mosaic Express is preconfigured with SPRY, Inc.'s World Wide Web home page. This is done so that you have a place to start looking for other WWW resources.

When you start AIR Mosaic Express, it automatically connects you to the SPRY home page. From there, you can begin browsing the Internet and begin connecting to other home pages. As you become an experienced browser, you can build a library of home pages that you like, using AIR Mosaic Express's Hotlist feature.

Start AIR Mosaic Express by clicking the AIR Mosaic Express icon. AIR Mosaic Express immediately begins connecting you to the SPRY *home page* (Figure 5-12). (You see the radar logo in the upper-right corner of the AIR Mosaic Express console spinning as the home page is retrieved.)

After you finish connecting to the SPRY home page, you can immediately begin browsing with Mosaic, as described in the next section.

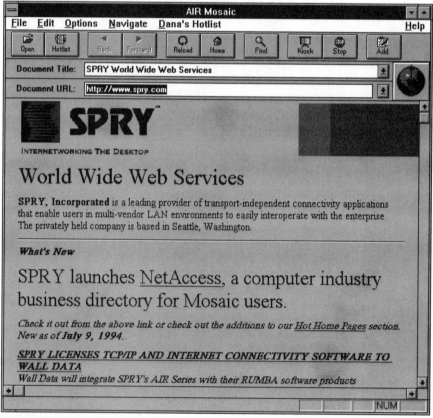

Figure 5-12: SPRY's home page.

You can easily define your own home page to connect to automatically on start-up. Use the Configuration option in the Options menu to set up a default home page. See "Configuring AIR Mosaic Express Options" later in this chapter for more information.

Exiting Mosaic

You can exit AIR Mosaic Express by choosing Exit from the File menu. You can also double-click the Windows System menu to exit AIR Mosaic Express.

 If you are currently retrieving a new Mosaic document, it is recommended that you wait to exit until that document is retrieved, or stop retrieving the document by clicking the Stop button or choosing Cancel Current Task from the History menu.

The AIR Mosaic Express Console _____

The AIR Mosaic Express Console is described in the following paragraphs.

The *toolbar* at the top of the Console contains buttons that serve as shortcuts for AIR Mosaic Express menu items. You can change the toolbar style between *Picture & Text*, *Picture only*, and *Text only* by choosing Toolbar Style from the Options menu.

The *status bar* at the bottom of the Console displays the locations of resources you connect to, as well as indicating when a transfer is in progress or a graphic is being loaded.

You can show or hide both the toolbar and the status bar by checking or unchecking Show Status Bar or Show Toolbar using the Configuration option in the Options menu.

Below the toolbar is the document title bar, containing the Document Title and Document URL drop-down lists. The two lists contain a listing of the last several documents you've accessed. The lists are identical, but one shows the title of the document (such as "SPRY Home Page") and the other shows that document's URL (http://www.spry.com). You can go back to any of the displayed documents by choosing its title or URL from the lists. You can change the number of documents that are displayed in these lists using the Configuration option in the Options menu.

The document title bar also contains the *radar retrieval icon*. This icon moves when a document is being loaded or a graphic is being transferred (roughly, it indicates that AIR Mosaic Express is busy). You can disable the animation of this icon by unchecking Animate logo using the Configuration option in the Options menu.

Using Kiosk mode

Kiosk mode is available with AIR Mosaic Express; you can use Kiosk mode to hide all the Console information except the actual document (in other words, the toolbar, status bar, and document title bar and the menu items and commands are hidden). This mode may be useful when you're giving Mosaic presentations (it shows a lot of the screen) or when setting up Mosaic on an unattended workstation.

1. Click the Kiosk button on the toolbar, or choose Kiosk Mode from the Options menu. AIR Mosaic Express changes into Kiosk mode.

You can move around in Mosaic as you would normally, except that the toolbar buttons and menu options are not available to you. The shortcut movement keys of F (for Forward) and B (for Back) are very helpful to you to move when in this mode, because the Forward and Back commands are not available.

2. Press Esc or Ctrl+K to exit Kiosk mode.

Browsing with AIR Mosaic Express

The World Wide Web uses *hyperlinks* (also referred to as *anchors* or *hot spots*) to enable you to jump to other resources. Hyperlinks are indicated by blue underlined text, or by graphics surrounded by a blue border (you can change the color that is used). Another way to tell that you are on a hyperlink is to highlight the text or graphic with your mouse. The mouse turns into a pointing hand, as shown in Figure 5-13.

You can then click a hyperlink to connect to another Mosaic document. The new document is then opened (you see the radar indicator in the upper-right corner of your AIR Mosaic Express Console begin to spin). If at any time you need to stop loading in a document, you can click the Stop button or choose Cancel Current Task from the Navigate menu.

You can continue to browse through WWW documents by simply clicking the hyperlinks you find in the document. You can also travel through documents you encounter as described in the following sections.

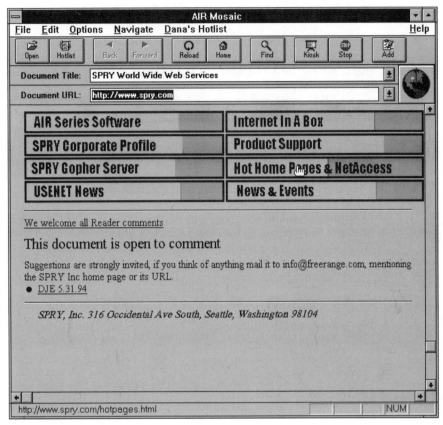

Figure 5-13: Hyperlinks.

Jumping back and forward

You can click the Back button (the third button on the toolbar) to move back to the last document you viewed. The Forward button (the fourth button on the toolbar) can move you forward after you have moved back. You can also press B for Back or F for Forward, or choose Back and Forward from the Navigate menu.

Opening previous documents

The Document Title: and Document URL: drop-down lists, located under the toolbar, contain a listing of the last several documents you've accessed in this session. The lists are identical, but one shows the title of the document (such as "SPRY Home Page") and the other shows that document's URL (http://www.spry.com). You can go back to any of the displayed documents by choosing its title or URL from the lists.

You can also click History to access the History dialog box. The History dialog box enables you to access documents you've already accessed in this session. Using it is equivalent to using the drop-down lists, above. Select the document you want to go back to, and click the Load button.

At any time, you can click the Home button on the toolbar, or choose Home from the Navigate menu to return to the document defined as your *home page*. When you start using Mosaic, the SPRY, Inc. home page is defined as your home page; you can set up a new home page (or set AIR Mosaic Express to start *without* opening a home page) using Configuration in the Options menu.

You can reload the current AIR Mosaic Express document at any time by clicking the Reload button or choosing Reload from the Navigate menu. You might want to reload if the document did not load properly.

Using Hotlists

One of AIR Mosaic Express's strongest features is its capability to organize the information that you find on the World Wide Web. There are so many documents out there with useful jumps to resources you might be interested in that it is common to want to access these documents again and again. You can save these documents and open them again later (see "Saving Documents in Mosaic" later in this chapter), but AIR Mosaic Express provides an easier way to reaccess documents.

You can use AIR Mosaic Express's Hotlists to remember WWW document locations so that you can easily locate and access them. You can group Hotlists by subject (Games, Sports, Weather, Fun Stuff) or by any other criteria (if several people use one computer, they might each have Hotlists).

Hotlists you create can then be accessed two ways: you can access them using a couple of mouse clicks from the convenient Hotlists dialog, or you can make Hotlists into drop-down menus so that you can choose them directly from the AIR Mosaic Express menu bar.

NCSA Mosaic users: You can convert any menus you created in NCSA Mosaic to Hotlists. See the end of this section for information.

The Hotlists dialog box

You work with Hotlists in the Hotlists dialog box (accessed by clicking the Hotlists button or by choosing Hotlists from the File menu). The Hotlists screen initially shows all the different Hotlists you have (Figure 5-14). AIR Mosaic Express comes with one default Hotlist preloaded: the Starting Points Hotlist. Other Hotlists are included in your \AIR\DATA directory; you can load them or, of course, you can make your own.

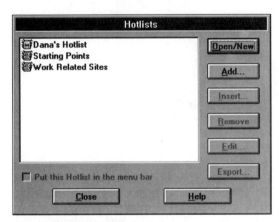

Figure 5-14: Hotlists dialog box.

The Hotlist itself is shown as a flaming document in the Hotlist dialog box. Initially, Hotlists may be shown *closed;* you can open up (expand) the Hotlist by double-clicking the Hotlist icon. Each Hotlist can contain many WWW documents, or it can contain folders that contain additional documents (you can use folders and subfolders to organize your documents any way you want). You see the documents and folders listed in a hierarchy similar to the Windows File Manager.

In the Hotlists dialog box, you can create new Hotlists, add new Hotlist items, edit your existing items, or delete them.

At any time, you can check Use Hotlist as menu item to have a Hotlist added as a menu item. (See Figure 5-15.) You can add as many menu items as can fit in your AIR Mosaic Express menu bar. When you choose this option, the Hotlist icon in the Hotlist dialog box changes to a dialog containing the letter *H*. If you add a Hotlist as a menu item, any folders within that Hotlist appear as menu items that have submenu items beneath them.

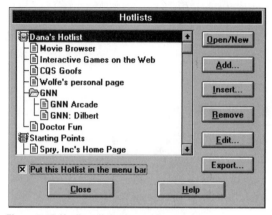

Figure 5-15: Hotlists dialog box with menu items.

Creating a new Hotlist

Select File⇨Hotlists, or click the Hotlist button on the toolbar. The Hotlist dialog box, described earlier, appears.

Click the New/Open button. You will see a Windows File Open dialog box. (You could specify the name of an existing Hotlist at this point, to open and load it into the Hotlist dialog box.)

Choose a filename for your Hotlist, and click OK. This name must be a legal DOS filename (using up to eight characters) with an HOT extension.

The next dialog box asks you to specify a name for this Hotlist. It can be any name you want (keep in mind that you may want to use this Hotlist as a Mosaic menu (as in Figure 5-16), so you might want to keep the name short). Type a name and click OK.

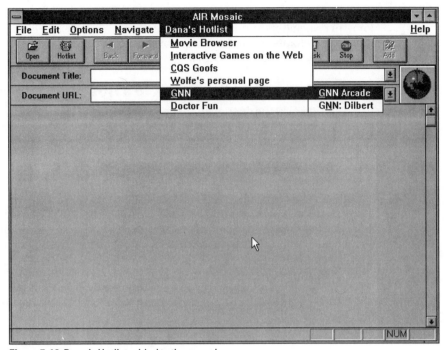

Figure 5-16: Dana's Hotlist added to the menu bar

The Hotlist is created, and you see it appear in the Hotlist screen (as a "flaming" document).

As mentioned earlier, you may want to create folders and subfolders to help organize your information. To do so, click Add with the Hotlist or folder highlighted, and specify Folder in the dialog box that appears. You are asked to name the folder. Name the folder, click OK, and the folder is created.

Now that you have a Hotlist, you can begin to add documents to it, as described in the next section.

Adding documents to a Hotlist

There are two ways to add documents to a Hotlist:

- Add the document to a Hotlist when you are viewing the document.
- Add the document to a Hotlist manually.

The first option is easier than the second option because you do not have to know or remember the document's URL (the document's address, described later in this chapter), but you do for the second option. These two options are described in the next two sections.

Adding the current document to a Hotlist

In Mosaic, display the document that you want to add to a Hotlist. You could do this by jumping to it from another document or opening it directly using its URL (as described later in this chapter).

You now have two ways to add the document to a Hotlist:

■ Clicking Add Document to Hotlist in the Navigate menu adds the document to the Hotlist you are currently using, which is the last Hotlist you selected. Open the Hotlist dialog box if you are not sure which Hotlist is currently selected. If no Hotlist is selected, this command may not work properly.

■ Using the Hotlists screen, as described in the following steps, enables you to specify exactly where you want to add the document.

1. Click the Hotlist button, or choose File➪Hotlist. You see the Hotlists screen.

2. Select the Hotlist to which you want to add the current document.

3. Click Add. You are asked whether you want to add a document or folder; select Document. You see the Add Document dialog box (see Figure 5-17). It should contain the Name and URL of the document you are currently viewing. If you want, you can change the name of the document. *Do not change the URL!*

Figure 5-17: Add Document dialog box.

4. Click OK. The document you specified is added to the Hotlist you selected.

Adding a document to a Hotlist manually

If you want to add a document that is not currently open to a Hotlist, you add the document manually. To do so, you need to know the URL (address) for each document; URLs are described in more detail in the next section. For example, someone may give you a list of WWW documents containing travel information. You can create a Travel Hotlist and add all the documents to it quickly — a one-step process. You create the Hotlist as follows:

1. Click the Hotlist button, or choose File⇨Hotlist to open the Hotlists dialog box.

2. Select the Hotlist to which you want to add a document by using your mouse to highlight the Hotlist name.

3. Click Add. You are asked whether you want to add a document or folder; select Document. You see the Add Document dialog box. If you currently have a document open, the information about that document appears in this dialog box. To add a different document to this Hotlist, you must type in the Name and URL of the document.

   For the *Document name:,* type any name you want. It should be a name that helps you recognize this file.

   For the *Document URL: (check)* field, type the Document's URL. Later in this chapter, you'll find more information on using URLs.

4. Click OK. The document you specified is added to the Hotlist you selected.

Importing NCSA menus as Hotlists

If you previously used NCSA Mosaic (by the National Center of Supercomputing Applications), you may have built up extensive menus of favorite home pages and resources; AIR Mosaic Express enables you to convert these menus to AIR Mosaic Express Hotlists so that you can use them just as you would use Hotlists created in AIR Mosaic Express.

To import an NCSA menu as a Hotlist

Click Import NCSA Menu as Hotlist in the Options menu. You see the Import NCSA Menu as Hotlist dialog box. (See Figure 5-18.)

In the INI file to import from field, specify the name and location of the MOSAIC.INI file where your NCSA menu information is stored. You can click the Browse button to browse the directories on your PC and select the correct file. After you've selected the file, you can confirm that it is the file you want by clicking the Open button.

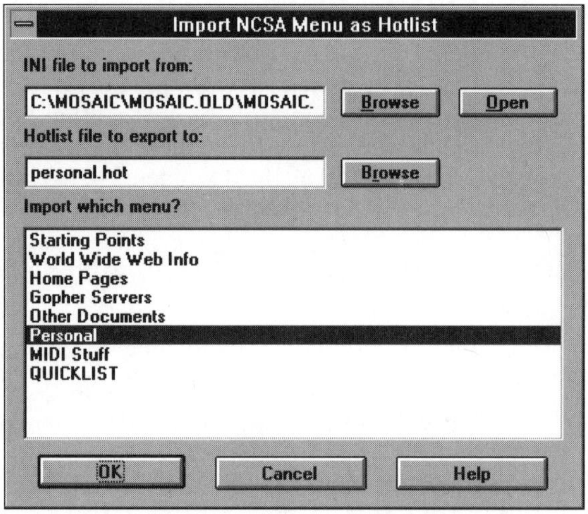

```
┌─────────────────────────────────────────────────────┐
│ ─            Import NCSA Menu as Hotlist             │
│ INI file to import from:                             │
│ ┌───────────────────────────┐ ┌────────┐ ┌────────┐ │
│ │ C:\MOSAIC\MOSAIC.OLD\MOSAIC.│ │ Browse │ │  Open  │ │
│ └───────────────────────────┘ └────────┘ └────────┘ │
│ Hotlist file to export to:                           │
│ ┌───────────────────────────┐ ┌────────┐            │
│ │ personal.hot              │ │ Browse │            │
│ └───────────────────────────┘ └────────┘            │
│ Import which menu?                                   │
│ ┌─────────────────────────────────────────────────┐ │
│ │ Starting Points                                 │ │
│ │ World Wide Web Info                              │ │
│ │ Home Pages                                      │ │
│ │ Gopher Servers                                  │ │
│ │ Other Documents                                 │ │
│ │ Personal                                        │ │
│ │ MIDI Stuff                                      │ │
│ │ QUICKLIST                                       │ │
│ │                                                 │ │
│ └─────────────────────────────────────────────────┘ │
│ ┌─────────┐   ┌──────────┐   ┌──────────┐           │
│ │   OK    │   │  Cancel  │   │   Help   │           │
│ └─────────┘   └──────────┘   └──────────┘           │
└─────────────────────────────────────────────────────┘
```

Figure 5-18: Import NCSA Menu as Hotlist dialog box.

You should then specify a Hotlist file for this menu. *Do not choose an existing Hotlist unless you want to overwrite the information in that file.* Again, you can use Browse to find a Hotlist file and a directory for the file.

Last, specify which menus from that NCSA MOSAIC.INI file you want to import (all the menus identified in that file should appear in a list). Click OK when you're ready to import the file.

The next time you open the Hotlists dialog box, the menu(s) you imported should be displayed. You can add them as menu items, if you like, using the Put this Hotlist in the menu bar command.

Opening Documents Directly in Mosaic

If you know a document's *URL* (Uniform Resource Locator; a standard address for WWW documents), you can access a document directly by typing the document's URL. If someone tells you the URL of a popular WWW site on the Internet, you can go to it directly using that URL. You also need to know a document's URL to set it up in a Hotlist or as a default home page. Opening documents using their URLs is described in the next section.

You can also create or save an HTML file directly to your PC and open it in AIR Mosaic Express. This is known as a *local file*. A local file should have an HTM extension. You can open a local file by choosing File⇨ Open Local File. Specify the name and path for the local file and click OK. AIR Mosaic Express then tries to open the file you specified.

Opening documents using URLs

Mosaic locates documents by using URLs. URLs are a standard notation for WWW resources, designed to be able to identify information stored on a variety of machines, in a variety of different ways. A URL can point to resources such as an HTML document (a WWW *home page*), an FTP server, a Gopher server, or a local document. When you access a document in AIR Mosaic Express, you see the URL for that document shown in the Document URL: field displayed below the AIR Mosaic Express toolbar.

URLs indicate the resource type and where it is located, as well as the resource name.

If you know the URL of a resource, you can access it directly, as follows:

1. Select File⇨Open URL. The Open URL dialog box appears, as shown in Figure 5-19.

Figure 5-19: Open URL dialog box.

The most common URL you specify in the Open URL dialog box is the URL for an HTML home page. It is always preceded by http:// followed by the address of the HTML document. For example:

```
http://www.spry.com/HotHomePages.html
```

2. Type the URL you want to connect to and click OK. If the URL is valid, AIR Mosaic Express should begin connecting to it.

Understanding URLs

URLs typically provide information about a resource type, location, and path. You might find a document called "Internet Web Text" with a URL of

```
http://www.rpi.edu/Internet/Guides/decemj/text.html
```

You can decipher this URL as follows:

```
http:    //www.rpi.edu    /Internet/Guides/decemj/text.html
```

or roughly

```
Resource Type  //Resource Location  /Pathname{/filename.ext}
```

These three portions are described in the next three sections.

Resource type

The resource type tells you the type of server on which the resource resides and what kind of protocol is used when retrieving the document.

Table 5-2	WWW Resource Types and Formats
Format	**Resource Type**
http://	HTTP Server (HyperText Transfer Protocol, used for WWW documents)
FTP://	FTP Server
file://	FTP Server or Local HTML File
telnet://	Telnet Server
gopher://	Gopher Server
wais://	WAIS Server
news:	Usenet news site

 The news: URL uses a slightly different format; it takes the format news:newsgroup.name because you already have a news server defined in Mosaic (using the Configuration option).

Resource location

The resource location is the Internet address of the machine where the resource resides.

In the previous example, www.rpi.edu is the World Wide Web server at Rensselaer Polytechnic Institute, a school in Troy, New York. Note that often you cannot figure out exactly where a resource is located.

Pathname {filename}

Depending on the type of resource you're accessing, the pathname either displays a path to the resource filename or a path to the most current filename. In most cases, the URL for a document or other resource contains a full pathname for the file. If you're familiar with DOS or UNIX pathnames, the path in a URL works similarly. (Paths in WWW always use the forward slash, /.)

In the previous example, the path is /Internet/Guides/Decemj/. If you're looking at the resource, you see that it is titled *Internet Web Text, by John December.* You might figure out that this is John December's personal directory on the Rensselaer Polytechnic Institute WWW server.

The following lines are some sample URLs:

```
http://www.spry.com/HotHomePages.html
http://www.rpi.edu/Internet/Guides/decemj/text.html
telnet://circe.spry.com:70
gopher://spinaltap.micro.umn.edu:70/11/fun/Movies
news:alt.tv.seinfeld
FTP://homer.spry.com
```

For advanced information on URLs, the URL primer is available from NCSA on the NCSA home page at http://www.ncsa.uiuc.edu/demoweb/url-primer.html.

Accessing FTP, Gopher, and More...

Although you may navigate principally between HTML documents (home pages) when using AIR Mosaic Express, you can also use it to access other Internet resources such as FTP and Gopher sites and Usenet news. The functionality of AIR Mosaic Express as an FTP, Gopher, or news browser is somewhat limited because the World Wide Web protocols used are not very sophisticated. For full-featured use of FTP, Gopher, and news, sophisticated applications such as the AIR Series Network File Manager (for FTP), AIR News, and AIR Gopher are recommended.

The following sections describe how AIR Mosaic Express works with these resources.

Accessing FTP and Gopher sites

Accessing FTP and Gopher sites is very easy with AIR Mosaic Express. Since AIR Mosaic Express incorporates both FTP and Gopher functionality, no additional tools are needed to retrieve files from these types of sites.

You may find an FTP or Gopher site when you're using AIR Mosaic Express, or you could connect to one directly if you know its URL (address), as described in the section "Opening documents using URLs."

The FTP or Gopher site is displayed in a hierarchical folder format (see Figure 5-20) on the AIR Mosaic Express screen. Using FTP and Gopher is very similar.

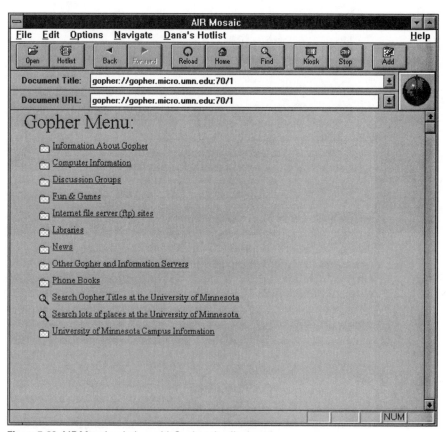

Figure 5-20: AIR Mosaic window with Gopher site displayed.

On an FTP site, you see only two types of items: folders (directories) and files. You can navigate through folders by double-clicking them to move deeper into the folders; if you want to move back, click the up arrow shown at the top of the folder list.

When you double-click the name of a file on an FTP screen, AIR Mosaic Express automatically downloads (copies) the file to your \AIR\DATA directory using the displayed filename.

 AIR Mosaic Express has an option for Extended FTP Directory Parsing, found in the Options menu. This option enables you to view additional information from UNIX FTP servers, such as file size and date, when available. Note that this option may cause some difficulty when you're using DOS-based FTP servers.

On a Gopher site, aside from folders and files, several other items are displayed on the screen: image files, sound files, search tools, and other Gopher resources.

Double-clicking a Gopher resource either downloads it to your \AIR\DATA directory or opens it, depending on whether you have a *viewer* for that resource configured on your PC, as described in the "Viewing Files You Find in Mosaic" discussion later in this chapter.

Accessing news

You can use AIR Mosaic Express as a very basic news reader for Usenet news. You cannot post any news articles using AIR Mosaic Express, however.

You have to access a *news server* to read news with AIR Mosaic Express. A news server address is provided with AIR Mosaic Express, so you can actually read news immediately, but you can see only a limited number of newsgroups when accessing this server. You need to find out the address of a news server to use; your Internet Service Provider may have one that you can access, or you may already have been using one that you can connect to. You can set up the news server address using the Configuration option in the Options menu.

Often you end up reading a Usenet newsgroup in Mosaic because you clicked a hyperlink in a WWW document that connected you to that newsgroup. Reading news on your own using Mosaic is not as simple. News can be directly accessed in Mosaic only by directly specifying the name of the newsgroup you want to subscribe to. If you don't know what newsgroups are available, this process can be difficult (a little bit like the "no job without experience," "no experience without a job" paradox). It is recommended that you use another news browser (such as AIR News) to familiarize yourself with the newsgroups on your news server before attempting this procedure.

To connect to a Usenet news newsgroup, you would specify the URL in AIR Mosaic Express dialogs (such as the Open URL dialog) in the following format:

```
news:newsgroup.name
```

After you're connected to news using Mosaic, you see news articles listed as bulleted items on the screen. Articles whose titles are not preceded by "Re:" are original _threads_ — they represent the initial article on a particular topic. Articles whose titles begin with "Re:" are responses to an initial article.

Mosaic displays only the last 20 articles in a newsgroup. To see earlier articles, click the "Earlier articles..." text. Mosaic then displays the preceding 20 articles. You can move back to the last 20 messages again by clicking the "Later articles..." text. (You can also use the Forward and Back buttons on the toolbar to do the same thing.)

To view an article, simply click its title. You see hyperlink text in the references section, as well as in the beginning of the article itself. Selecting this hyperlink text enables you to move to related articles in the news thread. You can then use the Back button on the toolbar to move back to the original article.

Accessing older WWW documents using HTTP/0.9

Some older WWW documents may require you to use an earlier version of the Transfer Protocol HTTP/0.9 to access them. In most cases, the hyperlinks to those documents warn you that HTTP/0.9 is required to read them. AIR Mosaic Express enables you to use this option in order to read these earlier documents.

Saving Documents in Mosaic _____

You might want to save WWW documents so that you can open them later (using the Open Local File command) or so that you can use the information in the documents (perhaps in word processing or other applications). When you save documents, you do not save the text exactly as you see it on the screen; any graphics on the screen are not saved, and the document is saved with accompanying HTML codes.

You can save documents two ways: you can use Load to Disk mode to save the document to disk as soon as you access it (as described in the following section), or you can save the document source code to disk directly using the Document Source command as described in the "Viewing Document Source" section at the end of this chapter.

Load to Disk mode

Turning on Load to Disk mode is like turning on a movie camera; everything that you encounter while in that mode is remembered. AIR Mosaic Express tries to save every document that you open until you turn off Load to Disk mode.

To enable Load to Disk mode, check Load to Disk Mode in the Options menu (a check mark indicates that the mode is enabled). The next time you load in a document by clicking a hyperlink, AIR Mosaic Express brings up a dialog asking you where you want to save the new document (the document is also opened on your screen). A name for this document is suggested; you can accept it or change it, and you can also change the directory where this document is stored. An extension of HTM, indicating that this is an HTML document, is suggested. Click OK to save the document to disk. To disable Load to Disk mode, uncheck the option.

Printing in Mosaic

You can print the information in a document by using File⇨Print. If you want to see how the output will look, choose Print Preview. The Print Setup command — as is typical of Windows applications — enables you to specify which printer you want to print to.

You can search a WWW document for particular text using the Find command. Click the Find option in the Edit menu, and type the text you want to search for in the dialog that appears. The search occurs from the top of the document to the bottom. If you want to search for additional occurrences of the text, choose Find Next from the Find dialog box.

Viewing Files You Find in Mosaic

AIR Mosaic Express internally provides support for text and inline graphics. However, some of the files you encounter using AIR Mosaic Express (image files such as GIF and JPEG files; MPEG movie files; sound files) require you to use *external viewers*, separate programs that can view graphics, play sounds, play movies, or otherwise interpret Mosaic resources. The Viewers feature (described in the next section) enables you to set up these viewers.

The URL of a resource gives you some indication of the file type by the file extension used in the resource's filename. Most commonly, you need external viewers to do the following operations:

- View GIF or JPEG graphics files

  Often you see inline graphics that you can double-click to retrieve the graphic to your PC; these require an external viewer. You also see hyperlinks called names like "Picture of the Louvre" or "LOUVRE.GIF."

  SPRY's AIR Series comes with an image viewer, ImageView, which enables you to view GIF and JPEG graphic files automatically. This viewer is already set up in AIR Mosaic Express.

- Play sounds

  If you have a sound card in your computer, you can play sounds that you find on World Wide Web. Microsoft Windows already includes an application called Media Player that can play sounds; AIR Mosaic Express is set up to use this application automatically to play sounds (your Windows documentation describes how to use this program).

- View multimedia movie files (MPEG)

  Multimedia movie files (almost always MPEG files) are found in many places on the World Wide Web. Usually, they are not identified with any symbol but are named with an extension of MPG (MOUNTAINS.MPG) or otherwise identified as movie files.

The AIR Series does not include an MPEG viewer, but you can find one on the SPRY FTP server: MPEGEXE.ZIP in the /MS-WINDOWS/VIEWERS/MPEG/APPS directory. *Note:* This application is freely distributed (by Xing™ Technology Corporation); it is not supported by SPRY. You can use any Windows-based MPEG viewer with AIR Mosaic Express.

The SPRY FTP Server's MS-WINDOWS/VIEWERS directory also contains shareware and freeware utilities for viewing PostScript, RTF, GIF, and JPEG files.

You can set up all your viewers for AIR Mosaic Express using the Viewers dialog box, as described in the next section, "Configuring AIR Mosaic Express Options."

AIR Mosaic Express also enables you to use external viewers for viewing PostScript, QuickTime, msvideo, rich text format, MIDI, and basic audio files, although you do not run into these types of resources as often on the World Wide Web.

Configuring AIR Mosaic Express Options

You can easily configure AIR Mosaic Express using the Configuration dialog box. This dialog box enables you to specify options for displaying elements in the AIR Mosaic Express Console, such as the toolbar, status bar, images, hyperlinks, and sounds; the default servers for AIR Mosaic Express; AIR Mosaic Express's fonts and colors: and which external viewers are used to view graphics and play sounds and movies. You can access the Configuration dialog box (see Figure 5-21) by choosing Configuration from the Options menu.

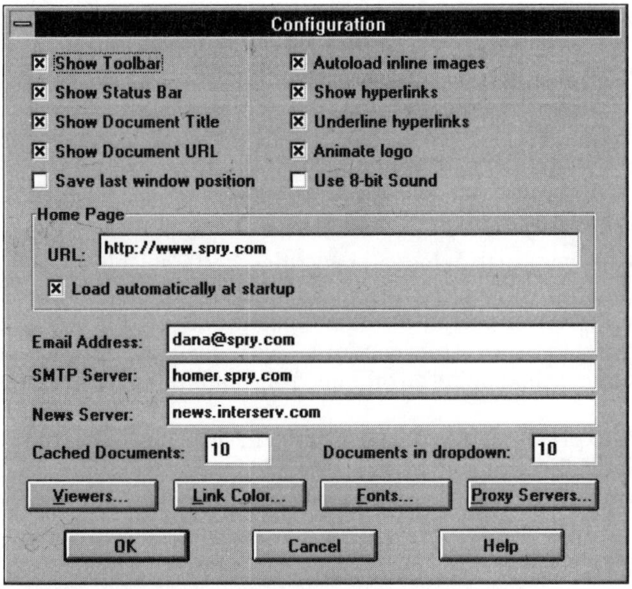

Figure 5-21: Configuration dialog box.

The Configuration options are described in the sections that follow.

General options

The General Configuration options shown at the top of the Configuration dialog box are described in the following short sections.

Show Toolbar and Show Status Bar

These options control whether or not the toolbar and status bar are displayed. You may not want to hide the status bar because it displays the locations of resources you connect to, as well as indicates when a transfer is in progress or a graphic is being loaded. By default, these options are displayed; check them again to hide them.

Show Document Title and Show Document URL

These options control whether or not the Document Title: drop-down list with the AIR Mosaic Express radar indicator, and the Document URL: drop-down list are displayed. You can show both options hide both options, or show only the document title bar. You cannot display only the Document URL: list. By default, these options are displayed; check them again to hide them.

Save last window position

You may want to resize the AIR Mosaic Express Console window during your AIR Mosaic Express session in order to see more (or less) of a WWW document. If you want these size changes to be saved and used during your next AIR Mosaic Express session, check this option.

Autoload inline images

By default, images (such as logos, fancy titles, and small photos) are automatically displayed on your system when you connect to a World Wide Web site. This is done by automatically downloading the image to AIR Mosaic Express, where it is kept in your system memory. This downloading process can be very time-consuming, depending on the speed of your Internet connection.

AIR Mosaic Express enables you to disable this feature so that the images are not automatically downloaded or displayed. Uncheck this option to stop viewing graphics. In the place of the graphics, you see graphic placeholders.

Show hyperlinks

This option enables you to hide the hyperlink jumps in a Mosaic document.

Underline hyperlinks

Typically, hyperlinks are displayed in blue and underlined. You may want to turn off the underlining. Removing the underline is a personal preference; it does not affect the speed that the document is retrieved in any significant way.

Animate logo

This option refers to the radar indicator on the document title bar. It may take additional time to animate this indicator logo. By default, this option is turned on because it offers you some useful information about whether or not a document or image is being retrieved (and gives your mind something to do while you wait — although you can always work in other Windows applications if a document is loading too slowly). The time you save by turning off the logo animation is not substantial; you will probably want to turn off this option only if your connection is very slow.

Use 8-bit Sound

AIR Mosaic Express features internal sound support for AU and AIFF files, using your sound card (if you have one). This option assumes you have a high-quality sound card. If these file types do not play properly or you have a lower quality (or 8-bit) sound card, choose this option.

Home Page

AIR Mosaic Express enables you to set up a default home page that you can quickly access using the Home button on the toolbar. Type the URL for the home page in the URL: field to set up this home page. See "Opening documents using URLs" for more information on understanding URLs.

You can also set up AIR Mosaic Express to load this home page automatically on start-up; if you want to see this home page whenever you start AIR Mosaic Express, check the Load automatically at startup option.

E-mail Address, SMTP Server, and News Server

These options are all used by AIR Mosaic Express when you are using some of Mosaic's extended functionality for news and sending mail.

You must fill out some information about your system in order for these options to work properly.

To send mail

You must fill out your e-mail address and SMTP server address.

E-mail address: This is the address others use to send you e-mail — for example, jwatson@moriarty.com. The installation may have already filled out this field with your e-mail address; if not, you should change it.

SMTP server: This is the mail server you use. A default mail server out on the Internet, relay.interserv.com, has been supplied for you. For optimum use, it is suggested that you use your own SMTP server. Specify the address for the server. An example would be an address such as mailserv.oz.com.

To read news

News server: You must fill out the address of your news server. It is the machine that you connect to in order to read news. The default news server news.spry.com, which is also supplied in SPRY's AIR News product, is supplied by default. If you have a news server you prefer to use to read news, type its name here.

Cached Documents

This item represents how many documents are cached, or kept active, in your PC's memory. If this number is 10, for instance, ten documents remain "available" to you; if you go back to them, they appear immediately and do not have to be loaded.

If you have a lot of available system memory, you may want to increase this number. Keep in mind that a high number for cache may affect other applications' performance, although Mosaic performance will probably improve quite a bit.

Documents in dropdown

This value indicates how many of your last-accessed documents will appear in the Document Title: and Document URL: drop-down lists (displayed beneath the toolbar). A value of 5 means that the last five documents you accessed display in these lists.

The three buttons at the bottom of the dialog box enable you to configure viewers, choose fonts, choose the hyperlink color, and define proxy servers. These features are described in the following sections.

Viewers

The Viewers button enables you to specify the external viewers you want to use for different resource types that you might run into on the World Wide Web. For instance, you may find multimedia movies in a WWW document and want to set up Mosaic with a movie player. The use of external viewers is described in more detail earlier in the section called "Viewing Files You Find in Mosaic."

When you click the Viewers button, an External Viewer Configuration dialog box (see Figure 5-22) that enables you to change the viewers and tools used to access AIR Mosaic Express resources opens.

When you pull down the Type drop-down list, you see a list of resource types (derived from the MIME multimedia specification) for resources that you are likely to find using AIR Mosaic Express. AIR Mosaic Express already has default viewers set up for all the resource types. However, it is unlikely that you actually have all the viewers that are set up (or, if you have them, that they are in the right location). Therefore, you may need to do some configuring to make sure that all the resources you find work properly in AIR Mosaic Express.

You can also define tools for Mosaic to do telnet, Rlogin, and tn3270.

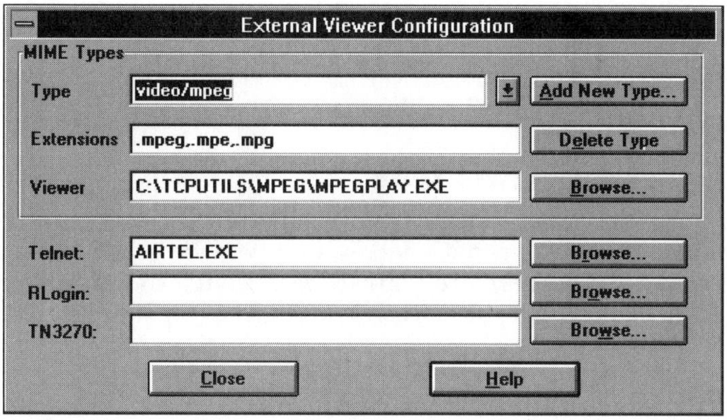

Figure 5-22: External Viewer Configuration dialog box.

Defining viewers and tools

AIR Mosaic Express includes an external viewer application called *Image View* that you can use to view graphics (this viewer is the one you are most likely to need).

The other external viewers that you are likely to already have on your system are

■ For sound (WAV, MIDI) files and MSVIDEO: Microsoft's Media Player

■ For RTF (rich text format) files: Microsoft Windows Write

These viewers are already set up on your system.

For the other viewer types (mpeg, PostScript, QuickTime, and Basic), if you have applications that can display or view them, you have to tell Mosaic where the viewers are located and what their application filenames are, as follows:

1. Choose the viewer from the drop-down list.

2. Type the full path and filename of the viewer you want to use in the Viewer field, or click Browse to find the viewer on your PC more easily (when you locate the viewer and click OK, the Viewer field is filled in automatically).

3. Click Save. Note that *you must click Save for every type you want to configure.* The changes are not saved until you do so. You can continue to configure viewers.

4. Click Close when you are done configuring viewers. The changes take place immediately.

You can also define the applications used by Mosaic for telnet, rlogin, and tn3270. To do so, type the application you want to use in the appropriate field (click Browse to search your disk for the correct file and directory name). When you close the dialog box, the changes you make are saved.

Adding a new viewer type

AIR Mosaic Express uses file extensions, found in the hyperlink that is created for the resource, to figure out what resource type the item is and, consequently, what viewer to use. Therefore, you can create your own resource types and link viewers to them so that you can use items that have resource types that aren't yet set up.

For example, you might be accessing a Gopher site with Mosaic and find some ZIP files. If you had an application that can read ZIP files (such as WinZip), you could define ZIP files, in AIR Mosaic Express, as a resource type associated with a viewer. You do so by clicking the Add New Type button in the Viewer dialog box.

You are asked to specify a name for the new type (for example, APPLICATION/ ZIP, but you could use any name).

You can then type in the extensions that you want to be considered as zipped files (.zip and .ZIP are used here), specify a viewer name, and save to store the new viewer type.

Color

The color is the color that is used to highlight Mosaic hyperlinks (jumps to other documents or document areas, or jumps to resources). Text hyperlinks are entirely highlighted, and graphics hyperlinks are surrounded by a highlight. The standard hyperlink color is blue.

1. To change the hyperlink color, click Color. The Color dialog box (Figure 5-23) appears.

2. Select the color you want to use for hyperlinks, and click OK. The hyperlink color is changed immediately.

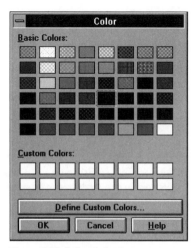

Figure 5-23: Color dialog box.

Fonts

You can change the fonts that AIR Mosaic Express uses to display documents. You can change the font that is used for a particular item or the font size. You might want to change fonts to make documents easier to read or to fit more information onto your screen.

Different items in documents use different font *styles* (similar to styles in word processors). Most regular text is displayed in *Normal* style, and headers are displayed in a *Header* style, such as *Header 1, Header 2, Header 3,* and so on.

You can change these font styles by clicking the Fonts button. You then see the Fonts dialog box.

If you want to change just one style, you can choose the style that you want to change from the drop-down menu, and you can define a font for that style by clicking the Change Font button. Specify the font type and style you want, and click OK. The style is changed until you change it again.

If you are not sure what style it is you want to change, you can do some experimenting. AIR Mosaic Express cannot tell you what styles are being used in a particular WWW document.

If you want to change all the styles in a document, you can choose Enlarge All or Reduce All to enlarge or reduce the styles. You can choose this option as many times as you like.

Click OK when you are finished changing styles.

Proxy Servers

AIR Mosaic Express enables you to specify any proxy servers that will be used for getting WWW, FTP, WAIS, and Gopher information past Internet *firewalls*. Click the Proxy Servers button and specify the addresses of your proxy servers to have AIR Mosaic Express use those servers (see Figure 5-24).

Figure 5-24: Proxy Servers dialog box.

Viewing Document Source _____

A Document Source command is provided in the File menu to enable you to view and save HTML document source code. Click Document Source to view the current document's source code (see Figure 5-25).

```
<HTML>
<HEAD>
<TITLE>SPRY World Wide Web Services</TITLE>
</HEAD>
<BODY>
<IMG SRC="sprylgo.gif"><P>
<H1>World Wide Web Services</H1>
<p>
<b>SPRY, Incorporated</b> is a leading provider of transport-independent
connectivity applications that enable users in multi-vendor LAN environments
to easily interoperate with the enterprise.  The privately held company
is based in Seattle, Washington.<p>
<p>
<hr>
<i><b>What's New</b></i><p>
<h2>SPRY launches <a href="netacc.html">NetAccess</a>, a computer industry business directory
for Mosaic users.</H2>
<I>Check it out from the above link or check out the additions to our
<a href="hotpages.html">Hot Home Pages</A> section.<BR>New as of <b>July 9, 1994.</b></I>.
<p>
<B><I><a href="http://www.spry.com/news10.txt">SPRY LICENSES TCP/IP AND INTERNET
CONNECTIVITY SOFTWARE TO WALL DATA</a></I></B><BR>
<I>Wall Data will integrate SPRY's AIR Series with their RUMBA software products</I>


<p>
<p>
<P>
<hr>
<p>
<p>
<a href="airserie.html"><IMG alt="The Air Series" align=top SRC="hpair1.gif"></a>
<a href="intabox.html"><img alt="Internet In A Box" align=top src="hpair2.gif"></a><br>
<a href="corpov.html"><IMG alt="Corporate Overview" align=top SRC="hpair3.gif"></a>
```

Figure 5-25: Document Source window.

You can now choose Save from the File menu to save the source code to a file.
Remember that all the HTML codes are also saved. You then are prompted for a
name for this file.

You can also choose Copy from the Edit menu to copy some or all of the HTML
text to the Windows Clipboard so that you can use it in other applications. (Use
the Select All command to select the entire document.)

Part III
Non-WinSock Internet Solutions

This part discusses some ways to access Internet information without actually connecting to the Internet: WinNET, The Pipeline, PowerBBS, WinCIM (CompuServe), and COM*t*.

What Is a Non-WinSock Solution?

Most of this book deals with solutions and applications that use TCP/IP to connect to the Internet. Your PC becomes a real Internet host. But being a host isn't for everyone! You can access some of the Internet's best features without the work of putting together an Internet host. You can use, for example, WinCIM to access CompuServe (with its technical support) to use Internet mail, newsgroups, and more.

Why Use a Non-WinSock Solution?

The Internet can be a bizarre and incomprehensible maze of interconnected hosts and services. While efforts are underway to clear the way for the non-hacker, much work must be done before most people will be comfortable navigating cyberspace. You can use a commercial service that guides you or distills the best information for you. If you want to play a part in creating an Internet gateway, check out PowerBBS, a bulletin board system that can offer Internet mail and news access.

One of the biggest advantages of using a commercial vendor like CompuServe or Pipeline is that you can expect a well-tested, popular, easy-to-use interface. There is no mystery about what you're getting, and technical support is readily available. After all, at rates commercial services charge for premium access, they should be doing most of the work *for* us!

WinNET Mail

WinNET is an electronic mail and newsgroup package designed to communicate with the Computer Witchcraft, Inc. host computers for access to Internet mail and newsgroups. When used this way, WinNET is free. WinNET is also a full-featured UUCP mail package, and can also connect to other UUCP-based mail hosts, but then WinNET costs you $99. Access to the Computer Witchcraft computer costs $8 per hour, but because you are really calling in only long enough to exchange e-mail and pick up the newsgroups you want to read, your actual connect time per month is low. Like Pipeline, WinNET can use an 800 number at a charge of 12¢ to 18¢ per minute based on the time of day.

If all you need is electronic mail and news feed access, then this might be just for you!

You can reach Computer Witchcraft via electronic mail at winnet@win.net.

The Pipeline

The Pipeline gives you point-and-click access to the Internet. It uses a proprietary protocol interface between your PC and the Pipeline host computers. It gives you access to key Internet features including mail, newsgroups, Gopher, WAIS (file searching), telnet, and FTP. The Pipeline will eventually offer World Wide Web access. With prices as low as $35.00 per month for unlimited access (as of November 1994), this is a reasonable deal. Even low-volume users pay only $2.00 per hour. Sprintnet dial-up access for the rest of the country adds $5.00 per hour during peak hours, and $2.50 per hour during off-peak hours. The Pipeline's biggest drawback is that you depend upon it for your services. If a new Internet service comes along, you'll have to wait for The Pipeline to support it before you can try it.

The Pipeline is on the Internet at

```
http://www.pipeline.com
```

PowerBBS

A great shareware program, PowerBBS — along with WinNET Mail — will get you started running your own BBS.

CompuServe via WinCIM

Like the Pipeline, WinCIM offers a point-and-click interface to computing services. Unlike Pipeline, most CompuServe users view the CompuServe computers as their ultimate destination. Although CompuServe will soon offer Internet access through their host computers, most users will probably never leave the CompuServe forums. Because of this, you may want to connect to CompuServe from the other direction: using WinCIM *from* the Internet. This part tells you how.

Naturally, WUGNET encourages you to visit the CompuServe WINCON forum to chat!

CompuServe is on the Internet at:

```
http://www.CompuServe.com
```

COM*t*

COM*t* is a program that fools communications programs into thinking that an Internet Telnet connection is actually a COM port on your Windows PC. So if your favorite COMM program, like PROCOMM for Windows, doesn't support TCP/IP, then you can slip COM*t* in the middle, and fake it out. COM*t* is simple to install and run, and is a really cool way to keep using existing communications programs. Of course, the computer you want to connect to must actually be on the Internet. This won't help you get to your favorite BBS unless they have an Internet connection.

Chapter 6
WinNET Mail

Overview

WinNET Mail lets you send electronic mail via modem to people who have a copy of WinNET Mail or to people who have an *Internet/Usenet* mail account. This process is very similar to sending mail by the post office, except that it's paperless, convenient, costs less, is more reliable, and happens more quickly!

WinNET Mail also provides complete access to the *Usenet News network,* a collection of over 5,000 subject interest groups covering every conceivable topic. Many users of the Internet/Usenet find Usenet News to be the most interesting and important service. "The News" links you to millions of correspondents worldwide — many foremost experts in their fields — and allows you to share your ideas, experiences, and opinions with a wider audience than can be achieved by almost any print medium.

Using WinNET Mail, you can also join any of the over 1,600 Internet Subject Information Groups (SIGs). These groups are similar to Usenet News but use the standard mailing capabilities of the Internet instead of Usenet conventions.

Features of WinNET

All the software you need to use WinNET Mail is included with the WinNET Mail distribution, including a program that allows you to automatically (and instantly) gain access to an unlimited Internet/Usenet account through Computer Witchcraft's Internet/Usenet service.

Windows Multiple Document Interface

WinNET Mail has a user-friendly, state-of-the-art Windows Multiple Document Interface, including a toolbar, status bars, and support for user-defined mail folders, address books, and database-like search facilities. The search facilities allow you to create subject folders easily for mail by creating search result folders. WinNET Mail has built-in support for storing mail in folders named after the senders of mail items, and for keeping your private mail compositions in a separate folder.

Facilities for easily replying to or forwarding mail and for posting and following up news articles (at a button click) are intelligently implemented.

Support for UNIX utilities

WinNET Mail supports a very integrated and user-friendly implementation of the UNIX uuencode/decode utilities for Internet/Usenet-compatible binary file transfer. These utilities allow the user to select a file of any size or data format to be included and mailed along with a message as an *attached binary file*. The recipient may then simply select a directory, using a file dialog box, as a location for storing the attached binary file.

Usenet News support

WinNET Mail's Usenet News support includes a context-sensitive toolbar for accessing news functions, automatic distribution of articles to separate subject folders corresponding to the correct group(s) for each article, conversational "threading" of articles, easy-to-use subscription management facilities for adding and removing newsgroups, search capability across newsgroups or within a single newsgroup, tools for copying news articles to mail folders, either singly or by thread, and support for automatic archiving of entire newsgroups.

Complete editor

WinNET Mail's editor is based on Computer Witchcraft's famous and widely distributed *Mega Edit* product. The editor can seamlessly handle files as large as virtual memory will allow, and fulfills completely the CUA interface standards published by IBM, including word wrap, cut and paste, text search/replace, go to, file import, support for printing, DOS shell, tab control, variable, sizable font support, and so forth. The editor can also be used to open and edit any files on the user's system, either for the purpose of constructing complex mail messages from multiple text files, or for any other purpose. The version of the editor integrated into WinNET Mail is tailored carefully to meet the needs of users preparing and editing Internet/Usenet mail, and has built-in support for various mail composition conventions.

Fast communications module

WinNET Mail's communications module is a high-performance implementation of the UNIX *uucico* utility (unix-to-unix-copy-in-copy-out). The communications module supports computer-to-modem interface speeds up to 57,600 bps, and Computer Witchcraft's systems are also configured to support a data link at 57,600 bps, with full v.42bis data compression. This can result in data through-put averaging significantly above the rated telephone line speed of 14,400 bps modems supporting compression protocols.

The communications utility runs smoothly in the background while other Windows applications may be active, and is very tolerant of disruptions by long processing cycles of other applications. The communications utility has a fault-tolerant mode of operation such that no possibility of losing a queued mail item exists short of a complete hard disk/system failure. It uses CRC error detection to guarantee faithful transmission of data, and will automatically monitor for error conditions and perform intelligent actions to ensure timely delivery and receipt of mail. It displays detailed transmission statistics as it runs, and records information about its activities in several detailed logs.

Additional utilities are provided for detailed scheduling of automatic, periodic connection to Computer Witchcraft's mail server, and for user notification of newly arrived mail.

Getting Technical Support

If you need additional help in resolving questions you have about WinNET Mail, you can receive free technical support by sending Internet e-mail to help@win.net.

 If you are having problems getting WinNET Mail to work properly enough to send e-mail, give us a call at

(502) 589-6800

For the purposes of written correspondence, our U.S. mailing address is

Computer Witchcraft, Inc.
P. O. Box 4189
Louisville, KY 40204
United States of America

You may also send a fax with questions or comments to our fax machine at (502) 589-7300. We would also appreciate hearing from you with any comments or general suggestions that you have about WinNET Mail or about Computer Witchcraft.

Browsing Mail

When you receive mail from another user, it is placed in a WinNET Mail folder called *Incoming Mail*. By default, the Incoming Mail folder automatically loads when you start WinNET Mail, so you can see your latest mail.

For each mail item in the Incoming Mail folder, there is a corresponding line in the list of items that shows the sender of the item, the date that the item was originally mailed by the sender, and the subject of the item. If you have not viewed a message, you will see that the line describing the contents of the message also has an *N* in the status column at the left margin. This means that the message is *New*.

Reading a message

To read a message, follow these steps:

1. Highlight the status line. To do this, you can use the ↓ key to move the highlight to the item.

2. To start the item in the mail reader, press Enter. Alternatively, you can double-click any item with the mouse to start it or you can single-click the item and press Enter.

Once you have opened a message, you will find yourself in the mail reader. The Internet address of the sender of the mail appears at the top of the mail reader, as in the following example:

```
Reply-To: megamail@win.net
```

This address is for your reference. It can be added to your address book (see the section of the on-line help file about address book (aliasing) for more information) for easy recall.

WinNET Mail's message reader performs auto-scrolling past the formal Internet mail header of all messages. Most users like to see the core of the message near the very top, as opposed to looking at the very cluttered header. If you want to look at the formal Internet header of a mail message, press Page Up or use the scroll bar to scroll up to the header.

After you get to the message reader, you can scroll through the message as you do in any Windows text editor, using either the keyboard or the scroll bar. Also, you can use the Edit⇨Copy command to move a selected region of the message into the Clipboard for pasting into a message you are composing, or into another file with WinNET Mail or another application. (See the section about the WinNET Mail Editor later in this chapter for more information about these operations).

Closing a message

When you are finished reading the message, you can either close the message by using the system menu for the message reader window, or if you have more mail in your Incoming Mail, you can click the Next Item button to view the next mail message. (You can also select this operation from the Mail menu.)

After reading one or more mail messages and returning to the Incoming Mail folder window, note that any new messages that you read now have an O, representing *Old,* in the status column.

When you click the Next button (or select Mail⇨Next), the viewer will some- times disappear and you will be returned to the folder containing the list of your messages. This occurs when you move from a series of new messages to an old message, as a way of indicating to you that you have already seen the next message. If you want to see the old message that follows, just click the Next button a second time.

Composing Mail

To compose a mail message, start the process by clicking the Compose button on the Control bar. (You also can choose Mail⇨Compose.) This will open the *mail composition* edit window as shown in Figure 6-1.

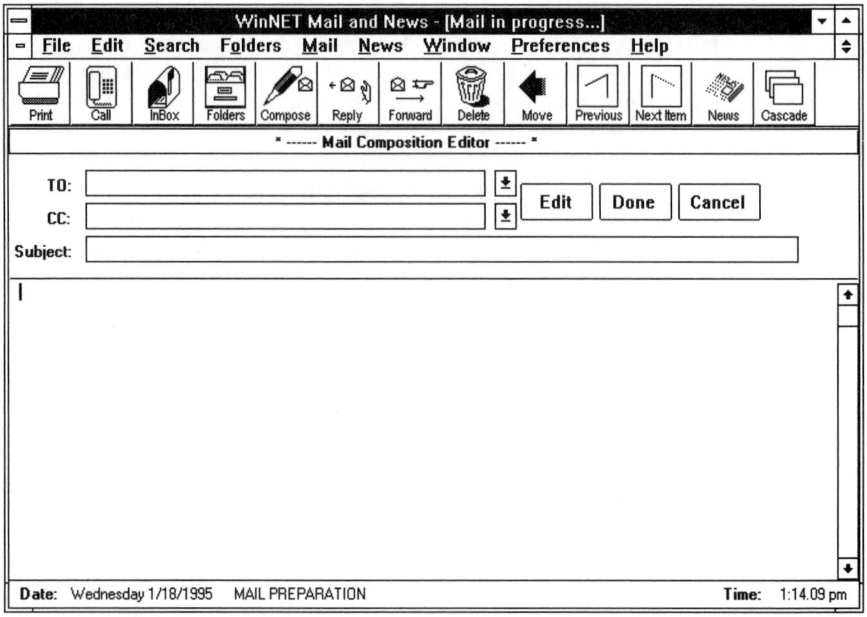

Figure 6-1: The Mail Composition Editor window.

Filling in the appropriate fields

Notice the fields at the top of this window, labeled To:, CC:, and Subject:.

The only required field is the To field. In the To field, you should put the Internet/Usenet e-mail address of the person for whom your mail is intended. Alternatively, you can click the little arrow box next to this field (or press Alt+↓) to pull down a list of address book entries that you have previously defined. You can then select the recipient from this list.

You also can type an address book entry into the field directly, if you know it by memory. You also have the option of entering multiple recipients in the To field, using either the direct e-mail addresses or address book entries, or a combination of both. To do so, make sure to separate each address or address book entry with a comma.

Another way of sending your mail to additional persons is using the CC (*carbon copy* or *courtesy copy*) field. The result of using the CC field is very similar to listing multiple addresses or entries in the To field. The only difference is that the formal mail header on the mail item that is sent will list these additional recipients as CC'd rather than in the main To field of the header. This has the same nuance for recipients of mail as with formal correspondence with internal office memos, and so on. It indicates that the item is sent primarily for the person(s) listed in the To field, but that it has also been posted to certain other persons for their reference.

The final field at the top of the Mail Composition Editor window is the Subject field. Although you are not required to put anything in this field, it is very polite in e-mail etiquette to do so. Putting a thoughtful, descriptive subject here will allow the recipient of your mail to know at a glance what your mail is about, and will also help the person later in categorizing mail items for assignment to different folders. It will also be used in replies to your mail to indicate the original subject when you receive a response to your mail.

Typing the contents of your message

Once you have filled out the desired fields in the top section of the mail composition editor, you are ready to type your message:

1. Tab to the Edit button (or just click it) to move into the editing area. (You can also just click in the editing area at any time to start writing your message.)

2. Once in the editing area, type the contents of your message. If the Preferences⇨Word Wrap command has been checked, word wrap is on and you don't have to worry about pressing Enter at the end of each line. In some cases, you may want to do your carriage returns manually. To turn word wrap off, just select Preferences⇨Word Wrap.

3. If you want to incorporate an existing text file into your mail message, you can use the File⇨Import command to bring up a file open dialog box to do so.

    You can also use the Edit menu's Cut, Copy, Paste, and Clear commands to add or excise additional material to/from other applications or the WinNET Mail system editor or mail message viewer to/from your mail item.

The WinNET Mail editor is very powerful. It can work with files of any size and has many easy-to-use features that facilitate complex editing tasks. For more information about WinNET Mail's editing facilities, see the on-line help.

Leaving the message area

When you complete your mail message, you can quit the mail composition editor by clicking the Done button in the top section of the editor. You also can press Esc, which will move the focus back to the top section, specifically, to the Done button, which appears highlighted. You can then select Done by pressing either the spacebar or Enter. If, before quitting, you want to edit the fields at the top of the editor, you can tab between the fields as with dialog boxes, and then tab back to the Done button and click it to exit. (You can use the mouse to accomplish these operations also.)

After selecting Done, you will see a message flash on the status line at the bottom of the WinNET Mail main display that says *SPOOLING MAIL, PLEASE WAIT*. This message indicates that your mail is being processed for sending.

Also, you will see a dialog box that asks whether you want to save a copy of the message in the Mail Sent folder. If you choose Yes here, a copy of the mail you are sending is saved in a folder named *Mail Sent* that is automatically created for you. You should choose Yes if the item you are sending is something you may want to review.

After a few moments, processing of your mail will be complete, and it will be properly set up on the system for Internet/Usenet mailing to your recipient at the time of your next communications session.

Sending the message

To actually send the mail on its way, you need to invoke the mail communications program, which calls up Computer Witchcraft's Internet/Usenet mail service, dropping off the message for delivery. You can do this immediately by clicking the Call button located on WinNET Mail's Control bar. (This button has a picture of a telephone.) However, it is not necessary to send the message right away if you don't want to. The messages will wait safely on the system for as long as you wish, and will go out the next time that you select the Call button, along with any number of other messages that you have created.

The next section covers calling the mail server and using the communications program.

Calling the Mail Server

To actually send mail you have composed on its way, you need to invoke the mail communications program, which calls up Computer Witchcraft's Internet/Usenet mail service, dropping off the message for delivery.

You can invoke the communications program immediately by clicking the Call button located on WinNET Mail's Control bar. (This button has a picture of a telephone). However, it is not necessary to send the message right away if you don't want to. The messages will wait safely on the system for as long as you wish, and will go out the next time that you select the Call button, along with any number of other messages that you have created.

 In order for the communications program to work properly, you must run the ACCOUNT.EXE program supplied with your WinNET Mail software to set up an Internet/Usenet account with Computer Witchcraft. Please see the file READ_1ST.TXT for information about setting up your Internet/Usenet account.

When the communications program connects with Computer Witchcraft, your outgoing mail will be dropped off. If any incoming messages are waiting for you at Computer Witchcraft, the system will send these messages to you. They will be placed into your incoming mail folder automatically.

Automatic calling

If you want, you can also set up the automated mail transfer features of WinNET Mail so that WinNET Mail will call Computer Witchcraft according to whatever schedule you desire. This way, you don't have to invoke the Call button directly. (For more information about the automated mail transfer features, see the section called "Automating Mail Transfer").

When you click WinNET Mail's Call button, the communications program starts up to convey all your outgoing mail messages to Computer Witchcraft's Internet/Usenet service, and also to pick up any messages that are waiting there for you.

On initialization, this program will open the communications port and connect to your modem at the interface speed you specified when you ran the WinNET Mail setup program. It will then configure the modem, also according to your specifications, take the phone off-hook, and dial Computer Witchcraft's UNIX computer system. Once connected, it will logon with your system name. After logon, the transfer of incoming and outgoing files takes place.

Mail statistics

When you select Call to start communications, the communications program initially shows at the bottom of your display as an icon (a telephone). You can double-click this icon to see a display of various messages and statistics as the program operates.

The statistics show such things as the number of files transferred in each direction, the speed on a file-by-file, real-time basis of the progress of the transfer, broken down in several time units, bad-packet errors detected either on incoming or outgoing packets, and the total number of bytes transferred during the session. The session's starting time (defined as the point at which login has succeeded) and the session length are displayed at the bottom.

There are also two message fields. The field on top, labeled *Latest Error,* displays information about the most recent error that has occurred, if any. The lower field, labeled *Most Recent Event,* displays messages about various milestones that have transpired during the current session, such as opening port, connected to server, establishing protocol, queuing file, sending file, file successfully sent, reversing role, becoming receiver, and so forth.

The communications program is designed to be *fault tolerant,* which means that it has smarts that allow it to compensate for error conditions. With the proviso that a program-compatible modem is properly configured, you should almost never experience communications failures, and data will always be transmitted with perfect fidelity to the original. This latter is accomplished by a system known as Cyclic Redundancy Checking (CRC Error correction), whereby a formula is applied to each outgoing packet resulting in a number sent along with the packet and verified by the receiver. If the CRC numbers do not correspond, the receiver will request retransmission of the data until the CRC numbers are in agreement on each side.

In the unlikely event that communications do fail, there is a final fail-safe in that spooled files are never destroyed until sender and receiver have agreed, by a robust series of mutual acknowledgments, that the file has been faithfully sent and received in its entirety. Thus, after a failed session, mail files continue to be present on both systems until the next communications session is initiated, at which time the transfer is retried. This situation will continue until successful transfer of the files is achieved.

Many of the statistics that the communications program displays are also saved in log files that you can view with a text editor. The files are on the directory where you installed WinNET Mail. The files created and maintained by the communication's program, and their contents, are described here:

File	Description
StdEvt.Log	Contains all the messages that appear in the Most Recent Event field of the communication's program display. The log thus serves as a record of significant events that transpire during each communications session.
Error.Log	Contains all the messages that appear in the Most Recent Error field of the communications program display.
XStats.Log	Contains a file-by-file record of the number of bytes transmitted (during either send or receive), the number of seconds required, and an average statistic for bytes transferred per minute. Additionally, there is a summary for each session of the previous statistics for all files transmitted.

Watch how much space is used on your hard drive by STDEVT.LOG and ERROR.LOG. These files grow and may take up more valuable disk space than you want to give up.

 You can also view these files when the communications program is running by clicking the corresponding buttons on the surface of the communications program's display window.

Replying to and Forwarding Mail

WinNET Mail makes it easy to reply to or forward a mail message.

These operations are both represented by buttons on the Control bar and both operations can be invoked either from any folder window, or from the mail message viewer.

To reply to a mail message from a folder window:

1. Select the line relating to the message to which you want to reply. You can use either the mouse or the keyboard to select the item. The message should appear highlighted.

2. Click the Reply button or select Mail⇨Reply. You will then see a dialog box that asks you whether you want to copy the original message into the mail composition editor.

   If you select Yes here, the item is copied, and each line from the original message has a chevron > character in front of it. This is the Internet mail convention for referring to or quoting another message. It indicates to the recipient of the mail that these lines are not written by you but are quotations from the original message (or, in some cases, multiple quotations from a chain of several exchanges of messages).

3. The reply operation will also automatically fill out the fields at the top of the mail composition editor and put the cursor in the editing area. It will also pick up the original subject line of the message and use it as the subject of the message you are creating, prefaced by *Re:*. You can edit all the header fields, if you want to, before or after creating your reply.

4. Once the mail composition editor is active, edit your message as described in the section entitled "Composing Mail," and select Done when you have completed your reply.

To forward a mail message from a folder window:

1. Select the item relating to the message that you want to forward.

2. When the item is selected, click the Forward button, or select the Mail⇨Forward command. The Forward command always copies the entire selected message into the mail composition editor.

3. The forward operation will automatically fill out the Subject field in the top section of the mail composition editor, but you will have to fill in the To field, and, optionally, the CC field.

4. Once the header fields are set, click the Edit button to add any text you wish to the forwarded message. When the message is readied, click the Done button to process the mail.

The process of replying to or forwarding a mail message from the mail viewer is essentially the same as working from a folder. When you click the Reply or Forward buttons (or select one of these choices from the mail menu), the command operates on the message that you are currently viewing and will set up your reply or forwarded message in the mail composition editor in the same way as described for starting the operation from a folder.

You can also reply to (by mail) or forward a news article. The functions work the same way when working with news articles as they do with mail messages. More details on replying to and forwarding news articles is found in the help index in "Usenet News."

Folder Management

WinNET Mail supports a very detailed and carefully designed system of folders for storing users' categorized mail messages. In combination with the database-like search folders functions, you can build very specialized storage locations for specific types of mail that you send and receive.

Within the WinNET Mail environment, it is possible to work with several predefined folders that have special functionality, as well as creating both user-defined folders and search result folders. (Search result folders are described in the section "Searching Folders").

Opening a folder

Opening a new folder is simple. You can use the mouse to click the Folder button on the Control bar, or alternatively, select Folder⇨Folder List. You will then see a window containing the names of all the currently defined folders as in Figure 6-2.

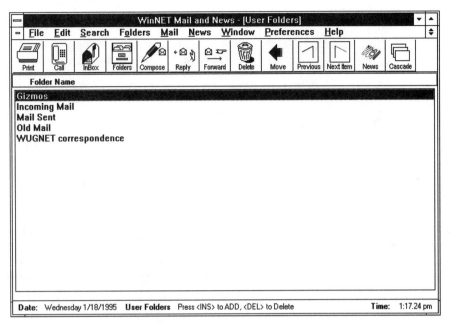

Figure 6-2: Currently defined folders.

This list will include any predefined folders that have items in them, as well as any folders you have defined. To actually open the folder, double-click the name of the folder you want to open, or select the name using the keyboard and press Enter.

Creating, deleting, and renaming folders

You can create new folders from the folder window by either pressing the Ins key or by selecting Folder⇨Create. When you create a new folder, you are prompted for a folder name. Folder names can be up to 128 characters long, so feel free to be descriptive.

You can delete whole folders from the folder window by pressing Del or by selecting Folder⇨Delete.

You can rename any folder by highlighting the folder name and selecting Folder⇨Rename.

Reading folder messages

Any item that a folder contains can be opened for reading by double-clicking the item or using the keyboard to move to the item and pressing Enter.

Deleting folder messages

You can delete any message in a folder. First highlight the message you want to delete, and then click the trash can icon on the Control bar. You also can press Del or select Mail⇨Delete. When you delete a message, it does not disappear from the list right away. Instead a *D* appears in the status column for the message.

If you change your mind about deleting the item, highlight it again at any time before closing the folder or quitting WinNET Mail, press Del again, select Mail⇨Delete again, or click the trash can icon again. This procedure will preserve (undelete) the item. Items are really deleted when you close a folder or quit WinNET Mail.

If the item that you marked for deletion is the only copy of the item in any folder, the mail item will be deleted from the WinNET Mail system. If another copy exists in another folder, only the copy in the folder that was marked for deletion will be deleted, and the copy in the other folder will remain.

Moving or copying folder messages

Except for search folder results, any item in a folder can also be moved or copied to another folder. These two operations differ in that *moving* an item means you remove the item from one folder and place the item in another folder, whereas *copying* an item places a duplicate of an item in another folder and the item is still in the originating folder.

You may move an item to another folder by selecting it and either clicking the Move button on the Control bar or by selecting Mail⇨Move. (The only exception to this is that you cannot move or copy a message into the Incoming Mail folder, which is reserved for new items.) After initiating the move operation in one of these ways, you will see a dialog box that asks you for the name of the folder to which you would like to move the message. Type the name of a new folder to create for the message, or select the name of a preexisting folder from the list of folders that follows.

To copy an item to another folder, select Mail⇨Copy. (Not to be confused with Edit⇨Copy, which copies text to the Clipboard). You will see a dialog box that asks you for the name of the folder to which you would like to copy the message. Type the name of a new folder to create for the message, or select the name of a preexisting folder from the list of folders that follows.

Folder sorting order

Items in these folders are stored in chronological order. Whether this order is from oldest to newest or newest to oldest can be set in the dialog box that is invoked by selecting the Preferences⇨Options command.

The order of items in any folder, with the exception of Incoming Mail, can be reversed by selecting Folder⇨Reverse List.

Predefined Folders

Predefined folders are the folders that come already defined in WinNET Mail. In some cases, you can turn off these features so that these folders do not appear. Each predefined folder is described in the following sections.

The Incoming Mail folder

The Incoming Mail folder is automatically loaded when you start up WinNET Mail, unless you turn off this feature with the Preferences⇨Preferences dialog box. This is where all your incoming mail messages are placed a few moments after new messages arrive on your system. (If WinNET Mail is not running when you receive new mail, the messages will appear in the Incoming Mail folder as soon as you start WinNET Mail.)

The Incoming Mail folder maintains the items in its list according to a convenient chronological scheme. Newly arrived mail items always get added to the list immediately after any other unread mail in the folder. The purpose of this is to keep older, unread mail at the top of the list. Mail that has been read previously is then listed from newest to oldest after the unread items.

As items pile up in your Incoming Mail folder, you may eventually want to use WinNET Mail's automated features for storing these messages in other folders.

Clearing messages from the Incoming Mail folder

On the Folder menu, a command called Clear Incoming Mail has a submenu containing two choices, *To Old Mail* and *Assign to folders named after senders*. This latter choice is selectable only when the Incoming Mail folder window is the active window.

If you select Clear Incoming Mail/To Old Mail, all unread messages not marked for deletion will be moved to another predefined folder called Old Mail. Making it a habit to move items periodically from Incoming Mail to Old Mail is a simple way of organizing mail into just two categories. The items in your Incoming Mail folder are more recent, and items in Old Mail are older. This may be all the organization that many people, who just want to keep it simple, require.

If you select Clear Incoming Mail/Assign to folders named after senders, all unread messages not marked for deletion are moved to folders named after the senders of the mail items. Most Internet mail programs, including WinNET Mail, follow a convention of putting a line in mail message headers with the format:

```
From: user@machine.net (FirstName LastName)
```

WinNET Mail will attempt to parse out the (FirstName LastName) part of the From line in the header to create the folder names. If this is not possible, the user address in the mail message header is used to create a folder name.

The folders created when you use this operation are considered *user-defined folders*, and have the functional characteristics of user-defined folders, described in the section entitled "User-Defined Folders."

The Mail Sent folder

Whenever you use the mail composition editor to create a mail message and then select the Done button, you are prompted about saving a copy of your outgoing mail in your Mail Sent folder.

This predefined folder is similar to other folders. However, instead of the list items in this folder showing who the mail is from, this folder shows the name or address of the person to whom the mail has been sent. WinNET Mail derives this name in one of two ways. If you have defined an address book entry (alias) for the recipient of the mail, WinNET Mail uses the address book name that you have defined for the recipient to derive the recipient name. Otherwise, WinNET Mail uses the address that is put in the header of the file when the item is processed for posting.

Because it is probably more desirable to see an address book name for these items in the list, it is a good idea to create address book entries for persons with whom you often correspond. (For more information about the address book, see the section entitled "The Address Book (Aliasing).")

The Old Mail folder

This folder has already been discussed. It is created the first time that you use the Folder⇨Clear Incoming Mail/To Old Mail command. This folder is just a standard folder with no special functions.

User-Defined Folders

User-defined folders can be created in a variety of ways. One of the most common methods is using the Folder⇨Clear Incoming Mail/Assign to folders named after senders command. This command creates individual folders named after and containing correspondence from each person from whom you have received mail.

You can also create user-defined folders directly from the folder list window by pressing the Ins key or by selecting Folder⇨Create when the folder list window is the currently active window.

Also, when you either move or copy items from a folder, you can create a user-defined folder simply by typing the name of a new folder into the name field to answer the prompt about the name from the folder (instead of picking a previously defined folder from the list).

The Address Book (Aliasing)

The address book lets you create a database of the names of people with whom you regularly correspond. You then use the book to fill in the To or CC fields of the mail composition editor instead of using formal Internet addresses. Address book entries simplify the addressing of mail and help you to avoid mistyping formal Internet addresses, which can sometimes be rather long and hard to remember.

For example, if you regularly send mail to the president of Computer Witchcraft to discuss your suggestions or observations about WinNET Mail, you normally have to address such messages to tague@cwinc.win.net. You might want to create an address book entry for this address. A logical choice for the address book entry is Computer Witchcraft's president's real name, which is Michael Tague, or more simply still *tague* or *mt.*

Creating address entries

To create address book entries, select Mail➪Address Book Management. This will bring up the Address Book Management dialog box as shown in Figure 6-3. The Address Book Management dialog box allows you to edit the address book database and to add new entries.

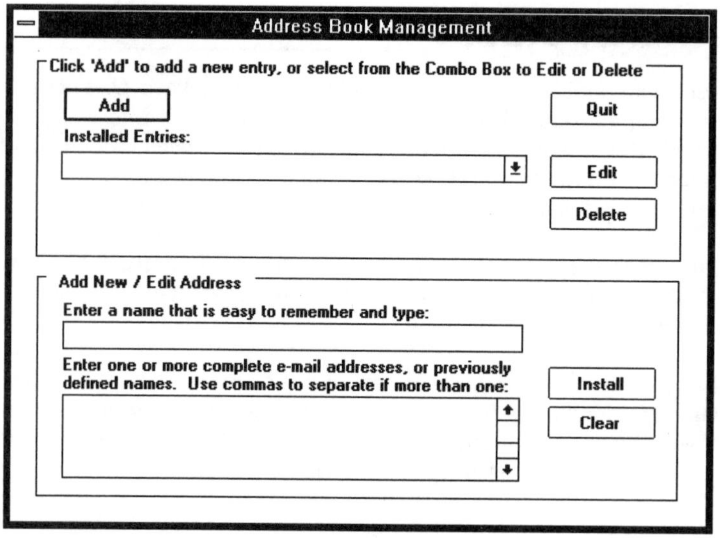

```
┌─────────────────────────────────────────────────────────────────┐
│ ▭              Address Book Management                           │
│ ┌─Click 'Add' to add a new entry, or select from the Combo Box to Edit or Delete─┐
│ │  ┌──────────┐                                      ┌──────────┐ │
│ │  │   Add    │                                      │   Quit   │ │
│ │  └──────────┘                                      └──────────┘ │
│ │  Installed Entries:                                             │
│ │  ┌──────────────────────────────────────┬─┐     ┌──────────┐  │
│ │  │                                      │▼│     │   Edit   │  │
│ │  └──────────────────────────────────────┴─┘     └──────────┘  │
│ │                                                 ┌──────────┐  │
│ │                                                 │  Delete  │  │
│ │                                                 └──────────┘  │
│ └─────────────────────────────────────────────────────────────┘ │
│ ┌─Add New / Edit Address──────────────────────────────────────┐ │
│ │  Enter a name that is easy to remember and type:             │ │
│ │  ┌──────────────────────────────────────────┐               │ │
│ │  │                                          │               │ │
│ │  └──────────────────────────────────────────┘               │ │
│ │  Enter one or more complete e-mail addresses, or previously  │ │
│ │  defined names.  Use commas to separate if more than one:  ┌─────────┐
│ │  ┌──────────────────────────────────────┬─┐              │ Install │
│ │  │                                      │▲│              └─────────┘
│ │  │                                      │ │              ┌─────────┐
│ │  │                                      │ │              │  Clear  │
│ │  │                                      │▼│              └─────────┘
│ │  └──────────────────────────────────────┴─┘                    │
│ └─────────────────────────────────────────────────────────────┘ │
└─────────────────────────────────────────────────────────────────┘
```

Figure 6-3: The Address Book Management dialog box.

If you want to add a new address book entry, follow these steps:

1. Click the Add button that appears in the top-left part of the Address Book Management dialog box. The cursor will move to the lower section of the dialog box, into the field labeled *Enter a name that is easy to remember and type:*.

2. Press the Tab key or use the mouse to move to the box immediately below the name field, which is labeled *Enter one or more complete e-mail addresses, or previously defined names....* In this area, type the person's real address.

3. This completes the process of creating a simple entry, so now click the Install button.

   After you click Install, the fields will clear, and the cursor will appear again in the field labeled *Enter a name which is easy to remember and type:*. This field enables you to add additional names.

4. To verify that the entry was successfully entered, you can navigate at this point (with the mouse or by pressing Tab several times) back to the top portion of the Address Book Management dialog to the drop-down list control labeled *Installed Entries*.

   By clicking the small down arrow, or by pressing Alt+↓ on the keyboard, you can pull down the contents of this list. You should see the name you entered earlier in this list. If you then select this item, using the keyboard or the mouse, you can then click the Edit button. Clicking the Edit button copies the selected item from the Installed Entries list down to the name field in the lower portion of the dialog box, and will also show in the address field the Internet address which is associated in the database with this name.

5. You can then proceed to edit/modify either of these fields, and then click Install again to store your modifications.

   You can also select an item from the Installed Entries list, and click the Delete button to remove the name and address from the address book database.

6. Whenever you are finished working with the Address Book Management dialog, click the Quit button to close the dialog box.

The address book allows you to create compound entries that consist of multiple addresses associated with a single name. To do this, click Add to begin the process in the usual way. When you move to the field labeled *Enter one or more complete e-mail addresses or previously defined names,* enter each address that you want associated with the name, and be sure to separate the addresses *with commas.* You can also put previously defined address book entries in this field, which may also be compound, as long as you put commas between every logical entry.

The address book entries that you create using the Address Book Management dialog become immediately accessible to the drop-down lists associated with the To and CC fields of the mail composition editor. When composing mail, just click the small down arrows next to these fields to access the list of address book entries. You can select an entry by double-clicking with the mouse or by using the cursor (arrow) keys. If you use the arrow keys, you have to press the Tab key to fold up the list and move to the next field.

You can add new entries to the address book even while the mail composition window is active. As soon as you click the Install button and quit the address book, the new address book entry is transferred to the drop-down list controls in the mail composition editor.

Sending and Receiving Binary Files

Most of the mail traffic on the Internet is in the form of plain ASCII text, with no control characters or extended graphics characters. This is true because mail must sometimes pass between many relay computer systems to get to its destination. Plain ASCII text is the common data format that guarantees proper processing for all systems in the network. Using the WinNET Mail editor ensures that your messages meet this requirement.

But what if you want to mail a word processing document or a graphics file or an executable program to someone? (These files are called *binary files* because they consist of bytes that can have any values in addition to those of the standard ASCII character set of letters, numbers, and punctuation marks.)

Never fear! WinNET Mail enables you to mail any file type that you want!

This process is accomplished by translating binary files into a sequence of bytes that are pure ASCII and then retranslating them back to their original format at the other end. You don't need to understand the details of this process to use it. Mailing and receiving binary files is very easy with WinNET Mail — much easier than when using traditional communications packages.

Sending a binary file

To mail a binary file:

1. Start the mail composition editor by clicking the Compose button on the Control bar or by selecting Mail⇨Compose.

2. Fill out the fields in the top section of the mail composition editor as you normally do to send a regular message, as described in the section called "Composing Mail."

3. You can then add some text to your message, perhaps describing in some detail the binary file you are mailing. It is not necessary to add any text.

4. Incorporate the binary file into your mail message by selecting Mail⇨Attach Binary File. A dialog box appears asking you to select a file from somewhere on your system. Use this dialog box to find and select the binary file that you wish to attach. Click the OK button when you find the file.

5. That's it! After you have attached the file, click Done. You will be asked, as usual, if you want to keep a copy of the file in your Mail Sent folder. You might want to select Yes if you added some text to the message that included the binary file. When you select Yes, only the text portion of your message is saved in your Mail Sent folder. The binary part is not saved. Instead, a line such as

```
Attached File: FILENAME.EXT
```

appears at the top of the copy of the message.

You can send only one binary file per mail message. If you want to send more than one binary file, the most convenient approach is to use a DOS archiving program to process several files into an archive before attaching it to a mail message. This has the added advantage of compressing the data that is to be sent, reducing the transfer time. Computer Witchcraft recommends PKWARE'S PKZip program for this purpose. You can find this shareware program on just about all BBSs.

Receiving binary files

When you receive a binary file from another WinNET Mail user, the first line of the message indicates that a binary file is attached, similar to the following:

```
Attached File: FILENAME.EXT
```

If you receive a binary file from a standard UNIX Internet mail site, this line does not appear, but the user will generally indicate in the text part of the message that an encoded file is attached. Also, you'll see a long section of characters after the text part of the mail message that is not legible, preceded by a line that appears something like:

```
begin 666 filename.ext
```

This is the encoded binary file data.

When you receive an attached binary file, you can reconstruct the binary file from the mail very easily:

1. Select Mail⇨Detach Binary File. You then see a dialog box asking you to select a directory where you would like the binary file to be stored. Use the dialog box to locate the correct directory, and double-click the directory. Then click OK to select the directory.

The hourglass cursor comes up while the binary file is being unbundled from the mail item. When the process is complete, a message box appears informing you that the file has been successfully processed. The reconstructed binary file is now stored in the directory you selected. If the file is an archive, you may have to then go to the DOS prompt to unarchive the files it contains. The sender of the item should provide instructions in the text part of the message if anything unusual is necessary.

Reconstructing multipart binary files

If you subscribe to Usenet newsgroups, you may subscribe to a group that disseminates binary files (for example, comp.ms-windows.binaries, or the various groups that have graphics files). Because many systems on the Internet/Usenet network do not allow files to be larger than approximately 100,000K in size, larger files distributed in these groups are frequently cut into more than one piece, and the pieces arrive separately as single files. If you receive a collection of such files, it is necessary to reconstruct them into a single file so that it can be decoded to the original binary file.

To do this, follow these steps:

1. Start by opening a new file by selecting File⇨New.

2. Open the first of the multipart binary files that you received. Toward the beginning of this file, look for the *begin* line of the encoded material that it contains. This line usually has a format such as

   ```
   begin 666 filename
   ```

3. Place the cursor at the beginning of the begin line, and click to move the caret there. Press Ctrl+Shift+End to highlight (select) the remainder of the file.

4. Adjust the selection by holding down the Shift key and using the arrow keys so that only the last line of encoded material is selected. (Pressing Ctrl+Shift+End selected everything to the end of the file, and you do not want to copy any material that is not part of the encoded material — usually, there is a line of dashes at the bottom of such files with the embedded comment — *Cut Here* — this last line should not be selected.) Make sure that the last line of encoded material is selected in its entirety. Press Ctrl+C to copy your selection.

5. Move back to the new file that you opened in the first step. Press Ctrl+V to paste the copied material into the new file. After pasting, position the caret so that it is at the beginning of the next (blank) line so that when you return to this file to paste again, the caret is in the right position.

6. Open the next in the series of the multipart binary files. Place the caret at the beginning of the first line in the file that contains encoded material. Cut the line with dashes as you did before. Once again, press Ctrl+Shift+End and then adjust the selected text as described previously so that the extraneous material at the end of the file is not selected.

7. Repeat steps 3, 4, and 5 until you have pasted the contents of each of the parts of the binary file into the file you opened in step 1.

When working with the last file in the series, make sure to include the last line of the encoded material that says *end*. This end line is part of the encoded material and must be present at the end of the reconstructed file you have put together.

8. You can now detach the reintegrated attached binary file by selecting Mail⇨Detach Binary File.

File binary notes

You can rename attached binary files to anything you like in the dialog box that comes up when you select Detach Binary File.

If you select the File⇨Run DOS Shell command after a Detach Binary File command, WinNET Mail will automatically make the directory where you detached the binary file the current working directory in the following DOS session.

If you receive a binary file from a non-DOS user, the original filename of the attached file may not conform to the rules for MS-DOS filenames. WinNET Mail handles this by creating a default filename, UNIXNAME.XXX, that does correspond to the rules for DOS filenames. This filename appears in the Choose Directory dialog box that comes up when you select Detach Binary File. You can change the name in the dialog box to something more suitable, if you know what the file contains and have a better name in mind.

You may sometimes receive files from non-DOS users that are in a format created by special compression or archiving utilities from those systems. The most common of these are the UNIX *compress* and *tar* (tape archive) utilities. In the event that someone sends you a file formatted by these utilities, you can acquire MS-DOS equivalents of these programs from CompuServe. You can download both programs from the UNIXFORUM section of CIS.

Searching Folders

One of WinNET Mail's most interesting and powerful features is the support it has for database-like searching of your collection of mail messages for a search-text. This search can be configured according to some simple rules, which help to refine the outcome of the search. The immediate result of searching folders is a search results folder. The search results folder appears after the conclusion of the initial search, with the same list format as regular folders and containing the mail messages that meet the search criteria.

You can also search through newsgroup folders. See the section "Searching News Folders" in the "Usenet News" topic in the Help Index for more information about news searching facilities.

Shrinking and growing the search results

Once an initial search has been performed and a search results folder has been created, it is possible to run subsequent searches to shrink or grow the search folder results by excluding or including additional items according to new rules that you define for each separate search. You can run as many shrinks and grows as are needed to satisfy the criteria you have in mind. At any time, you can view the messages that your search results folder contains by double-clicking a mail message to start the mail reader just as you do from a regular folder. If an item doesn't belong in the search results folder, you can delete the item. After all searches have been run and the search results folder contains precisely the items that you want, you can save the search results folder as a regular folder with a name that you supply.

Using the Search folder's operations, you can conveniently create subject-oriented folders that contain correspondence related to specific areas of interest.

Conducting a search

To begin a search operation, select Search⇨Search Folders. At this point, a dialog box appears for you to define the search operation. See Figure 6-4.

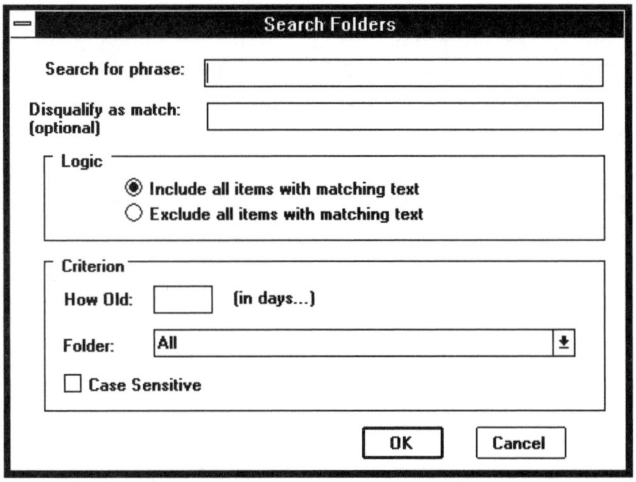

Figure 6-4: Search Folders dialog box.

■ The first field is labeled *Search for phrase*. This is where you put the search text. The text can be up to 80 characters long.

■ The next field, which is optional, is labeled *Disqualify as match*. The purpose of this field is to provide text that can mistakenly be matched in the search operation. For example, you've decided to search for all references to WinNET Mail. However, you know that the term *Mailer: WinNET Mail for Windows* is in the header of every mail message. You can enter **Mailer: WinNET Mail** in the Disqualify as match field to eliminate references made to WinNET Mail in the headers.

■ The next section of the search dialog box is labeled *Logic* and consists of two radio buttons labeled *Include all items with matching text* and *Exclude all items with matching text*. If you are trying to create a folder of items that include the text you put in the Search for phrase field, select the Include all items with matching text radio button. If you are searching for all items that do not contain your search phrase, select the Exclude all items with matching text radio button.

■ The next section of the Search Folders dialog box is called *Criterion* and allows you to further confine the scope of the search.

■ The first item in the Criterion area is a field labeled *How Old: (in days)*. If you put a number here, the search is confined to messages no older than that many days. If you don't put anything here, the search ignores the age of the message.

- The second item in the Criterion area is a drop-down list containing all the folders defined for your mail system. If you want to confine your search to a specific folder, you can select a folder from this list. If you do not select a folder, the search is not confined to a particular folder; it checks all mail messages in the system for a match.

- If you check the third item in the Criterion area, *Case Sensitive*, the search is limited to the exact uppercase and lowercase combination of letters entered in the Search for phrase field and Disqualify as match field.

When you have filled out the fields of the Search Folders dialog box to your satisfaction, click OK. The dialog disappears and you see a message at the bottom of the WinNET Mail display (in the status line area) that reads *Conducting background search for...* (... is the phrase you picked). If you want, you can now continue working with other tasks within WinNET Mail or other applications while the search is conducted.

When the search is complete (which may be quite a while if you have thousands of messages in your folders and your search criteria were not very exclusive), WinNET Mail produces the Search Results Folder window that contains the messages that met your search criteria. You can then open any of the files it contains for examination.

The standard editor Search facility is preloaded with your search phrase; you can select Search⇨Find or Search⇨Find Again to go to the search phrase immediately. You can also save the search results folder as a regular folder by selecting Search⇨Save. If, on the other hand, you close the search results folder by selecting Windows⇨Close, the results of the search are not saved.

If you want to further expand or shrink the contents of your search results folder, you can use the Search⇨Grow and Search⇨Shrink commands to do so. You can perform as many grows and shrinks as you like.

Selecting Search⇨Grow allows you to configure another search, using the same dialog box that you used to do the initial search. You can put completely new criteria for the Grow command, however, in order to create a folder that includes whatever messages you wish. The Grow command will not duplicate any mail item messages found in previous operations.

Selecting Search⇨Shrink allows you to configure a search *within the search results folder only*. The purpose of Shrink is to eliminate unwanted items from the contents of the search results folder. It has the same dialog box as the other search folder operations, but, because it operates only on the contents of the search results folder, it always produces a subset of the original folder's messages.

Whenever you feel satisfied with the list of items that you have produced with the various search folder tools, you can save the folder as a regular folder by selecting Search⇨Save.

Accessing Usenet Newsgroups_____

Overview of news

One of the richest properties of the Internet/Usenet is the provision it makes for discussion groups covering a staggering array of topics. Currently, more than 5,000 interactive newsgroups cover almost every academic and scientific discipline, the arts, personal issues, recreation, politics, government, education, and all major aspects of computer science, including many groups devoted to specific systems and software, such as UNIX, MS-DOS, Macintosh, and Windows. When you join one or more newsgroups, you will begin to receive articles that have been published by other participants in the newsgroups.

As a WinNET user, you can subscribe to any number of newsgroups. You can easily add or remove newsgroups any time, using the Subscription Management dialog box. (See Figure 6-5.) This feature allows you to try out different groups to find the discussion areas that are of the most interest to you.

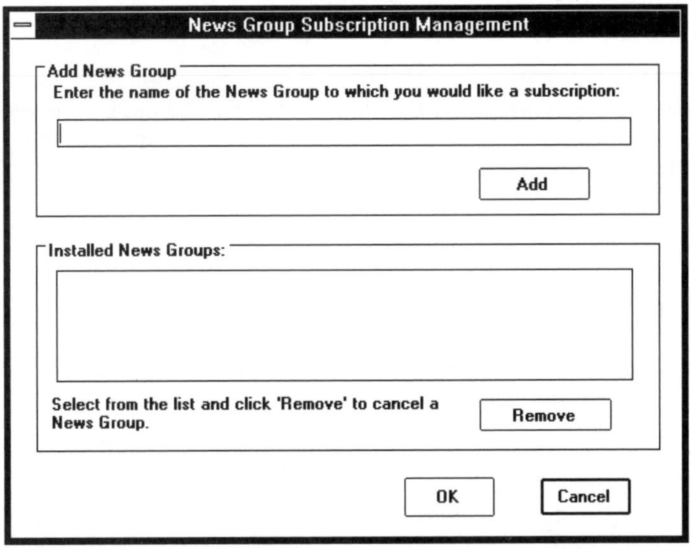

Figure 6-5: Subscription Management dialog box.

Computer Witchcraft's WinNET service also gives you access to the Clarinet newsgroups. Clarinet is an organization that provides professionally edited news articles, in the traditional sense of covering national and international events, sports, weather, syndicated columnists, financial markets, and so forth. The Clarinet groups are very popular with WinNET users.

Summary of news features

- Automatic electronic subscription to individual newsgroups. Groups may be added or removed with a simple dialog box. Mail messages are generated to the subscription management software at CWI that takes care of adding and removing groups from the user's receive list.

- Categorization of articles by newsgroup. As the user's system receives new articles, the articles are automatically delivered to folders corresponding by name to the proper newsgroups.

- Master newsgroup list. Like the folder list, this window displays all newsgroups that have articles in them, with groups having unread articles at the top (along with an indication of the number of unread articles).

- Ordering of news articles by conversation threads. Articles can then be browsed so that fidelity to the chronological order of the conversation is consistently achieved.

- Support for posting original articles. The user can select Post News from the News menu to activate the News Composition Editor. (The News Composition Editor has drop-down lists from which newsgroups can be selected for posting and which also designates a Followup-To: group.) Articles may be *cross-posted* (sent to more than one newsgroup).

- Support for *following up* (responding in a newsgroup to another article). The original newsgroups are automatically designated, or, in the case in which the original article suggests a follow-up group, the follow-up group is automatically designated.

- Support for reply by mail.

- Support for copying news articles to mail folders.

- Support for marking articles as seen en masse so that uninteresting articles can be dispensed.

- Support for copying articles from news folders to more permanent mail folders. Articles can be copied individually or by conversational thread.

- Communications batch processing of news articles and mail for increased data-throughput.

- Cleanup utility. This utility enables you to delete old news and mail. With a configuration file, optional archiving of news can be performed.

Getting the lists of newsgroups

After you have looked at the lists and have decided which groups you want to add to your subscription, write down the names of the groups carefully so that you can add them correctly during the subscription process.

If you want a list of just Comp, Misc, and News (Computing, Miscellaneous, and News) groups, include a subject line of *News List 1* in the mail you send to request@win.net.

If you want a list of Alt, Bionet, Bit, and Biz groups (Alternative, Biology-Net, Bitnet, and Business), include a subject line of *News List 2* in the mail you send to request@win.net.

If you want a list of Rec, Sci, Soc and Talk groups (Recreation, Science, Sociology, and Talk), include a subject line of *News List 3* in the mail you send to request@win.net.

If you want a list of Clari, GNU, IEEE, K12 and "other" groups (Clarinet professionally edited news, GNU software foundation, Institute of Electrical Engineers, Kindergarten through 12th grade education), include a subject line of *News List 4*.

The request@win.net server is part of the WinNET's service. Other files are available via this address. If you want a complete list of files that you can request, send mail to request@win.net with a subject line of *Help*.

Subscribing to newsgroups

To subscribe to one or more newsgroups, follow these steps:

1. Start WinNET Mail. Choose News⇨Subscriptions.

2. In the field labeled *Enter the name of a newsgroup to which you would like a subscription*, type the name of one of the groups you want to receive.

3. Click the Add button. You will see that the name of the newsgroup is added to the listbox in the lower part of the dialog box.

   You may continue to add as many groups as you wish in this way.

4. When you have completed adding the groups you want, click OK. WinNET Mail initializes and builds a database that is news ready, as well as creating several mail messages to Computer Witchcraft. The next time you call Computer Witchcraft, your requests to receive newsgroups are processed. Computer Witchcraft's system then sends you mail confirming that the groups have been successfully added to your receive list, and notifying you that you will be receiving the newsgroups soon.

5. In the event that you make a typing error when entering groups in the subscription dialog box, or if the group you specified no longer exists in Usenet, the return mail from Computer Witchcraft may indicate an error. If you receive notice from Computer Witchcraft that an error occurred, you should open the News/Subscriptions dialog box again and remove the newsgroup from your list.

Canceling a newsgroup

You can use the following steps to cancel your subscription to any newsgroup at any time:

1. Select News⇨Subscriptions and locate the newsgroup that you want to cancel in the listbox that contains the names of your current groups.

2. Highlight the newsgroup name by clicking it once or selecting it with the arrow keys.

3. Click the Remove button. You can remove one or several groups in this way.

4. When you've finished pruning your subscription list, click OK. WinNET Mail removes the newsgroup(s) from your list of groups, and generates mail to Computer Witchcraft indicating that you have canceled your subscription to the group(s). Computer Witchcraft in turn sends you a mail message indicating that the group(s) have been removed from your receive list.

Reading Usenet newsgroup articles

After you have signed up for one or more newsgroups, you will begin receiving articles from other Usenet News users throughout the world written in these newsgroups. (The time between requesting a group and receiving articles may vary from a few hours to two days, depending on the volume of traffic of the group and when Computer Witchcraft receives a batch of news for that group).

When these articles arrive on your system, they are not processed in the same way as e-mail. Instead of appearing in your incoming mail folder, news articles are processed directly to news folders pertaining to the specific groups. To access the news folders, you can click the News button on the Control bar or you can select News⇨News Group List. If you select News Group List before you have actually received any news, the display will be empty because only groups containing articles are shown. However, if you have articles, you will see each newsgroup containing articles listed in alphabetical order. The left column of the display will also show how many new (unread) articles are present in each particular group.

Note that when you click the News button or choose News⇨News Group List, the Control bar buttons change so that various buttons needed for accessing News functions become visible. (If you want to return to the Mail context, click the button labeled Inbox). The buttons that are present on the Control bar in the news context include a Post button (to post a news article), a Follow-up button (to follow up an article), a Copy button (to copy an article to a mail folder) and a Mark button (to mark an article as having been seen, or to mark an entire newsgroup of articles seen all at once).

To open a news folder, double-click its entry in the News Group List. A new window opens, displaying information about the contents of each article that is in the newsgroup folder. To read a specific article, double-click its entry. You may also click the Control bar Next Item button to read articles sequentially.

Articles are organized in conversational order so that you can easily follow the thread of the discussion from one article to the next. Unread news articles are placed sequentially at the top of the list when you first open it. If you click the Next Item button on the Control bar to move from article to article, upon reaching the last new article, the Next Item button will close the viewer at that point so that you know you have reached the last of the new articles in the group. If you want to review old articles, just click the Next Item button again, and it will permit you to continue reading through previously seen material.

The Mark Button

If you do not wish to read a news article, you can click the Mark button on the Control bar. When you click the Mark button, the currently highlighted article's status indicator will change from new to old so that it will not appear grouped with new articles the next time you open this newsgroup.

Also, if you have selected Hide Old Articles in the Preferences dialog box (see the section "Preferences" in the Help Index for more information about Preferences), old articles will not appear in newsgroups when you open them. Also, if you close the currently open newsgroup and select the name of the newsgroup from the master list of newsgroups and then click the Mark button, all the articles in that newsgroup will be marked as seen.

You cannot delete or move articles from a news folder. This is because the conversational "hierarchy" of articles must be retained by WinNET so that when new articles arrive, they can be placed in context. If you wish to prune your newsgroup system, you should run the supplied CLEANUP.EXE program. This program allows you to remove old news from your system. Please read the section entitled "Cleaning up Old News" from the Usenet News Help Index for more information about CLEANUP.EXE.

Posting news articles to Usenet

You may eventually want to contribute your own articles to groups in which you participate.

To post an original article (that is, an article that is not written specifically in response to another article), click the button labeled Post on the Control bar, or select News⇨Post News.

A window appears that is subdivided into a header part and the editor section. The header part includes two drop-down boxes and an edit field.

The first drop-down box (NewsGroup(s):) is where you put the name or, if you are cross-posting to more than one newsgroup, names of the newsgroup(s) where you would like to publish your article. You can click the small arrow next to the drop-down box if you want to select the newsgroup from the list of newsgroups to which you subscribe, or, if you like, you can type the name(s) in from the keyboard.

Cross-posting, or posting an article to more than one newsgroup, may sometimes get you in trouble with other members of the Usenet community, particularly if you post to groups that are not closely relevant to the subject material of your article. Although Computer Witchcraft takes no particular stand on this issue, users are warned that strong feelings about this are prevalent on the network. It is possible that another user or several users from the network might take it upon themselves to send you e-mail reviling you for what they consider to be inappropriate cross-posting!

In the second drop-down box (labeled Followup-To:), you can optionally specify one or more groups to which follow-up articles to your article should be posted. If you are posting to only one newsgroup, it is generally best to leave the Followup-To: area blank, as all Usenet news reading software defaults to the current group(s) if no Followup-To: field is specified. However, if you do post your article to multiple groups, it is generally considered polite to specify one and only one follow-up group so that continuation of the conversation can take place in one newsgroup only, or a few closely related groups at most.

Finally, in the third field (labeled Subject:), put a carefully thought-out, brief description of your article's contents. It is even more important than with mail to attach a careful subject line to a news article.

When you have filled out the header area, click the Edit button and write the contents of your article. Click Done when you finish the article and wish to dispatch it for publication on the network. WinNET will then publish your article in the appropriate newsgroup on your system, and will put the article in queue for delivery to Computer Witchcraft and subsequent distribution to the Usenet!

Following up articles posted by other authors

If you read an article in a newsgroup to which you would like to publicly publish an article in reply, select the article in the news folder or open the article and then select News⇨Follow-up.

You will then see a window subdivided in the same way as the Post News window. In this case, however, the NewsGroup(s) field and subject fields are carried over from the original posting automatically. You might want to have a look at the NewsGroup(s) and check for which groups are listed in terms of cross-posting. If only one group is shown, there is no problem. If, however, there are a number of groups, and some of them seem inappropriate, in your judgment, you can edit this field and remove some or all but one of the groups. You can also specify a Followup-To: group if you want.

As with composing mail or posting news, when you have completed your article, click the Done button to process your article and distribute it to the network.

Replying to/forwarding articles by mail

In many cases, you may not want to post an article publicly to reply to an article of interest. Instead, you may wish to contact the author privately by e-mail.

In this case, select the article to which you wish to reply from the new folder where it appears, or open the article for reading. Choose Mail⇨Reply to or click the Reply button on the Control bar. WinNET automatically sets up the original article for reply by mail. For more information on using WinNET's e-mail facilities, see the appropriate entries in the on-line help system.

Copying news articles to mail folders

Sometimes you will read a news article or follow a conversation (thread) that contains information that you would like to store permanently in a mail folder. This can be done easily.

To copy a single article to a mail folder, just highlight or open the item that you want to save to a mail folder and click the Copy button on the Control bar. A dialog box opens that shows you a list of all your user-defined folders. Select the folder to which you'd like to copy the article, or enter the name of a new user-defined folder; then click OK.

To copy an entire conversational thread to a mail folder, select any article that is part of the thread that you'd like to copy from the newsgroup list. Next, select News➪Copy Thread. A dialog box opens that shows you a list of all your user-defined folders. Select the folder to which you'd like to copy the thread, or enter the name of a new user-defined folder and click OK.

Using the Search News command

Using the News➪Search News command, you can conveniently create subject-oriented folders that contain articles containing a specific search text. See the section entitled "Conducting a search" to learn how to do this.

Removing old news articles from your system

From time to time, you will want to clear old news from your system. For this purpose, you must run the News Cleanup program. This is a separate program (CLEANUP.EXE) installed in your WinNET Mail Program Manager Folder when you installed WinNET Mail. Its icon is a picture of a garbage can.

The cleanup program has two main purposes. First, it deletes news articles older than a user-definable number of days. Second, it controls and takes care of archiving of the newsgroups that you specify.

The News Cleanup program has its own help file that you can invoke by pressing F1. When you want to expire old news articles, double-click the Cleanup Icon in Program Manager. If you have never run cleanup before or want to set up news archives for the first time, please press F1 and carefully read the Help for Cleanup.

Setting WinNET Mail Preferences

WinNET Mail has a Preferences menu that allows you to modify various aspects of the way the program works to suit your personal options.

Word Wrap On/Off

Choosing this command toggles WinNET Mail's word wrap feature on and off. If word wrap is currently on, a check mark appears by this command. You can set the right margin where wrapping occurs via the Preferences➪Preferences dialog box . The Preferences➪Preferences dialog box also lets you set a default start-up behavior for word wrap.

Set tab

Choosing this option lets you set the value of tab stops in WinNET Mail. Tab stops are positioned at a columnar interval across the editing area, and the value you supply here when prompted sets this interval, the unit being the width of a character. You can set the default start-up tab interval via the Preferences dialog box.

Colors

Options on this pop-up menu let you choose between three different color sets for the editing area of WinNET Mail:

- Choosing *Standard Colors* causes the editing area colors to correspond to the colors set in your SYSTEM.INI file. These colors can in turn be controlled via the Windows Control Panel, or some other utility that allows you to tailor Windows various system colors. Standard Colors is the factory default, and allows you to customize colors for certain types of monitors which support color irregularly or which only have monochrome colors (such as laptops).

- Choosing *Metallic Colors* causes text to appear as black on a silver background. Additionally, the reverse video highlight colors will be white text on a dark gray background. This color combination is attractive and very easy on the eyes, and is recommended for VGA or better CRTs.

- Choosing *Maize and Blue* causes text to appear as gold on a sky blue background. Highlight colors are red text on a powder blue background. Another attractive color set for VGA CRTs.

Change Font

This pop-up menu allows you to customize WinNET Mail's text fonts to best suit your taste, viewing conditions, and text format. The four settings are as follows:

- Choosing *Courier Font* selects WinNET Mail's most flexible font, the Courier font. It is the only font supported that allows you to use the Options/Enlarge and Options/Reduce font controls to adjust the font for maximum visibility. Courier is an ANSI font. To view/edit files that have IBM-extended ASCII characters, you should select the OEM (IBM) font.

- Choosing *ANSI Font* selects the Windows ANSI font.

- Choosing *OEM (IBM) Font* selects a font modeled after the IBM DOS text font. The Windows OEM (IBM) font supports most of the extended character set that is part of the OEM font, and is useful for viewing files produced with DOS applications that might have these characters (mostly line and box drawing characters, along with a variety of special symbols). OEM extended characters will appear as the corresponding characters from the ANSI character set if one of the other fonts is selected, but they will probably not match the original symbols in the OEM font.

- Choosing *System Font* selects the Windows fixed-width system font. This is the same font used by the Notepad utility supplied with Windows.

Enlarge Font

This option can be selected only when you have set the default font to Courier from the Options/Change Font pop-up menu. Selecting this option causes a magnification of the display of the Courier text of your document. You can select this option repeatedly until the maximum amount of magnification has been reached. It is easier to control this operation by using the keyboard accelerator, Ctrl+Numkeypad Plus.

On some systems, eliciting this choice once may not produce a change in the size of the font. Try pressing Ctrl+Numkeypad Plus repeatedly until a change in the font size occurs.

Reduce Font

This option can be selected only when you have set the default font to Courier from the Options/Change Font pop-up menu. Selecting it will cause a decrease in the size of the display of the Courier text of your document. You can select this option repeatedly until the minimum display size of the font has been reached. It is easier to control this operation by using the keyboard accelerator, Ctrl+Numkeypad Minus.

On some systems, eliciting this choice once may not produce a change in the size of the font. Try pressing Ctrl+Numkeypad Minus repeatedly until a change in the font size occurs.

Preferences

Choosing Preferences invokes a dialog box that allows you to set some default behaviors of WinNET Mail to best suit your use of the product. When you modify values in the Preferences dialog box and click OK to exit, your changes are retained from one editing session to the next, until you again invoke this dialog and make changes.

The following features appear in the Preferences dialog box:

Preference	Description
Tabs: Default setting	The value you supply here becomes the default Tab interval set when you start up a WinNET Mail session. You can also change this value on the fly by modifying the value here or with the Options/Set Tab command.
Word Wrap: Start up in Word Wrap Mode	If this check box is checked, WinNET Mail will start up assuming that you want the word wrap feature turned on for all documents. You can override the default during a particular editing session by selecting Options⇨Word-Wrap On/Off to toggle the word wrap feature to the desired state. If you unselect this box, WinNET Mail will start up assuming that you do not want to use the word wrap feature in each new document. Again, override the default at any time by toggling the feature with the Options⇨Word-wrap On/Off command.
Word Wrap: Right Margin At	The value you enter here indicates the character position which text should be wrapped to the next line when the word wrap feature is on. This value is measured in character width units. In effect, the value here represents the maximum line length in characters.
Default Windows	This area lets you select which default WinNET Mail folders should be automatically loaded and displayed when WinNET Mail starts up. The default is to load the Incoming Mail folder only.
Mail item sorting order	This setting controls whether mail items in folders are sorted and displayed from newest to oldest or from oldest to newest. *Note:* The incoming mail folder has its own algorithm for sorting, which is not affected by this setting. Items in the incoming mail folder are always sorted with the unopened items at the top, in oldest to newest order, and with the opened items that follow, from newest to oldest order.

Preference	Description
Default Search Criteria	The states of these various check boxes determine the default configuration that appears preselected in the dialog box that appears when you select Search⇨Find.
Default Replace Criteria	The states of these various check boxes determine the default configuration that appears preselected in the dialog box that appears when you select Search⇨Replace.
Default File Mask	The *default file mask* is the wild-card text that appears by default in all dialog boxes that involve opening new files for loading or importing into WinNET Mail. This mask can be used to derive a specific subset of files from the entire list of files that would appear in the Files listbox of these dialog boxes.
	The factory default of *.* selects all files, without filtering. A mask text of *.TXT filters all files in the current directory except those with the extension .TXT.
Maximize new windows	If you check this box, new windows opened by opening new folders, viewing a message, or starting the mail composition editor, and so forth, will automatically maximize to the full size of the work area. If you uncheck this box, new windows will be positioned and sized in a cascaded manner so that you can see the title bars of each open window.
Hide Old News Articles	When checked, this option causes news articles that you have read not to reappear in newsgroup folders when you reopen them to read new articles.

The WinNET Mail Editor

The WinNET Mail editor is a Common User Access (CUA) compliant editor (IBM standard). In function, it is very similar to the Windows Notepad editor, but with several significant enhancements that make it more powerful. The most notable of these enhancements is that the WinNET Mail editor can allocate all of Windows virtual memory to accommodate a file, compared with the approximately 35K that Notepad can allocate. Generally, the amount of virtual memory available in Windows is approximately three to four times the amount of physically installed RAM. So, if your computer has 4MB of physical RAM, you should have about 12 to 16MB of virtual memory. (You can check this figure by selecting Help⇨About Program Manager from Windows.) For this reason, you will find that WinNET Mail's editor can accommodate very large files.

The WinNET Mail editor is actually implemented within WinNET Mail with several different variations, as follows:

- The most generic version of the editor is called the *system editor*. The system editor can be invoked by selecting either New or Open from the WinNET Mail File menu. If you select File⇨New, a system editor window will open with an empty file. This file is initially named *noname*. If you select File⇨Open, you can use a standard Windows File Open dialog box to load any ASCII file on your system.

  You can do any normal editing operations that you wish to compose an ASCII text file in this editor, just as with Notepad. These functions include the various Windows editing commands, located on the Edit menu, and also the standard Find, Find again, and Search and Replace functions, which can be found on the Search menu.

- The second variation of the WinNET Mail editor is the *mail composition editor*. This editor is described in some detail in the section about composing mail. It is very much like the system editor, except that it has several fields in the top part of the window area that are used to address mail messages.

  Another feature of the mail composition editor that is not found in the system editor is the Paste Quote function, which, when the mail composition editor window is active, becomes available from the Edit menu. This function works just like the standard Paste function, except that each pasted line will be preceded by a > chevron character to indicate that the pasted material is a quotation of, or reference to, statements made in another item of mail.

  It should also be noted that you can include an existing text file into a mail message by using the File⇨Import File command. This operation opens a standard File Open dialog box. After you select a file, it will be pulled into the current mail message you are composing, at the position of the caret. This is convenient for constructing mail messages from already existing files.

Be careful to distinguish the File⇨Import File command from the Mail⇨Attach Binary File command. Import File is used to pull ASCII text into a file that is being edited, whereas Attach Binary File is used to attach binary files to mail messages. (You can of course attach text files to messages, but if you do, the recipient of your mail will have to detach the text file to read it.)

■ The *read-only* version of the editor is invoked when you read a mail message. It is more limited than the other editors because it does not support the editing of files. This is to protect your mail messages from accidental modification. However, it fully supports copy operations, so you can select and copy all or part of a mail message and then paste the contents that have been transferred to the Clipboard to one of the other WinNET Mail editors or to another application for editing. The mail reading editor also allows you to save a mail message with a different filename anywhere on your system. You can do this by selecting File⇨Save As.

Your Signature File

It is customary with Internet mail to include a few lines of information showing such things as your home and work addresses, a telephone number where you can be reached, and your Internet and/or other network e-mail addresses. You include this information normally at the bottom of each mail message that you send. Some people also like to include some words of wisdom or something humorous. These informational lines are called the *personal signature*.

This information serves a couple of purposes:

■ Sometimes, it helps sysops find you when they discover your mail in the "lost-and-found" and they want to get your mail back to you. (Mail sometimes is "lost" on the Internet, usually because it was improperly addressed.)

■ Also, your recipient may not know how to use the local mail programs to return a reply, so your address or telephone number can provide another way to do this.

WinNET Mail provides a mechanism whereby this information can be automatically included in every message that you send without your having to think about it. To automate the addition of a personal signature to your outgoing mail, you must create a text file called PERSONAL.SIG and put it in your WinNET Mail home directory.

Use the WinNET Mail system editor to make the file by selecting File⇨New. Here is an example of a simple signature file:

```
James T. Kirk  Internet: jkirk@newworld.win.net
Starship Enterprise  CIS UserID: 77777,000
Quadrant 3, Sector 72
(415)-555-1212 "Beam me up Scotty!"
```

Some automatic mailing list servers on the Internet require that your personal signature file start with two or more dash characters on a single line. If you set up your signature file this way, as in the previous example, it can prevent occasional problems with rejections of your submissions to a few of the SIG mailing lists. Also, you should probably avoid putting rows of + (plus) characters in your personal signature file, as these can sometimes trick Hayes-compatible modems into thinking that an escape sequence has been issued, which causes these modems to hang.

When you have finished creating the file, select File⇨Save and save the file as PERSONAL.SIG in the \USR\YOURNAME subdirectory of the directory where you installed WinNET Mail.

Automating Mail Transfer

If you want to, you may automate the process of having your computer call Computer Witchcraft's Internet mail service to drop off your stored messages and pick up your incoming mail messages. The automated mail transfer utility will call Computer Witchcraft at the times you schedule on the surface of the WinNET Mail Daemon program that will start up every time you start Windows.

Starting the Daemon program

You will probably want to start the program that handles automatic scheduling of calls to Computer Witchcraft by adding its program icon to your Program Manager Startup folder. This special Program Manager folder loads any files installed in it whenever you start a new Windows session. (For more information about the Program Manager and the Startup folder, see your Windows documentation.) Alternatively, you can list the program on the load= line of your WIN.INI file. Finally, you can also start the program directly from the WinNET Mail folder of Program Manager, if you elected to have the install program create a Program Manager group for WinNET Mail files.

Configuring your schedule

Once the daemon utility is installed, you will want to configure your automated mail service schedule. The Daemon icon has a large red cursive *D,* and has two small yellow *M* characters superimposed. Double-click the icon to bring up the scheduling grid. You will see that this grid has three separate schedule sets, one each for Saturday, Sunday, and Weekdays. To the left of each schedule set are the initials AM and PM to designate morning and afternoon, and at the top of each schedule set are twelve numerals representing the hours from 1 to 12.

To configure the schedule, use the mouse to punch out the hours in each of the schedule sets that you want to have the daemon automatically call Computer Witchcraft to drop off and pick up mail. When you have completed this process, click the Save Settings button if you want these settings to be the defaults that are selected every time you start Windows. If you do not click the Save Settings button, the settings will obtain for the current Windows session only, and when you start a new Windows session later, the program's schedule will revert to whatever settings you have most recently saved.

Finally, you might want to click the App Note button to read the text message that is invoked. This message explains that Computer Witchcraft will not be called exactly on the hours you selected with the scheduling grid, but rather at the number of minutes past the hour that was recorded when you started your Windows session. This is to prevent too large a volume of calls to the Computer Witchcraft service at or very near each hour, which could potentially over-whelm the service's capabilities.

To clarify this point, assume that you set your scheduling grid for 8 a.m. every weekday, and that you started your most recent Windows session at 3:22 p.m. on Sunday. When the daemon program detects that the 8 a.m. hour of the weekday has commenced (as of Monday morning), it will not immediately call Computer Witchcraft. Instead, it will wait until the number of minutes (22) past the hour when you started the current Windows session. At exactly 8:22, the daemon program will place the call. This same delay is applied to every other hour that you have scheduled for automated transfer.

Even if you have the automated transfer utilities installed, you can invoke the communications program to pick up and deliver mail any time by simply clicking the Call button on the WinNET Mail Control bar.

Optimizing Communications _____

After you have installed WinNET Mail on your system and have established a Computer Witchcraft Internet Account using the ACCOUNT.EXE program, you can use the WinNET Mail setup program, SETUP.EXE, to optimize communications settings.

When you run SETUP.EXE after it has already been run once to install the WinNET Mail files on your computer, the default option is Setup communications parameters for modem. (Make sure to run the installed copy of the SETUP.EXE program, rather than the copy of the program that you used when you first set up WinNET Mail on your system.) If you click OK to move into the Communications Setup dialog box, you can change several of the default settings to enhance WinNET Mail's communications performance. These settings are described in the following sections.

Interface speed

The interface speed controls how fast your computer sends data to your local modem and how fast your local modem sends data to your computer. Ideally, this speed should be set to the highest setting with which your modem is capable of working. This allows for an increase in local data throughput, which in turn contributes to an overall throughput increase. Your modem's manual should specify its highest interface speed. Interface speed is often referred to in technical manuals as *DTE/DCE speed* (Data Terminal Equipment/Data Communications Equipment).

Unfortunately, the quality of serial ports with which many IBM compatible systems are originally equipped can vary considerably. Most systems have an 8250 UART equipped serial controller. This type of serial port controller is frequently inadequate to run Windows communications software at DTE/DCE speeds higher than 19,200 bps. In some cases, only 9,600 bps speeds can be set reliably. Please take this into account when trying out faster DTE/DCE speeds with WinNET. Also, see the upcoming discussion about upgrading to the 16550B type UART serial controller.

Increasing the interface speed will also contribute to optimization of transfer speed when using a modem with data-compression features. (Your modem manual should specify if your modem has data-compression capabilities.) When a data-compressing modem can negotiate a compression protocol with a remote modem, it can take outgoing data and add it to a processing buffer where the data is compressed by replacing redundant sequences of bytes with codes. The best of these data-compression strategies, called V.42bis, has a theoretical maximum compression ratio of 4:1.

The data can then be transmitted over the telephone line in this compressed format and decoded on the other side by the remote modem. This technique allows the speed of the transfer to occur at a higher rate than the actual telephone line speed. To make sure that the modem receives data fast enough to keep up with its compression processing, an interface speed setting higher than the line speed is required.

Please check your modem manual to see whether your modem supports data compression. If it does, look for the manufacturer's suggestion for what interface speed best allows the modem to take advantage of data compression.

 Unfortunately, data compression techniques are imperfect, and there is much variance in the efficiency of the protocol in dependence on the data format of the material being transmitted. Plain text files and graphics files benefit the most from data compression, whereas executable programs and previously compressed data (like PKZipped files) benefit less. In fact, data compressing modems often transmit zipped files more slowly than the line speed because the compression is nearly ineffective and the overhead of compression processing results in a net loss of throughput. The V.42bis compression protocol is supposed to test data to see whether it is compressible before attempting to use data compression, but in practice the protocol is easily deceived and will often go, inappropriately, into a data compressing mode. If you use WinNET Mail to do a lot of binary file transfers of archived ("zipped") material, it is recommended that you turn off the data-compression features of your modem. The Hayes-compatible command for doing so is &Q6. You should check your manual to see whether &Q6 is supported and add this to your "Modem setup AT commands" with WinNET Mail's setup program, if you wish to disable data compression.

Packet window size

All data communications protocols send data in generally consistently sized units called *packets,* and require that, sooner or later, the receiver acknowledge that each packet is received and that the data it contains is not corrupted. (This acknowledgment is called an ACK, and negative reports are called NAKs, indicating that a packet was received but with corrupted data.)

WinNET Mail's communications protocol, called *uucico,* is designed as a *packet windowing protocol,* which means that the sending side is allowed to get ahead of the receiver's acknowledgments by a certain number of data packets, thereby reducing the bottleneck that can result when the send-acknowledgment cycle is kept on a short leash. The number of packets, called the packet window, is negotiated at the start of the uucico session. The larger the packet window, the more efficient the transfer of data. The maximum size of the window supported by the protocol is seven packets. However, as the packet window size gets larger, the chances of the two sides losing synchronization increases, especially over a noisy telephone line. In most cases, with modern telephone systems, loss of synchronization is not a problem. If you experience reliable communications when the packet window size is set to the default of five packets, it is recommended that you increase this setting to the maximum of seven. This will typically result in a data throughput increase of approximately 20 to 40 percent.

CPU utilization

This setting determines the extent to which your computer's processing resources are taxed when running the WinNET Mail communications program.

At the Low setting, WinNET Mail's communications program will run in a very cooperative mode, allowing other applications generous amounts of attention from the CPU (Central Processing Unit). This will make your work with multiple applications quite smooth when running WinNET Mail communications in the background. However, data communications throughput may not be optimal on many systems at this setting.

At the Very High setting, the communications program will assume very high priority over other applications. Other applications will still run, but their performance will be relatively poor. However, data communications throughput will approach absolutely optimal.

Whether this setting has a significant effect varies from system to system. Generally, if you have a very fast modem (14,400 or 9600 baud with v.42bis) supporting the higher interface speeds of 19,200 and 38,400, or 57,600 combined with a slower computer, (286 or 386sx), this setting will have more impact on performance than if you have a very fast 486 computer. The Very High setting has very little effect on systems with 2400 baud modems (even v.42bis) because the CPU can easily keep up.

You can experiment with this setting to determine the best results for your equipment.

Support for full connect statistics

When WinNET Mail's communications program connects with Computer Witchcraft's Internet/Usenet service, some statistics are displayed near the bottom of the communications program's display window. They show information about the speed of the connection. The communications program intercepts information from the modem to display these statistics, and the information provided by the modem depends on how certain modem registers are set.

Most modems, as configured at the factory, will show only the interface speed and line speed of the connection. To get full statistics, which usually include the error-correcting mode and data compression, you must add an additional Hayes AT command to the Modem setup AT commands field in setup. For most recently manufactured modems that support error correction and data compression, the following command requests the modem to emit full connect statistics:

```
S95=44
```

Please be sure to check your modem manual to see whether this register setting is supported by your modem. If it is supported, you can append this Hayes command to your Modem setup AT commands field in setup.

Taking advantage of a 16550B UART

Your computer's serial communications port is controlled by a *UART* chip. If you have an internal modem, the UART control chip is built into the modem. Otherwise, it is integrated into your computer's serial card.

Until recently, the standard UART control chip was known as the 8250. This chip has some significant limitations, however, the most severe being that it cannot maintain more than one character of data in its incoming data queue. When the 8250 receives a character, it immediately requests that the computer pick up that character and pass it to the control software. If the computer is busy, the character will be lost as it is replaced by the next incoming character.

In DOS, a single-tasking operating system, this isn't so much of a problem because the computer almost always can respond to the request to pick up the character, even when the communications port is configured for very high speed operation. However, in Windows and other multitasking operating systems, it is more likely that the computer will fail to answer a request from the communications port, and character loss begins to occur. This is especially true of computers with underpowered CPUs when the communications port is receiving characters at 9600 bps or higher.

To overcome this problem, a new UART called the *16550B* has been developed. This UART is capable of holding on to many characters while waiting for the computer to respond to their presence in the port's queue.

If you have a newer error-correcting internal modem, it may already have a 16550B UART. Also, recent model IBM PS/2 computer systems use this chip. But most other serial ports sold with other computer systems have the less expensive 8250 chips. If you have one of these serial cards, you might consider upgrading to a 16550B UART serial card.

Windows Version 3.1 supports the special capabilities of the newer 16550B chip. Additionally, you have to modify your SYSTEM.INI file to notify the Windows software that it should use the capabilities of the 16550B. You should add the line

```
COMxFIFO=1
```

to the [386enh] section of SYSTEM.INI if you have a 16550B UART. (Replace x in the example by the number of the communications port used by your modem.)

If you operate the software at high speeds, the use of a 16550B UART will reduce transmission errors in WinNET Mail communications sessions. (Please note that the communications program will remedy these errors if they occur in any case, but preventing them from happening in the first place by installing a 16550B UART will increase overall performance.)

Interfacing with CompuServe

CompuServe supports an Internet mail gateway. This means that, using WinNET, you can send mail messages to CompuServe users at their CIS IDs, and CIS users can send you messages at your WinNET address.

To send a mail message to someone at CompuServe, address the mail to the user's CIS ID with the following syntax:

```
777.7777@CompuServe.COM
```

where 777.7777 stands in this example for the CIS user ID of the person to whom you are sending a message.

Please note that instead of the usual comma in the CompuServe user ID, use a period.

CompuServe users can send mail to you from CompuServe by addressing mail with the following format:

```
>internet: you@.yoursys.win.net
```

where *you@yoursys.win.net* stands in this example for your complete Internet mail address.

The CompuServe user should make sure to include **>internet:** as the prefix to the e-mail address.

WinNET Mail Registration Form

Name _____

Company _____

Address _____

City _____

State _____   Country _____

Zip _____   Phone _____

Please be sure to include your full name as it appears on the "Help/About" box on win NET Mail and News, as well as your e-mail address in the "Help/About" box. For more information, see the REGISTER.TXT file on the CD-ROM.

Remit to:

Computer Witchcraft, Inc.
P.O. Box 4189
Louisville, KY 40204

Pricing

❏ $39.95 + $3.50 shipping and handling (US)
(Kentucky residents add sales tax.)

Chapter 7
Pipeline for Windows

This chapter contains specific instructions and general tips for using Pipeline™ for Windows. Also, you can get context-sensitive help for Pipeline by placing the cursor on a button or command and then pressing F1; or just choose Help from the menu.

Pipeline for Windows is a program that connects you to the global Internet. You need only a computer running Microsoft Windows and a modem. Using the Pipeline software, you dial into the Pipeline's host computer, which in turn is your gateway to every service and information source on the entire Internet. In other words, Pipeline is your on-ramp to the Information Superhighway.

The Pipeline Itself

Who, what, and where we are

The Pipeline itself lies in geographical space inside a Sun Microsystems computer network situated just off Wall Street in the heart of New York's Telecommunications District (formerly Financial District). In cyberspace, Pipeline is at an Internet node known simply as pipeline.com, roughly as near and as far (give or take a few milliseconds) as any other place on the Internet.

The Pipeline's founder is James Gleick, author of *Chaos: Making a New Science*. He grew obsessed with the Information Age and, at the same time, was frustrated by the hurdles that seemed to exist for normal, interested, non-university, non-UNIX-speaking individuals like himself.

Its administrator, chief programmer, and resident genius is Uday Ivatury, a Bombay native who cut his teeth on (and survived) the world of IBM mainframes. He has set himself a formidable challenge with the Pipeline: a joining of the seemingly alien cultures of UNIX workstations and DOS or Apple personal computers.

Getting Started _____

Create a new user

You need to create a new user (you) before connecting with the Pipeline. Choose File⇨Create New User from the main menu, or, if you have opened the Dial window, click the New button. Pipeline prompts for a user name and your full name. Enter them, and Pipeline sets up the necessary files and directories on your computer.

This copy of Pipeline for Windows lets you create as many different users as you want. In other words, you may share the program. Each user has a mailing address, so each needs an account at the Pipeline.

Dialing in

Choose Dial! from the main menu (or press Alt+D). Make sure your user name is selected.

Type your password and press Enter (or select Dial).

How to avoid long distance charges

If you are not in the New York metropolitan area, and if you happen to have access to another Internet connection, you can still use Pipeline for Windows as your interface.

In the Dial Options screen (available under the main Options menu), choose "Dial another site and log in remotely." Now, when you Dial, you will be asked to enter a phone number for your local site. If you have already entered it, you may just select it from the drop-down list.

Pipeline will connect you to the number you enter. A plain terminal window will appear to let you log into your site.

Now enter a command that connects you to the Pipeline via the Internet itself. The most standard command is rlogin -8 pipeline.com. (If it doesn't work, you may need to ask your local system administrator for help.)

As soon as the connection to the Pipeline is made, select Activate from the menu. The software takes over and logs you in automatically, using your Pipeline password. From here on, your session continues as if you had dialed the Pipeline directly.

About Passwords

If you have an account, you already have a password or will soon choose one in consultation with our staff. Unfortunately, in the Wild West frontier of the Internet, passwords are even more important than they are on private on-line services.

In the Dial window, you can show your password or hide it (click the Show or Hide button) depending on whether busybodies tend to be looking over your shoulder. The Pipeline remembers your preference.

You can change your password at any time. You will be connected directly with our host computer, and you will be prompted to enter your new password. Twice. You can also tell the software to remember your password from session to session so that you don't have to keep typing it. But this is risky. For either of these choices, select Options from the main menu.

What makes a good password?

Six to eight characters that can (and should) include numerals and punctuation. Case matters: If your password is "abcDef," then "abcdef" does not work.

Unfortunately, if your password is easy to remember, it's probably a bad password. Here are a few rules of password selection, some of which Pipeline may enforce automatically:

- Dictionary words and names are no good.
- Dates, social security numbers, and telephone numbers: no good.
- Sequences with patterns of a few characters: nope.
- Most important of all: A password you use anywhere else in the electronic universe is no good. We know this rule is a nuisance, but it's a necessary one. (Can you imagine how many passwords we've gone through ourselves?)

Kinds of Sessions

Full

You remain on-line until you decide to sign off by selecting Goodbye! from the main menu or by exiting the program.

Mail only

You will log on just long enough to receive any waiting mail and send any messages you have written off-line.

News and mail

Besides mail, you also get any News articles you have selected off-line and update the subject headings in your News folders.

Setting up your modem

You can set a variety of dialing options by choosing Options⇨Set Up Modem from the main menu. We hope you won't need to think about most of these options. Pipeline can usually figure out what it needs to know (software that forces you to find the manual that came with your modem is our idea of bad software). Nevertheless, here they are.

Do I want to...

Dial the Pipeline directly or log in from a remote site? Usually, you will just dial Pipeline. But if you're out of town and you have access to another Internet connection, then you may want to select the second option to take advantage of our Remote Connection Capability.

Your area code

We need to know whether you're calling from out of Pipeline's area, so we can dial the phone correctly.

Dial prefix

If you need to dial 9 to get an outside line, check the Dial 9 box. If you need to dial something more complicated, type it into the Other Prefix box. If, for some reason, you don't want to dial 1 (you're making a credit card call, for example), here's where you tell us that, too.

Dial suffix

You may need to add something after the number, usually for billing reasons at an office. If so, you probably know it.

Communications port

What communications port or serial port is your modem attached to? Pipeline thinks it knows, but in case we're wrong or you want to overrule us (have two modems?), you may choose 1, 2, 3, or 4.

Modem speed

Again, Pipeline has tried to get your modem to tell us. Nevertheless, you may choose any of the listed baud rates. By the way, we support the highest speeds and best compression schemes generally available: we recommend using a modem that takes advantage of them.

Type of dialing

Tone (you know, touch-tone, with musical buttons) or Pulse (the little clicks you get when you turn the rotary dial with your finger). Which kind of phone do you have? We assume tone until you tell us otherwise.

Init string and hangup string

Few people will need to touch these. But if you are having trouble connecting with the Pipeline or disconnecting, you might try changing them. You may have to look at your modem's documentation (sorry).

Pathways into the Internet

The list that appears in the middle of the main program screen is the Pipeline Gopher:

- The Pipeline: Information and Today's News
- Internet: Guides and Tools
- (and so on)

These items are like the main branches of a never-ending tree. If you double-click any item, a new list will appear … and so on.

Soon, though, you will start to see items that are not lists, but other things: text files, picture files, or even live connections to other sites. These items are like the leaves at the ends of the branches. They are marked with icons that show to which Gopher Type they belong.

It's not quite a tree, really, because many paths lead to the same destinations, though often by roundabout routes. You can issue a command to search all Gopherspace by choosing Veronica from the main Services menu. However you choose to do it, the idea is to explore.

Where is all this stuff?

At first, most of what you see is (physically) on the Pipeline's main computer. Soon, though, you will find yourself connecting to other computers around the globe. The whole thing is always evolving: even the main Pathways list changes and is refreshed each time you log in.

Gopher list

Every time you double-click on a new list, you move further through the Internet and find new resources. Double-click an item (or select the item and press Enter) to get the item, show it, search it, or connect to it.

Sometimes you will be prompted to enter a word or phrase. It might be an address of a person you want information about or a site you want to connect to. It might be a subject for a search. The next time you select the same item, the program remembers your previous choices and shows them to you in a drop-down list (click on the down arrow or press the down arrow on the keyboard to display them). Select one, or enter a new one.

If you find a resource you want want to use again, select Bookmarks! from the menu to add it to your permanent Bookmark list. Keyboard shortcut: To back up to a previous list, type **U**.

What if these lists are getting out of control? Bookmarks!

Often you will come upon a resource or service deep in the heart of Gopherspace that you know you will want to find again. Select it in the Gopher list and use the Bookmark! menu item to add something to the main Pipeline menu. Then you will be able to reach it next time with a single command.

A few sample Bookmarks are included with the program, and you may delete them (from the main menu) and substitute your own.

Search

Pipeline prompts you for a word or phrase to use for searching a database that may be anything from a dictionary to a collection of recipes to a library catalogue to a shelf of books.

The rules for searches vary because the searches are being carried out by many different computer systems. You may have to experiment, but usually if you "enclose a phrase in quotation marks," the search will look for exactly that. Some sites let you use the logical connectors **and, or,** and **not** to join two words.

Search Gopherspace with Veronica

What if you want to search in a single step through all the electronic resources connected through our "Pathways into the Internet"?

Choose "Search Gopherspace with Veronica" from the main Services menu. Enter a word to search for. You will get a list that (depending on your word) is likely to be an amazing mixture of useful, useless, fascinating, and irrelevant items.

Oh, and why "Veronica"? We hate to say it, but here's another far-reaching acronym:

Very Easy Rodent-Oriented Netwide Index to Computerized Archives.

Gopher (the rodent), defined again, from the software fathers of Gopher at the University of Minnesota:

> **gopher** n. 1. Any of various short-tailed, burrowing mammals of the family Geomyidae, of North America. 2. (Amer. colloq.) Native or inhabitant of Minnesota: the Gopher State. 3. (Amer. colloq.) One who runs errands, does odd-jobs, fetches, or delivers documents for office staff. 4. (computer tech.) Software following a simple protocol for tunneling through a TCP/IP Internet.

Glad you asked?

The Mail Manager

This will usually be the first new window you see when you connect to the Pipeline. You can always bring it up (whether you are connected or not) either by clicking on the mailbox icon in the mail Pipeline window or by choosing Mail/Services from the main menu.

Receiving mail

If mail is waiting for you, it quickly arrives in your Inbox. (The status bar at the bottom of the main Pipeline window shows the transfers in progress, but be warned: they may flash by too quickly for you to see.)

This window is basic, but if you are used to other on-line services, it may surprise you at first. The point is, you don't have to do anything to get your mail: if you are on-line, and the Mail Manager is running, your mail just comes.

Sending mail

To start a new letter, click the New button or choose File⇨New.

To reply to a letter's sender, click Reply or choose File⇨Reply. (Sometimes you may want to quote the text of the original letter in your reply. To do this, check the Quote box before you reply.)

The top of the mail window will now show fields where you can fill in information about your new letter: they are labeled To, CC, and Subject. (If you are replying, the To and Subject fields are filled in for you, but you can change them as you desire.)

To send (or CC) mail to more than one person, enter a list of names separated with commas. The To and CC fields also contain drop-down lists, so instead of typing a name, you can select one from your address list.

The address list can be opened and edited directly through the Addresses item on the menu.

The Address List

As a convenience, Pipeline lets you store e-mail addresses in your Address List. To work with this list directly, choose Addresses from the Mail menu.

You can define short nicknames — *aliases* — for any address. For example, if you correspond regularly with the President of the United States, you may find the nickname **Bill** more convenient to type (and easier to remember) than the full address. Just define a nickname in the Address List.

This feature becomes even more useful when you need to send mail to groups. The full version of a nickname need not be just a single address: it can be a list of addresses, separated by commas (with no spaces in between). These addresses can themselves be nicknames.

For example, you can define beatles as ringo,john,paul,george and sg as simon,garfunkel. Then if you define music as beatles,sg you can send mail to all six people with the single nickname.

Handling mail off-line

If you want to keep your on-line time to a minimum, you can work with your mail off-line. Start the Mail Manager (by clicking on the mailbox icon or selecting Services⇨Mail). Write as many letters as you like. Pipeline adds them to a queue and saves them in your Outgoing folder.

The next time you connect with the Pipeline, the queued mail will be sent. In the meantime, if you want to edit it, you may do so by selecting the Outgoing folder. When you dial, if you want to send outgoing mail quickly and receive mail that may be waiting, you may choose the Mail Only option in the Dial windows.

Sending files by mail

To insert text into letters, use the Windows Paste command. But you can also insert whole files, whether they are text or binary files. To do this, click the Insert button or choose File⇨Insert. Pipeline asks whether your file is ordinary text or a binary file.

For experienced users: Pipeline sends binary files by the Internet-standard uuencode method. If your recipient is a Pipeline user, the process will be transparent. The file will be processed automatically and saved to the recipient's disk. If your recipient is elsewhere on the Internet, he will have to know how to handle such files. By the same token, someone on the Internet who wants to send you a binary file should uuencode it; then the Pipeline software processes it for you automatically.

Mail window basics

The mail window has two main parts. At the top is the Table of Contents, the list of your mail items. At the bottom is the text of the selected item.

The Table of Contents contains four pieces of information about each item. A small icon shows whether the item is old or new (notice how the icon changes after you read a piece of mail); the name of the sender, the date and time, and the subject follows.

To navigate through this list, use the up- and down-arrow keys to move one item at a time, the PgUp and PgDn keys to move one page at a time, or click your mouse on the scroll bar to scroll through the list.

To adjust the width of these fields, use the mouse to drag the thin black line that separates them. Similarly, you can drag the border between the Table of Contents and the message text.

You can scroll or page the message text with the arrow and PgUp/PgDn keys, but first you must move the cursor to the text with the mouse or with the Tab key. You can select text to be copied to the Clipboard in standard Windows fashion. You cannot change the text. (This makes Edit⇨Cut effectively the same as Edit⇨Copy).

Using the buttons at the bottom of the mail window or the menu commands at the top, you can

- Reply to the sender
- Reply to the sender quoting the original

   If the quote check box is checked, the text of the letter you are reading (or a portion you have selected) will be inserted for you at the top of your reply. Each line beginning with a > character indicates the line is quoted material.

- Forward a letter to someone else
- Save a letter to a new folder
- Save a letter to a file on your disk

- Print a letter
- Delete a letter
- Search for the sender or subject of a letter. Choose Edit⇨Find from the menu or press Ctrl+F. To repeat your last search, press F3.

Until you delete a piece of mail or save it to a new folder, the mail remains in your Inbox.

Mail options

You can change several of the ways in which the Mail Manager behaves to suit your own way of working. Select Options from the Mail menu.

Hide headers and line breaks

On the Internet, mail comes with long, complicated, hard-to-read header information. Most of this is used by UNIX software to decide how to process the mail. Also, lines are broken every 60 or 80 characters because UNIX mail programs usually don't wrap lines intelligently. For Windows users, these features are annoyances. You probably don't want to see the headers, and you want text to wrap freely in your Mail window (which you can resize as you see fit). We remove them for you. If you want them back (for example, to see who has been CC'd on a letter), click this item to remove the check mark.

Beep for new mail

Pipeline makes a sound to alert you when new mail arrives. If you don't like the sound, click this item to remove the check mark.

Show message for new mail

Pipeline can put up a message to alert you when new mail arrives. If you want it, click this item to add a check mark.

Save outgoing mail in Sentmail folder

Pipeline saves copies of all letters you send in the Sentmail folder. If you don't want a copy saved, click this item to remove the check mark. You can also change this before you send any letter by checking or unchecking the box on the Mail window.

Confirm deletions

When you delete a letter or cancel one you're writing, Pipeline puts up a message asking you whether you're sure. It gives you one last chance to avoid losing data. On the other hand, maybe you don't want to waste an extra mouse click. If you don't like the prompt, click this item to remove the check mark.

Signatures

Some Internauts like to use a fancy standard signature at the end of their Mail and News postings. Enter one here. Our paternalistic advice is: Don't overdo it; the jokes get tiresome. But that's your problem.

Lost mail

We consider lost mail a serious calamity. If you delete a letter by accident, or if you suspect you didn't get a letter you should have, or if (God forbid) a program or communications flaw causes you to lose mail, please let us know right away (check the CD for information on contacting Pipeline). The Pipeline keeps secure copies of all mail that crosses its electronic threshold for at least a few days, and we will do everything we can to help you recover your mail.

Mailing lists

One of the fastest growing Internet phenomena is the mailing list. It's an interactive discussion group carried on entirely in your mailbox and the mailboxes of everyone else on the list. There are too many mailing lists to count, and they change daily. A list of mailing lists and a tool for finding and subscribing to mailing lists on particular subjects are available in the Pathways section under Internet. A list of mailing lists is also often available in the news.lists newsgroup.

Rules vary, but one way to join (or unjoin) a list is to write, not to the list itself, but to the list with "-request" appended to it. So to join the list whose address is somelist@someplace.org, you write to somelist-request@someplace.org. Include your own e-mail address (username@pipeline.com) in the letter.

News: an overview

News may seem like an odd name for the more than 4,000 (and increasing) discussion groups carried on continuously on the Internet. But the content of these groups is news in the most ancient sense of the word: tidings, rumors, bulletins, opinions, argumentation, and amusement. The News items or *articles* are posted by millions of individuals and transmitted around the globe in a sort of electronic chain reaction.

To activate the Pipeline's News system, click on the icon or choose News from the main Services menu.

Categories

Categories are broad, covering overall topics. At the Pipeline, we begin with a local category called *In Town*. Then a special category, *ClariNews,* follows;

ClariNews contains live News (current events, in the modern sense) from the wires of United Press International. Then seven major categories follow: *alt, comp, news, rec, sci, soc, talk,* and a catchall called *other.*

Groups

Within each category are many groups. Group names consist of words separated by periods; each part of the group name is a subcategory of the one before, like this:

```
rec.music.indian.classical
```

That group's sister group includes `rec.music.indian.misc` and many cousin groups, from `rec.music.a-cappella` to `rec.music.video`.

The best way to think of the structure is as a tree. In fact, that is how the Pipeline displays the groups to you.

Threads

Within each group are many topics of discussion, or *threads.* You will see lists of subjects, displayed as a sort of table of contents. These threads can last for months or die out within hours.

Articles

Within each thread are one or more articles. When someone replies to an article, the new message is listed under the old.

News: getting started

When you click on News, the first window you see contains a list of your folders. Some folders are provided to help you get started. Each folder contains several newsgroups. You can open, edit, delete, or start a new folder by clicking the appropriately marked button.

It is useful to organize folders by subjects that interest you. You might want to create one for all your baseball groups or all your music groups. A quick way to do that is to search for particular subjects when you are creating or editing a folder.

Searching for newsgroups on a subject

You may follow the updates of newsgroups in a folder daily or even hourly (news flows into the Pipeline around the clock). Or you can check the newsgroups for updates on a weekly or monthly basis (if the volume of articles is not too huge).

A recommendation: We've found that it's often easier to use a lot of folders with each tracking two, three, or a half-dozen newsgroups apiece. This is easier than stuffing everything into one or two huge folders.

Reading and posting news: open a folder

After clicking on News to start the News manager, create or edit a folder. Type in a word that might be part of the name of the group or groups that interest you. Click the Search command button. (If you already know the exact name of a group, you can add it to the folder by pressing Add.)

In a moment, you will see all of the 4,000+ groups that match your word or phrase. Add any or all of them to your folder by clicking the Add Group button. Then search again for something else.

You can also browse manually through the lists of newsgroups. To see the groups in one of the ten major categories, click on the folder tab. The list is organized as a tree. To expand a heading (and see the items it contains), double-click on the heading, or select the heading and press Enter.

Reading and posting news

After you open the News manager, a list of the latest articles from the newsgroups in your folder begins to arrive. Their progress displays in the status bar. Until all the articles finish downloading into your folder, the names of the newsgroups are grayed (disabled).

For a small group, or a group you are following regularly, this process will take just seconds. For a group with a thousand or more articles, it may take several minutes. (You can limit the number of headings that will be received by setting a number in the main Options menu.)

The Tables of Contents display a plus sign (+) next to the name of each group with messages and a minus sign (–) for groups with no new messages.

The news folder: how the screen is organized

This list of newsgroups is in the upper-left corner of the window. A Table of Contents appears in the upper-right corner. You can see the Table of Contents for any group by clicking on the group's name.

The Table of Contents shows a list of topics. At the beginning of each topic is a number in brackets, showing how many articles are listed for that topic, as in the following sample:

```
[4] Why is this man smiling?
```

That entry shows four articles about the smiling man. To expand the heading (that is, to show the items), double-click the heading, or highlight the heading and press Enter. This shows the names of each article's sender.

The bottom part of the screen shows the selected article's text. Use the mouse or the arrow keys to move through the Table of Contents and show new articles.

 Use the mouse to drag the borders between these portions of the screen and adjust the sizes until they suit you best.

Replying and posting

Using the buttons at the bottom of the window or the menu commands at the top, you can do one of these five exciting things:

- Mail a reply to the sender of an article.
- Post a public reply.
- Save an article to your disk as a file.
- Forward a copy of an article by mail.
- Write and post your own article.

User options

Find (current news)

Pipeline subscribers have special access to the United Press International news wire with a full feed of national, international, local, sports, financial, arts, and entertainment news. There are urgent bulletins and weekly features (from Dave Barry to Miss Manners). Find lets you search our archives of all this material for names, subjects, or phrases of particular interest to you.

Enter your search word or phrase at the prompt, and you will receive a list of items that match your query.

Unlike most of the Internet services available through the Pipeline, this re-source is not free, though it is free for you. We pay a fee to the ClariNet service for the right to distribute the UPI material to you, our subscribers. You may use it freely, but you may not redistribute it because this material is copyrighted.

If you want to browse this current news as it comes in, rather than search it, you may do so through News. All the UPI material is organized into the newsgroup format there.

How (our on-line help system)

The question-mark icon takes you to an interactive on-line help system. This system has direct hooks into a variety of frequently used features. If you don't know how to do something, look here first.

Talk

The Internet is live, not canned. There is no better reminder of that than the Talk feature. You can "phone" people anywhere on the globe, and if they are connected to the Internet, they will instantaneously get a message indicating that you want to chat. If they accept your call, a window will open on your screen and on theirs. Anything you type appears in one part, and anything they type appears in another.

You can receive calls, too. A message will appear alerting you that, for example, bclinton@whitehouse.gov wants to Talk. If you accept, the Talk window will appear.

Conference calls

You are not limited to two people. If a third (or fourth ...) person calls, you can add him or her to an ongoing conversation, and your screen is divided again to allow for more windows.

Beyond the Pipeline

Keep in mind that non-Pipeliners do not have your lovely windowed interface. When they receive a call, it interrupts whatever they may be doing (assuming they are doing something that can be interrupted), and they may not be able to respond immediately.

Furthermore, the UNIX talk programs around the Internet come in a variety of flavors, some more reliable than others. Nevertheless, you will soon find that you can carry on live conversations with people in Sweden or Japan. And it's free.

Options: user preferences

You may customize the appearance of most windows by changing their Fonts (type styles) and Colors from the Options menus of those windows. Pipeline will remember your choices next time. If you change the size or placement of most windows, the program will also remember where you left them.

A variety of other useful options can be changed from the main Options menu. You may never need to touch them, because they come set to useful values. But if you like making adjustments, read on!

Password

Change it. You should change it every so often, inconvenient though that may be.

Save it. If you're tired of having to type your password every time you log in, check this option. The software will remember your password from session to session. This is not without risks! Keep in mind that anyone who uses your computer will be able to get your password. So if someone you don't trust can access your computer, don't use this option.

Pipeline windows

Problem: Maybe you have lots of windows scattered all about your screen, and you need to navigate quickly among them. Solution: Use the Show floating window list option to display a little list of all your windows. This list floats above everything else. You can click on any window name, and you go directly to that window.

If Minimize all windows together is checked, then when you minimize the main Pipeline window (turn it into an icon at the bottom of your screen), everything else minimizes with it — another anti-clutter device. On the other hand, if you like complete control over what is minimized and what is not, then just leave this option unchecked.

News

When the Pipeline sends the new headings for all the articles in a newsgroup, is there a maximum number you would like sent each time? The How many entries at most option lets you set a number for this. A small number will keep you from seeing everything in a large or very busy group. A large number can take a while (several minutes or more) for retrieving the data. (Our suggested value is 100.)

The Organization name option is the identifying name attached to your news postings, so readers can see where you're from. Our suggestion is "The Pipeline." However, if you work for, say, the National Security Agency, you may wish to use that instead.

Pathways into the Internet

Pathways into the Internet shows how many open lists you have at once. If you burrow deeper and deeper, clicking on list after list, your screen gets cluttered. If this clutter bothers you, use a smaller number here. If you use 1, you'll see only one list at a time. (The most recently used list closes when you open a new one. You can always back up and see the list again, even if it has vanished, by typing **U** or **B**.) Our suggested value is 4.

Every so often you'll run into a list that doesn't have a nice, friendly number of items. If it has hundreds, it can take a long time to retrieve. Set How many list items at most to a low value, and you won't wait for them all (but then again, you won't get them all.) Our suggested value: 40.

Download directory

What directory would you like files to arrive in? Our suggestion: pipeline\user\username\download.

Word processor

When you receive a very big text file, our little text window cannot display it. Pipeline tosses the file over to your word processor instead. By default, we use Write, which every Windows user has. If you have another word processor that you prefer to use, enter the name here.

Font for printing

This option is where you change the typeface and point size used when you print something.

Today

This option is where we keep local weather, important breaking news and sport scores, and Pipeline bulletins that are not quite crucial enough for us to force on you.

The icon, when you are connected, shows the state of the current short-term forecast for the New York City area: fair, clouds, rain, or snow. If the National Weather Service happens to change its mind while you are on-line, you will see the icon change, too.

Files (FTP and Archie)

This feature lets you find all kinds of files from all across the Internet. Files may be computer programs for your PC, interesting texts of all sorts, pictures, or just about anything else you can imagine.

If you happen to know the exact location of a file that you want, you can enter the site address. When you press Enter, a directory list appears. You can then browse subdirectories by clicking on them, or choose files by clicking on them. Pipeline sends them directly to your computer and stores them in your download directory.

If you happen to know the file's name, you can enter that, too, and when you press Enter, Pipeline sends the file to your computer. This transfer is known as *FTP*.

But maybe you just have a filename in mind, or even an approximate filename. Pipeline will search the Internet for you. Enter a full or partial name, leaving the site blank, and a search begins. When it is complete, a list will appear, showing files stored in archives anywhere in the world that match your query. This search is known as Archie.

How Archie works (approximately)

Several computer centers on the Internet (and the Pipeline will soon be one of them) maintain Archie servers: systems that regularly poll computers around the network for lists and descriptions of publicly available files. It is a complicated business because millions of files are out there, and they're always changing.

Your search request is sent to one of these servers for processing. Sometimes the results can be instantaneous; at other times there can be delays, depending on the complexity of your search and the amount of traffic on the Internet.

Advanced features

You can make your search case sensitive. You can also search for either exact matches or partial matches. Check the appropriate boxes depending on your preference.

You can limit the number of matching files that will be returned. A smaller number speeds the process. You can choose the computer center that will process your search. We normally do this for you, making a judgment about which Archie server is likeliest to produce a quick and comprehensive result. But if you are having trouble connecting, or want to try a different site, choose one from this list.

Find someone

This command is available on the main Services menu. It uses one of the several methods available for finding someone in the vast, tangled electronic space of the Internet: it searches a huge database of Usenet news messages.

As many Internet authorities have pointed out, the best method may be to pick up the telephone and call. Many hours have been wasted because people were too embarrassed or too interested in exploring to avail themselves of this expedient method. Of course, you may truly not know.

A procedure known as *Whois* searches a database of companies, organizations, and individuals with registered Internet addresses. You can find this in Pathways into the Internet, in the Internet Tools category.

There are a growing number of on-line directories of many different kinds. If your missing person is affiliated with a university or other large organization, it's likely that you can find one of these directories. Netfind is the name of another, occasionally useful method, and many experimental directories are under development. All these tools are available through the Internet category of Pathways.

How do I ... ?

Now that you're a Pipeliner, what can you do? And how? Table 7-1 provides some random examples to help you get started:

Table 7-1	Examples of What You Can Find on the Internet by Using Pipeline
How do I ...	*Under Pathways, explore ...*
Get into the Library of Congress?	Government
Look up News in the Oxford English Dictionary?	Reference
Find lyrics to "Satisfaction"?	Arts and Leisure
Look up the ZIP code for Kalamazoo?	Reference
Buy books?	Shopping
View the latest electronic art projects?	Arts and Leisure
Check today's earthquake reports	Weather
Check White House press releases	Government
Find the Nielsen TV ratings	Arts and Leisure

More about Pathways into the Internet

Let's say you've explored for a while and come upon something wonderful. How will you be able to find it again? Answer: If you find a resource you will want to use again, select Bookmarks! from the menu to add it to your permanent Bookmark list.

Pink Slip™

A note about communications behind the scenes:

Pipeline for Windows stands out among on-line interfaces with its capability to transparently multitask many different windows (sessions, in effect). We have implemented our own proprietary packet-transfer protocol, invented by Uday Ivatury. It is called Pink Slip™, and it intelligently manages multiple data streams over an ordinary modem connection.

The process is transparent: you never see or know about Pink Slip. But it is always working behind the scenes. When you are downloading a large file, for example, Pink Slip automatically adjusts the speed of the transfer and the priority given to individual packets, depending on what else you are doing. If the user is reading or replying to mail or News, the background transfer is fast. If new mail arrives, or the user opens a new window and begins playing a game, those data streams take priority and push the file transfer into the background.

Glossary

Check the glossary of terms included in the on-line help file, beginning with *alt* through Veronica.

Easy Installation

For instructions on installing the CD, see Part I, "Getting Started." Run SETUP.EXE. If you know what that means and how to do it, you're done.

More detailed installation instructions are included on the program's README file.

Basically, you need to set up Pipeline in a directory on your hard drive. There should be about 50 files.

After loading Pipeline's SETUP.EXE, the program will groan, click, beep, and whistle, and finally display a box asking you where (that is, in which directory) you want to install the Pipeline software. We suggest C:\PIPELINE, but you can use any valid MS-DOS directory name.

Unless some errors are detected, the software returns (in a while) and tells you that the installation is complete. At this point, you see that we have added a group to your desktop Program Manager. It is the Pipeline group. Installation is complete.

Getting started

The Pipeline icon appears in the Pipeline group on your desktop. Double-click the icon to get started. Pipeline asks you whether you want a demo, or whether you have been assigned a valid user name and password (assigned by our staff at the Pipeline). After you answer, Pipeline sets up a new user ID for you, using either your user ID or the Demo user ID. Now all you need to do is set up the phone (Phone Setup) and Dial.

Phone Setup is easier than you think. From the Pipeline Main window, click on Options. From the proffered list, click on Dialing and modem setup.

You can just accept the option that says "Dial directly." If New York is a long distance call for you, you'll save money by choosing "Dial SprintNet data network" instead. There's a surcharge for this service of $5.00/hour during peak time and $2.50 nights and holidays, but it's still a lot cheaper than long distance.

Click on the appropriate buttons for Modem Speed and Comm Port. If you do not know what values to use, click on Don't Know.

Dialing the Pipeline is even easier. From the main Pipeline window, click Dial. If you have been assigned a user ID, create it now by clicking on the New button. Otherwise, select your user ID (or select Demo). Click on Dial.

After more clicks, hums, and whirrs, you will find yourself connected to the Pipeline.

Uh-oh

If you are having trouble getting started, call us at 212-267-3636. If you like, send e-mail to staff@pipeline.com, instead.

Some problems you may run into, and solutions to those problems, are described in Table 7-2.

Table 7-2	Troubleshooting Pipeline
Problem	**Solution**
Out-of-date copy of *xxx* when attempting to start the Pipeline.	This problem probably means that another application has created a copy of *xxx* in the Windows directory. The safest thing to do is call us. If you prefer, you can rename the offending file (to get it out of the way) and try again.
Modem won't dial.	Play with the following settings: Modem Speed, Modem Port. Click Don't know for either, if you like. The software tries to guess your modem's port. Try the Modem Setup String that you normally use with your modem. Or call us.
Modem dials but hangs up after the connection is made.	We've seen this problem with a few modems. This is usually a problem with the speed or with the Modem Setup String. Make sure that you have a modem rated for the speed you are trying to use. Lower the speed and try again. Refer to your modem manual for the correct setup string. Call us.

Some basic commands

Table 7-3 describes some basic Pipeline commands.

Table 7-3	Pipeline Commands
Command	**Action**
/quit	Quit IRC
/help	Get help
/help *xxxxx*	Get help about command *xxxxx*
/help newuser	Get info of interest to new users
/list	List every channel, with users and topic
/flush	Stop long output, such as the output from /list
/list -min *N*	List all channels with at least *N* users
/join *#yyyyy*	Join channel called *#yyyyy*
/set novice off	Lets you join more than one channel
/leave *#yyyyy*	Leave channel *#yyyyy*
/nick *zzzzz*	Change your nickname to *zzzzz*

Command	Action
/who *user*	Display info about person with nickname *user*
/whois *user*	Display more info about *user*
/who #*aaaaa*	List who is on channel #*aaaaa*
/who *	Show who's joined to the current channel
/msg nicknames text	Send private message to specified people
/msg , text	Send message to last person who sent you a message
/msg . text	Send message to last person you sent a message to
/query nicknames	Send all your messages to specified people

The Pipeline for Windows Registration Form

Name _____

Company _____

Address _____

City _____

State _____ Country _____

Zip _____ Phone _____

Remit to:

The Pipeline for Windows
150 Broadway, Suite 1710
New York, NY 10038

Pricing

Toe in the Water	❏ $15/monthly
20/20 Plan	❏ $20/monthly
IIMO (The Internet Is My Oyster)	❏ $35/monthly

(See information on CD for full details about these options.)

Chapter 8
PowerBBS for Windows Version 3.5

Getting Started

The default installation of PowerBBS provides you with the ability to run your own BBS. Although you can put this default installation on-line in a very short time, it is better to take your time and plan your installation. You will have many decisions to make: Do you want your BBS to be centered around files? Messages? Teleconferencing? Games? Do you want to allow minors to use your BBS or only adults? Will your callers have to pay to use your system? How many nodes (lines) will your BBS have?

As you can see, you have a lot to think about. Take your time. Sketch out a plan for your BBS. Use it as a guideline when configuring PowerBBS. You can always change settings later, but it is best to do things right the first time (isn't it always?).

Technical support

Before posting a message, scan or search the messages to see whether your question has already been asked, which is usually the case. You will get your answer immediately instead of waiting for a response from technical support.

Product Support BBS:	(516) 822-7396 (up to 14400); (516) 822-7568 (up to 28800)
Internet:	Support: James_Carr@PowerBBS.Win.Net; Product Information: Russell_Frey@PowerBBS.Win.Net
Voice Support Line:	(516) 938-0506
Orders only line:	(800) 242-4775 U.S.; (713) 524-6394 Local and international calls; (713) 524-6398 Fax
U.S. Mail:	Russell Frey, 35 Fox Court, Hicksville, NY 11801

Use a QWK Mail reader

The Support BBS offers QWK Mail downloading and uploading. Shareware QWK Mail readers are available on the Support BBS and almost every other BBS. QWK Mail allows you to download mail from the Support BBS. You can then read the mail off-line and compose messages to send back. You will then call back and upload your replies. This process is very fast. With a 14400 modem, the whole process of downloading and uploading mail will take just a few minutes. And if you can afford a 28800 modem, you'll soon be glad that you bought one. CompuServe and some other service providers are moving toward the 28.8 V32 specification.

If you have a question or problem, call the Support BBS and download all of the messages in the related forum and read the messages off-line. Chances are very good that you will find the answer you are looking for without having to leave a message!

Hardware considerations

At the very least, you need a 286 CPU with 4MB of RAM to run PowerBBS. If you intend to run DOS doors, you must have at least a 386 with 4MB of RAM. We recommend that you have at least 8 to 10MB of RAM on your computer for optimum performance. The more RAM your machine has, the faster and easier the application will run. For each node of PowerBBS that will receive outside callers, you need a separate phone line and modem. Contact your phone company and ask them about special lines for BBSs.

Software considerations

You must have Windows 3.0 or higher to run PowerBBS. You may also use Windows for Workgroups. PowerBBS for Windows has been known to function in Windows NT. However, we do not directly support sysops using Windows NT. We will do our best to assist you if you have a problem. Be aware, however, that PowerBBS has not been thoroughly tested for Windows NT. At this time, a Windows NT version of PowerBBS is not planned.

AUTOEXEC.BAT and CONFIG.SYS

Edit your path statement in AUTOEXEC.BAT to include the directory in which you install PowerBBS. For example,

```
PATH C:\;C:\WINDOWS;C:\DOS;C:\POWRBBS
```

The only entries you may need to make to AUTOEXEC.BAT are those required by third-party programs such as FrontDoor and external file transfer protocols.

In CONFIG.SYS, you must increase your FILES setting to at least 90. PowerBBS uses lots of files, as will some of the doors you will run. Add another 15 to the FILES statement for each additional node of PowerBBS. You will also need to load the DOS SHARE.EXE program to prevent PowerBBS and other programs from modifying the same files at the same time, which may cause errors in your BBS. For example,

```
FILES=90
INSTALL=C:\DOS\SHARE.EXE /L:50
```

Test your installation

Before starting PowerBBS, take a quick look at the program properties for that icon. Click that icon and then select File⇨Properties from the menu. If you have installed PowerBBS on your C: drive, you see the following information:

```
Name:   PowerBBS
Command Line: POWRBBS.EXE C:\POWRBBS\POWRBBS.DAT
Startup Directory:   C:\POWRBBS
```

The important thing to note here is the command line. It starts PowerBBS with a data file (POWRBBS.DAT). This data file comes with PowerBBS. You will edit it with the configuration program. POWRBBS.DAT contains all of the settings for PowerBBS. If you add an additional PowerBBS node, you must create a second icon to start PowerBBS. Its command is similar except that it uses a different configuration program. You will start an additional copy of PowerBBS for each node on your system. Click OK to close the Program Properties dialog box.

Start it up

Double-click the PowerBBS icon to start up PowerBBS. Figure 8-1 shows the main menu you receive when you start the program. The default installation of PowerBBS is not set up to use a modem, so you don't have to have a modem to get started.

The following mini-table lists the buttons on the main menu and their functions.

Button Name	*Function*
Local Logon	Allows you to logon to your BBS the same way your callers do.
Reset Modem	Resets your modem. Because PowerBBS resets the modem each time you start it up and between each call, you rarely need this button.
Quick Logon	Allows you to get into your BBS quickly. It will automatically enter your sysop name that you entered in Config under Sysop. You are asked for your password, which you entered when you installed the software. After you enter your password, the main menu appears.
Shut Down Node	Shuts down that node of PowerBBS. If that node of PowerBBS is set to use a modem, you are asked whether you want to take the modem off-hook so no one can call in.

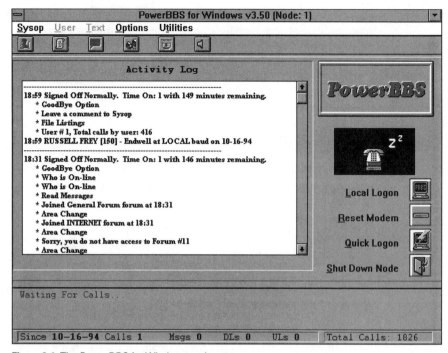

Figure 8-1: The PowerBBS for Windows main menu.

Go ahead and logon

Click the Local Logon button and logon to your BBS. You will see the opening screen and be asked for your name and password.

Proceed with the logon until you are at the main menu. By default, you have the security level automatically given to new users. However, you're in the big time now. You're a sysop! So go ahead and make yourself a sysop.

User Record

Click the first button on the toolbar at the top of the screen or select User⇨User Record from the menu. This is the screen you use to update your callers while they are on-line. Click the Pick List button next to access and select 150 as your new security level. Set your Expiration Access to 150 as well. Finally, set your Expiration Date as 00-00-00, which means your access never expires.

While you're here, take a look at the other options. You can increase or decrease the current caller's time on-line and give the caller credits (if you run a credit system). The check boxes along the bottom are used to give callers access to private forums, which is discussed later. The information in the top section of this screen is for informational purposes only. You cannot modify that information from this screen. Click OK to save your changes.

Sysop menu

Click the Sysop menu. You will see several options. The options that are gray are not available while a caller is on-line. Notice that these options are the same as the four buttons along the side of the local screen. Click the Node Status option. This shows you the status of all of the currently running nodes. Because you are running only one node right now, you will see only your name listed here. Double-click the control menu button in the upper-left corner of this dialog box to close it. You can also use the fourth button from the left on the toolbar to see the Node Status screen.

Click the Sysop menu again and select View Activity Log. Each node of PowerBBS has a separate log that tells you what's been happening on your BBS. You see the information about what you have done so far during this call. Click the OK button to close this dialog box. By the way, when a caller is not on-line, the local screen displays the contents of the activity log.

PowerBBS will display only the last 200 lines of your activity log. If you need to see more, you need to use a text editor. Look in Config under File Locations #1 for the name and location of this file.

If your activity log seems to be off by a single character, chances are the log is getting too large. Use the Del button from Sysop, View Activity Log, to delete it and start a new one. However, you may want to use PKZip to zip up this file before deleting in case you need it later.

User menu

The first option on the User menu is Chat. Use this option to interrupt the current caller and enter a split screen chat. The third button from the left on the toolbar does the same thing.

The next option is Time. Use the option to quickly add or take away time from the current caller. User Record will display the graphical User Record screen you learned earlier.

The last option is Hang Up Caller. Use this option to hang up on the current caller. You see a dialog box with three options: *Yes* sends a message to the caller that you are disconnecting him or her from the system and hanging up the caller. *No* still hangs up on the caller, but it sends "trash" characters to the caller as if it was line noise that broke the connection instead of you. The last option is *Cancel,* which does not do anything to the caller. You can also use the fifth button from the left on the toolbar to hang up on the caller.

Text menu

The first option is Paste from Clipboard. If you have copied text from another program, you can paste that text to the current caller. However, the caller must be able to receive the text, such as when entering a message.

The next option is Paste from File. This option allows you to paste the contents of a text file to the caller. The last option is Capture to File. This option captures the current screen to a text file.

You cannot block off and copy text from the PowerBBS local screen.

Options menu

There is only one option at this time: *Pager*. If Pager has a check mark next to it, your callers can page you using the Page Sysop command. If it doesn't have a check mark next to it, the caller will be notified that you are not available and will have a chance to enter a message. Notice that the last button on the toolbar at the top of the screen toggles the pager as well.

Utilities menu

You can use the Utilities menu to start either the Config, File List Manager, or PowerEdit programs that come with PowerBBS.

PowerEdit comes with the Professional version of PowerBBS. If you have the shareware version of PowerBBS, you must either register the professional version or register PowerEdit directly from Bill Ebina on the Support BBS.

The Last menu

When a caller is on-line or you are in a local logon, PowerBBS displays the options for the current menu along the left side of the screen. You can use these options to control the menus or type the actual letters. It is up to you.

While a caller is on-line, you can take over the keyboard. Just type. PowerBBS accepts input from the local keyboard or from the caller.

Caller information

While callers are on-line, you can see their current information listed at the bottom of the screen. At the very bottom of the local screen are the statistics for that node since you last started the program.

Sysop's Menu

The default installation of PowerBBS places Menu Command 33, Sysop's Menu in your main menu. This command is displayed only to callers with security

level 150 or higher. This is a special feature of PowerBBS. The default installation of PowerBBS uses 1 to access this menu. Because you have already upgraded
your status to sysop, logon locally and select 1 to start the sysop's menu.

DOS utilities

The Drop to DOS function starts a batch file called REMOTE#.BAT in which # is
the number of the node you are on. If PowerBBS does not find a REMOTE#.BAT,
it runs REMOTE.BAT. If it doesn't find that, it doesn't do anything. Drop to DOS
allows you to shell out to the DOS prompt. You need a program called Doorway
to be able to drop to DOS. This shareware is available on the Support BBS. The
following code segment is a sample REMOTE.BAT file:

```
****REMOTE.BAT****
C:
COPY C:\POWRBBS\DOORS\LIVE1\DOOR.SY C:\DOORWAY
CD \DOORWAY
DOORWAY SYS /B:MZ /V:D /C:DOS
```

You must have Doorway to use this batch file. Check the CD for more information about DOOR.SYS!

Perform DOS Function command

Perform DOS Function does not require Doorway. Select this option and then
enter a DOS command. PowerBBS shells out to DOS and runs the command.
When it is finished, PowerBBS displays the results, if any, of that command. You
can see what is happening. You'll just have to wait until it's done.

Type a File command

Type a File allows you to have PowerBBS type the contents of any file on your
system to your screen.

File maintenance

This option allows you to edit your file listings remotely. Basically, you can add,
remove, move, or edit each of your file lists remotely. Because PowerBBS
comes with a Windows-based File List Manager, you hardly ever need to use
this option on the sysop's menu. The commands within this option are self-
explanatory.

Sysop menu

This option brings you to the heart of the sysop's menu. From here, you can
view the activity log of any of the other nodes in the system. Use this option to
check up on your BBS when you return from being away. The List Users
command allows you to view a list of your callers by security level or search for
a user.

You will spend the most time in the Update User option. From here, you can edit the information on your users' accounts. To change an item for a user, enter the number of the item you wish to change. PowerBBS then asks you for the new information for that field.

If you have private forums on your BBS, use option 24 to give your callers access to those forums. You must do this if you have private forums. Place an asterisk under the appropriate forum number to give a caller access to that forum. Remove the asterisk to prevent a caller from accessing that private forum.

Use the Add option to add another user. This option is handy to set up an account for friends who don't have to fill out the information when they call. Be sure to tell your friends their passwords!

Use Find to find a caller. You must type the full name of the caller to search. Use Jump to jump to a certain caller. Each caller has a unique number. If you press Enter, you move to the next caller.

You cannot update a caller who is currently on-line!

Putting your BBS on-line

Play with PowerBBS

Before you start configuring your BBS, play with PowerBBS for a while. Get a feel for how all of the commands operate. Decide what things your callers might or might not want. Read over the menu commands discussed in the documentation. The default installation of PowerBBS doesn't install all of the commands.

Read the manual

Before you start playing around, read the documentation here and on the CD-ROM. I've tried to make the reading light and informative. Pay close attention to the Notes. They always include important information. Build your BBS a step at a time. Start with forums. Decide what types of messages you want on your BBS. Then move to files. Decide how you want to organize your files. Messages and files are related to forums. Be sure you have a thorough understanding of this relationship.

Pay very close attention to the chapters on modems and configuring Windows. It seems that 90 percent of the problems people experience are related to these two areas. Read over those sections at least twice. It will be time well spent.

Pick a theme or leitmotif

Leitmotif? I've always liked that word. It simply means a dominant theme. The default screens that come with PowerBBS sort of follow a 3-D look. Although many people consider this a sleek look, myself included, it is hardly original. Try to come up with your own ideas. Call other BBSs and look around. If your BBS has a unique look, you attract and keep more callers.

For example, you may call your BBS the Sleepy Hollow Inn. Instead of calling a command Enter a Message, call it Drop a Note. Instead of Comment to Sysop use Note to Manager. Instead of having a Doors option, call it the Recreation Area. Instead of using Who's On-Line, use Lovers' Lounge. You get the idea!

Color schemes

Even though you have many choices of colors, you should pick two or three and use them throughout your BBS. Doing so gives your BBS a smooth and attractive look. After you decide on a color scheme, drawing your screens is easy. But take your time. Use the default screens until you have a chance to create your own.

Charging for access

Although you may be tempted to charge for access to your BBS to cover your expenses, wait a little while before charging. Wait until you have worked out the kinks before asking for donations or subscriptions. Who wants to pay to use a work-in-progress BBS? Give new callers free trial memberships.

Be fair and responsive

On a BBS, there's nothing worse than a sysop who doesn't read mail. If a caller is kind enough to leave you a message, you should respond as soon as possible. After all, a BBS is an extension of your personality. Your callers will be more likely to pay for access if they think they are getting a good deal. Part of a good deal is the service they receive from you, the sysop.

You may find you need to post rules on your BBS. That's fine, but don't post too many. Nothing turns away callers faster than a set of complicated rules. Because 98 percent of your callers will follow your rules whether you post them or not, you may choose not to post any at all. I simply tell my callers that if I get complaints about them or see them abusing the system, I will lock them out. Then I do. If they have paid me money, I give it right back.

Callers who drop carrier

Some callers are rude and simply hang up the modem instead of using the Goodbye command. The problem with that is you never know if it was their fault or your fault. Some sysops post HELLO screens telling people not to drop carrier. This can be a big turnoff to most callers, who logoff properly.

I have found an effective method for habitual *carrier droppers*. The first time they do it I leave them a private message of concern. I explain to them that if they drop carrier, I think something is wrong with my system. I politely ask them to respond and tell me if they dropped carrier. I also casually chide them about using the Goodbye command.

If they do it again, I send them a *public* message that everyone can read. This message is basically the same as the first, but a little stronger. If they don't respond, I assume that they are dropping carrier, not me. If they continue, I send them a message that they will be locked out of my system if they continue to drop carrier. If they still continue, I lock them out. I've never had to lock out a caller, and dropped carriers are not a problem on my BBS.

This approach works for me. It may not work for you.

A final note

A BBS is a complicated program of interlocking parts. It is very much like a spider web in which everything is connected in one way or another. I have attempted to bring these connections to your attention in this discussion. PowerBBS is very flexible and powerful, yet it is easy to set up and use. You may find, however, that some features seem a little confusing at first because there are numerous options to expand and customize your BBS the way you want it. Just take your time. It will all come together.

Internet connection

If you intend to connect your BBS to the Internet for exchanging mail, you must check this option in the Config section in the Options 1 button (see Figure 8-2). If you don't, your Internet portions of your BBS will not operate properly. See the next section, "The Internet," for more information.

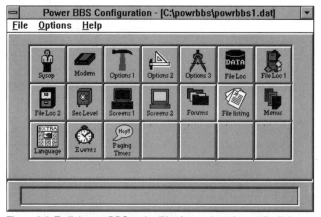

Figure 8-2: To link your BBS to the 'Net for exchanging mail, click Options 1 and select Mail from the screen.

The Internet

Overview

Before you embark on installing Internet access on PowerBBS, you need to have an idea of how it will all look when you're done. First of all, you will have two major software packages on your computer: PowerBBS for Windows and the WinNET Mail Server Package (also included in this book/CD package). Your users, however, see only PowerBBS for Windows. And for the most part, so will you!

After PowerBBS is set up for Internet access, your BBS looks a little different than it did before. Figure 8-3 shows the PowerBBS Message Menu. You will have one forum that your callers use to send/receive mail to/from the Internet. You might also have several other forums that your callers use to send/receive articles to/from the Internet. Over 6,000 newsgroups are available on the Internet right now. Many of those newsgroups will have many messages every day. Others will not have many messages at all. You have to start and stop many newsgroup subscriptions until you get it the way you want it.

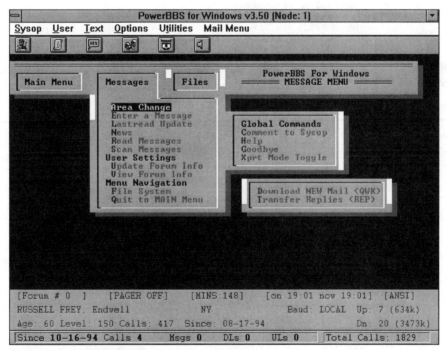

Figure 8-3: PowerBBS Message Menu lets you manage areas, users, and menus.

Every caller on your system will have an Internet address. When you set up PowerBBS to access the Internet, you will create a system name for your BBS. When anyone who has access to the Internet wants to send mail to one of your callers, he or she need only address the mail to *first_last@yoursystem.win.net*. The Internet and PowerBBS take care of the rest. If your callers want to send a message to someone who has an Internet account on another system, they need only leave a message in your Internet forum to *their_friend@theirsystem.whatever*. PowerBBS and the Internet handle the rest.

As for newsgroups, your callers can read the articles from a newsgroup simply by reading the messages in the appropriate forum on your BBS. It looks like normal mail except for the Internet header information at the top of the message. If they want to post an article to a newsgroup, they need only leave a message to ALL in that forum on your BBS. PowerBBS and the Internet handle the rest.

You, as the sysop, determine how often your system gets mail from the Internet. I have set up my BBS to get mail and news twice a day (6:00 a.m. and 6:00 p.m.). How often you move mail is your own decision. Just be sure to tell your callers what times you send and receive mail so they won't get upset when mail doesn't arrive when they think it should.

Internet addresses

Your callers might have only one name on your BBS (if you permit it) or two names. If they have one-word names, their Internet address is just their one word followed by an @ and your system name: Win.Net. For example, *grendyl@ladiesroom.win.net*. This is what people use to send mail to me on my BBS if I permit one-word names. If you allow only two-word names, the sender must use an underscore between the first and last name: For example, *james_carr@ladiesroom.win.net*. As long as the sender addresses the mail properly, your callers will get it!

To send mail to the following systems via the Internet, use these addresses:

CompuServe	User IDs on CompuServe are usually separated by commas. You need to replace the commas with periods to send mail to CompuServe. Example: *70562.3003@compuserve.com*.
America Online	User IDs on this system are usually handles. Example: *grendyl@aol.com*.
Prodigy	User IDs on this system are usually letters and numbers. Example: *shnb98b@prodigy.com*.

GEnie	User IDs on this system are usually letters and numbers. Example: *xty5787@genie.com.*
Delphi	User IDs on this system are usually handles. Example: *hendo@delphi.com.*

Setting up PowerBBS for Internet access

Following are the basic steps for making WinNET work with PowerBBS:

1. Download the latest version of WinNET.ZIP. It is available from the Support BBS as well as from America Online and other major BBS systems.

2. Install the WinNET mail program.

3. Create your account with the WinNET program. As of this writing, the cost of accessing the Internet via this service is $8 per hour. You can either pay the long distance charges, or you can use the 800 number to get rates a little below normal long distance rates. How much you spend depends on the volume of mail you move and the number of newsgroups you get. It is impossible to estimate this number, but expect to pay as little as $15 a month to as much as $100 a month. Most sysops find that they fall into the $25–40 range if they have several newsgroups. My best advice is to start small and grow gradually.

4. Subscribe to whatever newsgroups you wish. You can add and delete subscriptions via the WinNET mail program at any time.

 After you set up everything correctly, subscribing and unsubscribing to newsgroups is the only time you need to access the WinNET mail program manually.

5. Add or modify your existing forums in PowerBBS for the import and export of mail.

6. Create INTIMP.BBS and INTEXP.BBS files to tell PowerBBS how to import and export mail to and from the Internet server.

7. Create the IMPORT.BAT and INTEXP.BAT files that PowerBBS uses to move the mail in and out of your BBS.

8. Set up your event(s) for exchanging mail using the INTEXP.BAT file created earlier.

Let PowerBBS do the work for you: This is all you have to do!

Installing WinNET Mail

If you haven't already installed this file from the CD or previously downloaded it from your support BBS, AOL, CompuServe, or wherever, go do it now. I'll wait.

1. Create a *temporary* directory and copy the WNMAIL.ZIP file to this directory.

2. Run the PKUNZip program (commonly available shareware from PKWARE) to unzip the WNMAIL.ZIP file in this temporary directory.

3. From the Windows Program Manager File menu or directly from the Window's File Manager program, run the SETUP.EXE program supplied with the WinNET distribution. Use the More Information button to get more information on each screen

 You must install the WinNET mail server program on the same drive as PowerBBS. WinNET must also be installed in its own directory, usually \WNMAIL. Do not install it in the \POWRBBS directory.

4. Run the option to set up your account. This option asks you for billing and credit card information. The only item that is specific to PowerBBS is the *E-mail Name* used with WinNET. Be sure this is set to **Rfrey.**

   The *System Name* should be the name of your particular BBS. My BBS is called "The Ladies Room," so I call my system name *ladiesroom.* The system name you choose is what comes after the @ and before the *.win.net* in the address of the Internet mail sent to your system. After you have filled out this information, the program will call the Computer Witchcraft WinNET server and submit your account request. After a one-minute pause, the program calls back to verify that the account was accepted.

All account requests are accepted unless the System Name that you choose in SETUP is already taken by another WinNET customer. If the account request is not successful, you have to rerun SETUP, select a different System Name, and rerun the account program.

Although WinNET was originally intended as an application for an individual to connect to the Internet, PowerBBS uses WinNET to connect your entire BBS and all its users to the Internet! The only time you access this program directly is when adding and deleting newsgroup subscriptions. You get all of your mail and articles right from PowerBBS.

Newsgroup subscriptions

After you have set up WinNET and your account has been established, you are ready to add some newsgroup subscriptions. It's a good idea to get a book (I like *The Internet Directory* by Eric Braun) and learn about the various newsgroups. You can subscribe to newsgroups at any time, but now is as good a time as any. You can (and probably will) add and delete newsgroup subscriptions at any time. However, you must add and delete newsgroups subscriptions from within the WinNET Mail program.

Settings in Config

If you are setting up PowerBBS for Internet access, you should have one forum for private Internet mail. You can also have as many newsgroup forums as you want. The only restrictions are that you may *not* use forum #0 as an Internet forum, period. The forum you create for private Internet mail must be between forum numbers 1–199, inclusive. I use forum #1, but you can use any forum that you like. The newsgroup forums can be any forum(s) numbered from 1–999 (the current limit of PowerBBS forums).

The forums you use for the Internet must have special names. The forum for private Internet mail must be called INTERNET. Make sure the forum *you* set up for private Internet mail is not a *public messages only* forum. The forum names for the Internet newsgroups must begin with INTNN. For example, I subscribe to the newsgroup called alt.sex.stories. This forum is called INTNN Erotica on my BBS.

After you have established the new forums for the Internet, you must tell PowerBBS that you will be accessing the Internet. You have to do this by changing the start-up parameters for PowerBBS. Edit the properties of the icon for starting up PowerBBS (Alt-double-click the icon or File Properties). Add the /I command-line switch, like so:

```
C:\POWRBBS\POWRBBS C:\POWRBBS\POWRBBS.DAT /I.
```

You must do this to enable all the special features of PowerBBS to work with the Internet.

Getting Internet mail into and out of PowerBBS

First, you need to create a dummy user. Give that dummy user a security level of 150. For this example, call the dummy user *J. NET*. You can create a dummy user by either adding a new user from the Sysop menu or by logging in under this name. Regardless, you must give this user a security level of 150 (or whatever level you use as sysop of the system). Be sure to give this caller a password in case any of your callers get wise and try to use this name (they will see it from Who's On-Line if they logonto another node during an Internet mail run). If you intend to use J. Net for PowerMail, you should update this user's profile to be a QWK Mail user. You do not need to make any changes regarding maximum Internet messages per month for J. Net.

You have to create four files for PowerBBS to use for exchanging mail. Name the files as follows to avoid conflict with QWK mail. The first three entries that follow can have any name you choose. I chose these names to help me stay organized. The fourth entry must be called IMPORT.BAT. This may conflict with your QWK Mail routines, so you have to modify your QWK Mail routines to work around this limitation.

INTEXP.BBS — Tells PowerBBS from which forums to export mail and to what part of the Internet to send the mail.

INTEXP.BAT — The batch file that is set up as the event for your Internet connections. This batch file uses INTEXP.BBS and IN_OUT.EXE to export the mail from the BBS.

INTIMP.BBS — Tells PowerBBS what to do with the mail that WinNET gets from the Internet.

IMPORT.BAT — The batch file that PowerBBS uses along with INTIMP.BBS and IN_IN.EXE to move the mail into PowerBBS.

INTEXP.BBS

Use your favorite text editor to create the INTEXP.BBS file. PowerBBS uses this file to pull out messages from your BBS and send them to the Internet. The file *must* follow the format described in the following sample INTEXP.BBS file:

```
|10
;powerbbs
6,6,0
2,alt.bbs,0
```

The first line is a message counter. Set it to |**10** to start with. It must begin with a pipe symbol. PowerBBS uses this number to keep track of messages automatically.

The second line is the system name of your BBS that you created when you first set up WinNET Mail. (*;ladiesroom* is the system name that I used for my system.) Your system name will be different. Remember, when people send mail to your callers, this is the system name they will use: *first_last@ladiesroom.win.net*. Be sure to precede this line with a semicolon.

The rest of the lines are a little trickier (there are two here, but there can be many more). Each of these lines consists of three items separated by commas. The next section explains what each item means and then relates the items to the sample INTEXP.BBS file.

First Item: This item is the PowerBBS forum number from which you export mail. Remember the restrictions on forum numbers described previously. You will have one line for each Internet forum on your BBS from which you want to export mail.

You can import a newsgroup into a forum, but you do not have to export mail from that forum. It is up to you.

Second Item: This item can only be one of two things. If the first item on the line is the number of your forum for private Internet mail, this item must match the first item. In my case, my Internet forum for private mail is 6, so this entry in INTEXP.BBS is 6,6,0. In all other cases, this item will be the name of the Internet newsgroup to which you want to export mail.

Third Item: This item is the message pointer that PowerBBS uses to keep track of messages. Set this number to 0 to start with. PowerBBS will take care of it in the future.

Example #1:   6,6,0

This INTEXP.BBS entry is for private mail. *How can you tell?* Because the first two items are identical. The first item is a 6. It tells PowerBBS to export the mail from forum #6. The second item is also a 6. It tells PowerBBS to export the mail as private e-mail. Obviously, this sysop has chosen forum number 6 for the private Internet mail. The last item is a 0 because the event has never been run. After you run the event to send Internet mail, this number automatically increases one number for each piece of mail that is to be exported from this forum.

This INTEXP.BBS entry is for exporting a newsgroup. The first item tells PowerBBS that the mail to export is in forum #2. Item #2 tells PowerBBS to send this mail to the alt.bbs newsgroup. The third entry is a 0, which is just the message counter, as described previously.

Your INTEXP.BBS file will have entries only for the Internet forums from which you want to export mail. Do not list any forums that are not Internet forums. You will have one entry for your private Internet mail. The first two items for this entry in the INTEXP.BBS file will be the number for that forum. For all other Internet forums, it will be the number of the forum followed by the newsgroup name.

The following is another example of an INTEXP.BBS file from Adam Baker's BBS. As you can see, he has had many messages imported into his BBS (the message pointers are very high). Notice also that Adam uses forum #5 for private

Internet mail. We know this because the first two items on that line (5,5,720) are identical. His system name is *azbbbs*. The following is Adam's INTEXP.BBS file:

```
|1168
;azbbbs
5,5,720
2,rec.humor,4662
4,alt.fan.letterman,746
6,comp.os.ms-windows.misc,3506
7,alt.dragons-inn,16
8,alt.fan.mst3k,40
9,clari.news.almanac,37
```

INTIMP.BBS

Use your favorite text editor to create the INTIMP.BBS file. PowerBBS uses this file to place the messages from the Internet into your BBS. The file must follow the format followed in the following sample INTIMP.BBS file:

```
;ladiesroom
0,6
comp.bbs.misc,2
```

The first line is the system name of your BBS that you created when you first set up WinNET Mail. (*;ladiesroom* is the system name that I used for my system.) Your system name will be different. Remember, when people send mail to your callers, this is the system name they will use: *first_last@ladiesroom.win.net*. Be sure to precede this line with a semicolon.

The rest of the lines (there are two here, but there can be many more) are a little trickier. Each of these lines consists of two items separated by commas. This section explains what each item means and then relates the items to the sample INTIMP.BBS file.

First Item: The first item on this line will either be a 0 or the name of an Internet newsgroup. The 0 signifies private Internet mail. You will use the 0 on only one entry (the one for your private e-mail, of course). Otherwise, you will enter the name of the newsgroup for which you will be importing mail.

Please note the entry for private Internet mail is different than the INTEXP.BBS file's entry! In the INTIMP.BBS file, the first item for the line for private mail is always a 0.

Second Item: The second item is a PowerBBS forum number. Use this number to tell PowerBBS where to place the mail. The entry for private mail is the number of the forum you called INTERNET. For the rest of the entries, the number for the second item is the PowerBBS forum number of the corresponding *INTNN Name* forum.

Example: 0,6

This entry in the INTIMP.BBS file tells PowerBBS to place all private Internet mail directly into forum #6, which is called (remember?) INTERNET.

Example: comp.bbs.misc,2

This entry in the INTIMP.BBS file tells PowerBBS to place the newsgroup articles from comp.bbs.misc directly into forum #2, which is called INTNN Stuff About BBSing.

Your INTIMP.BBS file will have entries only for the newsgroups which you intend to import and for your private Internet mail. You will have one entry for your private Internet mail.

Another example

The following is another example of an INTIMP.BBS file from Adam Baker's BBS. Note that Adam's INTIMP.BBS and INTEXP.BBS files don't agree. He has elected to have several network newsgroups imported into the same forum. This can be done without any problems. Be careful, though, because users may not know exactly which newsgroup their posts will be sent to, if you will also be exporting mail from this forum. It's a good idea not to export articles from a forum that imports several different newsgroups. Folks on the Internet can get pretty uptight when they see articles about David Letterman in the Dungeons and Dragons newsgroup!

You can also have a network newsgroup as a read-only forum by just not adding its information to the INTEXP.BBS file. Sometimes you want your callers to be able only to read the articles from a newsgroup, not write articles to them. Usually, you do this to save money or if a newsgroup does not accept postings (like those in the ClariNet News hierarchy). Notice the entry for private Internet mail is 0,5. The 0 means private mail, and the 5 means put it in forum #5. The following is Adam's INTEXP.BBS file

```
;AZBBBS
0,5
comp.os.ms-windows.misc,6
alt.dragons-inn,7
alt.fan.mst3k,8
clari.news.almanac,9
rec.humor,2
rec.humor.funny,2
```

(continued)

(continued)

```
clari.news.interest.quirks,2
comp.protocols.misc,2
comp.society.cd-digest,2
alt.butt-keg.marmalade,2
alt.fan.letterman,4
```

INTEXP.BAT

You have to create an event in your Config Events Setup that will use the INTEXP.BAT file to export Internet mail. The import of the mail is then automatic. Use your favorite text editor to create your INTEXP.BAT file. In this running example, it will look as follows with all of the text being on one line:

```
in_out c:\powrbbs\powrbbs.dat J. NET ladiesroom
c:\powrbbs\intexp.bbs
```

Here is what it does. The first part of this line is in_out. This calls the program IN_OUT.EXE located in your \POWRBBS directory. This is the program that PowerBBS uses to export mail from the BBS.

The next part is C:\POWRBBS\POWRBBS.DAT. This is the name of the DAT file of the node for which you are running the Internet event. This node must be a node connected to an outside line.

The third part is J. NET. This is the name of the dummy user that you created earlier. Remember, this dummy user must have the same security level (usually 150) that you have as sysop. PowerBBS will use this dummy user to login to the BBS and get the mail out.

The fourth entry is ladiesroom. This is your Internet system name that you created earlier. This entry is needed for PowerBBS to convert the mail for the Internet properly.

The fifth and final entry is the full path and filename of the INTEXP.BBS file that you already created. This file tells IN_OUT.EXE what messages to take out of PowerBBS and where to send them on the Internet. In this case this entry is C:\POWRBBS\INTEXP.BBS. You must have this file in order for in_out to work properly. The following is an example INTEXP.BAT by Adam Baker:

```
c:\powrbbs\in_out.exe c:\powrbbs\powrbbs.dat J. NET azbbbs
c:\powrbbs\intexp.bbs
```

Notice that the only difference between the previous example and Adam's example is the system name. His system is called *azbbbs*. You must use your system name for your INTEXP.BAT. The true guts of the INTEXP.BAT file are contained in the INTEXP.BBS file.

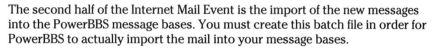

IMPORT.BAT

The second half of the Internet Mail Event is the import of the new messages into the PowerBBS message bases. You must create this batch file in order for PowerBBS to actually import the mail into your message bases.

Remember, this batch file must be called IMPORT.BAT.

In the current example, it will look as follows with all of the text being on one line:

```
in_in c:\powrbbs\powrbbs.dat J. NET ladiesroom
c:\powrbbs\intimp.bbs
```

Here is what it does. The first part of this line is in_in. This calls the program IN_IN.EXE located in your \POWRBBS directory. This is the program that PowerBBS uses to import mail into the BBS.

The next part is C:\POWRBBS\POWRBBS.DAT. This is the name of the DAT file of the node for which you are running the Internet event. This node must be a node connected to an outside line.

The third part is J. NET. This is the name of the dummy user that you created earlier. Remember, this dummy user must have the same security level (usually 150) that you have as sysop. PowerBBS will use this dummy user to login to the BBS and send the messages.

The fourth entry is ladiesroom. This is your Internet system name that you created earlier. This is needed for PowerBBS to properly convert the mail from the Internet to put into your BBS.

The fifth and final entry is the full path and filename of the INTIMP.BBS file that you already created. This file will tell IN_IN.EXE where to place the messages that have been received from the Internet by way of you WinNET Mail package. In this case, this entry is C:\POWRBBS\INTIMP.BBS. You must have this file in order for in_in to work properly.

PowerBBS takes the contents of the IMPORT.BAT file and combines it with its own commands to create an IMPORT1.BAT file (described next). In order for this process to work properly, you must press Enter after you type the last (or only) line in your IMPORT.BAT file.

The following is an example IMPORT.BAT by Adam Baker:

```
wait 120
c:\powrbbs\in_in.exe c:\powrbbs\powrbbs.dat J. NET azbbbs
c:\powrbbs\intimp.bbs
```

Adam imports a lot of information into his BBS. Therefore, he has added an extra line to his IMPORT.BAT file called wait 120. This line tells PowerBBS to wait two extra minutes (the *120* refers to 120 seconds, but it can be a higher or lower number) before importing the mail. You will see later that PowerBBS already waits three minutes. This entry makes PowerBBS wait a total of five minutes. You read later why this needs to be done. Notice that the only other difference for this example is the system name, which is azbbbs for Adam's BBS. You will put your system in this position. The real guts of the import routine are contained in the INTIMP.BBS file.

AUTOEXEC.BAT

The only entry you need to make here is to put your \WNMAIL directory into your path statement. That's it.

Putting it all together — setting up your event

You will set up an event on your BBS for one of your nodes. This event must run C:\POWRBBS\INTEXP.BAT. In the Events dialog box, you must check *Run Internet Connection After Event.* PowerBBS will run this event at the times you have specified.

You will not set up an event for the IMPORT.BAT file; PowerBBS runs that file after an Internet event, all by itself!

PowerBBS runs the INTEXP.BAT file at the time specified by your event. This essentially results in J. NET logging into your BBS and exporting all of the messages as specified in your INTEXP.BBS file. When this conversion is done, PowerBBS will automatically run the UUCICO.EXE program, located in your \WNMAIL directory *(not in the \POWRBBS directory as the original PowerBBS documentation had instructed!).* This program will dial the server (Computer Witchcraft) and send the mail you exported from your BBS and receive any waiting mail for your system. You don't need to do anything. Just let PowerBBS do its thing.

After the UUCICO.EXE program is done exchanging mail, the WinNET Mail program will pop up an icon on your system called Mail Manager (or "Mail Man") and convert all of the information into a recognizable format. Depending on how much mail you get, this process can take a few seconds or several minutes. At the same time WinNET is converting the mail, PowerBBS will pop up a DOS window (or an icon). In this DOS window, PowerBBS will be running a batch file called IMPORT1.BAT. If you've been paying attention, you might be wondering where IMPORT1.BAT comes from because I haven't made a file with that name.

Every time PowerBBS runs an event with *Run Internet Connection After Event* checked, it creates a file called IMPORT1.BAT (assuming you use node 1 for the event) in your \POWRBBS directory. You do not need to modify this file.

PowerBBS creates it automatically by adding a *wait 10* statement and adding in your IMPORT.BAT file. Basically, the IMPORT1.BAT file is a combination of IMPORT.BAT (that you created) and some internal stuff that PowerBBS adds. The IMPORT1.BAT file is created every time you run an Internet event. You never need to modify this file— actually, you can't modify this file because it is re-created every time you run an Internet event!

The WinNET system must take care of the exported messages before the import procedure is started. PowerBBS will not start IMPORT1.BAT until WinNET is done.

That's all there is!

After you have created the four files discussed here and set up your event, that's all there is. Remember, your event will simply run the INTEXP.BAT file. PowerBBS will take care of calling the server and then running the IMPORT.BAT file. Yes, it's that simple!

The Internet and your callers

User IDs on your system

When you set up your account with WinNET, you gave it a system name. All mail to users on your system must be *first_last@yoursystem.win.net*. My system name is *ladiesroom*.

To send mail to me on my system, address it to *james_carr@ladiesroom.win.net*. My system allows one-word names (this is different than the handle option). My wife has a one-word name she uses on our system called *sweetcheeks*. If you want to send her mail on our system via the Internet (to tell her what a great job I did on this documentation), address it to *sweetcheeks@ladiesroom.win.net*.

If anyone sends mail to your system using *whatever@yoursystem.win.net, your system* will get the mail. The Internet has no idea whether *whatever* is actually a user on your system. For example, if you sent a message to my system addressed to *wild_lover@ladiesroom.win.net* it will arrive on my system. I will see a message in my forum for private Internet forum addressed to *Wild Lover*. However, because there is no caller on my system, no one will ever get the mail. Only, I, the sysop, will be able to see it or kill it.

Likewise, if someone sends Internet mail to one of your callers and uses the proper system name, it will arrive on your system. However, unless you give that caller access to the INTERNET forum, he or she will not be able to see it. Personally, I limit access to my INTERNET forum using security levels. Thus, everyone on your system will have an Internet address, but it's up to you whether that person will actually be able to use it!

Telling your users their Internet addresses

I have modified my stats screen to display the current caller's Internet address. Because I allow one-word names on my system, I had to add the following:

```
If you have a one word name on our BBS, your Internet address is
|NAME|@ladiesRoom.Win.Net
If you have a two word name on our BBS, your Internet address is
|FIRST|_|LAST|@ladiesRoom.Win.Net
```

Notice that I use the underscore (_) character between the FIRST and LAST name macros. The only drawback here is that the caller will see two Internet addresses, a correct one and an incorrect one. Trust me, your users will understand!

Allowing Internet access for your users

You don't need to do anything special to give your users an Internet address. It's automatic. However, you do need to modify each user's account to allow a maximum number of Internet messages per month and provide access to FTP Mail. You can also set the number of maximum Internet messages allowed per month under Config, Data File Location under editing Security Level information.

Users are defaulted to 0/0 (meaning they cannot leave any Internet mail) and they are defaulted to not having access to FTP Mail.

Because you can make private forums or set a security level to access a forum, you have complete control over how your users access the Internet on your BBS.

Checklist for setting up the Internet and PowerBBS

Use this handy checklist to ensure that you have covered everything:

_____ Load the WinNET mail program.

_____ Install WinNET on the same drive as PowerBBS.

_____ Set up your account using the WinNET Mail program. Remember to select a unique system name for your BBS. Set the e-mail name to **RFrey**.

_____ If you want to have any newsgroup subscriptions, start these subscriptions using the WinNET Mail server program now. You can always change this later using the WinNET Mail package. Discussion about PowerBBS is currently happening in the comp.bbs.misc newsgroup. We hope to soon have our own comp.bbs.powerbbs newsgroup. Please join us on comp.bbs.misc. There's lots of good information out there!

_____ Use PowerBBS Config to create your forum for private Internet mail. Call this forum INTERNET. Set the security level high enough to suit your needs.

_____ Use PowerBBS Config to create your newsgroup forums. Call these forums INTNN Whatever Name. Again, decide on a security level to suit your needs.

_____ Create a dummy user called J. NET. Give this user a password and a security level of 150 or whatever your sysop security level is.

_____ Create your INTEXP.BBS file as described previously.

_____ Create your INTIMP.BBS file as described previously.

_____ Create your INTEXP.BAT file as described previously.

_____ Create your IMPORT.BAT file as described previously.

_____ Put the \WNMAIL directory in your path statement.

_____ Use PowerBBS Config to create an event for the Internet mail exchange. Be sure to use the INTEXP.BAT file as your batch file to run. Be sure to check the Run Internet Connection After Event option.

_____ Modify your icon for starting PowerBBS to include the /I switch to enable the Internet routines.

_____ Verify that UUCICO.EXE is in your \WNMAIL directory.

_____ Verify that IN_OUT.EXE, IN_IN.EXE, UUDECODE.EXE, and UUENCODE.EXE are in your \POWRBBS directory.

_____ Leave a private message in your private Internet forum to _james_carr@powerbbs.win.net_ and let me know if this documentation helped. It will be a good test. Also let me know your BBS name and phone number, and I'll see that you get added to the PBBS/Internet Sysops List, a group of PBBS Sysops on the 'Net who share tricks, tips, and lists of the most recent versions of useful PowerBBS applications.

Several hours before you are ready to test the system, leave a message to yourself via Internet. You can use America Online, CompuServe, GEnie, Delphi, Prodigy, or whatever. Just be sure to leave several hours lead time for the mail to be processed. You must have already established your account with WinNET. Your Internet address will be *your_name@yoursystem.win.net.*

Start PowerBBS and let the event run. If all goes well, you should get a message from yourself, and I should get a message. I reply to all messages I receive.

If it doesn't work, go over this chapter and the docs on the CD again. If you still get stuck, call the Support BBS and leave a message for James Carr telling me exactly where you think it is failing. Feel free to enclose the four files you created here.

PowerBBS for Windows Version 3.5

Name _____

Company _____

Address _____

City _____

State _____   Country _____

Zip _____   Phone _____

Remit to:

Russell Frey
35 Fox Court
Hicksville, NY 11801

Pricing

❑ PowerBBS 3.5 Standard $99   ❑ PowerBBS Professional $189

Please contact the author at the Support BBS or check the CD-ROM's registration file for more pricing information about add-ons, upgrades, and so on.

Chapter 9

QuickStart CompuServe Information Manager, Windows Edition

The CompuServe Information Manager for Windows — WinCIM® — brings new dimensions and a new look to using the CompuServe Information Service. WinCIM lets new CompuServe members quickly get acquainted with and use CompuServe more productively. (For information about a special discount on a CompuServe account, see the end of this chapter.) Existing CompuServe members can access, sort, and use the on-line information and services more effectively. Figure 9-1 shows the WinCIM main window.

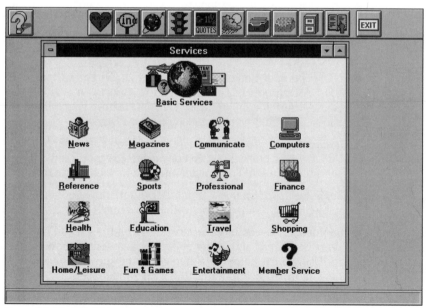

Figure 9-1: The WinCIM main window.

A WinSock edition of WinCIM will soon be available; see the sidebar "WinSock-compliant edition of WinCIM."

The usage instructions in this chapter are quite limited, and hit on only a few highlights of the program, giving you the opportunity to discover all the neato features on your own. The CD accompanying this book, however, includes a hefty amount of documentation for WinCIM. Detailed installation and usage instructions are included on the CD with the program, so you'll want to check the CD for answers to any other questions about using WinCIM.

WinCIM Features

WinCIM is the entry-level Windows 3.11 front end for accessing CompuServe. It is an interactive communications package, not an automated off-line navigator. WinCIM's most unique feature is the implementation of CompuServe's B+ file transfer protocol for error-free, optimized file transmission, and the HMI command protocol for optimized, asynchronous communications between remote and host. WinCIM's features include

- *Message maps* — A visual representation of message flow in a forum topic.

- *Electronic conferencing support* — A split-screen conferencing window. You can participate in more than one conversation at the same time.

- *Graphic Interchange Format (GIF) and JPEG support* — You can view GIF and JPEG images on-line or off-line.

- *INT14 support* — You can use WinCIM on LANs and with modem pools. NCSI/NASI support has been added to support connection to CompuServe via a LAN server configuration. This new feature is apparent only when you have NCSI/NASI drivers installed on your PC.

- *Enhanced "Copy To" functionality* — Lets you copy, via the Clipboard, to a MAPI message store. You can copy selected text directly to a mail message generated by a MAPI-compliant mail client, such as Microsoft Mail.

- *Simple mail attachments* — Not MIME-compatible for e-mail to Internet recipients. It is available only within CIS e-mail.

- *International keyboard characters (ISO Latin-1)* — WinCIM users can send CompuServe mail and forum messages that contain international characters. Using these characters involves some known limitations. For additional information about this topic, see the file WC8BIT.TXT in the "General" Library of the WinCIM Support forum (GO WCIMSUPPORT).

WinSock-compliant edition of WinCIM

WinCIM, WinSock-Compliant Edition, is a version of WinCIM that can use the WinSock 1.1 standard to connect to CompuServe's Internet Server on a TCP/IP connection. Official release should be early 1995. This version of WinCIM will let you connect to CompuServe running WinCIM as a telnet client to compuserve.com. It even lets you connect using a 56 kilobaud T1.

You can use WinCIM as a telnet client to compuserve.com by using COM*t* by Performance Systems (covered in Chapter 10). Use the COM*t*

Communications Port to telnet redirection utility. It lets you use any Windows asynchronous communications application as a telnet client on a WinSock 1.1 stack/connection.

A WinSock-compliant version of WinCIM lets the Internet user have WinCIM connected to CompuServe with all the benefits of CIS, and maintain links to the Internet. For example, you can run AIR Mosaic, WS_FTP, Hampson's Gopher, play a game of WinDoom, or finger microsoft.com.

- *Extended font support* — You can change the default Terminal font in WinCIM by accessing the General Preferences dialog box and clicking on the Fonts button.

- *Event sound support* — You can now associate sounds (WAV files) with WinCIM events (such as connecting, file transfer completion, and so on). Use the Windows Control Panel sound module to add and remove sounds.

WinCIM is supported on the WCIMSUP forum, which is free of on-line charges.

System Requirements

WinCIM Version 1.3.1, included with this book, requires

- At least 2MB of RAM (preferably more)
- Microsoft Windows Version 3.1, running in enhanced mode.
- 6MB of free disk space

A Hayes-compatible modem is recommended. (Also see the next chapter for information about using WinCIM with COM*t*.)

Connecting to CompuServe

You can connect using WinCIM, or using a terminal emulation program. WinCIM includes a terminal emulation program.

Connecting using WinCIM

The Connect to CompuServe dialog box lets you connect to CompuServe when you start up WinCIM without having to access WinCIM's initial desktop. To get here, choose File⇨Connect.

WinCIM displays the Connect to CompuServe dialog box the first time you start WinCIM. If you prefer, you can click on the large icon on the left to connect to CompuServe. It does the same thing as the Connect button to the right. This dialog box has the following controls:

Connect button — Connects you to CompuServe.

Continue button — Closes the dialog box without connecting you to CompuServe. If you modify the Show at Startup option and then click on the Continue button, WinCIM records your modification before closing the dialog box.

Show at Startup check box — If this check box is marked, WinCIM displays this dialog box for you each time you start up WinCIM.

Connecting using terminal emulation

The Terminal Emulation dialog box connects to CompuServe or to another host-based computer system using terminal emulation. To get here, select Special⇨Terminal Emulation.

Make sure the Manual Connect check box is not marked if you want to connect using the information recorded in your Session Settings dialog box. Click the Connect button to start the connection procedure.

WinCIM Menu Selections

Here is a brief explanation of the WinCIM menu commands. Many of them have toolbar counterparts, too.

File menu

The File menu has these commands:

New — Brings up your Windows Notepad, where you can create a text file.

Open — Lets you open a text or GIF file in Notepad.

Save — Saves information displayed in a text box, such as a forum or mail message or news article, into a file on your computer's hard disk or a floppy disk.

Save As — Saves information displayed in a text box, such as a forum or mail message or news article, into a file on your computer's hard disk or a floppy disk, with a name you choose.

Print — Lets you print information displayed in a text box, such as news articles and file abstracts, forum and mail messages, and so on.

Print Settings — Lets you modify your printer settings.

Leave — Exits an on-line area, such as a service or forum, without disconnecting you from CompuServe, and returns you to the Information Manager's initial desktop.

Disconnect — Disconnects you from CompuServe and returns you to the Information Manager's initial desktop.

Exit — Disconnects you from CompuServe and then exits the Information Manager.

Edit menu

The Edit menu has these commands:

Undo — Cancels your most recent editing action.

Cut — Moves a block of selected text from a forum or mail message you are composing into the Clipboard, overwriting whatever is there. Cut is useful when you want to move a portion of text from one place to another in your document, or from one document to another. Because the contents of Cut remain in the Clipboard even after you exit the Information Manager, you can use Cut to move text from one application to another.

Copy — Copies a block of selected text from an Information Manager text box, such as a news article or weather report or message composition box into the Clipboard, overwriting whatever is there. Copy is useful when you want to duplicate certain text in various parts of your document.

Paste — Inserts Clipboard text into a forum or mail message you are composing, at the current cursor position. Paste is usually used in conjunction with Cut and Copy, although it can also be used to insert text that was in the Clipboard before you started WinCIM.

Clear — Deletes selected text without writing it to the Clipboard. Undo can retrieve cleared text if used immediately after Clear.

Wordwrap — Enables or disables whether the words you type in text windows wrap to the next line without having to press Enter.

Select All — Selects all of the text in the active text window.

Fixed Font — Lets you control the appearance of type in your Information Manager windows.

Paste From... — Lets you specify the location of text to be pasted into a forum or mail message. You can paste your text from a text file on a disk or from an entry in your Filing Cabinet, In Basket, or Out Basket.

Copy To... — Lets you copy your selected text to a forum or mail message.

Help menu

The Help menu has these commands:

Contents — Lists help topics from which you can learn more about the Information Manager.

Search for Help on... — Lets you search for help on a particular topic. You provide a term for which you want help; the help system shows matching topics.

How to Use Help — Tells you how to use the help system.

CompuServe Directory — Lists categories from which you can learn about each service and forum.

About CIM... — Displays the Information Manager About WinCIM dialog box, which contains the version number of WinCIM you are using, the date and Port ID of your last access, and the amount of disk space available on your microcomputer.

Window menu

The Window menu has the following commands:

Tile — Displays windows on your desktop so that each window is the same size and the windows are displayed side by side.

Cascade — Arranges windows on your desktop in a layered, cascading fashion.

Arrange Icons — Rearranges the icons on your desktop into neat rows and columns.

Close All — Closes all windows on your desktop.

Mail menu

The Mail menu has these commands:

Get New Mail — Lets you read and delete mail messages or transfer them to your In Basket. If you are not connected to CompuServe, this command tries to make a connection.

Create Mail... — Lets you compose and address a mail message. The Recipient List dialog box appears; use it to assign recipient and carbon copies information from your Address Book. From there, access the Create Mail dialog box, where you compose the text of your message.

Send/Receive All... — Lets you send your outgoing Out Basket messages, as well as retrieve your incoming CompuServe mailbox messages into your In Basket.

Search New Mail... — Lets you search for messages in your mailbox.

Send File... — Lets you send a text or binary file to any CompuServe member. The Recipient List dialog box appears; use it to assign recipient and carbon copies information from your Address Book. From there, access the Send File Message dialog box, where you provide summary information about the file you are sending.

In Basket — Opens your In Basket, where you can read, edit, delete, forward, and reply to messages. This command also appears on the Mail menu on the initial desktop, the Special menu in CB, ENS, and Terminal Emulation, and the Messages menu in a forum.

Out Basket — Opens your Out Basket, where you can process your outgoing mail and forum messages. This command also appears on the Mail menu on the initial desktop, the Special menu in CB, ENS, and Terminal Emulation, and the Messages menu in a forum.

Filing Cabinet... — Opens your Filing Cabinet, where you can access, create, or remove folders and files stored there. This command also appears on the Mail menu on the initial desktop, the Special menu in CB, ENS, and Terminal Emulation, and the Messages menu in a forum.

Address Book — Opens your Address Book, where you can access, modify, add, and remove entries. This command appears on the Mail menu on the initial desktop, the Special menu in CB, ENS, and Terminal Emulation, and the Messages menu in a forum.

Forum Message menu

The Forum Message menu has the following commands:

Member Directory — Lets you find out information about other CompuServe members.

Browse — Lets you choose a forum section and learn and read the various section topics.

Search — Lets you find the messages you want. You provide a topic keyword, user ID, or message number, and the Information Manager looks for messages that match your information.

Get Waiting — Lists unread messages addressed to you. When no messages wait for you, this command is dimmed. It is unavailable if you are not a member of the forum.

Retrieve Marked... — Lets you retrieve all the messages you marked during your forum session. This command is unavailable if you have not marked any messages during your forum session.

Set Date... — Lets you decide the oldest message to be included in your forum session.

Create Forum Message — Lets you compose a forum message without being connected to CompuServe.

Create Message — The same as Create Forum Message.

Messages Notice — Lists message board announcements from the forum's sysop.

Messages Descriptions — Shows a brief summary of message board functions.

Freshen Messages — Shows any changes that have occurred on the message board since you entered the forum.

Forum Conference menu

The Forum Conference menu has these commands:

Enter Room — Enters a conference.

Who's Here... — Lists members currently in the forum and lets you start a private conversation.

Set Nickname... — Changes your conference name.

Ignore... — Blocks conversation, for whatever reason, from people you specify.

Invite... — Invites others to join a private group.

Notice — Lists any conference announcements.

Descriptions — Displays conference room function summaries.

Terminal Emulation Mode menu

The Terminal Emulation Mode menu has the following commands:

Special View Buffer — Reviews your recent on-line activities.

View Terminal — Exits the capture buffer and returns you to wherever you were before.

Record on Printer — Toggles your CompuServe dialog box's printing state. The first time you choose this command, the Information Manager prints the subsequent dialog box between you and CompuServe — everything you type and everything CompuServe displays. When you choose this command again, printing stops.

Record in File — Toggles your terminal logging state. The first time you choose this command, the Information Manager records your subsequent terminal emulation activity — everything you type and everything CompuServe displays — in a special file on your computer. When you choose this command again, logging stops.

Set Function Keys... — Lets you assign certain key combinations and special instructions to your function keys.

Clear Buffer — Empties your capture buffer.

General Usage

Ribbons

The desktop ribbon shows pictures of services and features that you might use frequently. To customize ribbon icons and their actions, choose Special⇨Preferences⇨Ribbon. The ribbon's appearance depends upon whether you are on-line with CompuServe.

The Modem button appears on the ribbon when you issue a command involving a transfer of data between your computer and CompuServe. The number above Cancel is the number of seconds WinCIM waits before canceling the command if no data is received in that time. You can also click on the Modem button to deliberately cancel the transfer.

Figure 9-2 shows the ribbon as it looks when you're not connected to CompuServe.

Figure 9-2: WinCIM's off-line ribbon.

While you are connected to CompuServe, WinCIM keeps track of your connect time, displaying it on the ribbon for the duration of your Information Manager session, as shown in Figure 9-3. If you disconnect from CompuServe without exiting WinCIM, and then reconnect to CompuServe, the counter continues to accumulate connect time. The ribbon also displays the word *Basic* or *Extended* above the connect time to reflect which type of service you are using at the time.

Figure 9-3: WinCIM's on-line ribbon.

The following table describes ribbon icons.

Icon	*Command*	*Function*
♥	Favorite Places	Launches the Favorite Places dialog box.
	Find	Launches the Find dialog box, where you can search for CompuServe services.
	Top	Brings up CompuServe's top-level services.
	Go	Launches a Go dialog box, from which you can access services by name.
	Quotes	Launches a Stock Quotes dialog box, in which you can get stock quotes from a personalized list of ticker symbols.
	Weather	Launches the Weather dialog box, in which you can get weather forecasts from around the world.
	In Basket	Brings up your In Basket, in which you can process your incoming messages.
	Out Basket	Brings up your Out Basket, in which you can process your outgoing mail and forum messages.
	Filing Cabinet	Brings up your Filing Cabinet, in which you can access, create, and remove folders and files.

(continued)

(continued)

Icon	Command	Function
	Address Book	Opens your Address Book.
EXIT	Exit	Disconnects you from CompuServe and exits WinCIM.
	Help	Gives you interactive WinCIM help. Equivalent to pressing F1.

Going directly to a service

The Go dialog box enables you to access a service quickly, but you must know the unique term for that service to type in the Go dialog box. To see the Go dialog box, choose Services⇨Go or click the ribbon's Go icon.

Type the unique service name in the box beside Service, such as WINNEW for the Windows New Users forum or HELP for the Member Support area on CompuServe. Then click OK. WinCIM brings up the service.

You can consult the CompuServe Directory (choose Help⇨CompuServe Directory) to learn a service or forum's service name. You can also list all CompuServe service and forum service names from the Go dialog box; type **QUICK** in the box beside Service, and click OK.

You can also go directly to a service from some other dialog boxes: the Search Results dialog box, after conducting a Find; a Favorite Places dialog box, if the service happens to be one of the services listed there; or a Display Menu dialog box, if you are browsing services.

Types of services and browsing

The Services window (Figure 9-4) is a pictorial menu of the major service categories on CompuServe. Just click an icon to access a list of services in that category. You see the Services window automatically when you start up WinCIM if the Browse option in the General Preferences dialog box has been set.

Basic Services — Brings up CompuServe's basic services, a basic group of the most popular CompuServe services, priced at a standard flat monthly rate. This means that you pay no connect time charges, no matter how much you use these services, although you do incur surcharges for connecting through some communications networks in some locations.

Figure 9-4: The Services window.

News — Contains a global news clipping service, business news, feature stories, sports scores and interviews, public and aviation weather, and even Hollywood gossip.

Magazines — Gives you access to electronic newsletters, computer magazines, electronic publishing forums, and more.

Communicate — Contains information on products that enable you to communicate with other CompuServe members. You can use CompuServe mail to send messages to specific people, forums to participate in discussions on specific topics, CB to type in real time with other CompuServe members around the world, and the CompuServe Classifieds to post ads.

Computers — Gives you support for virtually any software or computer on the market. Support includes direct links to software and hardware companies, libraries of on-line information and forums of knowledgeable users willing to help you solve your problems. Any time of day, you can logon and communicate with someone on-line or post messages, which are answered within 24 hours typically.

Reference — Accesses an extensive reference library that lets you gather vast amounts of current and historical information quickly and efficiently. The section includes large databases comprised of demographic information; articles from periodicals; directories of products, manufacturers, and households; trademark and legal information; government proceedings, information, and statistics; and consumer information.

Sports — Gives you fast-breaking sports news, information about sports medicine, and more. You can discuss your favorite sports topics in a number of sports-related forums.

Professional — Describes forums that enable professionals to exchange ideas and information with others in the same field. People interested in the law, medicine, business management, and other professional fields will find a forum to suit their professional interests.

Finance — Gives you an overview of the services that can help you with your financial interests. Though tailored for the individual investor, CompuServe's financial services are also used by many Wall Street firms. You can obtain quotes on stock prices, find information about companies and buy and sell securities. CompuServe invites you to use the H&R Block ticker symbol to practice and see the type of information each product provides. Type HRB at most company or issue prompts and get live information without a surcharge.

Health — Gives you relevant health information and access to forums pertaining to a range of health-related topics. Keep up-to-date with drug information, fitness, diseases, disabilities, and more.

Education — Gives you access to forums for education-related topics, such as computer training, education research, and foreign languages, as well as an electronic encyclopedia and information about colleges and universities.

Travel — Gives you air, hotel, car, tour, and cruise information. In addition, U.S. domestic and international information is available.

Shopping — Contains the CompuServe products that let you shop in the comfort of your own home. Depending on the merchant, you can order from on-line catalogs or have print catalogs sent to your home.

Home/Leisure — Contains information on diverse interests and hobbies, such as food, wine, genealogy, sailing, stamp collecting, pets, fishing, and health.

Fun & Games — Contains many different types of games. Some games are for one player against the computer. For others, like MegaWars I and III, you interact with other players, either as allies or enemies.

Entertainment — Contains entertainment services, such as Hollywood happenings, movie reviews, entertainment forums, and even an Entertainment Center.

Member Service — Helps you find your way around the CompuServe
Information Service. It provides information such as billing, logging on,
ordering and operating rules.

Mail

CompuServe includes an extensive electronic mail facility.

Sending mail

Creating a mail message

The Create Mail dialog box (Figure 9-5) lets you compose a mail message. To get
here, execute Mail⇨Create Mail, and complete the Recipient List dialog box that
appears.

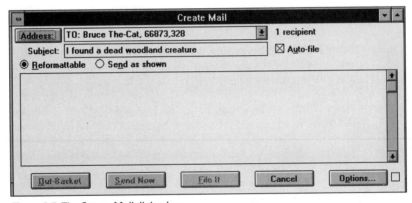

Figure 9-5: The Create Mail dialog box.

This dialog box has the following controls:

Address button — Brings up the Recipient List dialog box, in which you
assign recipient information. Your recipient address information appears in
the field to the right of the Address button after you click OK in the
Recipient List dialog box. TO: refers to the primary recipient., CC: refers to
a carbon copy recipient, and BC: refers to a blind copy recipient. You must
specify an address.

Subject: field — Type a descriptive word or phrase for the message. You must complete this field.

Auto-file check box — When this box is checked, and you send your message, WinCIM files a copy of your message in your Filing Cabinet.

Reformattable radio button — This button lets the message text wrap to the recipient's screen width.

Send as shown radio button — This button preserves your message's text format when the recipient reads it.

Untitled entry — Type or paste the body of your message (up to 50,000 characters) here. If this entry is incomplete, you can store the message in your Out Basket or Filing Cabinet, to be completed later.

Out Basket button — This button copies the message to your Out Basket and closes this dialog box. Available only when address, subject, and message text are supplied.

Send Now button — This button transmits your message. WinCIM connects you to CompuServe if you are not already connected. Available only when address, subject, and message text are supplied.

File It button — This button brings up the Filing Cabinet dialog box, in which you copy the message to your Filing Cabinet. Available only when address and subject are supplied.

Cancel button — This button cancels the message and closes the Create Mail dialog box.

Options... button — This button brings up a Message Options dialog box, in which you choose some options for your message.

Message options

The Message Options dialog box gives you some processing options for your outgoing CompuServe mail messages. To get here, create mail with Mail⇨Create Mail, and click the Options... button. This dialog box has the following controls:

Receipt check box — Mark this to receive confirmation when a recipient reads your message.

Reply Requested check box — Mark this to request a reply when a recipient reads your message. (Text and location vary from system to system.)

Importance selection button — Select the importance level for your message. Some systems deliver messages of high importance first.

Sensitivity selection button — Select the sensitivity level for your message.

Release Date: entry — Type the date on which you want CompuServe to send the message. The default is the current date.

Expiration Date: entry — Optionally, type a date for the message to be removed from the recipient's mailbox.

Sender Pays radio button — Mark this if you want the sender to be responsible for any sending surcharges.

Split Charges radio button — Mark this if you want to split the surcharge for sending and receiving messages.

Receiver Pays radio button — Mark this if you want the receiver to be responsible for any sending surcharges.

Addressing mail

The Recipient List dialog box (Figure 9-6) assigns recipient information to a mail message that you are creating. To see this dialog box, execute Mail⇨Create Mail or Mail⇨Send File.

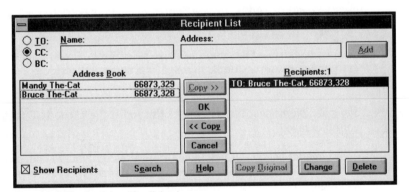

Figure 9-6: The Recipient List dialog box.

TO: radio button — Select this to identify a primary recipient. Every message must have at least one primary recipient.

CC: radio button — Select this to identify a carbon copy recipient.

BC: radio button — Select this to identify a blind copy recipient. Blind copy recipients receive a copy of your message but are not mentioned in any corresponding distribution list.

Name: entry — When the recipient is not already in your Address Book, type the recipient's name as you want it to appear on the message. Click the Add button to record Name and Address information under Recipients. If the recipient is already an entry in your Address Book, skip the Name and Address entries, and instead highlight the appropriate Address Book entry and click the Copy button.

Address: entry — When the recipient is not already in your Address Book, type the recipient's electronic mailing address. Select Add to record Name and Address information under Recipients. If the recipient is already an entry in your Address Book, skip the Name and Address entries, and instead highlight the appropriate Address Book entry, and click the Copy button.

Address Book entry — These are your Address Book entries. To use an entry as a message recipient, highlight it and click Copy.

Add button — Records Name and Address information under Recipients.

Delete button — Removes the highlighted entry under Recipients.

Copy>> button — Adds the highlighted Address Book entry to the Recipients list.

Copy << button — Adds the highlighted Recipients entry to the Address Book.

Recipients: entry — Lists your message's recipients. If you want to add an entry to your Address Book, highlight the entry and click the <<Copy button.

Show Recipients check box — Check this to list the TO and CC recipients in your message.

Copy Original button — Click this button when replying to a message to send the reply to each original message recipient. Unless you are replying to a message, Copy Original is unavailable.

Change button — Moves the highlighted Recipients entry to the Name and Address boxes, where you can edit the information.

Search button — Brings up a Search Member Directory dialog box where you can search the CompuServe Membership Directory for member addresses. You can add the member addresses directly to the Recipient List dialog box.

Selecting an address

The Select Address dialog box lists CompuServe members who meet your search criteria. These are the names and addresses that meet your search criteria. This dialog box has these controls:

Select button — Records the highlighted information in the Name and Address boxes in the Recipient List dialog box.

Open button — Brings up a Member Information dialog box where you can learn more about the highlighted entry and then add the name and address to the Recipient List dialog box if you still want to.

Searching for CompuServe members

The Search Member Directory dialog box (Figure 9-7) searches the CompuServe Member Directory for member information. To get here, choose Mail⇨Member Directory, or click the Search button in the Recipient List dialog box.

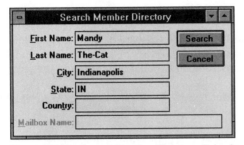

Figure 9-7: The Search Member Directory dialog box.

This dialog box has the following controls:

First Name: entry — If you know the person's first name, type it here. Unless you are sure of the name, you might want to leave this blank, as the person might have used a nickname when registering.

Last Name: entry — If you know the person's last name, type it here.

City: entry — If you know the city the person is registered in, type it here.

State: entry — If you know the state the person is registered in, type it here.

Country: entry — If you know the country the person is registered in, type it here.

Mailbox Name: entry — If you know the person's electronic mailing address, type it here.

Click Search to begin your search. If you accessed this dialog box by choosing Mail⇨Member Directory, Search brings up a Membership Search Results dialog box. If you accessed this dialog box by selecting Search from the Recipient List dialog box, you go instead to a Select Address dialog box.

Sending a file

The Send File Message dialog box lets you send a text or binary file that is stored on disk as a CompuServe mail message. To see this dialog box, execute Mail⇨Send File, and complete the Recipient List dialog box that appears. The Send File Message dialog box has these controls:

Address button — Brings up a Recipient List dialog box, in which you can assign recipient information.

Address entry — Use the Recipient List dialog box to complete this entry. Your recipient address information appears here after you click OK. TO: refers to the primary recipient, CC: refers to a carbon copy recipient, and BC: refers to a blind copy recipient. You must complete this entry.

Subject: entry — Type a descriptive word or phrase for your file. You must complete this entry.

Options button — Brings up a Message Options dialog box, in which you can assign some additional options to your message.

File button — Brings up a standard Windows Open dialog box, in which you can select a file from disk.

File entry — Specify a pathname for the file to send, either by typing it here or using the File button.

Text/Binary radio button — Mark this appropriately if the file is a binary file or text file. Text means that the recipient will see this file as an ASCII message.

GIF radio button — Mark this when sending a GIF file.

JPEG radio button — Mark this when sending a JPEG file.

Additional Information: entry — Type a comment, if you wish. Recipients will see your comment before retrieving your file message.

Out Basket button — Copies the message to your Out Basket and closes this dialog box. Unless you specify the appropriate information at this dialog box, Out Basket is not a valid selection.

Send Now button — Transmits your message. WinCIM tries to connect you to CompuServe if you are not already connected. Unless you specify the appropriate information at this dialog box, Send Now is not a valid selection.

Cancel button — Closes the dialog box without sending the file.

Receiving mail

Getting new mail

The Get New Mail dialog box lists mail messages waiting for you. To get here, choose Mail⇨Get New Mail. This dialog box has these controls:

Subject: entry — Tells what each message is about.

Name: entry — Tells who sent the message.

Size: entry — Tells how large the message is.

Get button — Displays the message associated with the highlighted entry. A Message dialog box appears. See the section "Reading and processing a mail message."

Get All — Moves all messages in your mailbox to the In Basket and closes the Get New Mail dialog box.

Delete — Removes the highlighted entry from the mailbox.

Undelete — Cancels the action when you have removed one or more entries from your mailbox without closing the Get New Mail dialog box. Undelete causes each previously deleted entry to reappear as an entry.

Depending on the kind of mail you have in your mailbox, WinCIM might display some message-related information here.

Reading and processing a mail message

The Message dialog box displays a CompuServe mail message. To get here, select Mail⇨Get New Mail and complete the Get New Mail dialog box, as described in the section "Getting new mail." This dialog box has the following controls:

Address button — Brings up an Add to Address Book dialog box, in which you can add the recipient list to your Address Book.

Address entry — When the message has more than one recipient, this entry lists them. It does not list blind copy recipients. If the message is addressed only to you, this box is empty.

From button — Brings up an Add to Address Book dialog box, in which you can save the sender's name and electronic mailing address in your Address Book.

Receipt check box — When marked, the sender receives a message stating that you have read the message.

Reply Requested check box — When this check box is marked, WinCIM asks you to reply to the message.

Priority check box — When this check box is marked, the message has high priority, and precedes lower priority messages in your mailbox.

In Basket button — Copies the message into your In Basket and brings up the Get New Mail dialog box. See the section "Getting new mail."

File It button — Brings up a Filing Cabinet box, in which you can copy the message to your Filing Cabinet.

Reply button — Brings up a Create Mail dialog box, in which you can compose and send a return message. See the section "Message options."

Forward button — Brings up a Create Mail dialog box, in which you can forward the message to one or more recipients, and type a note to introduce the forwarded message. See the section "Message options."

Delete button — This button removes the message from your mailbox.

Searching your mail

The Search New Mail dialog box finds mail messages in your mailbox that meet your search criteria. You can search by sender, subject, sensitivity, priority, or date. You get here by choosing Mail⇨Search New Mail. This dialog box has these controls:

From button — Brings up a Select Entry from Address Book dialog box, where you can select the address you want to search for. After you make your selection, WinCIM fills in the electronic mailing address in the box at the right. If you want to search for a particular electronic mailing address, type the address here. If you use From to select your search address, WinCIM puts it here.

Subject: entry — If you want to search for messages by their subject wording, type a word or phrase that makes up the subject you want to search for. Every word you specify must be part of the actual message subject for WinCIM to find the message.

Normal radio button — Select this if you want to search for messages of normal sensitivity only.

Personal radio button — Select this if you want to search for messages of personal sensitivity only.

All radio button — Select this if you want to search for messages regardless of sensitivity.

Sensitivity selection button — Select the sensitivity level for the messages you want to search for: Normal, Personal, Private, Confidential, or All.

Importance selection button — Select the importance level for the messages you want to search for: Low, Normal, High, or All. If you want to restrict your search to a date frame, type the oldest date here or type the most recent date here.

Search button — Conducts the search. WinCIM brings up a Get New Mail dialog box where you can view the messages that meet your search criteria. See the section "Getting new mail" for more information. If you think WinCIM should have found a message when it did not, you may want to double-check your search criteria.

Sending and receiving mail automatically

The Send and Receive All Mail dialog box automates your sending and receiving of mail. You get here by choosing Mail⇨Send/Receive All Mail. This dialog box has these controls:

Send Forum Messages from Out Basket check box — Mark this if you want WinCIM to send any forum messages stored in your Out Basket in addition to mail messages.

Disconnect when Done check box — Mark this if you want WinCIM to disconnect from CompuServe after sending and retrieving all messages.

OK button — Sends any outgoing mail in your Out Basket and retrieves any incoming mail that is waiting at your CompuServe mailbox, placing it in your In Basket. OK connects you to CompuServe if you are not already connected.

Cancel button — Closes the dialog box without sending or retrieving any messages.

Filing a message or a reply

The Filing Cabinet dialog box refiles a mail message that is already stored in your Filing Cabinet. It also files copies of your replies to forum and mail messages, as well as messages and ENS stories. To get here, execute Mail⇨Create Mail or Mail⇨Get New Mail and click the File It button. See the sections "Creating a mail message" and "Reading and processing a mail message" for information about these commands.

This dialog box lists your Filing Cabinet's folders. Highlight the one in which you want to file your message or story and select Store. If you want to create a new folder, select New. This dialog box has these controls:

Move radio button — Mark this if you want to put your reply into your Filing Cabinet to deal with later. If Move is selected and you select Store, the dialog box from which you requested the filing operation is automatically closed.

Copy radio button — Mark this if you want to make a copy of your reply and store it in your Filing Cabinet. If Copy is selected and you select Store, WinCIM returns you to the dialog box you were at before you requested the filing operation.

Store button — Moves or copies your reply to the highlighted folder and closes this dialog box. In this example, Auto-Filed is the folder that would be used.

New button — Brings up an Add New Folder dialog box, where you can create a folder.

Cancel button — Closes the dialog box without filing your message or story.

The Address Book

The Address Book lets you keep track of people with whom you correspond. Address Book entries are listed in alphabetical order by last name. You can make both individual and group entries. "Beth" is an individual entry. "Congressionals" is a group entry composed of three individual entries. To get here, select Mail⇨Address Book. The Address Book has these controls:

Add button — Lets you add an entry. See the section "Adding an entry."

Add Group button — Lets you create a group and specify group members.

Change button — Displays the highlighted entry for you to review or modify.

Delete button — Removes the highlighted entry.

Adding an entry

The Add to Address Book dialog box creates an entry in your Address Book. To get here, click Add in the Address Book dialog box. This dialog box has these controls:

Name: entry — Type or edit the name of the entry as you want it to appear. When you add an entry from a mail or forum message, the sender's name as shown on the message appears here.

Address: entry — Type or edit the electronic mailing address for the entry. When you add an entry from a mail or forum message, the sender's address appears here.

Comments: entry — Type a comment or two if you like.

The Change Entry in Address Book dialog box displays an Address Book entry so that you can review or modify it.

Adding groups

The Add Group to Address Book dialog box lists the entries in your Address Book so that you can combine one or more of them into convenient group entries. The Update Group dialog box displays a list of your CB friends for you to review or modify.

To get here, click Add Group in the Address Book dialog box. This dialog box has these controls:

Group Name: entry — Type the name of the address group you want to create. The entries currently in the address group you type are listed here.

Add button — Brings up a Select Entries from Address Book dialog box, where you can add entry information from your Address Book to the address group.

Delete button — Removes the highlighted entry from the address group.

Preferences, Parameters, and Settings ___

Modem control settings

The Modem Control Strings dialog box (Figure 9-8) lists your current modem parameters and lets you modify them. To get here, execute Special⇔Session Settings and click the Modem button in the dialog box that appears.

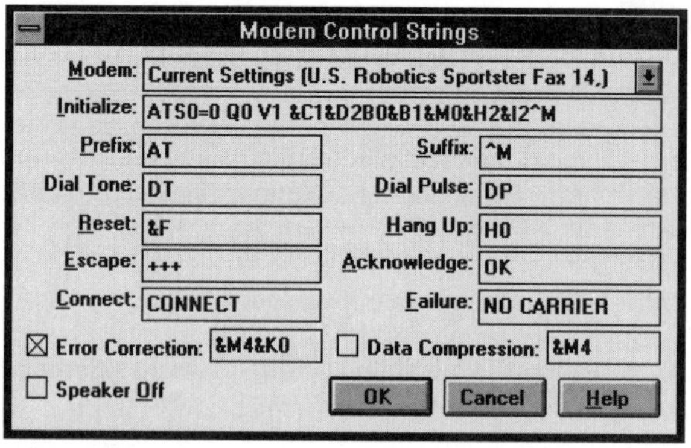

Figure 9-8: The Modem Control Strings dialog box.

This dialog box has these controls:

Modem: entry — Highlight your modem type in the list provided. If your modem type is not in the list and is Hayes-compatible, highlight Hayes. If this does not work, highlight Other.

Initialize: entry — Type your modem's initialization command string. If you highlight a modem in the list provided in the box beside Modem, that modem's initialization command string appears. Some modems require control characters in their control strings. WinCIM's notation for a control character is a caret circumflex (^) followed by the control character letter. For example, ^M is the notation for Ctrl+M, or carriage return.

Prefix: entry — Make sure that this is the correct prefix string, also known as the attention command.

Dial Tone: entry — Make sure that this is the correct string to initiate tone dialing.

Reset: entry — Make sure that this is the correct string to reset the modem.

Escape: entry — Make sure that this is the correct string to issue an Escape command.

Connect: entry — Make sure that this is the correct string or phrase displayed when connection is established.

Speaker Off check box — Mark this if you desire a silent operation (no dial tone, dialing, and connection sounds during logon) of a Hayes-compatible modem.

Suffix: entry — Make sure that this is the correct string to terminate a command.

Dial Pulse: entry — Make sure that this is the correct string to initiate pulse dialing.

Hang Up: entry — Make sure that this is the correct string to free the telephone line.

Acknowledge: entry — Make sure that this is the correct string or phrase displayed when a command is successfully received by the modem.

Failure: entry — Make sure that this is the correct string to or phrase to be displayed when there is no connection or the signal stops.

Error Correction check box — Mark this if you want to use error correction. Depending on the modem you have selected, the appropriate error correction command appears here. However, if you selected a modem for which information is not available, consult your modem's documentation to learn what to enter here.

Data Compression check box — Mark this if you want to use data compression. Depending on the modem you have selected, the appropriate data compression command appears here. However, if you selected a modem for which information is not available, consult your modem's documentation to learn what to enter here.

General preferences

The General Preferences dialog box displays your current Information Manager initial desktop options and preferences so that you can review or modify them. To get here, choose Special⇨Preferences⇨General. This dialog box has these controls:

About Box check box — Mark this if you want the About Box dialog box to be displayed each time you start WinCIM.

Browse check box — Mark this if you want the Services window to appear each time you start WinCIM.

Favorite Places check box — Mark this if you want the Favorite Places dialog box to appear each time you start WinCIM.

Prompt for Unsent Msgs check box — Mark this if you want WinCIM to remind you to send any mail in your Out Basket before you exit, or to send any forum messages that are in your Out Basket each time you leave a forum.

Show Graphic Menus check box — Mark this if you want WinCIM to display graphic menus for services rather than text menus, when graphic menus are available. Graphic menus have graphics, such as a company logo and one or more icons, that you can click on as menu selections.

Set Function Keys button — Brings up a Function Key Settings dialog box where you can assign a sequence of keystrokes to your function keys.

Support: entry — Type the directory in which you want to store WinCIM's support files, such as where you want to store the Filing Cabinet and Address Book.

Scripts: entry — Type the directory in which you want to store WinCIM's script files. WinCIM provides a number of these files which contain commands to automate routine functions such as connection and disconnection from CompuServe. You can learn more about scripts in the WinCIM Support forum on CompuServe.

Graphics: entry — Type the directory in which you want to store any GIF files you download. GIF files are graphics files that you can view and find in some forums and services on CompuServe. For example, certain weather maps are GIF files.

Cabinet: entry — Type the directory in which you want to store your Filing Cabinet files.

Fonts button — Brings up a Fonts dialog box, in which you can modify the fonts WinCIM uses to display information on your monitor.

Accesses radio button — Select this if you want the entries in your Favorite Places dialog box to appear according to their access frequency. In other words, the entry that you access most frequently is listed first, and the entry that you access least frequently is listed last.

Alphabetic radio button — Select this if you want the entries in your Favorite Places dialog box to appear in alphabetical order.

None radio button — Select this if you want your Favorite Places entries to appear in the order in which you add them.

Play Sounds check box — Mark this if you want to have certain WinCIM events accompanied by sounds that you specify. You specify the sounds that you want in the Sounds module of your Windows Control Panel. Your Windows Control Panel is probably in a folder called MAIN, although it could be elsewhere if you have rearranged or reorganized your Windows desktop.

Always Ask for File Name check box — Mark this if you want WinCIM to always prompt you for a destination filename whenever you mark or retrieve a file. The alternative is the forum filename.

Download: entry — Type the directory in which you want to store nongraphics files that you download.

Prompt for Unsaved Graphics check box — Mark this if you want WinCIM to prompt you about saving graphics that you view in your Graphics window. If Prompt for Unsaved Graphics is set and you attempt to close your Graphics window without saving the graphics image, WinCIM asks for confirmation before closing the window.

Changing your display font

The Fonts dialog box gives you some font-related options with respect to the way WinCIM displays text on your screen. To get here, select Special⇨Preferences⇨General and click the Fonts button in the dialog box that appears. This dialog box has these controls:

Dialogs radio button — Mark this to select a font for items in WinCIM dialog boxes.

Listbox Fixed radio button — Mark this to select a font for list menus displayed by WinCIM.

Editbox radio button — Mark this to select the font for Information Manager text boxes when a proportional font is required.

Editbox Fixed radio button — Mark this to select the font for Information Manager text boxes when a fixed font is required.

Printer radio button — Mark this to select a font for printing text that is displayed in a proportional font.

Printer Fixed radio button — Mark this to select a font for printing text that is displayed in a fixed font.

Terminal radio button — Mark this to select the font to be used when in Terminal Emulation.

Select button — Brings up a standard Windows Font dialog box where you can select a font, style, size, and so forth.

Default button — Returns all font settings to the default settings that originally came with WinCIM.

Mail preferences

The Mail Preferences dialog box displays your current mail options and preferences so that you can review or modify them. To get here, choose Special⇨Preferences⇨Mail. This dialog box has these controls:

Delete Retrieved Mail check box — Mark this if you want WinCIM to automatically delete mail messages from your on-line mailbox after you read them or retrieve them to your In Basket.

File Outgoing Messages check box — Mark this if you want WinCIM to automatically save copies of all outgoing mail messages to the specified Filing Cabinet folder. In this example, Auto-Filed is the name of the specified Filing Cabinet folder. However, you can specify any folder by typing its name in the box beside Folder.

Folder: entry — Used in conjunction with File Outgoing Messages, you can specify a Filing Cabinet folder here to store your filed messages. If you modify the folder name, messages previously saved will remain in the old folder, while messages subsequently saved will go to the new folder.

Do not retrieve radio button — When this button is selected and you choose Mail⇨Get New Mail, WinCIM retrieves only messages for which no postage is due.

Always retrieve — If this option is selected and you choose Get New Mail from the Mail menu, WinCIM will retrieve all messages from your mailbox, including those for which there is postage due.

Delete without retrieving — If this option is selected and you choose Get New Mail from the Mail menu, WinCIM will delete any messages for which there is postage due without retrieving or preserving them.

Terminal emulation preferences

The Terminal Preferences dialog box controls the size of your Terminal Emulation capture buffer. To get here, choose Special⇨Preferences⇨Terminal Emulation. This dialog box has the following controls:

Number of Buffer Lines: entry — Type the number of lines you want WinCIM to allot in its capture buffer before starting to overwrite them. You must specify a value of 20 or greater.

OK button — Records your changes and closes this dialog box. This button is available only when the value specified in the box beside Number of Buffer Lines is 20 or greater.

Cancel button — Closes the dialog box without recording any of your changes.

Strip High Bit check box — Mark this if you want to access CompuServe through any communications network other than CompuServe's own network. After you connect to CompuServe, if you want to access a service that uses extended characters — characters with accents, umlauts, and so forth — unmark Strip High Bit to ensure that such characters will be interpreted and displayed properly.

Function key settings

The Function Key Settings dialog box customizes your WinCIM session. You can assign a series of keystrokes or commands that you use frequently to up to ten Alt key combinations. If you wish, type a label for the Alt key combination. Whenever the key combination is available to you in WinCIM, you will see the label you assigned, rather than the default Alt+ wording that appears at the bottom of your screen.

Type the sequence of keystrokes you wish to automate (up to 80 characters). Type **^M** for a carriage return, and **^J** for a new line. For example, you could assign this to the Alt+4 Function key combination: **Morning, all! Anybody up for a chat? ^M^J.** Once assigned, you could send that greeting each time you entered a channel in CB by pressing or clicking on Alt+4. Similarly, you could assign **EF OH ^M^J** to the Alt+5 key combination in order to automate requesting an extended weather forecast for Ohio in the Weather service.

Session settings

The Setup Session Settings dialog box shows your current connection information, such as your User ID number or baud rate, so that you can review or modify it. To get here, choose Special⇨Session Settings. This dialog box has these controls:

Name: entry — Type your real name as opposed to your handle or nickname.

Network: selection button — Highlight the network you want WinCIM to use to connect to CompuServe. If you select Direct under Dial Type, there is no need to specify a network.

Baud Rate: selection button — Highlight the baud rate you wish to use. Make sure your modem supports the baud rate you select.

Redial Attempts: entry — Type the number of times your modem will attempt to redial if the first attempt to connect fails. A reasonable value is 10. If you select Direct under Dial Type, you don't need to specify retries.

Phone: entry — Type the CompuServe local access telephone number.

Session: selection button — If you have multiple Session Settings sets and want to use a specific set, highlight the name of the set. To add a set to the Session list, type a name for the set in the box beside *Session*; then complete the dialog box. When you click OK, WinCIM records your information in the Session list.

User ID: entry — Type your User ID number if you were already a member when you installed WinCIM. If you are a new member, use the User ID number you received during the sign-up process until you receive your permanent User ID number.

Password: entry — Type your CompuServe password. This is optional. If you do not type a password in Session Settings, WinCIM asks you for it when you attempt to connect to CompuServe. You cannot see your password in Session Settings.

Secondary Network: selection button — Highlight the network you want WinCIM to use to connect to CompuServe if the Primary Network is not available. If you select Direct under Dial Type, there is no need to specify a network, and the list arrow for Secondary Network will be dimmed.

Baud Rate: selection button — Highlight the baud rate you wish to use in your Secondary Connection. Make sure your modem supports the baud rate you select.

Redial Attempts: entry — Type the number of times your modem will attempt to redial if the first attempt fails in your Secondary Connection. A reasonable value is 10. If you select Direct under Dial Type, you don't need to specify retries, and Retries is unavailable.

Phone: entry — Type the access telephone number you use to connect to CompuServe.

Connector: selection button — Highlight the communications port on your computer to which your modem is attached. Most computers use COM1, although some laptops use COM2.

More button — Brings up a dialog box where you can specify the number of seconds WinCIM will wait for a response from CompuServe before canceling a command, as well as additional logon information that might be necessary for your network.

Current: selection button — Select the session settings set to be used to connect to CompuServe.

New button — Brings up a New Session Name dialog box, where you specify a name for a new set of session settings. The new settings are those currently specified at the Setup Session Settings dialog box. The new set is added to the collection of sets listed in the box beside *Current*.

Delete button — Removes the highlighted session settings set from the collection listed in the box beside *Current*.

Alternate: selection button — Select the session settings set to be used if the set specified for Current is unable to connect you to CompuServe. Once you select an alternate session settings set, the set will remain linked to the set specified for Current until you select a different set. If you do not want to specify an alternate session settings set, select [None].

Modem button — Brings up a Modem Control Strings dialog box, where you can review or modify modem specifications or provide special initialization strings.

LAN button — Brings up a LAN Session Settings dialog box where you specify the communications port through which your computer accesses the LAN or modem pool that connects to CompuServe for you. LAN will not be a valid selection unless you specify INT14 in the box beside Connector.

Dial Type: selection button — Highlight the dial type you wish to use. Select Direct only if your computer is hard-wired to another computer system which provides the connection for you.

Logon parameters and timeout settings

The More Session Settings dialog box contains some additional connection settings for rare situations. To get here, execute Special⇨Session Settings and click the More button at the dialog box that appears. This dialog box has these controls:

Logon Parameters: entry — These are special instructions appended to your User ID number. You should type only information when so directed by a CompuServe Customer Service representative.

HMI Timeout: entry — Type the number of seconds you want WinCIM to wait for a response from CompuServe before canceling the command. In this example, 30 seconds has been specified. If you frequently receive timeout messages, you might want to increase your current timeout value. The value you specify cannot be greater than 255.

Enable Carrier Detect check box — If this check box is enabled, your connection software will attempt to detect when your modem loses carrier. Your modem must support this feature in order for the Enable Carrier Detect option to work reliably. Enable Carrier Detect is enabled by default. If Enable Carrier Detect is enabled and you experience a problem connecting, disabling the Enable Carrier Detect option might solve the problem.

OK — Records your changes and closes this dialog box.

Cancel — Closes the dialog box without recording any changes.

Special CompuServe Offer _____

CompuServe is only $9.95 a month for unlimited connect time to a full package with more than 100 basic services — news, stock quotes, travel arrangements, movie and restaurant reviews, and 90 e-mail messages a month are just part of what's available on CompuServe. You can also choose from many other services that are available for nominal additional charges.

With your purchase of *Internet GIZMOS For Windows,* you're entitled to a **FREE** Introductory membership to CompuServe which includes the following:

- A **FREE** one month membership to access all of CompuServe's Basic Services.

- A $15 introductory usage credit to explore CompuServe's other extended and premium service offerings.

- A private ID and password.

- A complimentary subscription to *CompuServe Magazine*, CompuServe's monthly computing publication.

To receive your **FREE** Introductory membership, call 1-800-524-3388 and ask for Representative #426; Outside the U.S. and Canada, call 614-529-1349.

Chapter 10
COM*t*: The Telnet Modem

Version 1.02, copyright © 1994, Performance Designs.

Introduction

COM*t* is the perfect solution for underpowered Windows telnet client programs. COM*t* lets you use your favorite Windows communications program (PROCOMM Plus for Windows, Crosstalk for Windows, and others) to communicate over TCP/IP.

COM*t* does this by installing itself ahead of the standard Windows COMM driver (COMM.DRV), and intercepts accesses to the COM ports of your choosing, routing them to TCP/IP. Requests to access other ports are passed on to the original COMM driver, letting you continue to use those devices.

COM*t* also emulates a Hayes™-compatible modem, so your existing Windows communications programs will have no trouble interfacing to TCP/IP.

In addition, COM*t* can also access network modems, assuming you have modems available via a TCP connection. See the "Auto initialization" section later in this chapter for more details.

System requirements

COM*t* requires an IBM-PC compatible system with the following:

- Windows 3.1, Windows for Workgroups 3.1, or Windows for Workgroups 3.11
- 286 processor, but a 386 or greater is preferred for best performance
- 4MB RAM
- 256K free disk space
- WinSock 1.1-compliant TCP/IP software

Registering this software

This program is shareware. It is not free software. If you got this copy either from a BBS or a friend, then you are using an *unregistered* copy. You may run the program for an evaluation period of one month. After this time, if you wish to continue using the program, you must register by filling out the registration form and sending in the registration fee. This helps guarantee that the program is well supported and enhanced in the future. The shareware copy of COM*t* presents a registration reminder dialog on the first usage of a telnet port.

Currently, the price to register COM*t* is U.S. $15.95, payable by VISA, MasterCard, check, money order, or in the SWREG forum of CompuServe. Please see the REGISTER.WRI file for more details.

Getting technical support

Technical support for COM*t* is available via e-mail. You can reach us at one of the following e-mail addresses:

CompuServe: 73017,1375

MCI Mail: 572-1706

GEnie: PERFORM.DES

Internet: comt@world.std.com

Installing COM*t*

COM*t* comes with an automated installation utility. To use this utility, copy the distribution files to a floppy or temporary directory then start Windows File Manager and double-click on the INSTALL.EXE file.

The installer first gives you the opportunity to read the README.TXT file. It then asks you to choose a directory in which to install the COM*t* files. Enter a directory name, or click OK to keep the default of C:\COMT. The installer then copies the distribution files to the directory you chose, with the exception of the COMMT.DRV file, which it copies to the Windows SYSTEM directory.

After the installer has copied all the files, it asks you whether you want to create Program Manager icons. Letting the installer create the icons is recommended. After the icons are created, the installer displays a dialog box that lets you choose the COM port numbers to assign to be telnet ports. Choose any unused ports. You can change these settings after installation using the COM*t* configuration program.

This completes the installation. To begin using COM*t*, restart Windows. If the installation fails at any point, see the README.TXT file for instructions on manual installation.

Configuring COM*t*

You can configure COM*t* to provide telnet connections on up to eight COM ports (COM1–8) by running the COM*t* configuration program. Double-click the COM*t* Config icon in the Windows Program Manager. COM*t* Config then asks you to check off which COM port number you want to use. Select the desired ports and click OK. You can also use this program to uninstall COM*t* from your system. Please see the file README.TXT for complete details. Any changes you make to the port assignments do not take effect until you restart Windows.

It is best to choose *all* port numbers that you are not using. This way, you get the maximum number of possible simultaneous telnet connections. A particular COM device does not have to have a physical port to use it for telnet connections. In fact, you should *not* select ports that *do* have devices attached (that is, a modem) because you won't be able to access that device while COM*t* is installed. If you have a serial mouse connected to a COM port, you can't use that port number for COM*t*.

As mentioned earlier, COM*t* can provide telnet connections on the ports COM1 through COM8. Unfortunately, because of a limitation in how Windows operates in 386 Enhanced mode, most machines can use only COM1 through COM4. You may be able to use the higher port numbers if you have a multiport board that was provided with a 386 Virtual Device Driver (usually serial.386) which supports port numbers higher than 4.

Some machines may create problems when redirecting COM3 and COM4. Certain terminal programs (PROCOMM Plus for Windows, in particular) try to be intelligent about which ports can be accessed without causing hardware conflicts, and may either give unnecessary warnings or refuse to access the port altogether. To overcome this problem, add the following lines to the [386Enh] section of the SYSTEM.INI file:

```
COM3Irq=11
COM3Base=3E8
COM4Irq=15
COM4Base=2E8
```

If any of the above lines already exist in the [386Enh] section of the SYSTEM.INI file, especially if you have real hardware attached to COM3 and/or COM4, do *not* replace them with the above lines. Doing so may cause you to be unable to access the physical port. If, after adding the above lines, the problem is not rectified, you may find that it's necessary to adjust the numbers given above.

Using COM*t*

To use COM*t*, instruct your communications program (such as Windows Terminal) to use one of the COM ports you selected to access telnet. Because COM*t* emulates a Hayes-compatible modem, configure your application to use the Hayes Smartmodem, the OPTIMA, or the ULTRA modem. Set the connection to any baud rate, with 8 bits, no parity, and 1 stop bit.

Instead of specifying a phone number to make a connection, specify either the actual IP address of the host to which you wish to connect (such as 13.104.22.1) or the name of the host (such as world.std.com). When you use a host name, some terminal programs may try to outsmart you by substituting the tone equivalents for each letter in the host name. (Windows Terminal does this. Since *when* have people used their modem to dial 1-800-24PIZZA?) When this happens, use the IP address instead. Also, if your host name begins with t or p, you might need to insert either a space or a comma in front of the name for it to work properly.

To connect to a port on the remote host other than the telnet port (port number 23), add the port number in brackets after the IP address. For example, specifying a phone number of 123.456.222.111[25] connects you to the SMTP server on that host.

If you want your remote host to recognize a particular terminal emulation automatically, add a section to your modem initialization string which reads S1000="*terminal*" in which *terminal* is the terminal type you are using. See the "Hayes-compatible modem emulation" section for more details on S-registers.

 You can specify any baud rate for the telnet port, but COM*t* informs the remote telnet server of the baud rate you chose. For this reason, choose either a very high baud rate (that is, 38400 or 57600) for TCP connections through a network or the actual baud rate you are using for your SLIP or PPP connection.

Hayes-compatible modem emulation

To work as seamlessly as possible with standard modem-oriented programs, COM*t* provides a Hayes-compatible modem emulator. If your application lets you select a modem type, select the Hayes Smartmodem, the OPTIMA, or the ULTRA modem. This ensures that the program initializes and dials the modem emulator properly.

The modem emulator supports the standard AT command set. Most AT commands are ignored because they are relevant only when controlling a real modem. The next section lists the active AT commands.

Modem emulator AT command set

D — Dial command

Syntax: D *address*

The D command tells the modem emulator to try to establish a connection to the named host or IP address. This works similarly to a modem, except that a network address is specified instead of a phone number. The T and P (tone or pulse) modifiers can be included, but COM*t* ignores them. The modem emulator tries to connect to the specified host, returning a *CONNECT* response string on success or *NO CARRIER* upon failure. If the connection fails, an additional error message beginning with *WINSOCK:* is returned, providing more detail as to why the connection failed. As with a normal modem, if you press any key while the connection attempt is in progress, the connection aborts and *NO CARRIER* is returned.

E — Command-mode echo

Syntax: E0 or E1
Default: E1

This command enables or disables character echoing while the modem emulator is in command mode — that is, while it accepts AT commands. E1 enables echo and E0 disables echo.

F — On-line echo

Syntax: F0 or F1

This command enables or disables character echoing while the modem emulator is in on-line mode — that is, actually connected to a remote host. F1 enables echo and F0 disables echo.

H — Go off-hook

Syntax: H0 (H1 is *not* supported)

This command is valid only when the modem emulator has established a connection and causes the emulator to close the current connection.

O — Return to on-line mode

Syntax: O

This command is valid only when the modem emulator has established a connection; this command also causes the emulator to exit command mode and returns control of the serial line to the current telnet connection.

S*r* = *n* — Write to an S-register

Syntax: S*r* = *n*

This command writes a value *n* into the S-register numbered *r*. The list of S-registers supported is listed later. Any write to an unsupported S-register is simply ignored.

S*r*? — Query an S-register

Syntax: S*r*?

This command returns the current value of the S-register numbered *r*. The list of S-registers supported is listed later. Any write to an unsupported S-register causes the word *ERROR* to be output, and parsing of the current command line is terminated.

W — Negotiation progress messages

Syntax: W0, W1, or W2
Default: W0

In addition to the *CONNECT* response string, this command turns on the *CARRIER*, *PROTOCOL*, and *COMPRESSION* messages that are available with some MNP or v.42 modems. W0 and W2 disable the extended progress messages, and W1 enables the *CARRIER* and *PROTOCOL* messages. A value other than zero in register S95 overrides this setting. Also because no compression or transmission protocols are actually being used, they are always reported as *NONE*.

Z — Reset

Syntax: Z

This command resets the modem emulator to use the default settings and closes any open connection.

&C — Data Carrier Detect options

Syntax: &C0, &C1, or &C2
Default: &C1

This command controls how the modem emulator reports the Data Carrier Detect (DCD) line. &C0 causes the emulator to always report the DCD line as *ON*. &C1 causes the emulator to report the DCD line as *OFF* while there is no connection, is switched to *ON* immediately after the *CONNECT* message and *OFF* again when the connection is lost. &C2 causes the emulator to report the DCD line as *ON* while there is no connection, and as *OFF* while a connection is being established, and then *ON* again once the connection is made.

&D — Data Terminal Ready options

Syntax: &D0, &D1, &D2, or &D3
Default: &D0

The command controls how the modem emulator interprets control of the Data Terminal Ready (DTR) line by an application. &D0 causes the emulator to ignore the DTR line. &D1 causes an ON-to-OFF transition of the DTR line to put the emulator in command mode while maintaining any open connection. &D2 or &D3 causes an ON-to-OFF transition of the DTR line to close any open connection (issuing a *NO CARRIER* response if one was open) and puts the emulator in command mode.

&F — Factory defaults

Syntax: &F

This command acts exactly like the "Z" command.

&S — Data Set Ready options

Syntax: &S0, &S1, &S2
Default: &S0

This command controls how the modem emulator reports the Data Set Ready (DSR) line. &S0 causes the emulator to always report the DSR line as *ON*. &S1 causes the emulator to report the DSR line as *OFF* while there is no connection opened, switches it to *ON* when attempting to open a connection, and then *OFF* again once the connection is closed. &S2 causes the emulator to report the DSR line as *OFF* while there is no connection opened, switches it to *ON* when a connection is opened, and then *OFF* again once the connection is closed.

&V — View current settings

Syntax: &V

This command displays the modem emulator's current settings. A sample output (using the default settings) is shown below:

```
ACTIVE PROFILE:
E1 F1 W0 &C1 &D0 &S0
S02:043 S03:013 S04:010 S05:008 S12:050 S95:000
S1000:000
S1001:002 S1002:000 S1003:001 S1004:001 S1005:003
```

Modem Emulator S-registers

S2 — Escape Sequence character

This register holds the ASCII value of the escape character used in the escape sequence. The escape sequence is defined by a period of silence (as defined in S12) followed by three escape characters followed by another period of silence. This causes the modem emulator to switch from on-line mode to command mode while a connection is open. The default is 43 (the + character).

S3 — Carriage Return character

This register holds the ASCII value of the character understood and output as a carriage return. The default is 13.

S4 — Line Feed character

This register holds the ASCII value of the character understood and output as a line feed. The default is 10.

S5 — Backspace character

This register holds the ASCII value of the character understood and output as a backspace. The default is 8.

S12 — Escape Sequence Guard Time

This register holds the value of the silence period required when issuing an escape sequence, in $1/50$ of a second increments. The default value is 50 (1 second).

S95 — Negotiation progress messages

When this register's value is not zero, COM*t* ignores the W command's setting, which specifies how the emulator reports connection progress. Setting bit 2 of the register enables the CARRIER message. Setting bit 3 of the register enables the *PROTOCOL* message. Setting bit 5 of the register enables the *COMPRESSION* message. The default is 0.

Modem emulator extended S-registers

To set telnet-specific options, the modem emulator supports an extended set of S-registers, numbered 1000 through 1005.

S1000 — Terminal type

This register accepts both a numeric *and* a string value. If you set this register to a value other than zero, when the remote telnet server queries terminal type, COM*t* answers with the value of this register. When this register has a string value (for example, ATS1000="vt100"), the verbatim string is reported. When this register has a numeric value (for example, ATS1000=5), the numeric value (presumably a well-known terminal ID) is reported. The default is 0.

S1001 — Interpret IAC characters

The telnet protocol is based on an escape character (ASCII 255) known as the IAC character. This register controls whether COM*t* interprets and delivers these escape sequences. Setting this register to 0 causes the client to treat the IAC character as any other. Setting this register to 1 causes COM*t* to always interpret IAC. Setting this register to 2 causes COM*t* to interpret or ignore IAC, based upon the requested port number. If a connection to port 23 is made (the default in the D command, and the standard telnet server port), then IAC escapes are interpreted. If a connection to any other port number is made (by using [*nn*] in the D command), then IAC characters are treated like any other. The default is 2.

S1002 — Request Binary connection

The telnet connection can be used either in Terminal and Binary modes. This register controls whether COM*t* requests a Binary connection. When this register is set to 0, COM*t* *never* requests a Binary connection. When this register is set to 1, COM*t* *always* requests a Binary connection. When this register is set to 2, COM*t* requests a Binary connection only if the port was opened using a byte length of 8 bits. The default is 0.

S1003 — telnet echo

The telnet server can be operated in either echo or non-echo modes. This register controls whether COM*t* requests an echo mode connection. When this register is set to 0, COM*t* *never* requests an echo mode connection. When this register is set to 1, COM*t* *always* requests an echo mode connection. The default is 1.

S1004 — Verbose connection failure

This register controls whether COM*t* reports the *WINSOCK:* error message before the *NO CARRIER* response. Setting this register to 0 disables the *WINSOCK* message, and setting it to 1 enables the message. The default is 1.

S1005 — Carriage return padding

The telnet protocol specifies that all carriage return characters (ASCII 13) that are sent without a line feed character (ASCII 10) should be sent as "CR NUL" (ASCII 13 followed by ASCII 0). Setting this register to 1 causes COM*t* to strip away any NUL character received which follows a carriage return. Setting this register to 2 causes COM*t* to add NUL characters to any outbound carriage return which is not directly followed by a line feed. Setting this register to 3 enables both inbound and outbound translations, and setting it to 0 disables both. S1001 overrides this setting, such that when IAC characters are not processed, neither are carriage return characters. The default is 3.

Auto initialization

COM*t* includes automatic initialization, which lets you specify a string to send to the modem emulator upon opening the port. The modem emulator can be always initialized to a known state each time it is opened. In addition, this feature can be used as the basis for accessing remote network modems.

For example, to initialize the modem emulator automatically when COM3 is opened, add a line to the [COMt] section of SYSTEM.INI which reads:

```
COM3init=AT &C1 &D2 S1000="vt100"
```

Every time an application opens COM3, DCD and DTR handling are enabled (as described in the previous section), and reported terminal is set to vt100.

To illustrate using COM*t* to access networked modems, assume that a remote server (IP address 123.456.789.111) has a modem that can be accessed by connecting to port 4006. To cause an application to be connected automatically to that modem every time COM3 is opened, add the following line to the [COMt] section of SYSTEM.INI:

```
COM3init=AT &C1 &D0 S2=0 D:123.456.789.111[4006]
```

Note the colon after the D command. It is very important because it causes COM*t* to hold the port until the connection is made, making the connection transparent to the application. Also note the S2=0 command, which disables local interpretation of the escape sequence so that an escape sequence can be used for the remote modem.

 Because the application won't see the true status of the network modem's status lines and will be unable to manipulate that modem's control lines, some applications may not work correctly when used with this feature.

Application Notes

Using WinCIM

COM*t* works with CompuServe's WinCIM; you need either WinCIM Version 1.3.1 or the latest support files. Luckily, WinCIM is included in this book/CD package. The version of WinCIM you use must be able to dial using the network setting of Internet. If that option is not available in your copy of WinCIM, you need to either upgrade to Version 1.3 or get the latest support files from CompuServe.

To use COM*t* with WinCIM, change the Session Settings as follows:

```
Phone: compuserve.com
Baud Rate: 9600
Network: Internet
Connector: (one of the telnet Modems)
```

Also, set the Modem Control String as follows:

```
Initialize: AT&F &C1 &D2 S1005=1 S1002=1^M
```

Transferring Binary files

Transferring Binary files through a telnet connection can be problematic because the interpretation of Binary mode and carriage return padding varies a great deal among telnet implementations. To get Binary file transfer to work properly, you may need to experiment with S1002 and S1005 to find the best settings. On at least one SPARC-based telnet server, S1002=1 and S1005=0 work best with Binary files, although many files will transfer fine with S1002=0 and S1005=3. As noted above, S1005=1 and S1002=1 work best for the HMI protocol used by WinCIM. The YMODEM protocol also sometimes works better than ZMODEM.

Using Smartcom for Windows

COM*t* can work with Hayes' Smartcom for Windows. Select the "Use reduced command set" box in the Modem Settings. Failure to do so will prevent dialing using COM*t*.

Using Reflection

Reflection uses its own datacom driver, bypassing COM*t* and the Windows COMM driver. To get COM*t* to work with Reflection, issue the following command in the Reflection Command window:

```
SET ENHANCED-SERIAL-DATACOMM NO
```

COM*t* Version 1.02 Registration Form

Name _____

Company _____

Address _____

City _____

State _____ Country _____

Zip _____ Phone _____

Remit to:

Performance Designs
P.O. Box 1005
Concord, MA 01742

Pricing

❑ $15.95 for single use license (MA residents add $.80 state sales tax)
See the REGFORM.TXT file on the CD for other registration information.

Part IV
Windows E-Mail GIZMOS

E-mail is the electronic counterpart of regular mail. It generally has the same purpose as regular mail: saying hello, sending business communications, writing home for the holidays, that sort of thing. E-mail can be more powerful and cost-effective than regular mail because it's faster and can include attachments like word processor files, spreadsheets, and graphics. The disadvantage is that it can lose some of the personable feeling of a handwritten message. Also, until encryption and authentication programs are widely accepted, electronic mail cannot be considered secure from snooping. E-mail also is not generally accepted as a legal document.

E-mail is composed of the following elements:

- An E-mail address
- The body of the message
- An attachment (optional)

An attachment can be any valid binary or ASCII file. Although binary files are exchanged freely among users on on-line services, they cannot be sent reliably over the Internet. Three encoding schemes— uuencode, MIME, and BINHEX— have been developed to translate these files into ASCII versions for reliable transmission. Some or all of these encoding schemes are built into most e-mail packages used exclusively for the Internet and all the e-mail packages included on this book's CD-ROM.

Understanding the E-Mail Address

You need an e-mail address to be able to send or receive e-mail. When you establish an account with an on-line service, such as CompuServe or America Online, your account number is your e-mail address. Internet addresses are a little more complicated but revolve around three parts. An e-mail address on the Internet is composed of the following items:

address@provider.type

where *address* is your account name (identifies you), *provider* identifies who provides you access, and *type* indicates what kind of organization your provider is.

For example, this book's authors have the following addresses:

76702.1023@compuserve.com

sobel@libertynet.org

76711.1205@compuserve.com

lbudnick@mcs.com

Your Internet service provider will assign you an address. In the case of Howard Sobel's address, *libertynet* is the provider. The *org* extension identifies the provider as a nonprofit organization. The *type* portion of the mail address is usually one of the following valid extensions if you are in the U.S., depending on who is providing you with your Internet account:

Provider type	Extension
Business or commercial	com
Network	net
Academic or educational facility	edu
Military site or installation	mil
Government facility or site	gov
Nonprofit organization	org

It is very easy to send e-mail from the Internet to the most popular commercial services. The chart below demonstrates how to address mail from the Internet to a number of commercial systems.

Service	Account Address	Service Address	Full Address
CompuServe	76702,1356@	compuserve.com	76702.1356@compuserve.com The "." is necessary
America Online	HOWARDS697@	aol.com	HOWARDS697@aol.com
Prodigy	HOWARDS@	prodigy.com	HOWARDS@prodigy.com
BIX	HOWARDS@	bix.com	HOWARDS@bix.com
GEnie	HOWARDS@	genie.geis.com	HOWARDS@genie.geis.com

How Does E-Mail Travel?

You compose a message with an e-mail program on either your computer or a remote computer you access with a terminal emulation program. The e-mail program sends the message to an Internet mail router, a computer your service provider runs, using a standard protocol, usually *SMTP* (Simple Mail Transfer Protocol).

The definition of the SMTP protocol can be found in the Internet RFC-821. Use anonymous FTP to get RFCs from any of several sites, including ftp:// ds.internic.net. Many RFCs deal with SMTP issues.

The mail router sends the mail either directly to the host specified in the Service Address field or to as many mail routers as needed. Finally, the mail arrives at the destination host system — which may not be the PC of the person you are writing to. In that case, your computer calls your Service Provider's computer using a protocol called POP3, which stands for *Post Office Protocol version 3*. The POP3 protocol checks for mail, and transfers mail messages to your PC, where you read them with a mail client.

The definition of the POP3 protocol can be found in the Internet RFC-1460.

Protocols aplenty

Another protocol commonly used to send electronic mail as well as binary files is *UUCP* (UNIX-to-UNIX Copy). The name tells you that the protocol comes from UNIX-based computers. Many mail networks are still UUCP based. Even if your mail package doesn't use UUCP, your message will probably pass through a UUCP-based network on its way.

Local area networks (LANs) and privately networked LANs use other protocols, such as Novell's MHS or Microsoft's MAPI.

E-Mail Privacy

E-mail is not particularly secure from inquiring eyes. Others can read your mail. It's not hard for another person to type a mail message and claim you sent it to them. A great deal of work to find ways to make e-mail secure and to verify the sender is under way. One popular way to protect e-mail is to use an encryption method that is humbly called Pretty Good Privacy, or PGP for short. PGP uses a *one-way cipher* using a public key. If someone wants to send you a piece of encrypted e-mail, he or she can use a PGP encoder and your encryption key that is known to the public. Once encrypted, the same key cannot decrypt the mail — only your *private* key can decode the message. Public servers hold public keys so everyone can see them. If someone tampers with your public key, everyone will know. You could send your public key to the recipient of your e-mail, but so could someone trying to impersonate you. Thus, public key servers are the best solution. Some companies that use similar encryption mechanisms actually publish their public keys in a major newspaper every time they change.

Signing mail works similarly, but in reverse. To verify to a reader that you wrote a message, you encrypt your signature using a private key. The reader of a mail message can decrypt your signature with a public key.

Encryption legal pitfalls

Encryption involves some tricky legal issues. First, virtually every decent encryption scheme is patented. If you want to use encryption in a commercial product, you must pay a license fee. You can use PGP free for personal, noncommercial use only, through a deal struck between MIT and the RSA, a company that holds many encryption and authentication patents. ViaCrypt has a commercial version of PGP available for $98 per copy list price. Look up the on-line Internet resource at www.lcs.com (referenced in this commentary) for more information about ViaCrypt.

Second, although you can get a copy of the PGP source and executable code for your personal use, if you reside in the U.S., then you must not distribute that code outside the U.S. Export of encryption algorithms outside the U.S. is a crime in the same category as exporting bombs. Interestingly, if you reside outside the U.S., you can also get a copy of PGP from non-U.S. sources. Presumably, someone was allowed to export it, right?

An in-depth discussion of data encryption and authentication is outside the scope of this book. For more information, check out these good on-line resources:

```
http://draco.centerline.com:8080/~franl/crypto.html
http://www.lcs.com
http://bs.mit.edu:8001/pgp-form.html
http://www.rsa.com
http://www.quadralay.com/www/Crypt/PGP/pgp00.html
```

Also, look at the newsgroup alt.security.pgp.

Common E-Mail Problems

Should your message encounter a delivery problem, the destination's *postmaster* will probably return the message to you. This electronic postmaster is adept at finding incorrectly addressed mail. For example, when you're sending a message over the Internet to a CompuServe user, if you forget to change the comma to a period in the address (76702,1356 becomes 76702.1356@compuserve.com, remember), your mail returns with a message similar to the following:

```
Posted-Date: Thu, 15 Sep 94 08:52:09 -0400
Return-Path: <MAILER-DAEMON@noc1.dccs.upenn.edu>
Date: Thu, 15 Sep 94 08:52:09 -0400
From: MAILER-DAEMON@noc1.dccs.upenn.edu (Mail Delivery
Subsystem)
Subject: Returned mail: User unknown
To: <sobel@libertynet.org>
```

Check the e-mail address of your intended recipient closely for signs of an incorrect address. If any portion of the user address is incorrect, chances are that your mail will be returned. In that case the subject line may state "Addressee unknown."

Automated Mail Services

Mail servers, daemons, knowbots, and listservers

You can send mail to computer programs to make them perform a variety of services for you. You can have one of these mail robots search for files and programs and then send them to your mail address.

A mail archive server automates the process of searching a remote computer and can be initiated by your e-mail request. Your e-mail request to the mail server results in a response back to your e-mail address, depending on the kind of mail server you query.

For instance, I was able to find the author of one of the programs on the book's CD by sending a query to a large database of archived messages of people who have contributed to Usenet discussions. The mail server replied within a half-hour, saving me hours of on-line searching.

A successful mail server search looks like this:

```
From: mail-server@rtfm.MIT.EDU
To: sobel@libertynet.org (Howard Sobel)
Subject: mail-server: "send usenet-addresses/Howard Sobel"
Reply-To: mail-server@rtfm.MIT.EDU
Precedence: junk
X-Problems-To: owner-mail-server@rtfm.mit.edu
—cut here—

sobel@libertnet.org (Howard Sobel) (Mar 18 94)

—cut here—
```

To get instructions about how to search a mail server for a Usenet contributor send an e-mail inquiry as follows:

Send e-mail addressed to mail-server@rtfm.mit.edu
In the body of your message: help index

Send e-mail addressed to mail-server@rtfm.mit.edu
In the body of your message: usenet-addresses/help

To search the mail server at rtfm.mit.edu for a Usenet contributor:

Send e-mail addressed to mail-server@rtfm.mit.edu
In the body of your message: send usenet-addresses/"lastname or fullname"

FTP by e-mail

You can have files from FTP sites sent to you via e-mail. However, these files must be broken up into several 64K chunks to pass through certain gateways on the Internet that restrict e-mail message size. To find out how to do this, send e-mail to mail-server@pit-manager.mit.edu. In the message body, type

send usenet/news.answers/finding-sources. The server will send you a text file with instructions about how to obtain files through e-mail.

Currently, an Internet e-mail message cannot be larger than 64K. E-mail messages sent through CompuServe's Internet gateway can be no larger than 50K; e-mail messages sent through America Online's Internet gateway can be only 27K.

Mailing lists

You can subscribe to any of the more than 1,500 available *mailing lists* and newsletters. For example, you can subscribe to Microsoft WINNEWS and get the latest news from Microsoft by sending mail to enews@microsoft.nwnet.com, with the text SUBSCRIBE WINNEWS as the message body.

If you want to discover what new lists are available, send e-mail to listserve@vm1.nodak.edu, with the text SUBSCRIBE NEW-LIST *firstname lastname* as the message body, where *firstname* is your first name and *lastname* is your last name.

Remember to write down instructions on how to unsubscribe to any mailing list you join so you can quit when you want or need to!

In This Part

This part describes three e-mail packages on the CD-ROM: Eudora, a freeware e-mail client from QUALCOMM; RFD Mail, a shareware client that can access commercial services in addition to doing standard Internet e-mail; and Pegasus, which features NetWare MHS mail compatibility and private password mail encryption. Private password encryption means that you'll need to let the recipient of the e-mail know what the password is before the recipient can decode it, and there is only a single password.

The CD-ROM also includes two encoder/decoders to handle binary file encoding and decoding. Because the Internet e-mail doesn't handle binary (non-ASCII) files, you need to encode binary files before attaching them to your e-mail. These two handy utilities will do the job nicely.

Don't forget that some of the commercial samplers discussed in Part II also include e-mail clients in their commercial packages. You can call or write those vendors to see if they'll part with an evaluation copy.

Chapter 11
Eudora

Getting Started

This is the free version of Eudora and is provided *as is*. For information about the commercial version, e-mail eudora-sales@ qualcomm.com or call 1-800-2Eudora.

System requirements

As a Windows user, in order to use the QUALCOMM Eudora electronic mail (e-mail) program, you must have these minimum hardware requirements:

- An Ethernet card or a DDP/IP gateway or modem
- An account on a computer with a Post Office Protocol Version 3 (POP3) server
- IBM PC compatible machine.
- Windows Version 3.1
- WinSock Version 1.1 compliant TCP/IP stack
- At least 750K free disk space (more depending on mailbox sizes)
- Microsoft-compatible mouse (highly recommended)

Installing Eudora

To install Eudora, follow these steps:

1. Create a new directory for the Eudora files (C:\EUDORA is a good choice).
2. Copy the executable file into the directory you created in step 1 with this command:

   ```
   WEUDORA.EXE
   ```

3. Add the following environment variable to your AUTOEXEC.BAT file. (*TMP* represents a temp directory.)

   ```
   SET TMP=C:\TMP
   ```

Make sure that the TMP directory exists before attempting to add the environment variable to it.

4. PC Eudora makes use of several different TCP/IP services, and has default port numbers for these services. Most sites put these services on the default ports, but some may not. Contact your site network administrator to make sure that the following services listed in this step indeed have the default port numbers. If they don't, you'll have to make some changes to some files on your PC (usually to a SERVICES file).

A list of the services that PC Eudora uses follows, and what the list might look like in a typical services file. The names of these services must be exactly as named here (for example, the entry for the POP3 service must be *POP3* and not *POP-3*). Make sure that you make any changes necessary for your TCP/IP package to specify the location of the SERVICES file.

Service	*Port Number*
To receive mail	pop3 110/tcp
To send mail	smtp 25/tcp
To use Ph	ns 105/tcp
To use Finger	finger 79/tcp
To use the Change Password function*	epass 106/tcp

5. Run MS Windows and add PC Eudora as a Program Item to a new or existing Program Group.

If you want your mail files to reside somewhere other than where the executable resides, you can set the mail directory by specifying the directory as the first parameter on the command line of the Program Item that you create for PC Eudora.

Doing so is useful if you want to keep the executable on a server, but each user has individual mail hierarchy. It also works when you want to have multiple users on one PC. Always keep the help file in the same directory as the executable.

PC Eudora uses the directory on the command line first. If that isn't present, Eudora uses the directory where the executable resides.

The first time you run PC Eudora for Windows, you have to edit some of the configuration information in order to be able to send and receive mail. Do the following:

1. Select Configurations from the Special menu. The fields you need to review are

   POP Account. This required field should be set to the address where you receive your mail. Then you must type the entry in the following form:

   ```
   username@machine_name
   ```

   SMTP Server. This field should be set to the address of a machine that supports SMTP. If the machine that your POP account is on supports SMTP, you need not fill this in (Eudora uses the machine your POP account is on to deliver mail also).

   Return Address. Here you type the return address that appears on all mail that you send. If your POP account (as shown previously) is also your return address, you can leave this field blank.

   Real Name. You enter your real name here, and it is appended to the return address in messages you send, enclosed in parentheses.

Eudora configuration

After you install Eudora, double-click its icon to open the program. Before you can actually use Eudora, you must give it some necessary pieces of information. To enter this information, select Configuration from the Special menu. The Configuration dialog box appears, as shown in Figure 11-1.

To use Eudora, you must have an account on a computer that runs a POP3 server. This is the account to which your e-mail messages are delivered before they are transferred to the Eudora program on your PC. Fill in the appropriate fields:

1. In the POP account field, type your login name for this account and the full (domain) name of the computer, separating them with an @ sign. For example, if your assigned login name is Carolyn and the name of the computer where you receive e-mail is uxh.cso.uiuc.edu, you type **carolyn@uxh.cso.uiuc.edu** in this field.

2. In the Real Name field, type your real name. Your name, as it appears here, is displayed in parentheses after your return address in your outgoing mail. It is also displayed in the sender column of all messages sent by you.

3. If you are using Eudora with a network connection, select TCP/IP as the connection method. If you are using a modem or other serial connection, select Communications Toolbox as the connection method. Then select the Communications dialog box from the Special menu and choose the appropriate modem/serial communications settings.

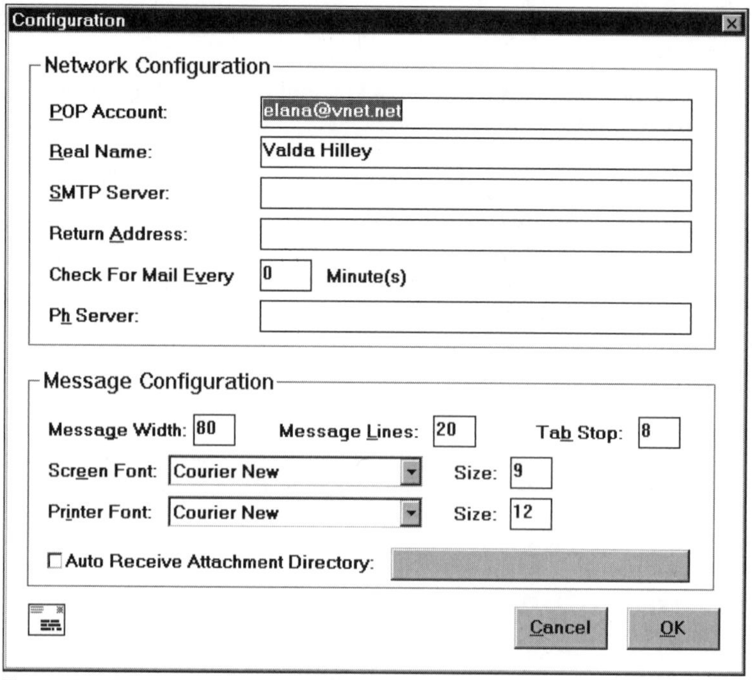

Figure 11-1: The Configuration dialog box.

4. At this point, it is best to leave the other items unchanged and click OK.

You are now ready to use Eudora.

Using Eudora

Creating an outgoing message

An outgoing message is a message you send to someone else.

To create an outgoing message, select New Message from the Message menu. A new composition window entitled <<No Recipient>>, <<No Subject>> appears with the blinking insertion point situated at the start of the To field (see Figure 11-2). The composition window consists of the title bar, the icon bar, the message header, and the message body.

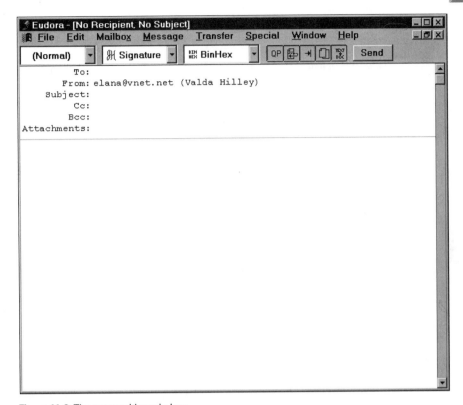

Figure 11-2: The composition window.

The title bar

The title bar provides information about incoming and outgoing messages, including the name of the sender (if it is an incoming message) or addressee (if it is an outgoing message), the time and date the message was delivered or sent, and the message subject. New messages are labeled <<No Recipient>>, <<No Subject>> until they are sent or queued. Messages get time stamps when they are sent, or if they are queued for timed delivery.

The icon bar

The icon bar consists of a series of objects displayed under the composition window title. It allows you to control your message's priority, override some of your preference settings for that message only, and send or queue the message. You see one pop-up menu and five icons. You can choose any of the five icons by clicking your preference. A check mark symbol appearing next to the icon denotes that the icon is active. The pop-up menu and icons are described next.

The default settings for the icon bar are determined in the Switches dialog box (see the section entitled "The Switches dialog box").

Icon Bar Option	Purpose
Priority/Attachment Type pop-up icon	The Priority portion of this pop-up menu is on top. If you want to indicate that your message is of a higher or lower priority than a normal message (blank), use this menu to make the desired selection. Priorities are discussed in the "Assigning message priorities" section.
The Attachment Type icon	Allows you to select what format documents that you attach to outgoing messages are encoded in MIME or BinHex. BinHex is most compatible with old Windows mailers and previous versions of Eudora.
The Always As Documents option	Selected when sending attachments between PCs, as this keeps the attachments in their original PC format. However, when sending a document to another platform, deselecting this option allows Eudora to convert the attachment into the format most likely to be understood by other platforms.
Signature	If this icon is checked, your signature file is automatically attached to the end of each message you send. Signatures are discussed in the "Creating a signature" section.
Word Wrap	If this icon is checked, a carriage return is not required at the end of each line you type in an outgoing message; Eudora automatically wraps text to the next line, with line breaks at roughly 76 characters per line.
Tabs in Body	If this icon is checked, pressing Tab within the message body results in Eudora inserting enough spaces to move the insertion point to a multiple of 8 characters from the start of the line. This mimics the way tabs work on many terminals. If this icon is not checked, pressing Tab returns the cursor to the To field of the message header.

The Tab icon also controls the handling of tabs in text pasted into the message window and in plain text attachments that are sent as documents (not BinHexed). If Tabs in Body is checked, tab spacing is replaced by blank spaces; otherwise, the tabs are included in the text.

Keep Copy	If this icon is checked, a copy of each sent message is kept in the Out mailbox (summaries are marked with an "S" in the far-left column of the Out mailbox window, indicating that the messages have been sent). These messages are saved until they are deleted or transferred to a different folder.
Quoted-Printable Encoding	If this icon is checked, quoted-printable encoding may be used when sending messages that contain long lines of text or special characters. When selected, it is used for all plain text attachments. It is recommended that this icon always be checked.
Send or Queue	If the Immediate Send option in the Switches dialog box is on, the rightmost button in the icon bar is labeled Send. Clicking the Send button immediately sends the message. Otherwise, this button is labeled Queue, and has the same function as the Queue for Delivery command in the Message menu (when you click this button, the message window closes and the message is held in the Out mailbox, marked ready for delivery).
Message Header	Outgoing message headers consist of six fields: To, From, Subject, Cc, Bcc, and Attachments. Each field holds a different piece of information. The To, Subject, Cc, and Bcc fields can be edited.
	To move the insertion point from field to field, press Tab or click the desired field. When entering information into the fields, use the standard Windows text-editing tools provided in the Edit menu. Here is a brief description of the intended contents of each field:
To	The intended recipient's e-mail address, or a nickname you have defined (see the "Creating and using nicknames" section). Multiple addresses are allowed, but must be separated by commas.
From	The sender's e-mail address. It is usually your POP account plus your real name. You can use a return address other than your POP account by entering the desired address in the Return Address field of the Configuration dialog box (see the section entitled "The Configuration dialog box").
Subject	Brief text indicating the contents of the message. This field can be blank (although it is a breach of e-mail etiquette to do so).
Cc	E-mail address or nickname of person to whom a copy of the message is to be sent. Multiple addresses are allowed but must be separated by commas. This field may be left blank.

(continued)

Icon Bar Option	Purpose
Bcc	"Blind" carbon copy. Like addresses listed in the Cc field, addresses listed here receive copies of the message. Unlike addresses listed in the Cc field, addresses listed here do not appear in the message header of the recipients. This is useful when you want to send a copy of a message to someone without everyone else knowing you did so. Multiple addresses are allowed but must be separated by commas. This field can be left blank.
Attachments	List of documents being sent along with the message. Specify them through the Attach Document command under the Message menu. To delete an attachment from a message, select it and press Delete. You cannot enter information directly into this field. This field can be blank.
Message Body	After filling in the fields, move the insertion point to the space below the message header. Type the body of the message here. Feel free to use the standard Windows text-editing tools provided in the Edit menu.
	If the Word Wrap icon on the icon bar is checked (or the Word Wrap option in the Switches dialog box is on), you don't need to press Enter at the end of each line of text. The text wraps to the next line automatically. If this option is not set, be sure to press Enter at the end of each line, or your message may not be legible on the recipient's computer. To use tabs in the message body, check the Tabs in Body icon in the icon bar.

Saving an outgoing message for later changes

Sometimes it is convenient to save an outgoing message either as a safeguard when typing long messages, or so you can return to it later to edit or add more text.

To save the message while the outgoing message window is open, select Save from the File menu. The message window does not close, but the current version of the message is saved in the Out mailbox. You might notice that the title appearing at the top of the message window changes from <<No Recipient>> << No Subject>> to whatever you typed in the To and Subject fields of the message.

If you now close the message (by clicking the close box in the upper-left corner of the message window or by selecting Close from the File menu), it can be reopened from the Out mailbox for further changes. As with any message summary listed in a mailbox window, it can be identified by the contents of its To and Subject fields. A small black dot, or bullet, to the left of a message summary listed in the Out mailbox indicates that the message is being indefinitely held there and is queueable. Such messages remain in the Out mailbox until they are queued and sent or deleted.

A sendable message saved in the Out mailbox

If you try to close an outgoing message window without specifically saving that version of the message, an alert is displayed asking whether the message should be saved or the changes discarded. If you select Discard and the message has never been saved, the message is deleted.

Methods for sending messages

If the Immediate Send option in the Switches dialog box is on, select Queue for Delivery from the Message menu to send a current message immediately . Alternatively, the rightmost button appearing in the icon bar at the top of the current message window is labeled Send. Click this button to send the current message.

Clicking the Send button

If the Show Progress option in the Switches dialog box is on, a progress window is displayed momentarily at the top of the screen indicating the progress of the transmission.

Clicking the Queue Button

Some people may prefer to compose many messages and transmit them all at once. This capability is possible only if the Immediate Send option in the Switches dialog box is off.

To accomplish the first step for any outgoing current message, select Queue For Delivery from the Message menu. The button appearing in the icon bar at the top right of the current message window is labeled Queue. Click this button to queue the current message for later delivery.

Either of these selections closes the message window (if it was open), saves the message in the Out mailbox, and marks it as *queued* (ready to be delivered). Queued messages are marked by a *Q* in the far-left column of the Out mailbox.

A queued message in the Out mailbox

For the second step, select Send Queued Messages from the File menu. Doing so sends the queued message (or messages). If the Show Progress option in the Switches dialog box is on, the progress window is displayed momentarily at the top of the screen indicating the progress of the transmission.

Timed messages

It is possible to tell Eudora to send a message at some specific time in the future. To do this for the current outgoing message, select Change Queueing from the Message menu. The Change Queueing dialog box then appears.

If you choose Right Now, the message is sent immediately upon clicking the OK button. If you choose Next time queued messages are sent, the message is sent the next time queued messages are sent. If you choose On or After, you can use the time and date fields to fill in the time when the message should be sent. The message is saved in the Out mailbox with a Q in the status column, just as if it were a normal queued message. However, the message is not actually sent until the specified time arrives.

For the message to be sent at the correct time, Eudora must be running when you tell the message to send. If Eudora is not running, the message is sent the first time you start Eudora after the selected time has passed.

Sending queued messages on check

If the Send on Check option in the Switches dialog box is on, every time a manual or automatic mail check occurs, all queued messages are sent, thus saving you the step of selecting Send Queued Messages.

Quitting with queued messages

If you quit Eudora after you have queued messages but before you send them, Eudora gives you the opportunity to send the messages before you quit.

Quitting with timed messages

If you quit with timed messages and the messages are due to be sent within the next 12 hours, Eudora warns you and gives you the opportunity to send them.

Editing a queued message

To edit a queued message, open the Out mailbox and double-click the desired message summary to open its composition window. Make the necessary edits and requeue the new version of the message with the Queue For Delivery or Change Queuing commands from the Message menu or the Save command from the File menu. You may also requeue the message using the Queue button on the icon bar. The message is returned to the Out mailbox with a queued status. If you close the changed message without choosing one of these options, an alert appears asking you to verify the changes.

Changing the status of a queued message

A message that is queued but unsent may be unqueued using the Change Queuing command. Open the Out mailbox and select the desired message summary. Then select Change Queueing from the Message menu and click Don't Send. This changes the message status from queued (Q) to saved (S). The message is held in the Out mailbox until it is either deleted or requeued and sent.

You can also send a message immediately or change it to timed send using the Change Queuing command.

Keeping copies of outgoing messages

Once a message is sent, it is placed into the Trash mailbox unless the Keep Copies option in the Switches dialog box is on or the Keep Copy icon in the icon bar is checked. In these cases, the message is left in the Out mailbox and is annotated with an *S* in the status column of the Out mailbox indicating that the message has been sent.

Password protection

There is password protection on mail checks to your account on the POP server. Each time the Eudora program is opened, your password is requested prior to the first mail check, whether it is conducted automatically or manually. If automatic checking is set (see the section entitled "The Configuration dialog box"), a dialog box requesting your POP server account password is displayed upon first opening Eudora. If automatic checking is disabled, the same dialog box is displayed at the time of your first mail check.

Type your password and click OK. If you make a mistake before clicking OK, simply backspace and enter the password correctly.

If your password is rejected, an error message is displayed indicating that you have entered the wrong password (see the next section). Select Check Mail from the File menu to redisplay the Password dialog box.

Remember that the Eudora password is case sensitive, so you must type it exactly as you first entered it, or it is rejected.

As long as it is running, Eudora remembers your password. If you don't want it to remember (when, for example, you are away from your PC), choose Forget Password from the Special menu. At your next mail check, you are prompted for your password again.

Another password-related option is Save Password, which is in the Switches dialog box. This option makes Eudora remember your password from one session to the next (you *never* have to enter your password again, even if you quit and restart Eudora). This option should be used only if your machine is in a secure location.

Finally, the Change Password command in the Special menu can be used to change your POP server password if your POP server machine is running a compatible password-change server. You'll be asked to enter your old password once and your new password twice (see Figure 11-3).

Figure 11-3: Changing a password with Eudora.

Checking for and receiving mail

The POP server is the machine where your mail is received and stored until it is transferred to the Eudora program on your Windows system. Your POP server account is specified in the POP Account setting in the Configuration dialog box (see the section entitled "The Configuration dialog box").

To best understand the functioning of the POP server with respect to Eudora, see the section entitled "Mail transport."

There are two methods to check your designated POP server to see whether you have new mail. One method is automatic and the other is manual. Both methods deliver any mail addressed to you from the POP server to your PC. Before any checks are made, however, the POP server requests your account password.

Automatic checking

Eudora automatically checks for mail if you tell it how often to do so. From the Special menu, select Configuration. The Configuration dialog box has a field entitled Check For Mail Every ? Minute(s). Type a value and Eudora automatically checks for mail at the desired interval whenever it is running (even if you are using other applications in Windows). For example, if you type **15**, Eudora checks for mail every 15 minutes. In fact, 15 minutes is a good minimum interval, as checking mail more frequently puts an unnecessary load on your POP server.

If automatic checking is set, the Check Mail command in the File menu displays the next time that an automatic check is scheduled.

When Eudora performs a mail check, you can be notified of new mail in one or all of four different ways: an alert dialog box, a special sound, a flashing mail flag icon in the menu bar, or the opening of the In mailbox. These options are on or off in the Switches dialog box (see the section entitled "The Switches dialog box").

When you receive notice that new mail has arrived, select Eudora from the applications menu. Mail always arrives in the In mailbox. The messages are listed in the order they are received, with the most recent message listed last.

Unread messages in the In mailbox

If the In mailbox is not already open, select In from the Mailbox menu. Unread messages are designated by a small black dot, or bullet, on the left side of the message summary. Double-click anywhere on a message summary to open the message. Incoming messages are saved in the In mailbox until they are deleted or transferred to another mailbox.

Manual checking

You may check for mail manually at any time by selecting Check Mail from the File menu. If you haven't successfully entered your password since opening the Eudora program, you are prompted for it.

If the Show Progress option in the Switches dialog box is on, the Progress window is displayed momentarily at the top of the screen as the POP server is checked.

If there is no mail waiting at your account on the POP server, the *You have no new mail* message is displayed. Click OK. You may check for mail again later.

If there is a problem reaching the POP server, an error message is displayed. To rectify the problem, review the POP server settings in the Configuration dialog box.

Error while checking mail

If there is new mail, it is transferred automatically from the POP server to Eudora on your Windows system. If the Show Progress option in the Switches dialog box is on, a progress window is displayed at the top of your screen, allowing you to monitor the mail transfer.

If the Get Attention By Alert option in the Switches dialog box is on, the new mail dialog box is displayed, stating that new messages have been delivered.

Depending on your settings, the In mailbox window may appear. Mail always arrives in the In mailbox. Unread messages in the In mailbox are designated by a small black dot, or bullet, on the left side of the message summary. Double-click anywhere on a message summary to open the message. Incoming messages are saved in the In mailbox until they are deleted or transferred to another mailbox.

During a mail check, Eudora normally transfers your incoming messages from your account on the POP server to Windows and then deletes them from the POP server. This may prove awkward for people who sometimes want to read mail from a secondary PC. It results in nonconsolidated storage of messages—if you read mail through a secondary PC, you aren't able to act on that mail from your primary PC.

The Leave Mail on Server option in the Switches dialog box solves this dilemma. If this option is on, Eudora transfers all of your new messages from the POP server to the PC you are presently using (presumably a secondary PC), while keeping copies of those messages in your account on the POP server. On the next mail check from the secondary PC, Eudora ignores the copies of previously read messages and looks for new ones.

If the Leave Mail on Server option in the Switches dialog box is on, the progress window appears on-screen when Eudora transfers the new mail.

When using your primary PC, you should turn off the Leave Mail on Server option so that all messages (new ones as well as copies of old ones you read through other systems) are transferred to and consolidated on the primary system. The Leave Mail on Server option should be used with care because it can result in a buildup of messages on the POP server machine.

Eudora looks for a Status: R header to determine whether a message has been read. Your POP server must cooperate for this to work; most do.

Skip Big Messages option

If the Skip Big Messages option in the Switches dialog box is on, Eudora does not download large messages (40K or larger). Instead, it downloads only the first few lines of such messages and adds a note at the bottom stating that the whole message has not been transferred. This capability can be useful on slow connections.

Eudora requires some help from your POP server to make Skip Big Messages work properly. Specifically, Eudora expects your server to add a Status: header once Eudora has downloaded the first few lines of the message. Eudora uses that line as a signal that it already has the first few lines and doesn't need to download them again.

Stopping a mail check

If you want to stop a mail check in the middle (because it is taking longer than anticipated), hold down the Ctrl key and type a period (.).

Opening a mailbox to read a message

To open a mailbox, select the desired mailbox from the list of mailboxes in the Mailbox menu. The Mailbox window then appears.

Opening a mailbox window

To open a *nested* mailbox (one that is contained within a mail folder), select the outermost folder from the Mailbox menu (folders are designated by an arrow next to their names). This displays the submenu of mailboxes and/or folders within the outer folder. Select the desired mailbox (or continue selecting subfolders until the mailbox can be selected).

Opening a mailbox in a Mail Folder

If any messages are stored in the mailbox, they are listed as individual message summaries. A message summary usually consists of the message status and priority, the sender/recipient of the message, the date it was received, its size, and the subject heading. See the "Anatomy of a mailbox window" section for descriptions of these fields.

Message summaries are listed in the In mailbox. To open a message, double-click its message summary or, if the message summary is current (highlighted), select Open from the File menu or press Enter.

Creating mailboxes and mail folders

There are two ways to create new mailboxes and mail folders. You can create mailboxes and folders using the Mailboxes dialog box in the Special menu, and you can create mailboxes and folders using the New option in the Transfer menu (see the "Creating a mailbox during transfer" section). The Mailboxes window is most useful if you want to create several mailboxes at one time. The New option is most useful if you want to create a mailbox and simultaneously transfer a message or messages into that mailbox.

Anatomy of a mailbox window

Mailbox windows are one of the most important elements of Eudora. See Figure 11-4 for an example window.

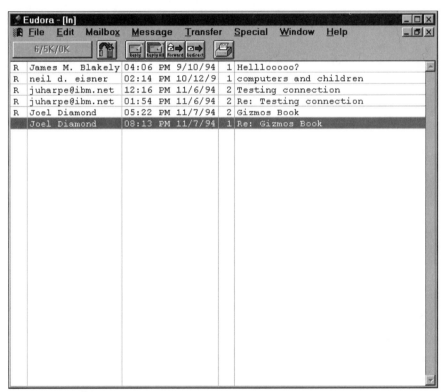

Figure 11-4: A mailbox window.

Message summaries

Each line in a mailbox window represents one message and is called a message summary. To select a message summary, click it. There are several ways to select more than one summary. You can select a summary and drag through the ones you want to select. You can select one summary, hold down the Shift key, and select another summary to select both summaries and all the summaries between them. Finally, you can hold down the Ctrl key and select individual summaries. This way, you can make nonsequential selections.

Mailbox window columns

A mailbox window (and hence each message summary) is divided into five columns: Status/Priority, Sender/Recipient, Date, Size, and Subject.

The Status/Priority column displays two separate items. The first is the message status, which is one of the following:

Message Status	Meaning
<blank>	The message has been read (all mailboxes except Out), or is not yet able to be queued because it has no recipients (Out mailbox only).
R	Reply has been chosen for the message.
F	Forward has been chosen for the message.
D	Redirect has been chosen for the message.
S	The message has been sent (outgoing messages only).
-	The message was transferred from the Out mailbox before being sent.

For more information on message priorities, see the section entitled "Assigning message priorities."

The Sender/Recipient column shows the sender of the message (for incoming messages) or the recipient or intended recipient (for outgoing messages).

Bugs in some POP servers/mail transport systems may result in Eudora displaying the sender of incoming messages as ???@??? because the required From header is missing.

The Date column displays the date and time the message was sent or, for timed messages, the date and time the message is scheduled to be sent.

The date is formatted according to the short date format in current use by your PC, and the time is formatted according to the current time format.

The Size column displays the size of the message in K. The Subject column displays the subject of the message. This information was typed into the message header by the sender.

Resizing columns

You can resize any column in a mailbox window. Move the mouse pointer until it is over the dotted column divider to the right of the column you want to resize. The pointer turns into the column resize cursor.

Simply press the mouse button, drag the divider to the position you desire, and release the mouse button. The column divider moves to the new location, and the mailbox is redrawn.

You can shrink a column only as far as its left divider. If you do so, a double divider line is displayed in place of the column, and its contents are hidden. To redisplay the column, drag the right divider line to the right.

Mailbox size display

The lower-left corner of each mailbox window displays size information for that mailbox. Three numbers are displayed. The first is the number of messages in the mailbox; the second is the total amount of space those messages require; and the third is the amount of disk space that is wasted in the mailbox. Eudora occasionally recovers this wasted space on its own. To force Eudora to recover this space from all mailboxes, select Compact Mailboxes from the Special menu. To compact an individual mailbox, hold down the Ctrl key and click the mailbox size display.

Deleting a message

As a safeguard against inadvertent deletions, two steps are required to delete a message in Eudora. For any current message, choose Delete from the Message menu. This does not actually delete the message, but transfers it to the Trash mailbox. To delete messages from the Trash mailbox, select Empty Trash from the Special menu. Quitting the program also empties the contents of the Trash mailbox when the Empty Trash on Quit option in the Switches dialog box is on. Finally, if you want to delete just a few messages from the Trash mailbox, highlight them and select Delete from the Message menu. Deleting a message that's already in the Trash removes it from Eudora.

Also, unless the Easy Delete option in the Switches dialog box is on, any attempt to delete a message that you have not opened (or a Queued message that hasn't been sent) results in Eudora asking for confirmation before proceeding with the deletion.

Compacting mailboxes: recovering storage space

Even after a message has been deleted with the two-step process described previously, the storage space used by that message is not freed. Normally, Eudora recovers this space automatically when it needs to. However, if disk space is very tight, you can force this to happen earlier than usual. In order to reclaim the storage space, select Compact Mailboxes from the Special menu. To compact an individual mailbox, hold down the Command key and click the mailbox size display (see the "Mailbox Size Display" section).

NOTE

Eudora compacts mailboxes automatically when you close them in either of two conditions. Mailboxes are compacted if the amount of wasted space in the mailbox is greater than the amount of space the messages in the mailbox use, or if the amount of space wasted in the mailbox is greater than 5 percent of the free space on the volume that contains it.

Transferring a message to a different mailbox

Messages may be transferred between any two mailboxes. For any current message, select the mailbox to which the message should be transferred from the Transfer menu. The message is removed from its previous location and stored in the selected mailbox.

NOTE

If you hold down the Alt key while transferring a message, the message is copied into the new mailbox instead of transferred. This approach is useful if you want to file a message in more than one mailbox.

Creating a mailbox during transfer

To create a mailbox and transfer the current message into it at the same time, select New from the Transfer menu instead of the name of a mailbox. The New mailbox dialog box shown in Figure 11-5 appears.

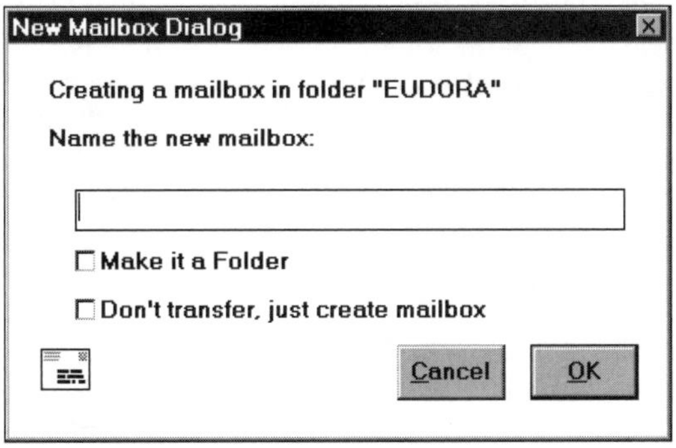
New Mailbox Dialog
Creating a mailbox in folder "EUDORA"
Name the new mailbox:
Make it a Folder
Don't transfer, just create mailbox
Cancel
OK

Figure 11-5: The New mailbox dialog box.

Type the new mailbox name and click OK. The mailbox is created and added to the Mailbox and Transfer menus. The current message is also transferred into the new mailbox. However, if you check the Don't transfer, just create mailbox option, the mailbox is created, but the message isn't transferred into it.

You can also create mailboxes using the Mailboxes dialog box in the Windows menu. The Mailboxes window is most useful if you want to create several mailboxes at one time.

Creating a mailbox folder during transfer: Eudora allows you to create mail folders in which you may keep one or more mailboxes and even other subfolders that hold additional mailboxes. In other words, not only can mailboxes be organized into folders, but folders can be contained one within another. To create a new mail folder during message transfer, select New from the Transfer menu instead of the name of a mailbox. The New Mailbox dialog box is displayed. Type the name of the new mail folder and check the Make it a Folder option. Click OK to create the folder.

Creating a mail folder: The new folder name is displayed at the bottom of the list of mailbox names under the Mailbox and Transfer menus. There is an arrow next to the name designating it as a folder and not as a mailbox. Your message can't be transferred, however, because messages must be in mailboxes and you have not yet created a mailbox. Therefore, the New Mailbox dialog box is displayed again. Now type the name of the mailbox you want to create within the newly created folder and click OK to complete the transfer.

Mailboxes and mail folders provide a structured way for Eudora users to organize received messages. The Mailboxes window allows you to create new mailboxes and folders and to remove and rename them. You may also want to move mailboxes and folders from one folder to another one.

To accomplish any of these tasks, choose Mailboxes from the Special menu. The Mailboxes window appears.

The window has two identical listings with scroll bars, each entitled Eudora Folder (or whatever the name of the folder holding your mail is.) They list the names of the mailboxes and folders you have created (folders are identified by an arrow to the right of the name). This list is similar to that displayed in the Mailbox and Transfer menus, except that the In, Out, and Trash mailboxes aren't included. Underneath each of the lists are buttons labeled Rename, New, and Remove. Between the lists are two additional buttons labeled Move, each pointing from one list to the other.

Double-clicking any of the mailboxes in a list opens that mailbox window on-screen. Individual messages can be selected, opened, and otherwise manipulated from there.

Finding the mailbox or folder

If the Mailbox window isn't big enough to display all of your created mailboxes and folders, use the scroll bar on the right side of either list to view the rest of the mailboxes and folders.

Double-clicking a folder (denoted with an arrow to the right of its name) changes the current title of the list from Eudora Folder to that of the chosen folder. The contents of the list also change to the names of mailboxes and subfolders contained in the chosen folder.

Opening a mail folder: To move back out of the subfolder to the folder that contains it, select the inner folder's title above the listing of its contents. A pop-up menu is displayed listing the available folders. Choose one of the folder names in this pop-up menu to change the list to reflect that folder's name and contents.

Removing a mailbox or folder: With the Mailboxes window open, use the scroll bar and selection tool to locate the name of the mailbox or folder that you want to remove.

You can perform this function using either of the two lists in the Mailboxes window. It is not necessary to locate a mailbox or folder in both lists before deleting it.

Once the desired mailbox/folder is found, click it once to select it. Then click the Remove button that is located below the list. A dialog box is then displayed asking you to confirm the mailbox removal. Click the Remove It button to remove the mailbox.

If you press the Ctrl key while selecting from a list of mailboxes/folders, you can select more than one mailbox or folder simultaneously. When you click the Remove button, the Mailbox Removal dialog box is displayed to verify the removal. The dialog box contains the name of the first mailbox you have selected. If you click Remove It, Eudora removes that mailbox and then displays another dialog box for the next mailbox. If you click Remove All, the selected items are removed without any further prompts.

If you choose to remove a mailbox in which messages are still stored, or a folder in which other mailboxes or folders are stored, all messages/mailboxes/folders contained within the selected mailbox are also removed.

Renaming a mailbox or folder: With the Mailboxes window open, use the scroll bar and mouse pointer to locate the name of the mailbox/folder that you want to rename. Once the desired mailbox/folder is found, click it once to select it. Then click the Rename button that is located below the list. A dialog box is then displayed requesting the new name. Type in the new name and click Rename to rename the mailbox/folder.

You can perform this function using either of the two lists in the Mailboxes window. It is not necessary to locate a mailbox or folder in both lists before renaming it.

Creating a new mailbox or folder: New mailboxes and folders can be created using the Transfer menu, as described in the "Creating mailboxes during transfer" section, or they can be created using the Mailboxes window. To create a new mailbox or folder, select Mailboxes from the Special menu. Double-click the folder in which the new mailbox/folder is to be created to open it. Its name is displayed above one of the lists, and its contents are displayed therein. Click the New button that is located below the list.

You can perform this function using either of the two lists in the Mailboxes window. It is not necessary to locate a folder in both lists before creating a new mailbox or folder inside it.

Naming a new mailbox: Type the new name, check the Make it a Folder option if you want to do so, and click OK. The new mailbox/folder is displayed in the designated folder's listing. The newly created mailbox/folder is also added to the Mailbox and Transfer menus.

The Mailboxes window provides the means for moving mailboxes and folders to other folder locations. This is why there are two lists in the window.

To begin, locate in one of the lists the folder or mailbox you want to move. In the other list, find and open (by double-clicking the name) the destination folder so that its name is displayed above the list and its contents are displayed. Then select the mailbox or folder you want to move. Now click the Move button that points from the list containing the item you want to move to the list displaying the destination folder. The mailbox/folder is moved to its new location.

Adding attachments

Any file or document can be attached to and sent with a Eudora message. To attach a document to a current outgoing message, select Attach Document from the Message menu. A standard file dialog box is displayed. Once the desired document is located, select it and click the Open button to attach the document to the message.

Attaching a document

The attached document functions like a "rider" to the e-mail message, and thus it does not appear within the message text. Instead, the name of the document and the disk from which it was copied is displayed automatically in the Attachments field of the message header.

A document cannot be attached to a message through manual editing of the Attachments field.

When the message is sent, if the chosen document is not a plain (ASCII) text file, it is formatted in the selected attachment format and sent with the message. This way you can send any kind of document through the mail, even Windows applications.

If the chosen document is a plain text file (and if the Always As Documents option in the Switches dialog box is off, or Always As Documents is not selected in the icon bar), it is not encoded in any special format before being sent, but rather it is added to your message as though you had typed it manually.

Multiple attachments

Multiple documents may be sent with a single message, but each document to be attached must be selected as described previously.

Detaching a document: To detach a document before the message is sent, click anywhere on the name of the document in the Attachments field of the composition window. Then press Delete or select Clear from the Edit menu.

Receiving an attachment: There are two primary ways you can receive an attached document from another Eudora user. One way prompts you to choose what folder the attachment should be placed in and to assign the attachment's name. The other way automatically receives all attachments in a specified folder on your disk. Both ways are described next.

Manual receive of attachments: Unless you choose Automatically save attachments to in the Configuration dialog box, whenever you receive a message with an attachment from another Eudora user, a standard file dialog box is displayed. Use this dialog box to choose where to put the document and what to call it.

Manually receiving an attachment: Eudora automatically decodes the attachment, and it arrives on your disk just the way it left the sender's.

Saving attachments automatically: The most convenient way to save attachments is to a specified folder on your disk. To set this up, select Configuration from the Special menu. In the dialog box, click the large button beneath Automatically save attachments to. A dialog box is displayed in which you may choose a folder in which arriving attachments are automatically saved.

Selecting an attachments folder: Double-click the name of the folder into which you want Eudora to put attachments (its name should be displayed in the menu above the list). At this point, click the Use Folder button. The dialog box then closes, leaving the Configuration dialog box displayed. The name of the folder you just selected to receive attachments is now shown in the button. If you ever want to specify a different folder to receive attachments, simply click this button, and the dialog box for choosing an attachments folder is redisplayed.

In order for the folder to be used, the Automatically save attachments to: option must also be checked. Eudora checks this for you when you select a folder.

 If at some future time Eudora cannot find your selected folder (perhaps because the volume that contained it is not available), it unchecks the Automatically save attachments to: option. However, the name of the folder remains in the button until another folder is selected.

When you choose this option, attachments are decoded automatically and saved directly into the selected folder. The name given your attachments is recorded in the message from which they came. If you receive multiple attachments with the same name, a number is added to each attachment's name.

Not saving an attachment: You may choose not to save the attached document. You click the Cancel button in the previous dialog box. In such a case, the attachment is included in the body of the message. The document has to be saved to a file and decoded manually to appear in its proper format.

Replying to, forwarding, or redirecting an incoming message

This section describes the Reply, Forward, and Redirect commands found in the Message menu. These commands are different from the Reply To, Forward To, and Redirect To commands found in the same menu. This latter set of commands is used with the Quick Recipient list (see the "Quick Recipient List" section for descriptions of these commands).

Replying to a message

To reply to a current message, select Reply from the Message menu. A new message window is displayed, with the original sender's address automatically placed in the To field of the header. The original sender's text is also automatically included in the message body (prefixed by > at the beginning of each line). This text may be edited as needed. Additional text can be added to the reply just as to any outgoing message, and the reply can then be sent or saved for further changes.

An incoming message for which the Reply command has been used is identified by an *R* in its message summary.

There are several variations of the Reply command, which are listed in the following mini-table.

Command	*Meaning*
Reply all	If you hold down the Alt key when selecting Reply from the Message menu, the reply message is sent to the sender of the original message and to everyone who received it. This is useful for carrying on group discussions electronically. However, if the Reply All option in the Switches dialog box is on, Reply all is the default, and you must hold down the Alt key to reply only to the message sender.
Don't include self	If the Include Self option in the Switches dialog box is off, Eudora does not include your return address in the Reply all.
Quote selection only	In some cases, you may want to respond to only a portion of the sender's message. First highlight the desired text in the sender's message. Then hold down Shift when selecting Reply from the Message menu. Only the highlighted text is quoted in your reply message.

Forwarding a message

You may want to relay, or forward, messages to other users. To forward a current message, select Forward from the Message menu. A new message window is displayed, with your address automatically placed in the From field of the header. The original sender's text is also automatically included in the message body (prefixed by > at the beginning of each line). This text may be edited, and more text can be added to the message. Type the address of the person to whom you want the message forwarded in the empty To field of the header. The message can then be sent or saved for further changes.

An incoming message for which the Forward command has been used is identified by an *F* in its message summary.

Redirecting a message

Eudora provides a way to redirect messages that you decide were more appropriately sent to someone besides yourself. To redirect a current message, select Redirect from the Message menu. A new message window is displayed. The address in the From field is that of the person who originally sent the message, by way of your address. In addition, there are no > markers at the beginning of each line of the original text. However, you may edit or add more text to the message. Type the address of the person to whom you want the message redirected in the empty To field of the header. The message can then be sent or saved for further changes.

An incoming message for which the Redirect command has been used is identified by a *D* in its message summary.

Easy repeat (canned) messages using Redirect: If you find yourself sending the same message over and over again to different people, you can keep a "canned" copy of that message and send it easily using the Redirect command. To do this, first compose a new message as you normally do but leave the To field blank. Save the message and, if desired, use the Transfer menu to move it from the Out mailbox into another mailbox (named "Canned Messages" perhaps). When you want to send the message to someone, locate the message and open it (or simply highlight it in the mailbox window), select Redirect from the Messages menu, fill in the To field, and send the message.

Redirect and signatures: When you use Redirect, your signature file (described in the "Creating a signature" section) is not added to the message when it is sent, unless the message was originally created by you. Eudora considers the message to be originally from you if the address in the From field exactly matches your return address.

Creating and using nicknames

When you're addressing messages, Eudora supports the use of nicknames in place of full user names. A nickname (sometimes called an *alias*) is an easily remembered, shorter substitute for an actual e-mail address or group of addresses. Typically, nicknames are created for persons with whom you have repeated correspondence, and hence serve as a typing and reference shortcut. Eudora allows nicknames to be used in place of proper e-mail addresses in the To, Cc, and Bcc fields in the headers of outgoing messages.

To create, edit, or remove a nickname, select Nicknames from the Special menu. The Nicknames window is then displayed. This window is divided into three main fields. The Nickname field lists all your nicknames; the Address(es) field displays a selected nickname's expansion (the addresses that the nickname represents); and the Notes field contains your private notes on a nickname.

Adding new nicknames: To add a new nickname, click the New button. The New Nickname dialog box is displayed prompting you for the name of the new nickname. (See Figure 11-6).

Type the name of the new nickname. If you want this nickname to show up on the Quick Recipient list under the Message menu (see the "Nicknames and Quick Recipient list" section), click the Put it on the recipient list option. Then click OK. The new nickname is displayed in the Nicknames field of the Nick-names window, and the insertion point is placed in the Address(es) field. Type the complete e-mail address of the person to be represented by the nickname.

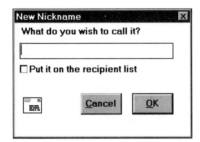

Figure 11-6: The New Nickname dialog box.

Entering an address for a nickname: If you'd like to add someone's proper name to the address that you specify, just put it in parentheses after the e-mail address. You may also type a series of many e-mail addresses (and even other nicknames), separated by commas or returns, in the Address(es) section. These multiple addresses are represented by the single entered nickname. In this way, a nickname can be used for a group mailing list. The Notes field can be used to enter any text you'd like to associate with a nickname, such as the addressee's company, title, or phone number.

 Be aware that the proper name is put in the To field of mail messages along with the full address.

 The Nicknames window is the only place where it is permissible to press Enter to separate addresses. Everywhere else you must use commas.

One nickname can point to another nickname, which can point to still another, and so on; eventually, however, the nickname must end in a real address or group of addresses. For example, Eudora contains John in its expansion, and John is itself a nickname for jnoerenberg@qualcomm.com.

One nickname using another nickname: Once you've finished typing addresses and notes, you can click the New button again to make another nickname. When finished making additions or changes, select Save from the File menu to save the changes. If you close the Nicknames window without saving the changes, a dialog box appears asking whether the additions/changes you just made should be saved or discarded.

 Your nicknames are saved in the Eudora Nicknames file. This file is a plain TEXT file in UNIX .mailrc format.

Changing and removing nicknames: To change a nickname, select Nicknames from the Special menu. Click the desired nickname in the Nickname field to select it. Then click the Rename button. A dialog box appears and allows you to change the nickname. You can also add or remove the nickname from the Quick Recipient list using the Rename dialog box. Just check or uncheck the Put it on the recipient list option. Once the changes are completed, click OK.

Renaming a nickname: To change a nickname's corresponding e-mail address(es) and notes, click the desired nickname to select it. The addresses and notes associated with the nickname are displayed in the Address(es) and Notes fields, and may be edited.

Changing a nickname expansion: To remove the nickname, click the desired nickname to select it. Click the Remove button.

When you are finished editing or making deletions, select Save from the File menu to save the changes. If you close the Nicknames window without saving the changes, a dialog box appears asking whether the additions/changes/deletions you just made should be saved or discarded.

Make Nickname command: The Make Nickname command can be used to make a nickname in two different ways.

From the Nicknames window itself, use Command-click to select several different nicknames, and then choose Make Nickname from the Special menu. The New Nickname dialog box is displayed prompting you for the name of the new nickname. Once you have entered the name, click OK to create the new nickname with the selected nicknames in the Nicknames window as its address-ees. This is an easy way to make a group nickname out of existing nicknames.

Alternatively, you can make a nickname out of the address list of a current message. Open a mailbox and click the desired message to make it current. Select Make Nickname from the Special menu. The New Nickname dialog box is displayed prompting you for the name of the new nickname. Once you have entered the name, click OK. If the current message is an outgoing message, its To, Cc, and Bcc fields are used for the nickname's addressees. If the current message is an incoming message, its From field is used for the nickname's addressees. If multiple messages are current (you have several message summaries selected in a mailbox window), addresses are taken from each message and all are put in the new nickname's expansion.

When an incoming message is current, Make Nickname pretends to do a Reply to the current message, and then takes all the recipients from the reply message and uses them in the nickname expansion. This means that Make Nickname acts just like Reply in regard to the Include Self and Reply All options in the Switches dialog box. That is, if the Reply All option in the Switches dialog box is on (or you hold down the option key), the nickname is made for all of the recipients of the messages plus the sender, not just the sender. Similarly, if the Include Self option in the Switches dialog box is off, your address is not included in the new nickname's expansion.

Using the nicknames window to address mail: The To, Cc, and Bcc buttons in the Nicknames window can be used to start mail messages or to add addressees to existing current messages. To create a new message from the Nicknames window, select the nickname to which you want to address the mail (you can select multiple nicknames by holding down the Ctrl key and clicking each nickname). Then click the To button. A new composition window is displayed with the selected nickname(s) inserted the To field.

Once the composition window is displayed, use the To, Cc, and Bcc buttons to insert additional nicknames into the corresponding fields.

If you hold down the Option key when addressing messages using the Nickname window To, Cc, and Bcc buttons, the full nickname expansion is inserted into the appropriate message field rather than just the nickname.

The Nicknames window can also be used to address existing messages, or new messages created by selecting New from the Message menu. Make sure the desired message is current (topmost), open the Nicknames window, and use the To, Cc, and Bcc buttons to address the message.

When the Nicknames window Nickname field is selected (indicated by the bold square around the field), you can type the first few letters of a nickname to select that nickname. If the bold square isn't around the Nickname field, click the list to select it.

Nicknames and the Quick Recipient list

Nicknames and the Quick Recipient list are two separate entities. Nicknames are used as an abbreviation for an address or a list of addresses. The Quick Recipient list is used to add addresses to messages via the Message menu. Nicknames do not need to be on the Quick Recipient list, and not everything on the Quick Recipient list needs to be a nickname.

However, you may have nicknames to which you often send mail, and it makes sense to add these nicknames to the Quick Recipient list. This is easily done from the Nicknames window.

Examine the Nickname field in the Nicknames window. Notice that there is a margin between the first letter of each nickname and the edge of the field. Now select a nickname and place the mouse over the margin between the nickname and the edge of the field. The cursor changes into a miniature image of a menu. Click the mouse once and a bullet (•) is displayed in the margin area. This bullet indicates that the nickname has been added to the Quick Recipient list.

Click again and the bullet disappears, removing the nickname from the Quick Recipient list. The Quick Recipient list is discussed further in the "Quick Recipient list" section.

Double-clicking a nickname also puts it on or removes it from the Quick Recipient list.

If you rename or remove a nickname that is also on the Quick Recipient list, the name on the Quick Recipient list is also changed or removed.

Finish Nickname command

The Finish Nickname command in the Edit menu is another nickname-related function designed to save typing in header fields. It allows you to type only a portion of a nickname in the To, Cc, or Bcc fields of a message, with Eudora completing the typing task.

To use this option, type only the number of characters in the nickname that make it unique with respect to other nicknames in the appropriate field of the message header. Then select Finish Nickname from the Edit menu. The partial text of the nickname is automatically completed in the header field.

For example, if you type an **S** in the To field and you have only one nickname that starts with the letter S, the Finish Nickname function completes the nickname in the message header.

If you hold down the Alt key while finishing a nickname, the nickname's expansion is inserted instead of the nickname.

Quick Recipient list

It may be more convenient to address a message by selecting a nickname or full address from a predetermined Quick Recipient list. This eliminates the need to type frequently used nicknames or addresses in the fields of outgoing message headers. If you select a nickname or address from the Quick Recipient list, the address or nickname is automatically entered in the desired field. The list may also be used to reply to, forward, or redirect messages more easily.

Eudora uses a single Quick Recipient list that can be accessed via the New Message To, Reply To, Forward To, and Redirect To selections in the Message menu, the Insert Recipient selection in the Edit menu, and the Remove Recipient selection in the Special menu.

Creating the quick recipient list: The Quick Recipient list should consist of the nicknames or addresses of common correspondents. To add a nickname to this list, choose Nicknames from the Special menu (see the "Creating and using nicknames" section for more details). The Nicknames window is displayed. Select the desired nickname or nicknames from the Nickname field. Then click in the margin between the first letter of the nickname and the left side of the field. This places a bullet in the margin and adds the nickname(s) to the Quick Recipient list.

To add a full e-mail address to the Quick Recipient list, select the desired text that makes up the full address from any current message header. Then select Add As Recipient from the Special menu.

Using the Quick Recipient list: The Quick Recipient list is displayed when you select New Message To, Reply To, Forward To, or Redirect To from the Message menu. To utilize the list, select a recipient using one of these commands. Releasing the mouse button performs the action (new message, reply, forward, redirect), and the chosen recipient is automatically inserted in the To field of the new message header.

Starting a message with the Quick Recipient list: More than one nickname or address from the Quick Recipient list can be added to the To, Cc, and Bcc fields of any message. To do this, first place the blinking insertion point in the field where you want the nickname/address to be inserted. Then select the desired recipient from the Insert Recipient list in the Edit menu. The chosen nickname/address is placed at the insertion point, and a comma is added (if necessary) to separate the new address from the ones previously placed in the field.

Removing a Quick Recipient from the list: To remove a nickname/address entry from the Quick Recipient list, select it using the Remove Recipient option in the Special menu. When you release the mouse button, the selected recipient is deleted.

Removing a nickname from the Quick Recipient list does not delete it from the Nicknames window, but removing a nickname from the Nicknames window deletes it from the Quick Recipient list.

Finding specified text within messages

Eudora incorporates a Find function that searches for specific text within a single message, multiple messages, or even multiple mailboxes. To display the Find commands, select Find from the Edit menu.

Finding text within one message: To search for text within a single message, open the message and make sure it is current. Then select Find from the Edit menu and select the Find command. The Find dialog box then appears, with the blinking insertion point located in the text field.

Type the text you want to find in the text field. When finished entering the desired text, click the Find button. Starting at the insertion point of the open message, Eudora searches the current message for the specified text. If no match is found, the *Not Found* message is displayed. If the search is successful, the message is scrolled to the first point where the match is found, and the matching text is highlighted.

To continue searching in the same message for the next occurrence of the text, click the Find button in the Find dialog box, or select the Find Again command. These commands are equivalent and limit the search to the same message. Repeating these commands cycles through the matches in the open message only.

Use the Find button or Find Again command to search within the topmost message only.

Enter Selection command

If you don't want to actually type the text in the Find dialog box (for example, the text is very long or complex), highlight it in an existing message, and then select Enter Selection from the Find submenu. This automatically inserts the selected text at the insertion point in the Find dialog box. Then select the Find command from the Find submenu to start the search.

Finding text among multiple messages and mailboxes: The Next, Next Message, and Next Mailbox commands are located in the Find submenu (in the Edit menu) or as buttons in the Find dialog box (see Figure 11-7).

Next command: The Next command allows you to search for the next match of the specified text until it is found either in the same message or among all messages in the current mailbox. Use Next to find the next occurrence of the text string in or after the topmost message.

 The Next command initiated in an open mailbox (even with messages selected) searches for the specified text among all messages contained in that mailbox. The search begins with the first selected message.

Next Message command: The Next Message command begins the search at the message after the current message. Eudora continues to search until it finds a matching character string, even if it has to open more than one message or a new mailbox. Use Next Message to skip the rest of the occurrences of the text string in the current message and search the next message(s)/mailbox(es).

Next Mailbox command: The Next Mailbox command begins the search for the specified text in the mailbox following the current mailbox. The search is conducted among all messages in that mailbox and any subsequent mailboxes, including the In, Out, and Trash mailboxes. The search includes all mailboxes, even if they are contained in mailbox folders or subfolders.

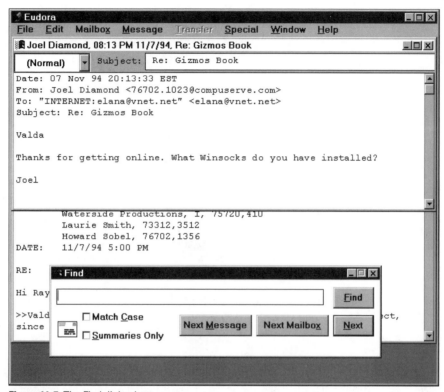

Figure 11-7: The Find dialog box.

Mailboxes are searched in the order they are listed in the Mailbox menu until the current mailbox is reached.

Use Next Mailbox to skip the rest of the occurrences of the text string in the current mailbox and search the next mailbox(es).

When the character string is found in a message, the mailbox containing that message is checked in the Mailboxes menu. This identifies the location of the message.

Summaries Only: If you know the text you are searching for is included in a message summary, check the Summaries Only option in the Find dialog box. When you click the Find button, Eudora searches for the text only in the Sender and Subject fields of message summaries as they appear in mailbox windows. Eudora searches much faster when this option is checked.

Match case: Normally, Eudora ignores capitalization when searching. If you want Eudora to consider capitalization when searching, check the Match case option in the Find dialog box. When this option is checked, Eudora searches for exact matches of character strings, including any capitalization.

Stopping a find: If you want to stop Eudora from continuing a search, hold down the Ctrl key and type a period (.).

Sorting messages within mailboxes

It is possible to sort the message summaries in a mailbox window according to their status, priority, sender, date, or subject. These commands are listed in the Sort submenu in the Edit menu.

The Sort submenu: To use any of these commands, first open the mailbox to be sorted. Then select the appropriate command from the Sort submenu. The mailbox's messages are sorted when the mouse button is released.

Eudora sorts in ascending order; the smallest item first. To sort in descending order, hold down the Alt key while choosing the desired command from the Sort submenu.

Eudora's sorting algorithm is "stable." This means that sorting on a particular column leaves items of the same value in the same order as they were before the sort. This feature allows you to sort based on multiple criteria by using multiple sort commands. For example, if you want your messages sorted by subject and within each subject you want messages sorted by date, first choose Sort by Date and then Sort by Subject.

Sometimes Eudora does not sort by date properly. This happens if the mail was stored in an old version of Eudora and the table of contents was rebuilt, or the messages have incorrectly formatted date fields or unknown or incorrect time zones.

Saving a message to a file

Eudora allows you to save a current message(s) to a separate text file on your PC. To do this, first display the desired message or highlight its summary in the mailbox window. Then select Save As from the File menu. The Save As dialog box is displayed allowing you to choose a name and location for the file.

Note the two options at the bottom of the Save As dialog box. Guess Paragraphs instructs Eudora to remove extraneous carriage returns from the message, leaving returns only at the ends of paragraphs. In addition, it converts multiple spaces into tabs.

Include Headers instructs Eudora to retain the message's header information in the saved document. If this is unchecked, only the body of the message is saved. Once you've made your choices, click the Save button in the dialog box.

Saving a message to a text file

If you select multiple messages from a mailbox window and select Save As, all of the messages are saved to a single file.

When Eudora receives a very large message from the POP server, it splits that message into multiple smaller messages. If you need to reassemble the original message, use the Save As command.

Choosing an application for saved messages: When you save a message to a file using the Save As command, the new text file is formatted as basic ASCII text. The document type is determined by the program you select using the Application TEXT files belong to setting in the Configuration dialog box.

To do this, select Configuration from the Special menu. The Configuration dialog box is then displayed (review Figure 11-1).

Near the bottom of the dialog box, click the large button beneath the Application TEXT files belong to prompt. An alert is displayed prompting you to choose the application you want to use to open messages saved as text files. A standard file dialog box is also displayed. Using this dialog box, search through your disk to locate the desired application (probably your favorite word processing program). Select the application and then click Open.

The selected application is then displayed in the Configuration dialog box, and the desired application is selected.

Resending rejected messages

Mail Transport Agents are computer programs responsible for routing e-mail messages through networks. If for some reason an e-mail message can't be delivered to an intended recipient, these programs return the message to the original sender. A message is typically rejected because of an error in the recipient's address, although many other reasons are possible.

The message sent back from the mail system usually includes cryptic information that may allow you to determine the reason for the message being rejected. It also includes the text of the original message.

Eudora deletes the error messages and added text and recovers the original message so that you can make any corrections and resend it. To do this for the current message, select Send Again from the Message menu. Choosing this option eliminates the inserted extra text and reformats the message as it originally appeared. You can then make changes or additions and resend the message, if desired.

Assigning Message priorities

Eudora allows you to assign priorities to your messages. These priorities are for sender/recipient reference purposes only, and they do not affect the way Eudora handles the messages.

There are five priority levels available, each represented by a small icon. Priorities range from 1 (highest) to 5 (lowest). Priority 3 is assumed for messages that have no assigned priorities, and it is not displayed.

Message priorities are displayed in the Status/Priority column of the mailbox window.

To change the priority of a message, open the message and choose the desired priority from the Priority pop-up menu on the icon bar. The selected priority icon is then displayed in the pop-up window. You can also change the priority of the current message(s) by holding down the Command key and pressing a number key from 1 to 5 (1 = Highest, 5 = Lowest).

When you receive mail with a priority other than Normal, Eudora adds an X-Priority: header to the mail. The header lists the assigned priority.

All new messages are created with Normal priority, even replies to messages whose priority you have changed. The exception is that, if the sender of a message gives it a priority other than normal, Eudora insists on giving your reply the same priority. You can, however, change the priority of your response by reassigning it manually.

Editing message subjects

Sometimes the subject of a message is not clear or descriptive. Eudora allows you to edit the subject of any incoming message.

After they are sent, the subjects of outgoing messages (messages sent by you) cannot be edited. However, prior to being sent, outgoing message subjects can be changed by editing the Subject field in the message header.

To edit the subject of an incoming message, open it from its mailbox window. Notice that the subject is displayed below the title bar and above the message proper. You may edit this text as you would any other text. When editing is complete, press Enter or close the message. The new subject is displayed in the message summary. The contents of the Subject field of the message header remain unchanged.

If you reply to the message, the original subject is used for the reply, not your changed subject. This gives you the freedom to put information useful to you into the summary, without fear of your private notes being revealed to your correspondents.

Printing messages

Eudora can print a current message or messages, a plain text window, or the contents of the Ph window. To print from within Eudora, select Print from the File menu with the message or item displayed. If you have text selected in any of the previous windows, you can print just the selected text using the Print Selection command under the File menu.

Eudora automatically prints headers and footers on each page, giving the window title, page number and your return address.

Using the Ph window

Eudora can access two different directory services, Ph and Finger, via the Ph window. To display the Ph window, select Ph from the Special menu.

The Ph window has two buttons (one for Ph and one for Finger) and two text fields (one where you type your query and one where you see the response).

To use the Ph protocol, the name of a Ph server must be entered in the Ph Server field in the Configuration dialog box. To use Ph, type the name of the person you want to look up in the query field and click the Ph button. The server's response is displayed in the response field.

You can type any Ph command in the query field, except login commands or commands requiring login.

Using Finger

To use the Finger protocol, type your query into the query field. This query should be in the form *name@domain*. If you omit the @domain segment, Eudora assumes you mean your SMTP server host. Once the name is entered, click the Finger button.

The Finger query is sent to the host specified in the @domain part, and the response is displayed in the response field.

Creating a signature

A *signature* is a brief message automatically added by Eudora to the end of outgoing messages. It should consist of a few lines giving the sender's full name and e-mail address. Other pertinent details, such as phone number, postal address, or place of employment, are also sometimes included.

To create the signature, select Signature from the Special menu. A blank Signature window is displayed. Type your signature text in this window. When you are finished typing the signature, close the Signature window. An alert is displayed asking whether you want to save the changes to your signature. Click Save. You may modify your signature at any time by repeating this procedure.

In order to activate your signature on an outgoing message, click the signature icon on the icon bar. The signature text is not displayed at the end of messages you create, but your recipients see it.

In order for Eudora to work correctly, the program must be configured by providing it with some basic, though important, information. To enter this information, select Configuration from the Special menu. The Configuration dialog box is displayed (see the next section).

The Configuration dialog box

The Configuration dialog box is divided into three segments: top, middle, and bottom. Each of the fields in the dialog is described next. The default settings are listed in brackets after the name of each Configuration setting. Figure 11-8 shows the Configuration dialog box again.

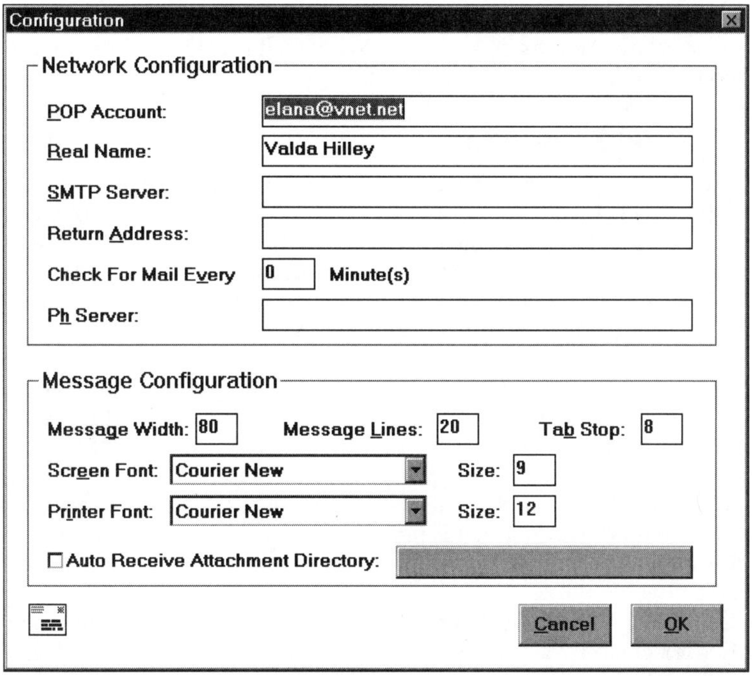

Configuration

Network Configuration

P̲OP Account:	elana@vnet.net
R̲eal Name:	Valda Hilley
S̲MTP Server:	
Return A̲ddress:	
Check For Mail E̲very:	0 Minute(s)
P̲h Server:	

Message Configuration

Message Wi̲dth: 80   Message Li̲nes: 20   Ta̲b Stop: 8

Scr̲een Font: Courier New   Size: 9

Pri̲nter Font: Courier New   Size: 12

☐ Auto Receive Attachment Directory:

C̲ancel   O̲K

Figure 11-8: The Configuration dialog box.

In order for Eudora to function correctly, the correct information must be entered into the fields in the top segment of the Configuration dialog. New users can safely ignore all fields below the top segment.

The top segment

POP account (none): To receive mail with Eudora, you must have an account on a computer that runs a POP 3 server. This is the account to which your e-mail messages are delivered before they are transferred to the Eudora program on your PC. Enter your login name for this account, followed by an @ sign and the (domain) name of the computer.

For example, if your login name for your POP account is carolyn and the name of the computer is uxh.cso.uiuc.edu, type **carolyn@uxh.cso.uiuc.edu** in this field.

Real Name (none): Enter your real name here. It is placed in parentheses after your return address in your outgoing mail. It is also displayed in the Sender column of messages you send.

The middle segment

SMTP Server (none): To send mail, a computer with an SMTP (Simple Mail Transfer Protocol) server program is necessary. You need not have a login on this computer, but you must have access to it through your network. If the computer on which you have your POP account is also an SMTP server, leave this field blank. Otherwise, specify the name of the computer which you want to use as your SMTP server.

Return Address (none): Normally, Eudora uses your POP Account as your return address. If you wish to use a return address other than your POP account, enter it here.

If you do enter an address in the Return Address field, first test the address to be sure that mail sent to it is indeed delivered to you. If you use an invalid return address, no one can reply to your mail.

Check For Mail Every ? Minute(s) (none): If you enter a number in this field, Eudora checks your POP server for new mail at regular intervals and transfers any mail addressed to you to your Windows. The number you enter specifies the number of minutes between checks of the POP server. It's a good idea to set this option at no less than 15 minutes. Checking mail more frequently puts an unnecessary drain on your POP server. This option works only when Eudora is running. Leaving this field empty disables automatic checking.

Ph Server (none): Enter the host name of your Ph name server here.

The bottom segment

Message Window Width (none): This field specifies the width of new and received message windows (in characters). If you leave this field blank, the default value is 80. This setting has no effect on what your mail looks like when it is sent. When mail is sent, Eudora wraps at or before 76 columns.

If you use a proportional font, Eudora sets the window width based on the width of the "0" character.

Message Window Height (none): This field specifies the height of new and received message windows (in lines). If you leave this field blank, the default value is 20.

If the Zoom Windows option in the Switches dialog box is on, received messages window heights are automatically adjusted to the length of the message text.

Screen Font, Size (Mishawaka): This pop-up menu allows you to select a screen font to be used for displaying the text of your Eudora messages and mailbox windows. Type the size (in points) of the font you want to use in the Size field.

Printer Font, Size (Courier): This pop-up menu allows you to select a font to be used when you print messages using the Print command.

Application TEXT files belong to: When you choose Save As from the File menu, Eudora creates a Windows document that is saved for the application named in this field. That is, when you double-click the saved file, this application is used to open it. You may want to set this option to your favorite word processing program. To change the setting, click the application name button . A dialog box is displayed allowing you to select the application (see the "Choosing an application for saved messages" section).

Automatically save attachments to (off, none): If this option is checked, Eudora automatically places file attachments that come with messages into the specified folder. To change the setting, click the application name button (the default is blank). A dialog box is displayed allowing you to select the folder (see the "Saving Attachments Automatically" section).

The Switches dialog box

You may tailor many aspects of Eudora to your own needs and preferences. Some of these are set with the Configuration dialog box described in the previous section. Others are set with the Switches dialog box, shown in Figure 11-9. If the setting can be either on or off, it's in the Switches dialog box; if a choice beyond on or off is required, it's in the Configuration dialog box. To display the Switches dialog box, choose Switches from the Special menu.

The Switches dialog box is divided into seven groups of options, with a descriptive heading above each group. A check in the box next to the option indicates that the option is on. Each of the options is described next. The default settings are listed in parentheses after the name of each option.

Composition options

Many of the Composition options can be turned on and off for individual messages using the icon bar displayed at the top of the message composition window. However, setting them here establishes these settings as the icon bar defaults for all new composition windows.

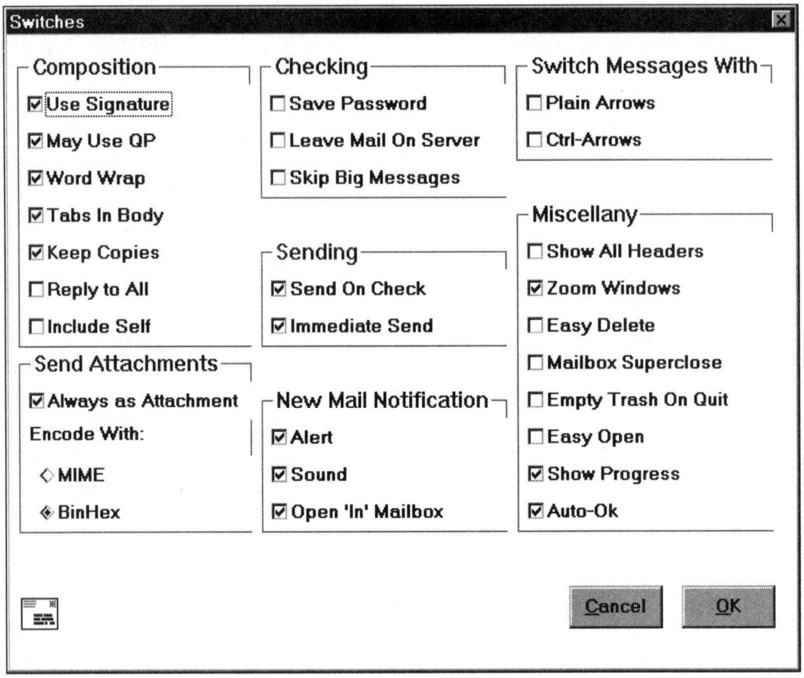

Figure 11-9: The Switches dialog box.

May Use QP (on): If May Use QP is on, Eudora uses quoted-printable encoding when necessary, such as when messages that contain long lines of text or special characters are sent. If this option is off, quoted-printable encoding is not used.

Word Wrap (on): If Word Wrap is on, a carriage return is not required at the end of each line of type in an outgoing message. Eudora automatically wraps text to the next line, with line breaks at roughly 76 characters per line. This makes your mail more legible to recipients using line-oriented mail systems. It is strongly recommended that you turn this option on.

Tabs in Body (on): If Tabs in Body is on, pressing Tab within the message body results in Eudora inserting enough spaces to move the insertion point to a multiple of eight characters from the start of the line. This mimics the way tabs work on many terminals. If this option is off, pressing the Tab returns the cursor to the To field of the message header.

This option also controls the handling of tabs in text that is pasted into the message window and in plain text attachments that are not sent as documents. If Tabs in Body is on, tabs in such texts are replaced with the previously mentioned number of spaces, as though you had typed them in.

This option also controls what Eudora does with tab characters that appear in mail downloaded from your POP server. If the option is on, Eudora replaces these with the appropriate numbers of spaces, like it does for typed or pasted text. It is suggested that you keep this option on. Otherwise, you may get messy results when receiving mail that contains tab characters.

Keep Copies (off): If Keep Copies is on, a copy of each sent message is kept in the Out mailbox (their summaries are marked with an *S* in the Status/Priority column of the Out mailbox window). If this option is off, Eudora moves outgoing messages to the Trash mailbox after they are sent.

Use Signature (on): If Use Signature is on, Eudora automatically attaches your signature file (if you have one) to the end of outgoing messages.

Reply to All (off): If Reply to All is on, selecting Reply from the Message menu creates a message addressed not only to the sender of the original message, but also to all of its recipients. If the option is off, Reply addresses the new message only to the sender.

You can use the Alt key to reverse this setting for any given reply. That is, if this option is off, holding down the Alt key while choosing Reply replies to all, and vice-versa.

This option setting also affects the Make Nickname command (see the "Make Nickname command" section).

Include Self (off): If Include Self is on, when you do a reply all (as described) your address is left in the address list of the new message and you receive a copy of your own reply. If this option is off, your address is removed from the reply message.

To determine who you are, Eudora uses the "me" nickname, if you have one. If not, it uses the contents of the POP Account and Return Address fields from the Configuration dialog box.

This option setting also affects the Make Nickname command (see the "Make Nickname command" section).

Send Attachments options

These options define the way attachments are sent.

Checking options

These options determine the way Eudora checks for and receives mail.

Save Password (off): If Save Password is on, you never have to enter your password to check your mail (even if you quit Eudora and restart it) because your password is stored in Windows. Use this option only if your PC is in a secure place.

Leave Mail on Server (off): Eudora normally transfers your incoming messages from your account on the POP server to Windows and deletes them from the POP server. If Leave Mail on Server is on, Eudora transfers incoming messages to Windows and also keeps copies on the POP server (see the "Leave Mail on Server option" section).

Skip Big Messages (off): If Skip Big Messages is on, Eudora does not download the entire texts of very large messages from the POP server, but only downloads the first few lines. This can be useful on slow connections.

Sending options

These options determine the way Eudora sends mail.

Send on Check (on): If Send on Check is on, Eudora automatically sends any messages that are queued in the Out mailbox whenever it checks the POP Server for new mail.

Fix Curly Quotes (on): If Fix Curly Quotes is on, Eudora replaces all "smart" quotes in message text or attachments with "conventional" quotes prior to sending the message/attachment. The "smart" quotation marks are special characters, and this option allows messages to be sent without using quoted-printable encoding.

If your recipients have MIME, there's no reason to use the curly quotes option. Turn it on only if most of the people you correspond with don't use MIME.

Immediate Send (on): If Immediate Send is on, the rightmost button in the icon bar of the message composition window is labeled Send. Clicking this button immediately sends the message to the POP server. If this option is off, the button is labeled Queue, and clicking it places the message in the Out mailbox marked ready for delivery (Q).

New Mail Notification options

These options determine what Eudora does when it is running in the background and wants your attention, or when new mail arrives.

Alert (on): If Alert is on, Eudora uses an alert to notify you when new mail is received.

Sound (on): If Sound is on, Eudora makes a noise when it needs you. There are two different sounds: one for the arrival of mail and one for everything else.

Flash Menu Icon (on): If Flash Menu Icon is on, Eudora flashes an icon in the menu bar when it needs you. Eudora uses two different icons: a Mail flag when you have new mail and an envelope with an exclamation point in it for everything else.

Open "In" Mailbox (on): This option applies only to the arrival of new mail. If Open "In" Mailbox is on, Eudora automatically opens the In mailbox when new mail arrives. It also scrolls to the end of the mailbox and selects the first unread message of the last unread batch of messages, or FUMLUB. If this option is off, Eudora doesn't open the In mailbox when new messages arrive.

Switch Messages With options

These options allow you to activate the Windows keyboard arrow keys as a method of toggling through messages.

Plain Arrows (off): If Plain Arrows is on and there is a message window open on the screen, the Windows keyboard arrow keys can be used to close the current message and open the next or previous message in the mailbox. The up- or left-arrow key opens the previous message; the down or right arrow key opens the next message. If this option is off, the arrow keys can be used to move the insertion point in messages.

Even if Plain Arrows is on, the arrow keys do not switch messages if there is a message composition window topmost on the screen.

Ctrl-Arrows (on): If Ctrl-Arrows is on, message switching using the arrow keys (as described in the "Plain Arrows" section) is permissible only when you press the Ctrl key.

The Ctrl-Arrows keystrokes do work when composition windows are open on the screen.

Miscellany options

These options control miscellaneous Eudora functions.

Show All Headers (off): If Show All Headers is on, Eudora displays the complete header, including routing information, with the message. If this option is off, Eudora withholds this additional information.

 If you want to see all headers for just one incoming message, close the message and reopen in with the Option key held down.

Zoom Windows (off): If Zoom Windows is on, new mailbox and message windows automatically open to their zoomed size. The zoomed size is computed on a window-by-window basis. For mailbox windows, zoomed size is just wide enough to display the widest summary, and just long enough to display all the summaries (but no longer than the Windows display screen). For message windows, zoomed size is just long enough to display all of the message (but no longer than the Windows display screen), and as wide as the Message Window Width setting in the Configuration dialog box. Composition windows zoom to the height specified by the Message Window Height setting in the Configuration dialog box.

Easy Delete (off): If Easy Delete is on, Eudora does not alert you when you are deleting messages you haven't read or transferring queued messages out of the Out mailbox.

Mailbox Superclose (off): If Mailbox Superclose is on, closing a mailbox window closes all open messages from that mailbox.

Empty Trash on Quit (on): If Empty Trash on Quit is on, Eudora empties the Trash mailbox whenever you quit the application. If this option is off, Eudora empties the Trash only when you select Empty Trash from the Special menu.

 If you want to remove some messages from the trash but don't want to empty it entirely, highlight the summaries you want to delete and select Delete from the Message menu. The selected messages are deleted.

Easy Open (on): If Easy Open is on, deleting or transferring the current message opens the next message in the mailbox, but only if it is unread.

Show Progress (on): If Show Progress is on, Eudora displays a Progress window at the top of your screen to advise you of progress made when making a network connection, transferring mail or some other long operation.

Auto-OK (On): Many network problems are temporary. When a problem occurs while Eudora is transferring or checking your mail, you are notified in the same way you would be if you were receiving new mail (see the "Get Attention By options" section). If Auto-OK is on, these notifications automatically go away after a couple of minutes. This allows Eudora to try the communication again. This setting is most useful if you have a non-zero value for the Check for mail every ? minute(s) setting in the Configuration dialog box.

 Turning this option on may cause some Communications Toolbox connection tools to give you less progress information and feedback.

Mail Storage: The first time you start Eudora, it creates a Eudora folder within your System Folder. Even though you do not need to access the Eudora folder during normal operation, this section is provided to show you where Eudora stores your mailboxes and messages.

In, Out, and Trash: These files hold your mail. You'll see files like these for every mailbox you create. These files are in UNIX mail format.

IN.TOC, OUT.TOC, and TRASH.TOC: These files are the tables of contents for your mailboxes. They make it much faster for Eudora to access your mail. You'll see files like these for every mailbox you create.

Eudora Log, Old Log: Eudora keeps records of all mail transfers. These records are kept in the Eudora Log and Old Log files. The Old Log file is overwritten and a new Eudora Log file is created when the Eudora Log file reaches its approximately 100K maximum size.

Eudora supports the use of aliases for mailbox and .TOC files that, for some reason, you have moved to a location outside the Eudora folder. This allows you to open these mailboxes from within Eudora. Place Eudora aliases in the Eudora folder or a subfolder within the Eudora folder.

Sharing a PC with other users: If you are sharing a PC with other users, make a copy of the Eudora Folder for each user. The copies can be named whatever you like, and put anywhere you like, including on floppies or network volumes. To tell Eudora which folder to use, launch Eudora by double-clicking the Eudora Settings file in that folder.

Quitting Eudora

To quit the Eudora program, select Quit from the File menu. If you have queued messages or timed messages due to be sent in the next 12 hours, you are asked if you want to send them. If the Empty Trash on Quit option in the Switches dialog box is on, quitting Eudora also empties your Trash mailbox.

A word about memory

Eudora alerts you if it is running low on memory.

When this alert is displayed, quit Eudora and assign it additional memory. To do this, use the Finder to locate the Eudora application file and click it to select it. Select Get Info from the Finder's File menu to display the Eudora Info dialog box. Type the amount of memory you want Eudora to have in the Current size field. Then close the window and restart Eudora.

Changing Eudora's memory size

You can see Eudora's estimate of how much memory it needs at any given time by choosing About Eudora from the main menu with the Eudora application running. Eudora estimates the amount of memory it needs based on your open windows and the size of the In, Out, and Trash mailboxes (which are constantly in use). The best way to reduce how much memory Eudora needs is to clean up these mailboxes regularly or use other mailboxes for long-term mail storage.

 There's no harm in giving Eudora more memory than it asks for. Eudora is giving you the minimum suggested memory when it suggests size.

Summary of Eudora menu commands

File

This menu provides basic file and mail program functions, as listed in this table.

Command	Purpose
New Text Document	Creates a new text file.
Open	Opens the selected message summary, a text file, or a Eudora Settings file.
Close	Closes the current window.
Save	Saves changes to the contents of the topmost window. This applies to composition windows, text windows, and the Nicknames window.
Save As	Saves the current message(s) to a plain text file.
Send Queued Messages	Sends all messages that have been queued for delivery.
Check Mail	Picks up new mail from the POP server.
Page Setup	Sets printing options.

Command	Purpose
Print	Prints the current message(s), text window, or Ph window.
Print Selection	Prints the current selection from a message, text window, or Ph window.
Quit	Quits the Eudora application.

Edit

This menu provides text editing and sorting tools.

Command	Purpose
Undo	Reverses the last editing action taken on a piece of text.
Cut	Deletes selected text and places it on the Clipboard.
Copy	Copies selected text and places it on the Clipboard.
Paste	Places contents of Clipboard at chosen insertion point in message.
Paste as Quotation	Places contents of Clipboard at insertion point, with > characters at the beginning of each line to denote quoted text.
Clear	Deletes selected text.
Select All	Selects entire contents of message or mailbox.
Show Insertion Point	Scrolls selection or insertion point into view.
Wrap Selection	Inserts returns into the current selection, in the same way as Eudora does when it sends mail. With the Option key, unwrap text the way Save As does when Guess Paragraphs is on.
Finish Nickname	Completes the partial text of a nickname in the field of a message header.
Insert Recipient	Inserts the chosen nickname/address from the Quick Recipient list at the insertion point.

Find

Searches for designated text or a character string within message(s).

Command	Purpose
Sort submenu	Sorts message summaries in a mailbox. Hold down the Option key to reverse the order of the sort.

(continued)

Command	Purpose
Mailbox	This menu lets you open a mailbox or bring an open mailbox to the front.
In	Opens the mailbox where incoming messages are stored until deleted or transferred to another mailbox.
Out	Opens the mailbox where messages you compose are stored, and where queued messages are held until actually sent, and where copies of sent messages may be initially stored.
Trash	Opens the mailbox where deleted messages are stored.
[Your Mailboxes]	Mailboxes you create are also displayed in this menu.

Message

This menu lets you create and delete messages.

Command	Purpose
New Message	Opens the new message composition window.
Reply	Replies to the sender of the current message.
Forward	Forwards the current message to someone else.
Redirect	Forwards the current message to someone else but makes the return address the person who originally sent the message.
Send Again	Resends a message rejected by the mail system. Be sure to fix whatever caused the problem before you queue the message.
New Message To	Sends a message to someone on the Quick Recipient list.
Reply To	Replies to the current message but sends the reply to someone on the Quick Recipient list.
Forward To	Forwards the current message to someone on the Quick Recipient list.
Redirect To	Redirects the current message to someone on the Quick Recipient list.
Queue For Delivery	Saves the message in the Out mailbox and marks it as queued or ready to be delivered.
Change Queueing	Queues a message, unqueues a queued message, or sets a message for timed send.
Attach Document	Attaches file(s) to the current message.
Delete	Transfers the current message to the Trash mailbox; also used for deleting messages from the Trash mailbox.

Transfer

This menu lets you transfer current message(s) to the selected mailbox.

Command	Purpose
In	Transfers the current message(s) to the In mailbox.
Trash	Transfers the current message(s) to the Trash mailbox.
New	Displays New Mailbox dialog box to create a new mailbox; current message(s) may be transferred into that mailbox.
[Your Mailboxes]	Transfers the current message(s) to the selected mailbox that you previously created.

Special

This menu provides additional Eudora functions.

Command	Purpose
Ph	Displays the Ph window.
Add As Recipient	Adds selected text to the Quick Recipient list.
Remove Recipient	Selects a recipient from this menu and the recipient is removed from the Quick Recipient list.
Empty Trash	Deletes all messages from the Trash mailbox.
Compact Mailboxes	Reclaims unused space in mailboxes.
Mailboxes	Displays the Mailboxes window.
Configuration	Displays the Configuration dialog box.
Switches	Displays the Switches dialog box.
Communications	Displays the Communications Toolbox settings (not needed when using MacTCP).
Signature	Displays the Signature window.
Nicknames	Displays the Nicknames window.
Make Nickname	Creates a nickname for an address or addresses in the current message.
Forget Password	Makes Eudora ask for your password the next time it checks for mail.
Change Password	Changes your password on the POP server computer. This requires a special server.

Window

All Eudora window titles are listed in this menu. Select one to open it or bring it to the front.

Command	Purpose
Send to Back	Sends the topmost current window to the back of all displayed windows.
[Mailbox Windows]	Toggles between open mailboxes.

Shortcuts

Modifier keys

Many operations in Eudora can be affected by holding down one or more "modifier" keys. Eudora uses the Shift, Alt, and Ctrl keys as modifiers. The Shift key is usually used to "constrain" things—to keep them from happening or make them happen in a limited way.

■ Shift + Opening Eudora stops Eudora from checking for mail at start-up, even if you have a mail checking interval set.

■ Shift + Reply instructs Eudora to copy only the selected body text to the new message. This is sometimes easier than having Eudora copy it all and then deleting what you don't want.

■ Shift + Delete or Transfer disables Easy Open for that operation; Eudora won't open the next message.

■ Shift + To, Cc, or Bcc in the Nicknames window does not bring the composition window to the front after inserting the name.

■ Shift + Check Mail instructs Eudora to check for mail and resets the checking interval (normally, checking mail manually doesn't affect when the next automatic check is done).

■ Shift + Print instructs the printer to print the selected text only.

The Alt key is usually used to make an operation to reverse option settings.

■ Alt+ Insert a nickname inserts the full nickname expansion in the specified field.

■ Alt + Finish a nickname inserts addresses instead of nickname.

■ Alt + Queue or Send button brings up Change Queuing dialog box.

■ Alt + Save instructs Eudora that all open windows are to reopen automatically at the next start-up.

■ Alt + Reply toggles the "Reply to all" option in the Switches dialog box. If the Reply to all option is on, Alt + Reply generates a reply to the sender only. If the Reply to all option is off, Alt + Reply generates a reply to all addresses in the message header.

■ Alt + Transfer sends a copy of the current message to the selected mailbox and retains the original message in the original mailbox.

■ Alt + Open a message shows all headers.

The Ctrl key is also sometimes used as a modifier. Ctrl + Drop a document onto Eudora attaches the document to a message, even if the document is one Eudora could have opened.

Other important keys

The arrow keys, depending on the settings in the Switches dialog box, can move you from one message to another in a mailbox. If the Plain Arrows or Ctrl+Arrows option in the Switches dialog box is on:

■ Up/left arrow or Ctrl + up/left arrow takes you to the previous message.

■ Down/right arrow or Ctrl + down/right arrow takes you to the next message.

Enter performs several different functions:

■ It selects the outlined button in any dialog box, alert, or window.

■ It opens the selected message(s).

■ It lets you begin or end editing the subject of a message.

Escape (or Ctrl + .) stops any operation currently in progress.

If you have an extended keyboard, the following keys are also useful:

■ F1 is Undo.

■ F2 is Cut.

■ F3 is Copy.

- F4 is Paste.
- Delete deletes the character to the right of the insertion point.
- Home scrolls the window to the beginning.
- End scrolls the window to the end.
- PgUp and PgDn scroll up or down through the window.

Ctrl + key equivalents

Command Key	Purpose
Ctrl + .	Stops Eudora 's current action
Ctrl + A	Selects all
Ctrl + B	Moves window behind another window
Ctrl + C	Copies
Ctrl + D	Deletes message
Ctrl + E	Queues an outgoing message
Ctrl + F	Opens the Find window (searches for message)
Ctrl + G	Finds again
Ctrl + H	Attaches a document to outgoing message
Ctrl + I	Opens the In mailbox
Ctrl + J	Filters messages
Ctrl + K	Makes a nickname
Ctrl + L	Opens the Nicknames window
Ctrl + M	Checks your mail
Ctrl + N	Creates a new message
Ctrl + O	Opens a message
Ctrl + P	Prints a message
Ctrl + Q	Quits Eudora
Ctrl + R	Replies to a message
Ctrl + S	Saves a message without sending
Ctrl + T	Sends queued messages
Ctrl + U	Opens Ph window

Command Key	Purpose
Ctrl + V	Pastes
Ctrl + W	Closes message
Ctrl + X	Cuts
Ctrl + Z	Undoes

Mail transport

Eudora uses Simple Mail Transfer Protocol (SMTP) to transfer your outgoing mail to your SMTP server machine, which in turn uses SMTP to send your mail to the world at large. Mail from the world at large arrives on your Post Office Protocol (POP) server, where it waits for Eudora to pick it up with Post Office Protocol Version 3 (POP3). The mail Eudora sends and receives is constructed in accordance with RFC 822 and RFC 1341 (MIME).

Outgoing mail

When you send an e-mail message to someone, Eudora uses SMTP to send the mail to your local SMTP server computer. That computer then sends the mail to your addressee's computer, also (usually) by means of the SMTP protocol.

Why doesn't Eudora talk directly to your addressee's computer? For one thing, it would take a lot longer for your mail to leave Windows because Windows would have to call up each addressee's computer and deliver your mail. For another, some computers are "hard to find;" it's much better to let another computer "hunt" for your addressee than to make Windows do it. Finally, sometimes your addressee's computer isn't available when you want to send mail. The SMTP server handles this by holding your mail until the other computer is ready to accept it, eliminating the inconvenience of having unsent messages hanging around in Windows.

Incoming mail

When somebody sends you mail, other computers use the SMTP protocol to deliver the mail to your POP server. Your POP server puts mail in your "mail drop," where it stays until the Eudora program picks it up. When you check your mail, Eudora uses POP3 to pick up your mail and move it to Windows.

Why doesn't Eudora use SMTP to receive your mail? SMTP works best when the computers it knows about are always ready for mail. Unless you wanted to run Eudora and Windows 24 hours per day, seven days a week, SMTP wouldn't work very well for you.

More information

If you want to know more about SMTP, RFC 822, POP3 and MIME, the official standards are

- RFC 821, "Simple Mail Transfer Protocol," by Jonathan B. Postel
- RFC 822, "Standard for the Format of Internet Text Messages," by Ned Freed and Nathaniel Borenstein
- RFC 1225, "Post Office Protocol, Version 3," by Marshall Rose
- RFC 1341, "Multipurpose Internet Mail Extensions," by Dave Crocker

You can find the RFCs by anonymous FTP to nic.ddn.mil; see Internetworking with TCP/IP for details.

Dialup Eudora

Eudora is designed for dialup to Cisco terminal servers. It can be used with other dialup connections as well. Complicated setups are likely to be unreliable, but if the setup commands to connect are simple, Eudora works well.

These instructions assume you are familiar with ResEdit, your communications equipment, and your hosts. It is suggested that one person make these changes to Eudora and then redistribute the customized version to other users at your site.

Requirements

Eudora needs a "transparent" connection to your POP, SMTP, and (optionally) Ph servers. Transparent means primarily two things:

1. Characters Eudora sends should *not* be echoed back to Eudora. Most systems do echo characters, so something special may need to be done to achieve this.

2. You must pay close attention to how carriage returns are treated. UNIX systems routinely translate carriage returns into linefeeds; you must either disable this on your system or teach Eudora how to deal with it.

Navigation

Eudora has a very rudimentary scripting system built in. This capability is called "navigation" to separate it from the rather sophisticated connotations of "scripting."

Introduction

Navigation is simple; Eudora uses a list of strings which it sends out the serial port one at a time. After each string, it waits until there is no output from the remote system for two seconds or until a given string is matched, after which Eudora continues with the next string.

There can be three sets of navigation strings contained in STR# resources: one is used when connecting (Navigate In); one is used when disconnecting (Navigate Out); and one is used when switching from SMTP to POP (Navigate Mid). You may use ResEdit to manipulate these resources. Any of the resources may be absent, in which case Eudora skips the navigation it would otherwise have done with that resource.

For each function, Eudora selects an appropriate resource in the following manner. First, it takes the name of the connection tool currently in use; then it appends a space and the current type of navigation. Eudora looks for an STR# resource with that name. If that is not found, Eudora looks for an STR# resource named after the navigation type. Finally, it looks for specific resource IDs. The first STR# resource found is the only one used.

Navigation resources can be in the Eudora application itself, in your Eudora Settings file, or in a plug-in file. The latter is a file with type "rsrc" and creator "CSOm" placed in your Preferences folder; use of a plug-in file is highly recommended. Plug-in files go in the Preferences folder.

Special sequences in Navigation resources

Eudora provides a set of special character sequences for use in Navigation resources. These sequences are all two characters long, the first character being a backslash. They are either replaced with items from your Eudora settings, or they modify the Navigation process.

Replacements

These special characters are replaced with strings. They can appear at any place in a navigation string.

\u	POP account user name.
\h	POP account host name.
\p	POP account password.
\s	SMTP server host name.
\U	Dialin user name.
\P	Dialin password.
\n	A linefeed (ASCII 10).
\r	A carriage return (ASCII 13).
\\	A single backslash character.

Modifiers

\b	Hide from Progress window.
\D	Delay.
\B	Break.
\e	Expect something.
\b	When this character appears as the first character in a given a string, Eudora won't print the string in the Progress window when it is sent. This is useful for passwords or other state secrets.
\D	Should be the first character in the string and followed by digits. The digits are taken as a number of seconds to delay (for example, "\D2" is a two-second delay). As with other strings, Eudora will wait for output to stop for two seconds, or for an expect string, before proceeding.
\B	Should be the first character in the string and followed by digits. The digits are taken as the number of ticks (60ths of a second) to send a break signal (for example, "\B30" is a half-second break). As with other strings, Eudora waits for output to stop for two seconds, or for an expect string, before proceeding.
\e	Makes Eudora expect to see a specific string in the output from the dialup server. Eudora sends whatever comes before the \e and then waits for whatever comes after it to occur in the data sent from the host. There are two caveats to this. First, Eudora only matches on the first 7 bits; the high bit of each character is ignored for matching. This is needed for systems that use parity. Second, Eudora's matching is fast and sloppy; highly repetitive data streams and long expect strings might fool it (for example, Eudora wouldn't see "Login:" if your server said: "LogLogin:").

Eudora follows its normal time-out process when looking for an expect string. That is, after 45 seconds Eudora asks you if you want to keep waiting or cancel the process. If you cancel, the connection process is stopped.

If you use either of the password replacement sequences ("\p" for your POP account password or "\P" for your dialup password) in the same string as an expect, Eudora assumes the password is wrong if the expect string isn't found. This causes Eudora to ask for your password the next time it tries to connect.

Connecting to servers

Once the navigation is done, Eudora issues a command to connect to the proper port of the server you are using. Once this command is sent, the connection must be transparent, as discussed; no echoes and no carriage return translation. Eudora comes configured to send this command:

```
telnet hostname portnumber /stream<return>
```

The <return> means a carriage return in this document only; you must type actual carriage returns in ResEdit. A template for the command is kept in 7400.13 (7400.13 is short for STR# resource id 7400, string 13). The template begins life as *telnet %p %d /stream\n*. The %p is replaced with the hostname and the %d with the port number. It is acceptable to change this string however you please, except that %d, if it is used, must come after %p. The best way to change this string is not to modify it but to override it. You can do this by creating an 'STR ' resource of id 7413 and putting the string you want Eudora to use in that.

A return by any other name

When Eudora is communicating with your POP or SMTP server, it's important that they agree on what constitutes a line. The Internet specification stipulates that a line ends with a carriage return followed by a linefeed. Most UNIX systems will "helpfully" translate carriage returns into linefeeds. If you can't turn that feature off, it may help to make Eudora send only a carriage return, and not the carriage return/linefeed pair. You may edit 6000.17 to be what you want Eudora to send at the end of a line. The best way to change this string is not to modify it, but to override it. You can do this by creating an 'STR ' resource of ID 6017 and putting the string you want Eudora to use in that.

An example: direct connection to a UNIX box

Here's a suggested connection method if your Windows has a serial line to a UNIX machine, or if there are modems on your Windows and UNIX machine.

1. Install the srialpop program on your UNIX system. The source code to this is part of the Eudora distribution program.

2. Put the following strings in the "Navigate In" resource.

    1: \r\r\r\egin:

    2: \u\r\eword:

    3: \p\r\r\r\e%

    4: exec srialpop

3. Put one empty string in the "Navigate Mid" resource.

That's it. Srialpop takes care of the terminal settings for you.

 A plug-in with these strings in it is part of the Eudora distribution. The filename is "Direct UNIX Navs."

Need more options?

If Eudora's scripting doesn't cut it for you, a couple of alternatives are available. One is the Calypso connection tool. It lets you use CCL scripts for the connection/disconnection process. Calypso can be found on major archive sites. The other is the Simon Fraser University version of Eudora, which has a powerful built-in scripting language. This is available for anonymous FTP from ftpserver.sfu.ca.

Chapter 12
RFD Mail Version 1.22

RFD Mail, an application designed to run under Microsoft Windows, is an easy-to-use, graphical front end to many dial-up e-mail services. Important features include

- Easy, graphical editing and browsing of letters
- Transparent handling of multiple mail services
- An Address Book for easy access to often-used addresses
- Backup and restore folders
- Automatic checking for mail
- Support for more than one signature
- Connectivity through TCP/IP connections in addition to dial-up mail
- Support for SMTP/POP accounts

With RFD Mail, you can

- File letters into folders for future reference
- Search easily for filed mail
- Send carbon copies of letters within a single mail service
- Send letters individually or in batches via the Out Box

RFD Mail currently supports many Internet and information services. To use this program, you should have an account with supported services. RFD Mail includes scripts for dial-up UNIX and VMS systems. Also, the RFD Mail staff can help you configure the software to access a local BBS. Supported services include CompuServe, Delphi, MCI Mail, GEnie, The Direct Connection, World UNIX, MV Communications, Panix, The WELL, The Portal System, Netcom Online Communications, CRL, and The Internet Access Company.

If you belong to an unsupported information service (that is, a local BBS), you can customize RFD Mail to support it. Write a new script file and add a new mail service to the Post Office. Before you write a custom script, it is helpful to have some experience with other communication script languages, such as Crosstalk or Procomm. Dial-up UNIX and VMS users should read the UNIX.WRI or VMS.WRI files. If you use another Internet provider, read the INTERNET.WRI file. If you use TCP/IP or SMTP/POP, read the SMTP.WRI file.

This program is shareware. It is not free software. You may run the program for an evaluation period of one month. After that you must register by filling out the program registration form (at the end of this chapter) and sending in the registration fee. See the REGISTER.WRI file for pricing information and limitations.

CompuServe members can register RFD Mail electronically. Type **GO SWREG** at any ! prompt and look up RFD Mail under the keyword *RFD*. See the on-line help topic *Program Registration* for more information.

Installing and Upgrading Requirements

This section explains requirements for first-time installation and upgrading of RFD Mail Version 1.22.

RFD Mail distribution files

The RFD Mail distribution contains the files listed in Table 12-1.

Table 12-1	RFD Mail Distribution
File	*Description*
INSTALL.EXE	Installation program
INSTALL.BIN	Installation program
INSTALL.INF	Installation script
INSTALL.BMP	Installation bitmap
RFDMAIL.EXE	The main executable for RFD Mail
RFDMAIL.HLP	Help file for RFD Mail
POSTOFFC.DAT	Initial Post Office file
ADDRBOOK.DAT	Initial Address Book file
BIGLIST.DLL	Drag-and-drop support library
BWCC.DLL	Borland Custom Controls Library
CSERVE.SCR	Script file for transferring mail to and from CompuServe
CSERVE_A.SCR	Alternate script file for transferring mail to and from CompuServe

File	Description
DELPHI.SCR	Script file for Delphi
GENIE.SCR	Script file for GEnie
MCIMAIL.SCR	Script file for MCI Mail
TDC.SCR	Script file for The Direct Connection (United Kingdom)
UNIX.SCR	Script file for World UNIX
MV.SCR	Script file for MV Communications
UNIX_CIS.SCR	Script file for World UNIX via the CIS Packet Network
VMS.SCR	Script file for a VMS machine
ISMENNT.SCR	Script file for accessing ISMENNT.IS site (see script for details)
PANIX.SCR	Script file for Panix
NETCOM.SCR	Script file for Netcom Communications
TIAC.SCR	Script file for TIAC
WELL.SCR	Script file for the WELL
CRL.SCR	Script file for CRL
HKSUPER.SCR	Script file for Hong Kong SuperNET
PORTAL.SCR	Script file for The Portal System
GREEN.SCR	Script file for GreenNet
GMUMASON.SCR	Script file for George Mason University
SMTP.SCR	Script file for SMTP and POP
UNIX.WRI	Information on using the UNIX script
VMS.WRI	Information on using the VMS script
INTERNET.WRI	Information about RFD Mail support for Internet sites
OVERVIEW.WRI	General information about RFD Mail
WARRANTY.WRI	Warranty information about RFD Mail
LICENSE.WRI	License information about RFD Mail
ORDERFRM.WRI	Registration form
BUGS.WRI	List of known bugs as of Version 1.22
HELPME!.WRI	Troubleshooting pointers and information
GENIE.WRI	More information about GEnie support
CSERVE.WRI	More information about CompuServe support

(continued)

Table 12-1 *(continued)*

File	Description
DELPHI.WRI	More information about Delphi support
MCIMAIL.WRI	More information about MCI Mail support
TDC.WRI	More information about The Direct Connection support
WORLDUNX.WRI	More information about World UNIX support
SMTP.WRI	More information about SMTP/POP and TCP/telnet support
INSTALL.WRI	The unedited text of this document

System requirements

- Windows 3.1 (Version 3.0 is insufficient)
- 2MB of RAM minimum (4MB recommended)
- 1.5MB free disk space (the more the merrier)
- 80286 processor or higher
- Hayes-compatible modem
- WinSock 1.1-compliant TCP/IP stack if TCP/telnet connectivity is to be used
- Any display except CGA, although this program has not been tested on monochrome displays

First-time installation

Run the supplied INSTALL.EXE program from the CD-ROM. You will be asked for the location to install the program (C:\RFDMAIL is recommended) and which components you want to install. Browse the list of Internet script files and select those which you are interested in. When the installation is finished, double-click the RFD Mail icon to start RFD Mail. To get further help on setting up RFD Mail, pull up the Contents help topic from the Help menu, and read both the Overview and Getting Started help topics.

Upgrade installation

If you have been using Version 1.11, 1.12, or 1.2 of RFD Mail, delete the *.SCC files from the RFD Mail directory because the format of those files has changed since those versions. The next time you log into your configured Mail Services, RFD Mail regenerates these files. If you are not upgrading from a previous version of RFD Mail, follow the instructions in the last section.

For more information about RFD Mail Version 1.22, please see the *Improvements Since Version 1.21* and *Documentation Errata* sections supplied in the INSTALL.WRI on the CD.

Uninstall instructions

To remove RFD Mail from your system, simply remove the entire directory that you originally installed it into (for example, remove C:\RFDMAIL) and then remove the RFDMAIL.INI file from the WINDOWS directory.

File directory

RFD Mail maintains the following files in its directory:

Table 12-2	RFD Mail Directory Files
File	*Description*
*.SCR	Script files for Mail Service entries
*.SCC	Compiled script files
*.DTX	Index files for folder databases
FOLDER??.DAT	Mail folder database files, one for each mail folder
BNDL??.DAT	Mail bundle database files, one for each mail bundle
FOLDERS.DAT	Directory of existing mail folders
LETTERS.DAT	Database for all letters currently on the Mail desktop
INBOX.DAT	Database for all letters currently in the In Box
OUTBOX.DAT	Database for all letters currently in the Out Box
POSTOFFC.DAT	Database of all Mail Services currently defined
ADDRBOOK.DAT	Database of all Address Book entries currently defined
SIGNAT.DAT	Database of all Signatures currently defined
_MAIL.DSK	Mail desktop window layout

RFD Mail also may create RFDMAIL.INI in the WINDOWS directory (usually C:\WINDOWS). This file stores the current preferences (as set in the Preferences dialog box) for the program.

Improvements in Version 1.22 from previous versions

A comprehensive list of improvements is included in the INSTALL.WRI file; if you're upgrading from a previous version of RFD, check out this file.

Documentation errata

To fine-tune your installation of RFD Mail or to check on common errors, see the INSTALL.WRI file under the *Documentation errata* section heading.

Internet Support

RFD Mail supports several dial-up Internet-access sites, including World UNIX, MV Communications, Islenska menntanetid, The Portal System, George Mason University, GreenNet, Netcom Online Communications, Panix, The Internet Access Company, The Direct Connection, The WELL, CRL, and Hong Kong SuperNET. The supplied Post Office comes set up with entries for World UNIX, MV Communications, and The Direct Connection. Support for one of the other services can be easily added by creating an entry using one of these supplied script files:

Table 12-3	RFD Mail Supplied Script Files
Script File	*Supported Site*
PANIX.SCR	Panix
NETCOM.SCR	Netcom Online Communications
TIAC.SCR	The Internet Access Company
WELL.SCR	The WELL
CRL.SCR	CRL
HKSUPER.SCR	Hong Kong SuperNET
ISMENNT.SCR	Islenska menntanetid
PORTAL.SCR	The Portal System
GREEN.SCR	GreenNet
GMUMASON.SCR	George Mason University
SMTP.SCR	SMTP/POP Mail (see the SMTP.WRI file)

All these script files, except ISMENNT.SCR and SMTP.SCR, are very similar to the UNIX.SCR FILE, with only simple changes to aliases in the beginning of the file needed for prompts and messages sent by each system. All transfer mail using the ZMODEM file transfer protocol; we recommend that you set the flow setting in the Post Office entry to Xon/Xoff to prevent overrunning either the host or your computer. If you have difficulties with file transfer, you can configure the scripts to use either XMODEM or YMODEM.

You can use script aliases to modify the script files. For example, if you use a shell other than /bin/csh (bash, for example), change the script's prompt alias to accommodate your shell's prompt. This and other options are documented within the script files.

CompuServe

RFD Mail uses CSERVE.SCR or CSERVE_A.SCR to interact with CompuServe. (A version of CompuServe is included on the *Internet GIZMOS for Windows CD-ROM.*) CSERVE.SCR downloads and uploads mail using the XMODEM file transfer protocol, reportedly not a particularly efficient error-correcting protocol. If you are using an error-correcting modem (MNP, v.42, and so on), use CSERV_A.SCR to improve the performance of mail transfers. It uses a simple ASCII file transfer protocol, which is very efficient but is not error-checked. Use CSERVE_A.SCR only when your modem provides an error-free connection.

Users of high-speed modems (9600 and above) should consider using the normal script or dialing CompuServe at 2400 baud. At 9600 baud, CompuServe may have trouble downloading the file, especially if the system is heavily loaded. This can pause the transfer. When this happens, RFD Mail incorrectly assumes that CompuServe has finished downloading the file and truncates the download.

To use the CSERVE_A.SCR script, edit the Post Office entry for CompuServe and set the Script File field to be CSERVE_A.SCR. In addition, set the Flow field to be Xon/Xoff.

Alternate access

The scripts are initially set up to dial directly to CompuServe Packet Network, which is essentially a direct connection to CompuServe. If you access CompuServe through either TymNet or SprintNet, the script can be modified to login through those networks. See the CSERVE.SCR and CSERVE_A.SCR files for details.

Delphi

Use the DELPHI.SCR script file to interact with Delphi. This script downloads and uploads mail using the XMODEM file transfer protocol. The script also supports file transfers using the more efficient ZMODEM protocol, but Delphi's implementation of ZMODEM has proved to be less reliable in our testing. See the DELPHI.SCR file for details on switching file transfer protocols.

Alternate access

The script is initially set up to dial directly to Delphi. If you access Delphi through either TymNet or SprintNet, the script can be modified to login through those networks. See the DELPHI.SCR file for details.

GEnie

RFD Mail uses the GENIE.SCR file to interact with GEnie. This script downloads and uploads mail using a simple ASCII file transfer protocol, which is very efficient but is not error-checked. You should use an error-correcting modem (MNP, v.42, and so on) to exchange mail using GEnie.

The script file also assumes that your break character is set to ASCII 3 or Ctrl+C. This is the default setting for all new GEnie accounts. If you have changed this setting in your GEnie User Profile, you either need to change it back or change all occurrences of the string Control C to Control x in GENIE.SCR, in which x is the value of your break character. Failing to do this may cause the script to abort when it tries to upload a letter.

Avoid sending mail beginning with an asterisk. These are assumed to be commands issued by GEnie. At best, GEnie skips that line; at worst, the mail is not delivered.

MCI Mail

Use the MCIMAIL.SCR script file to interact with MCI Mail. This script downloads and uploads mail using the ZMODEM file transfer protocol; we recommend that the flow setting in the Post Office entry for MCI Mail be set to Xon/Xoff to prevent overrunning either MCI Mail or your computer. If you have trouble transferring mail, configure the script to use the Kermit transfer protocol. See the MCIMAIL.SCR file for details.

RFD Mail supports the delivery of mail to MCI Mail addresses (that is, to people who have MCI Mail accounts). MCI Mail does support delivery to outside mail systems other than the Internet (such as CompuServe or X.400 mail).

To send mail from MCI Mail to Internet addresses, specify the 'Net address (for example, *user@company.com*) followed by the letters *EMS*. When you reply to mail from Internet accounts, you will note that only their address appears in the To field. You must manually add EMS to the address when replying.

MV Communications

Use the MV.SCR script file to interact with MV Communications. This script downloads and uploads mail using the ZMODEM file transfer protocol; we recommend that the flow setting in the Post Office entry for MV Communications be set to Xon/Xoff to prevent overrunning either MV Communications or your computer. If you have trouble with the script, contact rfdmail@world.std.com to get further assistance.

The MV.SCR file can be modified through script aliases. For example, if you use a shell other than /bin/csh (bash for example), you can easily adjust the script to accommodate your shell's prompt by changing the prompt alias. You can also select a transfer protocol other than ZMODEM if you are having difficulties uploading or downloading. These and other options are documented within the MV.SCR file.

TCP/IP Support

In addition to connectivity through a modem, RFD Mail can communicate to your mail service by using a TCP/IP network connection. Your computer needs to either be directly connected to a network running the TCP/IP protocol, or connected to a TCP/IP host over a modem using the SLIP or PPP protocols. In either case, the networking software (sometimes referred to as the TCP/IP Stack) needs to be WinSock 1.1-compliant. Check with your network vendor or network documentation to verify this.

To connect using TCP/IP, you need to adjust the Connect and Phone Number setting in the Post Office entry for your mail service. If you normally connect to your mail service by using a telnet program and logging in to a shell account (in the same way that you would connect to a service), then follow these four steps:

1. Set the Connect field to telnet.

2. Set the Phone Number field to either the name of the host you connect to, or the actual IP address of that host. Check with your system administrator or service provider if you need help with this step.

3. Set the Baud field to the approximate throughput of your connection, or 38400 for network connections.

4. Set the Length field to 8, the Parity field to None, and the Stop field to 1.

The remaining fields should be set as described in the Mail Service Dialog topic.

SMTP/POP Mail

RFD Mail also supports the *SMTP* (Simple Mail Transfer Protocol) and *POP* (Post Office Protocol) protocols for the delivery and fetching (respectively) of e-mail. To use this support, your computer needs to be configured for TCP/IP (see the preceding section for details). The script file for SMTP/POP is SMTP.SCR. To add a Mail Service for SMTP/POP, create a new Post Office entry with the following five settings:

1. Set the Connect field to telnet (direct).

2. Set the Phone Number field to either the name of the host you connect to, or the actual IP address of that host. Check with your system administrator or service provider if you need help with this step.

3. Set the Baud field to the approximate throughput of your connection, or 38400 for network connections.

4. Set the Length field to 8, the Parity field to None, and the Stop field to 1.

5. Set the Script File field to SMTP.SCR.

You must properly set the Mail-Address and Your Name fields because RFD Mail uses them to specify your return e-mail address and name in outgoing messages. In particular, if you incorrectly set the Mail-Address field, your mail recipients won't be able to reply to your e-mail. All other fields should be set as described in the Mail Service Dialog topic.

The SMTP.SCR script file contains several important aliases that you may need to set for proper operation. Refer to the SMTP.SCR file for more details.

The Direct Connection

Use the TDC.SCR script file to interact with The Direct Connection in the United Kingdom. This script downloads and uploads mail using the ZMODEM file transfer protocol; set the flow setting in the Post Office entry for The Direct Connection to Xon/Xoff to prevent overrunning either The Direct Connection or your computer.

If you have modified your login procedures, the script file may not work out of the box. If not, contact either helpdesk@dircon.co.uk (Direct Connect) or rfdmail@world.std.com to get further assistance.

UNIX.WRI

RFD Mail Version 1.22 includes the UNIX.SCR script file, which supports UNIX accounts. A new Post Office entry for a UNIX account can be created by using this script, which is currently the script used to support World UNIX (part of *Software Tool and Die*) but should be modified easily for other UNIX systems, according to RFD Mail staff.

Alias statements at the beginning of the script determine where the script will look for various commands (rz, sz, and so on), and what types of prompts are expected at various times. In most cases, changing the prompt alias and a few others should be enough to make the script work.

To use this script, your UNIX account must support the following:

- The rz and sz commands — to receive and send files via the ZMODEM protocol
- The standard /usr/ucb/mail or /bin/mail program (also in your path)
- A command-line prompt more unique than just %
- If you are using a 9600 baud or above modem, the remote system should support Xon/Xoff flow control, and you should set this in the Post Office entry for this system

If your account meets this criteria, you should refer to the script file for more instructions on customizations that will let you use RFD Mail with your UNIX account.

VMS.WRI

The VMS.SCR script file supports VAX/VMS accounts using standard VAX Mail. You can use this script file to create a new Post Office entry for a VMS account.

Because VMS configurations vary widely, this script probably will not work without some modification to support your particular account. For this reason, this script file is provided without any warranty or support. *Use it at your own risk.*

Alias statements at the beginning of the script determine where the script looks for various commands (rz, sz, and so on) and which types of prompts are expected at various times. In most cases, just changing the prompt alias and a few others should be enough to make the script work.

To use this script, your VMS account must support the following:

- The rz and sz commands (and you must set the sz and rz aliases in VMS.SCR to their location) — to receive and send files via the ZMODEM protocol

- Xon/Xoff flow control, when you use a 9600 or greater baud modem. You should also set this in the Post Office entry for this system

- The ability to set the LAT to pass all characters, if you use a LAT. This can be a very tricky task, so it is best to discuss this with your system administrator *before* doing it.

If your account meets this criteria, refer to the script file for more instructions on customizations that will let you use the script with your VMS account.

World UNIX

World UNIX, part of the Software Tool and Die system, is a public-access UNIX service providing access to Internet mail, newsgroups, file transfer, and more. The Script File used to interact with World UNIX is UNIX.SCR. This script downloads and uploads mail using the ZMODEM file transfer protocol; set the flow setting in the Post Office entry for World UNIX to Xon/Xoff to prevent overrunning either World UNIX or your computer.

If you have trouble with the script, contact either staff@world.std.com or rfdmail@world.std.com for help.

Alternate access

You can access World UNIX via the CIS Packet Network. If you are not local to the Boston area, you may find this to be an economical way of accessing your account. To do so, change the phone number in the Post Office entry to a local CompuServe access number, change the script file from UNIX.SCR to UNIX_CIS.SCR, and change the flow setting to None. This alternate script file uses ZMODEM to download mail, but Kermit is used to upload mail due to limitations of the CIS Network. Kermit is known to be extremely inefficient over a packet network, but it is the only protocol that works at all in the upload direction.

Other options

You can modify the UNIX.SCR file through script aliases. For example, if you use a shell other than /bin/csh (tcsh, for example), change the prompt alias to adjust the script to accommodate your shell's prompt. You can also select a transfer protocol other than ZMODEM if you are having upload or download trouble. The UNIX.SCR file documents these and other options.

RFD Mail Version 1.22

Name _____

Company _____

Address _____

City _____

State _____   Country _____

Zip _____   Phone _____

Remit to:

Performance Designs
P.O. Box 1005
Concord, MA 01742

Pricing

❑ $29.95 (+ $1.50 tax for MA Residents)
Please see the REGISTER.WRI file for RFD Mail on the CD-ROM for more payment information.

Chapter 13
Pegasus Mail

Welcome to Pegasus Mail! Before you begin using the program, you must provide Pegasus Mail with a small amount of information about your system and its configuration. This information tells Pegasus Mail who you are and where to store your mail folders, address books, and other mail-related files. You need to provide a Home mail path, indicate a user name, and save your user name in your WIN.INI file, as described in the following paragraphs.

The Home mail path field contains the DOS path to the directory in which your home mail folder is located. The default value is C:\PMAIL\~8. Pegasus Mail replaces ~8 with the first eight letters of your user name before it uses the path.

If you enter Peter as your user name, for example, Pegasus Mail sets your home mailbox location to C:\PMAIL\PETER. Using the special substitution this way means that more than one person may use the mail system on the same machine and ensures that their mail is kept separate. If you prefer not to use drive C for your mail, or if for any other reason you need to change the path, you may do so as long as the path you enter is legal. We recommend that you use the default value, however, unless you have good reasons to change it. If the path you supply does not exist, Pegasus Mail creates it.

In the Your user name field, enter the name by which Pegasus Mail will recognize you. You can tell Pegasus Mail to use the first eight characters of this name as a way of identifying your home mailbox. Use only letters and numbers in your user name — it must not contain spaces or special characters.

When you start Pegasus Mail, it opens a small dialog box asking for your user name. If you are the only person using this system, bypass this step by telling Pegasus Mail to store your user name in the Windows setup file, WIN.INI. After you have done this, the system always uses the name you supply. Do not check this control if other people are using this system for mail as well. You also can specify the user name Pegasus Mail should use in the DOS-environment variable PMUSER.

Addressing Your Pegasus Messages _____

Just as the postal service needs an address to deliver a letter, Pegasus Mail needs an address to send your electronic mail. Depending on your system and network, you may be able to use any of several kinds of addresses, each slightly different. The following are the types of addresses Pegasus Mail recognizes, which you can enter in the To, CC, or BCC fields.

Local addresses

Using the standard NetWare syntax (that is, user name, or server/user name), you can enter the NetWare user name of any user on your file server or on any other file server to which Pegasus Mail can deliver. Look up local users with the `user lookup` function.

Internet addresses

If your system has an SMTP gateway, you can enter any valid Internet address in the address fields.

NetWare MHS addresses

If your system has an MHS gateway, you can enter any valid NetWare MHS address in the address fields. If you are using an advanced MHS transport, you can access MHS directory services from the Addresses menu.

Addressing tips

You also can prepare distribution lists or lists of addresses you use frequently.

The To field of a message indicates the primary recipient of a message.

A CC (*carbon copy*) recipient of a message is someone you want to listen in to the message you are sending to the primary recipient. CC recipients receive the message normally but their addresses do not appear in the To field of the message.

Use a BCC (*blind carbon copy*) when you want to send a copy of your message to someone other than the primary recipient without the primary recipient knowing that you have done so. When you use BCC, the primary recipient's copy of the message does not show that you have copied anyone in the BCC list. BCC is very handy for office politics.

An SMTP gateway lets you send mail to machines on the Internet or to machines that use the Internet RFC821/822 message protocols. Almost all UNIX systems and many mainframe and minicomputer systems can receive mail using this protocol.

NetWare MHS is Novell's messaging system. Several versions are available for both NetWare and non-NetWare environments.

Pegasus Mail supports all versions of NetWare MHS, including NetWare Global MHS. Ask your system administrator if you're unsure whether this option is available on your server.

Composing a Message

The Subject field

Figure 13-1 shows a message editing window. Enter a short summary of your message in the subject field. Because the recipient may use the subject line as a filing key, you should try to make it as descriptive and helpful as possible. When you're replying to a message, Pegasus Mail automatically formats the subject for you as *Re: the original subject.*

The subject field can be up to 64 characters long.

Reading confirmation

If you want to be notified when the recipient reads your message, check the confirm reading box in the message editing window. A small message is sent back to you when the message is read.

The recipient must be using a version of Pegasus Mail for reading confirmation to work. Some MHS mailers also may provide receipt confirmations.

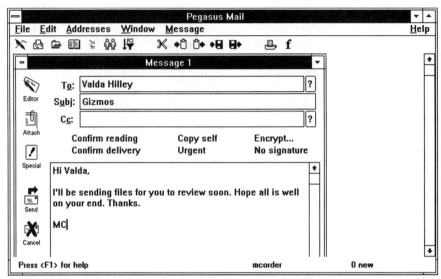

Figure 13-1: Message editing window.

The system administrator can allow users to refuse reading confirmation because many people feel that it is an invasion of privacy. If you try to mail to a local user who will not provide reading confirmation, a small dialog box appears when you send the message advising you of this. If you mail to a nonlocal Pegasus Mail user who does not permit reading confirmation, you do not receive any notification.

Delivery confirmation

Checking the confirm delivery box in the message editing window tells Pegasus Mail to ask for confirmation that your message has been delivered successfully. Delivery confirmation differs from reading confirmation in that you are only advised that the message has been delivered to the recipient, not that it has been read.

Delivery confirmation is always available if you are using NetWare MHS. You never get delivery confirmation on local mail, however, because Pegasus Mail tells you immediately if it fails to deliver your message. With Internet mail, you may or may not receive delivery confirmation, because there are no guaranteed ways of asking for it.

Keeping a copy of your message

If you want to keep a copy of the messages you send, check the copy self box in the message editing window. Pegasus Mail files a copy of your message in a folder called *Copies to self*, which it creates.

If your Copies to self folder becomes too full, you can force Pegasus Mail to create a new copy self folder by renaming the existing one. Note that you must change the short name as well as the long name when doing this.

Urgent messages

Check the urgent box in the message editing window if you want your message to be sent at the highest priority available on the message transport your system uses. The effect of setting this flag varies from system to system. Many MHS mailers recognize it, as do some Internet mailers. Pegasus Mail displays urgent messages at the top of the new mail folder in red text and sends a different new mail notification to the recipient to indicate that the message is urgent.

You should use the urgent flag with care: Urgent messages can be annoying, and overuse of the feature seriously affects its usefulness.

Encryption

If your message contains sensitive or private information, you may want to encrypt it. An encrypted message is scrambled and can only be read by someone who knows the correct password.

To encrypt your message, click the encrypt button in the message editor. A small dialog box opens, in which you should enter the password for the message. The password should have from five to eight characters and is case sensitive (FOOBAR and foobar are different passwords). Press OK to add the password or Cancel to remove it. Pegasus Mail encrypts the message using your password when it sends it.

The recipient must know the password, so you need to agree in advance on a suitable choice. Don't forget the password! If you forget it, you can never read your message again; even the author of Pegasus Mail cannot break the encryption method it uses.

Signatures

A signature is a small fragment of text that Pegasus Mail automatically adds to the end of messages you send. You should usually put your name, address, and phone/fax number in your signature; some people like to place a witty saying or other text there as well.

Pegasus Mail supports separate signatures for each type of message you can send — local, Internet, and MHS. You can create and edit signatures by choosing File⇨Preferences.

To suppress the addition of a signature to a message, click on the no signature button in the message editing window. You may need to omit your signature when sending mail to some Internet list servers.

Editing your message

Edit your message in the large message box at the bottom of the message editing window. The message text word-wraps when it reaches the right-hand margin, but you can press Enter to end a line at any time. Use the Edit menu to cut text from and paste text into your message.

Spell check

To check your spelling, position the cursor at the point in the message where checking should begin and select Edit⇨Check spelling.

Delete

Pressing Ctrl+Y deletes the current line in the message; pressing Ctrl+T deletes the word to the right of the cursor.

Formatting

Pressing Ctrl+B reformats the current paragraph so that all its text falls between the left and right margin. Pressing Ctrl+D opens the Indenting dialog box, which contains commands that let you reformat your text with indented left and/or right margins. You can also select these reformatting commands from the Message menu.

Glossary

You can store abbreviations for commonly used text in Pegasus Mail's glossary. You can expand the glossary at any time by pressing Ctrl+/.

Send

To send your message, click the Send button or press Ctrl+Enter.

Attachments

You can attach files to your mail message by clicking on the Attach button in the message editing window. A dialog box appears, letting you choose files and control the way Pegasus Mail deals with them.

The way Pegasus Mail handles your attachments depends upon the message's destination. You can have considerable control over this process, although Pegasus Mail's automatic handling is usually more than adequate.

Selecting files to attach

Before you select files to attach to your message, make sure that the File type and Attachment encoding fields in the dialog box are set correctly. Then use either of the following methods:

- Usename adds it to the attachment list with the current settings of the File type and Attachment encoding fields. Type the name (including an optional DOS path) of the file in the filename window. When you press Enter or click Add, Pegasus Mail adds the file to the attachment list.

- If you have entered a directory name, Pegasus Mail changes the file and the file and directory lists at the bottom of the window (which you use to navigate your disks). Double-click the file and directory list boxes to reflect the new directory.

To remove attachments from the attachment list, highlight them and click Remove. You cannot change an attachment's settings after you have added the attachment to the list — instead, remove the attachment and then add it again.

File type

You can tell Pegasus Mail which type of file you are attaching by choosing from a predefined list of file types. The file type information is optional and is currently used only for informational purposes — the recipient usually sees the file type when examining the list of files attached to the message.

Future versions of Pegasus Mail will probably use the file type information to provide attachment viewing facilities or to launch the original application with the attachment, so you should get into the habit of filling it in.

If you are uncertain of the file type, use Unknown, the default choice.

Pegasus Mail does not convert files. That is, Pegasus Mail does not convert a Microsoft Word file to WordPerfect even if you indicate WordPerfect format here — it simply conveys the wrong information.

Attachment encoding

When you send an attachment, it cannot always be transmitted as is. Sometimes it is necessary to package the attachment in a particular way so that the mail transport system or the recipient's mailer can understand it. Pegasus Mail always makes sensible default choices about attachment encoding; you won't need to change the attachment encoding except in very special cases. Pegasus Mail supports the attachment encoding options described in Table 13-1.

Table 13-1	Attachment Encoding Options
Option	**Description**
Pegasus Mail decides	Tells Pegasus Mail to do whatever is appropriate based on the way it sends the message. Attachments to local and MHS addresses are not encoded in any way, while attachments to Internet addresses are UUencoded prior to transmission. The default setting.
No encoding	Tells Pegasus Mail not to encode the attachment at all. This is an extremely dangerous choice in some cases, particularly for Internet mail. Use it only if you know that the attachment is a plain text file with no high-bit characters.
ASCII text	Indicates that the file is plain text with no formatting or high-bit characters. Pegasus Mail actually sends the attachment as a separate message rather than as an attachment.
UUencoding	A scheme used widely on the Internet. If you are mailing via the Internet or to a user on a UNIX or mainframe system, this encoding is a good choice.
BinHex	A scheme used heavily in the Macintosh world. BinHex is a good format, containing a certain amount of error checking and compression. Because it is not widely used outside the Macintosh world, you should check in advance that the recipient can deal with BinHex-encoded files.
MIME Encodings	MIME (*M*ultipurpose *I*nternet *M*ail *E*xtensions) is an Internet standard for multimedia mail; it allows different mail applications to exchange a variety of types of information. If you select any of these MIME encodings, Pegasus Mail attaches the information necessary so that other applications can decode the file. You must choose an appropriate translation — selecting GIF image for a TIFF file does not cause Pegasus Mail to convert the file: it simply is sent in the wrong format. Pegasus Mail chooses basic MIME encoding automatically if you set encoding to *Pegasus Mail decides* and check the Use MIME features control in the Special screen of the message editing dialog box.

Other message options

When you choose Message⇨Other message options or click on the Special button in the message editing dialog box, the screen changes to a dialog box that lets you control less frequently used features for your message. Table 13-2 describes other Pegasus message options.

Table 13-2	Other Pegasus Message Options
Option	*Description*
BCC	Enter any BCC addresses in this field.
Send replies to	If you want replies to your message to go to an address other than your own, enter that address in this field.
Message is obsolete after	If your message is only meaningful for a certain length of time, enter the time after which it is obsolete in this area. Obsolete messages appear gray in the folder window. A browser command lets you purge all obsolete messages. Obsolete mail also can be purged by utilities run by the system manager.
Message width	This field lets you specify the average length of a line of text in your message. Pegasus Mail adjusts the margin of the message editor so that approximately the number of characters you specify fits on a line. You cannot enter a width wider than the current width of the editing window. Click Use as default to use the value you enter for all future messages.
Average tab width	By default, Pegasus Mail obeys the standard Windows Tab key convention (pressing Tab moves you from field to field in a dialog box). If you enter a width in this field, however, Pegasus Mail inserts the Tab characters in the message instead. You can only change the tab width if tabs were enabled when you started the message. You can enable tabbing for all future messages by clicking Use as default. The width you enter is an average based on the average width of characters in the current font; it will be exact only if you use a monospace font, such as Courier.
Use MIME features for Internet and local mail	MIME is an Internet standard that allows mailers on different systems to exchange binary data and messages using International characters. If you check this control, Pegasus Mail uses MIME encodings to represent accented and special characters and to package attachments so that other MIME-compatible mail systems can read and convert them. MIME is a very powerful standard. The only time you should not check this control is if you believe your correspondent may not be using a MIME-compatible mail system.

Importing text from other sources

You can add text from other applications to your message in two ways.

- You can use the standard cut, copy, and paste commands on the Edit menu to move text around within Windows.

- The Message⇨Import file into message option lets you read a text file into your message. The dialog box that appears lets you navigate by using standard file and directory lists or typing the name of the file in directly.

The file must be a text file for the latter option to work. Word processor files are usually not text files.

Distribution Lists

Pegasus Mail can accept up to 180 characters in any address line. If you need to send a message to more addresses than will fit in this space, or you have lists of users to whom you mail regularly, you can create distribution lists.

A distribution list can be any text file containing addresses, one per line, but it's generally easier to use Pegasus Mail's distribution list manager, which you can access by pressing the button on the button panel, pressing F6, or choosing Addresses⇨Distribution lists.

Creating a distribution list

To create a distribution list, press F6 and click on the New button in the selector window (see Figure 13-2). A dialog box opens, prompting you for a long name for the list and an optional filename. Complete the dialog box and then click OK. You are returned to the selector window.

Now, highlight the list you created and press the Edit button. A window opens, where you can create and control your distribution list. The title you gave your list when you created it appears in the Title field.

To add addresses to your distribution list, click in the address list area and either type in the addresses or select them from address books or the local user list. Make sure that you have only one address per line in the list. Any valid address can be entered in the list.

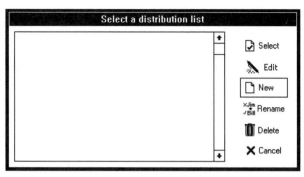

Figure13-2: Selector window.

Distribution list options

You can control and customize the operation of your distribution lists in several ways, as described in Table 13-3.

Table 13-3	Distribution List Options
Option	*Description*
To field	Entering an address in this field forces Pegasus Mail to suppress enumeration of addresses when you use the list. Instead of showing every member of the list, the To field contains only what you enter here.
Reply to	If you want to direct replies to list mailings to a particular address, enter them here. A Reply to field you set in the list overrides any in the message.
Confirm reading, confirm delivery, urgent, no signature	These controls duplicate the same features in the message editor. If you set them for the distribution list, they override the values you use when you compose the message.

Using a distribution list

Tell Pegasus Mail to use a distribution list in one of two ways:

■ While composing your message, open the distribution list selector by clicking the button in the button panel, pressing F6, or choosing

Address⇨Distribution lists. Then double-click on the address you want to use. Pegasus Mail pastes the appropriate filename into the message's address field.

■ Type @ and the DOS path to the file containing the distribution list. This method may be more convenient if you have a mailing list in a format that was not created in Pegasus Mail.

Glossaries (Abbreviations)

Pegasus Mail lets you store abbreviations for commonly used text strings that you can expand at any time with a single keystroke. To create a glossary entry, choose Edit⇨Glossary⇨Create/edit. Figure 13-3 shows a Glossary dialog box.

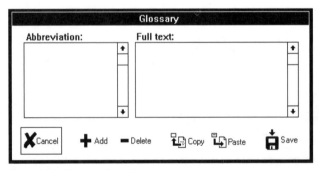

Figure 13-3: Glossary dialog box.

In the Glossary dialog box, a list of abbreviations appears on the left-hand side of the screen, while the full text of the currently selected abbreviation appears in the edit window to the right. To change a glossary entry, select it in the list and edit it in the editing window. To add a glossary entry, click the Add button, provide an abbreviation, and edit as before. You can copy and paste into your glossary texts by using the buttons in the dialog box.

To expand a glossary entry in your message, type the abbreviation, make sure that the cursor is at its end, and then press Ctrl+/. In Pegasus Mail 1.0, you can only expand glossary entries in the message editor. Future versions will let you expand them in any text field.

Browsing mail

The folder browser lets you manage the mail you receive. You can move, copy, delete, forward, print, and reply to messages. Special options and functions for sorting folders are located on the Folder menu, which appears at the end of the menu bar when a folder window is on top.

A *mail folder* is a place where mail messages are stored. The *new mail folder* is a special folder that changes as you receive, read, and delete mail, but you also can create other folders for long-term storage of messages you wish to keep. Folders can have long descriptive names to aid in filing.

The folder selector

When you ask to open a folder, or if you select the Move or Copy options in the folder window, the folder selector opens. In this dialog box, you can create new folders, rename existing ones, and delete folders you no longer require. You can also create *trays*, which are a special kind of folder that can contain folders and other trays. Trays let you organize your mail into a hierarchy or to group-related topics and folders in their own areas.

The folder selector lists all the folders and trays available to you. Folders in the list that appear in blue are *system folders* — you can read from them, but you might not be able to alter their contents.

You can select items from this list by using the mouse or typing the first few characters of their names. To open a tray, highlight it and press Enter. Or click on the Open button. Its contents appear in the list indented one level.

At the right-hand edge of the entry for each folder is a pair of numbers, representing the number of messages in the folder and the number of unread messages in the folder, respectively. Unread mail can appear in folders as a result of new mail filtering rules or when you copy a message you have not read from the new mail folders. Folders containing unread mail appear in the list in green.

When you click the Special button in the folder selector, a pop-up menu offers four options, as described in Table 13-4.

Table 13-4	Folder Selector Special Options
Option	**Description**
Reindex folder	From time to time, a folder's index file may become corrupted, which can result in errors when you try to open it. To force Pegasus Mail to rebuild the index file, highlight the folder and select Reindex folder. Reindexing works reliably if the actual messages in the folder are intact but may result in the loss of some status information (such as whether you have replied to a message or forwarded it). A side effect of rebuilding a folder is that some deleted messages may reappear the next time the folder is opened.
Compress folder	When you delete a message from a folder, Pegasus Mail does not immediately reclaim the space it occupies; instead, it waits until you have deleted around 20,000 characters from the folder. Pegasus Mail then recovers all the space in a single pass. This deferred compression improves the performance of the program at the cost of some disk space. Select Compress folder to force Pegasus Mail to compress a folder. Compression is always a safe option and does not result in the loss of information.
Move entry	Select Move entry if you want to move a folder or tray to another tray. The highlighted folder or tray is removed from the list and information about it is saved in a disk file (called TRAYSAVE.PM) in your home mailbox. Once you have chosen the Move command, each time you click the Special button again, the Move option is replaced by a Retrieve option, letting you insert the moved entry into the list. Navigate to the place in your tray hierarchy where you want the item to appear and then choose Recover from the Special menu; Pegasus Mail inserts the saved item for you. It is safe to exit from Pegasus Mail without recovering the entry — you can do so at any time after you have moved it.
Check tray list	If you create folders by using an old version of Pegasus Mail after you have run Pegasus Mail 1.1, the folder does not appear in the tray list because Pegasus Mail stores the tray structure in a way that the old version of Pegasus Mail does not understand. Selecting Check tray list tells Pegasus Mail to compare its tray list (the list of all folders and trays that it maintains) with the folders that actually appear in your home mailbox. If it finds any folders that are not in the tray list, it adds them to the main tray for subsequent use. This command is completely safe and may be used routinely if you wish.

 You can dismiss the pop-up menu without selecting a choice by pressing Esc or clicking the mouse outside the menu.

Copying and moving messages

If you want to make a copy of a message in a mail folder or move the message from the current folder to another, click on the Copy button or the Move button. The folder selector opens, listing the available folders. You can create a new folder or double-click on the destination folder.

If the message you are copying has not been read, the folder's unread messages counter that appears in the folder selector increases by one.

Deleting messages

To delete messages you no longer need, highlight them in the folder and click the Delete button (or press the Del key).

Pegasus Mail has a preferences option (Deleted message tracking) that lets you recover mail messages you delete accidentally. If you have checked Preserve deleted messages until exit in your preferences, Pegasus Mail does not delete messages from the folder; instead, it moves them to a special folder called *Deleted messages*, which it creates as necessary. When you exit from Pegasus Mail, the Deleted messages folder is removed and the messages are deleted once and for all. Any time up to the point when you exit from Pegasus Mail, you may open the deleted messages folder and move or copy messages you wish to recover to other folders.

 You should not enable Deleted message tracking if you are running in an environment with low or restricted disk space.

Forwarding messages

If you wish to refer a message to another person, then highlight it in the folder list and click the Forward button (or press *F*). A small dialog box opens, prompting you for the address to which the message should be forwarded. If you click Edit before forwarding, then a message editor opens, letting you change the contents of the message before it is sent; otherwise, it is forwarded at once.

 With Pegasus Mail 1.0, you cannot pick addresses from address books or other lists in the forwarding window. You can only type the address in. According to the software authors, this restriction is temporary and will be removed in the near future.

Printing messages

You can print messages from the message reader or from the folder list by pressing Ctrl+P or selecting File⇨Print. The message reader also has a Print button.

When you ask to print a message, the Printer setup dialog box appears, showing the last settings you used. Pegasus Mail remembers your print settings from session to session. The currently selected printer (or the default Windows printer if this is the first time you have printed your message) appears in the list control. You can select other installed printers by clicking on the down arrow at the right-hand end of the control. From the Printer setup dialog box, you can adjust the options described in Table 13-5.

Table 13-5	Printer Setup Dialog Box
Option	**Description**
Margin fields	Margin fields let you specify a printing margin for the Top/Bottom and Left/Right of the page. The default is 20mm (one inch = 25.4mm) all around. Pegasus Mail does not let you set margins narrower than 10mm.
Font button	The Font button lets you select a font from those supported by your printer.
Setup button	The Setup button brings up the standard Windows Printer setup dialog box, which varies from printer to printer.

The Folder menu

When a folder window is on top, a Folder menu appears at the right of the menu bar. The Folder menu contains options which are less frequently used or are more specialized than the button functions in the window.

The last entry on the menu, Special folder options, lets you select the font the folder window uses to display the list. This setting is global to all folders and is remembered from session to session. You cannot choose very large fonts for the folder display without truncating some of the information it shows. A 14-point font is normally adequate.

Searching for text in a folder

The Find and Find again options on the Folder menu let you search the contents of the current folder for a piece of text. Type the text you want to look for in the editing field. The text can contain * and ? wild-card characters. Unless you use wild-card characters, the search is case sensitive (that is, *Pegasus Mail* and *pegasus mail* are regarded as different).

If you want Pegasus Mail to restrict its search to the special headers at the start of the message, check the Search message headers only box. Searching headers only is considerably faster than searching the whole message; this method is appropriate if you are interested in the subject of a message or whom it is from.

Usually, Pegasus Mail opens a message reader and displays the first message it finds that matches your search criteria. If you want to select all messages in the folder that match your criteria instead of reading them, click the Mark all matching messages box. This option is handy if you want to tag all messages on the same subject for moving or copying.

If you want to search only for a particular header containing your search string, make sure that Search message headers only is checked and then enter the search text. For example, when you only want messages in which the From field contains the word *Otago*, enter the following search text:

```
From:*otago*
```

A *wild-card character* is one that matches any character or group of characters in the text searched. In Pegasus Mail, the ? character matches any single character (that is, *?illy* matches both *Willy* and *Billy*), while the * character matches any number of characters (that is, *j*on* matches *johnson, johnston,* or *john's son*).

Extracting messages to files

Select the Extracting messages to files command if you want to save the text of a message or messages to files on your hard disk or file server. What happens when you select this option depends on whether you have selected more than one message in the folder.

If you have selected only one message, Pegasus Mail simply asks you for a filename and saves the contents of the message to that file.

If you have more than one message marked, then Pegasus Mail opens a dialog box asking you to choose from three options:

- If you choose the *Extract all messages to a single file* option, Pegasus Mail asks you for a filename and saves the text of all the marked messages in the same file, one after the other in the order they appear in the folder.

- Choose the *Extract messages to separate files, asking for names* option and Pegasus Mail asks you for a filename for each marked message. Use this option when it is important that you control the names of the files containing the message text.

■ If you choose the *Extract to separate files, creating unique names for each* option, then Pegasus Mail asks you to enter a single filename. It then takes the filename you supply and creates unique filenames based on it, saving the text of each message in a separate file. Pegasus Mail creates the unique names by removing any file extension you supply and adding a numeric extension starting at 000, adding 1 to the extension for each file. Using this command, you can extract a maximum of 999 messages to files.

Sorting folders

The second group of entries on the Folder menu lets you specify how the folder should be sorted. The default for folders is Sort by date. A check mark appears next to the entry that indicates how the folder is currently sorted.

Pegasus Mail remembers the last sorting option you selected from session to session.

Special folder options

The last entry on the Folder menu has a submenu containing some specialized functions, described in Table 13-6.

Table 13-6	Special Folder Options
Options	**Description**
UUdecode message	Sometimes Pegasus Mail cannot recognize that a message is actually an attachment sent using a special encoding method called *uuencoding*. This scenario usually arises if the attachment was sent across the Internet by someone using a mail system other than Pegasus Mail. If you receive such a message, you can force Pegasus Mail to decode it by highlighting it in the list and selecting the UUdecode message option. Pegasus Mail prompts you for a filename and tries to decode the message for you.
Un-BinHex message	BinHex, commonly used on Macs, is another special transmission format, like UUencoding. If you receive a BinHexed message that Pegasus Mail does not recognize as BinHexed, you can force it to unpack it by using this option.
Add sender to distribution list	When you select this command, Pegasus Mail opens the distribution list selector and prompts you to select a list. The addresses of the sender of every marked message in the folder are added to whichever distribution list you select. Pegasus Mail does not duplicate an address that already appears in the list.

Options	Description
Remove sender from distribution list	This command removes the sender of every marked message in the folder list from whichever distribution list you select.
Delete all expired messages	Pegasus Mail lets you set an *expiry*, or obsolescence date for a message — in other words, a date after which the message is meaningless. Messages that are past their expiration dates appear gray in the folder window. The Delete all expired messages command, which instructs Pegasus Mail to delete all expired messages from the folder, only works in the New Mail folder.

BinHexed files from Macintosh users may be useless to you on a PC. The Macintosh has a filing system quite unlike that of any other computer, and its files are often only usable on other Macintoshes. Some programs such as WordPerfect and Excel create data files which are compatible on both platforms, but not all do. If you find that you cannot use the attachment when you extract it, this may well be the reason.

Address Books _____

Pegasus Mail's address books let you store e-mail addresses and other information about people with whom you correspond. You can create as many address books as you wish, and the system administrator also can create address books that everyone can see (these appear in blue in the address book selector window). (See Figure 13-4.)

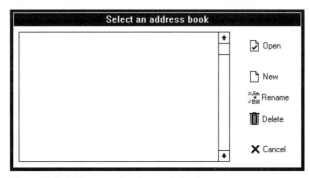

Figure 13-4: Address book selector dialog box.

The address book selector

When you click on the Address books button, or choose Addresses⇨Address books, the Address Book Selector dialog box will open. In this dialog box, you can create new address books, rename existing ones, and delete address books you no longer require.

The selector shows a list of all the address books available to you. Address books in the list that appear in blue are systemwide address books available to all users: you can read from them, but you may not be able to alter their contents.

To open an address book, either double-click its entry or highlight it in the list and click on the Open button.

Naming address books

When you create an address book in the selector, you can give it any name, using as many as 50 characters. There are no restrictions on the names you can use in the address book long name. If you choose to specify the short name (or filename) for the address book, you must enter a legal DOS filename — no longer than eight characters — with no extension. Usually, you should leave the short name field blank and let Pegasus Mail choose a filename for you.

Creating address book entries

After you open an address book, a window opens, listing the contents of the book in an abbreviated form. If you click on an entry in the list, all the details from that entry appear in the information pane at the bottom of the address book window.

To add an entry to your address book, click the Add button. A simple data-entry dialog box opens, presenting you with a blank entry template. After you fill in the fields, click the OK button. The fields that you must complete in this screen are described in Table 13-7.

Table 13-7	Fields for Adding an Address to your Address Book
Field	*Description*
Name (alias)	The person's name. You can use what you enter in this field as an address in any address field. It is generally easier to remember that someone is called *Peter Smith* than to remember his address. This use of the name as an address is called *aliasing*. This field may not contain a comma.
Key	A short search key for the entry. Pegasus Mail lets you sort the address book either by name or key.
E-mail address	The person's e-mail address. Any single valid address can be entered in this field, including distribution lists and NetWare groups. You may not use an alias in this field.

All other fields in the address book are yours to use in any way you wish.

Using address book entries in your mail

You can use your address books in your mail in three distinct ways:

- You can double-click on an entry in your address book to start a new mail message using that address and any others selected in the book.

- When you click on the Paste button on the address book window, any highlighted addresses are copied into the last active field in the message you are editing.

- You can drag the address entries you want to use to any edit control and drop them there. Note that the edit control need not be in Pegasus Mail — it is possible to drag addresses from Pegasus Mail to edit controls in other applications, such as Windows Notepad.

Depending on the setting in the address book menu, Pegasus Mail pastes either the alias (the default) or the actual e-mail address into the destination field. You may use either approach.

Most address fields in Pegasus Mail can accept only 180 characters. If you have selected addresses with more characters than can fit in the field, Pegasus Mail issues a warning. When this happens, you may have to consider creating a distribution list.

Aliasing happens when you use the name field from an address book rather than the e-mail address. Pegasus Mail accepts either as an address: if you use the name, Pegasus Mail looks up the real e-mail address at send time. You may prefer to use aliases over e-mail addresses because it is generally easier to remember someone's name than his or her address.

Searching address books

The quickest way to search your address book is to type the first few characters of the name or key you want to find. Depending on the current sort order of the address book, Pegasus Mail moves the highlight to the first entry in the book with a key or name that matches what you type. This process is called *speed searching*.

For more comprehensive searching, the Address book menu contains a Find command that you can use to locate or select entries in your address books. When you choose Find, a small dialog box opens, asking what you want to search for. Enter the string you want to find. If you want Pegasus Mail to search the whole address book marking all entries that match your criteria, click the Select all matching entries button.

You can repeat the last search you made by selecting Find again from the Address book menu. The search text is global, so you can search in one book and then open another and choose Search again to continue your search in the new book.

The Address book menu

When an address book is the top window in Pegasus Mail, the Address book menu option becomes available at the right of the menu bar. This menu contains actions and commands specific to address books.

The first two commands, Find and Find again, let you search for text in the address book.

The next two options control the sort order for the address book. Unless the address book is a systemwide entry, the sort order is remembered for each address book separately between sessions. The sort order that is currently active has a check mark beside it in the menu.

The final three options on the menu control the way Pegasus Mail uses addresses from the address book. Like the sort order, these settings are local to each nonsystem address book and are remembered between sessions. The first two options in the group let you choose whether Pegasus Mail should paste the alias or the actual e-mail address into messages when you drag and drop or press the Paste button. The default is to paste the alias.

The last option on the menu lets you tell Pegasus Mail whether to resolve aliases in this address book. *Alias resolution* is the process of taking a name and finding the e-mail address that matches it from the address book at send time. Alias resolution can take quite a while if you have many or large address books, so you may want to disable it for some or all your books. By default, Pegasus Mail resolves aliases in all address books.

The button panel

Pegasus Mail's button panel is a set of tools that provides access to the most commonly used parts of the program at the click of a button. Depending on the setting you specify in your Button Panel Preferences (see under the File/Preferences menu), the button panel can appear as either a fixed toolbar beneath the main menu (the default) or as a small floating window in either horizontal or vertical format.

Pegasus Mail remembers the location and state (open or closed) of the button panel between sessions. You also can choose between having the button panel as a toolbar or as a floating window in vertical or horizontal format.

When the button panel is active as a toolbar, the buttons have the following functions:

Compose a new message
Read new mail
Open/manage mail folders
Open/manage address books
Open/manage distribution lists
Open the local user list
Open new mail filtering rules
Cut selection to the Clipboard
Copy selection to Clipboard
Paste the contents of the Clipboard
Save or write to disk
Retrieve or import from disk
Print
Select font

When the button panel is active as a floating window, the buttons are marked to reflect the following functions:

Start a new mail message
Browse your new mail folder
Browse other mail folders
Manage your address books
Manage your distribution lists

Preferences

Pegasus Mail lets you customize many aspects of its operation. These settings are called your Preferences and are stored in the file PEGASUS MAIL.PRO in your NEWMAIL directory.

Preferences fall into two classes:

■ *Implicit preferences*, such as the location of windows on the screen and the values you set in the controls in the message editor. Pegasus Mail automatically remembers implicit preferences.

■ *Explicit preferences*, or ones where you actually instruct Pegasus Mail to operate in a particular way. Explicit preferences are changed by choosing File⇨Preferences.

General settings

The following items can be changed in the General Settings dialog box:

Table 13-8	General Settings Dialog Box Options
Option	*Description*
Personal name	Pegasus Mail attaches whatever you enter here to your address when you send messages, making it easier for the recipient to identify who you are. Make this entry simple and clear. Your personal name should consist only of letters and digits.
Open new mail at startup	If you check this box, Pegasus Mail automatically opens your new mail folder for you when you run it.

Option	*Description*
Preserve deleted messages until exit	If you check this box, Pegasus Mail saves any messages you delete in a special folder called *Deleted Messages*, which is cleared when you exit. This option lets you save messages deleted accidentally.
Ask for confirmation before deleting	If you prefer that Pegasus Mail does not ask you to confirm that you really want to delete messages, uncheck this control. If you uncheck this control, you risk accidentally deleting messages you want to keep. As a result, if you uncheck this control, consider turning the Preserve deleted messages until exit option on.
Ask for NetWare password at startup	Check this option and Pegasus Mail prompts you for your NetWare password when you run it; Pegasus Mail does not run unless you enter the password correctly. This option adds security to your mail if you are away from your desk a lot. This control has no effect in non-NetWare environments and so is not available.
Offer advanced options for replies	Pegasus Mail has an alternative reply dialog box that lets you select particular addresses from the original message for your reply. If you want to use the advanced reply dialog box rather than the default simple reply dialog box, check this box.
Folder for copies to self	If you click on the Select button, Pegasus Mail opens the folder selector and lets you create or select a folder where your copies to yourself are stored. By default, the folder is called *Copies to self* (with the DOS filename COPYSELF).
Default reply address	If you want to specify an address that Pegasus Mail automatically copies to the Reply to field of every outgoing mail message, enter it here. There is usually no need to use this option. However, you may use it if you routinely prefer to receive your mail on another system.

NetWare MHS preferences

If a version of Novell's MHS transport is installed on your system, this option lets you configure the way Pegasus Mail interacts with MHS for you. In general, the options in this screen are quite complex, and you should change them only if instructed to do so by your MHS administrator. Table 13-9 describes the NetWare MHS preferences available in Pegasus.

Table 13-9	NetWare MHS Preferences Options
Option	**Description**
My NetWare MHS user name	The user name by which MHS addresses you. It may be the same as your NetWare user name but need not be. If you are using an SMF-71 transport, such as NetWare Global MHS, you can enter a full SMF-71 address (up to 128 characters long) in this field. You may need to enter a complete address here if you are not a member of the default MHS workgroup.
Mailbox name	The directory in the MHS tree where your MHS new mail folder is located. If you are using MHS 1.5, it is usually the first eight characters of your NetWare user name (this is the default Pegasus Mail uses), but it may be different; it is likely to be different if you are using an SMF-71 transport.
New mail folder	The name of the folder in your new mail folder where Pegasus Mail should expect to find your new mail. In technical terms, this field should contain the name of your preferred mailer, which may or may not be Pegasus Mail.
Check the MHS new mail folder	By default, MHS creates a new mail directory for every user called MHS and makes this directory the preferred mailbox for the user. Checking this control tells Pegasus Mail to check the MHS new mail folder, as well as any other you name in the New mail folder field. Checking this option is harmless at worst, but it may slow down checks for new mail a little bit.

Signatures

A signature is a small fragment of text that Pegasus Mail automatically adds to the end of messages you send. You should usually put your name, address, and phone/fax number in your signature, although some people like to place a witty saying or other text there as well. Pegasus Mail supports separate signatures for each type of message you can send — local, Internet, and MHS.

Home mailbox location

Your home mailbox is where all your mail folders, distribution lists, address books, and other Pegasus Mail-related files (except unread new mail) are stored. By default, it is located in a special directory on the file server, but you can specify an alternate location for it using this option.

Before using this option, make sure that all windows in Pegasus Mail are closed except the button panel (which can also be closed but does not have to be).

You may want to change your home mailbox location if you have limited space on the file server, if you are concerned about the privacy of your mail, or for other reasons. You also can have more than one mailbox and change between them by using this dialog box — you may want to do this if you received mail at your address for more than one person or organization.

To change your home mailbox location, type in the new path in either DOS or NetWare format. If you want to change the location but leave all your mail files where they are, make sure that the Move mailbox contents to new location button is not checked (this is how you would implement more than one mailbox). If you have moved your home mailbox but want to revert to the original location on the file server, press the Default button.

If you have chosen to move the contents of your home mailbox, Pegasus Mail does so as soon as you click OK.

Extended Features

Extended features are special Pegasus Mail features that you have only if the system administrator has explicitly granted them to you. If you have been granted access to extended features, then Preferences⇨Extended features is available; otherwise, it is grayed and you cannot select it. Choosing this option opens a dialog box that lets you change the following:

Autoforwarding

Pegasus Mail supports autoforwarding, or the redirection of your mail to another account. You can autoforward mail delivered to you from local addresses, mail received from the Charon or Mercury Internet gateway, both, or neither. It is possible to forward one type of mail but not the other. To set autoforwarding, place the forwarding address in either or both of the available autoforward fields. You can forward local mail to any address Pegasus Mail can understand, including NetWare groups and distribution lists. Internet mail can only be forwarded to simple local addresses or to Internet addresses. Table 13-10 describes autoforwarding options.

Mail arriving via NetWare MHS cannot be autoforwarded.

Table 13-10	Autoforwarding Options
Option	**Description**
Deliver mail even if autoforwarding	Check this box if you want Pegasus Mail to leave a copy of mail as well as forwarding it when you have autoforwarding addresses set. This option has no effect if you are not forwarding your mail.
Allow 'reading confirmation' requests	If you uncheck this box, then Pegasus Mail does not return confirmation that you have read messages when it is requested. Local users are told the moment they send the message that no confirmation will be supplied, but Internet and MHS mailers receive no such notification.
Advise of new mail via broadcasts	When this box is checked, Pegasus Mail sends a NetWare-style broadcast message to indicate that a new mail message has arrived. If you find the broadcast messages annoying but do not want to use the NetWare `castoff` command to disable them, uncheck this box.
Disable mail delivery to this address	If checked, it will not be possible to send mail to this address.

Reading Mail

To read a message in a folder, either double-click on it or select it and press the Open button.

While you are reading a message, a button bar with most of the options available in the folder window appears. Three other buttons also are available:

Print	Pressing this button has the same effect as choosing File⇨Print.
Next	Pressing this button replaces the message in the reader window with the next message from the folder.
Prev	Pressing this button replaces the message with the one before it in the folder.

 If you hold down the Shift key while you press the Next or Prev button, the message you are leaving is marked in the folder selector before the new one is loaded.

Choosing Edit⇨Copy copies lines from the message reader for pasting elsewhere. By pressing Ctrl while selecting lines, you can select separate groups of
lines simultaneously in the message and then copy them all with one command.

Options specific to the message reader appear in the Message menu (see the
next section).

The Message menu

While you're reading mail, the Message menu appears at the right of the menu
bar. The menu offers four options specific to the message reader, as described
in Table 13-11.

Table 13-11	Message Menu Options
Option	*Description*
Save window size	When you choose this option, Pegasus Mail saves the current size of the message reader window to your preferences. All future message reader windows then open at this size. You cannot save the location of a message reader window because doing so would result in messages overlapping on-screen, thus being difficult to select.
Show all headers	By default, Pegasus Mail displays only headers in the message that are meaningful to the reader, suppressing all others. If you need to see the message exactly as it was delivered, with its headers intact, select this option.
Extract message to file	If you want to make a copy of this message in a DOS text file, perhaps for inclusion in another program, select this option. You are prompted for a filename — when you click OK, Pegasus Mail extracts the contents of the message to the file.
Font	Use this option to change the font you use to view messages. This change is global — it affects all messages already open and subsequently opened in Pegasus Mail.
Headers	Headers are the special set of lines at the start of a mail message that contain addressing and other machine-readable information about the message. Headers are rigidly formatted and vary widely from system to system. Many headers in a message are only of interest to the mail transport system and are meaningless to a human reader.

Unlike the DOS version of Pegasus Mail where the Show all headers option is global and affects all subsequent messages, Pegasus Mail only applies this option to the current message.

The MHS Directory Service

If your system has an MHS SMF-71 message transport, such as Novell's NetWare Global MHS, then the directory service provided by that system (called the Extract File) is available to you from within Pegasus Mail. To open the MHS Directory Service, choose the entry from the Addresses menu.

The MHS directory service list behaves like a read-only address book: you can double-click on an entry to start a new message by using the entry as an address, you can drag addresses from the list window to any address field, or you can click on the Paste button to paste the selected addresses into the last address field you were using.

You also can speed-search through the list by typing the first few characters of the name you are looking for.

For technical reasons, you should close the extract file window as soon as you can after using it because NetWare MHS may not be able to update the list while you have the file open.

Built-In TCP/IP Network Mail Services

Pegasus Mail has built-in support for mail services accessed using TCP/IP (Internet) network protocols called POP3 (*Post Office Protocol*) and SMTP (*Simple Mail Transfer Protocol*). To access these services, you must have a TCP/IP network transport interface with a special Windows DLL called WINSOCK.DLL installed on your system.

POP3 services let you retrieve new mail held for you on another machine (usually a UNIX machine or a NetWare file server).

SMTP services let you send mail to the Internet; Pegasus Mail implements SMTP mail by using a relay service — that is, it asks a complete SMTP implementation (usually running on a UNIX machine) to send the mail on its behalf.

Configuring Pegasus Mail for Network Mail Services

If you have a valid WinSock implementation installed on your system, three extra options appear on your File menu. The first option lets you configure Pegasus Mail's use of these services.

POP3 host

The name of the machine where the account you wish to access is located. The address you provide here depends on your WinSock implementation; many let you enter a normal Internet name (for example, parnassus.pmail.gen.nz), but some may require that you enter the address in dotted notation (for example, 192.156.225.2). Consult your system manager or WinSock manual if you are unsure which form to use.

User name

The name of the account on the machine under which mail is being held for you. Pegasus Mail logs into the host using this account name and retrieves any mail waiting there.

Password

The password for the account on the host. The password is not displayed on-screen and is stored in an encrypted format in your configuration file.

Leave mail larger than

If you are connected to the mail host by a slow TCP/IP link (such as a SLIP link), downloading large messages can be very time-consuming. If you enter a value in this field, Pegasus Mail does not try to retrieve any mail larger than the size you specify (in kilobytes); that mail is left untouched on the host. A value of 0 in this field means no limit — Pegasus Mail downloads all mail.

Delete mail retrieved on host

If you check this box, Pegasus Mail deletes the host's copy of each mail message it successfully downloads, which will prevent it from being presented to you again the next time you retrieve mail. Leaving this box unchecked tells Pegasus Mail to leave the mail on the host even if successfully downloaded. Mail left on the server is retrieved every time you download mail.

Check when opening new mail

If you check this box, Pegasus Mail checks the host for new mail every time you open the new mail folder or click the New Mail button in the button panel. If you leave this button unchecked, then Pegasus Mail checks for new mail only when you explicitly choose File⇨Check host for new mail.

Relay host

Enter here the name of a machine that can process outgoing mail on your behalf. This is usually the same machine you entered as your POP3 mail host, and the address is subject to the same restrictions and rules.

Send mail at once (don't queue)

If you check this option, Pegasus Mail sends your mail messages to the relay host as soon as you click the Send button in the message editor. If you leave the box unchecked, Pegasus Mail queues your messages and sends them to the relay host only when you choose File⇨Send all queued mail. If you are using a slow TCP/IP link, you should probably leave this box unchecked.

Prefer for outgoing Internet mail

This option is only meaningful when you are running Pegasus Mail on a NetWare system that's also served by either the Mercury SMTP transport or the Charon Internet mail gateway. Checking this control tells Pegasus Mail to use its own built-in mail delivery routines instead of passing your outgoing mail to Mercury or Charon for processing. If you leave this box unchecked, then Pegasus Mail always uses Mercury or Charon in preference to its own SMTP delivery routines if either is available on the NetWare system to which you are connected. The setting of this control is ignored when you run Pegasus Mail in a non-NetWare environment.

Communication Protocols and Tools _____

Full details on using Pegasus Mail with WinSock, POP3 (*Post Office Protocol*, Version 3), and SMTP (*Simple Mail Transfer Protocol*) are offered in the Pegasus MAIL.TXT file included on the CD-ROM bundled with this book.

Pegasus Mail V 1.10

Name _____

Company _____

Address _____

City _____

State _____ Country _____

Zip _____ Phone _____

Remit to:

Pegasus Mail, c/o David Harris
P.O. Box 5451
Dunedin, New Zealand
or fax: (+64)3-453-6612

Pricing

Please see the Pegasus ORDER.FRM file on the CD-ROM for more information and Terms and Conditions.

❏   5-copy manual license for WinPMail $150 US

❏   Site-licensed manuals for WinPMail $325 US

❏   Site bundle Pegasus Mail/DOS and Windows $500 US

Chapter 14

Wincode: A Uucoder for Windows

Copyright Snappy_Inc. (1993,1994), written by George H. Silva

Wincode is a Windows 3.1 program that converts 7-bit ASCII (text) files to 8-bit binary (EXE, COM, GIF, and so on) files and vice versa through a process known as *uucoding*. This ASCII/binary conversion lets you send and receive binary files over any ASCII-based communications system, such as electronic mail. Wincode provides a quick and easy way to distribute programs all over the world.

Uucoding is also commonly used by many Internet newsgroups in which users wish to exchange binary data. If you spend any time on the Internet, you should own a uucoder. If you use Windows, then Wincode is for you.

I originally wrote this program for my own needs and released it to the public as freeware. I did not expect such a positive response to this small utility but have since been encouraged to upgrade and support it. However, remember this distinction: this program is freeware, not public domain. The author retains the copyright to the source code and to the use and distribution of the program. See the help file for further copyright and distribution information. I hope others find this program as useful as I do. If so, drop me a line at the address in the help file.

Wincode is 100-percent compatible with all standard uucoders. I have tried to incorporate as many extra features as possible to make the uucoding process painless. The average user may not need or use all of Wincode's features, but hey, they're free!

So why is such a great program free? Well, I guess I've found enough useful freeware utilities that I figured I'd make one myself.

I suggest that all users (novice and expert) carefully read this chapter. It contains all the information you need (and more) to run Wincode.

Wincode Features

Wincode is a full-featured Windows 3.1 program, written in TPW 1.5. Wincode has an integrated file-sorting companion program (separate executable for easier upgrading) that handles many types of file header formats. Wincode's features are described in Table 14-1.

Table 14-1	Wincode Features
Feature	*Description*
Bytes per File	You can encode into one large file or into several files of any length you choose (for e-mail systems that restrict file size). Wincode even shows you how many bytes the unencoded file is versus how many lines the encoded file has.
Close When Done	When this option is chosen, Wincode exits after completing a task.
Code Type	You can choose the code table Wincode uses for either encoding or decoding files. Choose UUE or XXE, or make your own. You can also include these tables in encoded files.
Create Report File	When this option is chosen, Wincode creates, for each en/decode, report files listing essential file processing information and output file errors.
Drag and Drop support for batch en/decoding	Use your favorite Windows file manager to choose the files you want, and drag them onto the Wincode window or icon.
Dump Files	Wincode can move encoded files it has decoded to your temporary directory so you can easily delete them.
EMBL File Compatible	You can en/decode files in the EMBL uucode format. This is useful for researchers who use the EMBL File Server.
Error Checking	You can check for errors in files which decode improperly. Wincode works faster with this option turned off, though.
File and Line Checksums	Wincode adds checksums to the encoded text to monitor data integrity.
File Directories	You can choose the working directory and the encoded and decoded file directories. You can place files Wincode encodes into the input file directory, a custom directory per file, or a fixed directory. You also set a temporary directory for Wincode to use when it en/decodes multiple files. You can erase files from the temp, encode, and decode directories from within Wincode.

Feature	*Description*
File Extension(s)	You can choose your own extensions for encoded or decoded files. For encoded files, choose the default and Wincode does the work. For decoded files, you can enter up to 20 custom extensions.
File Headers	Wincode encodes files with headers which include section numbers and a filename. You can turn this option off.
Filename(s)	You can choose your own filenames for encoded or decoded files as they are being created. Wincode can also choose them for you.
File Type	Choose the text file type Wincode creates for encoded files: MS-DOS, MAC, or UNIX.
Full-featured Windows 3.1 program	Written in TPW 1.5. Integrated file-sorting companion program (separate executable for easier upgrading) which handles many types of file header formats.
Multimedia Sound Support	If you have a sound card and have assigned new sounds to your Windows events, Wincode uses them. Otherwise, you hear the default beep for important events. You can turn this feature off.
Encode into one file or many files	You can encode a file into either one large file or up to 999 small files.
Run decoded files	You can set Wincode to automatically execute files that have just been decoded.
SMART decoding	Wincode decodes single files, multipart files, single files containing multipart files, and so on. Wincode also incorporates many error-bypass options and can correct improper output filenames when en/decoding.
Start As Icon	You can make Wincode start as an icon. Supports uu, xx, and user-defined en/decoding.
The Wincode package	Wincode now includes the Snappy Installer, which makes sure you install or upgrade Wincode correctly.
Command-line parameter at start-up	You can use the File Manager to associate Wincode with an extension (such as UUE) and start Wincode by double-clicking a file of that type. When Wincode is already running, the file you click is passed to the active copy.
Wincode client area responds to double-clicks	Double-clicking left mouse button pops up the File menu. Double-clicking the right mouse button pops up the Options menu. Double-clicking the middle mouse button, if it exists, pops up the Help menu.
Winsort	Winsort processes multipart files containing single files which are not ordered. See "Supported formats" for more information.
Winsort First	This option passes mixed multipart files containing single files to Winsort for processing before decoding.

It's all free. Browse the entire help file to discover Wincode's full potential. As always, I offer free support.

Requirements

- IBM compatible running DOS 3.3 or higher
- 286 or higher processor with at least 2MB memory
- Windows 3.1 running in standard or enhanced mode
- About 370K of disk space

Wincode now en/decodes files of up to 8MB.

Installing Wincode

Files

WINCODE.EXE	The main executable program
WINCODE.HLP	The help file
WINSORT.EXE	A companion file sorting utility
INSTALL.EXE	The install/upgrade program
INSTALL.INI	The installation information file
SUM.EXE	A bonus "sum -r/size" DOS utility
README.TXT	The unedited text of this chapter

Installation

If you have not already done so, expand the ZIP archive into a temporary directory (I suggest using a floppy disk). Start Windows, select File⇨Run from Program Manager or File Manager, and type the full path of INSTALL.EXE. The install program copies all the files to a directory you specify, overwriting older files. Upgrade WINCODE.INI if you are running an older version of Wincode. Now, install WINCODE.EXE as an icon (see the WINCODE.HLP file or your Windows manuals) or use Program Manager's File⇨Run option to run Wincode (type in the full path of WINCODE.EXE).

When you have Wincode running, chose Help⇨Contents and read the help file for information on using and configuring Wincode. Have fun.

All of the files listed previously must be present and in the same directory for the installer to function properly. If you want to move these files to other directories, run the installer before you do.

The install program checks each file's checksum to ensure you have an original version. If you receive a *Bad Checksum* message, you have a corrupted file or a virus-infected file. If you need any help, send information to the address(es) in the help file.

The help file explains all of Wincode's options.

Setting Up Wincode

First, make sure that your WINDOWS directory is in your path statement. Then, use the installer to copy the appropriate files to a directory of your choice (like C:\UTIL\WINCODE).

To make a Wincode icon

1. Choose File⇨New from the Program Manager.

2. Select Program Item and click OK.

3. For Description, type **Wincode**.

4. For Command Line, select Browse and highlight WINCODE.EXE or type in the file's full pathname.

5. Click OK. The Wincode icon appears in the group you selected.

6. To run Wincode, double-click its icon.

To run Wincode from the Windows command line

1. Choose File⇨Run from the Program Manager.

2. Type in the program's full pathname. Wincode starts with its default settings (Options⇨Configuration shows them to you). It creates a WINCODE.INI file in your WINDOWS directory as soon as you quit the application.

Configuring and Using Wincode

The following is Wincode's menu layout. Click on each highlighted menu choice for a detailed explanation of its function.

Encode

Choose Encode to encode a single file. A File Open dialog box, which lets you select a file for encoding, appears.

Use Options⇨Wincode⇨Working Directory to choose the default start-up directory. Wincode creates names for encoded files by appending a sequential number from 1 to 999 to the original file's name. Wincode truncates the filename so that it does not exceed the DOS eight-character limit.

When Wincode encodes a file, it displays an information window which shows you the input filename, the output filename, and the percentage of the input file Wincode has encoded. The window includes Stop and Quit buttons. Wincode encodes files of up to 8MB (8192000 bytes).

If you get a memory allocation error and you are sure that you have the required memory (that is, you have 4MB RAM and you're encoding a 3MB file), try setting a larger swap file size for Windows.

Helpful hints

- Wincode inserts file headers at the beginning and end of every file.
- Wincode lists file checksums immediately following the keyword end as sum -r/size checksum/filesize.
- Wincode also includes a code table.
- ASCII characters used to encode files vary with the code type selected.
- The default encoding mode is 644 (owner:rw-; group:r—; public:r—). See the "Mode" section in the documentation for details on changing this value.

See the "Make EMBL files" section for important information regarding differences in encoded file format.

Encode options

Bytes per file

This option lets you set the maximum number of encoded bytes per file. This does not include file headers or any other headers or trailers the encoding process creates, such as BEGIN and END lines.

When you select this option, the following text appears in a dialog box:

```
Click on any area to get more information:
This is where you enter the encoded file size in bytes.
Min.= 1 Byte; Max.= 8192000 Bytes
This shows an approximate conversion of bytes-per-file to
text-lines-per-file. The information is updated each time
you click recalculate.
This lets you check your output-file size prior to setting a
definite value.
```

Checksums

Wincode supports *line* and *file* checksums.

Line checksums add the ordinal value of every encoded character per line, modulo 64. Wincode places this character at the end of the encoded line. This type of data security is only necessary in cases of noisy communications.

File checksums involve using the UNIX "sum -r" 16-bit checksum algorithm. Every character (value and position in file) in the original file contributes to the checksum. This type of analysis is good for everyday use; it is turned on by default. The checksum result appears at the end of the encoded file as sum -r/ size. Wincode looks for checksum values as it decodes files when the error checking option is on.

The Bonus DOS utility provided performs this kind of checksum analysis on any size file.

Wincode creates checksums for *every* encoded line in the output file. Wincode creates sum -r/size checksums for the input file and list the results at the end of the output file.

Encode filename

This option lets you choose a new filename for every file Wincode encodes. Wincode uses the input filename to create the output filename. Created filenames usually differ only by extension and/or numbering to keep multipart files in order.

- To create the appropriate names for encoded files, W/ appears in the (Encode Info) Output File Name/Extension section of the Configuration dialog box.

- To create the names for encoded files yourself, Wincode asks you to rename the filename Wincode has chosen for every file being encoded (including each part). When this option is set, U/ appears in the (Encode Info) Output File Name/Extension section of the Configuration dialog box.

Encode file extension

This lets you choose the extension your encoded files will have. Generally, this is UUE, but it can be anything you want. If you choose the default, then Wincode automatically assigns UUE for uuencoded files, XXE for xxcoded files, and USR for user-defined table coded files.

Encode directory

This option lets you choose the directory in which your encoded files are created. You must specify a directory when entering this value.

Frequently check this directory and delete unnecessary files as they accumulate.

You create encoded files in the same directories as the original input file. Also, this option lets you choose the location of each encoded file before Wincode creates it. Wincode prompts you for a new directory for every file. To choose this option, select the Set radio button. When you double-click on the directory portion, a directory dialog box appears. Choose an existing directory or input a new directory for Wincode to create. This is the directory in which Wincode creates all WC_E_RPT files if the Create Report File option is set.

File headers

Choosing this option creates file headers for each encoded file. File headers mark the beginning and end of the file. They indicate a part number (for multipart files) and original filename for each encoded file.

Formats follow:

```
section xx/yy file filename.ext [Wincode v# ]
```

where `xx/yy` indicates the part number (`xx`) from the total parts (`yy`), `filename.ext` indicates the original binary file, and # indicates the Wincode version number.

Winsort relies on these headers to sort files. Leave this option on to benefit the receiver of your files.

Include table

With this option enabled, Wincode includes a code table before the encoded file's BEGIN line. The code table has the following format:

```
table
first 32 characters of table
second 32 characters of table
```

There are no spaces between the keyword table, the table lines, and the keyword BEGIN.

Single file

This option overrides the Bytes per File option and encodes the input file into one file. Wincode uses the original input filename, with the appropriate extension, as the output filename.

Make EMBL files

The European Molecular Biology Laboratory, Heidelberg (EMBL) supports a large database of scientific programs which run on a variety of platforms (DOS, Mac, UNIX, and so on). See the on-line help file for more details on this.

Helpful hints

A code table is included in every file. The code table is standard uucode; however, the space is not remapped to the back-quote.

For multipart files, a BEGIN keyword is in every file. In successive files, the BEGIN is followed by the keyword part indicating which letter part of the main file is being encoded.

An include directive at the end of multipart files lists the name of the next file part. Both Wincode and the EMBL decoder use this keyword to determine the next file in sequence.

Files are arranged by extension, not by filename. The ordering scheme is as follows:

1. The entire filename is retained, only the extensions change.

2. For single files, the extension is UUE. For multipart files, this extension varies as explained below.

3. Successive files are created by incrementing the last letter of the extension alphabetically (from *a* to *z*). The first extension is .UAA.

4. When *z* is reached, the middle letter in the extension is incremented alphabetically and the last letter is reset to *a*. The third step is then repeated for new file parts. This method essentially allows for 26×26=676 unique filenames based on extension.

A very important point is that every encoded line in each file ends with a lowercase letter used as a line check. The coding works in reverse alphabetical order (the first line ends in z) and continues cycling throughout and across multipart files. Wincode analyzes these line checks for file integrity. Interestingly enough, the line checks play a dual role:

■ To ensure file integrity by preventing the mailer from stripping spaces (#32)

■ To ensure the file is decoded correctly by acting as line sequence checks

When you're encoding EMBL files, these Wincode features are disabled:

Line Checksums
Encode Code Type
Include Table

Decode

Choose this option to decode single and multipart files. A File⇨Open dialog box appears; select from it a file to decode. To choose a default start-up directory for selecting files, use Options⇨Wincode⇨Working Directory.

When you select the file you want, click OK. Wincode begins processing the file as specified in your active configuration. Decoded files are created in the directory specified under the active configuration's Decode Info section (see below).

To decode a multipart file, select the first file in the series. Wincode opens the rest of the files as it needs them. Wincode interprets multipart files as such: If the input file does not contain the appropriate END message to stop decoding, Wincode keeps reading the file, searching for the rest of the encoded text.

If it finds nothing, Wincode checks to see whether the input-filename ends with a number. So, *filename*3270.UUE is as valid as *filename*1.UUE. Wincode searches the current directory for the next file in sequence by incrementing the number in the original input file.

If no file is found, Wincode asks you for the next file in sequence.

Wincode always reads a file from first to last byte. It can decode multiple files concatenated in a single file: the files can be pieces of a single file or multiple files. The only requirement is that the files be in order within the input file. However, with Winsort, you can overcome this limitation. When Wincode decodes a file, it shows an information window that lists the input filename, output filename, and the percentage of the input file Wincode has scanned and/or decoded. The window also includes Stop and Quit options. Wincode can encode files of up to 8MB (8192000 bytes).

If you get a memory allocation error and you are sure that you have the required memory (that is, you have 4MB RAM and you're encoding a 3MB file), try setting a larger swap file size for Windows.

Since displaying windows requires system resources, Wincode works considerably faster when it's an icon. See "SMART decoding" and "Winsort Introduction."

Decoding format

Wincode can decode EMBL encoded files.

To decode an EMBL file, pass *only* the *first* file to Wincode. Unlike standard multipart files, EMBL files all contain the keyword BEGIN, which fools Wincode if they are not recognized as part of the EMBL multipart sequence.

Wincode analyzes line checks as the file is decoded. If an error occurs, Wincode disables this feature. (The program calls line checks checksums. However, they are not true checksums.)

The Include directive is essential for Wincode to decode EMBL files.

Not all standard uucoders support the EMBL uucoding format. For more information on the EMBL File Server and the uucoding format, please contact them at

NETSERV@EMBL-Heidelberg.DE (e-mail) or 192.54.41.33 (Anonymous FTP)

Snappy, Inc. is in no way associated with EMBL.

Encode code type

This dialog box lets you set the kind of code table Wincode uses to encode files.

Wincode creates standard uuencoded files or xxencoded files. These files use a different encoding table and are not universally supported by all encoders/decoders.

This option forces Wincode to use the user-defined table to create encoded files. Unless you want to encrypt your files or just plain confuse people, turn the Include Table option on so that other decoders can read the file.

Not all decoders support alternate table selection.

File type

Text file formats can differ in the control codes used to terminate a line. This option lets you control which file type Wincode creates when encoding files.

Wincode can decode these file types:

- Wincode creates MS-DOS files. Lines terminate with a CR/LF (#13/#10).
- Wincode creates MAC files. Lines terminate with a CR (#13).
- Wincode creates UNIX files. Lines terminate with a LF (#10).

Decode options

Decode filename

When Wincode decodes files, it uses information from the input file to create appropriate output filenames (the original filename is part of the encoded information). This option lets you choose a new filename for every file that Wincode decodes.

Select this option if you want Wincode to create the appropriate names for decoded files. When this option is turned on, the Input File Name/Extension section of the Configuration dialog box contains W/.

Select this option if you want to create the names for decoded files yourself. Wincode asks you to rename the filename it has chosen for *every* file being decoded. When this option is chosen, the Input File Name/Extension section of the Configuration dialog contains U/.

Decode file extension

This option lets you set the file extension(s) Wincode recognizes as being an encoded file. Generally, this includes UUE for uuencoded files and XXE for xxcoded files. You can choose up to 20 valid extensions, however.

This file extension setting is important: When you select File⇨Decode, if you have set only *one* file extension, then only files with this extension appear in the File⇨Open dialog box; otherwise, *all* file types appear. Also, and more importantly, if you drag and drop files on the Wincode window or icon, *all* the files with the extension(s) chosen here are batch decoded.

The active ADD/DELETE window displays the current extension to be added or deleted.

The ADD extension is limited to a total of twenty (20) different extensions.

The DELETE extension requires at least one (1) valid extension at all times.

Temp directory

This option lets you choose a directory in which Wincode can write temporary files. When the Dump Files option is enabled, Wincode dumps the decoded files into this directory. This is also the directory in which Winsort creates its temporary files. Frequently check this directory and delete unnecessary files as they accumulate. See "Clean directories."

Decode directory

This option lets you choose the directory into which your input files are decoded. A valid directory must be indicated when entering this value. You can either browse through your drive to select a directory or input a new directory which Wincode creates for you.

Frequently check this directory and delete unnecessary files as they accumulate.

The decode directory lets you create decoded files in the same directories as the original input file. It also lets you select the location of each decoded file before Wincode creates it. Wincode asks for a new directory for every file.

To choose a decode directory, select the Set radio button. When you double-click on the directory portion, a directory dialog box appears.

You can choose an existing directory or input a new directory for Wincode to create. You can change the directory at any time without affecting the current selection. This is the directory in which all WC_D_RPT files are created when the Create Report File option is set.

Dump files

This option lets you move (dump) encoded files that have been decoded into a common directory so you can delete them easily. Wincode first reads the entire original file into memory while creating a copy (in the specified temporary directory) with the extension WCT. If the file copy is completed correctly, it erases the original encoded file and renames the WCT file in the temporary directory. Wincode warns you if duplicate filenames exist.

This option is incompatible with Winsort.

Run decoded

This option lets you run the newly decoded programs instantly. Wincode automatically scans your WIN.INI file for associations (by matching file extensions to executables) and runs the appropriate program with the newly decoded file as a command-line parameter. If no associations are found, it treats the decoded file as executable and tries to launch it. This can be useful for .GIF files, self-extracting files, and other files in which you don't want to switch back and forth between programs (that is, Wincode and File Manager) to decode and run.

Wincode prompts you before launching any files. Files do not execute after decoding if any of the following possibilities are true:

There was an error in decoding.

The file is invalid.

The file has no associations and is not executable.

Error checking

Wincode checks for several kinds of errors when en/decoding a file. However, to save time and user input, you can shut most of this feature off. If you encounter a problem with a decoded file, turn this feature on (by checking it) and try re-decoding the file. Wincode checks for the following kinds of errors:

- Memory allocation errors; that is, whether an input file exists and/or can be opened. If the file exists, Wincode lets you select a new filename, overwrite the file, or skip it.
- Error handling for temporary files (for the dump files option).
- Existence of a valid Mode value in the header.
- Existence of a valid Filename value in the header (provides option to change the filename to a valid DOS filename and prompts for the next file in the sequence if none found).
- Existence of BEGIN/END pair in encoded files being decoded.
- Number of characters per encoded line.
- Individual characters in each line are checked for validity.
- Line and file checksums, when enabled.
- Assorted errors for handling multipart files.

The level of error checking depends on how you select a file. By default, when you perform batch decoding, some error checking is off. When Options⇨Decode⇨ Error Checking is set, using File⇨Decode gives you the most error checking. See "Wincode errors and warnings."

Decode code type

This dialog box lets you choose the kind of code table Wincode uses to decode files.

Wincode decodes standard uuencoded and xxencoded files. These files use a different encoding table and are not universally supported by all encoders/ decoders.

Wincode decodes files using the standard uuencode table. If Wincode finds a valid code table before the keyword BEGIN, Wincode uses it to decode the file. If Wincode cannot find a valid table for a non-uuencoded file, an error results. Either edit the file to include the table, or set the User Code Type option.

This option forces Wincode to use the user-defined table to decode files. It lets you control which kind of file Wincode can decode (recognize as valid).

Working directory

Select this option to choose the default start-up directory that File⇨Encode NS File⇨Decode uses.

Wincode tries to create any directories you specify that do not exist.

Make table

This option lets you create a personal code table. Wincode uses this table whenever a Code Type User option is set in en/decode. You should also turn on the Include Table option to minimize confusion for other users.

The table must be the 64 ASCII characters from the space (#32) to ~ (the tilde, #126), in ascending order. The ASM routine used for decoding does not tolerate a non-ordinal code table. Use this option with caution, unless you are familiar with the ASCII character set.

Clean directories

This option lets you delete all the files that have accumulated in your temp, encode, and decode directories. Both Wincode and Winsort create and use temporary files. Wincode can also create report files in the en/decode directories. Delete needless files from these directories periodically to minimize wasted disk space.

Create report file

This option lets you create report files for either the encoding or decoding process (or both at the same time). The files are named WC_E_RPT.*number* for encoding, or WC_D_RPT.*number* for decoding, where *number* is from 001 to 999.

Wincode assigns the extension in increasing order to prevent over-writing report files. If, by chance, you reach 999 files, Wincode loops back to file number 001 and, if the file exists, overwrites it. Report files, by default, are placed in the directory specified by the set choice under the Options⇨En/Decode⇨Directories selection.

For encoding, the Report file contains the following information:

- The file it is encoding.
- The original (input) file size.
- The approximate encoded file size(s). This is generally accurate to within 10 bytes.
- The code type.
- The text file type.
- The file it is encoding into.
- The total number of encoded files.
- The type of checksums being created (if applicable).
- The checksum value (if applicable).
- Any error messages that arise.

For decoding, the Report file contains the following information:

- The name of the encoded file it is decoding.
- The input file size.
- The name of the file being decoded.
- The checksum status (if applicable).
- Any error messages that may arise.

See "Wincode errors and warnings."

Start as icon

This option lets you start Wincode as an icon. When you have Wincode set up as you want, you can drag and drop files onto it for en/decoding. This option is also handy if you set Wincode to Close When Done and run it by double-clicking associated files.

When you run Wincode as an icon, it encodes and decodes considerably faster.

Close when done

With this option turned on, Wincode does its job and exits. This is ideal if you need to quickly decode a file and you don't want Wincode to stay on your desktop. When you turn on this option and the Start As Icon option, you can decode as you go using File Manager and Windows associations, without being bothered by Wincode.

Sound effects

Wincode now supports multimedia sounds. If you have a sound card and have assigned new sounds to your Windows events, Wincode uses them to get your attention. If you have not reassigned your Windows sounds, Wincode uses the default Windows beep. This option lets you turn Wincode's sound effects on or off.

Winsort first

This option makes Wincode pass all files to Winsort before en/decoding. Read and understand Winsort's features before using this option (it does take extra time to sort the files).

This option is incompatible with the Dump Files option.

Configuration

Choose this option to see the active settings for Wincode. When you choose Save, Wincode writes these settings to WINCODE.INI, which is created the first time you run Wincode. When you choose Exit, your settings do not change. If you change an option, it is not written to disk unless you select Save, but any configuration changes during the active session appear in this dialog box.

If you change, but do not save, the configuration and then try to quit, Wincode asks whether you want to keep the changes.

Save also stores the current position of the Wincode window.

Reload from disk

Select this to reload the configuration from WINCODE.INI. If WINCODE.INI does not exist, the configuration is reset to program defaults.

About Wincode

This option displays the program name, version, and company name.

SMART decoding

SMART decoding manipulates input files so that you do the least amount of work. Wincode has the ability to decode:

> single files

> multipart files

> multipart single files

> multiple multipart single files

You don't need to remove "intervening" text from any file. Wincode figures out what is encoded and what is not. Generally, the only requirement is that the files be in order (see the note below). This means that for any type of multipart file, part one must precede part two, and so on, within the file. However, part three could exist in another file, provided the file is numbered and follows the first file.

Wincode comes with Winsort, an integrated file-sorting companion. Winsort lets you decode multipart files of any type that are not in order. For more information, read the Winsort section of this help file. See "Winsort Introduction."

Single file	This type of file contains a single encoded file from BEGIN to END.
Multipart files	This involves one encoded file split into several files.
Multipart single files	This kind of file contains multipart files concatenated into a single text file.
Multiple multipart single files	This involves enumerated multipart single files that are distributed among several files.

Stop

This option appears in the main menu when Wincode is either encoding or decoding a file. Stop terminates the en/decoding of the current file. When

Wincode is encoding, it finishes the current file and stops, except when executing a drag and drop (batch) process, when it begins encoding the next file. If Wincode is decoding, it stops decoding the current file but still searches through the rest of the input file for more encoded files.

If this is a batch process, Wincode continues to the next file when it finishes scanning. As a precaution, Wincode prompts for confirmation before stopping the current process.

Quit

This option appears in the main menu when Wincode is either encoding or decoding a file. Quit terminates the en/decoding of the current file, as well as all successive files in batch jobs. As a precaution, Wincode prompts for confirmation before quitting all jobs.

Drag and drop

The drag and drop feature allows batch en/decoding. To use this option, open a session with any file manager program that allows drag and drop file processing. Then select all the files you want to en/decode and drop them on the Wincode window or icon.

Wincode processes each file using the specifications of your active configuration. Wincode decodes all dropped files which carry the extension you set for decoded files (see "Decode file extension"); otherwise, it encodes them. For decoding multipart files, you need only drop the *first* file of the series; Wincode finds the rest. However, you can select an entire directory of files (single and multipart files to be decoded and files to be encoded) and Wincode correctly en/decodes all valid files (you will notice it searches through invalid files very quickly). When Wincode is batch processing (that is, you've dropped files on it), many default error messages are suppressed. If a decoded file appears corrupt, decode it again with File⇨Decode with Error Checking on. This lets Wincode report any errors.

Exit

Choose this to end the program. If your configuration has changed, a dialog box appears, giving you a chance to save the changes.

Wincode errors and warnings

Wincode separates the en/decoding problems it encounters into *errors* and *warnings*. An error is generally an unrecoverable problem which either causes Wincode to halt, or produces an error in the resulting output file. A warning is a problem which Wincode can try to fix or which you might easily remedy. Wincode also issues warnings as notifications of potential problems (that is, they are not real problems). The following list describes encoding and decoding problems you may encounter. A list of general Wincode problems is also provided.

Encode messages

ERROR 01	File Read/Memory Allocation Error	Wincode halts execution. There is an error in allocating global memory and/or reading the input file into memory. Wincode can handle files of up to 8MB.
ERROR 02	Memory Allocation Error	Wincode halts execution. There is an error in allocating global memory (see ERROR 01).
ERROR 03	Can't Open File	The input file is either corrupt, changed, has an invalid DOS filename, or does not exist.
ERROR 04	Can't Open File	The output file is either corrupt, changed, has an invalid DOS filename, or does not exist.
ERROR 05	Error writing to output file	Usually, there isn't enough disk space.
WARNING 01	SET directory is invalid	The directory selected for encoded output files has become invalid. The directory probably no longer exists.

Decode messages

ERROR 01	File Read/Memory Allocation Error	Wincode halts execution. There is an error in allocating global memory and/or reading the input file into memory. Wincode can handle files of up to 8MB.
ERROR 02	Memory Allocation Error	Results in Wincode halting execution. There is an error in allocating global memory (see ERROR 01).

ERROR 03	Error writing Temp file	The Dump Files option is on and there isn't enough disk space.
ERROR 04	Can't Open File	The input file is either corrupt, changed, has an invalid DOS filename, or does not exist.
ERROR 05	Error creating Temp file	The Dump Files option is on and there isn't enough disk space.
ERROR 06	Error deleting (MOVING) original input file	The Dump Files option is on and there is an error in disk-space allocation (that is, insufficient disk space).
ERROR 07	Error deleting UUE file	This problem arises when the Dump Files option is on and the file has changed, is corrupted, or does not exist.
ERROR 08	Improper Mode value	The input file mode value is incorrect or does not exist. Though errors are generally unrecoverable, this error can sometimes be bypassed.
ERROR 09	Illegal DOS filename	Wincode lets you choose a new filename.
ERROR 10	Can't Open File	The output file is either corrupt, changed, has an invalid DOS filename, or does not exist.
ERROR 11	Error writing output file	Usually, there isn't enough disk space.
ERROR 12	Next file number not found	Wincode can't find the next file of a multipart set. You are given the option to enter a new filename.
ERROR 13	New BEGIN found before END of previous encoded file	This error generally occurs in a multipart containing single file. The files may not be in order.
ERROR 14	Encoded line # checksums do not match disabling analysis	The file line checksums do not match. Wincode performs modulo 64 line checksums. Line checksum formats, however, differ from encoder to encoder, so you may get this error frequently. Wincode disables checking if this problem arises and the file decodes normally.

(continued)

(continued)

ERROR 15	Encoded line # of file filename is too long	The encoded file is corrupt and is generally unrecoverable.
ERROR 16	filename is empty	The input file size is zero (0).
WARNING 01	WCT File exists in Temp directory	This message alerts you to temporary file errors. WCT (Wincode Temporary) files are created to ensure file integrity when dumping files.
WARNING 02	UUE File exists in Temp directory	This message alerts you to temporary file errors.
WARNING 03	Too many characters per line (maybe line checksums or EMBL file)	This message alerts you to potential file line-length problems. Wincode recognizes and analyzes both line checksums (mod 64) and EMBL file line checks.
WARNING 04	Nothing to decode	This problem arises if the keyword BEGIN is not found within the file.
WARNING 05	Wincode default bypass of Mode value	This message appears in the Report file when Wincode runs with error checking off and a problem arises in the file header text.
WARNING 06	Skipping line # of file filename	This message appears in the Report file when Wincode encounters a line which may have confused it. The file usually decodes successfully.
WARNING 07	Encoded line # of file filename is too short. Disabling length checks.	This message replaces the Space-Replace option message. Wincode has found the first instance of a truncated line in the encoded file. The missing characters are automatically replaced with ASCII character #32 (a space). From this point on, Wincode handles space-replacing without warnings (disabled).
WARNING 08	Checksums do not match.	This message appears in the Report file. Wincode lists the calculated and expected file checksums. Checksum errors may indicate corrupt encoded files.
WARNING 09	Problem detected. Check encoded file.	File decoding was aborted unexpectedly.

WARNING 10	SET directory is invalid	Directory selected for decoded output files has become invalid. This problem generally arises when the directory no longer exists.
WARNING 11	Improper Code Table detected. Check encoded file.	Wincode requires a Table made of the ASCII characters in order from #32 to #126.

General Errors

ERROR: WINSORT.EXE not found.	The Winsort executable (EXE) file must be in the same directory as the Wincode executable file. This error is only reported if the Winsort option is selected.
ERROR: Invalid Working Directory. Using Wincode default.	This error is reported when Wincode is first started. It indicates a problem in the working directory saved in the INI file. The default is the current directory.
ERROR: Illegal filename.	The command-line filename passed to Wincode is invalid.
WARNING: No Files Sorted.	This error indicates a problem with Winsort. The files passed by Wincode were either not proper encoded files or of improper format.

Winsort Introduction

Winsort is an integrated file-sort companion designed to work with Wincode v2.1 and later. It functions behind the scenes (that is, no icon, and so on) to sort the various file-parts of any type of multipart file (that is, multipart files, multipart single file, multiple multipart single files, and so on). This lets you decode multipart files in which the parts are out of order, essentially removing the Wincode files-must-be-in-order restriction. Winsort currently supports seven known formats.

Future updates will only be created in response to user demand. If you know of a format you want supported, e-mail the information to me. Wincode controls Winsort execution.

The following list describes how both programs function together. (You must have the Winsort First option checked):

- Wincode creates a file list, which it passes to Winsort.

- Winsort checks each file extension. If the extension matches one found in the decode extension list, it processes the file. Otherwise, Winsort skips to the next file.

- Winsort reads through each valid file, searching for supported header formats.

- Headers are used to get the filename and section part number.

- Filenames and file parts are internally catalogued for sorting.

- Winsort creates logical DOS filenames for each file part and extracts the encoded information to these temporary files.

- Temporary files are created in the temp directory.

- Winsort creates a new file list and passes it back to Wincode.

- Wincode uses the information in the temporary files to decode.

- Winsort supports its own error checking. It is designed as a self-contained executable to facilitate future upgrades and support.

Things users should know

Three INI file options were added to allow some flexibility when calling Winsort. These options are not automatic; you must edit your WINCODE.INI file manually. Use these options only if you feel you need them. They are not necessary; Wincode functions just fine without them.

First, create a new section in WINCODE.INI called [Winsort]. Use the INI file you have now as a format example. Then you can add the following sections:

WinsortExe=	This lets you choose another filename for Wincode to recognize as the Winsort executable; the default is WINSORT.EXE.
WinsortDir=	This lets you choose the location of the Winsort executable. This directory *must* end in a backslash (\); the default is Wincode's start-up directory.
WinsortSwitch=	This lets you set a command-line parameter (switch) that will be passed to Winsort when it is executed. The only valid switches are FLEFT or FLEFT LOOP.

FLEFT or FLEFT LOOP	This option is for users who experience communications problems with encoded files. Sometimes, communications programs and/or various text file editors have the nasty habit of adding a space (#32) at the beginning of every line of a text file (this can also happen when transferring text files between different machines, such as Mac to PC). This destroys the encoded files' integrity. To compensate for this, Winsort can strip these spaces from the encoded files before it hands them back to Wincode, essentially making the text flush left.

The switches work as follows:

WinsortSwitch=FLEFT	This option turns off Winsort's sorting feature while enabling the flush left capability (strip-only mode). Wincode passes the files to Winsort as usual, but rather than sort the files, Winsort strips any spaces on the text's left margin. The new files are created in the Temp directory with the same name as the originals.
WinsortSwitch=FLEFT LOOP	This option works like FLEFT, except it lets Winsort sort the files.

The sequence of events is

1. Wincode passes the files to Winsort.

2. Winsort strips off any left-margin spaces.

3. Winsort passes the files back to itself and sorts them as usual.

4. Winsort passes the files back to Wincode for processing.

Helpful hints

If a file contains both supported and non-supported header formats, only the supported formats are sorted and passed to Wincode. You should be aware of this because it will seem that Wincode is ignoring portions of the file. Future updates of Winsort to support more header formats should fix this problem. Winsort does not delete the temporary files it creates in the temp directory.

You *must* have enough disk space for Winsort to create the temporary files and for Wincode to create the decoded files.

For multipart files, drop all file parts on Wincode so that Winsort can catalogue the multiple sections accordingly.

Winsort Version 1.1 requires Wincode Version 2.2 or greater to use the three WINSORT .INI file options mentioned in the preceding section.

Winsort is not compatible with the Dump Files option.

Supported formats

Winsort version 1.1 supports the file header formats of Wincode Version 2.0 and later.

Wincode headers

Wincode headers have been redesigned to list only vital information. Winsort requires that both the leading and the trailing header exist. It analyzes both headers to ensure that all the encoded information is intact. The part format is as follows:

```
section xx/yy file filename.ext [Wincode v# ]
(ENCODED INFO GOES HERE)
section xx/yy file filename.ext [Wincode v# ]2) uuencode by
R.E.M:
```

R.E.M. file headers

Winsort treats R.E.M. file headers much the same as Wincode headers. Since uuencode does not include a trailing header, Winsort uses the trailing "sum -r" information to signal the end of the encoded text. This method may be more error prone than having the dual checking listed above. The part format is as follows:

```
section xx of uuencode version # of file filename.ext by
R.E.M.
(ENCODED INFO GOES HERE)
sum -r/size sum-value section (from 'begin' to 'end')3)
xmitBin by Jim Howard:
```

Other file headers

Winsort processes any file whose headers match this format, whether or not they were created with xmitBin (it is listed for users who recognize the header format). Both the filename and the part number(s) must be in the first header.

Winsort looks for the keyword BEGIN and then gets the information it needs. It stops collecting information when it reaches the END keyword.

The following is a sample of the header format (the actual text may vary):

```
BEGIN — CUT HERE — Cut Here — cut here — filename.ext xx/yy
(ENCODED INFO GOES HERE)
END — CUT HERE — Cut Here — cut here — filename.ext xx/yy4)
Self Extracting Archive (shar) Files by 'post-bin':
```

Part and file lines

Winsort reads the part and file lines to get the information it needs. The keyword END signals the end of encoded information.

```
# (EXTRACTION INFO GOES HERE)
(EXTRACTION SCRIPT GOES HERE)
part=filename.ext
pfile=filename.ext
file=xx
(EXTRACTION SCRIPT GOES HERE)
BEGIN- filename.ext - xx/yy -
(ENCODED INFO GOES HERE)
END- filename.ext - xx/yy -
(EXTRACTION SCRIPT GOES HERE)5) POST V1.2.0:
```

Post

Support for Post is provided only for files which contain the END keyword. I have seen this with Version 1.2.0 but cannot guarantee other versions. Winsort gets the information it needs from the Post line and then uses the END keyword to stop. The format is as follows:

```
POST V1.2.0 filename.ext (Part xx/yy)BEGIN — Cut Here — cut
here
(ENCODED INFO GOES HERE)
END — Cut Here — cut here6) 'X-File' headers:
```

This format has been on the Internet, but I'm not sure of all the specs.

```
X-File-Name: filename.ext
X-Part: xx
(MORE INFO)
BEGIN- CUT HERE -
(ENCODED INFO GOES HERE)
END- CUT HERE -
7) 'Subject - EOET' headers:
```

This is actually a catchall form of sorting. Usenet groups contain header information which can be extracted with the file. If the Subject line of this header contains a valid DOS filename and a valid part number (in this format xx/yy), Winsort will consider it the start of the encoded information and start writing to the temp file. It stops writing when it encounters any of the above End Of Encoded Text (EOET) keywords (that is, END, section, sum, SHAR_EOF,etc).

The general format is as follows (it varies depending on how you access the Internet):

```
Group: alt.binaries.pictures.utilities, Item xxxx etc, etc
Subject: filename.ext (xx/yy)
From: silva@tethys.ph.albany.edu (silva)
Date: 3 Jan 94 2:20:00
(OTHER NET INFO, IF ANY)
(USER INSERTED INFO, IF ANY)
(ENCODED INFO GOES HERE)
(EOET KEYWORD GOES HERE)
```

For Winsort to get the correct file info from the Subject line, a) at least one period must be in the line that is part of the FILENAME.EXT information; b) a slash (/) must be in the part number (that is, even if there is only one file, 1/1). If the two conditions are not met, Winsort keeps looking for another filename/ part indicator (that is, options 1–6 above). This method of sorting is the first option Winsort tries since the Subject line precedes all other types of headers.

Winsort problem solving

If you experience problems with Winsort, check the temp files (if any) it created. Sometimes the problems involve file ordering, which can easily be fixed by renaming files.

Problem: Wincode is accepting files, but Winsort is ignoring them.

Solutions: The files being passed to Winsort are either non-encoded files (based on the file extensions recognized by Wincode) or they contain unsupported header formats. Problem: Wincode is not decoding the entire encoded file.

Winsort will sort only internal file parts containing supported header formats. All other information is not passed to Wincode. Try decoding the file without Winsort.

Snappy Installer _____

Introduction

The Snappy Installer installs Wincode correctly while ensuring proper file integrity. It was created for three main reasons:

1. To let users easily upgrade from older versions of Wincode (the INI file structure changed from version to version, which caused many problems when upgrading) while retaining their previous configuration.

2. To create a program to ensure that all files are being distributed intact and to perform simple virus checking.

3. To create a programmable program. The Installer is configured entirely from the INI file. Future updates (bug fixes) of Wincode need not include all files.

Using the installer

Before running the installer, make sure all program files (as listed in the README.TXT) are located in the same directory (try copying all the files to a floppy). Using Program or File Manager, run the INSTALL.EXE program.

When the install program is executed, you see a full-screen display with a centered dialog box.

Installation progress is displayed graphically as each file is copied and the checksums are calculated. Snappy Installer also properly date- and time-stamps each file it transfers. The time stamp can be used to quickly determine a Snappy program version; for example, a file stamped 2:10:00 is actually Version 2.1, and so on. The user is notified of any errors detected during installation.

Unsuccessful installation

A log file (INSTALL.LOG) is created in the SOURCE directory. If install fails for any reason, check the contents of this file. The following should be noted:

■ A *Bad Checksum (CS) Error* indicates a corrupt file. This could be due to virus infection or incorrect data transmission.

Do *not* use these files. Please contact the shareware author for a replacement.

- If one of the required files is missing, Installer indicates an *Unsuccessful Installation*. See note #4 below.

- A general error message is given if Installer encounters problems copying appropriate files (such as a full disk). Check your destination drive and try re-installing the software.

- Installer updates and maintains the VERSION section in the WINCODE.INI file. Any errors encountered during installation will set VERSION=ERROR. If you are sure that all files are correct and still receive an *Unsuccessful Installation* error (such as when a file is missing, and so on), manually edit your WINCODE.INI file to correct this value. Refer to the About dialog box for correct version info.

I will replace damaged files for free.

Files

INSTALL.EXE	The main executable program
INSTALL.INI	The INI data file

Use the installer to select a source directory which contains the files to be installed. By default, this directory is set to the INSTALL.EXE starting directory.

When selecting a destination directory for the program files, remember that any existing files in this directory are overwritten. You may enter a directory which does not exist; Snappy Installer tries to create it for you. You must choose a destination directory for installation to continue.

Use this option if you want Snappy Installer to create the default directories Wincode needs. This option overwrites previous configuration settings. Four subdirectories are created under the main program directory: DECODE, ENCODE, FILES, and TEMP.

When the installer is started, this button is disabled. Selecting a Destination directory enables this option. Installation begins immediately.

 If Installer finds a previous version of Wincode on your system, Installer warns you that installing (rather than upgrading) will overwrite your current configuration.

Sum Utility

With Wincode Version 2.1 and later, you receive a free DOS sum -r utility. This small program computes UNIX sum-r/size checksums on files of any size. At a DOS prompt, type **sum filename** (or just **sum** to see the program usage). Checksums are useful in monitoring file integrity. Sum -r checksums are calculated using each byte in a file relative to the next byte in sequence. This ensures that files remain unchanged (either by a virus or bad data transmission lines). Sum is written in Turbo Pascal with inline assembly to calculate the checksums.

Files

SUM.EXE is the main executable program.

Availability

In case the CD-ROM bundled with this book is missing, you can find recent versions of Wincode (or other Snappy_Inc software) at the following locations:

- The CompuServe WinShare forum (use keywords Snappy, Wincode, and so on)

- The Nebuolic Cheese BBS, SysOp Stephen Lau, phone (415) 949-1788. This BBS is located in the Los Altos, CA, USA area, and is an official Snappy_Inc. software release site for the West Coast. (I'm the East coast release site; see below.)

- The Internet (Okay, so this isn't *very* specific, but if you have access to the Internet, ARCHIE for WNCODE*XX*.ZIP, where *xx* is the version number; that is, WNCODE22.ZIP for Version 2.2)

Mailing List

I have been trying to maintain a mailing list of all users who have offered advice, reported bugs, or helped in beta testing. Being on this list entitles you to free upgrades (personally e-mailed prereleases) and support. In other words, you don't have to download Wincode. For more information, see the help file.

Part V
WinSock Client GIZMOS

In this part, you'll find a number of special-purpose tools you can use to explore the Internet. If you know what all these things are, then just jump to the chapter you're interested in. If you'd like to know what each tool can do for you, keep reading.

Gopher

Gopher is one of several Internet document-retrieval systems. Most World Wide Web browsers include Gopher.

The CD-ROM contains two Gopher clients: Hampson's Gopher (HGopher), named after the author of the program, Martyn Hampson; and BC_Gopher, in honor of Boston College. They are freeware, so you don't need to pay anything to anybody to use them. For on-line information about Gopher and to get Veronica, the tool to search Gopherspace, check out these references:

```
gopher://gopher.micro.umn.edu
gopher://veronica.scs.unr.edu
gopher://gopher.ncsa.uiuc.edu
gopher://gopher.uiuc.edu
```

HGopher is a Gopher+ client. Gopher+ is an extension of the Gopher protocol that includes additional information about a document so that your computer will know how to view the document.

 Internet RFC-1436 defines the Gopher system's protocol. RFCs can be obtained via anonymous FTP from a number of sites, including ftp://ds.internic.net.

Telnet

Telnet is the Internet terminal program. It is one of the oldest Internet services and is still widely used. You can probably use a telnet client to login to a computer provided by your service provider. Telnet clients do not usually include file transfer protocols because FTP meets Internet file transfer needs. (You can get around this limitation if you use CompuServe. Combine a CompuServe navigator like WinCIM with COMt, a program that makes a telnet session look like a COM port, and you'll be able to transfer files. You can find COMt in Part III of this book.)

In Part II, Chapter 3, you can find a telnet client program as part of the Distinct TCP/IP sampler. The CD-ROM also includes a 3270 telnet client useful when connecting to a mainframe that supports the TN3270 protocol, called QWS3270.

You can also get other telnet clients from one of the large WinSock software FTP sites, such as ftp://ftp.cica.indiana.edu. This particular site is very busy, but if you can't get through, it lists several alternate sites. Try any of them.

 Internet RFC-854 defines the protocol that is the basis of telnet. You can get RFCs via anonymous FTP from a number of sites, including ftp://ds.internic.net. Several other RFCs also deal with telnet issues, such as protocol options and negotiated settings.

FTP — File Transfer Protocol

Another one of the oldest services on the Internet — FTP — is the standard way to transfer files between computers.

This book discusses two of the many FTP programs available, one of which is in this part, and the other is a super file-manager-like graphical FTP in the SPRY Internet Sampler (called Network File Manager). Both are Windows clients, and both are very good. Try them both out and make your own decisions! If you are using a Microsoft-supplied TCP/IP protocol stack for any of the Windows products, you should already have a basic command-line FTP client. Also, all the available PC TCP/IP stacks include at least a basic FTP client.

Anonymous logins

By far the most common way to connect to an FTP server is using an *anonymous login,* in which you login with the user ID "anonymous," and supply your e-mail address as the password. Both of the FTP clients supplied with the book do this for you. Remember that even though the term is ANONYMOUS, it really isn't. When you connect to an FTP server, you offer up the actual Internet address of your PC, which can be logged and traced. This information is needed, since information coming from the FTP server to you must know how to find you in the Internet.

File transfer pitfalls

The most common file transfer error is to try to transfer a binary file with the ASCII transfer option set. A binary file is any nontext file. Most FTP clients default to ASCII transfers. The ASCII option exists because different computers represent the end of a line in different ways. When you choose the ASCII transfer option, your FTP program converts the end of each line in the file to the kind of line your PC understands well. The ASCII option is useless, though, when you transfer anything but a text file. Most of the time, you'll transfer nontext files, so choose the binary transfer option.

 Internet RFC-765 defines the File Transfer Protocol.

Finger

Finger is a client you can use to get information about a user on a remote system. Sometimes, you can find interesting information about a computer service by asking for information with Finger. This is done by *fingering* the user "info." For example, to get information about the Internet service provided by MCS in Chicago, finger info@mcs.com. This returns a lengthy description of all the services available from MCS.

Be careful about how you use the Finger utility. Computer operators are increasingly turning off the Finger service to protect their users' privacy. Some operators view a finger as an intrusion and will take steps to keep you from doing it again. In general, fingering the user "info" is not considered rude, but don't start fishing around, or you might make someone mad!

In this part you will find a Finger client program in Chapter 20, and a Finger server program in Chapter 21.

 Internet RFC-1288 defines the Finger protocol.

Ping

The Ping application checks connectivity and tracks down network connection. A ping sends a message to another computer that asks it to reply. Every computer that uses TCP/IP is required to support this service, so you can always use a ping to see whether your computer supports a path to another TCP/IP computer. Another name for ping is an ICMP Echo Request. All TCP/IP protocol stacks come with Ping, so you don't need to find another.

Internet RFC-793 defines the protocol used by the Ping command, as part of the Internet Control Message Protocol.

Plug-and-Play Clients

You'll read about a number of WinSock Internet clients throughout the book. A key feature of all of them is how they can work together, and how they can work over any WinSock 1.1 compatible TCP/IP protocol stack. Aside from Windows Sockets, the TCP/IP specification itself makes the Internet work as well as it does. For example, when you use an FTP client to connect to a remote host and transfer a file, TCP/IP lets you not know and not care what kind of computer you are actually connected to. A wide variety of software and hardware platforms support TCP/IP, including DOS, Windows, Windows NT, many kinds of UNIX-based systems including Solaris and UNIXWare, VMS, AS-400, Macintosh, Amiga, OS/9, and OS/2.

Not only can TCP/IP clients work together across a network, they can also work side by side at the same time on the same computer. They do so because each kind of service (FTP, telnet, and so on) is assigned a unique *port number* and *protocol*. The port number is used whenever a client wishes to make a connection to a remote computer. For example, to make a telnet connection, the telnet client requests a TCP/IP connection to port 23 on the remote computer. The remote computer understands that this is a telnet request because port 23 is reserved for telnet.

Most user services run on the TCP/IP protocol, which is why TCP/IP is the generic name for a protocol stack to operate over the Internet. The Internet predominantly uses three protocols: TCP/IP, UDP/IP, and ICMP. The term *TCP/IP* means *Transmission Control Protocol running over Internet Protocol,* and *UDP/IP* means *User Datagram Protocol running over Internet Protocol.* All vendors also support UDP/IP as well, which is a less reliable but very efficient protocol used in a variety of services, including Simple Network Management Protocol (SNMP), a network management protocol widely used on the Internet. ICMP is the Internet Control Message Protocol, used for low-level network management messages.

The following table lists a few of the many standard services that can operate over TCP/IP, as defined in Internet RFC-1060. This is a very short list of these services; refer to the standard for the complete list of hundreds of assigned ports.

Port	Keyword	Description
7	ECHO	Echo
13	DAYTIME	Daytime
17	QUOTE	Quote of the Day
20	FTP-DATA	File Transfer [Default Data]
21	FTP	File Transfer [Control]
23	TELNET	Telnet
25	SMTP	Simple Mail Transfer
37	TIME	Time
42	NAMESERVER	Host Name Server
43	NICNAME	Who Is
67	BOOTPS	Bootstrap Protocol Server
68	BOOTPC	Bootstrap Protocol Client
69	TFTP	Trivial File Transfer
71	NETRJS-1	Remote Job Service
79	FINGER	Finger
105	CSNET-NS	Mailbox Name Name Server
107	RTELNET	Remote Telnet Service
109	POP2	Post Office Protocol, Version 2
110	POP3	Post Office Protocol, Version 3
119	NNTP	Network News Transfer Protocol
161	SNMP	Simple Network Management Protocol

What this all adds up to is a collection of constantly expanding protocols that coexist peacefully in an ever-growing worldwide network. Cool, huh?

Utilities

In addition to the assortment of standard Internet tools found on the CD, there are two additional tools that can make your Internet exploring easier and more interesting. NetDial is a utility that makes dialing up your favorite Internet service provider more convenient. This program is particularly useful if you connect to more than one phone number, or you have trouble with busy phone lines. XRay is a nifty utility for tracing the actual information that is being sent over your Internet interface via WinSock. This capability can be extremely useful if you are a WinSock programmer, or if you want to dig around under the covers of WinSock communications.

Chapter 15
HGopher, a Gopher+ Client

*G*opher is an Internet-based document-retrieval system. A *Gopher client* runs on your PC and talks over the network to many Gopher servers.

Gopher servers provide useful documents that you may like to access. These documents can be about anything, from science papers to recipes for chicken soup. They may be text documents, images, sounds, or even video. They may not really be documents at all — they may connect to another computer or to a telephone/e-mail inquiry system and may let you search a large collection of documents by using keywords.

Gopher clients like HGopher present you with menus that they get from Gopher servers. You can move around these menus and fetch information you think looks interesting. You don't need to know where the information is coming from, and generally you don't have to supply any information (such as user IDs) to get it. This sounds great, and in fact, it is.

But how do you find what you want? Well, you have to be an explorer. Hopefully, your company or university has set up a local Gopher server. Connect to it first and start from there. Your local Gopher server probably has lots of information about local matters. After that, the world is your Gopher. Plan to spend a lot of time exploring GopherSpace because it's addictive. Additionally, there is an indexing system called *Veronica*. When you find a Veronica, it enables you to search the whole of Gopherspace using a keyword.

The best way for you to find out more about Gopher is to use Gopher. It seems to have more entries on Gopher than anything else. The comp.infosystems.gopher Usenet newsgroup is also another useful source of information.

Happy Gophering!

What Is Gopher+?

A Gopher client uses a computer protocol to talk to Gopher servers around the world. This protocol was defined some years ago and works well. But even if something is good, someone usually finds a way to make it better! So along comes the Gopher+ protocol.

The big improvement Gopher+ gives you over Gopher is something called *attributes*. Attributes are extra information associated with a document.

The most useful Gopher+ attribute is the *View* attribute. With normal Gopher documents (sometimes called *items*), the Gopher server says, "Here's a document. It's text or it's an image, but we don't know what kind of text or image, which is a major problem if we are trying to show it to you."

With a Gopher+ item, you are told exactly what kind of text item it is — for example, it's PostScript or it's plain ASCII. If it's an image, it could be a GIF or a JPEG or something else. So now we can invoke the right viewer so that you can see it.

Also, a Gopher+ item can have more than one view. For example, the item could be available in ASCII or PostScript form, so you can choose which one you want to see. It could be available in English or German.

There's more.... You can see Admin information, such as who wrote the document and when it was last updated. It may also provide an abstract you can read instead of the document. With Gopher+, a document can even ask you questions before you get to see it.

Attributes are also extensible, so expect new features to be coming along.

You will be pleased to hear that HGopher is a Gopher+ client, so it understands most, if not all, of the currently defined attributes. However, it gets these attributes only when it's talking to a Gopher+ server.

Jump Start Installation

Because you are reading this chapter, I'm assuming you have already installed the HGopher files from the *Internet GIZMOS for Windows* CD-ROM.

It is important to install the HGOPHER.INI file; without it, all kinds of things are missing. In Version 2.3 (and later), HGopher first looks for its HGOPHER.INI in your WINDOWS directory. If it does not find the file there, it looks in the working directory that it starts with (that is, the one in the Program Manager Properties dialog). Finally, if HGopher cannot find the file there, it tells you and refuses to run.

Whether HGopher works straight "out of the box" depends on your local setup. Either way, you need to configure your PC as follows:

1. Select Options⇨Gopher Set Up and configure the options in the Gopher Set Up Options dialog box (Figure 15-1).

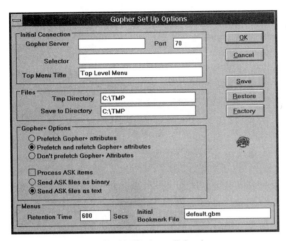

Figure 15-1: Gopher Set Up Options dialog box.

2. Select Options⇨Network Set Up and configure the options in the Network Setup dialog box (Figure 15-2).

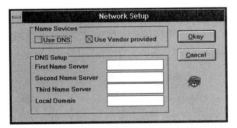

Figure 15-2: Network Setup dialog box.

3. Select Commands⇨Go Home and, voilà, you should have a Gopher menu. Double-click the text of the menu to move around and fetch items.

After you have played around a bit, you might like to read a bit more of the on-line help to see what else you can fiddle with. If you have problems with HGopher, read the section on bugs and queries.

You also find a bookmark file called DEFAULT.GBM as part of the ZIP package. If you have the correct working directory set, HGopher starts up using this bookmark file. These bookmarks are important places in GopherSpace that you may like to explore. See Figure 15-3 for an example Books Marks dialog box.

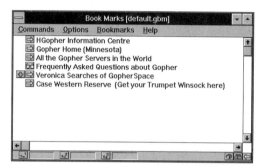

Figure 15-3: Book Marks dialog box.

One of these important places in the default bookmark file is the HGopher Information Centre. It is a place where you can pick up the latest HGopher release, get new viewers, test these viewers, and check for the latest details on HGopher.

Bugs and Queries

Report bugs and comments to m.hampson@ic.ac.uk. You can also discuss

- WinSock-related issues in the alt.winsock Usenet group.
- PC NFS-related issues in the comp.protocols.nfs Usenet group.
- Gopher-related issues in the comp.infosystems.gopher Usenet group.

Some common problems found while attempting to use HGopher include the following:

■ **HGopher won't start; it cannot talk to the network or gives a funny message about a DLL.**

Sounds like your WinSock is not set up correctly. Read "What Is WinSock?" consult your vendor manuals, or talk to the news group.

■ **HGopher cannot resolve any host names or only local host names.**

Sounds like a DNS problem. Check your network setup, your WinSock setup, or consult a local guru.

■ **HGopher does not seem to transfer any data. I am running PC NFS and Vista Exceed.**

Don't know what this problem is — but increasing the RTM heap size to 64 seems to solve the problem.

Basic Usage

The main HGopher window is split into four areas. The title bar tells you where you are and contains the normal Windows buttons for minimizing and so on. The menu area below contains pop-up menus that you can use to send commands to HGopher. At the bottom is a status bar that tells you about connections in progress. The rest of the window is the main viewing area, which typically shows you a menu (sometimes called a *directory*) of Gopher items that you can access.

Each Gopher item has one or more symbols that tell you what kind of item it is and some text describing it. If you double-click the text, HGopher attempts to get that item for you. This process is called a *fetch*.

If you fetch another directory using the right-pointing arrow icon, then HGopher replaces the one you are currently viewing in the main viewing area. You can cycle back through previous menus using the Previous command. If the Gopher item you fetch is something other than a directory, Gopher starts a viewer to display it for you. If you are a bit lost and want to start from the beginning again, use the Go Home command.

Note that to fetch an item, you double-click its *text*. Don't click its symbol because that does something else. Also, if you click the text, but all that seems to happen is that it is highlighted, you did not double-click fast enough — try again.

When you fetch an item, you may notice that one of the boxes in the bottom status line starts giving you some information. First, it tries to connect to the right Gopher server, and then it starts telling you how much of the document it has transferred.

You can find out what each bit of the main menu and status bar does by looking in the help section "Gopher Main Screen" and clicking different bits of the image. You might like to do that now. Don't worry if you don't understand it all — I am about to explain some more.

If you single-click the text of a Gopher item, HGopher highlights it. This item is then called the *currently selected item*.

Some commands work on the currently selected item. For example, if you pop up the Commands menu and choose the Fetch option, the highlighted item is fetched. This method is another way to get an item (but double-clicking is easier).

There is more than one way to *go home* as well. You can choose this option from the Commands menu, or you can click the house icon in the status bar.

In fact, there are four ways to get to the previous menu. One way is to use the Commands menu; another method is to fetch the previous menu item in the Gopher directory; and the third way is to click the • button in the status bar.

What is the fourth? Well, you can jump to any previous menu using the History command. If you select History from the Commands menu, you are shown a list of all the previous menus you have used. They are normal Gopher items, and you fetch them as normal. If you want to get out of the History menu and back to where you were, choose the Flip command or just press the right mouse button.

Finally, a connection may hang, or the document may be so big that you are getting bored waiting for it. You can *abort* a connection by pressing the Connection button (zig-zag arrow with 1 in the corner of the button) on the left of the box in the status bar.

Copying to a File

In addition to fetching documents and viewing them, you can tell HGopher that you want to copy them to a file. To do so, select Copy Mode from the Options menu or click the eye symbol in the status area. The eye symbol in the status area changes to a closed folder icon. This tells you that you are in Copy to File mode.

From then on, if you fetch a document, you are asked for a filename, and HGopher copies it to that file. Note that certain types of Gopher items are not affected by this. For example, directories are not copied to file and neither are telnet items. You can tell what type an item is by looking at its symbols.

Alternatively, if you want to copy many files, you may want to specify a directory and have HGopher dump files in there with an automatically generated filename. You can do so using Copy to Directory mode. You can select this mode directly from the Options menu, or you can click the closed folder icon, which then turns into an open folder icon. You can change the directory that HGopher writes such files to by using the Gopher Set Up dialog.

The eye button on the main screen can be used to cycle through the three modes: View, Copy to File, and Copy to Directory. The symbols on this button change to tell you what mode you are in.

Also note that some of the viewers you are using may also enable you to save to file or print. HGopher does not support printing, so you have to print through a viewer.

Gopher+ Usage

If a tri-colored button (that looks a little like the corner of a picture frame) or a plus sign pops up next to a Gopher item, then it's a Gopher+ item. If it's the plus sign, then you don't have the item's attributes yet. You can pretend you are using a non-Gopher+ client by ignoring the symbol and proceeding as normal, or you can tell HGopher to fetch the attribute by clicking the plus sign. Clicking the plus sign causes a pop-up menu to appear. Select the only option, Fetch Attributes.

If it's a tri-colored button, then you already have the attributes, and you can start doing funky things. Refer to "Gopher Set Up Dialog" in the help file to find how to tell Gopher to get attributes automatically.

Once you have the attributes, you can click the Type symbol to get a pop-up menu. It enables you to see Admin information and maybe an abstract for the item. Clicking the tri-colored button shows you the alternative views for the document. You can select any of them and have HGopher fetch it for you.

If you do a normal fetch (that is, double-click the text), HGopher brings back your preferred view.

Using Bookmarks

Using bookmarks is a convenient way of saving interesting items or directories so that you can go back to them easily without having to retrace the steps you took to find them.

HGopher supports saving and loading bookmarks from files, so you can save your work between sessions. Most of the action with bookmarks centers around the Bookmark menu, so you might want to have a look at it now.

To create a bookmark, select an item and choose Mark Item from the menu. You can also mark the current Gopher menu with the Mark Menu option. You can toggle between showing the Bookmark menu and the normal Gopher menu using the Show Bookmarks and Hide Bookmarks options; however, it's easier to just click the right mouse button.

To load and save bookmarks to a file, you also use the Bookmark menu; however, you can ask HGopher to load a particular bookmark file from the Gopher Set Up dialog when HGopher starts up. (Refer back to Figure 15-1, Initial Bookmark File field.)

Finally, if you know a bit about how Gopher items are constructed, you can build them from scratch using Create Bookmark, or you can edit an existing bookmark. Even if you are not an expert, you may still want to edit a bookmark in order to change its description to something you prefer.

Gopher Items That Are Not Documents

Some Gopher items are not really documents at all. The telnet type, the terminal symbol, is a good example of this. If you fetch such an item, HGopher starts its viewer. For example, with telnet, HGopher starts a telnet application and gives it enough information to connect to a host on the network. You may still have to login.

An Introduction to Viewers

Viewers are an important part of any Gopher client. HGopher makes use of internal viewers and special HGopher viewers called *Gophettes*. However, for the bulk of its document viewing, HGopher expects you to use existing Windows applications, buy applications, or find public domain/shareware applications off the 'Net. See Part VI of this book for some viewers.

A viewer is an application that processes a document that your Gopher has fetched for you. Text and image viewers show you information on-screen. Sound viewers play music to you. Some viewers may just do some background processing; for example, a viewer for the view type *file/zip* may unzip the file into a directory of your choice.

Take care when selecting viewers. Remember that your viewer is operating on an unknown document. Doing so can cause problems if your viewer treats the document as a program and runs it. It's the same as taking a program from a floppy disk and just running it — sooner or later, you get a virus if you don't scan everything for viruses before installing programs locally.

Fortunately, most viewers you use are simply displaying a document, so getting a virus isn't a problem. One to watch out for, however, is PostScript. Remember that PostScript is a programming language; the program normally displays pictures or text, but it could wipe out your files. Choose a PostScript viewer that prevents this kind of thing.

Setting up viewers

Setting up viewers involves using the Viewers dialog. See Figure 15-4. Select one of the possible Gopher *view types* and set up how you would like it processed. When HGopher gets a document with that view type, it follows your directions about what to do with the document.

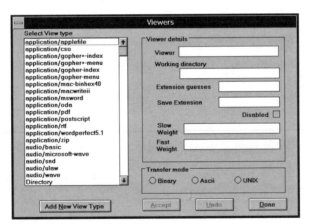

Figure 15-4: Viewers dialog box.

The basic thing to tell HGopher is which viewer to run for a view type. This is simply a command to run when HGopher gets a document. Normally, it displays your document for you. Viewers generally require information as to what to view. You give the viewer one or more parameters. The following parameters can be passed to a viewer by HGopher:

%f	Replaced by the filename
%h	Replaced by the host name
%I	Replaced by the host's IP address (if available)
%p	Replaced by the host's port number
%s	Replaced by the Gopher selector
%t	Replaced by the Gopher type
%d	Replaced by the Gopher description
%S	Replaced by the search string (if any)
%%	Replaced by %

For example, your viewer for ASCII text documents might be the Windows Notebook, in which case you use the command **notebook %f**. Your command for a telnet viewer is likely to look like **telnet %i %p**.

As released, HGopher has a number of viewers set up already but disabled (because I don't know if you have the applications). Some that use standard Windows applications are enabled. Note that I am not forcing you to use these viewers, nor am I recommending them. You can find some HGopher-compatible viewers from the HGopher Information Centre; see the section on obtaining viewers.

The view types available in HGopher represent Gopher+-defined view types. Non-Gopher+ documents have only a simple type indication. Non-Gopher+-item types are mapped into the base type of a Gopher+ item in most cases. For example, the item type text is mapped into the Gopher+ view type text. There are odd exceptions; for example, the item type telnet is mapped to terminal/telnet.

To get more out of non-Gopher servers, you can override this default mapping using extension guessing. If the Gopher server manager has given the Gopher item selector a file extension, you can use it to determine the view type. An example may make this situation clear.

Suppose you have defined a GIF viewer for the view type image. Now if you fetch an image item and it happens to be a JPEG, your GIF viewer may have a problem with this setup. What you can do is set up a JPEG viewer for the view type image/JPEG and configure it with an extension guess of JPG. If the selector on the JPEG Gopher item ends in JPG, your JPEG viewer is started by HGopher rather than the GIF viewer, and life is sweet. This method is a bit of a hack and depends on the Gopher server manager setting things up with reasonable extensions, but it seems to work in practice.

Gopher+ items, of course, ignore any extension guesses — they don't need them.

Another thing about view types is that they have up to two weights associated with them. This allows automatic selection of the type of view you prefer to see for Gopher+ items with multiple views. Refer to the "Setting preferred views" section for more information.

Adding new view types

Sooner or later, you are going to find a document with a view type HGopher does not already know about. Don't worry — you can extend the view types known by HGopher.

Let's say there is a new view type called *image/fractal* that you want to add. Go to the Viewer dialog and click the Add New View Type button. In the dialog box, type **image/fractal** and choose OK. You then can set up this newly added view type in the normal way.

Setting preferred views

This section applies only to Gopher+ items.

When a Gopher+ item has one or more view types associated with it, you can go to the tri-colored button and select any of the view types you want. However, you can also double-click the text as in a normal fetch and bring back your preferred view.

HGopher selects which view you want to see using a weight system. With this system, you can say things such as

- Always bring back PostScript if it's available.
- Always bring back PostScript from hosts on my fast local Ethernet, but for other machines get ASCII.

If you have a choice between a JPEG and a GIF, get the GIF unless it's bigger than the JPEG by more than 200K.

Weights with languages

If the document is available in French, I'd prefer that to English. This is how it works.

Various things can have a weight associated with them. This weight is generally an integer number. When HGopher has to pick one of many views, it *weights* each view type, and the one with the biggest weight is the one that gets fetched.

To select your preferred language, you need to invoke the Language dialog box (Figure 15-5). You can then set a weight for each language you prefer. For example, if you like to see things in French, failing that, German, and last of all English, you set the French weight to 10, the German to 5, and the English to 1. Now if the document is available only in English, you still get it, but the other languages are preferable.

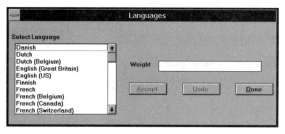

Figure 15-5: Languages dialog box.

Weights with view types

From the Viewers dialog, you can set two weights for a particular view type: one for machines designated fast and one for machines that are slow. If you specify only one weight, it is used for both types of machines.

Here's an example of setting view type weights. If you set image/JPEG to 1000 and image/GIF to 900, you always get a JPEG over a GIF if there is one available. Note that in order for the view type to be considered in the weighing, it must have a viewer command and not be disabled.

Now what is all this fast and slow stuff? Using the Server dialog, you can categorize all the hosts in the world into two camps: fast and slow. Then using the Viewer dialog, you can give different weights for each type. Note that fast/slow does not refer to the speed of the machine but to how fast or slow you think the network access to it is. A Cray might be the fastest machine in the world, but if it's on the end of a 2400 baud line to you, it's slow.

One more thing about a weight: Generally, it's an integer, but it can be an expression containing the symbols +, –, and $(SIZE). You should know what the first two mean already; the *$(SIZE)* represents the estimated size of the item in kilobytes as given by the Gopher server.

So now you are ready for a complex example. Let's say you have a viewer for GIFs and a viewer for JPEGs. Your JPEG viewer takes three times as long to show the image as the GIF viewer, so you prefer to get a GIF unless it's very big and going to take a long time to transfer. You have a local Gopher server called gopher.here.edu, which is directly connected to you by FDDI.

Here is a good setup. Using the Server dialog box, set up gopher.here.edu as a fast server and default to slow. Give the view type image/GIF a fast weight of 10000 and a slow weight of 10000-$(SIZE). Give the view type image/JPEG a slow weight of 9700-$(SIZE).

Now you always get a GIF over a JPEG from the high-speed machine gopher.here.edu. You get a GIF from all other machines unless the difference in size is greater than 300K.

Managing weights

You can do what you like with weights, but you might end up with some strange choices. It's a good idea to band your weights. For example, put all text weights in the range 20000 – 30000, your image weights in the range 10000 – 15000, and so on. Remember that you can always use the tri-colored symbol to get a view explicitly.

Internal viewers

You may notice that some view types have strange-looking viewers assigned to them by default that start with the string *internal-*. These viewers are internal viewers; that is, they are actually processed by HGopher itself, rather than by invoking an external program.

internal-directory

This internal viewer is used with Gopher menu view types and tells HGopher to process the information as a Gopher menu. This internal viewer also checks the base Gopher type, and if it is an *index* type, it treats the item as an index item.

internal-directory-only

This viewer is almost the same as internal-directory. However, HGopher does not check the base type to see if it's an index; that is, it is always treated as a straight menu. You can use this viewer if a server gives an item that has alternative views, one of which is an index and another is a directory. I don't know of any Gopher servers that support this type of viewer yet.

internal-index

This viewer is the companion viewer to internal-directory-only. It treats the item as an index item only.

internal-copytofile

HGopher fetches the item in Copy to File mode; that is, the item is copied to a file of your choice if you are in View mode.

internal-copytodir

HGopher fetches the item in Copy to Directory mode; that is, the item is copied to the directory you specified in Gopher Set Up if you are in View mode.

internal-messagebox

HGopher displays the item in a Windows message box. Note that you can use this viewer only on Gopher Info, Admin, Abstract, and Server info views. It is also the default for these types if you don't specify a viewer.

Ask Processing

Ask Processing is a Gopher+ extension and applies only to Gopher+ items.

The idea here is that a Gopher item can ask you questions and use this information in some way. What questions it asks you varies from item to item. It may also ask you for a filename that HGopher sends to the server. HGopher presents the questions using a Windows dialog box, so you should be able to use it easily.

Ask Processing is, by default, turned off because it can be dangerous. You can enable it from the Gopher Set Up dialog.

So why can Ask Processing be dangerous? Remember that you don't know to whom you are sending this information, so don't give away any sensitive information such as your password or home telephone number, or upload a file of undercover field operatives or your credit card numbers, and so on.

When transferring data in ASCII mode, Gopher uses a dot to mean End of File. This use can cause problems with files that have lines starting with a dot. Gopher puts extra dots in these lines to stop you from thinking you have reached the end. However, most implementations do not follow the specification on how to do this. You need this option when talking to such a Gopher server. HGopher works around the problem as best it can, but even then some lines can get corrupted.

The Gopher server you are talking to stuffs all lines beginning with a dot. It follows the spec. Hooray!

On the Show the multiview symbol radio buttons, clicking the Always radio button shows the Multiview symbol on all Gopher+ items with views defined. Clicking the Never radio button causes the Multiview symbol to never appear. I always get my preferred view, and the dots give me eye strain. Clicking on the On "interesting" items radio button means only show the Multiview symbol if the item is interesting to see. It's interesting if more than one view is available, and they are not just directories.

On the Show the Feedack meter bars radio buttons, clicking yes means I'd like to see the percentage complete feedback meter if you have an estimate of the size of the document. Clicking No means I don't want to see the percentage complete feedback meter ever.

The CSO Gophette

The CSO Gophette is called *hgcso* (or *hngcso* if you're using the PC NFS version). It is a simple read-only CSO client designed for use with HGopher, but it can be used as a standalone in a limited fashion.

Installation and setup

hgcso or hngcso comes in the HGopher ZIP file. The distributed HGOPHER.INI is preconfigured to use hgcso with the following command (for view type *application/cso*)

```
hgcso %i %p %d
```

If you are using hngcso, you need to change this line. Also, if the installation directory is not in your path, you need to add the path to the command. If you are using PC NFS, I recommend that you always use hngcso because there seems to be a problem with the PC NFS WinSock: After a few invocations of hgcso (the WinSock version), the whole network hangs.

You can pick up these viewers from the HGopher Information Centre.

hgcso takes command-line parameters to tell it what CSO server to use. The parameters are an IP address or host name, a port number, and a description to use as a caption. Using these parameters, you also can run hgcso from the Program Manager; however, it is able to talk to only one server (you could, of course, have a few hgcso icons in a group, each connecting to different servers).

Usage

hgcso pops up a little control box. The general idea is that you type in a name, select the Do Query button, and a few moments later the directory information for this name appears in a Notepad. You can, in fact, type in any ad hoc *ph* query in the control box — **smith phone=9100**.

From the Show Field menu, you can ask the server to display fields that fall into several categories.

Finally, you can tell hgcso whether to format the displayed text or not by using the Options menu.

The HGopher Information Centre

In the world of Gopher+, you are only as good as your viewers. Therefore, I am building a collection of HGopher-compatible viewers from which you can select your viewer portfolio. Around this collection, I have also created a few useful documents (such as a FAQ list) and the *HGopher Assault Course,* which contains many different types of documents you can test your setup with. I have called this collection the *HGopher Information Centre.*

Of course, you gain access to the Information Centre using Gopher. Here's the bookmark entry to get you there:

```
Type=1
Host=gopher.ic.ac.uk
Port=71
Path=1/HGopher Information
```

Note that this entry and a few other useful bookmarks are in the bookmark file DEFAULT.GBM, released with the distribution.

You can also get access to the HGopher and viewer distribution by anonymous FTP to

```
lister.cc.ic.ac.uk:/pub/wingopher
```

Of course, these viewers are not the only ones. As you wander around the Internet, you are sure to find other applications you can use. If you find any good ones, drop me a line.

HGopher is free public domain software, but your viewers may not be. Be sure to honor any licensing arrangements your viewers — or any shareware you use — may require.

Chapter 16

BCGopher

BCGopher is a Windows program for burrowing through Gopherspace on the Internet. This program is distributed freely on an *as is* basis. You may e-mail comments to ed@bcvms.bc.edu.

What Is Gopher+?

Gopher+ n. 1. Hardier strains of mammals of the family Geomyidae. 2. (Amer. colloq.) Native or inhabitant of Minnesota, the Gopher state, in full winter regalia (see PARKA). 3. (Amer. colloq.) Executive secretary. 4. (computer tech.) Software following a simple protocol for burrowing through a TCP/IP internet, made more powerful by simple enhancements (see CREEPING FEATURISM).

When you navigate Gopherspace, you encounter the following:

- Files
- Folders and links to other Gopher servers
- Indexed Search pointers
- CSO Phone Book pointers
- Telnet and TN3270 pointers

There are other operating system-based files also, such as the following:

- A BINHEX file
- A UUENCODED file
- A DOSBINARY file and straight BINARY

Included in the Gopher protocol is support for graphic images, sounds, and movies. These file types are also considered to be binary files. These files sometimes are in formats that multiple computers can read (such as GIF for images, AU for sounds, or QuickTime for movies).

Some extended item types are Hypertext Markup Language (HTML) used in the World Wide Web, MIME, and messages.

The term *Gopherspace* refers to the many different menus and services you can navigate through using a Gopher client.

A *file* is a document that contains text. This text can be in the form of ASCII-readable documents or other text encoded types. The value for an item of this type is 0.

A *folder* is an item that contains more files and/or folders. A folder can also be a pointer to a different Gopher server at another computer at the same site or at a different site. The value for an item of this type is 1.

The Indexed Search pointer service is a query engine that returns documents pertaining to the search string and the particular search. The value for an item of this type is 7.

A CSO Phone Book is server-developed at the Computer and Communications Services Office at the University of Illinois at Urbana and can be accessed by a client called a PH client. BCGopher has built into it the capability to query these phone books. In most cases, these phone books contain information about faculty, staff, students, or employees at a particular site. The value for an item of this type is 2.

Telnet and TN3270 are pointers that contain information for a telnet connection. BCGopher launches the telnet or TN3270 application you specify in the Application Associations section of the Configuration dialog box and automatically connects to the site pointed to. The value for an item of this type is 8.

A file with an HQX extension is a text file encoded in the BINHEX format. These files are typically for Macintoshes. Though BCGopher cannot decode these files, you can receive them in case you want to move them to a Macintosh later. The value for an item of this type is 4.

A file with a UUE extension is a text file encoded in the UUENCODE format. This file can be decoded on many types of machines. This is typically a UNIX file but can also be a DOS file. The value for an item of this type is 6.

DOS Binary and straight Binary files are files that cannot be displayed on your screen and must be captured directly to your computer. In most cases, they may be program files and will be operating system dependent. The value for an item of this type DOS binary is 5. The value for an item of this type binary is 9.

The Gopher protocol supports graphic pictures in binary form, usually in a graphics format readable by many different computers (such as GIF or JPG, or some other image form). With BCGopher, you need an external program to view this type of file, which you can set in the Application Association section of the Configuration dialog box. The value for an item of this type is I.

The picture icon specifically represents a GIF file, and the palm tree icon represents any kind of image. This format was added for compatibility's sake. The value for an item of this type is g.

A *sound file* is in binary form, usually in a sound format readable by many different computers (such as AU). With BCGopher, you need an external program to hear this type of file, which you can set in the Application Association section of the Configuration dialog box. The value for an item of this type is s.

A *movie file* is in binary form, usually in a movie format readable by multiple types of computers (suck as QuickTime). With BCGopher, you need an external program to view this type of file, which you can set in the Application Association section of the Configuration dialog box. The value for an item of this type is ; (semicolon).

If there was an error in transmission or a problem at the server, the Trash can may appear. If the item has been transmitted correctly, but the item is not supported by BCGopher, the bars appear. The value for an item of this type is 3.

Hypertext Markup Language (HTML) is the language used when creating Hypertext documents displayable on the World Wide Web (WWW), which is readable by the Mosaic suite of WWW viewers. The value for an item of this type is h.

MIME is an encoding scheme used in sending nontext documents through mail. The value for an item of this type is M.

An *Inline item* is an informational line that has no document associated with it. It can be used for short instructional messages. This type was first proposed by the Panda Project at the University of Iowa. The value for an item of this type is I.

Connecting to a Gopher Server (or Other Service)

If you have just started with BCGopher, you should have an empty window (see Figure 16-1). This window is where the Gopher menu items reside. To connect, you can select File⇨New Gopher, or you can have BCGopher connect to your favorite site every time you start it up. The way to do this is to check the Connect on Startup check box in the Configuration dialog box.

Figure 16-1: BCGopher main window.

After you are connected to a server, you see (in most cases) the top level of the server. This level typically consists of a file describing the server and a number of folders ordered by subject.

It is also possible to start up BCGopher with a series of command-line parameters informing it where you want to connect. This way, you can make static bookmarks in the Windows Program Manager. Following is the command-line usage:

Usage: **bcgopher -h***hostname* **-p***port* **-t***itemtype* **-n***name* **-s***selector*

-h*hostname* where *hostname* is the IP address of the host to connect to.

-p*port* where *port* is the port number of the host.

-t*itemtype* where *itemtype* is the single character type attribute (for example, ';' = image).

-n*name* where *name* is the name you want to associate with this item.

-s*selector* where *selector* is the item selector.

Refer to your Microsoft Windows documentation for more information about adding icons and command-line parameters to the Program Manager.

Selecting an Item_____

After you have successfully connected to a Gopher server, you are presented with the many different services available at that server.

The focus rectangle

By clicking a particular icon or title, you see a focus rectangle. This item is now selected. Any operations made refer to this particular item.

Selecting with the keyboard

It is also possible to use the arrow keys to move the focus rectangle around. To open the particular item, you can double-click the item with either the left or right mouse button, or press Enter. The left and right mouse buttons perform different functions depending on the type of item you have selected (refer to "Viewing items" for more information).

Using the binoculars to acquire Gopher+ information

If your menu appears with the binoculars icon, that item is a Gopher+ item. Notice that you can alternatively click so that the focus rectangle surrounds the item icon and title or just the binoculars. All functions work normally on the item icon and title, but now there is added functionality by using the binoculars to view other information. You can acquire some more detailed attribute information about that item by double-clicking with the left mouse button on the binoculars. If you double-click with the right mouse button on the binoculars, you receive a list of alternate views.

Jumping to items by letter

In general, Gopher servers alphabetize their menu listings. If you connect to a server or service that contains a long listing, you can press the first letter of the section you want (for example, **s**), and the Focus Rectangle jumps to the first occurrence of an item starting with **s** in the list. If the focus rectangle does not jump, there are no (more) items starting with that character.

The uppercase A is not the same as the lowercase a in the alphabetized menus, but they are when you press the character.

Gopher+ Attribute Information

Notice that the menu item descriptions may not contain all the information you may need or want to determine whether you really want to view a particular item. That is why Gopher+ has allowed for additional information. If you have connected to a Gopher+ server, you see the icon next to the item. If you click this icon with the left mouse button, you receive a dialog box containing the additional attributes.

The additional attributes that may be returned are as follows:

INFO: The detailed selector string that Gopher+ uses to fetch an item.

ADMIN: Admin. information about the administrator of the server the item is on.

Mod-Date: The modification date of this particular item.

VIEWS: Alternate views available for this one particular item. This information includes the sizes of the file in each particular view incantation.

ABSTRACT: A short (maybe three or four lines) detailed description of this particular item.

Generally, the INFO and ADMIN blocks appear with information; however, the VIEWS or ABSTRACT fields may not contain data, depending on whether there are any alternate views or an abstract for that item.

Gopher+ Alternate Views

A single item in a menu may have more than one representation. For example, if you have an important document that you want many people to be able to read, you may want to save it in a number of formats. You can save it in Microsoft Word for Macintosh for people accessing the server from a Macintosh. You can save it in Microsoft Word for Windows for people accessing the server with BCGopher. You can save it in RTF (Rich Text Format) for people who may have other word processors, or you can save it in plain text for the die-hard character cell terminal user or DOS user. Instead of having all four of these files show up in the menu, you can have just one item with many views. If you were to just double-click the item title, the file would be received using the first (which is the default) view.

If you don't want this view, you can double-click with the right mouse button on the filename, and you will receive a dialog box containing a listbox of the alternate views. If you select one and click the Retrieve View button in the dialog box, BCGopher receives that particular view of the document in question.

Navigating Gopherspace

Some of these services can lie on servers located in different places throughout the world. They can be anywhere from a different office at that site, a different site altogether, or maybe even in a different country.

Any item on the menu that is represented by a folder can be one of these services or can contain other information pertaining to a specific subject.

The term *navigating* refers to the ability to jump between different servers by using pointers to other servers. You can usually jump all around the country or even the world by starting at one site.

A rectangle surrounding an item can be dangerous because it indicates that it is the *point of focus*.

Viewing items

In most cases, everything that is not a folder can be viewed on your local system. To view a file, just double-click it or select the File⇨View Item. BCGopher enables you to customize the way in which you view documents. From the Configuration dialog box, you can specify which application you want to use to read different types of documents. If you double-click an item with the left mouse button, the item is brought up in the application you specified. If the document is large, the first part of the document is displayed, and you can use the Save As dialog box to name a file so that the entire document is saved to your local machine. If you double-click an item with the right mouse button, the document is saved in a file you name.

Other items may be binary files and, therefore, not displayable unless they are binary images, sounds, or movies. In these cases, if you double-click with the left-mouse button, the file is downloaded as a temporary file and opened up immediately for viewing, and the subsequent temporary file is deleted upon exiting BCGopher. If you double-click with the right button, a Save As dialog box asks you to name the file and then proceeds to download it to the local computer for permanent storage.

Index searches

A collection of files that pertain to the subject referred to in the title can be indexed by every "meaningful" word so that an interested party can do a quick search.

If you were to take all the e-mail messages sent to a computer support agent and put them in a database, a person who had a problem could read these messages looking for a problem that was similar to his or hers and the corresponding answer. This process, of course, could take quite a long time. If those messages were cross-referenced by the problem, the person would have to look only at the references to find the mail message that could help him or her. This is the essence of an *indexed search*.

On Gopher, the indexed search returns documents matching the particular search information in the form of a Gopher directory, thus returning a document without having to search manually through the entire hierarchical structure of a server.

CSO Phone Books

The CSO Phone Book is a different type of server. It was originally written to be talked to from a PH client. The PH-style client was written into Gopher to facilitate a way to do name look-ups. These phone books can contain detailed information about people at a particular location.

The simple search

When selecting a CSO Phone Book search, you are presented with a simple dialog box requesting the search string. If you enter a string, the subsequent database is searched for this string. There is no way, usually, to determine what fields exist or which fields are involved in the search. If you are looking for a name, the bet is pretty good that it will search for a name, but it may also pick up street addresses and e-mail addresses. There is also no control over which fields are returned to you. If the result of the search does not contain a field you were looking for, you can specify more information using the More button.

The detailed CSO dialog box

If you select the More button in the Simple Search, you receive the detailed CSO dialog box. This dialog box enables you to search on specific fields and for more than one item. You also can determine what the fields are and have fields returned to you with information that may not usually be included (such as a person's pager number).

The top part of the dialog box contains the search criteria. The leftmost drop-down menu enables you to choose the field to apply the search criteria. The site you connect to determines the list of fields you can search on. The center drop-down menu determines the type of search you can perform. It's possible to get an exact match, one that contains only the first part of the search string, or one that contains the search string anywhere in that field.

If you click the And check box, you can specify another field and string to search on, enabling you to narrow your search.

The bottom part of the dialog box contains the fields to be returned by the search. If the default radio button is selected, the default fields — which may not contain all the fields in the database — are returned. You can scroll the list to see what fields exist and which ones are returned. If you want any fields that are in the database but are not selected, you can choose the Return selected fields radio button, which enables you to change the selections in the listbox of fields.

Telneting

When you double-click an item associated with a telnet or TN3270 connection, you are presented with a dialog box informing you of any information you may need, such as a user name and/or password to log into that remote server. When you click the OK button, BCGopher launches the application associated with that specific type and connects you to the address pointed to by that item. When you are in the telnet or TN3270 application, you are no longer associated with BCGopher and can quit the application if you want.

File Menu

From the File menu, you can connect to a Gopher server, save an item, view information about an item, or exit the application. Following are the File menu options:

- New Gopher
- Save As
- View Item
- Alternate Views
- Attribute Info
- Exit

New Gopher

You can connect to a Gopher server by specifying the Internet address of the server in the Server Address box and the port number in the Server Port box. For Gopher, the port number is typically 70 (see Figure 16-2). Select the Connect button to start the process. The Configuration dialog box comes up with the default server specified. If you do not specify the server description, the address shows up in the title bar.

Figure 16-2: The New Gopher dialog box.

Save As

You can invoke the Save As function by either selecting File➪Save As from the File menu or by double-clicking the particular item with the right mouse button.

This menu item has two functions:

- If you have selected any item that is pointing to another item (such as a phone book or a directory), that item is added to the bookmark list.
- If you have selected any other item, you receive a Save As dialog box to save the particular document.

Exit

As you might guess, this menu item quits the application. When you exit, any changes you made to the configuration or the bookmark list are saved.

Edit Menu

Cut

There is no instance in the program (so far) that causes text to be removed.

Copy

When you select an item, you can copy the title into the Clipboard to use elsewhere. Using Copy does not copy the address.

If you want to copy the address or selector string, you can use the description box. When the description box is visible, you can select an item and use the Ctrl+C accelerator keys to do the copying.

Paste

You must first use the Copy command to copy something to the Clipboard before you can paste something from the Clipboard (refer to "Copy"). The only place in BCGopher that you can paste information is the Bookmark dialog box. You can, of course, paste into other applications.

Options Menu

The Options menu contains the different options you can alter. By choosing the appropriate menu, you can change information about where to connect and how to view documents, the font type, and observe information about items.

Configuration

In the Configuration dialog box shown in Figure 16-3, you can set the default information shown in the following sections.

Figure 16-3: Configuration dialog box.

Default Server Description

When BCGopher is first started, it uses this information for display along with the Default Server, whether this information is used to connect automatically on start-up or just as the information contained in the New Gopher dialog box. This description is placed in the title bar when you're connecting to the default server.

Default Server Address

The Default Server Address is the Internet address of your favorite Gopher server. It appears in the New Gopher dialog box when you're connecting to a new server. If you have checked the Connect on Startup check box, BCGopher connects to this server when the application starts.

Default Server Port

In some rare occasions, a Gopher server may exist at a port other than the "universal" default of 70.

Connect on Startup

Check this box if you want BCGopher to connect to your Default Server automatically upon launching the application.

Differentiate Gopher links

Check this button if you want links to other Gopher servers to appear different than directory items located on the same server.

Default Directory

The Default Directory is where the files that you receive when using Save As or double-clicking with the right mouse button are automatically placed.

Application Associations

The Application Associations section indicates how to associate different applications with certain item types and file extensions. See "Making Application Associations" for more information about making these associations.

Close Configuration

Clicking this button saves the current configuration to your BCGOPHER.INI file and closes the dialog box.

Cancel

Clicking this button does not save any changes made to the configuration, but it closes the dialog box.

Making Application Associations

There are many different item types (refer to "What Is Gopher?"). Each type can have multiple formats — thus the joy of multiplatform computing. For example, you can have a binary image file. This image file can be in GIF format, JPG format, TIFF, or any number of other formats. What do we do if we want to view any of these documents? We can find a single viewer that will recognize many formats, or we can get different viewers for each. If we were to use the former method, we could just open up the document in the viewer, and it would recognize the format and display it for you. However, what if we encounter a format that can only be read by one viewer and that viewer cannot read other formats? Well, in that case, what we can do is make an Application Association.

BCGopher has set up the ability to associate a specific application with both an item type and the possible extension of the file being received.

In the Application Associations listbox of the Configuration dialog, notice three columns: Extension, Item Type, and Application Path. The way in which BCGopher works is to attempt to resolve the application by searching the item types. If it finds more than one application for a single item type, it then attempts to locate a filename extension in the Item Title. In most cases, nice server administrators place the filename at the beginning of the Item Title if the item is meant for download. If an extension is found in the Item Title, then the item types are searched for a match with the file extension. If one is found, BCGopher takes the first eight characters of the Item Title and parses the extension to it. If no extension is found in the Item Title, BCGopher presents you with a Save As dialog box and gives you the opportunity to choose the extension to place on the filename (not to mention the ability to change the filename).

In the File Name box is the name of the target file. If you want to change any of this filename, you can. The different extensions, along with their associated applications, are listed in the Save File as Type box. The file extension is whatever you choose as the file type unless you choose the "(specified)" setting.

Adding and editing associations

If you click Add or select an item to edit and click Edit, you are presented with an Application Associations dialog box. The following sections describe settings you can make in this dialog box.

File extension

The three-character part of a filename located after the period. For example, TXT is the extension in the filename README.TXT. You can enter any three-character extension here (without the period).

Item type

Select which item type this extension is associated with. You can choose only from the list of predefined types.

Application path

The full directory path and filename location of an application. If you do not specify a directory path, the PATH environment variable will be searched for the application. It is possible to enter only the application name (for example, wingif) if that application is located in the DOS search PATH environment variable. If it is not, or you don't want to bother, you can click Browse and choose the application this way. When you return from the File Open dialog box, the entire application directory path and filename are placed in the edit box.

Application parameters

Some applications might need other information besides a single parameter. There is a way to pass more information to an application that may need more. In the case of a telnet application that needs a port number, you can tack on that information using the parameter parsing in BCGopher.

When we're passing parameters, we use the percent (%) convention. This means that we indicate the % sign and a number to show which parameter we may want passed:

%1   The Item Address.

%2   The Item Port.

%3   The Item Selector.

%4   The Item Description.

The following example is a command line for a telnet application you would use in the Program Manager:

```
wtnvt bcvmcms.bc.edu 23
```

Here is an application path and parameter for BCGopher:

```
wtnvt %1 %2
```

In this case, the %1 is replaced with the address, and %2 is replaced with the port number. All intervening information is kept. For example:

```
telnet /address=%1 /port=%2 /name="%4"
```

can expand to

```
telnet /address=bcvmcms.bc.edu /port=23 /name="Boston
College Quest System"
```

Here, all the other information is preserved.

Note for FTP's PC/TCP users

Execute application when download is complete: When you're double-clicking an item with the left mouse button, the associated application is executed when the information has been downloaded. The resulting file created to capture the information is deleted upon exiting BCGopher. However, if you double-click an item with the right mouse button, it is usually to save the information permanently to your local machine. The resulting file is not deleted, and in this case, you may opt not to activate the associated application when the download is complete.

If this item is checked and you double-click with the right mouse button, the application is activated. If it is not checked and you double-click with the right mouse button, the application is not activated.

If you double-click an item with the left mouse button, the application is activated whether this button is checked or not.

FTP's PC/TCP users

When you're using Version 2.2 and below of PC/TCP, you should have the following as your telnet command:

```
wtnvt -t vt100 %1
```

If you are using 2.3, you can have the following:

```
wtnvt %1 %2
```

Description box

The description box is a floating dialog box that informs you of the details of a specified item in a Gopher menu, including the file type, host name, host port, and selector string. You can use this information to create bookmarks or to add to Gopher servers you may have.

If the host or selector string is too long to show in the text field, you can click the field and scroll the string in the edit box. You can also select the string to copy and paste in other documents.

Because the box is floating, it always remains on top of your application. You can click any item in the menu even if the box is obscuring part of the window. If you can't find it or the box has been moved too far, you can use the Magnet button on the status bar to get it to return to the bottom of the main window. (*Note:* If the bottom of the main window is at the very bottom of your screen, the description box may be off the bottom of your screen and not visible. If you move the bottom of your Gopher window up and click the Magnet, the window appears so that you can move it using the menu bar.)

To remove the description box, you can reselect the Description Box item in the Options menu.

What Is a Bookmark?

So, you're reading a great book, and just as it gets to a good part, the phone rings. You just want to finish this sentence. The phone has now rung twice, and you go to put the book down but slip and grab the phone before the answering machine picks it up. You finally get the phone, and it turns out to be a wrong number. Unfortunately, you dropped your book and now aren't sure where you were. You thumb through it trying to find your place, having to reread things you've already read. Flipping a few pages ahead (because you're sure you were far past there), you start to read and realize that, not only are you a few pages too far, but you just read who the murderer was without the build-up. If only you had had a bookmark to put in your page!

I know, we all know what a bookmark is. But it can be just as frustrating maneuvering through Gopherspace. You find a site that has the one FAQ you've been looking for to quickly solve a problem that's been plaguing you for days. You start reading the file and instead of quitting the pager application, you mistakenly quit Gopher. You don't know what site you were connected to. You had spent all day threading yourself through any number of sites. If you were to make a bookmark of that site (or that specific document), you could go back there anytime you like.

If you create a bookmark to a site, it stores the host address, port, and selector string (if needed) so that you can return to that site any time you want by selecting it from the menu listing.

Bookmarks menu

Add (^Add)

After you have selected an item on your Gopher menu, you can select the Add item from the Bookmark menu. This item adds the currently selected item to your bookmark list. If you want to add the current site you are looking at, you can hold down the Control (Ctrl) key and select Add from the menu. When you select the Bookmark menu, you see a little hat (^, caret, up arrow) to indicate that you are adding the site and not a specified item. You can also add a bookmark by double-clicking with the right mouse button on certain items, such as a folder, Index Search, CSO Phone Book, or telnet link. Other file types are downloaded without being displayed in the pager.

The Bookmark dialog box

From the Bookmark dialog box, you can add, modify, delete, and go to bookmarks. A bookmark consists of a bookmark name, item type, host address, host port, and selector string. Table 16-1 describes options in the Bookmark dialog box.

Bookmark name

The Bookmark name is the name in which you remember what the service is you are connecting to. This name shows up in the Bookmark menu.

Item type

The item type is a number that informs the client what type of item the particular service is. For more information on item types, refer to "What Is Gopher?"

Host

The host is the Internet address of the server that contains the item.

Port

The port is the Internet port of the server that contains the item. If the item is a Gopher server, the port is typically 70.

Selector

The selector is a string, usually the pathname of the item. You use it to locate (or identify) the particular item on the server. If the bookmark is referring to a server, the string is blank.

Table 16-1	The Bookmark Dialog Box
Button	**Function**
OK	Saves changes to the current bookmark list and closes the dialog box.
Cancel	Discards any changes made to the bookmark list and closes the dialog box.
GoTo	Saves any changes made to the bookmark list, closes the dialog box, and connects to the current bookmark selected.
Add	Enables you to add any bookmark to the list by hand. When you choose Add, you should make sure that you have all the information you need to fill in the bookmark.
	Select the Add button again when you're finished adding, or select Cancel to not add it.
Modify	Changes a currently entered bookmark. You can change any part of the bookmark information.
Delete	Removes the currently selected bookmark from your list.
Move Up	Places the selected bookmark one level higher on the listing.
Move Down	Places the selected bookmark one level lower on the listing.
Bookmark Name	The name you want to give to this bookmark.
Item Type	The type of item the bookmark is pointing to. You can choose only from the items in the pull-down box.
Host	The Internet address of the server.
Port	The port of the server.
Selector	The selector string that describes the path of the item. If it is pointing to a server, you must leave the selector blank.

Selecting bookmarks

You can connect to a site saved by a bookmark in two ways:

1. Select it from the Bookmark menu.

2. Select it and click the Go To button in the Bookmark dialog box.

Returning to previous sites

Whenever you double-click a folder, the site that contains that folder is placed into the Recent menu. The menu contains all the places you have gone since the application was started. You can return to any of these places by selecting it from the Recent menu. A check mark is placed next to the name of the site where you are currently located.

Chapter 17
QWS3270 Telnet Client

QWS3270 is a telnet client application that lets a network-attached PC running Windows 3.1 connect to an IBM mainframe, using the Windows Sockets interface in 3270 mode (TN3270). The application was designed to take full advantage of the point-and-click Windows 3.1 environment.

QWS3270 is a WinSock 1.1-compliant application.

Installation

A properly installed WINSOCK.DLL must already be running on your PC. Refer to the "System requirements and restrictions" section, later in this chapter, for the WinSocks that support QWS3270.

1. Copy the distribution files to the directory of your choice.

2. The QWS3270.INI must be in the working directory. If it isn't, copy QWS3270.INI to the directory of your choice; add this line in your AUTOEXEC.BAT file to point to this file:

   ```
   set qws3270=c:\directory
   ```

   Then restart your computer for the `set` command to take effect.

3. Create a program item for QWS3270 by using the Program Manager⇨File⇨New method, or use the easy way: drag the program name out of the File Manager into the desired Program Manager window.

4. Customize QWS3270 by using the application's Setup menu.

QWS3270.HLP must be in your working directory or the WINDOWS directory.

Connecting to a Host

Using QWS3270, you can connect to a host in several ways:

- *Use the Connect menu item.* QWS3270 opens the Connect dialog box to allow you to enter the name or IP address of the host. This method is useful if you connect to many different hosts.

- *Use the Auto Connect option.* The Setup⇨Options menu lets you customize QWS3270 and specify the default host. If you set the Auto Connect feature to yes, QWS3270 automatically connects to the host when you select the icon from Program Manager. This is useful if you always connect to the same host and want to bypass the Connect dialog box.

- *Include a host on the command line.* You can include a host on the command line when you create the icon. The command line would be `c:\directory\qws3270` *host port*. The port is optional and defaults to the value in the QWS3270.INI file. When a command-line host is found, QWS3270 automatically connects to the host when you select the icon from Program Manager.

This last method is useful when you have a couple of hosts that you connect to frequently and want to bypass the Connect dialog box. Just create an icon for each host with the host name or IP address on the command line. Because QWS3270 can accept a host and port as command-line arguments, it can be used with Archie clients to connect to 3270 hosts.

System requirements and restrictions

QWS3270 is a WinSock-compliant application. You must have a properly installed WINSOCK.DLL already running on your PC. Listed in the next section are the WinSocks that are known to support QWS3270.

Development and testing is being done using the Trumpet Windows Sockets DLL Alpha #18 running on a Packard Bell 486SX/25 with a 101-key keyboard running Windows 3.1.

A Trumpet WinSock Stack Sampler is included in *Internet GIZMOS for Windows*. See Part II.

WinSocks supported

The first three items on this list are WinSock implementations that the developer has tested. Others are based on notes received by the shareware author from users of the application.

Trumpet Windows Sockets Alpha #16 , #17, and #18

PC/TCP 2.22 and WinSock 1.09 alpha 5

PC/TCP 2.3 and WinSock 1.10

Lanera TCPOpen

NetManage Chameleon 3.11n

Microsoft TCP/IP for Windows for Workgroups

Windows NT 3.1

PC/NFS Version 5.0

Novell LWP 4.1 with Novell's WinSock API

OS/2 2.1 with OS/2 TCP/IP 2.0 with DOS/Access Kit

Frontier Technologies Super-TCP WinSock DLL Version 3.68

Pathway 3.0 from Wollongong

Mainframe hardware/software supported

The first two items on the list are mainframe software that the developer tested. Others listed are based on notes received from application users.

MVS/ESA 4.3 with IBM TCP/IP 2.2.1

VM/ESA 1.0 with IBM TCP/IP 2.2

NCR's COMTEN boxes

Interlinks SNS/TCP

Known restrictions

Among QWS3270's known restrictions are the following:

- Does not support three terminal types: IBM-3278-5, IBM-3279-2, IBM-3279-3.
- Only supports 101-key keyboards.
- Three 3270 commands have not been implemented: `start field extended, modify field, set attribute`.
- Does not support the Cursor Select key.
- If you're using a Token Ring card, it must have at least 16K of shared memory.

■ QWS3270 has sporadic problems with some versions of Novell's WinSock stack. Several users have complained about error message *4e52*. The fix ensures that WINSOCK.DLL, WLIBSOCK.DLL, and NOVASYNC.EXE are all placed in the same subdirectory and that this subdirectory must be included in the path.

Features

Table 17-1 describes the QWS3270 Telnet Client application's features.

Table 17-1	QWS3270 Features
Feature	*Description*
Clipboard Support	QWS3270 includes support for the common copy and paste functions. It also provides an `append` function where data can be appended to data already in the Clipboard. A `print` function lets the Clipboard data be sent to the Windows printer.
Disabling Setup Menu Item	The setup menu can be disabled by adding a `disablesetup—yes` line in the `[qws3270]` section of QWS3270.INI
Mouse Support	The cursor can be positioned anywhere on the screen using a single click of the left mouse button.
Transparent Print Support	QWS3270 includes support for the transparent write feature available with IBM's 7171 ASCII Device Attachment Control Units. The transparent write feature is documented in the *7171 Reference Manual and Programming Guide* (manual number GA37-0021). Yale University offers a TPRINT package that can be used on VM systems to print files to a printer attached to your PC. You can get this package by issuing the following VM command: `tell listserv at yalevm get tprintv2 package`. When using the standard package from Yale, use the following commands: `tprint fn ft fm (vt100` causes the output to be sent to both the screen and the printer port, and `tprint fn ft fm (ibmpc noytp` causes the output to be sent only to the printer. This is the correct setting for QWS3270.

Feature	Description
Tektronix 4010 graphics emulator support	QWS3270 includes support for Tektronix 4010 terminal emulation.
Type Ahead Buffer	QWS3270 has a 64-character type ahead buffer. This allows keyboard input while waiting for the host to process the last attention key.

Keyboard mapping

3270 Key	PC Key Equivalent
ATTN	ATTN button
Back Tab	Shift+Tab
Cent Sign	Ctrl+\
Clear keypad	Plus (+) or Ctrl+C or Clear button
Delete	Delete
Dup	Dup button
Erase End of Field	Keypad minus (–) or Ctrl+E or Erase EOF button
Erase Input	Erase Input button
Field Mark	Field Mark button or Esc+;
Home	Home
Insert	Insert
New Line	Ctrl+N or New Line button
PF13 thru PF24	Shift+F1 through Shift+F12
PF7	Page Up
PF8	Page Down
RESET	Ctrl+R or Alt+R or Reset button
SYS REQ	Esc+V or Sys Req button
Tab	Tab

PC key definitions

Key	Description
Backspace	Move cursor one position to the left
End	Tabs to one position past the last nonblank character in the field
Page Down	PF8
Page Up	PF7

Menu commands

Connect

This item opens a dialog box that lets you establish a connection to a host. The dialog box contains the following fields:

Host	Enter the name or IP address of the host to which QWS3270 should connect. The default host that appears in this box can be changed by using the Setup⇨Options menu.
Port	Enter the telnet port number that QWS3270 should use to make the connection. The default port number that appears in this box can be changed by using the Setup⇨Options menu.
Language File	Enter the fully qualified name of the file (that is, *c:\directory\file.typ*) that QWS3270 should use to provide the character translation between the mainframe and the PC. This allows QWS3270 to use a different language translation table to provide support for international character sets. The default language file that appears in this box can be changed using the Setup⇨Options menu. Enter a value of English (U.S.) to use the default translation table that corresponds to the Country Extended Code Page number 037.

Close

This menu item lets you close the connection with the host. No attempt is made to logoff or sign off from the host before the connection is closed.

Exit

This menu item closes the window if no connection with a host exists.

Edit

This menu item accesses the Windows Clipboard functions:

Copy	Copies the marked contents of the screen to the Clipboard. To mark the area, hold down the left mouse button and drag the mouse until the desired area is marked. If the marked area spans more than one screen line, the last nonblank character of each screen row is followed by a carriage return and linefeed character. The data is sent as text. This menu item is deactivated after the first Copy or Copy All.
Copy All	Copies the entire contents of the screen to the Clipboard. A carriage return and linefeed character are inserted after the last nonblank character in each line. The data is sent as text. This menu item is deactivated after the first Copy or Copy All.
Append	Appends the marked contents of the screen to the Clipboard. To mark the area, hold down the left mouse button and drag the mouse until the desired area is marked. If the marked area spans more than one screen line, the last nonblank character of each screen row is followed by a carriage return and linefeed character. The data is sent as text. This menu item is activated after the first Copy or Copy All.
Append All	Appends the entire contents of the screen to the Clipboard. A carriage return and linefeed character are inserted after the last nonblank character in each line. The data is sent as text. This menu item is activated after the first Copy or Copy All.
Clear	Deletes any data currently in the Clipboard. Menu items Append, Append All, and Print are deactivated. Menu items Copy and Copy All are activated.
Paste	Retrieves the contents from the Clipboard and adds it to the screen starting at the current cursor position, just as if the data was typed from the keyboard. Embedded carriage return and linefeed combinations are treated as a `newline` function. Invalid characters in the retrieved data are ignored.
Print	Invokes the Windows Print Manager to send the contents of the Clipboard to the printer. The contents of the Clipboard are cleared. Menu items Append, Append All, and Print are deactivated. Menu items Copy and Copy All are activated.

Print Screen

This item copies the screen's contents to an attached printer. To activate it, use the mouse or press Ctrl+P. This function invokes the Windows Print Manager.

Setup

This menu item lets you customize QWS3270. To disable the setup menu, add a
disablesetup= yes line in the [qws3270] section of the QWS3270.INI

Options

This menu item lets you set QWS3270 options to your preference:

Default Host	The default host that appears in the Connect dialog box. It can be a host name or an IP address.
Default Port	The default port number that appears in the Connect dialog box. The default is 23.
Auto Connect	When set to yes, QWS3270 automatically attempts a connection to the default host and port when you double-click on the icon from the Program Manager. The default setting is no.

Button bars

Line 1	When set to yes, QWS3270 displays a row of mouse-activated button bars for the following 3270 keys: Clear, Erase end of Field, Newline, PA1, PA2, and PA3. The default setting is Yes.
Line 2	When set to yes, QWS3270 displays a row of mouse-activated button bars for several 3270 keys: ATTN, Dup, Erase Input, Reset, and Sys Req. The default setting is no.
Exit on Close	When set to yes, QWS3270 automatically closes the window when the connection to the host is closed. The default setting is no.
Language File	Lets QWS3270 use an external file as the character translation table to provide support for international character sets. Enter the fully qualified name of the file (that is, *c:\directory\file.typ*) that QWS3270 should use to provide the character translation between the mainframe and the PC. Enter a value of English (U.S.) to use the default translation table that corresponds to the Country Extended Code Page number 037.
Message Beep	When set to Off, QWS3270 suppresses the beeps that the host sends to the PC. The default setting is On.
Terminal Type	This lets you choose the 3278 terminal type that QWS3270 uses when negotiating terminal types with the host. The listbox shows the valid values. The IBM-3278-2 is a 24-line by 80-column display. The IBM-3278-3 is a 32-line by 80 column display. The IBM-3278-4 is a 43-line by 80-column display. The default is the IBM-3278-2.

Yale Null Processing	When set to On, QWS3270 translates all null characters to blanks before sending the screen data to the host. Most 3270 emulators have Yale Null Processing turned on. When this parameter is Off, QWS3270 simulates a true 3270 terminal. The default setting is On.

Currently, QWS3270 includes the following language translation files:

ENGLISH.LAN	CECP page 037 English (U.S.)
BELGIAN.LAN	Belgian language translation file, based on CECP page 500.
DANISH.LAN	language translation file for Denmark/Norway based on CECP page 277. (Not all of CP277-1 has been implemented.)
DUTCH.LAN	Dutch language translation file.
FRENCH.LAN	French language translation file.
GERMAN.LAN	German/Austrian language translation file, based on CECP page 273.
HEBREW.LAN	Hebrew language translation file.
ITALIAN.LAN	Italian language translation file.
NORWEGN.LAN	Norwegian language translation file.
PORTUGUE.LAN	Portuguese language translation file.
SPANISH.LAN	Spanish language translation file.
SWEDISH.LAN	Swedish language translation file.
UK.LAN	English (U.K.) language translation file.

If you create a new language file, the shareware author asks that you contact him with the appropriate documentation if you want it included as part of the distribution. See the on-line help file for further instructions.

Colors

Lets you customize the QWS3270's colors. You can select a color for three items:

Background	Select the background color. The default is black.
Unprotected / Protected Fields, Normal	Select the normal intensity color. The default is white for unprotected and yellow for protected fields.
Unprotected / Protected Fields Bright	Select the high intensity color. The default is cyan for unprotected and red for protected fields.

Fonts

This menu item invokes the Windows-supplied Font Selection dialog box, letting you choose the font that QWS3270 should use to display the text on the terminal. This dialog box only shows fixed pitch screen fonts. The default font is FIXEDSYS.

Printer

This menu item invokes the Windows-supplied Printer Setup dialog box, enabling you to choose the printer that QWS3270 should use for all printer output. This setting is saved in the INI file for future use.

Help

Provides access to the following QWS3270 help features:

Help	Provides access to the Windows help file for QWS3270.
Keyboard Mapping	Provides information on special 3270 keys that do not have PC keyboard equivalents.
About	Provides information about QWS3270, including the author, version number, and the e-mail address to use when reporting bugs.

Availability and Pricing

This version is functionally stable and is no longer being enhanced. If you need more function or have suggestions for enhancements, contact the author.

QWS3270 is available free to anyone who wants to use it *as is* (that is, no guarantees whatsoever). These programs are not to be sold or distributed with other programs that are for sale without the express written permission of the shareware author.

QWS3270 Telnet Client Registration Form

Name _____

Company _____

Address _____

City _____

State _____ Country _____

Zip _____ Phone _____

Remit to:

Jolly Giant Software
56 Chartwell Crescent
Kingston, ONT, Canada K7K 6P3

Pricing

❏ $35 (U.S.)

Please include your e-mail address and FTP site information as well. Contact the author for site licensing.

Chapter 18
WS_FTP, Windows Sockets FTP

WS_FTP is a File Transfer Protocol (FTP) client application for Windows Sockets designed to take full advantage of the point-and-click Windows 3.x environment. WS_FTP is easy for the beginner to use but includes a full set of functions for the power user. WS_FTP remembers site profiles and supports multi-file transfer using standard Windows methods.

WS_FTP conforms to the WinSock interface specification, making it a WinSock-compliant application.

For more information on FTP and FTP sites, refer to the many different Usenet newsgroups or check out some of the recent books about the Internet.

This program is distributed freely for noncommercial use. For commercial use, contact Ipswitch, Inc., at info@ipswitch.com or call 617-246-1150.

Installation

Place WS_FTP.EXE, WS_FTP.HLP, and WS_FTP.INI in your WINDOWS directory or in any directory you choose.

The easiest way to add WS_FTP to your Program Manager is to drag the program name out of the File Manager into the desired Program Manager window. Alternatively, you can select File⇨New to create a new program item.

Enter a command line with the full path to WS_FTP.EXE and set the working directory as desired. Click OK.

You must install WS_FTP.HLP and WS_FTP.INI in either your working directory or the WINDOWS directory.

The WS_FTP Screen

The left half of the main WS_FTP window contains local information. The right half of the main window contains remote information. In each half of the main window are two listboxes. The upper box lists directories, and the lower half lists files. Just to the right of the two listboxes is a column of buttons. Below the listboxes are two status lines. You can double-click in this area to expand this listing.

This screen has these controls:

ChgDir button	Use the ChgDir button to change directories. If a name is highlighted in the directory listbox, the system changes to that directory. If no name is highlighted, WS_FTP asks for a directory name. Some systems do not use directories, so a failure here does not necessarily mean the WS_FTP has failed.
MkDir button	Use the MkDir button to create a directory, if possible. WS_FTP asks for a directory name. You must supply a name valid for the current system. Some systems do not let you make and delete directories remotely, so a failure here does not mean that WS_FTP failed.
RmDir button	Use the RmDir button to remove a directory, if possible. WS_FTP asks you for a directory name. Some systems do not let you make and delete directories remotely, so a failure here does not mean that WS_FTP failed.
File Mask	Here you supply a file mask that is valid for the system that you are using. You can use "-altr" in the remote side if you are connected to a UNIX host to receive names in date sequence. Any argument string that is valid on the remote system may be used on the remote side at the end of an "ls" command in a command-line FTP client.
Display button	Use the Display button to see an ASCII file using whatever viewer you have defined in the Options dialog box.
Exec button	Use Exec to execute a file according to the standard File Manager extension associations. If you select the remote Exec button, the file is downloaded to the WINDOWS temporary directory (defined with the DOS TMP environment variable). If an association does not exist, WS_FTP lets you provide that association at execution time. Files are automatically downloaded in binary mode when the Exec button is used.

When you click on a filename in the local side and then click Exec, the file executes using the same rules as if it were executed in the File Manager. |

If you click on a remote filename and then click on Exec, it is transferred in binary mode to the Windows temporary directory and is executed from the current directory using the same rules as if executed in the File Manager.

If the filename has an extension other than EXE, COM, BAT, or PIF, then WS_FTP uses the file associations from the File Manager. If the extension has no association, you can specify the association at runtime. This association is saved in the WIN.INI file in the Extensions section and is also valid for the File Manager.

You can set associations by selecting the Options and then selecting Associations.

Rename button	Use Rename to rename a file, when possible. Enter the new name for the item and click Rename, or click Cancel to leave the item intact. Not all systems let you rename files and directories remotely, so a failure here does not mean that WS_FTP failed. Other systems will let you rename a file over the top of an existing file. You may also be able to move a file from one directory to another by specifying a full or relative path with the filename.
Delete button	Use Delete to delete a file, when possible. Click Yes to delete the item, No to cancel. Some systems do not let you delete files remotely, so a failure here does not mean that WS_FTP failed.

Connecting

WS_FTP contains a remote host profile feature. After you have entered the profile information, you can connect to a remote host by clicking Connect, choosing the host from the name list, and then clicking OK.

Advanced profile parameters

Profile Name	This profile or configuration name can be anything you want to identify the connection you're creating. The length of this name is restricted because it is used as a section name in the WS_FTP.INI file.
Remote Host Name	This is either a fully qualified Internet host name or an IP address.

(continued)

Remote Host Type	If you know the host type, select it from the drop-down list. If you don't know, try "auto detect." If you can connect to a remote host but don't get a directory listing, try changing the host type in the Options dialog box. I am still working on auto detect. It takes care of about 90 percent of all hosts.
User ID (userid)	Enter the user ID that you wish to use for this configuration, or click on the Anonymous Login check box to enter anonymous automatically as the user ID.
Password	Enter the password that you wish to use for the user ID that you entered. When logging in anonymously, enter a minus sign (–) followed by your full electronic mail address. Instead of entering your password for anonymous logins, click the Anonymous Login checkbox.
Firewall Password	Enter the password for the firewall host for the user ID that you entered.
Account	When the remote host requires an account, enter the account to use for the user ID that you entered. The account is used for VM/CMS hosts for the initial password to the user's default directory. When you change a directory on a VM/CMS host, the host prompts you each time for the password to connect to that directory.
Timeout	This is the number of seconds before WS_FTP times out waiting for a host response to a command. *Your WinSock DLL determines the initial connection timeout.* Setting this value higher does not have any effect on the initial connection to the host. Setting to less than the amount of time that your WinSock DLL uses causes the connection to fail in that number of seconds. When connection is lost, file transfers do not time out. To end the transfer, cancel it.
Port	This is the port to connect to on the remote host. This is normally 21, but when you go through a firewall, it may be different.

Anonymous login

Checking this box enters *anonymous* as your user ID, and then you enter your e-mail address as the password.

Most FTP sites support *anonymous* logins, to let you access the system's files without having an account there. The user ID is usually the word *anonymous,* and the password is your full e-mail address. You can usually place a minus (–) sign in the password before your e-mail address to reduce the number of messages that come from the host FTP process.

Firewall

Some organizations separate their networks from the rest of the world but still let certain users access resources outside of that organization's network. This access is provided through a *gateway* or *firewall* host system and is generally unidirectional.

If you are behind a firewall host, click this box. You must ensure that the firewall information has been correctly filled out. You can specify a port to be used for the firewall. WS_FTP supports five kinds of firewalls, described in Table 18-1.

Table 18-1	Firewalls That WS_FTP Supports
Firewall Type	**Login Requirements**
SITE hostname	Firewall host, user id, and password are required. User is logged on the firewall and the remote connection is established using SITE remote_host.
USER after logon	Firewall host, user id, and password are required. User is logged on the firewall, and the remote connection is established using USER remote_userid@remote_host.
USER with no logon	Firewall host is required; user id and password are ignored. USER remote_userid@remote_host is sent to firewall upon initial connection.
Proxy OPEN	Firewall host is required; user id and password are ignored. OPEN remote_host is sent to firewall upon initial connection.
PASV Mode	There is another kind of firewall, which is not specifically configured. A router-based firewall allows connections to be established in only one direction. The router itself is invisible to the user. However, the default mode within FTP is that the server, rather than the client, establishes data connections. To work with a router-based firewall requires using FTP's PASV mode. Use the Options screen to turn on PASV mode.

Save password

Check this box only if you are the only user of your computer and no one else has access to your WINDOWS directory. Passwords are stored in the WS_FTP.INI file and even though they are encrypted, it is an easy encryption to break (especially since the source file is distributed).

Save/Delete buttons

The Save and Delete buttons help you manage configurations. If the Auto Save Config option is checked, *a configuration is automatically saved when you select the OK button,* and you can make limitless connections.

The Delete button removes unwanted entries, and the Save button saves an entry without trying to actually connect to the host. The Cancel button exits the dialog box without saving any changes to the current configuration.

Transferring files

File uploads and downloads do *not* timeout. You must cancel the operation in the event that you lose the connection to the remote host.

During the transfer of files, the Help button changes to Abort if the hash option is off, or an Abort dialog box is displayed if the hash option is on. The current transfer may be cancelled by clicking Cancel or Abort. File uploads are cancelled immediately, but file downloads may take up to 30 seconds to be cancelled. In both cases, the partial file is not automatically deleted.

Command-Line Options

Items enclosed in [brackets] are optional.

WS_FTP -i *inifile* [other_args_as_required]

WS_FTP [**-i** *inifile*] **-p** *profile_name* (not valid with other args)

WS_FTP -ask (prompt for command-line arguments)

WS_FTP *file://hostname/pathname/filename* [**local:**/*pathname/filename*] [**-ascii**]

WS_FTP *ftp://hostname/pathname/filename* [**local:***/pathname/filename*] [**-ascii**]

WS_FTP *//hostname/pathname/filename* [**local:***/pathname/filename*] [**-ascii**]

WS_FTP *hostname:/pathname/filename* [**local:***/pathname/filename*] [**-ascii**]

WS_FTP **local:***/pathname/filename //hostname/pathname/filename* [**-ascii**]

WS_FTP **local:***/pathname/filename hostname:/pathname/filename* [**-ascii**]

Hints

Changing the default directory

To set the default local start-up directory to be something other than where WS_FTP is located:

1. Highlight the WS_FTP icon and press Alt+Enter (or select File Properties) in the Program Manager.
2. Change the Working Directory to your desired directory.

Overcoming name-conversion problems

If you have problems with remote-to-local filename conversions, check the Prompt option in the Options dialog box. WS_FTP shows you the proposed filename and lets you change it.

Changing directories

To change directories, click the desired directory and click the ChgDir button.

If you want to change to a directory without traversing the full tree, make sure no name is selected in the list box and click ChgDir (works with RmDir also). When changing drives on a remote system, you usually have to enter a directory name in addition to the drive letter.

You also can double-click on a directory name to change to that directory.

Double-clicking

You can double-click on a directory name to change to that directory, and double-click on a filename to transfer or execute that file.

File transfer modes

Use ASCII mode to transfer text files. Use Binary mode to transfer all other files.

If you know that the host that you are transferring to or from is the same as your local host, you can always use Binary mode and never use ASCII.

Transfer modes are ASCII, Binary, L8, and Auto Detect.

Saving a viewed file

If you use View to display a remote file and then wish to save that file and have the viewer set to Notepad, select the Save As menu option and save the file to whatever name you want.

Transferring multiple files

To transfer multiple files, use the Shift or Ctrl keys when selecting filenames.

To select two or more items in sequence, click the first file that you want to select and drag the mouse pointer down, releasing the mouse button on the last file in the group. You can also click the first file that you want to select, and then press and hold down Shift while you click the last file in the group.

To select two or more items out of sequence, press and hold down Ctrl while you click each file.

To cancel a selection, press and hold down Ctrl while you click the selected file.

After selecting the desired files, press the desired transfer direction button.

Dragging and dropping

You can drag one or more files from the Windows File Manager and drop them anywhere on the main window or WS_FTP icon, and WS_FTP uses the current transfer mode to transfer them to the current directory of the remote host.

You cannot drag and drop directories, nor can you drag or drop from the remote host to another application.

Directory display problems

If you can connect to a remote host but don't get a directory listing, try changing the host type in the Connect or Options dialog boxes. Some hosts may not be auto-detected properly and must be set at connect time. I am always working on the auto-detect and host types. They work for 90 percent of the hosts.

Debug menu

To pop up a menu, click the right mouse button when the cursor is pointing at the main window's gray area. This gives you access to some additional FTP commands. These commands are not recommended for beginners.

Program Options _____

Options available in the Program Options dialog box affect the WS_FTP display and operation for all configurations.

Alternate Screen Layout	This option controls the main window display layout. The alternate layout has the local directory and file list on top and the remote directory and file list on the bottom. Directories are on the left, and file lists are on the right.
Buttons on Top	This option controls the placement of the buttons that are normally across the bottom of the window.
Show Directory Information	When this option is turned on, additional file information is shown when possible. This option does not support all kinds of hosts. The client does not attempt to decipher or interpret this information.

(continued)

(continued)

Auto Save Config	When this option is checked, WS_FTP saves the Session Profile when you click OK in the Session Profile dialog box. Even though this option also appears in the Session Profile dialog box, its state is only saved in the Program Options dialog box.
Verify Deletions	When this option is checked, WS_FTP prompts you for confirmation before deleting files.
Auto Connect	This option controls whether or not WS_FTP displays the Connect dialog box when WS_FTP starts.
Debug Messages	This option enables extra debug messages in the message window, which appears at the bottom of the main window. These messages generally don't help you; all error messages are displayed even when this option is off.
Text Viewer	This option specifies the program that is invoked for LongDir and Display buttons. The default value is Notepad.
E-Mail Address	This option specifies the default password for anonymous logins as required by most anonymous FTP sites. Place a minus (–) sign as the first character of your e-mail address to turn off descriptive messages on the remote host.
ListBox Font	This option specifies the listbox font. SysVar is the default system font and is a variable font. SysFix, the fixed system font, improves the alignment of columns in the boxes. AnsVar is the ANSI Variable Font, which is a narrower font than the System font. AnsFix is the ANSI Fixed Font.
Scale Fonts	This option, when checked, reduces the font outside the listboxes when the window size reduces. The font used is always ANSI Variable.
Double Click Transfer	If this option is checked, when you double-click on a file on the local side, WS_FTP uploads it to the remote system. When you double-click on a file on the remote side, WS_FTP downloads it to the local system.
Double Click Execute	When this option is checked, when you double-click on a filename, the file executes using the same rules as if double-clicked in the File Manager. When you double-click a remote file, WS_FTP transfers it in Binary mode to the Windows temporary directory and executes it from the current directory using the same rules as if double-clicked in the File Manager.
Double Cick Nothing	When this option is checked, when you double-click on a filename, nothing happens.

Receive Size	This option controls how many bytes are read from the network in each read (recv). This option can have a value from 80 to 4096. You should see the best results with this value set to 4096. The actual number of bytes read in each pass is determined by the underlying TCP/IP stack and by the amount of information available.
Send Size	This option controls how many bytes are written to the network in each send. This option can have a value from 80 to 4096. The optimum value to place here will depend on your underlying TCP/IP stack. If you have a direct connection, I suggest setting this to 4096. If you have a SLIP or PPP connection, you probably want to set it to the MTU size.

Session Options

These options reflect the options in use for the current session and are specific for the configuration. If you want to make the options the default for all sessions, click the Save as Default button. Sessions can still be nondefault by setting the option in this dialog box and clicking Save. Only options that are different than the default options are saved for the session. If you change the defaults later, you may want to recheck the session options for a configuration.

Auto Update Remote Directories	When this option is not checked, WS_FTP does not update the remote directory list after it uploads a file, deletes a file or directory, or creates a directory. To refresh the list, click the remote side Refresh button.
Show Transfer Dialog	When the option is on, an Abort dialog box appears during file transfers to show transfer status. The Percent Done bar appears only during receives when the remote host sends the file size.
Use PASV Transfer Mode	PASV mode forces the client, not the server, to establish data connections. PASV Mode may be required for users behind a router-based firewall.
Send Unique	This option causes the transmitted filenames not to conflict with existing files when the remote host supports the STOU FTP command. The remote host determines the new filename.
Receive Unique	This option causes the received filenames not to conflict with existing files. The new filename is changed so that the sixth though eighth character of the filename is a number from 000 to 999.

(continued)

(continued)

Prompt for Destination	This option enables local/remote filename prompting. For each file that is transferred, WS_FTP shows you the proposed destination filename and lets you change it. You can enter a full pathname to a different directory if you want.
Sound When Transfer Done	When this option is on, a bell sounds at the end of each file transfer. If you have a sound card and Enable System Sounds is selected in the Control Panel Sound setup, this is the Default Beep sound.
Sorted Listboxes	If this box is checked, the Remote File Listbox is automatically sorted. Otherwise, the files are presented in the order the remote host transmitts them.
Send PORT Command	This causes the *PORT nn,nn,nn,nn,nn,nn* command to be sent to the remote system each time a file is transferred. Always leave this option on. This option is *not* saved with the other program options. This option no longer appears in any dialog boxes.
ASCII	Used to transfer text files. The end-of-line character is different on different types of computers. This will ensure that the end-of-line character is translated properly. If you know that the host that you are transferring to or from is the same as your local host, you can always use Binary mode.
Binary	Used to transfer nontext files. Executable programs, word processing documents, spreadsheets, databases, graphics files, and sound files are some examples of files that must be transferred in Binary mode. If you know that the host that you are transferring to or from is the same as your local host, you can always use Binary mode.
L8	Used for VMS nontext file transferring.
Auto Detect	When this option is selected, WS_FTP checks the WS_FTP.EXT file for the file's extension. When WS_FTP.EXT contains the extension, WS_FTP transfers the file in ASCII mode. Otherwise, WS_FTP transfers the file in Binary mode. Note that extensions can be up to ten characters long and can contain periods and other special characters. These are not DOS extensions, but the ending characters of a filename. If you expect it to match on a period, you must include the period.

Download

Transferring a file *to* your local workstation *from* a remote host or workstation.

Local file name	Enter a valid MS_DOS filename as *filename.ext,* where *filename* is a maximum of eight characters consisting of the letters A–Z and digits 0–9, and *ext* is a maximum of three characters consisting of the letters A–Z and digits 0–9. Use standard extensions, such as .TXT, .ZIP, .DOC, .WKS, and so on.
Remote file name	Enter a valid filename for the remote system. Many systems allow names longer than those MS-DOS allows. Also, some systems allow characters that MS_DOS does not. WS_FTP does not check or filter the name you enter here.
Remote directory name	Enter a remote directory name. Naming conventions must match the remote system. Refer to the remote system's documentation for help. On most systems, a directory must be empty before it can be deleted. Not all systems let you make and delete directories remotely, so a failure here does not mean that WS_FTP failed.
SITE Command	To access this command, click the right mouse button. Enter a remote site specific command. The client prefixes your entry with the word SITE, and sends your unedited entry to the remote system. It is up to you to determine valid input for this command by reading the remote system's documentation.
QUOTE Command	To access this command, click the right mouse button. Enter any command that you want. WS_FTP sends it unedited to the remote system. You must determine whether the command syntax is correct for the host you are connected to. Do not send any commands that open a secondary channel.

Chapter 19
NetDial

Welcome to NetDial. NetDial is an Internet dial-up program for Microsoft Windows. With NetDial, you can connect to an Internet provider with just a click of the mouse. NetDial has many features:

- Can be configured for up to five separate connections
- 300–256K baud support
- Easy-to-use login scripting with user-specified timeout value
- Can redial up to 99 times or be set to 0 for call until connected
- On-line timer
- Log option to maintain a record of calls made, time spent on-line, and so on
- Built-in call log viewer/editor
- Cumulative timer window
- Up to five start-up programs that can be shut down on hangup/exit (if desired)
- Can parse IP and gateway address for users with dynamic addressing

This program has been painstakingly written to be the best, easiest to use dial-up package available today. I hope you enjoy using it.

Program Registration

NetDial is shareware, which means that if you continue to use this program for more than 30 days, you are required to pay for it. Following are a few good reasons to register NetDial:

- Registration gets rid of the nag/guilt conscience trigger screen.
- Registered users are entitled unlimited technical support and discount prices on future versions of this program.
- It gives the author (me) reason to develop future versions of this program, and to develop more quality shareware programs.

■ It gives you another cool program to add to your collection.

■ It gives you a warm, fuzzy feeling to be supporting the shareware concept.

How to register

The cost of registering NetDial is only $20 (U.S.) or £15 (U.K.). NetDial can be registered in either of the following ways:

You can register NetDial on-line through CompuServe's Shareware Registration Forum (GO SWREG). NetDial's registration ID is 3528.

You can mail in your order and pay by check or money order. To register, fill out the registration form at the end of this chapter and send it with your registration fee to one of the following addresses:

United States

James Sanders
NCTS PSC 802
Box 44FPO AE 09499-1200

United Kingdom

James Sanders
49 West End Lane
Pinner, Middlesex
HA5 1BU

Miscellaneous information (legal stuff)

■ Each copy of NetDial registered may be used by only one person at a time.

■ Site licenses can be negotiated for company discounts.

■ The registered version may *not* be distributed.

Program Operation

NetDial main window

Figure 19-1 is a snapshot of NetDial's main window.

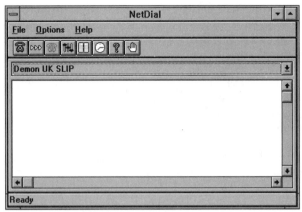

Figure 19-1: The NetDial main window.

Refer to Figure 19-1 to understand the following descriptions:

Menu bar: This is NetDial's menu bar. Each menu item (File, Options, and Help) can be activated by holding down the Alt key and pressing the underlined letter of the desired menu item. For a list of the menu commands, see "Menu commands" in the "Reference" section, later in this chapter.

Toolbar: NetDial's toolbar contains buttons for the most often used commands. These are (from left to right):

This is the Dial button. Click this button to call the number currently displayed in the connection box (the drop-down box directly below the toolbar), connect, login, and run your TCP/IP package.

Note: If a call is already in progress, the Dial button is disabled.

This is the Cycle Dial button. Click this button to dial each connection configured for Cycle Dial until a connection is established with one of them.

Connections are configured as Cycle Dial entries in the Call Settings section of the configuration window.

Note: If a call is already in progress, the Cycle Dial button is disabled.

This is the Hang Up button. Click this button to hang up and reset the phone line.

Note: If a call is not in progress, the Hang Up button is disabled.

This is the Configure button. Click this button to invoke the NetDial Configuration window, where you set up/edit all your Internet connection settings and options. See the section "Configuring NetDial," later in this chapter, for configuration/setup options.

This is the Call Log button. Click this button to view/edit the NetDial call log. This button is disabled if you don't have the Log Connections option turned on (this option can be set in the General section of the configuration window), or if the log file has been deleted.

This is the Cumulative Timer Statistics button. Click this button to invoke the Cumulative Timer Statistics window, where you can view/reset total on-line time to date.

This is the Help button. Click this button to receive help on using NetDial's main window (the help topic you are currently viewing).

This is the Exit button. Click this button to terminate NetDial. If a connection has been established, NetDial hangs up before exiting.

Every window in NetDial has a Help button. Click the Help button to receive help on the current area of NetDial that you are in. You can also select various help items from NetDial's main window Help menu command by pressing Alt+H.

Connection listbox: In the connection listbox, you select which connection you want to work with. When you click the Dial button, the connection displayed here is the connection NetDial calls.

Status window: In the connection status window, all information coming in and going out of your modem is displayed. This window displays modem/connection information until a successful connect/login sequence is completed. This window is cleared every time a new connection is attempted.

Status bar: In the NetDial's status bar, information relating to the progress of a connection will be displayed here. Common messages displayed here are Ready, Line Busy, No Answer, and Dialing.

Configuring NetDial

The NetDial Configuration window is the heart of NetDial. It is where all elements of a connection are configured. Several miscellaneous program options also can be tailored here.

The Configuration window has five separate sections marked by tabs. Each section contains configuration information about a particular aspect of NetDial. In the following section, "Configuration window (Preferences)," the entire Configuration window is explained. However, for the remaining sections, only the items for the associated section are discussed.

Configuration window (Preferences)

A snapshot of NetDial's Configuration window (Preferences section) is displayed in Figure 19-2.

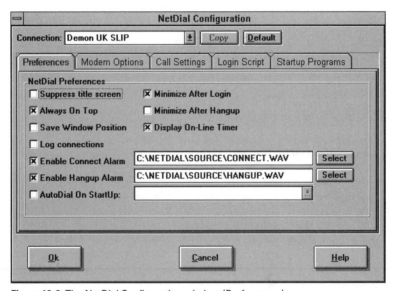

Figure 19-2: The NetDial Configuration window (Preferences).

Refer to Figure 19-2 to understand the following descriptions.

The following items pertain to *all* sections of the Configuration window:

Connection: This box displays the connection you are currently working with (you can have five). Click the down arrow to select a different connection to edit.

Preferences and Modem Options are global settings. They can't be made different for each connection.

Copy button: Click this button to copy the currently displayed configuration section to another connection. The following sections can be copied from connection to connection: Call Settings, Login Script, and Startup Programs. If you are not in one of those sections, this button is disabled.

Default button: Click the Default button to restore the current configuration section to default values.

Preferences tab: Clicking this tab brings up the Preferences section of NetDial's Configuration window. This is the section that is currently open in Figure 19-2.

Modem Options tab: Clicking the Modem Options tab brings up the Modem Options section of NetDial's Configuration window, which is where you specify various modem options such as the modem initialization string, modem type, speaker options, and so forth.

Call Settings tab: Clicking on the Call Settings tab brings up the Call Settings section of NetDial's Configuration window, which is where you specify various connection information such as connection name, phone number, port settings, and so on.

Login Script tab: Clicking on the Login Script tab brings up the Login Script section of NetDial's Configuration window, which is where you specify your Internet host login script commands.

Startup Programs tab: Clicking on the Startup Programs tab brings up the Startup Programs section of NetDial's Configuration window, which is where you specify programs to run upon successful login (such as your TCP/IP start-up program, and so on).

OK button: Click OK to save any changes you have made and return to NetDial's main window.

Cancel button: Click Cancel to discard any changes you have made and return to NetDial's main window.

Help button: Click Help to receive on-line help for NetDial's configuration window.

The remaining items pertain to the Preferences section:

Suppress title screen: If this option is turned on, the NetDial "splash screen" is not displayed on start-up. If this option is turned off, the splash screen is displayed for approximately five seconds on start-up.

Always On Top: If this option is turned on and NetDial is minimized, its icon stays on top of all other windows. If this option is off, the NetDial icon can be covered up by other windows.

Save Window Position: This option dictates whether or not NetDial's main window position is saved when you exit NetDial. If this option is turned on, the window position is saved for later sessions. If this option is turned off, NetDial starts up centered on your screen.

Minimize After Login: If this option is turned on, the NetDial main window is minimized to an icon after the login script for the current connection has completed.

If NetDial is minimized when you exit the program, the window position is *not* saved.

Minimize After Hangup: If this option is turned on, NetDial minimizes to an icon when the Hangup button is pressed. If this option is turned off, NetDial's main window stays active.

Display On-Line Timer: If this option is turned on, NetDial displays an On-Line Timer once a successful login has been completed. If NetDial is minimized, the on-line timer is seen under NetDial's icon. If NetDial isn't minimized, the on-line timer is displayed in NetDial's title bar.

Log Connections: If this option is turned on, connection information is logged to your hard drive. This log file can be viewed/edited by selecting File⇨View Log from NetDial's main window.

The log filename is NETDIAL.LOG, and it resides in the same directory as the NetDial program files. If you don't want to use NetDial's built-in log editor, the file can be viewed/edited with any text editor. If this option is turned off, no connection information is logged.

The NETDIAL.LOG file will not exist if this option is never turned on.

Enable Connect Alarm: If this option is turned on, the wave file displayed in the box to the right is played when a connection is established. If this option is turned off, no sound plays upon connection.

Alarm Text Box: This is the wave file that is played upon connection. To choose a different wave file, click the Select button to the right of the text box.

Enable Hangup Alarm: If this option is turned on, the wave file displayed in the box to the right is played when NetDial hangs up. If this option is turned off, no sound plays upon disconnect.

Hangup Alarm Text Box: This is the wave file that is played upon hangup. To choose a different wave file, click the Select button to the right of this text box.

AutoDial On Startup: If this option is turned on, NetDial automatically dials the connection selected in the combo box to the right. If this option is turned off, the combo box to the right is disabled.

AutoDial Box: This combo box enables you to select which connection NetDial automatically dials when the program is started. If the AutoDial On Startup option is turned off, this combo box is disabled.

Configuration window (Modem Options)

A snapshot of NetDial's Configuration window (Modem Options section) is displayed in Figure 19-3.

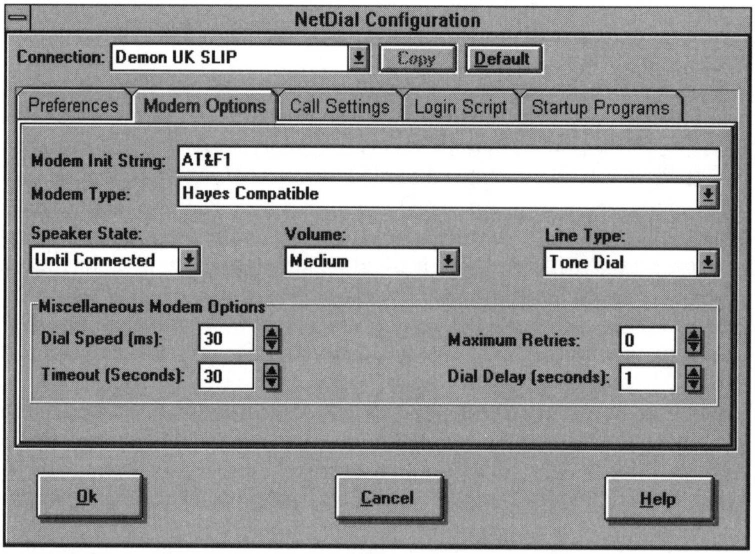

Figure 19-3: The NetDial Configuration window (Modem Options).

Refer to Figure 19-3 for an illustration of the options defined in the following descriptions:

Modem Init String: This text box allows for a user-defined modem initialization string. The default initialization string is AT&F1 but can be changed to suit your particular needs. If you are unfamiliar with the Hayes modem command set, it is best to leave this initialization string *as is*.

Modem Type: Click here to select an appropriate modem type. Currently only two selections are available: Telebit 2500 and Hayes Compatible. Unless you have a Telebit 2500 modem, leave this at Hayes Compatible.

Speaker State: The Speaker State options tell NetDial how to set your modem's speaker once a connect attempt has started. Select Off if you want the modem's speaker to always be off. Select Until Connected if you wish to hear your modem's progress until it establishes a connection. Select Always On if you want the modem's speaker to remain on at all times after a connect attempt has begun.

Volume: This tells NetDial how loud you want your modem's speaker to be. Select the speaker volume desired. If Speaker Settings is set to OFF, this setting has no effect.

Line Type: This tells NetDial which dialing method to use. Select Tone Dial for touch-tone dialing or Pulse Dial for pulse dialing.

Dial Speed (ms): This tells NetDial how fast to transmit phone number digits (as in, 555-5555) to your modem . The Dial Speed value is set in milliseconds (ms). This value can range between 15 – 95. A value may be entered by keyboard or by using the up/down arrows to the right of this box. If you use the up/down arrows, clicking the up arrow increases the value by 5; clicking the down arrow decreases the value by 5.

Timeout (Seconds): This tells NetDial how long (in seconds) to wait after dialing for a connection to be established. This value can range between 15 – 95. A value may be entered by keyboard or by using the up/down arrows to the right of this box. If you use the up/down arrows, clicking the up arrow increases the value by 5; clicking the down arrow decreases the value by 5.

Maximum Retries: This tells NetDial how many times to try and connect to the number it's dialing. If the line is busy, or if no dial tone is detected, or if there is no answer, NetDial attempts to make a connection up to the number of times specified in this box. Values can range from 0 – 99.

The value 0 instructs NetDial to retry until a connection is established. A value may be entered by keyboard or by using the up/down arrows to the right of this box. If you use the up/down arrows, clicking the up arrow increases the value by 1; clicking the down arrow decreases the value by 1.

Dial Delay (Seconds): This tells NetDial how long to wait (in seconds) for a dial tone before dialing. This value can range from 1 – 60. A value may be entered by keyboard or by using the up/down arrows to the right of this box.

If you use the up/down arrows, clicking the up arrow increases the value by 1; clicking the down arrow decreases the value by 1.

Configuration window (Call Settings)

A snapshot of NetDial's configuration window (Call Settings section) is displayed in Figure 19-4.

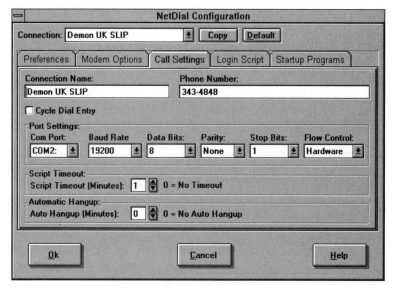

Figure 19-4: The NetDial Configuration window (Call Settings).

Refer to Figure 19-4 to understand the following descriptions:

Connection Name: Enter a name for the connection here. This text replaces the currently displayed name in the connection box if you choose to save your changes.

Phone Number: Enter the phone number for this connection here. The phone number can be preceded by call waiting disable commands. For example, you could enter ***70 555-5555**.

Cycle Dial Entry: Turning on this option allows this connection to be used with Cycle Dial. Turning off this option tells NetDial not to use this connection with Cycle Dial.

Cycle Dial calls each connection configured for Cycle Dial until a connection is established.

Com Port: This is the COM port selection listbox. Select the port that your modem is connected to.

Baud Rate: This is the baud rate listbox. Select a baud rate supported by your modem. Baud rates supported by NetDial are 110, 300, 600, 1200, 2400, 4800, 9600, 19200, 38400, 57600, 128000, and 256000.

Note: Baud rates above 57600 should work fine but could not be tested due to lack of appropriate hardware on the author's behalf. Therefore, if baud rates above 57600 do not work, drop it down to 57600!

Data Bits: This is the data bits listbox. Choices available are 7 and 8 data bits.

Parity: This is the parity listbox. Choices available are Even, Mark, None, Odd, and Space parity.

Stop Bits: This is the stop bits listbox. Choices available are 1 or 2 stop bits.

Flow Control: This is the flow control listbox. Choices available are hardware (CTS/RTS) and software (XON/XOFF) flow control.

Script Timeout (Minutes): This tells NetDial how long to wait (in minutes) for each command in the associated login script to complete.

- Setting this option to 0 disables script timeout (NetDial waits indefinitely to complete the login procedure).
- Setting a timeout value instructs NetDial to hang up if a command isn't executed within the number of minutes specified.

The Script Timeout value can range from 0 – 99. A value may be entered by keyboard or by using the up/down arrows to the right of the box. If you use the up/down arrows, clicking the up arrow increases the value by 1; clicking the down arrow decreases the value by 1.

Auto Hangup (Minutes): This tells NetDial how long to wait (in minutes) after a connection has been established before automatically hanging up. Setting this option to 0 disables auto hangup. This value can range from 1 – 95. A value may be entered by keyboard or by using the up/down arrows to the right of this box. If you use the up/down arrows, clicking the up arrow increases the value by 1; clicking the down arrow decreases the value by 1.

Configuration window (Login Script)

A snapshot of NetDial's configuration window (Login Script section) is displayed in Figure 19-5.

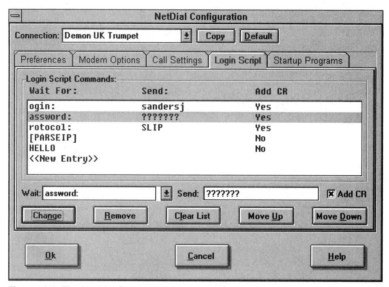

Figure 19-5: The NetDial Configuration window (Login Script).

Refer to Figure 19-5 to understand the following descriptions:

Login Script Commands list: This listbox contains the login script commands. The last entry in the listbox is always <<New Entry>>.

Select <<New Entry>> to add new entries, or select an existing entry to edit it. The command buttons directly below the listbox handle adding, editing, removing, and arranging the login script commands.

Wait text box: Enter word(s) that NetDial should wait for from the remote computer in this box. After NetDial receives the word(s) from the remote computer, it sends the word(s) specified in the Send box directly beside the matching Wait box.

If you want to send word(s) or a carriage return (CR) without waiting for anything, leave the Wait box empty and fill in the Send box and/or check the Add CR box. An example for this procedure would be if you need to send a CR on connect.

NetDial also has the following login script commands which can be entered or selected from the drop-down list:

- [PARSEIP] — To retrieve dynamic IP address
- [PARSEGATE] — To retrieve dynamic gateway address
- [SLEEP] x — Pause login for x (1 – 60) seconds

These commands are explained in greater detail in the next section, "Login script commands."

Send text box: Enter word(s) that NetDial should send to the remote computer once the matching Wait word(s) have been received.

Add CR: This option instructs NetDial to add a carriage return (CR) to the end of the Send line. If this option is turned off, the Send line will be sent without a CR.

Add button: This button works as an add/edit button. If you are entering a new login command line, it will read ADD. If you are editing an existing login command line, it will read CHANGE.

Clicking Add takes the information from the Wait box, Send box, and Add CR box, creates a new login command line, and adds it to the login script command list. Clicking Change takes the same information and updates the currently highlighted login command line.

Remove button: Click this button to remove the currently highlighted login command line from the listbox. If no login commands are defined, this button is disabled.

Clear List button: Click this button to remove all login commands from the listbox. If no login commands are defined, this button is disabled.

Move Up button: Click this button to swap the currently highlighted login command line in the listbox with the login command line directly above it. This button is enabled only if such a swap is possible.

Move Down button: Click this button to swap the currently highlighted login command line in the listbox with the login command line directly below it. This button is enabled only if such a swap is possible.

Login script commands

Besides wait/send login scripting, NetDial provides three login commands. These commands are as follows:

[PARSEIP]: This command is useful if your Internet host designates a different IP address for you every time you call, which is referred to as *Dynamic IP Addressing*. If you use Trumpet, NetDial automatically passes your IP address to TCPMAN when this command is used. To use this function, do the following:

■ In the Login Script section of the configuration window, enter **[PARSEIP]** as a Wait item (or select it from the drop-down list). Ensure that this command is placed in the appropriate area of the login script.

■ In the Startup Programs section of the configuration window, make TCPMAN.EXE your first start-up program.

Ensure that your TCPMAN setup has an IP address of 0.0.0.0

[PARSEGATE]: This command is useful if your Internet host designates a different gateway address for you every time you call. If you use Trumpet, NetDial automatically passes the gateway address to TCPMAN when this command is used. Set up this command in the same manner as [PARSEIP] above.

[SLEEP]: This command may be used to pause NetDial for a specific amount of time. One use for this command is to make NetDial wait a few seconds after connecting before sending any data (like a carriage return). To use this command, do the following:

In the Login Script section of the configuration window, enter **[SLEEP]** *x* (where *x* is a number from 1 – 60) as a Wait item (or select it from the drop-down list). Ensure that this command is placed in the appropriate area of the login script.

Configuration window (Startup Programs)

A snapshot of the NetDial Configuration window (Startup Programs section) is displayed in Figure 19-6.

Refer to Figure 19-6 to understand the following descriptions:

Startup Program(s) listbox: This listbox contains the start-up programs. Up to five start-up programs can be selected. If fewer than five programs are configured, the last entry in the listbox is <<New Entry>>.

Select <<New Entry>> in order to add new entries, or select an existing entry to edit it.

Start-up programs must be BAT, EXE, or COM files.

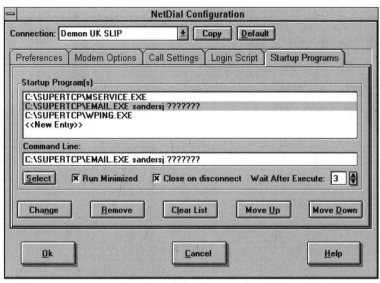

Figure 19-6: The NetDial Configuration window (Startup Programs).

The command buttons directly below the Startup Program(s) listbox handle adding, editing, removing, and arranging the start-up programs.

Command Line: Enter a program to run on this line. Any switches or parameters can also be appended to the program name. You can also use the Select button below to find and select a file.

Select button: Click this button to find and select a start-up program. The program selected is placed in the Command Line box. The Command Line box can then be edited to include any desired switches or parameters.

Run Minimized: If this option is turned on, the program currently highlighted in the listbox is run minimized (as an icon) upon successful login script completion. If this option is off, the program runs in its default window size.

Close on disconnect: If this option is turned on, the program currently highlighted in the listbox is shut down (closed) upon hangup or exit (if a session is in progress). If this option is off, the program has to be shut down manually before hangup or exit(if a session is in progress).

Wait After Execute: This tells NetDial how long to wait (in seconds) after executing the program currently highlighted in the listbox before executing the next start-up program. This value can range from 0 – 99. A value may be entered by keyboard or by using the up/down arrows to the right of the box.

If you use the up/down arrows, clicking the up arrow increases the value by 1; clicking the down arrow decreases the value by 1.

Add/Change button: This button works as an add/edit button. If you are entering a new start-up program, it reads Add. If you are editing an existing start-up program line, it reads Change.

Clicking Add takes the information from the Command Line box, Run Minimized box, Close on disconnect box, and Wait After Execute box, creates a new start-up program line, and adds it to the start-up programs list. Clicking Change takes the same information and updates the currently highlighted start-up program line.

One of your start-up programs should be your TCP/IP start-up program.

Also Note: There is a maximum limit of five start-up programs. If five programs have been selected, the <<New Entry>> line goes away, and only editing of existing start-up program entries is possible.

Remove button: Click this button to remove the currently highlighted start-up program from the listbox. If no start-up programs are defined, this option is disabled.

Clear List button: Click this button to remove all start-up programs from the listbox. If no start-up programs are defined, this button is disabled.

Move Up button: Click this button to swap the currently highlighted start-up program with the start-up program above it. This button is enabled only if such a swap is possible.

Move Down button: Click this button to swap the currently highlighted start-up program with the start-up program below it. This button is enabled only if such a swap is possible.

View NetDial Call Log window

A snapshot of the View NetDial Call Log window is displayed in Figure 19-7. Access this window by selecting File⇨View Log from NetDial's main window.

Refer to Figure 19-7 to understand the following descriptions:

Text window: The NetDial call log file is displayed in this text box. All standard editing functions are available.

Exit button: Click this button to exit the call log window and return to NetDial's main window. If you have made any changes to the log file, NetDial queries you to save your changes.

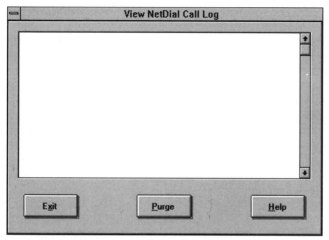

Figure 19-7: The View NetDial Call Log window.

Purge button: Click this button to purge the call log of all data.

Help button: Click this button to receive on-line help for NetDial's call log window.

NetDial Cumulative Timer Statistics window

A snapshot of NetDial's Cumulative Timer Statistics window is displayed in Figure 19-8. Access this window by selecting Options⇨Time To Date from NetDial's main window.

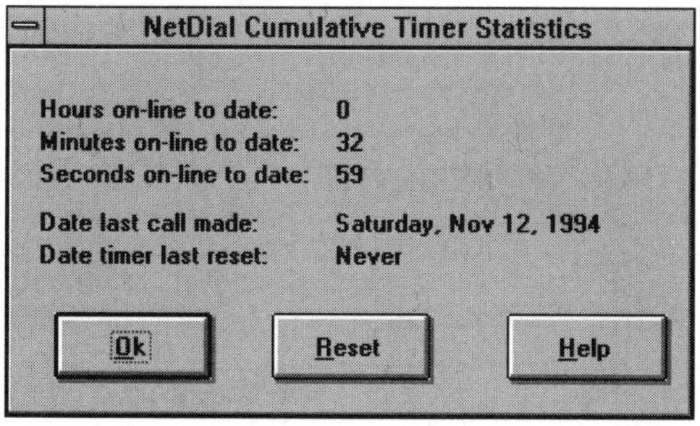

Figure 19-8: The NetDial Cumulative Timer Statistics window.

Refer to Figure 19-8 to understand the following descriptions:

Information display: The timer window details your total on-line time to date. Total hours, minutes, and seconds on-line are displayed here. The date of your last call and the date the timer was last cleared are also displayed.

OK button: Click this button to save any changes made and return to NetDial's main window.

Reset button: Click this button to reset the timer statistics. Hours, minutes, and seconds are reset to 0, Date last call made is set to Never, and Date timer last reset is set to the current date.

Help button: Click this button to receive help on NetDial's cumulative timer statistics window (the help topic you are currently viewing).

Command-line arguments

NetDial supports the following command-line arguments:

Numbers 1 through 5: The NetDial command line may be appended with a number from 1 – 5 (as in **C:\NetDial\NetDial.Exe 1**). The number instructs NetDial as to which connection to call. Thus, if you want, you can set up five NetDial icons (because only five configurations are possible), each with a different command-line argument. This command-line argument overrides the AutoDial On Startup selection.

CYCLE: The NetDial command line may be appended with the word *CYCLE* (as in **C:\NetDial\NetDial.Exe CYCLE**). The command tells NetDial to begin the Cycle Dial process — where all connections configured for Cycle Dial are called until a connection is established — on start-up. This command-line argument overrides the AutoDial On Startup selection.

Reference

Menu commands

To activate any of the menu bar menus, hold down the Alt key and press the underlined letter of the desired menu item. A drop-down list of choices for the selected menu item appears. The following is a breakdown of each top menu item:

File menu

Dial: This dials the number for the connection currently displayed in the connection listbox directly below the button bar.

Cycle Dial: This dials each connection configured for Cycle Dial until a connection is established.

Hang Up: This hangs up and resets the phone line.

View/Edit Call Log: This brings up NetDial's Call Log Viewer window where you can view/edit the log file.

Exit: This terminates your NetDial session.

Options menu

Configure: This invokes NetDial's Configuration window.

Time To Date: This invokes NetDial's Cumulative Timer Statistics window.

Help menu

Contents: This brings up NetDial's on-line help at the Table Of Contents.

Search for help on: This allows you to do a keyword search of NetDial's on-line help.

How to register: This brings up NetDial's on-line help at the Registration topic.

About NetDial: This brings up an information window about NetDial.

Keyboard shortcuts

Some of NetDial's commands may be executed by entering a simple key combination. These shortcuts are as follows:

File commands

Ctrl+D: Dial.

Ctrl+H: Hang Up.

Ctrl+V: View/Edit call log.

Ctrl+X: Exit NetDial.

Options commands

Ctrl+C: Invoke Configuration window.

Ctrl+T: Display Cumulative Timer Statistics (total time on-line to date) window.

Troubleshooting

You should have no problems whatsoever running NetDial. However, you should keep some things in mind. Following is a breakdown of potential problems and solutions:

TCP/IP Package won't run after connecting with NetDial

Your TCP/IP package must support a *direct line* option and be configured to operate as such.

Trumpet users: For Trumpet to support a direct line, you need to run TCPMAN and then select Options⇨Dialer⇨No automatic login. (A Trumpet Sampler is included in *Internet GIZMOS for Windows.* See Part II.)

Chameleon Sampler users: The Chameleon Sampler doesn't support a direct line option and thus is unusable with NetDial. To use NetDial with Chameleon, you need the full Chameleon package.

Chameleon users: Custom needs to be configured for No Modem, and all login script/phone number data must be removed prior to using NetDial. Also, when NetDial runs Custom, you still need to select Connect from Custom's menu.

The COM port settings for your TCP/IP package must match *exactly* how you have them set up in NetDial. For example, if you have call settings in NetDial configured for 19200 baud, 8 data bits, no parity, 1 stop bit, and hardware flow control, your TCP/IP package must be configured exactly the same.

Some TCP/IP packages support user-defined settings up to 19200 baud and also allow a *use win.ini* setting. With that in mind, there is a good chance that if you have your COM port set up for greater than 19200 baud in the Windows Control Panel, the TCP/IP package *downsizes* the baud rate to 19200. Therefore, you may want to set up your TCP/IP package using user-defined COM port settings and then set your NetDial settings the same.

Dynamic IP/Gateway Parsing problems

Currently, dynamic IP and gateway parsing *only* works with Trumpet. If someone can give information on how to make other packages handle dynamic
addressing, NetDial will be enhanced to accommodate them.

For dynamic addressing to work with Trumpet, run TCPMAN, select File⇨Setup,
and set the IP address to 0.0.0.0 before using NetDial.

NetDial reports "Com *x* not available" on dial

This message tells you that the COM port you are trying to use is *not* the COM
port that your modem is connected to. Change the COM port setting via the Call
Settings window.

NetDial reports "Could not initialize modem"

Make sure you have the right modem type selected. Modem type is set in the
Modem Options section of the NetDial Options window. If you have a Telebit
2500 modem, make sure you have `Telebit 2500` selected. Otherwise, use the
Hayes Compatible setting (default).

At the beginning of each dial attempt, NetDial sends the modem initialization
string (defined in the Modem Options section of the Netdial Options window) to
the modem. If the modem doesn't respond with an OK, you receive this message. Ensure that the modem initialization string defined works with your
modem and change if necessary.

NetDial won't exit or hang up

NetDial attempts to shut down any specified programs that were executed after
login (Startup Programs). If NetDial can't close these applications, they have to
be shut down manually. Any TCP/IP programs that were started manually have
to be shut down manually as well.

"Call To Undefined Dynalink" error message

It is very unlikely that you will see this error. But if you do, it means that you
have an old WINSOCK.DLL file (that isn't for the TCP/IP package you are
running) in your WINDOWS directory. When NetDial starts up your TCP/IP

package, it first looks for WINSOCK.DLL in your WINDOWS directory. If the file it finds isn't the right WINSOCK.DLL, NetDial displays the error and terminates. To fix this problem, remove *all* old WINSOCK.DLL files from your C:\WINDOWS and C:\WINDOWS\SYSTEM subdirectories.

"CTL3DV2.DLL not properly installed" error message

You receive this message if the file CTL3DV2.DLL is *anywhere* on your hard drive other than in your C:\WINDOWS\SYSTEM directory. Remove all instances of CTL3DV2.DLL from your hard drive(s) *except* for the one in your C:\WINDOWS\SYSTEM directory. If the file doesn't exist in your C:\WINDOWS\SYSTEM directory, put it there, and there *only.* This is not a "fatal" error message. NetDial still runs after displaying it, but you won't get lovely, stylish 3-D message/dialog boxes.

NetDial compatibility

This program has been thoroughly and successfully tested with the following TCP/IP packages:

- Frontier Technologies SuperTCP for Windows

- NetManage Chameleon

- Peter Tattam's Trumpet WinSock

Any TCP/IP package that supports a direct connection should be compatible with NetDial.

Technical Support

If by chance you *do* have problems with NetDial, and none of the preceding tips help or pertain to you, please feel free to contact me! I can be reached at the following e-mail addresses:

Internet mail: Sandersj@sandersj.demon.co.uk

CompuServe: 74640,3352

Any comments or suggestions about NetDial would be greatly appreciated.

NetDial Registration Form

Name _____

Company _____

Address _____

City _____

State _____ Country _____

Zip _____ Phone _____

Remit to:

In the United States:

James Sanders
NCTS PSC 802
Box 44FPO AE 09499-1200

In the United Kingdom:

James Sanders
49 West End Lane
Pinner, Middlesex
HA5 1BU

Pricing

❑ $20 (U.S.)
❑ £15 (U.K.)

Chapter 20
Finger 3.1: A Windows Sockets Finger Client

Finger 3.1 is a Windows Sockets finger client. Use Finger to query for users on a remote host. The Finger 3.1 distribution builds two finger clients: Finger and MFinger. These clients have the same user interface and differ only in their network interface. Finger uses Berkeley-style synchronous blocking calls, whereas MFinger uses the asynchronous Windows Sockets extensions. Table 20-1 describes the Finger 3.1 program files.

You can reach the author, Lee Murach, at lee@nrc.com, or via CompuServe at 71161,651.

Table 20-1	Program Files
File	*Description*
makefile	The make file for building the distribution.
finger.c	MFinger's user interface. This module processes all user input, and displays query results and errors.
dsplist.c	The display list module. This module lets the network module hand off the finger query results in a form meaningful to the user interface.
netwrkm.c	MFinger's network module. It isolates the network interface from the rest of the program and uses asynchronous WS calls to query the remote host.
netwrkb.c	Finger's network module. It has the same external call interface as netwrkm.c but uses Berkeley-style synchronous WS calls.
*.ico	*Dirty Bert,* or the finger icon. It is a matter of hysterical convention.
other.ico	Can be used in place of finger/mfinger.ico if you prefer a more conventional icon.
*.def	The .def file describes executable output to linker.
finger.dlg	Defines dialog boxes.
finger.rc	Specifies resources.
readme.*	You're reading a version of it now.
m/finger.exe	The executables.

Requirements

To run Finger, you need access to a remote host that runs a Finger server.

Because Finger dynamically links to the WinSock DLL and builds with the winsock.h, .def, and .lib files, you need a TCP/IP implementation that provides a Windows Sockets interface.

The 3.1 distribution was built with the Microsoft C/C++ 7.0 compiler and the Windows 3.1 SDK.

Release Notes

The netwrkm.c module now calls WSAAsyncSelect( ) with FD_READ | FD_CLOSE flags to detect the end-of-stream. Actually, the module considers the zero recv( ) return to definitively indicate end-of-stream.

Netwrkm.c now checks for the WSAEWOULDBLOCK error that connect( ) usually returns. It isn't actually an error but merely indicates that the connection request is still pending completion.

The host dialog now (optionally) queries for a user login ID, along with the host name/address.

The 3.0 MFinger would crash if given a host IP address. This problem has been fixed.

By default, the release now builds for Windows Sockets rev 1.1.

Chapter 21

WSFNGRD, Winsock Finger Daemon, Version 1.3

Tidewater Systems, Copyright (c) 1994

WSFNGRD is a shareware WinSock finger daemon for Microsoft Windows 3.11. It was developed in C and is based on my interpretation of RFC1288. Some of the code in WSFNGRD is based on source code published in *UNIX Network Programming* by W. Richard Stevens and *Programming Windows 3.1* by Charles Petzold.

Developers Ian Blenke and John A. Junod are also to be thanked for making their source code available, as it is an invaluable resource when trying to figure how things work in Windows.

This is a shareware product and as such you are free to use and evaluate the program for 30 days. At the end of the evaluation period, register the product or remove it from your system. See REGISTER.FRM, use the form at the end of this chapter, or see the registration topic in the help file for more details.

This archive may not be distributed in any commercial product without the express permission of Tidewater Systems. The copy of WFNGRD13.ZIP contains the following:

WSFNGRD.EXE

WSFNGRD.HLP

IDLE.DLL

FIXINI.EXE

WSFNGRD.TXT

REGISTER.FRM

LICENSE.TXT

Installing WSFNGRD

You install WSFNGRD by copying WSFNGRD.EXE, WSFNGRD.HLP, and IDLE.DLL to a subdirectory of your choice. Using Program Manager, create a new program item in a group of your choice.

The first time you run WSFNGRD, an INI file (WSFNGRD.INI) will be created in your WINDOWS directory. A dialog box will be presented for you to fill in the information returned when your machine is fingered.

To hide the WSFNGRD icon, add **h** to the command line field of the WSFNGRD property. When you're running WSFNGRD in the hidden mode, it will not be listed in the Windows task list. It will be, in effect, resident until you end the Windows session.

Setting Up the SERVER

To set up the SERVER, you need to select single-user or multiuser mode. In single-user mode, all finger requests are serviced with information about the *default user.* In multi user mode, each finger request is parsed, and if there is a user name match, then information about that user is returned.

In Plan File Directory, type in the full path for a directory in which *all* plan files will be kept (that is, C:\PLANFILE). This provides support for multiple users and maintains security.

In Log File, type in the full path and filename of the file to which you want finger requests logged (that is, C:\TEMP\FINGER.LOG). This file is made up of single line entries.

An entry is added for every finger request received. Each entry has the following information:

Date (in local format)

Time

The requesting machine's host name or IP address

The user that was fingered

Default plan

Type in the name of a default plan file to return in response to a finger request with no data when in multiuser mode. If you leave this line blank, the following message will be returned:

```
** specify user+@<hostname>
```

Default user

This is a list of users defined by you. The *user* selected here is used in single-user mode. It can be ignored if operating in multiuser mode. This list is empty until at least one user is defined.

Log finger requests

Toggle logging on/off.

Return Idle Time

Toggle Idle on/off.

Adding users

Fill in the field under User Setup: Username (required), Full Name, Email, Phone, Plan. Click the Add button to commit user information to disk. All fields, with the exception of Username, can be left blank. If a field is left blank, it will not be returned when a finger query is serviced.

Changing a user

Select the user from the Username list, update the user's information, and click the Change button. If you change the user name, WSFNGRD will not be aware of it and will actually create another user with the new user name. You then have to delete the old user name, as described in the following section.

Deleting a user

From the Username list, select the user that you want to delete. Click on the Delete button.

Limitations of WSFNGRD

This version services only one finger request at a time. Idle time will reset if idle for more than 49 days.

Bug Reports and Enhancement Requests

Send bug reports and enhancement requests to one of the addresses listed in the on-line help under "Contacting the Author."

Registration

You can choose from three ways to register this software. Print and fill out REGISTER.FRM from the program files, or if you prefer, photocopy the form at the end of this chapter. In either case, send the completed form with check or money order to the address listed on the form.

You can also register this product through the Shareware Register Forum on CIS (GO SWREG), #3421.

WSFNGRD Version 1.3 Registration Form

Name _____

Company _____

Address _____

City _____

State _____   Country _____

Zip _____   Phone _____

Remit to:

Tidewater Systems
207 Glen Avenue
Salisbury, MD 21801

Pricing:

❏ $10 (US) - single user
    MD residents add $.50 sales tax.

Chapter 22
X-Ray/WinSock, The WinSock Debugger

This software was developed and published by Systems Software Technology Inc., Charles Eaton,Copyright 1994. X-Ray/WinSock traces Windows Socket (WinSock) function calls.

Installing X-Ray/WinSock

Create a directory for X-Ray/WinSock, such as C:\XRAY. Unzip all the files contained in the ZIP file on the CD and place the files in the directory that you created. To run the X-Ray demonstration, select File⇨Run in the Program Manager and type **C:\XRAY\XRAYWINS**.

Compatibility

X-Ray has been tested with Novell WinSock 1.1, IBM TCP/IP for OS/2, and the shareware Trumpet WinSock version 1.0 Rev A. However, X-Ray fully complies with the Windows Sockets Specification 1.1, and should work with WinSock libraries from any vendor that adheres to that specification.

Product Modifications

Single files can be dragged from the Windows File Manager and dropped on the X-Ray window or the X-Ray icon. The specified EXE file launches when the trace is started.

The WINSOCK.HLP public domain is included with X-Ray/WinSock and has hypertext links to the API functions that appear in the trace log. By pressing Shift+F1 in the main window or clicking the Call button in the Details dialog box, you can get detailed help on that WinSock function.

Send and receive buffer display options can be specified by clicking the Buffers button in the Filters dialog box.

The Hide/Show Title Bar option has been removed from X-Ray. Any references to it in the manual or help file should be ignored.

Using X-Ray

The first time you run X-Ray/WinSock, use the following procedure:

1. Select Trace⇨Options to set your trace preferences. Alternatively, press Ctrl+O, or select the Trace icon in the toolbar. See the "Setting your trace preferences" section later in this chapter for more information.

2. Select Trace⇨Filters to set trace functions and tasks. Alternatively, press Ctrl+F, or select the Filters icon in the toolbar. See "Selecting filters" later in this chapter for more information.

When the menu bar appears, you can access help on any menu item. Highlight it and press F1.

The version of X-Ray for WinSock stores no more than the last 30 trace records. The monochrome, file, and printer log options in the Options dialog box are disabled. The WinSock help facility is disabled. All other features are fully functional.

This demonstration does not require WINSOCK.DLL on the system in order to execute, but without it, the demonstration won't amount to much.

Setting your trace preferences

To access the Trace Options dialog box, select Trace⇨Options, press Ctrl+O, or select the toolbar's Trace icon.

Setting output options

Trace log — Displays trace information to only a window.

Monochrome — For a monochrome monitor.

Display — This option is grayed if you do not have a monochrome video card installed in your computer.

Printer — Outputs trace information to your printer.

DBWin — Outputs trace information to DBWin, a sample debugger available with Microsoft Windows SDK and Microsoft C/C++ (Visual C++). This option also supports output to WinScope by Periscope. X-Ray is compatible with any program capable of displaying messages sent by the function `OutputDebugString( )`. This option can slow your system down if many trace events are being logged.

File — Outputs trace information to a log file. The default log file is C:\WINSOCK.LOG. You can enter another file in the Log File text box, or choose another log file by selecting the Browse button. The default is "Append to existing file," which appends new trace information to the log file you specify. If you deselect the default and run a trace or other function, the log file is deleted and a new file is created.

Log — Select this option if you want Exception to log WinSock 2 functions that are return errors only.

Level of detail — Select High to output information to a printer, DBWin, or the file you specified in the File option. Select Low to display only two lines of information to the Event Details dialog box.

Stop trace — Stops the trace when you activate the X-Ray activated window.

Setting the Log File — If you selected File in the Output Options field, and if you do not want to accept the default C:\WINSOCK.LOG, enter the name of the file to which you want trace information stored, or choose another log file by selecting the Browse button.

Setting buffer options

The number in parentheses below the Buffer Size option is the amount of memory in kilobytes.

Buffer Size — Enter the number of records, between 25 to 2000, that you want to buffer.

Circular — When the number of records is one more than the number you specified in the Buffer Size option, the buffer drops the oldest record, giving the appearance of an endless buffer. The larger the buffer size, the more records it can hold before losing the oldest record.

Stop when filled — The buffer stops accepting records when the number of records you specified in the Buffer Size option is reached. The trace is automatically stopped.

To set your preferences and exit the dialog box, click OK or press Enter.

Selecting filters

To set filters, select Trace⇨Filters, press Ctrl+F, or select the Filters icon in the toolbar. The Filters dialog box appears.

Selecting trace functions

Select the trace functions you want to run in the API Functions list box. To select all functions in the list box, select the Select All button. To cancel the functions you selected, select the Clear button. For more information about these functions, refer to the documentation that accompanies the WinSock API. X-Ray does not trace the WinSock function `WSAGetLastError( )`.

Selecting tasks

Select the applications for which you want trace information in the Active Application(s) list box. To select all tasks in the list box, select the Select All button. To cancel the tasks you selected, select the Clear button. Select "Launch specified application" to run a trace on an application that is not displayed in the Active application(s) list box. To select the application, click the Choose application button or enter the command line of the application.

Skip if **WSAWOULDBLOCK**

`WSAWOULDBLOCK` is returned when the `recv`, `recvfrom`, `send`, and/or `sendto` functions fail because no data could be received or sent. Select this option if you do not want `WSAWOULDBLOCK` logged.

Exiting the filters dialog box

To exit the dialog box without setting any filters, click Cancel. To set your filters and exit the dialog box, click OK or press Enter.

Running traces

After you have set your trace preferences and filters, you can run traces.

Starting a trace

To start a trace, select Trace⇨Start, press Ctrl+S, or select the Start icon in the toolbar.

Pausing a trace

To pause tracing, select Trace⇨Pause, press Ctrl+A, or select the Stop icon. Alternatively, if you selected the "Stop trace when activated" option in the Trace Options dialog box, tracing stops when you activate X-Ray/WinSock.

Viewing trace event details

To see trace event details, select Trace⇨Event Details, double-click a trace record in the X-Ray/WinSock window, press Ctrl+E, or select the Details icon in the toolbar. The Event Details dialog box appears. It can remain on the screen as long as the trace buffer is not cleared. To clear the trace buffer, select the Clear icon or select Trace⇨Reset Events.

Using the Event Details dialog box

The Event Details dialog box contains a window that shows the specified trace's detail. You can specify the trace for which you want more detail by double-clicking on a trace record in the X-Ray window, or by entering a number in the Record text box and pressing the Get button. Alternatively, you can scroll through the list box or select the Animate button to view other records.

The following information is displayed for every trace detail:

A summary of the function, including record number, function, and the time it was called.

Parameters Before Call — Parameters in the code before the function is executed.

Returns — Error codes or values WinSock returns.

Parameters After Call — Values that WinSock may have changed.

Close button — Click this button to close the dialog box.

Help button — Click this button for help on the dialog box.

Start button — Click this button if you want to automate scrolling through the detail list box. To set the animation delay, enter the number of seconds delay in the seconds text box.

Speed — Enter a number from 1 to 15. The higher the number, the slower the animation (that is, automated scrolling through the detail list box). The range of values equates to .2 through 3 seconds. To start animation, select the Animate key.

Errors Only — Select this option if you want to view error messages while animation is enabled.

Backwards — Select this option if you want to animate backwards.

Find button — Click this button to find a record. The Find dialog box appears. You can search by any numeric or alphabetic characters. If you search alphabetically, you can do a case-sensitive search by selecting the Match Case option. You can also search up or down through records.

Get button — Click this button to retrieve details for a trace you specify in the Record text box. The record is the first field that is displayed in the X-Ray window. You can also use the scroll buttons to scroll backward and forward through record numbers.

Errors scroll buttons — Select these scroll buttons to scroll backward and forward through errors.

Continuing a trace

Select Trace⇨Continue after you have stopped/paused the trace to save the current trace and continue tracing events.

Clearing the trace log and buffer

Select Trace⇨Reset Events or the Clear icon to clear all events from the trace log and buffer. If you select this command or the Clear icon, and the Event Details dialog box is displayed, the dialog box closes.

Tips

Tracing Borland Turbo Pascal for Windows applications: When an API error is detected, the Stack Trace listbox has only one entry. This happens because Borland manipulates the stack in a nonstandard way. Borland C/C++ programs do not behave this way.

Tracing applications with large send and receive buffers: X-Ray consumes much more memory when you trace applications that send and receive data in large packet sizes (2048, 4096, and so on.). To minimize memory usage, click the Advanced button in the Filters dialog box. Set a limit for buffer sizes, or turn off the buffer display altogether. Alternatively, you can set the trace buffer size to a smaller value, typically half the current buffer size.

Level of detail settings (Options dialog box): Remember that this option does not change the format of the X-Ray main window. This option affects either the File or Printer output options.

OS/2 Users: If you want to debug a Windows application running on the OS/2 desktop, the application must be launched by X-Ray itself so that X-Ray and the Windows application share the same memory space. OS/2 creates a separate instance of Windows for each application that is launched from the OS/2 desktop.

X-Ray/WinSock Registration Form

Name _____

Company _____

Address _____

City _____

State _____ Country _____

Zip _____ Phone _____

Remit to:

Systems Software Technology, Inc.
Dept. CS
5727 Canoga Ave., #283
Woodland Hills, CA 91367

Pricing

☐ $79.95

Please call or e-mail for information about other products, 818-346-2784, sstinc@netcom.com.

Part VI

World Wide Web Tools and GIZMOS

The World Wide Web (also known as theWeb, WWW, or W3) is, like the Internet itself, a collection of thousands of computers around the world, each linked in some way with another. Quoting from one description of the World Wide Web project:

> From http://info.cern.ch/hypertext/WWW/TheProject.html

> The World Wide Web (W3) is the universe of network-accessible information, an embodiment of human knowledge. It is an initiative started at CERN, now with many participants. It has a body of software, and a set of protocols and conventions. W3 uses hypertext and multimedia techniques to make the web easy for anyone to roam, browse, and contribute to. Future evolution of W3 is coordinated by the W3 Organization.

> Everything there is to know about W3 is linked directly or indirectly to this document.

Lately, not only has the W3 been an "embodiment of human knowledge," it is also becoming an "embodiment of all advertising"! Much of the recent growth in the W3 is from the addition of thousands of company sites promoting their products and services. The good news in all of this is that it is up to you to go to the W3 site you are interested in — these companies don't come pestering you.

On the CD-ROM, there is one sample viewer for the W3, AIR Mosaic Express, in the SPRY Internet Applications Sampler in Part II. You can choose from many more that are not on the CD-ROM, including the free NCSA Mosaic. You will also find LView Pro 1.8 an add-on graphics viewer, and WHAM, an add-on sound player, in this part of the book.

NCSA Mosaic

The original client program for accessing the W3 is *Mosaic,* developed by the University of Illinois, Urbana-Champaign by the National Center for Supercomputing Applications. The NCSA has released freeware versions of Mosaic for Windows workstations, the Apple Macintosh, and many types of UNIX-based workstations. In addition, the source code for the Windows version has been licensed to a number of companies who have added their own touches to the basic program. SPRY's AIR Mosaic is an example of this. NCSA still owns a piece of each copy of the software sold, so whenever SPRY (or anyone) sells or gives away a copy of a commercial version of Mosaic, a royalty goes to NCSA.

The viewers for W3 are evolving quickly, and none of them are perfect the way they are. If we had included a bunch of them on the CD-ROM, by the time you got it, the versions would probably be obsolete.

So instead, we've provided a sample copy of AIR Mosaic — AIR Mosaic Express — that you can get started with.The following section lists places to pick up more samples, as well as fully functional freeware W3 viewers.

World Wide Web Viewers for Windows _____

This section describes where to get other World Wide Web viewers for Windows.

Mosaic for Windows: The original Mosaic. Requires Windows 95, Windows NT, or win32s with Windows 3.x. It comes with a great getting-started list of "hot" sites.

ftp site:	ftp://ftp.ncsa.uiuc.edu
directory:	/WEB/MOSAIC/WINDOWS
information:	http://www.ncsa.uiuc.edu/SDG/Software/WinMosaic/HomePage.html

Netscape for Windows: A very fine W3 viewer not based on Mosaic code. A multithreaded-like connection scheme allows you to start reading the document before everything is loaded; no initial hotlist.

ftp site:	ftp://ftp.mcom.com
directory:	/PUB/NETSCAPE/WINDOWS
information:	http://mosaic.mcom.com/MCOM/products_docs/index.html

EINet WinWeb: Stable viewer that comes with some support programs; no initial hotlist.

ftp site:	ftp://ftp.einet.net
directory:	/EINET/PC/WINWEB
information:	http://galaxy.einet.net

SPRY AIR Mosaic: W3 Viewer with great user interface, built in support for DDE and a full-screen mode. The best initial hotlist around. The demonstration program included with this book — AIR Mosaic Express — is limited to six URLs per invocation.

ftp site:	ftp://ftp.spry.com
directory:	/VENDOR/SPRY/DEMO/AIRMOSAICDEMO
information:	http://www.spry.com

Spyglass: The commercial version of Mosaic, this product is available only through certain OEMs. You'll see this product popping up at various corporations and in their products.

information:	http://www.spyglass.com

Great! I've installed a W3 viewer. I'm done, right?

Well, that depends! None of the viewers in the preceding list contains every tool you'll need to access every document on the W3. There are a variety of document types to view on the W3. There are several different types of audio, video, graphics, and picture files. Some viewers handle the common types internally, but all of them require some type of support for viewing special file types. For your convenience, we've included two viewers in this book/CD package, LVIEWP18.EXE and WHAM.EXE, which are covered in Chapters 24 and 25. At the end of this section, we've listed a few more viewers that should put you well on your way to viewing all the common document types.

 You can get started without any special viewers. Most W3 documents are supported entirely by the W3 viewers, so go ahead and get started — you can add the special viewers as you find you need them.

Some common types of files and viewers for Windows are

Audio WAV files	WPLANY.EXE, WHAM.EXE
Audio AU files	WPLANY.EXE, WHAM.EXE
PostScript files	GSWIN.EXE with GSVIEW.EXE
Video MPEG	MPEGPLAY.EXE
Picture JPEG	LVIEWP18.EXE
Graphics GIF	LVIEWP18.EXE
Graphics TIFF	LVIEWP18.EXE
Movie QuickTime	QuickTime Viewer
Graphics BMP	LVIEWP18.EXE

All of these are available through the NCSA server. Go to the

```
http://www.ncsa.uiuc.edu/SDG/Software/WinMosaic/viewers.html
```

for pointers to each of the viewers mentioned. Once you put the viewers on your computer, you update the initialization information for the W3 viewer you are using.

HTML: The HyperText Markup Language

The World Wide Web is based on a special language called the Hypertext Markup Language, or HTML for short. Actually, calling HTML a language is a bit of an overstatement. It is really a way of taking plain text and adding some special control strings that tell the W3 viewer how to display the text. The SPRY W3 home page (see chapter 5 for a figure SPRY's home page), located at http://www.spry.com, was created by the following HTML code:

```
<HTML>
<HEAD>
<TITLE>SPRY World Wide Web Services</TITLE>
</HEAD>
<BODY>
<IMG SRC="http://www.spry.com/sprylgo.gif">
<P>
<p>
<H1>World Wide Web Products and Services</H1>
```

```
<p>
<b><i>SPRY, Inc.</b> is a leading provider of transport-
independent connectivity applications for personal computers
that enable consumers and corporations to easily take
advantage of the power of on-line communications.
</i><hr><i><b>What's New (updated 11/16/94)...
</b><i><p>SPRY's <b>AIR Mosaic Express</b> has been chosen
as Mecklerweb's <b>publishing interface</b> to the World
Wide Web. Read the <a href="http://www.spry.com/
mos_meck.html">press release</a>.<p><h5><img align=middle
src="http://www.spry.com/mosexbmp.gif"><b>SPRY Releases New,
Improved Version of AIR Mosaic Express</b></h5>
<p>
SPRY has released a new version <b>AIR Mosaic Express</b>
for Windows.  Version 1.1 offers World Wide Web users
additional functionality, greater speed and improved
stability.  You may view instructions on <b><a href="http://
www.spry.com/download.html">how to download a demonstration
copy</a></b> of Version 1.1, or <b><a href="http://
www.spry.com/upgrade.html">how to obtain a free upgrade
</a></b> for an existing installation of AIR Mosaic Express
Version 1.0.  You can also find answers to <a href="http://
www.spry.com/mofaqs.html"><b>frequently asked questions</b>
(FAQs)</a> about AIR Mosaic Express.</h5>
<h5><b><a href="http://www.spry.com/choice.html"><img
align=middle src="http://www.spry.com/pcmag.gif"></a>SPRY
Wins Editors' Choice Award for Internet Tools</b>
</h5><p><p>In its October 11th issue devoted to Internet
connectivity, <i>PC Magazine</i> chose SPRY's AIR NFS prod-
uct as its top pick among eight tools reviewed.  Read the
<a href="http://www.spry.com/choice.html">full text</a> of
their review.
<p>
<b><i>Also...</i></b>
<p>
SPRY announces point-and-click access to the Internet with
the release of <b>Internet In a Box&#153 </b>, combining the
easy access of an on-line service with the full resources of
the Internet.  Read the <a href="http://www.spry.com/spry/
Press/iboxpr.html">press release</a>, or get answers to
<a href="http://www.spry.com/intabox.html">frequently asked
questions</a> about the product.</h5>
<p>
<HR>
```

If the picture of this screen were transmitted as a bitmap, there would be about 280,000 bytes of information to send. As an HTML document, the amount of information is 2,247 bytes of HTML text, plus another 17,600 bytes for the graphics. Even with the rather large graphics files, this is still a significant reduction in the amount of information.

Picky persons note: Okay, so the graphics image of the entire screen shown could be compressed down to about 16,000 bytes total, which is less than the sum of the parts, but in the HTML version, there is additional information about the meaning of the various parts of the page, plus the hypertext information.

Without spending a lot of time going through each part of the HTML text, you can quickly take a look at the markup to see that paragraphs are marked with a <p>, italics with a <i>, hypertext links with a <a>, and so on. Take special note of the <a> anchor markup, which creates a hypertext link. This markup encloses the text that is underlined in the displayed image, and includes the URL (Uniform Resource Locator) that gives the destination of a jump if you click on the underlined text. Because the URL can point to any computer, anywhere, you can see how easy it is to jump all over the globe from a single W3 page.

Images are included by reference, too, which is why you can turn "inline images" off: the viewer reads the text first and then goes back to get the graphics if you want it to.

Even though this isn't very complicated, there are plenty of references available to help you understand HTML. For starters, check out:

`http://www.ncsa.uiuc.edu/General/Internet/WWW/HTMLQuickRef.html`

for a quick overview;

`http://www.ncsa.uiuc.edu/demoweb/html-primer.html`

for a tutorial, and:

`http://info.cern.ch/hypertext/WWW/MarkUp/MarkUp.html`

for the HTML reference.

Creating your own HTML pages

Many of the service providers have given their users the ability to add *home pages* to their own computer. All you need to do is create an HTML page with all the elements you want. Fortunately, there are several HTML editors available that can help you do this! In this part of the book and CD-ROM, we've provided four solutions for creating HTML: CU_HTML, a template add-on for Word for Windows 2.0; and three self-contained HTML editors: SoftQuad HoTMetaL, HTML Assistant, and HTML Writer. These three programs have vastly different user interfaces, so give them each a try and see what you think.

In addition to creating the HTML text for a home page, you may want to include pictures, graphics, or audio. There are two tools included in this part, LViewPro for images and WHAM for sound files that can be used to edit and convert from formats you may have on your Windows PC into the popular W3 formats. The most common format for Audio on the World Wide Web is the AU file format, and inline images are always GIF files. Be very careful what raw material you use, because most anything you find that you didn't create yourself is already copywritten, which means you'll have to get permission to use it. Also, don't put really big graphics inline, since anyone with a slow link (like a modem) will wait forever to open your page.

Running your own HTTP Server

HTTP servers are the systems that are W3 hosts. HTTP is the *Hyper-Text Transfer Protocol* that delivers HTML pages to callers. If you think you'd like to try this, see Part IX.

Chapter 23
HTML Editor GIZMOS

Keeping an accurate record of Internet journeys is not a trivial task. In fact, one of the major criticisms about using the Internet is that information is not well organized, and it is therefore difficult to retrace your steps if you want to repeat a search. Many (if not most) Internet users find themselves using computers to scan the Internet for information while keeping a pencil and paper at hand so that they can make notes about the places they have been.

Some Gopher and WWW browser packages permit saving place markers by using *bookmarks* or a *hotlist* to collect address information. As useful as these are, after several searches or browse sessions, these collections quickly become a potpourri of tags, markers, and pointers to a varied assortment of Internet places that have no particular relationship to each other.

What Is a URL?

URL is an abbreviation for *Uniform Resource Locator*. URLs are the pointers to information in a hypertext link. They tell the browser how to obtain information and where it is located.

URLs enable a single WWW browser program to incorporate many of the functions that normally require several other software packages, including FTP, news, e-mail, and Gopher.

 The general format of a URL is *prefix host.domain[:port]/path/filename*. The space after the word *prefix* is used only for clarity. In a URL, there is no space following the prefix.

The port number may be omitted from the URL, unless it differs from the recognized standard port for the indicated service. Table 23-1 describes some commonly used URL prefixes, along with their functions.

Table 23-1	Commonly Used URL Prefixes
URL Prefix	**Function**
ftp://	Retrieves a file from an FTP server.
http://	Retrieves a file from a World Wide Web server.
file://localhost/	Retrieves a file that resides on the same computer as the browser; a *local* file.
gopher://	Retrieves a file from a Gopher server.

The following URLs do not use the double slash (//) in their prefix:

URL Prefix	**Function**
mailto:	Requests the browser to enable the transmission of an e-mail message.
news:	Retrieves a Usenet news message.

The following are examples of properly constructed URLs:

```
ftp://ftp.cs.dal.ca/htmlasst/htmlasst.zip
```

The preceding URL is used in an HTML document to enable a browser to retrieve the file HTMLASST.ZIP from an FTP site.

```
file://localhost/c:/www/myfile.txt
```

The preceding URL causes the browser to retrieve and display the file MYFILE.TXT from the user's local disk drive. And finally, the following URL

```
http://www.cfn.cs.dal.ca/Media/News/TodaysNews.html
```

results in the retrieval and display of an HTML file from a WWW server.

Collecting URLs

World Wide Web browsers use URLs to find and access all forms of information on the Internet — including text files, newsgroups, mailing lists, Gopher directories, HTML documents, program files, images, sounds, movies, and so on.

To use *HTML Assistant* as an aid to organizing your WWW experience, you first need to begin collecting the URLs that point to the WWW sites that interest you.

Two MS Windows browsers, *Cello* and *Mosaic*, both permit transferring the URLs they use for Internet access to the Windows Clipboard. From the Clipboard, they can easily be copied to any Windows text editor.

With Cello, use the mouse to point at a link on Cello's main display page, and then click the mouse to bring up a dialog that will permit you to copy the link's HTML code to the Clipboard.

 Mosaic has a URL text display that can be copied by selecting the text (using the mouse and dragging across it) and pressing Control+C — the standard Windows key sequence for copying text to the Clipboard. Later versions may also include a copy function in one of the menus. A version of SPRY's AIR Mosaic is included in this book/CD package. See Chapter 5, "SPRY Internet Applications Sampler," for more information.

After the URL text is on the Clipboard, the text can be pasted into a text file using a simple text editor like *MS Notepad* (supplied with Windows) or *HTML Assistant*. Be sure that there is an end-of-line following the URL. An *end-of-line* is a carriage-return/linefeed pair added when you press Enter after inserting text. That is all that is required to begin collecting URL links for use by HTML editing tools.

HoTMetaL

SoftQuad HoTMetaL is a freely distributed professional SGML editor especially for HTML files.

The version of HoTMetaL included in *Internet GIZMOS for Windows* is a public domain edition and is an entry-level tool for creating HTML World Wide Web compatible compound documents. SoftQuad will not provide support for HoTMetaL 1.0. You are encouraged to upgrade to HoTMetaL Professional, SoftQuad's commercial edition. If you want to upgrade to SoftQuad HoTMetaL Pro, contact SoftQuad Inc. at

SoftQuad Inc.
56 Aberfoyle Crescent
Toronto, Ontario
CANADA M8X 2W4

Phone: +1 416 239 4801
Fax: +1 416 239 7105

Mail: hotmetal@sq.com — for HoTMetaL
sales@sq.com — for other products

Installing HoTMetaL

HoTMetaL requires at least 4MB of Windows 3.1 memory, although 8MB is recommended. You will also need 5MB of memory to successfully install the documentation in PostScript as PS files on the book's CD. Printed in PostScript, the manual is approximately 60 pages. The HoTMetaL installation creates a directory called HOTMETAL, but you can move this directory to anywhere on your configuration. From the \HOTMETAL directory, type **hotmetal**, which unpacks the archive.

After you have unpacked the HoTMetaL archive, you can run the executable by changing to the \HOTMETAL\BIN directory and clicking SQHM.EXE. To set up a Program Manager icon, use this SQHM.EXE as the command executable, but make your default directory C:\HOTMETAL.

For the purposes of making the HoTMetaL editor as productive as possible, I suggest that you associate files with the extension HTM with the SQHM executable in the \HOTMETAL\BIN directory. This lets you load an HTML file directly into HoTMetaL if HoTMetaL is currently loaded, or launch HoTMetaL with the associated selected HTML document. Obviously, you may not want to associate HTM extension files if you already associate HTML files with Mosaic or another WEB browser.

HTML Assistant — Freeware Version _____

Copyright ©1993,1994, by Howard Harawitz and Brooklyn North Software Works.

HTML Assistant is a freeware HTML editor developed in Visual Basic. You are not obligated to register or pay any fee for personal use. A full commercial version, HTML Assistant Pro, is available from the developers.

The author, Howard Harawitz, and Brooklyn North Software Works disclaim any liability for special, direct, indirect, incidental, consequential or any other damages believed to have been caused by the use of HTML Assistant or any files derived from its use.

Users of HTML Assistant are encouraged to contact the author, Howard Harawitz, with suggestions, support questions, and news about upgrades/new versions of HTML Assistant Pro by e-mail at *harawitz@fox.nstn.ns.ca* or by telephone/fax at (902) 835–2600.

What is HTML Assistant?

HTML Assistant is a text editor with extensions to assist in the creation of HTML hypertext documents. HTML Assistant also includes many special functions that help you to organize the information you gather during your Internet experiences, and to keep track of URLs, the pointers to information that you discover on the World Wide Web.

The version of HTML Assistant on this book's CD features:

- Context-sensitive help for all menu items and controls through F1.

- Dynamic status bar with command indicators for all controls and menus.

- An *emulation mode* to test and view your work with WWW browsers of your choice at the click of the mouse — without leaving the editor.

- Full support for Windows MDI (multiple document interface), allowing for multiple file-editing and browsing.

- Inclusion of special HTML Assistant URL example files for organizing and quickly combining URLs from different sources — including Cello bookmarks, NCSA Mosaic menus, and hotlists.

- A unique URL Editor that permits rapid editing and compilation of URLs from any number of these sources.

- Automatic one-step conversion of HTML Assistant URL files, Cello bookmarks, and Mosaic INI files to HTML text.

- User-defined toolkits with the capability to save user-defined tools to files for repeated access.

- Support for automatic conversion of UNIX text files to DOS text files.

- Option of straight printing of text.

See the section titled "What is HTML Assistant Pro?" for information on the features in HTML Assistant Pro.

You can subscribe to the *HTML Assistant Newsletter,* a free e-mail newsletter that includes announcements, bug reports, and new version updates and tips submitted by the program's author and users. The newsletter also covers general-interest news items on learning HTML, new WWW sites, commentary on the Web, and customer feedback. To subscribe, send e-mail with the word *subscribe* in the *Subject:* field to *harawitz@fox.nstn.ns.ca.* You may also include comments or suggestions in the text field of your message.

Using HTML Assistant for your Web activities

If you are serious about using the World Wide Web, you can save URLs by creating bookmarks (if you are using Cello) or adding to the *hotlist* (if you are using Mosaic). *HTML Assistant*'s *URL file editor* permits you to convert Cello bookmark files and URLs collected in Mosaic's menus and hotlists to *HTML Assistant URL files. HTML Assistant* makes it easy to create URL files that combine information collected with both browsers.

 Files containing URLs should be saved with the extension URL. Although this isn't absolutely necessary, it does make it easier for you (and HTML Assistant) to identify URL files.

Editing and organizing URLs

After you have collected URLs that point the way to the places you have visited, the next step is to select and organize the URLs into separate files that suit your particular needs. For example, you may want to create a file containing URLs that can help you learn about Internet resources, interesting art exhibits, or animal breeding.

HTML Assistant provides two ways to organize your URLs. Use whichever works best for you:

- The most familiar way for most people is to open a new edit window (by selecting File⇨New) for each subject and then copy and paste the selected URLs (and their optional comments) from your general URL collection or other URL files to the new one. Figure 23-1 shows a new edit window.

- The second method involves using the URL file edit pop-up window (Figure 23-2) that can be viewed by selecting Edit/Build URL Files from the URL menu. This enables you to combine commented URLs from different sources and to use scrolling lists for editing.

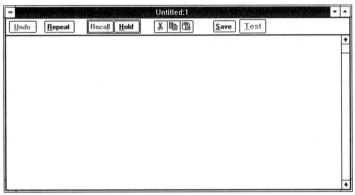

Figure 23-1: HTML Assistant new edit window.

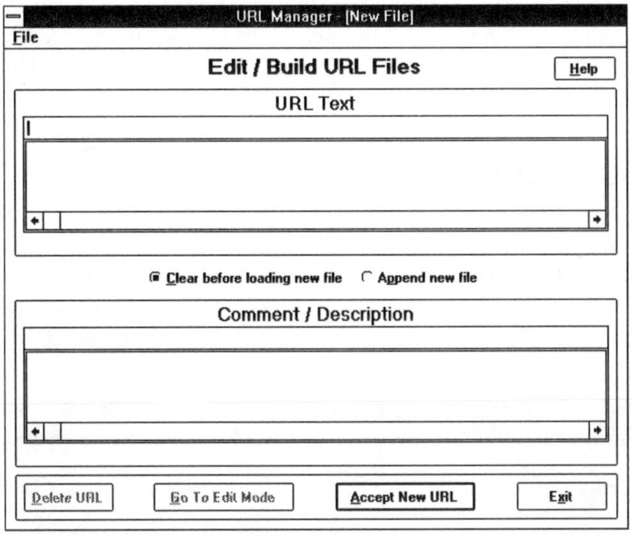

Figure 23-2: URL file edit pop-up window.

Building browser pages

The URLs you have collected are pointers to the places you visited on your Internet journeys. The final step in organizing your personal Internet experience is to incorporate selected URLs into HTML documents to be used as WWW browser pages. These pages become tour guides for you, and others, to retrace your steps. With HTML Assistant, you can easily create browser pages with titles, headings, descriptive text, and hypertext links to Internet resources.

HTML Assistant can quickly convert URL files to HTML hypertext links. For information on how to do this, see the section titled "Direct conversion of files to HTML text."

Using HTML Assistant tools and editing functions, you can easily format your links into formatted lists (numbered or unnumbered), intersperse them with descriptive text, and create headers in various sizes and styles to highlight your page.

HTML Assistant Pro includes an *automatic page creator* that makes this part of the job very easy. It guides you through the process of creating a title, headings, and descriptive text for your page, and enables you to incorporate a list of URLs (from a file of your choice) which becomes the links to the places you want to visit. With the click of a button, your new page is automatically created and displayed in an edit window. All you have to do is save it as an HTML document.

Using local files with HTML

As you create your own HTML files with links to remote sites, you may also want to create other browser pages consisting of links to these local files. By doing this with successive generations of locally created files, you can create a hierarchical system of *menu pages* for organizing and indexing your work.

For example, you could build separate files (with remote links) about the following subjects:

Using HTML

WWW and related FAQs

Selected sites via CERN

You may want to create a menu file concerned with general WWW topics that includes the previous files as selectable links.

Creating a menu page

You can build such a file one step at a time, as described here:

1. Open a new edit window and create a local file link for each file using the Link button. When the Link pop-up appears, select the FILE://LOCALHOST/ prefix from the prefix listbox.

2. Enter the name of a file or use the Browse button to select a filename from a File Select dialog box.

3. Click OK (on the Link pop-up). HTML Assistant will create the URL (and insert it in the edit window) for a link to the file you selected. It looks something like the following line:

```
file://localhost/C:/html/myfile.htm
```

You can continue in this manner to add additional URL links. Using HTML Assistant's list formatting capability, you can select and format the file links as one or more lists (numbered or unnumbered).

4. When the process of adding and formatting file links is finished, you can complete your menu page by using HTML Assistant's HTML formatting tools to add a title, headers, and explanatory text.

Overview of HTML's menus

Not all menus or menu options are visible upon start-up. The menu bar and the contents of most menus change when at least one document window is open. To view all the menus, open a file or a new document.

HTML Assistant's menus may seem formidable at first. There are a number them, and each one presents many options.

Although this bewildering array of choices may seem confusing at first, after you become familiar with the menu structure, you will learn that the menus present many opportunities for you to simplify and speed up the creation of your HTML documents.

Many of the options, such as those in the File and Edit menus, will already be familiar to you because they are found in commonly used word processors and text-editing software.

The fastest way to learn any of the menu options is to try them. Just be sure that you have a backup copy of the document with which you are experimenting.

While learning, you can use the Hold button on the text window to keep a snapshot copy of the current state of your document. Clicking the Recall button brings it back, just as it was immediately before you decided to hold it. The next section is devoted to explaining how to use the menu features that are unique to the creation of HTML documents with HTML Assistant.

Tips for using HTML Assistant

Inserting a file at the cursor: This permits you to load and insert an existing HTML document wherever your cursor is on the blank page. Great for using predefined boilerplate text throughout your pages (e-mail addresses and FTP sites).

Set test program name: One of HTML Assistant's unique features is the capability to designate your favorite Windows-based browser to autoload the open document on which you are working, without leaving HTML Assistant. You designate which browser using the File⇨Set Test Program dialog box. Completing all the path information allows you to set this browser as your permanent test program browser.

HTML Assistant comes preconfigured for Cello's DDE: Using the options menu, you can designate Cello as your test browser for your HTML pages. The program uses a DDE command to activate or launch Cello with the loaded HTML page for viewing. After Cello is loaded, you do not have to close Cello to test other pages.

Unfortunately, Cello does not always refresh itself if your file is changed. Changes to your open document are not reflected in Cello. Use Cello's reload document to refresh the document.

Autosave file before test: If you choose Options⇨Autosave Before Testing, your work is saved before it is tested. New files must be saved manually before they are tested the first time.

Configure paragraph button: This selection in the Options menu displays a submenu with choices to insert HTML newlines in the text whenever the button that inserts a new paragraph tag is clicked. This option affects how your text is displayed only in the editor, not in the browser.

Use lowercase HTM: If you have text selected and you choose this option, all text in HTML markings becomes lowercase. HTML is not case sensitive, so you have the option of working in all uppercase or all lowercase.

Default font: This option permits selection of the font and font characteristics (bold, font size, and so on), which are used as the default for all new text windows. The font for text in an individual window that is already displayed can be changed by using the Font (current window only) command on the Edit menu.

Custom User Tools menu: HTML Assistant features options for customizing the various tools available to you when editing an HTML document. The User Tools menu allows you to customize the tools you can invoke from the menu for quick access.

Hide lower toolbar: Selecting and deselecting this option toggles the display of the main window's lower toolbar, or button bar. The small button at the right end of the main toolbar (with a *T* on it) performs the same function.

Creating formatting links: One can create custom-formatted links in HTML Assistant as follows: Suppose you have a WWW link *www.nsac.ns.ca/,Agricultural College Site.* This would be converted to <A HREF="www.nsac.ns.ca/">Agricultural College Site</A>. Note the comma (",") separating the URL from the clickable text in the original line. This comma is required, unless there is no clickable text.

Autoconvert file to HTML: This option brings up a submenu with options for selecting file types from which URLs and their associated clickable text are automatically converted to HTML text. The HTML text is displayed in a document window. You may convert URLs from Cello bookmark files, AIR Mosaic's MOSAIC.INI file, or HTML Assistant format .URL files.

HTML Assistant editing and tools

HTML Assistant's tools can be accessed by means of two toolbars at the top of the program's main window. There is also a menu item labeled HTML that permits the insertion of HTML tags. The top toolbar is always visible. The lower one, called the *button bar,* can be hidden by clicking the small button marked *T* in the lower-right corner of the upper toolbar. The button is a toggle. Clicking again restores the lower toolbar. Figure 23-3 shows both toolbars.

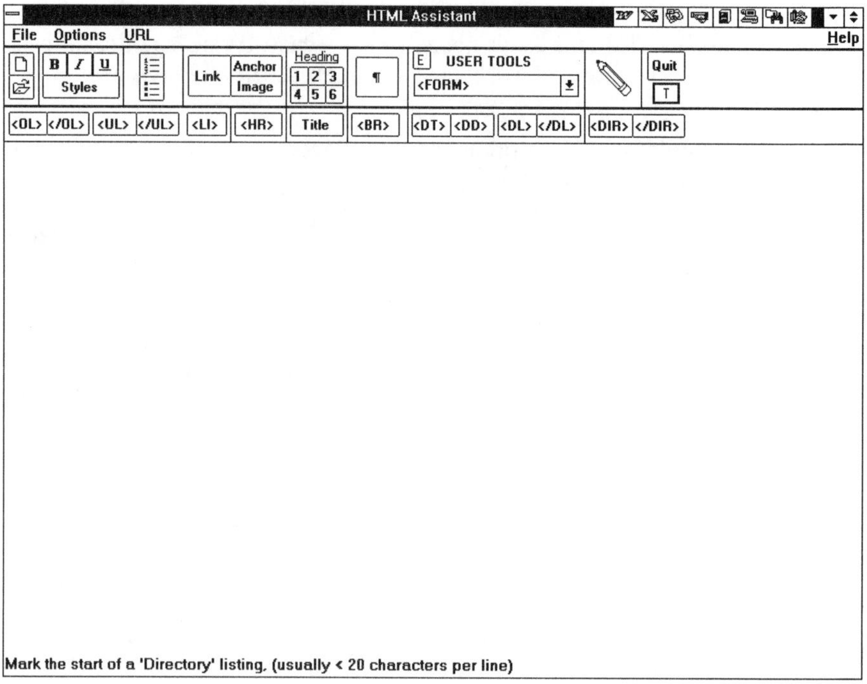

Figure 23-3: HTML Assistant toolbars.

The tools are basically of two types:

- Tools that normally involve the selection of text, and that mark the selected text by bracketing it (*type 1 tools*).
- Tools that insert HTML elements at the cursor (*type 2 tools*).

The tools accessible on the upper toolbar are, with one exception, type 1 tools that involve the selection of text. The exception is the button marked *<P>*, which inserts a paragraph mark at the cursor.

To use the type 1 tools, highlight the desired text by dragging the text cursor across it. Then, with the mouse cursor over a toolbar button, press the left mouse button to view a pop-up menu. Selecting a menu item will cause the appropriate HTML markings to bracket the selected text.

The tools listed on the HTML menu are type 2 tools that insert HTML markings at the cursor. Clicking a menu item causes the displayed HTML text to be inserted.

As you enter and use URLs in your documents, they are saved and appear in the URL listbox whenever the URL data entry window pops up. You may save the contents of this listbox to a file and retrieve the contents of a saved file to the listbox by accessing the URL File menu on the URL pop-up window.

Editing User Tools

The User Tools list can be changed by clicking the Edit User Tools command in the Options menu, or by selecting the small button (labeled *E* for Edit) adjacent to the User Tools list. Either of these actions will cause an Edit User Tools dialog box to appear (see Figure 23-4).

The buttons on the right side of the dialog box, along with the contents of the text box at the top, are used to modify the contents of the User Tools list. Use the buttons to delete, insert, append, and replace list items (whenever the mouse cursor is passed over it, the function of each button is described on the main window's status bar).

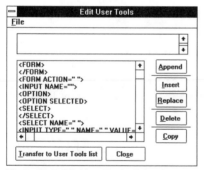

Figure 23-4: Edit User Tools dialog box.

Click the Transfer to User Tools list button to copy the edited list to the User Tools list on the main window toolbar. Selecting the Close button closes the Edit dialog box *without* altering the User Tools list on the toolbar. The contents of the Edit window's listbox *are preserved* until you quit the program.

When you exit HTML Assistant, the User Tools in the toolbar list is automatically saved for use in future editing sessions.

User Tools files

The File menu on the Edit User Tools dialog box permits you to save your lists of User Tools as files and to reload them for later use. In this way, you can build sets of special-purpose user tools as the need arises. For example, you might have a set of tools for creating forms and another for a specialized application that involves tables. An option in the File menu permits you to combine different User Tools files by appending to the listbox.

User Tools files have the suffix .UT. A file called DEFAULT.UT is automatically loaded to the User Tools list when HTML Assistant starts. The User Tools list is saved to this file when the program ends.

Edit/Build URL files

Selecting Edit/Build URL Files from the URL menu permits you to edit and combine commented URLs from different sources.

For example, you may quickly combine selected URLs from Cello bookmark files with other URLs automatically extracted from Mosaic menus and hotlists. While perusing news groups and mailing lists, you might cut and paste URLs into text files (with Notepad or HTML Assistant) and then later combine them with other files.

Of course, once the URLs and comments from various sources are loaded into the editor's listboxes, they may be edited and supplemented with new URLs that are manually typed in. If they are saved as HTML Assistant URL files (the default type), they can later be loaded into an edit window for more extensive editing and reorganization.

You may also convert and save any combination of URLs from any of these sources into a Cello bookmark file.

Operation of the URL editor

When the Edit/Build URL Files option is chosen, a window with two listboxes, two text boxes, and some control buttons pops up.

When a file is loaded, any necessary conversions (for Cello bookmark) or extractions (for MOSAIC.INI files) are performed, and the listboxes are filled with the URLs from the file (the actual files remain unchanged). One listbox contains a list of all the URLs found in the selected file. The other listbox, in corresponding positions in the list, contains comments or descriptions of the URLs in the first box.

You may create your own files or add to the contents of existing files by clicking the Add New URL button and entering URLs and comments into the corresponding text boxes. When an entry is complete, use the Accept New URL control button to save the new data into the listboxes.

Clicking a data item in either listbox causes the URL and its associated comment (if any) to be copied to corresponding text boxes. The contents of the text boxes may be edited and the changes can be saved. Clicking the Accept Edited Text button makes the changes part of the file. Saving the file makes them permanent. You may add and delete URLs and comments by clicking the appropriate control buttons.

Direct conversion of files to HTML text

When you select the Autoconvert File to HTML option in the URL menu, HTML Assistant permits you automatically to convert certain files that contain URLs (along with optional comments or descriptions) directly into HTML text in a new HTML Assistant text-editing window. This is a quick and easy way to build HTML files for editing, testing, or browsing.

When you select a file type (from the pop-up submenu), you are presented with a file selector box from which you may select a file to convert (or you may cancel the operation).

As soon as a file of the appropriate type is selected, the conversion process begins. In a few seconds conversion is complete. The URLs that were found in the file, now properly converted to HTML text separated by paragraph marks, are automatically inserted into a new text window for further editing or testing.

You can elect to convert data in the following types of files to HTML:

- Cello bookmark files (*.BMK)
- HTML Assistant URL files (*.URL)
- Mosaic initialization files (*.INI)

HTML Assistant URL files (*.URL)

HTML Assistant URL files are text files containing URLs and possibly descriptions or comments. Each record, or line, in the text file contains a URL optionally followed by a comma and a description.

An uncommented line looks like this:

```
http://info.cern.ch/example.html
```

A commented line looks like this:

```
http://info.cern.ch/example.html,Sample Page
```

Because HTML Assistant can automatically convert these files into an HTML text document, they provide an excellent way to store or capture interesting-looking URLs for later perusal.

For example, if you see a URL for an interesting home page while you are browsing newsgroups, mailing lists, or the World Wide Web, you can simply copy the URL from the document and paste it into a text file using Notepad (or HTML Assistant).

If you want, you may enter a comma after the URL (but before pressing Enter), followed by a description or comment. The comment will appear as the live, or clickable, item in the HTML file when viewed by a browser. If you don't enter a comment, HTML Assistant adds a copy of the URL (for display as the live selectable item) to the HTML file at conversion time.

Just be sure you press Enter at the end of each line. Make sure that the URL and its comment (separated by a comma) appear on one logical line. It may look like two or more lines if the editor window is narrow, but as long as you press Enter only at the end of the URL-comment combination, the item is a single record and will be processed properly.

Mosaic initialization files (MOSAIC.INI)

The Mosaic WWW browser uses an initialization file with the name MOSAIC.INI for storage of setup parameters. Included in this file are lists of menu items that contain descriptions and URLs that can be executed by Mosaic when the descriptions on the menus are selected. (A version of SPRY's AIR Mosaic is included in this book; see Chapter 5.)

Also included in the file is a hotlist of user-selected URLs gathered during browsing expeditions on the Web. These URLs do not have descriptors associated with them.

The URLs in Mosaic initialization files are converted to HTML text by HTML Assistant. If the URLs come from menu items, their associated menu captions are displayed as the selectable on-screen text. Hotlist items are displayed with a copy of the stored URL as the on-screen text.

What is HTML Assistant Pro?

 HTML Assistant Pro is constantly being revised and improved. Contact *harawitz@fox.nstn.ns.ca* for the latest information about its features.

HTML Assistant Pro is an advanced version of *HTML Assistant* that adds advanced features to the base *HTML Assistant program.* See the ordering information later in this section for information about ordering HTML Assistant Pro. HTML Assistant Pro provides

- A printed manual with a "Beginners' Guide To HTML" plus a step-by-step tutorial for creating HTML pages.

- An *automatic page creator* that enables rapid creation of HTML text pages for use with WWW browser programs. Minimal knowledge of HTML is required, and attractive screens with your own selected hypertext links can be created in a few seconds. This makes it easy to create *menu pages* on your hard drive so you can systematize and organize URL links by subject, date, and so on.

- The capability to remove HTML markings and to use special reformatting filters to transform hard-to-decipher HTML files into clear, readable text.

- The capability to extract and copy URLs from HTML files quickly and automatically, such as NCSA's "What's New" page, for easy organization and compilation into your own documents.

- File-search features — you can search your hard drive and locate files by file extension (for example, *.HTM or *.TXT) that contain key words that you select.

- Capability to load files that are larger than 32K. Large (>than 32K) files may be loaded in segments.

- An option to save DOS text files as UNIX text files.

- An option to extract (without altering the original file) all the link URLs from an HTML text file and display them in a text edit window. Files can be any size. The URLs are displayed in HTML Assistant format: URLtext, Clickabletext. The displayed URL text can be edited and saved as HTML Assistant .URL files.

- Support for the ISO-Latin character set. It can automatically convert ISO ASCII codes in text files to displayable HTML.

- Full technical support, including availability of enhancements and upgrades.

HTML Assistant Pro — Automatic Page Creator

The Automatic Page Creator, supplied with HTML Assistant Pro, permits very rapid creation of HTML text pages for use with WWW browser programs. Minimal knowledge of HTML is required, and an attractive screen with your own selected hypertext links can be created in a matter of seconds.

For WWW information providers, this makes it quite easy to create pages for others to view. For active collectors of information on the World Wide Web, the automatic page creator (as well as HTML Assistant Pro's other features) makes it easy to organize links to information in ways that make sense. You can quickly select links from different pages and files and combine them into a single page with headings and descriptions of your choice.

Be your own Internet organizer

The automatic page creator makes it a snap to organize your Internet experience. It becomes a simple matter to create hierarchies of menu pages that access other pages stored on your local disk drive. All of these can be annotated with text of your choice.

The automatic page creator allows you to put together presentation pages quickly on any topic. Together with the URL File Editor/Builder, you can organize links to WWW data by subject, date, or in any other way that suits you.

With HTML Assistant Pro, you can easily build attractive and pleasing layouts that incorporate headers, divider lines, text, and links to other pages and graphics on your own hard drive or at remote sites.

HTML Assistant Pro makes keeping track of your work on the Internet not only manageable, but an enjoyable and aesthetically pleasing experience.

Ordering HTML Assistant Pro

You can order HTML Assistant Pro via e-mail, mail, telephone, or fax. The fastest ways to order are by fax, telephone, or e-mail with a credit card. Payment may be made by money order, check, VISA, or MasterCard.

Contact Brooklyn North Software Works as follows:

e-mail: *harawitz@fox.nstn.ns.ca*

Telephone/fax: (902) 835-2600

CU_HTML.DOT (Version 1.5) _____

by Kenneth Wong and Anton Lam, The Chinese University of Hong Kong.

CU_HTML.DOT is a Word for Windows document template (for Word 2.0 and 6.0) that allows users to create HTML documents inside Word in a WYSIWYG manner and generate a corresponding HTML file.

You can assign different formatting tags to the paragraphs by simply pointing and clicking. You can also insert inline GIF images and specify hyperlinks by choosing the target file from a dialog box. The inline GIF images also appear in the Word document.

By using the template, you can create HTML documents with little knowledge of the HTML syntax. Existing word processor features such as spell checking, printing, cutting and pasting, macro automation, and so on, can be used. And you can avoid many errors by using the template instead of typing the HTML manually.

Copyright and warranty

The software is provided *as is*. There is no warranty and no support in any form will be entertained. You use this software at your own risk. You can send comments and wishlists to *anton-lam@cuhk.hk*.

The Computer Services Centre of The Chinese University of Hong Kong holds the copyright of CU_HTML.DOT, GIF.DLL, and CU_HTML.DLL. It may not be distributed in conjunction with any commercial or for-fee product. This copyright notice must be distributed together with the software. Send mail to

Anton Lam (anton-lam@cuhk.hk)
Computer Services Centre
The Chinese University of Hong Kong

CU_HMTL features

The following text outlines some of the features of CU_HMTL:

- Easy to use. Intuitive for existing Word users.
- WYSIWYG (*almost*). Inline GIF images can be displayed inside Word.
- Supports standard HTML tags, including the following:

  <H1> - <H6> Heading 1–6

  <OL> Numbered (Nested) list 1–4

  <UL> Unnumbered (Nested) list 1–4

  <ADDRESS> Address

  <PRE> Preformatted text

  <TITLE> Title

  <HR> Horizontal rule

  <IMG SRC...> Inline .GIF image

  <A HREF...> HREF

  <B><I><U> Bold, italic, and underline

 Line break

  <P> Paragraph break

Installing CU_HTML

Get the most updated copy of CU_HTML.ZIP from *ftp.cuhk.hk*. Unzip the file to an empty directory. CU_HTML requires you to copy CU_HTML.DLL, CU_HTML.INI, and GIF.DLL to the default Windows directory (for example, C:\WINDOWS). All other files must be copied to the appropriate Word default directories on your configuration.

For Word 2.0 users, copy CU_HTML2.DOT as CU_HTML.DOT to the default Word template directory. For Word 6.0 users, copy CU_HTML6.DOT as CU_HTML.DOT to the default Word 6 template directory.

Creating a new document

Follow these steps to create a new document:

1. Start Microsoft Word. Choose File⇨New.

2. Type **CU_HTML** in the New Document dialog box. You'll see six new buttons on the toolbar and eight new items in the Tools menu.

   In addition, a number of new style names are available in the Style pull-down list.

Converting an existing document

The safest way to convert an existing document is to copy and paste the contents of the old document into a new one that uses CU_HTML.DOT. You should delete all the styles that do not come with CU_HTML.DOT, or you may get unexpected results.

Inserting inline images

To insert an inline GIF image, place the cursor at the position where the GIF should be; then click the Graphics button (the button with a circle, square, and triangle on it) on the toolbar. Proceed to select your GIF file from the listbox. The GIF file must exist in your file system; only then will you see the actual GIF file in your open HTML document in Word.

To delete an inline GIF, just click to select it and press Delete.

Specifying hyperlinks

Links are inserted by first selecting a *hotword,* which can be text, graphics, or both. Once you highlight the hotword, you can choose Link button to link to another HTML page, sound file, or video clip (assuming that you have the required multimedia setup on your system).

After you select a target file, CU_HMTL completes the link and designates a blue character hotword to show a successful link.

Link to another HTTP server, FTP, or Gopher

Your URL document can have an associated link to another URL page on another Web server. To do this, click the URL button, and you are prompted to enter the full HTTP path and name of the target document.

Link to another part in the same document

A hotword source can be designated to jump to another part in the same document. This is done by using Word's Insert Bookmark command.

After a bookmark is in your document, you can use CU_HTML's Document Link button to associate the target bookmark.

Deleting hyperlinks

You select a configured link (designated in blue) and use the Delete button to delete this link.

Generating a final HTML

If you save your HTML document to a Word DOC file, then press the HTML File button, you're saving the document as an HTML file. The HTML file will have the same name as the Word document, with an HTM extension.

CU_HTML tips

Save your new document at least once before inserting any links or images: The directory relative to the current document will be saved, so you must know where the current document is saved first. If the document is C:\WWW\HTML\ INDEX.HTM and the inline GIF is C:\WWW\HTML\GIF\LOGO.GIF, the path GIF/ LOGO.GIF is saved. If the document is C:\WWW\HTML\INDEX.HTM and the inline GIF is X:\OTHERDIR\GIF\LOGO.GIF, the path ../../OTHERDIR/GIF/ LOGO.GIF is saved.

Put all the files in the same directory: Many people will put their HTMLs on UNIX, if all documents were saved in one directory (and the subdirectories inside). The HTMLs are easier to maintain.

All the filenames should be in lowercase: If you are going to put the HTMLs on a UNIX, Windows NT, Macintosh, or OS/2 server, the HTML filenames should be in lowercase and conform to the DOS *filename.ext* format (eight-character filename limit, three-character extension) because the names are converted to lowercase. But for the URLs you entered directly in Insert URL, what you type is what you get.

Always add an extra carriage return at the end of document: Otherwise, you may encounter strange results when selecting the whole last line and insert a linkage file to it.

Don't add extra colors: The blue color added for the hotwords is meaningful to the program. Don't try to modify (shrink/extend/delete/change) the color. If you want to delete the link from a hotword, select the hotword and press the button.

You can edit the hotword as usual, as long as it remains blue.

View field codes: In case of any doubt on the links or inline images, choose View⇨Field Codes, or choose Options from the Tools menu and turn on the Field Codes check box. You see the actual filename that will be saved. Don't modify characters other than the filename inside the fields.

Use picture placeholders: Use picture placeholders only if you feel your computer is slow. Select Tools⇨Options, and then check the Picture Placeholders check box in the View category.

Resize your document window before generating the HTML file: Make the document window as small as you can. Again, only if you feel your computer is slow. This is to minimize the area Word needs to redraw. For a slow display card, the time difference is significant.

If there are errors in writing the final HTML: Bugs are unavoidable, so if you encounter errors generating the HTML (endless loops or an error dialog box pops up), press Esc to stop the macro and discard your document. Always save your original document before doing this. If possible, mail the document to me (*anton-lam@cuhk.hk*) for error diagnosis. I will respond if I can, but don't expect this to be *official* support. The software is provided *as is.*

Test with Windows Mosaic: Select File⇨Open Local File in Windows Mosaic to test the generated HTML. You will instantly know that what you see in Word is *almost* what you get in Mosaic.

Why the document in Mosaic is different from the one in Word: The styles defined in CU_HTML.DOT are based on the default font and styles used in Windows Mosaic. Mosaic users may have their choice of fonts.

There is no convenient support of bullet or numbered list in Word 2.0. Word 6.0 has it now.

You will find more differences when viewing from X Window or Mac Mosaic.

HTML Writer

HTML Writer is an easy-to-use, Windows-based authoring tool for creating or editing HTML documents.

Introduction

HTML Writer is an easy-to-use Windows text editor specifically designed for the creation and editing of HTML documents. It was developed by Kris Nosack using Visual Basic 3.0. I am continually improving and refining HTML Writer. If you have a suggestion or think you have found a bug in this program, please let me know by sending me an e-mail message to the address that follows. Any questions or comments may be directed here as well.

Internet: `html_writer@byu.edu`

CompuServe: `INTERNET:html_writer@byu.edu`

HTML Writer is *donationware*. Because you probably haven't heard of this concept — mostly because it's something I came up with on my own ;-) — I'll explain how it works. This program is yours to use as long as you want with no restrictions (no 30-day evaluation period, no nags or threats). In other words, you can use HTML Writer — guilt free — for as long as you want. If you like HTML Writer and you feel like rewarding me for writing this program, by all means send me $5 or $10 as your way of saying thanks.

A mailing list supporting a newsletter for HTML Writer is also available by contacting the author through his e-mail address. HTML Writer's home page can be found on WWW at

`http://wwf.et.byu.edu/~nosackk/htmlwrit.html`

Donations should be forwarded by mail to Kris Nosack, 376 North Main Street, Orem, Utah, 84057.

Installation and setup

After decompressing HTML Writer, copy HTMLWRIT.EXE, HTMLWRIT.HLP, and the data file, HTMLWRIT.DAT, to a directory of your choice, for example, C:\WINDOWS\HTMLWRIT.

Because HTML Writer is a VB 3.0 application, you must have VBRUN300.DLL, CMDIALOG.VBX, COMMDLG.DLL, and TOOLBARS.VBX in the default WINDOWS SYSTEM directory. (usually C:\WINDOWS\SYSTEM). Be careful to examine the default versions of these files that may already exist in your directory.

To launch, just execute the file HTMLWRIT.EXE.

Figure 23-5 shows the main HTML Writer window.

HTML Writer maintains an initialization file HTMLWRIT.INI, which is created the first time you change any settings within HTML Writer. Maintain this file in the default WINDOWS directory.

The first time you test a document in either Mosaic or Cello (by selecting File⇨Test or the Test button), you are prompted for the location (drive and directory) of your Mosaic or Cello executable (for example, MOSAIC.EXE or CELLO.EXE). This location information is stored in the HTMLWRIT.INI file, so you should have to do this only once.

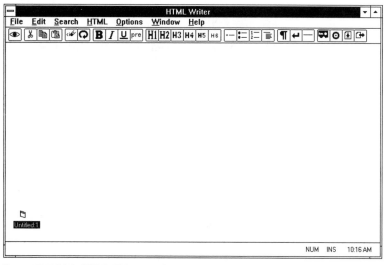

Figure 23-5: Main HTML Writer window.

Tips for using HTML Writer

Defining an Inline Image

To add an *inline image* (a picture that appears in your document), follow these steps:

1. Position the text cursor (the short, flashing vertical line) where you want the image to appear.

2. Click the toolbar button that looks like a small picture of a landscape. The Inline Image dialog box should appear (Figure 23-6).

Figure 23-6: Inline Image dialog box.

3. In the Resource heading, click the small button with the down arrow on it and click the File item in the list that pops down.

4. Skip over to the path heading and enter the directory where you have a GIF file, or enter any made-up path if you don't have a GIF file.

5. Enter the filename (with the GIF extension) of a GIF file that is in the directory you just entered. If you don't have a GIF file, enter a made-up filename. When you're done, click OK.

You should now see the following tag in your document:

```
<img src="file:///c:\vb3\projects/my_pic.gif">
```

Testing your document in Mosaic

To test your document in Mosaic, follow these steps:

1. If you have Mosaic installed on your computer, select File➪Test from the pull-down menu. (You can also initiate the test function by clicking the left-most toolbar button that looks like an eye.) Remember, if you don't already have Mosaic, Chapter 5 covers AIR Mosaic, also in this book/CD package.

2. If this is your first time testing a document in Mosaic from HTML Writer, you are prompted for the location of the MOSIAC.EXE file on your system. (This location is saved, so you should have to do this only once.)

3. HTML Writer should now save your document as $TEMP.HTM, launch Mosaic, and load your document into Mosaic where you can look it over and make sure it is formatted correctly. If something doesn't look right, just switch back to HTML Writer and change it.

That's pretty much it! Of course there are many more HTML tags and functions of HTML Writer for you to explore and use, but this should help get you started.

The Insert Menu command

Choosing File➪Insert Menu also brings up the file selector dialog box, but the selected file is inserted into the currently active document (window) at the position of the text cursor instead of opening up a new window.

The text cursor is the flashing bar that locates your position in the text of a document.

The Test command

Choosing File➪Test loads the currently active document into Mosaic or Cello for evaluation. The currently active document is saved as $TEMP.HTM and is then loaded into Mosaic or Cello, depending on which test program is selected in the Options menu.

You may also elect to have HTML Writer save your document before it is loaded into Mosaic or Cello by choosing Options⇨Save on Test.

Tips for using HTML Writer's main menu

The HTML Writer main menu pops up if you click the right mouse button.

If a particular menu item supports a shortcut key, it is presented in parentheses next to the menu entry name in this on-line help. Holding down the Shift key while selecting an HTML menu item or toolbar button causes a paragraph tag (<p>) to be added to the end of the tag (for example, my text<p>).

The actual HTML tags inserted by HTML Writer are presented to the right of the menu item names in this on-line help.

The "..." indicates that the HTML tag is double-ended (it inserts a beginning and ending tag, such as ...). Any text that is highlighted before you select these double-ended tags in HTML Writer has the beginning tag added to the front of the selected text and the ending tag added to the end of the selected text.

Selecting the Remove Codes menu item causes all of the HTML codes (tags) that begin with the < character and end with the > character to be deleted from the selected text in the currently active document. To delete all the HTML codes from the currently active document, choose Edit⇨Select All and then choose HTML⇨Remove Codes.

The HTML hyperlinks

Inline Images

Inline Images will bring up an edit box requiring the following information defining the URL or other attributes for an inline image.

Example: Inline Image... <img {*options*} src="*URL*">

The *Resource, Host, Port, Path,* and *Filename* fields are used to specify the URL for the inline image file (usually either a GIF or XBM file). If a Resource is not specified, HTML Writer assumes that you want to construct a relative URL; otherwise, an absolute URL is constructed. Here are examples of each:

Absolute URL: *Resource* - http

Path - my/home/dir

Filename - my_page.html

Resulting URL - http:///my/home/dir/my_page.html

Relative URL: *Path* - my/home/dir

Filename - page_two.html

Resulting URL - my/home/dir/page_two.html

The *Alternate* field allows you to enter some text that will appear when the program reading/displaying the HTML file is either not capable of displaying inline images or is not set up to display them.

The *Alignment* buttons determine where the text following the inline image is placed. Selecting the Middle or Top alignment options inserts an *align=middle* or *align=top* option code. Bottom alignment is the default, so no align option code is inserted when Bottom is selected.

Clicking the *Paste* button will generate an inline image tag in the active document with the Clipboard text inserted in place of the URL argument in the previous example. This is useful for grabbing interesting URLs of other inline images from other sources (newsgroups, e-mail messages, and WWW browsers) and incorporating them into your document.

Using the Paste option merely copies the text from the Clipboard verbatim with no attempt made by HTML Writer to verify that the text is or is not a valid URL!

Target... <a name="*anchor_name*">...</a>

Brings up a dialog box for defining a hyperlink target (named anchor) for Local and Remote hyperlinks to jump to. Simply enter a name for the target in the Target Name field. This name is inserted in place of *anchor_name* in the previous example. All target names entered in this dialog appear in the drop-down list of the Local hyperlink dialog box (see the next section).

Local... <a href="#*anchor_name*">...</a>

Brings up a dialog box for entering the URL and other attributes used in defining a local hyperlink. You can either enter a target name or select one from the drop-down list accessed by clicking the button with a down arrow on it.

Remote... <a href="*URL#anchor_name*">...</a>

Brings up a dialog box for entering the URL and other attributes used in defining a remote hyperlink. Any text highlighted before selecting this function appear in place of the ... argument in the heading example and is used as the trigger that initiates the hypertext jump.

The *Resource, Host, Port, Path,* and *Filename* fields specify the URL for the resource to which you want to create a jump.

You may also use this dialog box for specifying *relative jumps.* Once the user has jumped to the first HTML document, subsequent jumps need specify only the new URL information. If a *Resource* is not specified, HTML Writer assumes that you want to construct a relative URL; otherwise, an absolute URL is constructed. (See the examples in the previous section "Inline Images.")

For example, if all your HTML documents are in the same directory and a remote user jumps to your home page, subsequent jumps from your home page to other documents in that directory need supply only the filename.

The *Target* field allows you to enter a target name (named anchor) in the destination HTML file you want to jump to (see "Target"). So not only can you jump to another HTML document, you can also jump to a specific location in that document.

Clicking the *Paste* button generates a remote hyperlink (anchor) tag in the active document with the Clipboard text inserted in place of the URL argument in the previous example. This is useful for grabbing interesting URLs from other sources (newsgroups, e-mail messages, and WWW browsers) and incorporating them into your document.

Using the Paste option merely copies the text from the Clipboard verbatim, with no attempt made by HTML Writer to verify that the text is or is not a valid URL!

Special Character < > &

Because the greater than (>), less than (<), and ampersand (&) characters are used to denote HTML tags in a document, this menu (and submenus) will insert the HTML codes representing these special characters into the active document at the position of the text cursor. Here's how it works:

Submenu	HTML Code	Interpretation
<	<	<
>	>	>
&	&	&
"	"	"

ASCII Character... &#xxx

Inserts the HTML code for displaying an ASCII character. The *xxx* placeholder is the decimal number for the ASCII character you want to display (for example, &#136 causes the caret symbol ^ to appear).

Comment <!— ...>

Inserts the HTML comment tags into the active document. Any text enclosed by this tag (put in place of the "...") is not shown when interpreted by an HTML document viewing program. This is so you can put comments into a document that will not be seen by the reader.

Uppercase Tags

Selecting this menu item causes all subsequent HTML tags inserted by HTML Writer to be in uppercase (for example, <B>some text</B>).

Save as UNIX Text

Selecting this option causes the text file written to disk by HTML Writer to use UNIX-style line termination. DOS and Windows use a carriage return and linefeed pair to indicate the end of a line of text. UNIX uses only a linefeed to terminate its lines of text. Enabling this option tells HTML Writer to end each line of text with only a linefeed.

Most FTP programs — when set to ASCII transfer mode — correctly change line-termination codes when transferring text files to/from UNIX and DOS/Windows systems. If your FTP (or other transfer program) program handles this translation properly, you probably do not want to use the Save as UNIX Text option.

Test in Mosaic or Cello

When this option is selected and the File➪Test command is used, HTML Writer tests the active document in NCSA's Mosaic. The Test in Cello option allows you to use Cello to test the active document.

Chapter 24

WHAM — Waveform Hold and Modify Utility

WHAM (Waveform Hold and Modify) is a Windows 3.1 application for manipulating digitized sound. It can read and write Windows 3.1 WAV files, raw eight-bit digitized sound files, and files of several other formats. It can perform various operations on sounds of any size, restricted only by memory.

WHAM Version 1.31 is an Internet Windows Viewer utility you can configure to work with a WinSock-compatible Gopher, World Wide Web (WWW) browser, or FTP client. As long as you associate WAV files in your Windows File Manager and maintain WHAM in an open path, WHAM launches whenever you execute a designated WAV file on the Internet or your local hard disk. As long as WAV files are associated with WHAM, you can also drag WAV files and drop them onto WHAM to play the WAV files.

WHAM accepts command-line arguments, so you can play any WAV file from the Program Manager or File Manager File⇨Run window. WHAM looks in the executable's directory for sound format drivers.

WHAM also features sound recording for those who have a Windows MPC-certified sound card and a Windows sound driver. WHAM uses file format reading through DLLs, which lets you add more formats without changing the WHAM utility.

WHAM also reads a variety of sound-encoded formats, including 16 bit WAV files. If you use WHAM as your default sound player with MS Viewer applications, WHAM now supports custom RIFF WAV files. WHAM can also read and write Creative Voice VOC files, Amiga IFF/8SVX sound files, Sun/NeXT AU (8-bit linear and Mu-Law) files, and Apple/SGI AIFF files, making it even more valuable for WWW and Gopher navigation.

WHAM also supports a number of sophisticated sound editing features, including stretching and shrinking large sounds. If you use WHAM to create or edit sound files, you can also embed description information in sound files, including title, copyright, date, software, artist, engineer, technician, comments, and so on.

Be careful when using WHAM with Microsoft's Sound Speaker or offshore sound cards. Performance and quality depends fully on what card and driver you use. For those who do not have a 16-bit sound card, WHAM will not play 16 bit WAV files. It's best to reduce such WAV files to 8 bits with WHAM's editor.

About the Author

Andrew Bulhak created WHAM. The program is in the public domain, but the author invites any user of WHAM to send a donation of $20 or $30 and forward it to the following address:

Andrew Bulhak
21 The Crescent
Ferntree Gully Vic 3156
AUSTRALIA

For WHAM support, e-mail acb@yoyo.cc.monash.edu.au

Warranty Disclaimer

Andrew Bulhak ("The author") makes no warranty of any kind, express or implied, including any warranties of fitness for a particular purpose. In no event will the author be liable for any incidental or consequential damages arising from the use of, or inability to use, this program.

Menus and Controls

The button bar

The button bar is near the top of the WHAM window (Figure 24-1). It contains buttons that cause certain functions to be performed when they are clicked. In addition, some buttons will show a menu of other buttons when clicked with the right mouse button. These buttons are as follows:

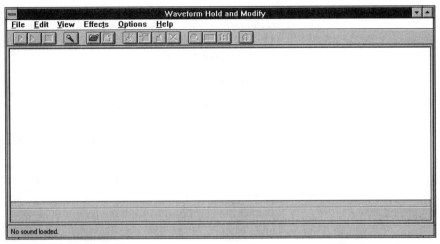

Figure 24-1: WHAM window.

Play	This button causes the current sound to be played in its entirety.
Play from cursor	This button causes the current sound to be played from the position of the cursor to the end. It is only present when nothing is selected.
Play selection	This button causes the selected portion of the current sound to be played. It is only present if part of the sound is selected.
Stop	This button causes playback to stop. It is enabled only if a sound is currently being played.
Record	This button invokes the recording dialog box, allowing you to record a sound through your sound card.
Open	This button brings up a dialog box prompting you to select a sound to load into memory.
Save	This button causes the current sound to be saved to disk.
Save As	This button is displayed when the Save button is clicked with the right mouse button. This button brings up a dialog box, prompting you for a new name to save the current sound under.
Cut	This button causes the current selection to be copied to the Clipboard and removed.
Copy	This button causes the current selection to be copied to the Clipboard.

(continued)

Paste	This button causes the contents of the Clipboard to be inserted into the current sound. If it is clicked with the left mouse button, a dialog box is displayed, prompting you for the method of insertion. If clicked with the right mouse button, three buttons appear:
	Paste at cursor/selection: If this button is clicked, the contents of the Clipboard will replace the currently selected portion of the current sound, if any part is selected, or else they will be inserted at the cursor position.
	Paste at start: If this button is clicked, the contents of the Clipboard will be inserted at the start of the current sound.
	Paste at end: If this button is clicked, the contents of the Clipboard will be appended at the end of the current sound.
Delete	This button causes the current selection to be removed.
Zoom in	If this button is clicked, WHAM will zoom in on the current selection.
Zoom out	If this button is clicked, the entire sound will be displayed.
Actual size	If this button is clicked, the current sound will be displayed at actual size.
Information	If this button is clicked, you will be prompted with a dialog box allowing you to see and change information about the current sound.
System information	This button invokes the system information dialog box which displays information about your hardware.

The status line

The status line is the area at the bottom of the WHAM window. When a sound is loaded, it displays information in several compartments, as follows:

Size of sound	This is the physical size of the current sound in bytes.
Length of sound	This is the length of the current sound in seconds.
Sample rate	This is the rate at which the current sound is played back, in kilohertz.
Resolution	This is the resolution of the current sound, in bits per sample.

Viewing scale	This is the scale at which the current sound is shown.
Modified flag	If the current sound has been modified since it was last written to disk, the word "Modified" appears here.
Selection/cursor position	When part of the current sound is selected, this contains information about how much is selected and whence; otherwise, it contains the position of the cursor, as an offset from the start of the sound.

Finally, the rightmost portion of the status line contains information about any operation in progress, such as "Playing"; normally, it is blank.

WHAM menus

The following tables describe WHAM's File, Edit, View, Effects, and Options menus.

Table 24-1	File Menu
Option	***Description***
Record new	Opens the recording dialog box, letting you record a sound through a sound card.
Open	Opens an existing sound file.
Save	Saves the current sound file to disk.
Save As	Saves the current sound file to disk under a different name.
Information	Lets you view and change information about the current sound, such as the title and copyright information.
System information	Displays information about your hardware; this includes sampling/playback rates and maximum resolutions.
Exit	Exits WHAM.

Table 24-2	Edit Menu
Option	**Description**
Cut	Puts the selected part of the current sound into the Clipboard and removes it from the sound. Any previous Clipboard contents will be replaced. If nothing is selected, the entire sound will be cut into the Clipboard.
Copy	Places a copy of the selected part of the current sound into the Clipboard. Any previous Clipboard contents will be replaced. If nothing is selected, the entire sound will be copied into the Clipboard.
Paste	Inserts sound from the Clipboard into the current sound. The new sound can be inserted at the start of the current sound, appended to the end, inserted at a selected point or be made to replace the current sound.
Clear	Clears the selected part of the current sound, replacing it with silence. If nothing is selected, the entire sound is cleared.
Delete	Removes the selected part of the current sound. If nothing is selected, the entire sound will be deleted.
Delete unselected	Removes all but the selected part of the current sound.
Copy to file	Saves the selected part of the current sound to disk.

Table 24-3	View Menu
Option	**Description**
Actual size	Displays the waveform at actual size. Each line on the display represents one sample.
1:2 scale	Displays the waveform at a 1:2 scale. Each line on the display represents two samples.
1:5 scale	Displays the waveform at a 1:5 scale. Each line on the display represents five samples.
1:10 scale	Displays the waveform at a 1:10 scale. Each line on the display represents ten samples.
1:100 scale	Displays the waveform at a 1:100 scale. Each line on the display represents 100 samples.
Zoom in	Displays the waveform at the smallest scale at which the entire selection is visible.
Entire sound	Zooms out to display the entire sound.
Full height	Displays the waveform at full height, adjusting the WHAM window's height.

Option	Description
Half height	Displays the waveform at half height, adjusting the WHAM window's height. Use this to conserve screen space.
Solid display	Displays the waveform in solid form.
Outline display	Displays the waveform as a line.
Blob display	Displays the waveform as a symmetrical blob.
Point display	Displays the waveform as a series of scattered points.

Table 24-4	Effects Menu
Option	**Description**
Change sign	Changes the sign of the current sound. This command allows signed sounds, such as Amiga sounds, to be converted to the Windows format.
Decode Mu-Law data	Converts the current sound from mu-law samples to linear samples. Be careful, because if the sound is not in mu-law format, this function will really make a mess of it.
Expand to 16 bits	Expands the current sound's resolution to 16 bits. This function is enabled only when the current sound has an eight-bit resolution.
Reduce to 8 bits	Reduces the current sound's resolution to eight bits. This function is enabled only when the current sound has a 16-bit resolution.
Reverse	Reverses the selected part of the current sound, causing it to play backwards. If nothing is selected, the entire sound is reversed.
Volume⇨Increase (200%)	Increases the volume of the selected part of the current sound, making it twice as loud. If nothing is selected, the entire sound's volume is increased.
Volume⇨Decrease (50%)	Decreases the volume of the selected part of the current sound, making it half as loud. If nothing is selected, the entire sound's volume is decreased.
Volume⇨Change	Changes the volume of the selected part of the sound by a user-specified percentage. At present, the percentage is rounded to the nearest 50%.
Playback rate	Changes the playback rate of the current sound. The playback rate is specified in kilohertz (kHz). The higher the playback rate, the faster the sound is played.
Stretch/Shrink	Physically changes the length of a sound. This allows a sound to be sped up or slowed down without changing its playback rate, or to be converted to a different playback rate.

Table 24-5	Options Menu
Option	**Description**
Can modify unselected	If this menu item is checked, then operations such as copying and reversing will be performed on the entire sound if nothing is selected. If this menu option is not checked, you have to select part of the sound before performing such an operation.
Save settings on exit	If this menu item is checked, the dimensions of the WHAM window and the vertical scale will be saved when WHAM exits. If you wish to save the settings immediately, hold down Shift and select Exit from the File menu.
Information defaults	Calls up a dialog box that allows you to select whether WHAM reads the DOS creation date of files.
Format defaults	Brings up the Format defaults dialog box, which allows you to set options specific to individual file formats.
Window options	Calls up a dialog box that allows you to specify how the WHAM window can be resized.
Display options	Brings up the Display options dialog box, which allows you to configure the way in which WHAM presents a sound on the screen.

Using WHAM

Changing the volume

You can increase or decrease the volume of the current sound, or of any part of it.

To double the volume of part of a sound:

1. Select the part of the sound. This step is not necessary if you want to double the volume of the entire sound.

2. Select Volume⇨Effects⇨Increase (200%).

If part of a sound is already very loud, increasing its volume will distort it.

To halve the volume of part of a sound:

1. Select the part of the sound. This step is not necessary if you wish to halve the volume of the entire sound.

2. Select Volume⇨Effects⇨Decrease (50%).

To change the volume of part of a sound by a percentage:

1. Select the part of the sound. This step is not necessary if you wish to change the volume of the entire sound.

2. Select Effects⇨Volume⇨Change....

3. Enter the percentage to change the volume and click OK or press Enter.

   For example, 300% triples the volume and 50% halves it.

If part of a sound is already very loud, increasing its volume distorts it.

Clearing part of a sound

You can clear part of a sound. This erases that part of the sound, replacing it with silence. To clear part of a sound:

1. Select the part of the sound that you wish to clear.

2. Select Effects⇨Clear.

Converting Amiga sounds

You can convert signed sounds, such as Amiga sounds, to the unsigned format used by Windows. You can also convert sounds to signed format.

To convert the current sound from signed to unsigned format (or vice versa), select Effects⇨Change sign.

Copying sound to the Clipboard

You can copy the current sound, or part of it, to the Clipboard. From there, you can insert it into other sounds. To copy part of a sound to the Clipboard:

1. Select the part of the current sound to copy. If you want to copy the entire sound, select nothing.

2. Select Edit⇨Copy, or click the Copy button.

To copy part of a sound to the Clipboard and delete it:

1. Select the part of the current sound to copy. If you want to copy the entire sound, select nothing.

2. Select Edit⇨Cut, or click the Cut button.

Deleting part of a sound

You can delete part of a sound. That part is removed and the sound becomes shorter. To delete part of the current sound:

1. Select the part of the sound that you wish to delete.

2. Select Edit⇨Delete.

To delete all but part of the current sound:

1. Select the part of the sound that you wish to keep.

2. Select Edit⇨Delete unselected.

Editing sound information

Sounds stored in the RIFF Waveform and IFF formats can contain information about their contents. You can inspect this information, modify it, or enter your own information. To view or edit the current sound's information, select File⇨Information. A dialog box appears, containing information about the current sound. You can change this information.

Inserting sound from the Clipboard

You can append sound from the Clipboard to the end of the current sound or insert it into the current sound at any point. You can also replace the current sound with sound from the Clipboard.

To insert sound from the Clipboard at the start of the current sound:

1. Select Edit⇨Paste, or click the Paste button.
2. In the dialog box that appears, select the Insert at start option button and click OK.

To append sound from the Clipboard to the end of the current sound:

1. Select Edit⇨Paste, or click the Paste button.
2. In the dialog box that appears, select the Add to end option button and click OK.

To insert sound from the Clipboard into the current sound:

1. Select the part of the sound that you wish to replace.
2. Select Edit⇨Paste or click the Paste button.
3. In the dialog box that appears, select the Replace selection option button and click OK.

To replace the current sound with the contents of the Clipboard:

1. Select Edit⇨Paste, or click the Paste button.
2. In the dialog box that appears, select the Replace waveform option button and click OK.

Loading a sound from disk

You can load an existing sound file, such as one of the sounds provided with Windows, into WHAM. To load a sound file from disk:

1. Select File⇨Open, or click the Open button.
2. Select the filename from the list. You can change directories and drives through the dialog box. You can also select the type of files that you want to load.

Playing a sound

You can play the current sound, or a part of it, through your sound output device.

■ To play the current sound, press P or click the Play button.

■ To play part of the current sound, press Ctrl+P, or click the Play selection button.

Recording a sound

If you have a sound card that supports sound recording, you can use WHAM to record sounds.

To record a sound:

1. Select File⇨Record New, or click the Record button. The recording dialog appears (Figure 24-2).

2. Press the dialog box's Record button.

   The dialog box should display the message *Allocating memory* above the buttons. Please note that recording will not start immediately, as WHAM first tries to allocate as much memory as it can.

   When the line above the buttons reads *Recording commenced*, WHAM starts recording sound.

Figure 24-2: Record sound dialog box.

3. If you are recording through a tape or compact disc, press "Play" on the device; if you are recording through a microphone, speak (or sing or yodel, or whatever) into the microphone.

4. When you are finished recording, click the dialog box's Stop button.

   WHAM stops when it runs out of memory, even if you're not finished recording.

5. To listen to your sound, click Play.

   If you like it, click OK. This closes the dialog box and lets you edit your sound in WHAM. If you do not like it, you can try to record it again, or you can discard it and close the dialog box by clicking Cancel.

Reversing part of a sound

You can reverse the order of part of a sound, which causes that part to be played backwards.

To reverse part of a sound:

1. Select the part to reverse. If you want to reverse the entire sound, select nothing.

2. Select Effects⇨Reverse.

Saving a sound to disk

You can save the current sound to a file on disk. This file can be in one of the several formats WHAM supports.

To save the current sound to disk:

1. Select File⇨Save or click the Save button.

2. If the sound has not been given a name, WHAM prompts you for one.

   You can also select the format in which it is saved and, in some cases, the encoding.

To save the current sound under a different name or in a different format:

1. Select File⇨Save As.

2. WHAM prompts you for a name for the sound.

   You can also select the format and, in some cases, the encoding in which it is saved.

Saving part of a sound to disk

You can select part of a sound and save it to disk as a separate sound. To save part of the current sound to disk:

1. Select the part of the sound to save.

2. Select Edit⇨Copy to file.

3. Enter the name for the new file in the dialog box that appears.

   You can also select the format (and in some cases the encoding) to save the sound in.

Selecting part of a sound

You can select part of the current sound. Then you can play the selection, copy it to the Clipboard, or modify it. If you are not satisfied with how much you have selected, you can move the start and end of the selection.

To select part of the current sound:

1. Position the mouse cursor over the start of the part of the waveform that you want to select.

2. Hold down the left mouse button and drag to the end of the part that you want to select.

3. Release the left mouse button.

The selected part of the sound is displayed inversed.

To change how much is selected:

1. Position the mouse cursor over the marker beneath the start or end of the selected area.

2. Hold down the left mouse button and drag the marker to its new position.

3. Release the left mouse button.

Hint: To see whether you have selected the right part of the sound, press Ctrl+P, or click the Play selection button.

Speeding up or slowing down a sound

You can change the speed at which the sound plays. The speed is specified in samples per second, or hertz (Hz). The default speed is 22,050 Hz, or approximately 22 kilohertz (KHz). Windows can handle any speed between 4000 and 44,100 Hz.

To change the playback speed of the current sound:

1. Select Effects⇨Playback Rate.

2. Enter the new speed.

   Type the new speed in Hertz, type the new speed in Kilohertz followed by the letter K, or select a standard speed from the drop-down list.

3. Click OK, or press Enter.

Frequently Asked Questions about WHAM ____

Q: Can I transfer sound between WHAM and Sound Recorder?

A: You can transfer sound from the Sound Recorder to WHAM but not from WHAM to the Sound Recorder. The Sound Recorder is an OLE application and was not intended to transfer data by other means. Of course, you can save a sound in WHAM and open it in the Sound Recorder.

Q: What do I do if a sound sounds noisy and distorted?

A: If the sound sounds dirty and the waveform looks messy, then sound is probably in signed format (as used on the Amiga). Before playing it, convert it to unsigned format by selecting Effects⇨Change Sign.

If the sound sounds slightly distorted and the waveform display shows many curved (parabolic or hyperbolic) patterns, then the sound is probably in Mu-Law format. You can convert this to linear format by selecting Effects⇨Decode Mu-Law data.

Q: I have a program that cannot read WAV files created by WHAM. Is this a bug in WHAM?

A: No. WHAM implements the RIFF format as defined in the official Microsoft/IBM specification. The other program has a bug. Some programs cannot handle RIFF waveform files containing anything but the sound and its header. If you want WHAM to write RIFF files without additional information, select Options⇨Format defaults, select the RIFF Waveform format, and change its options to omit the INFO chunk from RIFF waveform files.

Q: Can WHAM handle Macintosh sound formats?

A: Unfortunately not. I would have liked to have put in SND resource read and write capabilities, but I can't find the Macintosh sound resource format. I have only seen programs that write this format on the Macintosh, and I have heard that they use some system functions.

If you wish to convert your favorite Windows sounds to Macintosh files, you must first save them to an intermediate format and then use a Macintosh utility to do the conversion. To do this, I save files in IFF format and use a Macintosh program called AmigaSndConvert to convert them to Macintosh sound files.

Q: How does WHAM handle signed and unsigned samples?

A: There are two ways of storing digitized sound: with signed samples and with unsigned samples. Signed samples are values ranging from –128 to 127 and centered around 0. Unsigned samples are centered around 128 and range from 0 to 255. Windows uses unsigned samples.

Q: What are samples and markers?

A: Digitized sound is a series of samples. A sample is a single reading of volume. A marker is a small triangle, immediately below the waveform display, representing the start or end of a selection. By dragging a marker, you can change the selection.

Q: What sound file formats does WHAM support?

See Table 24-6.

Table 24-6	Sound File Formats Supported by WHAM
Sound Format	*Description*
RIFF Waveform	The Microsoft Windows WAV sound format. This format is used for Windows system sounds. RIFF Waveform files have the extension .WAV. RIFF Waveform sounds may be of 8-bit or 16-bit resolution.
Raw 8-bit sample	Sound files in this format consist of nothing more than the samples that they are comprised of.
Creative Voice	This is the SoundBlaster sound format and has the VOC extension. WHAM can currently deal only with uncompressed VOC files. The WHAM VOC format driver can handle only 8-bit VOC files.
Amiga IFF	This is the standard Amiga 8-bit sound (8SVX) format. These files are often given the extension IFF. These files contain only 8-bit sounds.
Sun/NeXT sound	This is the standard sound format of the Sun and NeXT workstations, and traditionally have the AU extension. These formats can contain either 8-bit or 16-bit linear or Mu-Law samples.
AIFF	This format was developed by Apple and is also used by Silicon Graphics (SGI) workstations. The AIFF file structure is based on the Amiga IFF tagged file structure, although it is *not* the same as the IFF (8SVX) format. AIFF files may be of 8-bit or 16-bit resolution.

Q: What are linear and Mu-Law samples?

Most sounds are stored using linear samples. Here, the amplitude readings are conventional, linear numbers. Mu-Law samples are another way of encoding sounds. Mu-Law sounds have logarithmic, rather than linear, samples. This gives 14-bit resolution, but uses only 8 bits. Mu-Law encoding is used mainly on workstations.

Most sound drivers for Microsoft Windows 3.1 do not directly support Mu-Law encoding, which is a shame. This means that sounds currently have to be converted to linear samples in order to be played from Windows. However, Microsoft has released an updated RIFF sound file specification that includes support for Mu-Law encoding. I will add full Mu-Law support to WHAM as soon as I have a Windows sound driver (for the Gravis UltraSound) that complies with the updated specification.

Chapter 25
LView Pro 1.8

Copyright 1994 Leonardo Haddad Loureiro

LView Pro 1.8 is an image file editor for Microsoft Windows 3.1, Windows for Workgroups 3.11, Win32s, and Windows NT. It loads and saves image files in JPEG JFIF (JPG), GIF 87a/89a (GIF), TIFF (TIF), Truevision Targa (TGA), Windows and OS/2 bitmap (BMP), ZSoft's PCX (PCX), and PBMPLUS' PBM, PGM, and PPM (PBM, PGM, PPM) formats. LView Pro is one of the most popular Internet-based image viewers for viewing, manipulating, and printing bitmap images from FTP sites, World Wide Web (WWW) pages, and Gophers. If you send and receive a lot of images through e-mail, LView Pro can display almost anything you want.

The version included on the *Internet GIZMOS for Windows* CD is *shareware* from the same author of the *freeware* version of LView, Leonardo Haddad Loureiro. Contact him at mmedia@world.std.com. Send mail and registration forms to him at

Leonardo Haddad Loureiro
1501 East Hallandale Beach Boulevard, #254
Hallandale, FL 33009
USA

About LView Pro

Image file formats

LView Pro supports the following image file formats:

JPEG	Joint Photographers Expert Group, JFIF. Reads baseline compliant JPEG/JFIF files. Writes JPEG/JFIF files in 3 or 1 (grayscale) bytes per pixel, 2H2V subsampling.
BMP	MS Windows and OS/2 bitmap. Reads and writes BMP files with 1, 4, 8, and 24 bits of color information per pixel.

(continued)

TIFF	Aldus' Tagged Image File Format 6.0. Reads TIFF files with 1, 4, 8, and 24 bits of color information per pixel, in strip or tile format, uncompressed or compressed with PackBits, Next compression, Thunderscan, or LZW compression. Writes TIFF files with 1, 4, 8, and 24-bits of color information per pixel, always in strip format, either uncompressed or using LZW compression.
TGA	Truevision Targa. Reads TGA files with 8, 15, 16, and 32 bits of color information per pixel. Writes TGA files with 8 or 24 bits of color information per pixel, uncompressed.
GIF	CompuServe's GIF87a and GIF89a. Reads and writes GIF87a and GIF89a formats. Writes transparent color and background color information when using GIF89a format.
PCX	ZSoft's PCX. Reads all PCX versions, with 1, 4, 8, or 24 bits of color information per pixel. Writes PCX Version 3.0, with 1, 4, 8, or 24 bits of color information per pixel.
PBM, PGM, and PPM	Jef Poskanzer's PBMPLUS formats. Reads PBM (Portable Bitmap, monochrome), PGM (Portable Graymap, grayscale), and PPM (Portable Pixmap) in both ASCII and RAWBITS formats. Writes PPM files in RAWBITS format.

Additional file formats may be added in future versions.

Hardware requirements

LView Pro 1.8 requires a 386 or better CPU and a true color SVGA card, although the software will run under most cards and Windows video configurations. A mouse is required for performing most editing functions, including drag-and-drop functions.

You can get a registered version of the software for the 486 or Pentium CPUs. Write to the address on the registration form at the end of this chapter.

Software requirements

The shareware version of the software is a 16-bit application targeted to Microsoft Windows 3.1 and Windows for Workgroups 3.11. The software has been tested to run under Windows NT 3.5. We recommend that Windows NT users use the 32-bit registered version. Registered versions of the software may be obtained for the Win32s extension of Windows 3.1.

Package contents

Table 25-1 lists the files in the LView Pro 1.8 directory on the CD-ROM.

Table 25-1	LView Pro 1.8 Files
File	*Purpose*
LVIEWP18.EXE	LView Pro 1.8 executable file
LVIEWP.HLP	LView Pro 1.8 help file
README.1ST	General information about LView Pro 1.8
IREGISTR.TXT	Individual user registration form
SREGISTR.TXT	Site license registration form
CHANGES.TXT	Summary of version changes

Menus

File menu

New — This command prompts for image dimensions and then creates a new image for editing. The new image background is painted with the color defined in the Options⇨Background Color command. This command is useful for creating a (blank) image and then defining its contents with the Edit⇨Add Text command and/or the Edit⇨Paste command.

Open — Use this command to select the filename containing an image to be loaded into LView Pro for viewing or editing. Regardless of the filename extension, LView Pro examines the file's contents and determines the internal file format among the supported formats. If loading is successful, the File⇨Save command uses the same filename. This command is also available on the toolbar.

Reopen — This command reloads the last file loaded by LView Pro. This may be useful after previewing a JPEG file and switching to Normal decompression mode. See Options⇨Jpeg I/O for an explanation about decompression modes. This command is also available on the toolbar (click the *right* mouse button).

Save — Saves the current image using the filename from the last File⇨Open execution. If this filename doesn't exist or is invalid, LView Pro uses File⇨Save as. This command is also available on the toolbar (click the *right* mouse button).

Save as — This command prompts for a filename to which to save the current image. Select a format from among those provided. This command is also available on the toolbar.

Delete — Use this command to delete the last file you specified in File⇨Open or File⇨Save as. If the delete is not successful, LView Pro displays a message saying so.

Print — Use this command to configure printing options and then print the current image. Use the File⇨Printer Setup and Options⇨Printer commands to customize other printing options.

Printer Setup — Use this command to select and configure the target printer. The File⇨Print command also lets you do this. Use this command in conjunction with Options⇨Printer to customize image printout.

Exit — This command ends LView Pro's execution. If the current image has been edited, LView Pro offers to save it before exiting.

Edit menu

Undo — Use this command to undo the last edit made to the current image. When undoing is not possible, this command is dimmed. To free memory allocated to undo buffers, use the Options⇨Interface dialog box and disable undo operations. This command is also available on the toolbar.

Cut — This command cuts the image or current selection area and places it in the Clipboard. The Options⇨Interface command lets you choose the Clipboard image format. When you delete a selection area, it is replaced with the color selected in Options⇨Background Color. This command is also available on the toolbar.

Copy — This command copies the image or selection area to the Clipboard. The original image or area is left unchanged. The Options⇨Interface command lets you choose Clipboard image format. This command is also available on the toolbar.

Paste — This command is enabled whenever DIB or DDB data is present in the Clipboard. The Paste operation is performed differently depending on the current state of LView Pro. If no image is currently loaded, the pasted image becomes the current image. If an image is being edited and no selection area is defined, the pasted image is placed in a detached selection area. If an image is being edited and a selection area is defined, the pasted image replaces the selection area contents, maintaining the selection area dimensions. This command is also available on the toolbar.

Delete — This command deletes the current image (not the file) or the current selection area. When a selection area is deleted, it is replaced with the color selected in the Options⇨Background Color command.

Capture — This command captures elements from the desktop into LView Pro's window. Capturing modes are as follows:

- Window — Use the left mouse button to select a window. The contents of the selected window, including caption and frame, are captured.

- Client Area — Use the left mouse button to select a window. The client area of the selected window (excluding caption and frame) is captured.

- Desktop Area — Click the left mouse button to determine a corner of an area on the desktop, drag the mouse pointer to define a rectangular area, and release the button when done. The area is captured.

- Desktop — The whole desktop is captured.

  If no image is currently loaded, the captured image becomes the new current image. If an image is already loaded, the captured image becomes a selection area. If an image is already loaded and a selection area is defined, the captured image replaces the selection area contents, maintaining the area's dimensions.

Resize — This command lets you change the dimensions of the current image or selection area. Choose from among the predefined dimensions, or enter custom values for Columns and/or Rows. Special options in this dialog box include

- "New size/Current size ratio" scroll bars — Let you enter resize ratios for the new image dimensions. For example, scroll to 0.5 to reduce one dimension to $1/2$ of its original value, or scroll to 3.0 to enlarge one dimension three times its original value. When "Preserve aspect ratio" is checked, scrolling one scroll bar moves the other scroll bar to preserve the aspect ratio.

- Fit to desktop — Resizes the image to occupy the maximum desktop area. The resulting window contains scroll bars because the window caption, menu, and frame are not counted. The image is fully visible (without being resized) in full-screen mode.

- Fit to max client — Resizes the image to occupy the maximum client area size. The image is fully visible without scroll bars.

- Preserve aspect ratio — Alters the selected Column or Row value to keep the original image aspect ratio

   This command is also available on the toolbar.

Redimension — This command is similar to Edit⇨Resize. Redimension does not change the image's aspect ratio but adds or takes columns and rows from or to the current image or selection area.

Crop — This command is only available when a selection area is defined. It replaces the current image by the contents of that area. This command is also available on the toolbar.

Undefine — This command undefines the current selection area.

Apply — This command is available when the selection area is detached. It tiles the selection area over the editing image at its current position.

Add Text — This command lets you add a string of text to the current image. Text is always added to a detached selection area that can be moved, applied, or deleted after closing this command's dialog box. When no area is defined, this command creates a default selection area in the upper-left corner of the current image. The dialog box lets you define characteristics for the text to be added, such as color, background color, orientation, positioning, font, and text background transparency. You can also move and resize the selected area while defining the text to be added by using the Modify selection area scroll bars. This command is also available on the toolbar.

Flip Horizontal — Flips (mirrors) the image horizontally. If a selection area is defined, LView Pro flips only that area. This command is also available on the toolbar.

Flip Vertical — Flips (mirrors) the image vertically. If a selection area is defined, LView Pro flips only that area. This command is also available on the toolbar.

Rotate Left — Rotates the image counterclockwise, transforming rows into columns and vice versa. If a selection area is defined, LView Pro rotates only that area. This command is also available on the toolbar.

Rotate Right — Rotates the image clockwise, transforming rows into columns and vice versa. If a selection area is defined, LView Pro rotates only that area. This command is also available on the toolbar.

Retouch menu

Gamma Correction — Use this command to specify the amount of gamma correction to apply to all image pixels. Use gamma correction to brighten or darken the image. If Lock RGB Scroll bars is checked, moving one scroll bar moves the other two. Otherwise, you can set gamma correction values individually for red, green, and blue components. Values above 0 brighten the corresponding color component on all pixels, values below 0 darken the corresponding color component on all pixels. Gamma correction may not be suitable for all images. Retouch⇨Exp Enhance, Retouch⇨Log Enhance, and Retouch⇨SineH Enhance can also brighten your image.

Editing in true color mode is a slow process. In this mode, when Lock RGB Scroll bars is not checked, changes are performed only when you click the Exec button, so you can alter more than one parameter before waiting for command execution.

Click Cancel to discard any changes you have made. Click OK to confirm the changes. This command is also available on the toolbar.

Color Balance — Use this command to specify increments or decrements for red, green, and blue color components. The values specified are added to each pixel in the image. For instance, a pixel whose current value is RGB (10, 10, 10) becomes RGB (20, 10, 10) if you move the red scroll bar to 10 and keep the others at 0. The maximum value for a color component is 255, and the minimum, 0. LView Pro truncates invalid results.

Editing in true color mode is a slow process. In this mode, changes are made only when you click the Exec button, so you can alter more than one parameter before waiting for command execution.

Click Cancel to discard any changes you have made and terminate the dialog box. Click OK to confirm the changes and terminate the dialog box. This command is also available on the toolbar.

Contrast Enhance — Use this dialog window to alter the image contrast. Contrast enhancement is obtained by brightening darker pixels and darkening brighter ones (to reduce contrast) or doing the opposite (to increase contrast). Contrast offsets vary from –64 (no contrast) to +64 (maximum contrast).

Click Cancel to discard any changes you have made. Click OK to confirm the changes. This command is also available on the toolbar.

HSV Adjust — Use this dialog to edit the hue, saturation, and value components for all pixels in the image. Hue is a circular value denoting the dominant color tendency among red, green, and blue. Saturation is the amount of color in the image; 0 saturation produces a grayscale image. Value is a measure of lightness. For saturation and value, scrolling to positive values increases the component. For hue, the scrolling extremes take you back to hue = 0. HSV editing may be useful to reduce or increase the amount of color in certain images by varying the saturation control. You can use the value control to brighten or darken an image, although the Retouch⇨Log Enhance, Retouch⇨Exp Enhance, Retouch⇨SineH Enhance, and Retouch⇨Gamma Correction usually do a better job. Hue is useful to adjust some images that were originally scanned with excess yellow or green (due to bad scanner setup).

Editing in true color mode is a slow process. In this mode, changes are made only when you click the Exec button, so you can alter more than one parameter before waiting for command execution.

Click Cancel to discard any changes you have made. Click OK to confirm the changes. This command is also available on the toolbar.

YCbCr Adjust — This command lets you adjust Y, Cb, and Cr values for all pixels in the image. The YCbCr color system is used for color TV broadcast in Europe. Y is known as the *luminance* component, and affects pixel luminosity. Cb and Cr are known as the *chrominance* components, and together they define the color for each pixel. Roughly speaking, Cb and Cr represent the balance between blue and red in relation to green. As in the Retouch⇨HSV Adjust command, YCbCr editing may be useful to correct images that were poorly scanned (in terms of color balance). While the Y component can darken or brighten the image, Retouch⇨Log Enhance, Retouch⇨Exp Enhance, Retouch⇨SineH Enhance, and Retouch⇨Gamma Correction usually do a better job.

Editing in true color mode is a slow process. In this mode, changes are made only when you click the Exec button, so you can alter more than one parameter before waiting for command execution.

Click Cancel to discard any changes you have made. Click OK to confirm the changes. This command is also available on the toolbar.

Interactive RGB — This command lets you define and execute arbitrary user-defined transformation maps for the red, green, and blue color components of all pixels in the image. Transformation maps are functions of a single variable yielding a single result. An example of a map is 2*x, which doubles the value of original color components. This command treats red, green, and blue like real (floating point) numbers ranging from 0 to 1.

If you do not want to define a map in algebraic terms, you can still use the mouse to draw a curve representing the desired transformation and uncheck the Use Functions check box.

LView Pro stores up to 20 map definitions in its initialization file. The first 10 maps are predefined by LView Pro, but they can be edited and customized by the user. Interactive RGB comes in handy when dealing with images for which none of the predefined Retouch Menu commands produce satisfactory results. Mappings for some of the Retouch commands (Retouch⇨Log Enhance, Retouch⇨Exp Enhance, and Retouch⇨SineH Enhance) were actually discovered through experimentation with Interactive RGB.

Options and tools in this command's dialog box include

- The Map Graph window — Shows a graphical representation of the selected map and allows for interactive definition (by drawing with the mouse) of a map.

- Ordering — Choose None if you do not want the mapping to be non-decreasing nor non-increasing. Choose Increasing if you do not want to allow f(x) < f(y) for x > y. Choose Decreasing if you do not want to allow f(x) > f(y) for x > y. Decreasing maps produce image photographic negative effects.

- Lock RGB Graphs — Check this box if you want a single function definition or if you want to use map drawing to be for red, green, and blue components. Uncheck this box if you want to define separate functions or map drawings for each component. Using different maps for different components may help correct color component unbalancing.

- Use Functions — This item is automatically unchecked whenever you draw in the Map Graph window. When this item is unchecked, LView Pro does not consider the current function expression shown in the Select Function listbox. When this item is checked, LView Pro uses the function definition exhibited in the Select Function listbox.

- Select Function listbox — Choose one of the predefined function's definitions for editing or to define the map in the Map Graphiwindow.

- Edit Function definition — Click this button to replace the function definition for the current item shown in the Select Function listbox.

- Color Component — Choose the color component function to show in the Map Graphiwindow. If Lock RGB Graphs is unchecked, each color component stores its own definition.

- Click Exec to execute the current Interactive RGB setup. Click Cancel to discard changes made to the image. Click OK to keep changes made to the image. This command is also available on the toolbar.

Exp Enhance — Use this command to set the desired level of exponential enhancement for all pixels in the image. Exponential enhancement brightens dark pixels in the image, while simultaneously reducing overall image contrast.

Exp Enhance may not be generally adequate for images, but it comes in handy for highly contrasted images. Click Cancel to discard any changes you have made. Click OK to confirm the changes. This command is also available on the toolbar.

Log Enhance — Use this dialog window to specify the desired level of logarithmic enhancement for all pixels in the image. Logarithmic enhancement brightens dark pixels, while keeping already bright ones from becoming too bright. It may not be generally adequate for images, but it often produces better results than Retouch⇨Gamma Correction for brightening dark images. Click Cancel to discard any changes you have made. Click OK to confirm the changes. This command is also available on the toolbar.

SineH Enhance — Use this dialog window to specify the desired level of hyperbolic sine enhancement for all pixels in the image. Hyperbolic sine enhancement brightens dark pixels, while simultaneously increasing overall image contrast. It may not be generally adequate for images, but it comes in handy for poorly contrasted images with dark areas. Click Cancel to discard any changes you have made. Click OK to confirm the changes. This command is also available on the toolbar.

Grayscale — This command transforms a color image into grayscale. Each pixel is transformed into the gray pixel (red = green = blue) with approximately the same luminosity. If undo operations are enabled in Options⇨Interface, restore the original image with Edit⇨Undo. This command is also available on the toolbar.

Negative — This command transforms a color or grayscale image into its photographic negative. Each pixel's luminosity is nearly complemented. If undo operations are enabled in Options⇨Interface, restore the original image with Edit⇨Undo. This command is also available on the toolbar.

Palette Entry — This command activates the Palette Entry Color dialog box, where you can select one of the palette entries for editing. When a palette entry is selected, the 24-bit Color dialog box appears next. Respecify the selected entry. When you click OK, the palette entry is altered to the new specification, and the image is redrawn. This command is only available for color palette-based images. To cancel this command, click Cancel in either color dialog box. This command is also available on the toolbar.

Color Depth — Use this command to redefine the current image's *color depth* — the maximum number of colors that can be used to display the image. This command's dialog box has the following controls:

- True color image — Displays up to 16.7 million colors. Your graphics card may not be able to show a true color image correctly.

- Palette image — Displays up to 256 colors. You can also determine the number of colors in the color palette.

- 256 colors (including Windows palette) — LView Pro creates a new palette for the image or adapts the current palette to hold 256 color entries. The default Windows colors are included in the resulting palette.

- Windows palette (16 colors) — LView Pro tries to represent the current image using only the 16 default colors (the colors Windows uses for caption bars, buttons, text, and so on).

- Black and White — LView Pro displays the image using only black and white pixels.

- Custom number of colors — Use this item if you want a palette-based image with fewer than 256 and more than 16 color possibilities. The default Windows colors are always included among the set of resulting colors.

  When you're changing the color depth of an image from true color to palette image, it is necessary to create a new palette of colors. Each pixel in the original image must then be mapped to one of the colors in that new palette. In the process of mapping, many colors in the image will not find a perfect match among palette colors. One approach in this case is to represent the color with the palette entry that best approximates it. Another approach is to try to represent non-matching colors using a group of pixels. These pixels (like color combinations in an impressionist painting) approximate the desired color. This last approach is called *dithering*, and LView Pro will use it when the Enable Floyd-Steinberg Dithering option is checked.

Image Filters — Use this command to execute an image filter and/or to define a new image filter specification. Image Filters perform averaging operations on color components of neighboring pixels. The resulting color components for any given pixel are calculated based on the current color components of its neighbors and itself. LView Pro defines some default filter specifications at the beginning of the Select Filter listbox. You can freely edit these default specifications and later restore them by clicking the Defaults button. For best results, apply image filters to true color images. To operate on a palette image, quantize it; but the resultant color information loss may be noticeable. This dialog box has the following controls:

- Selected Filter listbox — Select one of the filters in this list, either to edit its definition or to execute it in the current image.

- Affected Color Components — Only color components (red, green, and blue) that are checked are affected when the filter executes. In most cases, you should check all three components.

- Rename Current Filter — Lets you rename a filter specification to better describe its action. LView Pro initializes the first few filters in the list, while you must define (and rename) the rest. You can edit and rename all filters.

■ Filter Matrix — Each entry in this matrix contains a multiplier. When a filter is executed, the Filter Matrix is centered at each pixel in the image, and pixels in a 5x5 neighborhood of the center pixel (including the central pixel itself) have their color components multiplied by matrix entries. All 25 (5x5) products are added.

■ Division Factor — This value divides the sum from Filter Matrix above. Usually, this parameter is the sum of all Filter Matrix indices, but a slightly smaller or bigger value may be used to brighten or darken the image proportionally.

■ Bias — The final step in applying the filter is to add the Bias parameter to the result of the Filter Matrix sum divided by the Division Factor. This value replaces the color component of the central pixel.

■ Click Default to restore LView Pro's default filter specifications. This overwrites the first nine filters currently defined. Double-clicking on a filter name makes LView Pro execute that filter and end the dialog box. Click Exec to execute the filter currently selected in the Selected Filter listbox. Click Cancel to terminate this dialog box and discard any changes made to the image during dialog execution. Click OK to terminate this dialog and keep changes made to the image. This command is also available on the toolbar.

Options menu

Full Screen — Displays the image centered in the screen. The screen background is black. If needed, LView Pro shrinks the image to fit the screen. This mode can be automatically set when displaying images in a Slideshow. To exit this mode, click the left mouse button, or press the Esc key. This command is also available on the toolbar.

One keystroke — This command configures combo retouch operations. A combo retouch operation can perform up to eight preprogrammed retouch functions in sequence. The current combo retouch operation is started by a keyboard accelerator key (Ctrl+K). Available retouch operations are

    Retouch⇨Gamma Correction
    Retouch⇨Color Balance
    Retouch⇨Contrast Enhance
    Retouch⇨HSV Enhance
    Retouch⇨YCbCr Enhance
    Retouch⇨Exp Enhance
    Retouch⇨Log Enhance
    Retouch⇨SineH Enhance
    Retouch⇨Image Filters (available only for true color images)

Using one-keystroke retouch operations is useful when editing a series of similar images. If, for example, all images are too dark, low in contrast, and need color balancing, define a one-keystroke combo using Retouch⇨SineH Enhance, Retouch⇨Contrast Enhance, and Retouch⇨Color Balance in that order. Each operation is limited by values in the same range as in the scroll bars present in their dialog boxes. Image filter operations are limited by the (0-based) displacement of the desired filter in the Retouch⇨Image Filters dialog.

Use the Select retouch combo listbox to determine what retouch combo LView Pro uses in reply to the Ctrl+K keyboard accelerator. To edit the selected retouch combo, select up to eight retouch operations in the Combo retouch operations and parameters window. Select the operations and parameters suitable for the images to be edited. Select No operation to fill entries where no operation is desired. Click the Edit combo name button to rename the retouch combo currently selected.

LView Pro defines a few retouch combo operations. You can change these and then restore them by clicking Defaults. The predefined retouch combo operations may not produce the same effect in different video monitors and/or graphics cards.

Double-clicking on a combo operation makes LView Pro execute that operation and close the dialog box. Clicking on the Exec button closes the dialog box and executes the currently selected combo retouch operation. Clicking OK closes the dialog box, saving the changes made to the currently selected combo retouch operation. Clicking Cancel closes the dialog box and discards changes made to the currently selected combo retouch operation. Changes to a combo retouch operation are saved when another combo is selected, so Cancel does not discard these.

Interface — Several interface options are configured in this dialog window (see Figure 25-1). With few exceptions, these options are usually configured after installation and remain unchanged afterwards. Following is an individual description for each option:

- Enable undo — LView Pro reserves memory for undo buffers if this option is checked. In systems where main memory is relatively small, or if you edit very large images, leaving this option on will make LView Pro frequently run out of memory. The command Edit⇨Undo is not available when this option is off.

- Auto quantize setup — When this option is on, LView Pro chooses the adequate way for loading images in the current graphics mode. This setup is done every time LView Pro is loaded, and you are prompted to accept any necessary changes. If this option is off, LView Pro uses the parameters set in Options⇨Quantizing.

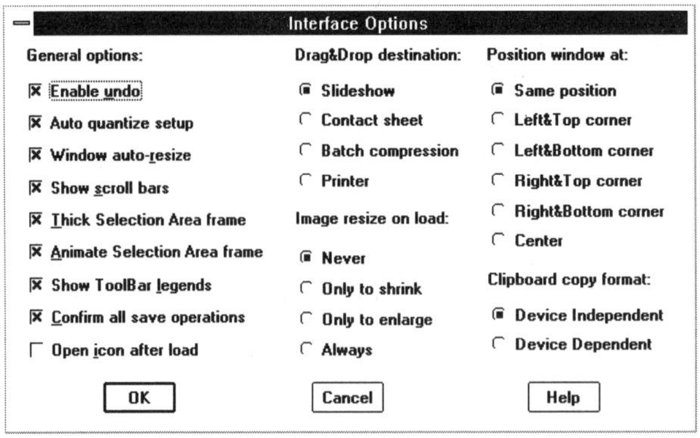

Figure 25-1: Interface Options dialog box.

■ Window auto-resize — Checking this option makes LView Pro resize its window to fit the current editing image dimensions. When a perfect fit is not possible and Options⇨Show Scroll Bars is checked, scroll bars are available. Unchecking this option prevents LView Pro from changing the dimensions of its window.

■ Show scroll bars — When this option is checked, LView Pro displays scroll bars whenever the current editing image cannot be fully displayed inside LView Pro's client area. When this option is unchecked, scroll bars are not used. You can still scroll while defining a selection area by using keyboard accelerator keys.

■ Thick selection area frame — This option controls the width used for selection area borders. Check it to specify a thicker and easier-to-move-and-drag area frame. When this item is unchecked, the selection area border width and height are one pixel.

■ Animate selection area frame — When this option is checked, selection area frames are animated for easier operation. Uncheck this option to turn animation off.

■ Show Toolbar legends — When this option is checked, LView Pro shows a legend explaining the function of toolbar buttons, whenever the mouse pointer stays positioned over one of these buttons for a short while.

■ Confirm all save operations — Check this option to receive a confirmation message from LView Pro before saving images to the disk. When this option is unchecked, LView Pro does not confirm before saving an image when you select File⇨Save or click the Save icon in the tool bar. When you're saving images in JPEG grayscale format, a confirmation prompt may be exhibited regardless of this option.

■ Open icon after load — Check this option if you want LView Pro to restore its window (if the window was minimized) when an image load operation is completed. Uncheck it if you prefer LView Pro to remain minimized.

■ Drag&Drop destination — Selects which Open Destination function processes multiple file selections dropped to LView Pro's window or icon.

■ Image resize on load — LView Pro may optionally resize images when it loads them. Check Never if you do not want to use this feature, Only to shrink if you only want to resize images larger or wider than the maximum client window, Only to enlarge if you want images smaller than the maximum client window to be enlarged, or Always to resize all images.

■ Position window at — Selects where LView Pro places its window every time an image is loaded or image dimensions are changed. Choose from the desktop corners and the desktop center. Select Same position if you do not want to use this feature.

■ Clipboard copy format — LView Pro may use one of two formats when copying images to the Clipboard. The Device Independent Bitmap (DIB) format is recommended to fully describe an image in terms of color resolution, independent of the current graphics mode. This is also the format used in Windows BMP files. Some applications do not support the DIB format. When generating a Clipboard image to be pasted into one of these applications, use the Device Dependent Bitmap (DDB) format. When you're pasting from the Clipboard, LView Pro will look first for data in DIB format. In the absence of DIB data, if a DDB is present, LView Pro will paste it and convert it into DIB format. This command is also available on the toolbar.

Background Color — This command opens the 24-bit Color dialog box when the current image has 24-bit/pixel color information or the Palette Entry Color dialog box when the current image has palette-based color information. The color you define is used to paint images created with the File⇨New command, and to paint image areas after the Edit⇨Cut or Edit⇨Delete commands are executed on a selection area. When the Edit⇨Redimension command increases the number of columns or rows, the new image area is also painted with this color. When you're saving an image to a disk file using either the GIF87a or the GIF89a format, LView Pro stores the background color that is currently selected in that file. This information is read the next time the file is loaded.

Quantizing — This command's dialog box is similar to the one associated to the Retouch⇨Color Depth command. Use it to configure the resulting color depth when loading images. When Auto quantizing setup in Options⇨Interface is checked, LView Pro sets the quantizing options adequate for your graphics card when it starts. Notice that black and white quantizing on load is not supported for JPEG images. When you're saving an image to a disk file using the GIF89a format, LView Pro stores the background color currently selected as the GIF's transparent color.

Jpeg I/O — Use this command to define JPEG input and output (compression and decompression) parameters. LView Pro offers two JPEG decompression modes: Normal and Preview. Set options that yield higher decompression quality for Normal decompression mode, and aim for speed when choosing Preview decompression options. Switching from one mode to the other is simple: use the *right* mouse button to click this dialog's button on the toolbar. The Toolbar button also provides visual information to tell which mode is currently set. When Normal mode is set, the button is painted blue. When Preview mode is set, the button is painted red. If you decide to reload a file, after loading it in Preview mode, use File⇨Reload. This command is also available on the toolbar, if you click the *right* mouse button on the File⇨Open button. In this dialog box, the mode for which options are being set is indicated at the "Jpeg decompression" title, as either Normal or Preview. To select options for the other mode, click either Switch to Preview mode or Switch to Normal mode, depending on which mode is currently being edited. The mode being edited when you click OK becomes the current decompression mode. Because JPEG decompression offers special quantizing and dithering options, it does not perform black and white quantizing on load (if specified in Options⇨Quantizing). To reduce color to black and white, use Retouch⇨Color Depth.

- Load grayscale — Check this box to force JPEG images to be loaded without color information. When this option is checked, JPEG decompression is faster. This feature may be useful in the Preview decompression setup.

- Fast upsampling — Check this box to select a faster but less precise upsampling algorithm. Uncheck it to slightly improve image decompression quality. Checking this option may be useful in the Preview decompression setup.

- 1-pass quantize — Check this box to select a faster but less precise quantizing algorithm. Uncheck it to improve image decompression quality. This option is useful in the Preview decompression setup.

- Fast dithering — Check this box to select a faster but less precise dithering algorithm. Uncheck it to improve image decompression quality. This option is useful in the Preview decompression setup.

- DCT method — Choose among three methods for computing discrete cosine transforms. Use Integer accurate for slower but accurate integer computation (recommended for the Normal setup). Use Integer fast for faster, less accurate integer computation (recommended for the Preview setup). Use Floating point for the most accurate computation, but note that it is slower than the integer methods.

- Scaling ratio — This option loads a JPEG file using its full dimensions (1:1) or scales its dimensions at load time, using a 1:2, 1:4, or 1:8 scaling ratio. Decompression speed rapidly increases as scaling ratio denominators grow, and this feature is certainly useful in the Preview decompression setup. This dialog box has these compression parameters:

Compression quality — Can assume values from 20 to 95. The lower/ higher the value, the smaller/bigger the resulting file, yielding greater/ smaller compression ratios. Notice that there is a tradeoff between compressed file size and posterior decompression fidelity to the original image. The bigger/smaller the compression quality, the better/worse the decompressed image.

Entropy optimization — When checked, JPEG compression takes longer but usually generates slightly smaller files.

Save grayscale — Check this option when compressing a grayscale image to JPEG format. Images stored in JPEG grayscale format produce smaller files and are decompressed faster than JPEG images stored with color information.

- Confirm before saving in grayscale format — Check this option to make LView Pro confirm each time an image is saved to JPEG format with the Save grayscale option checked. It is a good idea to leave this option checked, since it is possible to forget the Save grayscale option is checked after saving a grayscale image. When this option is checked, LView Pro prompts for confirmation before conducting the save operation. In the confirmation message, you have the choice of confirming the save operation (if you really want to save the image in grayscale format) by clicking Yes, canceling the save operation by clicking Cancel, or saving the image in color JPEG format by clicking No.

- Click OK to confirm the options you entered. Click Cancel to discard any changes you have made. This command is also available on the toolbar.

Slideshow — LView Pro can load and display a sequence of image files in a slideshow. You can select files for the slideshow with File⇨Multiple Open, or by using Windows File Manager to select the files and setting the "Drag&Drop Destination" to slide show. This command's dialog box customizes the slide show behavior. Its options include the following:

- Cycle slides — When this option is checked, the first file reloads after the last one is shown.

- View full screen — When this option is checked, images are displayed in full-screen mode.

- Interactive after mouse click — When this option is selected, an image is displayed until the *right* mouse button is clicked in LView Pro's client area (or on the desktop when in full-screen mode).

- Automatic after X seconds — When this option is selected, it loads the next image after the desired number of seconds.

■ To abort the slide show in full-screen mode, click the left mouse button. Otherwise, click the menu bar.

Printer — In this command's dialog box, you specify

■ Column enlargement/shrinking percentage *and* Row enlargement/shrinking percentage — Setting these to 100% produces an image in the actual printer resolution. Setting them to different values alters the aspect ratio on the resulting image. Values greater than 100% enlarge the corresponding dimension. Values smaller than 100% shrink the corresponding dimension.

■ Fit to printer page — When this option is checked, LView Pro enlarges or shrinks the image to maximize the printed area.

■ Center — When this option is checked, LView Pro centers the image printout.

Contact Sheet — A contact sheet is an image that groups smaller images. Use it to catalog related images. The smaller images are sometimes called *thumbnails*. This command's dialog box configures the contact sheet's text font, text size, text attributes and position, text color, text background, image background and image dimensions. These options are used when a multiple file selection is performed and the drag-and-drop destination in Options⇨Interface is set to contact sheet. File⇨Multiple Open can also build a contact sheet. Before building a contact sheet, LView Pro displays the Contact Sheet Preview dialog box.

Memory — When main memory is low, some functions may use secondary memory (temporary disk files). Use this dialog window to enable or disable temporary file usage and to specify the directory where temporary files should be created.

Load All — Use this command to restore all LView Pro configuration options from the initialization file.

Save All — Use this command to save LView Pro's current configuration options to the initialization file.

Default — Use this menu to reset all LView Pro's configuration options to their factory defaults. The options are set for the current LView Pro execution and are not saved to the initialization file. To make the default options available for later execution, use the Options⇨Save All command.

Help menu

Contents — This command starts the help system positioned at the help Contents topic. This command is also available on the toolbar.

About LView Pro 1.8 — This command opens a dialog window containing information about LView Pro 1.8. Related help topics are Package Contents and LView Pro 1.8 Licensing, Registration, and Distribution. This command is also available on the toolbar.

Registration & Distribution — Gives information about registering and distributing LView Pro.

Diagnosis — Use this command to get information about how to set up LView Pro for the current graphics mode.

Device Caps — Use this command to get information about the display driver installed in your system. LView Pro gets this information directly from the display driver.

The Toolbar

Each toolbar button selects a command also available in LView Pro's menus. To execute a button's function, click it with the left mouse button. Some buttons execute a different command when clicked with the *right* mouse button.

LView Pro may, optionally, exhibit a legend containing a short explanation about the function of individual toolbar buttons. To enable or disable this feature, use the option Show Toolbar legends in Options⇨Interface. When this option is enabled, a legend appears every time the mouse pointer stays positioned over a toolbar button for a short while.

The Toolbar window can be positioned in three locations: to the left of LView Pro's window, to the right of LView Pro's window, and at LView Pro's caption bar. The position of the toolbar is updated to the initialization file every time you exit LView Pro, and is retrieved the next time you start it.

To move the Toolbar window to either side, click the left mouse button on its caption bar. To place the Toolbar window at LView Pro's caption bar, click the button at the Toolbar window caption. To restore the Toolbar window from LView Pro's caption bar, click the tool icon at LView Pro's caption bar.

Selection Area Operations _____

Selection areas are image pieces that can be processed separately from the current image. Most commands in the Edit menu work on the current selection area, when one is defined. On the other hand, commands in the Retouch menu are only available when no selection area is defined.

Introduction

You can use a selection area to delimit an image area for cropping, to hold an image pasted from the Clipboard, to delimit an area of the editing image to be copied to the Clipboard, to duplicate or move parts of the current image, and more.

A selection area can be in one of two states: *defined* and *detached*. An area is said to be defined when it is visually represented by a red and white frame. Defined means that the user has delimited an area. When a selection area becomes detached, its frame is changed to blue and white. A detached selection area contains its own image information, independent of the current image.

Creating a defined selection area

Click either the left or right mouse button anywhere on the current image; then (without releasing the mouse button) drag the mouse pointer. A selection area frame appears, delimiting the rectangular area defined by the point where you first clicked the mouse button and the current mouse pointer position. There is no required order for selection area definition; the point where you initially click the mouse button may end up being any of the four corners defining the area, depending on where you release the mouse button. Release the mouse button when done.

The defined selection area frame has a handle at each corner. The handles are small squares outside the frame rectangle. To resize the selection area frame, click either the left or right mouse button and drag on one of these handles. To move a defined selection area, click either the left or right mouse button over one of its frame segments and drag the mouse pointer.

After a defined selection area is properly positioned and sized, you can detach it.

Creating a detached selection area

To create a detached selection area from a defined one, click a mouse button anywhere inside the area frame. This operation produces different results depending on the mouse button used. When you use the left mouse button, the original image area contained inside the area frame is erased and painted with the color defined in Options⇨Background Color. If you use the *right* mouse button, the original image is left unchanged, and the selection area holds a copy of it.

When you detach a defined selection area using the left mouse button by mistake, use Edit⇨Undo to undo the operation (when Options⇨Enable Undo is checked).

Moving a detached selection area

Detached selection areas do not have frame handles, and cannot be resized. To move them, click either the left or right mouse button anywhere on or inside the area frame and drag.

Applying a detached selection area

A detached selection area may be applied (tiled) anywhere over the current image. The original contents of the image are overwritten by the contents of the selection area, and the selection area is destroyed.

If you apply a detached selection area by mistake, undo it with Edit⇨Undo (when Options⇨Enable Undo is enabled).

Undefining a selection area

To undefine a defined selection area, click either the left or right mouse button outside the area frame. If the area frame covers the entire image, use Edit⇨Undefine.

To define a detached selection area, use Edit⇨Cut, Edit⇨Delete, or Edit⇨Undefine.

Additional topics on selection areas

The thickness of selection area frames can be adjusted in the Options⇨Interface dialog window.

Selection area frames are animated, by default, for improved visibility over color images. Sometimes the animation process makes it difficult to see the mouse pointer when it is positioned over or near a frame segment. This effect is more easily noticed when using a slower graphics card. For that reason, you can turn this animation off in the Options⇨Interface dialog window.

Performance Comparisons

The *shareware* version of LView Pro is a 16-bit application compiled for the i386 processor. *Registered* versions of LView Pro are available for different platforms, such as for the i486 and Pentium, and for Win32s and Windows NT. The overall performance of LView Pro is improved when switching from the shareware version to one targeted to a better processor or to Win32s/Windows NT.

For most operations, switching from the i386 version to the i486/Pentium version does not yield a significant gain in performance. On the other hand, the change from a 16-bit to a 32-bit version (Win32s/Windows NT) doubles the speed of most operations.

Frequently Asked Questions

Q. Why do colors look wrong when I load an image?

A. Your graphics card may not be able to do better than that. If your graphics card can display at least 256 simultaneous colors, you still have to check if the display driver selected at Windows' Setup allows for 256 color representation. Another possibility is that LView Pro is not trying to auto configure its quantizing options. See whether "Auto quantize setup" is checked in Options⇨Interface.

If everything else failed, LView Pro may not be receiving correct information from the display driver. If not, try unchecking "Auto quantize setup" in Options⇨Interface, and set Options⇨Quantize manually for characteristics you believe your card (and driver) are set to provide.

Q. Why is the command (and toolbar button) Retouch⇨Palette Entry always disabled?

A. Your graphics card must be operating in True or High color mode. Check Help⇨Device Caps for confirmation. If so, LView Pro is loading 24-bit/pixel images without (unnecessary) palette information. The Retouch⇨Palette entry command is only available when the current image is palette-based. (Check Graphics Mode for an explanation about these terms.) If you want to use this command, use Retouch⇨Color Depth to transform the image into a palette-based image. If the original image is stored in 24-bit/pixel format, image quality is lost in the process.

Q. Why is it better to use Retouch⇨Image Filters on True color images?

A. Image filters compute new color values for each pixel in the image. Even if the original image has only 256 colors (or fewer), the resulting image may be composed of thousands (or millions) of colors. When you use Retouch⇨Image Filters on a palette-based image, LView Pro assumes that the result should also be a palette-based image. To produce that result, LView Pro will quantize intermediate and final results to match the number of colors in the original image.

If your card can work in True or High color modes, and the image you are editing is palette-based (such as images produced from GIF files), you should first use Retouch⇨Color Depth and promote it to true color, and then use Retouch⇨Image Filters. LView Pro then assumes that resulting images should also be represented in true color, and it executes the image filters faster and with more precision. If you need to save the image in a palette-based format, you can always use Retouch⇨Color Depth after you are done with filter editing and transform the image back to palette-based format.

Q. Will image format XYZ be supported by LView Pro?

A. LView Pro already supports the most commonly used image formats in the Windows/PC environment. That doesn't mean that new image formats will not be added, but searching for good specifications on image file formats is time-consuming and the priority for these enhancements is not high.

If you want to contribute and produce either clear documentation about a particular file format, or provide source code to read and write files in this format into or from Windows DIB format, I'll gladly add it to LView Pro. It is very easy to plug in another file reader/writer module.

Q. Why are there so many commands to edit brightness and contrast?

A. Video monitors display images with different brightness and contrast sensibilities. The same image viewed on different monitors may look darker in one and brighter in the other. One solution is to regulate the contrast/brightness controls on the monitor. But, given the degree of flexibility provided LView Pro for image editing, it may be better to adjust the image representation instead. The problem is that a single algorithm is not effective for all images. That's why LView Pro provides many different algorithms for contrast/brightness adjustment. Some work only on brightness, like Retouch⇨Gamma Correction, or only on contrast, like Retouch⇨Contrast Enhance. Other commands alter both brightness and contrast, like Retouch⇨Exp Enhance, Retouch⇨Log Enhance, and Retouch⇨SineH Enhance. It is only though experimentation that you will learn which one should be used on a given image.

Brightness and contrast commands all use color mappings to produce their effect. You can develop your own mappings using the Retouch⇨Interactive RGB, either by drawing curves or by specifying algebraic functions. Exp, Log, and SineH enhancement commands were developed through experimentation with this command.

It is often a good approach to use more than one editing function on the same image. By combining the effect of different enhancement functions, one after the other, the resulting image may look more natural.

Q. Can LView Pro process files from the command line?

A. Yes. LView loads each file specified in the command and performs a Slideshow using the currently set Options⇨Slideshow options.

Q. How can I start a slideshow/contact sheet/batch compression/batch printout?

A. One way to perform these operations is by using Windows File Manager with drag-and-drop operations. See the help topic "Multiple File Selection" for more information. Another way is to use File⇨Multiple Open.

LView Pro 1.8 Registration Form

Name _____

Company _____

Address _____

City _____

State _____   Country _____

Zip _____   Phone _____

Remit to:

Leonardo Haddad Loureiro
1501 East Hallandale Bch. Blvd., #254
Hallandale, FL 33009

Pricing

(See the SREGISTR.TXT file on the CD-ROM for site licensing information.) Please provide operating systems and CPU information as well.

❏ $30 (U.S.)

Part VII

Conferencing Applications GIZMOS

Conferencing applications have recently become popular on the Internet. Conferencing occurs in many forms, as discussed in this part.

Shared Text

Shared text is perhaps the best known conferencing technique, because it involves straight text, which any PC or terminal can handle. CompuServe uses this kind of conferencing in its forums. In this kind of conferencing, everyone in the conference sees what everyone else types. In many text-conferencing systems, when more than two people are in a conference, a moderator grants write permission to only one person at a time so that things don't get too confusing.

The Internet version of this kind of conferencing is called Internet Relay Chat (IRC). You can find a shareware package available on several of the major anonymous FTP servers in the file IRCIIWIN.ZIP.

Shared Document Markups

Shared document markup conferencing lets conferees edit a document on-line. Users involved can talk over an audio bridge, usually a conference call over a regular phone system. They also access a single copy of the document on-line. As a discussion of the document takes place, conferees use the mouse and keyboard to add notes to the shared document. When they're finished, someone saves the notes so that the author can make the changes in the document.

Face*to*Face, in Chapter 26, is a shared document markup conferencing system.

Shared Blackboards

Shared blackboard conferencing is a system in which all conferees share a blank screen they can mark with text, lines, and images. Any conferee can save the screen at any time. The conference can be moderated or unmoderated.

Mr. Squiggle, WinSock Point-to-Point Blackboard, is a two-party shared blackboard conference application covered in Chapter 27.

Note Passing

Chapter 28 covers Sticky, an application that lets Internet users pass notes in a fashion similar to those familiar "yellow sticky notes." The recipients of such notes must also run the program so that their computers can accept the incoming messages. You post a note to one or more people, and almost instantly the note appears on their screen(s).

Video Conferencing

A few Internet-based computer-to-computer video teleconferencing applications exist. One of them is called CU-SeeMe, a shareware application available on several popular anonymous FTP servers. Recently, a multiparty, one-way video conferencing scheme called *Mbone* was introduced to the Internet. Mbone relies on Internet IP Multicast service, which needs to be specially configured on routers, and which requires a protocol stack on the endpoint computers that understands IP Multicast. Mbone also requires very high bandwidth and can severely impact performance on slower network links. When this book was written, no Windows implementation was available. If you are interested, you can get more information about Mbone at http://www.eit.com/techinfo/mbone/mbone.html.

Chapter 26
Face*to*Face

Document Conferencing Software for Macintosh and Windows Users

Face*to*Face is the world's first cross-platform document conferencing software for both IBM PCs and compatibles running Microsoft Windows and Macintosh computers.

This version of Face*to*Face provides features specifically for use with the TCP/IP network interface. The standard version provides interfaces to many other networks. In addition, this version functions for only 30 days after the initial installation date. See the coupon from Crosswise at the back of this book for a discount on Face*to*Face.

With Face*to*Face, you can use your telephone and desktop computer to share documents with anyone, anywhere in the world, on a moment's notice. You and your remote colleagues can simultaneously view documents, guide one another with electronic pointers, and make annotations using a simple set of drawing tools — all while you talk on the telephone. You do not have to be concerned about the computers, applications, or networks involved.

Today, people typically fax time-critical documents to one another for review. Face*to*Face offers a faster and more efficient way to accomplish this process. With Face*to*Face, you can send documents to others with a few mouse clicks. While talking on the telephone, you can view and manipulate identical, synchronized images of documents on your computer screens while you make annotations that appear instantly, as you create them. The result is a much faster and clearer review process. You don't need to guide one another through your documents verbally ("go to page ten, second paragraph, third line") or spend time describing comments to each other while taking notes. At the end of a Face*to*Face meeting, everyone walks away with a soft copy of the annotated document he or she can save, print, or forward to others by electronic mail.

Face*to*Face is easy to install and use. Unlike other remote meeting solutions, such as video conferencing, Face*to*Face does not require special hardware or network services. Within minutes, anyone with a telephone and a Windows or Macintosh computer can experience the fastest way to review documents at a distance.

Major Features

- Users in different locations can review and annotate documents in real time, using their desktop computers and telephones.

- Two users of any combination of Windows and Macintosh computers can conduct on-line, on-screen meetings.

- Macintosh users can select meeting participants from either the built-in Face*to*Face Address Book or an Apple PowerTalk Catalogue.

- Meeting participants work with complete documents instead of individual "screen shots" or "screen snaps."

- During a meeting, you can review documents created in any Windows or Macintosh application.

- Face*to*Face automatically distributes documents to each meeting participant. You can save these documents for subsequent review, printing, or forwarding to other users who were unable to attend the meeting.

- Face*to*Face includes a file transfer utility you can use to transfer any type of file, easily and automatically.

- Face*to*Face operates over a variety of networks, including NetWare, AppleTalk, TCP/IP (the Internet), ISDN, and modems (down to 2400 baud). (The version of Face*to*Face included in this book/CD package supports only TCP/IP.)

- Every standard product package includes a Listener version for both Windows and Macintosh that you can use to conduct meetings with any standard version of Face*to*Face. The Listener version's only limitation is that it receives calls only from remote Face*to*Face users — that is, you cannot initiate a meeting using the Listener version. Crosswise encourages you to distribute copies of the Listener to as many people as you like, free of charge. (The Listener is available only with the standard version.)

- Face*to*Face is completely software-based — it does not require special hardware.

Benefits

- Face*to*Face provides fast, efficient turnaround for reviewing and approving time-critical documents.

- Face*to*Face reduces the expense and inefficiency of faxing, courier services, and travel.

- Face*to*Face provides concise and accurate long distance communications.

Face*to*Face Services _____

The Meeting window

The Meeting window is the first window that appears when you launch Face*to*Face. It is the control center for Face*to*Face, the place where you designate with whom you intend to meet and what documents you intend to share. The Meeting window also indicates the network selected for the meeting, and who happens to be in control of the meeting at any given moment.

The Meeting window appears almost exactly the same whether you are using a Windows or Macintosh system. Figures 26-1 and 26-2 illustrate the Meeting window for Windows and Macintosh computers.

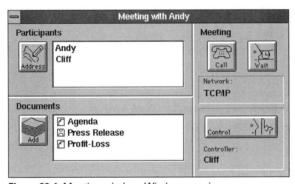

Figure 26-1: Meeting window, Windows version.

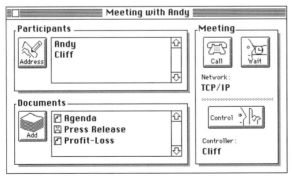

Figure 26-2: Meeting window, Macintosh version.

Meeting files

A Face*to*Face meeting file is the central repository for all documents and information about a given meeting. You normally have a separate meeting file for each meeting in which you participate.

The meeting file contains the names of the meeting participants, copies of all documents used during the meeting, and annotations made by the participants. The meeting file is a handy storage area for meeting information and an easy way to resume any meeting. Face*to*Face automatically creates a meeting file for every meeting you conduct and provides you with the option of naming and saving a file from the meeting.

You can prepare for a meeting in advance by creating a meeting file, complete with the documents you intend to share, and saving it for a later time when the meeting takes place. You can predistribute meeting files by any standard electronic mail or file transfer facility, so others can review the documents and make comments in advance.

The Address Book

Included with Face*to*Face is an Address Book for storing and retrieving the names, telephone numbers, and network addresses of people with whom you meet. To prepare for a meeting, you identify the remote user by name in your Address Book. The Address Book automatically retrieves the network specifics so that you need not remember telephone numbers or complex network addresses.

If you are using Face*to*Face on a Macintosh equipped with Apple PowerTalk, Face*to*Face automatically uses the PowerTalk catalogue as the Address Book and can use the messaging services of PowerTalk to e-mail meeting files.

The Documents list

Before calling a meeting, you specify the documents you will share by adding them to the Documents list in the Meeting window. Preparing the Documents list before the meeting improves performance because Face*to*Face exchanges the documents as soon as the meeting is established. However, if you choose, you can bring documents to a meeting already in progress. You can open any document in the Documents list during a meeting, or before or after a meeting while you work alone.

You can add two types of documents to the Documents list: Image Documents and Transfer Documents. You use the Face_to_Face Image Catcher to convert the documents you want to review or annotate into image documents. You can convert documents created in any Windows or Macintosh application into an image document. Using the Image Catcher is as easy as printing a document. While you're in the creating application (such as Word, Excel, and others), you simply use the creating application's native Print command to "print" to the Image Catcher. The Image Catcher then creates, names, and saves an "image" of the original document on your hard disk. You can use the resulting image document in any Face_to_Face meeting.

Transfer documents can include any file you want to send to another user. You cannot review or annotate transfer documents during a meeting. However, the recipient of a transfer document can use the Face_to_Face export feature to store transfer documents in their native format. This feature is a convenient way to exchange the original versions of documents in their native application format.

Click the Add button in the Meeting window (either before or during a meeting) to add image and transfer documents to your Documents list. Doing so displays a dialog box you use to select the document or documents you want to add to a meeting.

The Document window

When you open a document in the Documents list, it appears in a Document window. You and the person you are meeting with take turns controlling how it is viewed and annotated (Figure 26-3). The toolbar along the top of the Document window provides tools for working with documents. For example, you can enter extensive text annotations using the note tool and then cut and paste the contents back into the original document during or after the meeting. After the meeting, both you and the person you are meeting with automatically retain a soft copy of the annotated documents. You can print these documents, review them off-line, or send them to colleagues who were unable to attend the meeting.

Document layers

Face_to_Face helps you organize your comments on a document into independent document layers. Each document layer is like a transparency on top of the original document. When you draw or make any other change to a particular layer, it will not affect the contents of any other layer. For example, with layers, you can erase comments you have made to a document while leaving the original image intact. You can use document layers to separate comments made by different individuals, or comments made on different meeting dates, or by any other means you find helpful.

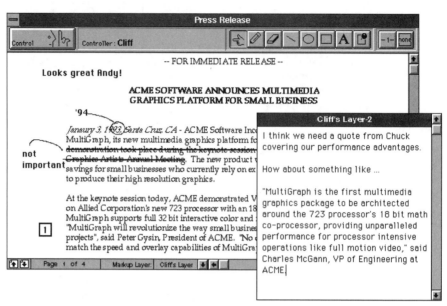

Figure 26-3: Document window, with annotations.

Installing Face*to*Face

This section explains how to install Face*to*Face on a Windows or Macintosh system. It makes the assumption that you have already inserted the compact disc in your CD-ROM drive and you know how to access it. Table 26-1 shows the Windows and Macintosh system requirements.

Table 26-1	System Requirements
Windows	**Macintosh**
Any 386 or 486 IBM PC/AT computer or compatible or IBM PS/2 computer	Any Macintosh except SE, Plus, or Classic
Minimum 4MB of main memory	Minimum 4MB of main memory
Hard disk	Hard disk
Windows Version 3.1 or higher and PC-DOS/MS-DOS 3.1 or higher	Macintosh system software Version 7.0 or higher
TCP/IP (Windows Sockets) Network Interface	TCP/IP (MacTCP) Network Interface

Installing on Windows systems

Start Windows if it isn't already running. Switch to the Program Manager if it isn't currently active. Choose File↵Run.

Locate the Setup program in the Face_to_Face folder on your CD-ROM and run the program.

The Setup program opens the Installation Read Me file. Read this file, and when you finish, choose Exit from the File menu to return to the Setup program. The Face_to_Face Custom Installation window appears.

In this window, *Install to* indicates the drive and directory where the Setup program plans to install the software. If you want to install it elsewhere, click *Set Location* and select the drive and directory you want. If necessary, Setup will create new directories.

Under *Installation Options*, select the Face_to_Face Program Files option and the System Files option. Please deselect the NetWare Files option to prevent these files from installing.

If Setup finds any files from a previous version of Face_to_Face in your WINDOWS or WINDOWS/SYSTEM directories, those files are renamed with a SAV extension and saved in the same directory in case you want to recover or reuse them.

Click Install to begin installation of the components. Click Exit to leave the Setup program.

When the Setup program finishes, read the Read Me file for important informa- tion that could not be included in this chapter. Click the Read Me file icon in your Face_to_Face program group.

When you return to your Windows desktop, you will find a new program group named Face to Face. This group contains the application program, the Read Me file, and the Installation Notes.

Installing on Macintosh systems

Locate the Face_to_Face folder on your compact disc and open its window.

Look for a Read Me document in the window. If the document is present, double-click its icon to open and read the document. The Read Me document contains last-minute information that could not be included in this chapter.

Launch the Face_to_Face Installer application, which is located inside the folder.

The Installer asks whether you want to install the Apple Basic Connectivity Tools. The Installer normally installs the current versions of the AppleTalk ADSP tool, Apple Serial tool, and the Apple Modem tool in your Extensions folder, inside your System folder. This will not be a problem unless you have other applications that rely on a specific (usually older) version of these tools. If you want to preserve your existing versions of these tools before continuing with the installation, do the following:

1. Quit the Installer at this point.

2. Move (do not copy) the existing tools from your Extensions folder to a different folder.

3. Relaunch the Face*to*Face Installer application. When asked whether or not you want to install the Apple Basic Connectivity Tools, click Install.

Upon successful completion of installation, your hard disk contains a folder named Face*to*Face. Inside this folder is the Face*to*Face application and supporting documents. Other software components have been installed in your Extensions folder, inside your System folder.

Using Face*to*Face on TCP/IP Networks

This version of Face*to*Face supports only the TCP/IP networks. To use Face*to*Face with any other network, please buy the standard version of the software. For more information on ordering, see the back of this book.

Using Face*to*Face for Windows on a TCP/IP network

To use Face*to*Face on Windows systems over a TCP/IP network, you need a third-party TCP/IP product installed on your system. Your third-party TCP/IP product provides the Windows Sockets interface. For Face*to*Face to use the Windows Sockets interface, your PATH statement in your AUTOEXEC.BAT file must include the location of the Windows Sockets dynamic link library (WINSOCK.DLL).

Using Face*to*Face for Macintosh on a TCP/IP network

To use Face*to*Face on a Macintosh over a TCP/IP network, you must have Apple Computer's MacTCP installed on your system. Face*to*Face works best with MacTCP Version 2.0 or greater.

Configuring Face_to_Face for use with TCP/IP

Before establishing a meeting across a TCP/IP network, you must properly configure Face_to_Face. In most cases, you need to configure only the first time you use Face_to_Face with TCP/IP.

To specify your network configuration, choose Edit⇨Setup to display the Face_to_Face Setup dialog box. Next, choose TCP/IP from the Connection Type pop-up menu.

On Windows systems, Face_to_Face deactivates the Connection Setup button when you choose the TCP/IP Connection Type. Click OK to continue.

On Macintosh systems, you can click the Connection Setup button to display the Connection Settings dialog box. However, Face_to_Face ignores anything you enter. Click OK in the Face_to_Face Setup dialog box to continue.

Adding TCP/IP names to your Address Book

When you click the New button in the Address Book window, the Address Book New Entry dialog box appears. Enter the TCP/IP address you want to use to meet with the person whose name you're entering. You can enter two forms of TCP/IP addresses: host names or IP addresses.

About Face_to_Face Meetings _____

A Face_to_Face meeting involves two participants: a Meeting Caller and a Meeting Listener. Most meetings take place as described here:

The Meeting Caller prepares a meeting file by selecting the Meeting Listener from his or her Address Book.

The Meeting Caller prepares and gathers documents he or she wants to use during the meeting. The Meeting Listener also does the same if required.

When the meeting is ready to begin, the Meeting Caller contacts the Meeting Listener by telephone to establish voice communication.

The Meeting Listener starts Face_to_Face and places the program in the Wait state.

The Meeting Caller establishes data communications with the Meeting Listener by initiating a call through the software on the TCP/IP network.

After establishing data communications, Face*to*Face distributes documents to the Meeting Listener and, if necessary, to the Meeting Caller.

The Meeting Caller receives control of the meeting.

The meeting can now begin.

Meeting Preparations

This section helps you prepare for a Face*to*Face meeting. It explains the following procedures:

- Starting Face*to*Face
- Selecting participants for a meeting
- Preparing documents for a meeting
- Assembling documents for a meeting
- Preparing Face*to*Face to operate on the network over which you intend to meet

Starting the Face*to*Face application

You can start Face*to*Face by double-clicking the Face*to*Face application icon.

This method starts Face*to*Face with a new Untitled Face*to*Face meeting file.

The Meeting window

The Meeting window appears first when you launch Face*to*Face. It is the control center — the place where you prepare and initiate a meeting. The Meeting window contains three major components:

Participants list: Lists the individuals who will attend an upcoming meeting.

Documents list: Lists the image documents you will review during the meeting and any transfer documents being distributed.

Meeting control panel: Use to initiate and control meetings.

You will read about the Participants and Documents lists later in this chapter.

Meeting files

Face_to_Face automatically creates a meeting file for every meeting you conduct. You can save and name meeting files and use them again whenever you want.

You do not have to wait until you conduct a meeting to create a meeting file. You will often find it far more efficient to create a meeting file ahead of time in preparation for the meeting. You can then distribute the meeting file to the other participant ahead of time over electronic mail or any other suitable distribution network. Doing so saves time distributing documents at meeting time. You can also use this method to allow others not involved in the meeting to review what transpired.

Saving meeting files

When you first open a new meeting file, it appears as an Untitled meeting and remains so until you save and name it.

To save a meeting file and give it a name:

1. Choose File⇨Save or Save As.

2. Use the dialog box that appears to enter a name for the meeting file and specify the directory where you want to store the meeting file.

Use File⇨Save to save a revised meeting file or to save the file periodically while you work. This command saves the file under its existing name.

Participants list

The Participants list holds the names of the people who will attend a meeting. Face_to_Face automatically places your user name in the list. Before you can call a meeting, you must add the other participant's name to the list. When someone else initiates a meeting and you are waiting, your Participants list does not need to contain any name other than yours.

To add a name to the Participants list:

1. Click the Address button, or choose Meeting⇨Participants. Face_to_Face displays your Address Book. (See the next section for information about working with your Address Book.)

2. Select a participant in the Address Book list; then click Add or double-click the name.

To remove a name from the Participants list:

1. Select the name in the Participants list, and choose Edit⇨Clear.

Address Book

To display your Address Book, click the Address button in the Meeting window.

Your Address Book stores information for contacting those individuals with whom you have meetings. It provides the means for selecting individuals who will participate in a meeting.

Your Address Book contains two listboxes. The one on the left shows the names currently in your Address Book. The one on the right side shows the names currently in the Participants list of your Meeting window.

Adding to the Participants list

To add a name to the Participants list:

1. Select the name in the Address Book listbox.

2. Click the Add button to move the name to the Participants list or double-click the name in the Address Book listbox to select and add it at the same time.

To remove a name from the Participants list:

1. Select the name in the listbox.

2. Click the Remove button.

To close the Address Book and return to the Meeting window, click Done.

Adding names to your Address Book

You can add as many names to your Address Book as you require. You must assign each individual in your Address Book a unique name.

To add a new name:

1. Click the New button in the Address Book window to display the New Entry dialog box.

2. Enter the person's name in the Name text box.

Your Address Book has room to store some additional information about your addressees. This information is optional — Face*to*Face does not use it. It is simply a way for you to record useful information about the other participant.

To store additional information:

1. Click the Extend button in the New Entry dialog box. Face*to*Face displays an extended version of the New Entry dialog box.

2. Enter whatever information you want to store in the Title, Company, Telephone, and Notes text boxes.

3. When you finish, click Done.

4. Click Short to return the dialog box to its shorter version.

5. Click New to clear all fields in this dialog box to start a new address entry.

Editing your Address Book

To make changes to an Address Book entry:

1. Select the entry you want to modify in the Address Book listbox.

2. Click the Edit button. Face_to_Face displays a dialog box that looks identical to the New Entry dialog.

3. Change whatever information you want.

4. Click Done.

Preparing documents for a meeting

You can include two types of documents in a Face_to_Face meeting: image documents and transfer documents. See "Assembling documents for a meeting" later in this chapter to learn how to include these types of documents in a meeting.

Image document

An image document is one you can review and annotate during a meeting. It is a replica of a document as it appears when printed. Any document you want to use as an image document during a meeting must first be converted into the format that Face_to_Face understands. Face_to_Face provides a special tool called the Image Catcher for converting documents to the required format.

Using the Image Catcher is as easy as printing a document. To convert a document into an image document, print it using the application you used to create it. The Face_to_Face Image Catcher intercepts the print process and enables you to convert and save the document to disk. See "Using the Image Catcher" later in this section for specific instructions.

The Face_to_Face Setup or Installation program installs the Image Catcher software for you automatically.

Transfer document

A transfer document is one you can send to another meeting participant. It differs from an image document because you cannot review or annotate it during a meeting.

You can export a transfer document from a Face*to*Face meeting file and subsequently use it with the application with which it was created. For example, you can send a Microsoft Excel spreadsheet to another participant as a transfer document. The other participant exports the transfer document (using the Face*to*Face Export command) and then opens the exported document using his or her copy of the Microsoft Excel application.

To include a transfer document in a Face*to*Face meeting, you simply add the document to your Documents list. Again, you will learn how to do this when you read the section "Assembling documents for a meeting."

Using the Image Catcher

You use the Image Catcher to convert a document to the image document format. You can then view and annotate the image document during a Face*to*Face meeting.

To convert a document with the Image Catcher:

1. Open the document you want to convert and share during a meeting. Open the document using the application (such as Microsoft Word or Aldus PageMaker) that created it.

2. Using the appropriate print command in that application, or the Macintosh Chooser, select the Face*to*Face Image Catcher as the current printer.

3. Choose File⇨Print to display the Print dialog box.

4. If the application has a print preview capability, use it to verify page breaks and margins.

5. Set the print options you want and click Print. A dialog box appears for you to name the image document and specify where you want to store it.

6. Enter a name and location for the image document; then click OK.

You have created an image document that you can use in any Face*to*Face meeting.

When used with Windows, image documents must have a DOI extension. If they do not, Face*to*Face adds them to the Documents list as transfer documents, not image documents. Filename extensions are not required for Macintosh systems.

Repeat steps 1 through 5 for all image documents you want to bring to a meeting.

You can convert documents to the image document format while a meeting is in progress. For this reason, you might want to leave the Image Catcher selected until after the meeting concludes. Select a different printer after the meeting concludes.

See the next section, "Assembling documents for a meeting," for information about including converted image documents in your meeting.

Assembling documents for a meeting

The Documents list in the Meeting window holds the names of all image documents currently available to share during a meeting and any transfer documents you have included.

Face_to_Face helps you distinguish image documents from transfer documents by assigning different icons in the Documents list.

The Documents list can be empty when you start a meeting. You can add documents to the list while the meeting is in session.

To add a document to the Documents list:

1. Click the Add button to display the Document Selector dialog box.

2. Locate the document you want to add to the list; then click OK.

Repeat these steps for each document you want to add.

To remove a document from the Documents list:

1. Select the document in the Documents list and choose Edit⇨Clear.

Conducting a Meeting _____

This section explains how to

■ Establish and control a Face_to_Face meeting

■ Distribute and work with documents

■ Save and print your work

■ Leave a meeting

■ Quit Face_to_Face

To establish a meeting, one participant waits for a call until the other participant makes the call. After the call is established, the meeting is ready to begin.

Placing a call

Before placing a call:

1. Make sure the other participant is waiting for your call. See the next section for instructions.

2. Add whatever documents you want to use during the meeting to your Documents list. You can add documents to the list while the meeting is in progress, so your Documents list can be empty when the meeting starts. However, it is more efficient to add documents beforehand whenever possible.

3. Make sure you have connected to the proper network, as specified in the Meeting panel of the Meeting window.

You can place a call to establish a meeting whenever your Participants list contains one name besides your own.

To place the call:

1. Click the Call button in the Meeting window, or choose Meeting⇨Call Meeting.

Waiting for a call

When you are waiting for a meeting to begin, you need to place your Face*to*Face software in the Wait state. You can do so by clicking the Wait button in the Meeting window, or by choosing Meeting⇨Wait for Meeting.

The Participants list in your Meeting window must contain your user name, but it can otherwise be empty. Your Documents list can also be empty. When the meeting starts, Face*to*Face might add documents to your Documents list from the person who initiates the meeting.

Distributing documents

Face*to*Face automatically distributes documents to both meeting participants when the meeting call is established. Face*to*Face also takes the necessary steps to ensure that all participants have an identical set of documents.

When distributing documents for a meeting, Face*to*Face does the following:

- Examines each participant's Document list and compares them for the presence of documents with matching names. If Face*to*Face finds the same name in both lists, it compares the contents of the two documents.

- If the documents have the same name and contain the same data, no further action is necessary.

- If the documents have the same name but contain different data, Face*to*Face asks the caller of the meeting to rename the document in his or her list. It then distributes the renamed document to the other participant.

Documents with the same name become a factor when you conduct multiple meetings using the same meeting file. For example, if you begin reviewing a document in one meeting and continue your review of the same documents with the same person in subsequent meetings, Face*to*Face recognizes that you are working with the same documents. In this case, the time it takes to establish your follow-up meetings decreases considerably because it is not necessary to redistribute the documents.

Controlling a meeting

During a meeting, you and the other participant take turns controlling the activities. The meeting Controller is the participant who *has the floor* and is in control of various functions of the shared workspace. Either participant can take control of a meeting and become the Controller at any time.

Only the meeting Controller can work with meeting documents. If you are not the Controller, the only thing you can do is take control.

After a meeting is established, the Controller button appears in the Meeting section of the Meeting window, and the name of the caller appears as the initial Controller. If you are not currently the Controller, you can take control of the meeting at any time by doing any of the following:

Enter the hot key — Ctrl+T for Windows and Cmd+T for Macintosh.

Click the Controller button in the Meeting window.

Choose Meeting⇨Take Control.

Click the Controller button in any open Document window, as described later in this section.

Once you gain control, your name appears as the Controller and Face*to*Face disables your Controller button.

Working with image documents

Once you capture an image document and add it to the Documents list, you can open it, review its contents, and make annotations. You can open any image document in the Documents list during the meeting, or before or after a meeting while working alone. However, only one image document can be open at any given time.

The Document window

To open a particular image document in the Documents list, select its name in the list; then choose Documents⇨Open or double-click the name in the list.

The image document opens in a Document window.

The toolbar at the top of the window contains four sections:

> Control Button: Click to assume control of the current meeting. Face*to*Face disables the button when you have control and hides it when you work alone.

> Meeting Status: Shows whether you are working alone or, during a meeting, shows the controlling participant.

> Annotation Tools: A series of tools for marking and writing on the current image document. Descriptions of the tools and how to use them follow in this section.

> Attribute menus: Pop-up menus for selecting attributes (that is, line width and fill pattern) for objects you draw, such as lines, rectangles, and circles.

The status bar at the bottom of the window also contains four sections:

> Page Turn Controls: Click the up arrow to move one page toward the top of the image document. Click the down arrow to move one page toward the end.

> Page Number Indicator: Shows the page currently displayed and the total pages in the image document.

> Document Layer Selection menu: Displays a pop-up menu for selecting the layer on which you want to work.

> Scroll Bar: Standard document scroll bar for moving the document left and right in the window.

Document window size

Face_to_Face fixes the size of the Document window on your screen — you cannot change the window size. Face_to_Face sets the window size according to the lowest screen resolution being used by either of the meeting participants. For example, if you are using a video driver with a screen resolution of 1024x768 and the other participant is using a video driver with a screen resolution of 640x480, Face_to_Face sets the window size to the 640x480 resolution for both participants.

The fixed window size ensures that both participants see the identical information at the same time. It also ensures that when someone moves the pointer on his or her screen, it cannot disappear from the other screen.

Working with document layers

Document layers are like transparencies laid on top of an image document. You can have multiple document layers. You can freely annotate on a layer without disturbing the contents of the image document or of other layers.

One way you might find document layers very useful is to assign a different layer to each meeting participant. This is a simple but effective way to keep track of which participant made various annotations to any given image document. Whenever any participant takes control of the meeting, he or she switches to his or her reserved document layer.

You'll undoubtedly find additional uses for document layers, such as assigning a different layer to each date when you received the document. This way, you can maintain a simple "history" of work done with the document.

Document layers are specific to each image document. So you can have different layers for different documents.

Selecting a document layer

The Document Layer Selection menu in the status bar is the most direct way to select the layer on which you want to work.

Face_to_Face disables the name of a layer in the menu if that layer is currently hidden.

Managing document layers

You use the Layers dialog box to initiate most of the remaining procedures for managing document layers. Choose Document⇨Layers to display the dialog box.

The listbox shows the names of the document layers that are currently available for the named image document. The Original layer is the image document itself. Face_to_Face creates the markup layer at the time you create the image document with the Image Catcher tool.

If a layer is hidden, Face*to*Face disables its name in the list. An icon precedes the current markup layer's name.

Adding new layers

You can add up to three document layers to an image document. When you add a new layer, it automatically becomes the current markup layer.

To add one or more layers:

1. Click New in the Layers dialog box.

2. Enter a name for the new layer; then click OK.

Repeat these steps to create other layers as required.

Hiding and showing layers

You can selectively hide and show layers. When you hide a layer:

■ Face*to*Face hides all annotations made on that layer.

■ Face*to*Face hides notes attached to the layer.

■ The layer's name is disabled (gray) in the Document Layer Selection menu and the layer list in the Layers dialog box.

■ If it is the current markup layer, Face*to*Face automatically selects a different layer to take its place.

To hide a layer:

1. Select the layer name in the layer list; then click Hide.

To show a hidden layer:

1. Select the layer name in the layer list; then click Show.

Choosing the markup layer

You can change the current markup layer by selecting any name in the Layers list and then clicking the Markup button. An icon precedes the name in the list, indicating it is the current markup layer. Its name will also appear in the Markup pop-up menu when you return to the Document window.

You can also change the current markup layer from the Markup pop-up menu in the Document window.

Removing an existing layer

To remove an existing document layer:

1. Select the layer name in the Layers dialog box.

2. Click Remove.

Removing a layer automatically discards any notes it contains.

Annotation tools

Pointer

Use the pointer to direct attention to a particular part of the document.

To use the pointer:

1. Select the tool; then move the cursor into the document work area.

2. Press and hold the mouse button while moving the pointer on your screen.

The pointer moves on the other participant's screen exactly as it moves on your screen, and it remains visible as long as you hold down the mouse button.

Pencil

Use the pencil just as you would to annotate a hard copy document. For example, use it to draw a check mark, or circle a word or graphic to which you want to draw attention.

To use the pencil:

1. Select the tool; then move the cursor into the document work area.

2. Press and drag to draw whatever image you want.

The pencil always draws with a single-pixel-width line.

Although you can write with the pencil tool, you'll achieve more legible results using the text tool, described later.

Eraser

Use the eraser to erase any portion of the image on the current document layer.

To use the eraser:

1. Select the tool; then press and drag it across the document layer to erase information on that layer.

If the eraser fails to erase data, it is most likely because that data is on a different document layer.

To erase everything on the current layer:

1. Select the eraser tool.

2. Double-click the eraser tool.

You cannot undo this action.

Line tool

Use the line tool to draw a straight line between any two points.

To draw a line:

1. Select the tool; then move the cursor into the document work area.

2. Click at the starting point; then drag to the end.

3. Release the mouse button.

See the description of the line width tool later in this chapter to learn how to set the width of the line you draw.

Oval tool

Use the oval tool to draw circles and ovals on the document layer.

To use the oval tool:

1. Select the tool; then move the cursor into the document work area.

2. Begin dragging from the upper-left corner where you want the oval to start.

3. Drag to the lower-right corner; then release the mouse button.

See the description of the line width tool later in this chapter to learn how to set the width of the oval's line. See the description of the fill pattern tool to learn how to specify a fill for the inside of the oval.

Rectangle tool

Use the rectangle tool to draw a square or rectangle on the document layer. Use this tool exactly like the oval tool described previously.

Text tool

Use the text tool to enter comments directly on the document layer. You can edit text entered with this tool on any layer except the document layer.

To use the text tool:

1. Select the tool; then click anywhere on the document layer. A blinking insertion pointer appears where you click.

2. Type your text.

Note tool

The note tool works like Post-It™ notes that you've probably attached to many different hard copy documents. The Face*to*Face note tool is useful for making annotations that you want to copy to or paste from another application. For example, you can enter text into a note during a meeting and then subsequently paste it from the note into the original document in the original application. In preparation for a meeting, you can copy text from some other application and paste it into a Face*to*Face note that you'll use during the meeting.

To create a note in an image document:

1. Select the note tool.

2. Click in the image document where you want to insert the note. Face*to*Face opens a Note window where you click.

3. Type your text in the Note window.

To close the Note window:

1. Click its minimize button or choose Document⇨Close Note. Face*to*Face displays a Note icon to indicate where each note is located.

You can drag a Note icon to any location, as long as it is on the same page of the image document.

To open a closed note:

1. Double-click its Note icon, or select the icon and choose Document⇨Open Note.

To delete a note:

1. If the Note window is open, click its close box. You can delete only closed notes.

2. Choose Edit⇨Clear.

Using the Clipboard to copy and paste note text

The Edit menu provides the standard Cut, Copy, and Paste commands for working with the Clipboard.

To place text on the Clipboard:

1. Select the text in the Note window.

2. Choose Cut or Copy from the Edit menu. Cut removes the selection from the window and places it on the Clipboard. Copy places a duplicate of the selection on the Clipboard.

The Clear command in the Edit menu removes the selected text from the Note window but does *not* place it on the Clipboard.

To place text from the Clipboard into a Note window:

1. Click in the Note window where you want the text to appear.

2. Choose Edit⇨Paste.

Line width tool

Use the line width tool to specify a line weight (or width) for drawing lines, ovals, and rectangles. You must specify a width *before* drawing — you cannot change line widths after drawing. Note that the line width tool shows the currently selected line width.

Click the line width tool and select a line width from the pop-up menu.

Fill pattern tool

Use the fill pattern tool to specify a pattern for filling ovals and rectangles. You must specify a pattern *before* drawing — you cannot change the pattern after drawing. Note that the fill pattern tool shows the currently selected pattern.

Click the fill pattern tool and select a pattern from the pop-up menu.

The white portion of each fill pattern is transparent. When you draw an oval or rectangle using a light pattern, you can see the data on the image document that is behind it.

Page turn controls

Click the down arrow (in the status bar) to go to the next page; click the up arrow to go to the previous page. To go directly to any other page, choose Document⇨Go To Page and enter a page number in the dialog box.

Saving your work

You should save your work on an image document periodically by choosing File⇨Save.

You can also save the current image document, along with all changes, to a separate image document. Doing so provides you with a copy of the image document under a different name. Choose File⇨Save Document As and enter a name for the new document.

Any time you save an image document, Face_to_Face automatically saves the current meeting file. The reverse is also true — any time you save the current meeting file, Face_to_Face saves all image documents that are part of the meeting file.

Printing a document

To print the document that is currently in the Document window:

1. Choose File⇨Print Setup to display the Print Setup dialog box and specify the options you want. Then close the dialog box.

2. Choose File⇨Print to display the Print dialog box.

3. Select the options you want to use for printing.

4. Click OK.

When printed, your image document contains the contents of all document layers that are currently visible.

If the document contains notes, Face_to_Face appends them to the end of the printed document and identifies each note with its note icon number.

Creating new image documents

There might be times when you find it useful to create a document for sketching ideas and storing supplemental notes.

To create a new image document:

1. Choose Document⇨New while you work in the Meeting window.

   Face_to_Face displays a single page, blank image document in a new Document window. It names the document <controller>-n — where <controller> is replaced by the name of the user currently in control, and n is a sequence number starting at one.

2. Use the blank document for whatever purpose you require. When you save the current meeting file, Face*to*Face also saves the image document.

You can create a new image document while working alone, or while you are the Controller of a meeting in progress.

Adding a document during a meeting

There will undoubtedly be a time when you need to make a document available during a meeting, but it is not currently in your Documents list.

You can add an image or transfer document to your list during a meeting. To do so, simply click the Add button and select the document you want.

Any time a meeting participant adds a new document to his or her list, Face*to*Face automatically distributes the document to the other meeting participant.

Exporting transfer documents

You need to export transfer documents distributed during a meeting from the Face*to*Face meeting file. The export procedure makes it possible to use the document with other applications. You can also export image documents for use in other meetings.

To export a transfer document:

1. Select the document in the Documents list.

2. Choose Document⇨Export to display the Export dialog box.

3. Enter a name for the document (use the correct filename extension) and click OK.

Leaving a meeting

You can leave a meeting in progress only when you are the Controller.

To leave a meeting:

1. Choose Meeting⇨Leave Meeting, or click the Leave button.

A dialog box appears asking you to confirm that you want to leave the meeting. If you respond affirmatively, Face_to_Face notifies the other meeting participant that you are departing.

Quitting

To quit the Face_to_Face application:

1. Choose Exit or Quit from the File menu.

   If you are in a meeting, you can choose Exit only if you are the Controller. Face_to_Face will ask if you want to save your work before quitting. Normally, you will save your work for future reference and follow-up.

Contacting Crosswise Corporation _____

You can contact us at the following addresses:

Crosswise Corporation
105 Locust Street
Santa Cruz, CA 95060
(800) 747-9060
(408) 459-9060
(408) 426-3859 (fax)

Technical support inquiries can be e-mailed to support@crosswise.com.

Product suggestions or comments can be e-mailed to marketing@crosswise.com.

Sales inquiries can be e-mailed to sales@crosswise.com. Also, see the coupon from Crosswise at the back of this book.

© 1994 Crosswise Corporation. All rights reserved. Crosswise, Face_to_Face, and Listener are trademarks of Crosswise Corporation. All other trademarks are trademarks of their respective holders.

Chapter 27
Mr Squiggle — WinSock Point-to-Point Blackboard

Mr Squiggle is a Windows 3.1/WinSock-based point-to-point electronic blackboard. It lets two people connected across the Internet share a common drawing surface, a bit like Microsoft's Paintbrush, but networked 'round the globe — as long as you are both running Mr Squiggle.

If you are one of the small group of people who can draw better than they can talk and who likes using a mouse to draw, then you might like Mr Squiggle.

The name *Mr Squiggle* (probably a registered name or trademark of the Australian Broadcasting Corporation) comes from a very popular children's program shown in Australia since the 1960s. Its star is a floppy sort of puppet with a very long pencil for a nose. Children mail in bits of paper with random sorts of *squiggles*. Then Mr Squiggle, with a few deft strokes from his nose/pencil, miraculously creates funny drawings, such as an elephant making a peanut-butter sandwich or a butterfly knitting a scarf. More often than not, the squiggle must be rotated before the picture becomes recognizable. There was probably a TV show like this when you were a kid, so you may know what this software is based on anyway.

This Mr Squiggle is a program written entirely in Microsoft's Visual Basic 3, Professional Edition.

Installation and Use

The release directory contains

SQUIGGLE.DOC	The full documentation
SQUIGGLE.ZIP	Windows 3.1 files in ZIP format

You must have successfully installed a WinSock TCP/IP stack before Mr Squiggle can run. See Chapter 4, "Trumpet WinSock Stack Sampler."

1. Copy SQUIGGLE.ZIP to your PC and unzip it into any directory.

2. Some Visual Basic v3 executables and libraries must be copied to the Windows system directory, as follows:

   ■ MSGBLAST.VBX (Ed Staffin's VB Windows Event hook)

   ■ THREED.VBX

   ■ CMDIALOG.VBX

   ■ VBRUN300.DLL

3. Copy the SQUIGGLE.INI file to the WINDOWS directory.

4. Define the Mr Squiggle executable (SQUIGGLE.EXE) to the Program Manager (no working directory is required).

On starting for the first time, define your local friendly name by using the Configure menu and add a few definitions for other users of Mr Squiggle that you can draw with.

A definition consists of:

■ A friendly name, which appears later in the open connection list box.

■ The machine name (as known to DNS or whatever else your WinSock program uses to resolve names).

■ The Mr Squiggle TCP/IP port number that you will attempt to connect to on the other machine (defaults to 4253).

Click Add to add a new definition to the list of other host definitions.

If you want to change an existing definition, click it and then click Modify (or double-click the definition). The definition is removed from the top list and is made available for editing. Don't forget to click Add to reinsert it in the list of other host definitions.

To make the changes permanent, press the big OK button on the bottom of the configuration form.

When starting Mr Squiggle, you should probably put it into listening mode so that other users can contact you. To do this, choose Connection➪Wait for Connection. This should happen automatically (see the `autolisten` parameter in the SQUIGGLE.INI file).

The little status message should change to *listening*, indicating that your WinSock stack is now waiting for a connection to your PC from the Internet. The port that you listen on defaults to 4253, but you can change it by editing your WINDOWS directory's SQUIGGLE.INI file.

If you want to start a connection with another listening Mr Squiggle user, choose Connection⇨Call Another Mr Squiggle. If you were previously in a listening state, you first must choose Connection⇨Disconnect to release the listening mode.

After you choose Call Another Mr Squiggle, a list box appears with the friendly names from the Configure panel. Click an entry and then click Connect. Mr Squiggle then tries to contact the previously configured machine and port. If it is successful, the status message changes to *Connected to machine name*, and the Blackboard form appears.

The Blackboard form is deliberately meant to look like the Microsoft Paintbrush program, but it doesn't have as many features. Still, you can draw lines, boxes, circles, select colors and fonts, and erase previous work. You can clear the drawing area and toggle a funny option (Draw Options, Overlay) that determines how shapes appear on top of one another.

When you are finished, click Exit on the Blackboard.

Availability

Written by Kent Fitch, ITSB, CSIRO Australia kent.fitch@its.csiro.au. Copyright CSIRO 1994, all rights reserved (must not be stolen or resold). Executables and documentation in the public domain; source code available for a donation to CSIRO. *Use at your own risk.*

CSIRO, the largest publicly funded scientific research organization in the world, operates a large variety of research programs at sites across Australia. The home FTP site for Mr Squiggle is commsun.its.csiro.au, in anonymous FTP directory CSIRO/WIN3/SQUIGGLE.

Known Bugs and Limitations

- Not all the Paintbrush tools are implemented.
- No notification is received when using a font not available on the other machine.
- Blackboard can't be resized.
- Undo remembers only the last drawing action and works only on some drawing tools.

- Character tool processing is very limited — no tab or backspace like in most character-mode UNIX programs. If you're familiar with UNIX, you may want to try pressing Ctrl+B to move back a character, Ctrl+F to move forward a character, and all the other usual suspects.

- Only 50 other Mr Squiggle hosts can be configured.

- Local friendly name is not transmitted to other host.

- Can't have more than two people talking at a time (no three-, four or more-way Mr Squiggle sessions).

- Current version does not work with versions of Mr Squiggle before Version 0.26.

- Occasionally, things go wrong — especially if user drags the transfer in progress box during a big bitmap transfer. So don't do that!

- .BMP/.ICO becomes white squares in SVGA with fewer than 256 colors, as tested by the program author with a Diamond Stealth 32 video card.

Chapter 28

Sticky

This simple VB3 WinSock was written in a hurry by Kent Fitch of the Commonwealth Scientific and Industrial Research Organization (CSIRO), ITSB, Canberra, Australia.

Sticky is a little application that enables very simple inter-PC communication using a metaphor of those millions of bits of sticky yellow paper — stickies — that so many people use. You can send a message over the Internet to any PC running Sticky Listen; you need to have WinSock TCP/IP stack installed on your PC before Sticky can be run.

Anyone can use the Sticky executable, but do not resell it. Source is available (but it's a bit scrappy); send e-mail to commprog@its.csiro.au. The program authors welcome donations to CSIRO, a government-funded not-for-profit organization that always needs more money. Contact kent.fitch@its.csiro.au for information about donations.

Installing Sticky

If someone has scarfed the disc that originally came with this book, the program files are available via anonymous FTP at commsun.its.csiro.au in csiro/msdos/sticky. From there, type **bin get sticky.zip** — remember to use lower-case on these touchy UNIX systems. Then use pkunzip (or some other such tool) to unzip STICKY.ZIP, producing these files:

File	*Purpose*
STICKY.INI	Move this file to C:\WINDOWS. Configure STICKY.INI, using the config option of STICKYT
VBRUN300.DLL	Move this file to C:\WINDOWS\SYSTEM
STICKYT.EXE	The Sticky Talk program — used to configure and send messages
STICKYL.EXE	The Sticky Listen program — used to receive messages

Copy the *.EXE files to any directory. Be sure to define them to Program Manager. The program authors recommend placing the icon files in the Startup group.

The authors have tested this version of Sticky with Trumpet WinSock Alpha 18 but not with any other WinSocks.

Using Sticky

When starting Sticky for the first time, define your local friendly name using the Configure menu and add a few definitions for other Sticky users to whom you can send Stickies. A definition consists of the following:

- A friendly name, which appears later in the open connection list box.
- The machine name (as known to DNS or whatever else your WinSock program uses to resolve names).
- The Sticky TCP/IP port number (defaults to "6711") on the machine to which you will attempt to connect.

Click Add to add a new definition to the list of other host definitions. To change an existing definition, click it and then click Modify (or double-click the definition). Sticky removes the definition from the top list and makes it available for editing. Don't forget to click Add to reinsert it in the list of other host definitions.

To make the changes permanent, click OK.

Using Sticky from UNIX

After you are connected to an Internet server, try sending a message from a UNIX session by telnetting to the PC at port (default) 6711. For example, type

```
0005Harry0007Go home!<enter>
```

See what happens! And see the CD for more information about Sticky.

Part VIII
Windows Internet Games

No book on the Internet is complete unless it includes a few games! The Internet offers plenty of entertainment, and lots of users take part. This part focuses on games you can play across the Internet. One fine resource for investigating recreation on the Internet can be found at: http://www.cis.ufl.edu/~thoth/library/recreation.html.

Internet Games

On the *Internet GIZMOS for Windows CD-ROM,* you'll find:

- FIBS, the International Backgammon Server Client
- WinChess, a network version of Chess
- WinGo, a Windows version of GO, a two-player strategy board game

Using the Go client, you can actually log into the Go server at hellspark.wharton.upenn.edu, login as guest, and observe any number of games currently underway.

These games are on the CD-ROM in the directory \FILES\PART08.

For more information about these games, you can check out the following:

Internet Chess Library — ftp://ics.onenet.net/pub/chess/HTML/homepage.html

The Go Page — http://www.cs.utexas.edu:80/go/

The WWW Backgammon Page — http://www.statslab.cam.ac.uk/~sret1/backgammon/main.html

Chapter 29
WinSock Chess

WinSock Chess lets two players play chess over a WinSock network. The program validates moves and disallows illegal moves.

WinSock Chess (or WinChess) uses GNU Chess as a basis for checking moves and as the underlying engine for the program. Figure 29-1 shows the main WinSock Chess window.

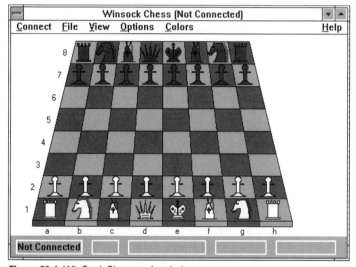

Figure 29-1: WinSock Chess main window.

Connection

To start a game, the first player should select Connect⇨Host. A dialog box appears, saying that the program is waiting for a connection.

The second player should then select Connect⇨Connect to Host. WinChess prompts the second player to enter the first player's host name or IP address. The name must be a valid network name in the host's file or available on a DNS. If a successful connection is established, the dialog box disappears, and you are ready to play.

Currently, there is no negotiation as to who plays what color — the host always plays white.

Select Connect⇨Disconnect to disconnect from your remote opponent.

File Menu

Save — Saves the game. WinChess prompts you for a filename. This command saves only the saving player's time.

Open — Opens a saved game. Select the file to load from the dialog box that appears. WinChess then asks your opponent whether he or she agrees to let you load the game. If your opponent agrees, WinChess loads the game on your machine and transmits it to your opponent's machine. The game then continues. Currently, you can select this option only when it is your turn. This command sets both players' times to the saved time.

New — Starts a new game. WinChess asks your opponent whether he or she agrees to let you start a new game. When your opponent agrees, WinChess resets the board on both sides. Currently, you can select this option only when it is your turn.

List — Saves a list of game moves in a text file. WinChess asks for a filename.

Connect Menu

Host — Use this command to start a game as host. The host always plays white.

Connect to Host — Use this command to play a game started by a host. You play black.

Disconnect — Use this command to disconnect from your remote opponent. Currently, you can select this option only when it is your turn.

Options Menu

Tone — Switches beep on receipt of opponent move on or off.

Co-ordinates — Switches display of algebraic coordinates on or off.

Review Game — Displays a dialog box showing a list box with all moves in the game so far.

View Menu

Reverse Board — Shows you the board from the opposite side.

Colors

This option lets you change the background color, the colors of the pieces, and the colors of the squares. You may also reset the colors to the default colors. When you choose this option, a standard color selection dialog box appears.

Chapter 30
Go — The Game

Playing Against Human Players

If you know the game of Go or have recently learned it by using the IGO.EXE program, you may like to try to play against human opponents. You can do so by joining a Go club.

See the RULES.MGT file on the CD-ROM for a graphic introduction to Go.

Using a Client with International Go Server (IGS)

A Go client — WIGC.EXE, (Windows Go Client) — is available on the CD-ROM bundled with this book. To use it:

1. Create a directory and unzip into that directory. (Read the author's documentation as well as this text.)

2. Create an icon for Go.

3. Dial and connect with WinSock in the normal way.

4. Double-click the WIGC icon.

5. Answer No if you do not want to register now. When you do register, registration is U.S. $5.

6. Select File⇨New Connection and supply *guest* (null password) when prompted. (You also may be prompted as WIGC warns that client mode is not set. That's fine, just accept it.)

WIGC then connects you with the IGS. If you are a guest user, IGS (Internet Go Server) restricts you in several ways. It is simple to register as a named user — type **help register** and follow the instructions. You have to supply your new name on the server and your e-mail address. IGS will mail you a password for your name. (While testing for this documentation, I received the mail in ten minutes.) When you get your password, you can set WIGC to use it and login for you.

There is an old guide to the IGS on the Go archive, but the only way to get up-to-date information is to read get help.

Some IGS Commands

channel	List the channels (chat areas)
games	List all games in progress
match *prams*	Use the match item in the pull-down menu
observe *nn*	Do not use this command with WIGC; instead, use the observe item in the pull-down menu
pass	A pass from each player ends the game
resign :)	Adjourn
say *txt*	Send *txt* to opponent (short form is ,)
shout *txt*	Send *txt* to all players (be careful)
tell *name txt*	Send *txt* to player *name* (after first tell, the short form is .)
undo	Undo your opponent's last move!
who	List all the logged-on players
who all 1	List a subset of the logged-on players; those with a ! are looking for a game
yell *nn txt*	Join channel *nn* (short form is ;)

Once registered, you use can use these additional commands:

stats	List your information and statistics
stats *name*	List another player's statistics
addr *addr*	Set your e-mail address so that you can be sent copies of the games you have played
info *txt*	A line about your style
toggle *flag*	Toggle a binary flag
kibitz *txt*	Send *txt* to other players
Kibitzing	Observe a game (short form is k)
rank <nn>	Set your rank
password <pw>	Set a new password

When you get your registered account, set (on WIGC) options, network preferences, and your user name and password. Then login to IGS and type **addr *name@addr* your email addr toggle automail on rank 25k** (or 20k if you learned quickly against IGO.EXE).

Do not be too modest and set a very low rank (for example, 30k). Players do not mind playing an overrated player: their rating rises and yours falls. We hate playing an underrated player: your rank rises and ours falls. Grrr.

How to Get a Game

To start a game, type

```
toggle open on
toggle looking on
```

This message tells other players that you are both open for games and actively looking for a game. To find available players and then ask one to play, enter

```
who all 1
tell name match with me (25k)
```

where *name* is a player near your strength with a ! by his or her name. If you have no luck, you can try

```
shout match anyone, me 25k
```

Advanced Use of WIGC

WIGC.EXE has many great features, most of which you can find yourself. One feature is colored messages, so you can see clearly what is happening. I have incoming set to bright red so that messages that are sent personally to me stand out clearly. The default board color is not the most appealing, so you may want to change it.

You can obtain the latest version of WIGC by FTPing to bsdserver.ucsf.edu in the directory /GO or ftp.mth.pdx.edu in the directory /PUB/GO.

If anyone does decide to join the IGS, let me know. I may play a game with you. Reach me at roger@fist.demon.co.uk, or skoda on IGS.

Contacting the British Go Association

You can contact the British Go Association as follows:

BGA Membership Secretary: Terry Barker
7 Brockelhurst Ave
Bury, Lancs BL9 9AQ
Phone 061-705-2040

You can try getting the list of the British Go clubs from the Internet Go archive: FTP to bsdserver.ucsf.edu in the directory /GO (or, from the mirror, ftp.pasteur.fr in the directory /PUB/GO).

This archive is full of interesting Go stuff, such as an FAQ and lots of problems and tutorial information. It is not the purpose of this document to duplicate the information at the Go archive, but I have given a couple of tasters in the form of MGT files (zipped up together with this file) which WINMGT.EXE can read.

A lot of text material in the Go archive is UNIX-compressed and shell-scripted. Unpack it with COMP430D.ZIP and UNSHAR.ZIP, both of which you can find in PUB/IBMPC/MISC.

As an alternative to a Go club, you can spend time (and money) going on-line and playing via the International Go Server (IGS).

WIGC Version 1.3 Registration Form

Name _____

Company _____

Address _____

City _____

State _____   Country _____

Zip _____   Phone _____

Remit to:
John Neil   ❑ $5.00 (U.S.)
Dept. of Mathematical Sciences
Portland State University
P.O. Box 751
Portland, OR 97207

Chapter 31

FIBS — The International Backgammon Server

The First International Backgammon Server (FIBS) is an Internet server that lets players all over the world use the Internet to play backgammon against human opponents.

This chapter is a brief tutorial about playing backgammon on FIBS.

FIBS provides an enormous variety of commands and options useful for playing backgammon. FIBS/W provides a user interface that lets you use some of those commands (in particular, those involved with actually playing a game) using a mouse- or menu-driven interface.

The first command to learn on FIBS is the help command, which shows you a list of available help topics. For information on any but the basic FIBS commands, please refer to the help files.

The first step toward playing is getting an FIBS account. Log in to FIBS as a guest by setting the FIBS Login Name field of the Options⇨Connect Script Settings dialog box to *guest* and connecting to FIBS. FIBS walks you through the account creation procedure.

After you have chosen an account and password, execute Options⇨Connect Script Settings, enter the name and password into the FIBS Login Name and FIBS Password fields, and reconnect to FIBS.

After you are connected using your new account, find people to play with and invite them to play. Choose Actions⇨Who, or type **who**, to see a list of all players currently connected to FIBS. Choose Actions⇨Who Ready, or type **who ready**, to see a list of players currently willing to play.

Before you can invite someone to play a match, or be invited yourself, you must tell FIBS that you are willing to play. To do this, choose Actions⇨Toggle Ready or type **toggle ready**. Having identified a player you would like to play with, and having toggled your ready status, you are now ready to extend an invitation.

To invite another player to join you for a game of backgammon, type

```
invite name number
```

where *name* is the name of the player you want to play and *number* is the number of points in the match you want to play. It takes longer to play a match on FIBS than it does in real life, so it's probably a good idea to start with a three-point match until you get a better feel for FIBS.

If the player accepts your invitation, you are ready to play backgammon! If not, try again. All FIBS players were once newbies, and thus, most are reasonably tolerant and willing to help.

Other FIBS commands you should know:

Command	Function
shout	Sends a message to all players connected to FIBS. (Use this command sparingly until you get a feel for FIBS culture and conventions for polite behavior.)
tell *name*	Sends a message to a particular player.
kibitz (or just k)	When playing a game, sends a message to your opponent and anyone watching your match at that particular time.

You also may watch other players' matches. Type **watch *name*** to watch a match that *name* is playing in. Type **show games** to list games in progress.

Once you have started a match, FIBS/W lets you perform most actions by using the mouse or issuing menu commands.

Happy backgammon playing. Good luck.

FIBS/W

FIBS/W is a Windows interface to the famous Internet First International Backgammon Server (FIBS).

The FIBS server lets backgammon players from around the world play backgammon against each other. FIBS also lets you watch some of the best backgammon players in the world play. Many top-ranked backgammon players frequent FIBS.

FIBS/W adds a graphical board to play on (rather than a text board) and lets you use a mouse to execute most game functions.

FIBS/W includes script files that automatically connect to FIBS via a variety of common host systems. If your system is not one of these, consult the "Script files and automated connection" section for details on how to write or modify login script files. If you are eager to try FIBS/W out right away, you can manually connect to FIBS, using the MANUAL.SCC login script.

When you are connected to FIBS, type **help** to get further information on FIBS commands and capabilities. When you're connected to FIBS and are using FIBS/W, type the command **set boardstyle 3** at the FIBS command prompt for FIBS/W to operate correctly. You can configure FIBS/W to do this for you when you login. See the section "Script files and automated connection" for information.

To use FIBS/W, you must have dial-up access to an Internet host system and the ability to use telnet capabilities from that host. FIBS/W does not currently support TCP/IP or SLIP connections to FIBS.

Configuring FIBS/W

To configure FIBS/W, choose and configure the serial port to use, and then choose and configure a login script file. After you have completed these steps, choose Communications⇨Connect to establish a connection with FIBS.

If you are connecting to FIBS for the first time, set the FIBS login name to *guest* and the password to blank; then follow the instructions that FIBS sends for registering and creating a new user ID.

Choosing and configuring a serial port

Use the Options⇨Modem Settings command to configure FIBS/W to use your modem, and to choose baud rate, number of data bits, parity, number of stop bits, and flow control. If you need help choosing these settings, please contact a service representative for your host system.

For FIBS/W to operate correctly, the COM port must be configured to use some form of flow control. If the modem is configured to use XON/XOFF flow control, then the modem initialization string setting should initialize the modem for XON/XOFF flow control as well. See the "Choosing a modem init string" section for important information on modem initialization strings if you intend to use XON/XOFF flow control.

The recommended configuration is to use hardware flow control, as most modems are configured this way by default. Unfortunately, default modem configurations are not standard, and there are no standard commands that configure the modem properly. If FIBS/W seems to drop characters or displays a lot of garbage, the modem is probably not configured to use hardware flow control. If this happens, see the "Choosing a modem init string" section for further instructions on how to configure the modem properly.

For more help on configuring the serial ports, click the Help button in the Modem Settings dialog box.

Choosing a login script

FIBS/W provides several login scripts that dial up the host system and establish a connection to FIBS via the host system. To choose a login script, choose Options⇨Connect Script Settings. The first field in the dialog box that appears lists login scripts with a brief description of the host systems they are intended for.

If your system is directly supported, you can either

- Use the manual connection procedure (see the next section).
- Modify one of the existing scripts for your system (see the section "Script files and automated connection").

If your system is directly supported, choose the login script for your system in the Options⇨Connect Script Settings dialog box. The scripts provided with FIBS/W let you omit some information from the Script Parameter fields.

Because it's not a good idea to store passwords in unprotected files, FIBS/W lets you enter passwords at password prompts if the Host Password or FIBS Password entries are left blank. The login scripts continue only when the passwords have been entered.

For more help on configuring the login script files, click the Help button in the Connect Script Settings dialog box.

Manually logging in

If the provided login scripts do not support your system, use the manual login script. This script dials the telephone number found in the Telephone Number entry of the Options⇨Connect Script Settings dialog box. You complete the connection to FIBS by typing commands for your host system.

If you choose to use the manual login script, then you must enter the command **set boardstyle 3** at the FIBS command prompt to get FIBS/W to work correctly. FIBS/W understands only backgammon boards sent when boardstyle is set to 3. If you continue to get text backgammon boards, you probably forgot to enter the boardstyle 3 command at the FIBS command-line prompt. Make sure that FIBS responds *Value of 'boardstyle' set to 3* when the command is issued.

Methods for connecting to FIBS vary among host systems. On UNIX host systems, typing **telnet 129.16.235.153 4321** usually establishes a connection to FIBS. This Internet address is, unfortunately, subject to change without notice. Issue the command appropriate to your system to establish a telnet connection with FIBS.

Once connected to FIBS, follow the instructions for logging on to the FIBS server.

After connecting to FIBS

For FIBS/W to work with FIBS, type **set boardstyle 3** at the FIBS command prompt. If this command is issued correctly, FIBS returns the message *Value of boardstyle set to '3'*. FIBS/W displays backgammon boards in text mode if this command has not been issued. Automated login scripts other than MANUAL.SCC send this command automatically.

After completing these steps, you are now ready to play backgammon on FIBS.

See also the "Script files and automated connection," "Modem Settings dialog box," "Connect Script Settings dialog box," and "Choosing a modem init string" sections.

Choosing a modem init string

Unfortunately, modem commands vary greatly from manufacturer to manufacturer, as do default modem configurations. Therefore, FIBS/W can't correctly configure all modems correctly all the time by default.

The best course of action is to use the following default modem initialization string:

```
ATE1V1Q0S0=0&D2
```

Most modems are configured to use hardware flow control by default. Therefore, unless you have a specific need to use a different form of flow control, the flow control field of the Options⇨Modem Settings should be set to hardware (CTS/RTS handshake).

Problems

If any of the following problems are encountered with this setting, you need to modify your modem initialization string. Consult your modem's user manual for information on choosing an appropriate initialization string for your modem.

- FIBS/W appears to drop characters or displays garbage on-screen (particularly ~ characters).

- FIBS/W appears to be using a nonerror-correcting connection on a modem connection that supports error-correcting communication protocols.

- FIBS/W does not hang up the line properly when exiting.

Setup

FIBS/W requires that the modem be set up as follows:

- The modem must return result codes for modem commands. This modem command is Q0 for most modems and is usually set by default.

- The modem must respond to modem commands and must respond in English rather than with numeric result codes. This modem command is V1 for most modems and is not always set by default.

- The modem should not answer the phone if it rings. This modem command is S0=0 for most modems and is usually set by default.

- The modem should hang up the line if FIBS/W terminates unexpectedly. This command is &D2 for most modems but is often something else. Most modems do not satisfy this condition in default configuration. FIBS/W should work without this setting, but the risk of leaving the modem online if Windows should crash makes it a good idea to include this modem command.

- The modem must be configured to use the same form of flow control as FIBS/W is configured to use. The modem configuration must match the FIBS/W setting in the flow control field of the Options⇨Modem Settings dialog box. The form of hardware flow control that FIBS/W uses is often referred to as CTS/RTS flow control. Most modems are configured to use hardware flow control by default. The default modem initialization string does not set this parameter. The modem command to configure a Hayes modem to use hardware flow control is &K3 but is known to be different on many common modems. The modem command to configure a Hayes modem to use XON/XOFF flow control is &K4. Please note that on some common modems, the &K command is used to select the communications protocol (v32/bis, MNP 5, and so on) instead! For example, on US Robotics modems, the initialization string must contain &H1&R2 instead of &K3 to configure the modem for hardware flow control.

Even though many high-speed modems use error-correcting communications protocols such as MNP, V.32, and V.42 variants by default, others must be explicitly configured to use these protocols. For example, if you are using a 14400 baud modem, and the modem connects at 9600 baud rather than 14400 on a line that should support 14400, the modem may not be properly configured.

Please consult your modem's documentation to determine the correct commands to configure the modem correctly. If you are using other communication packages that appear to work properly, it may be a good idea to copy the modem initialization strings and serial port configurations from those programs.

The FIBS/W Window

Toolbar icons

Table 31-1 describes the FIBS/W toolbar icons, from left to right, and their functions. Figure 31-1 shows the main FIBS/W window.

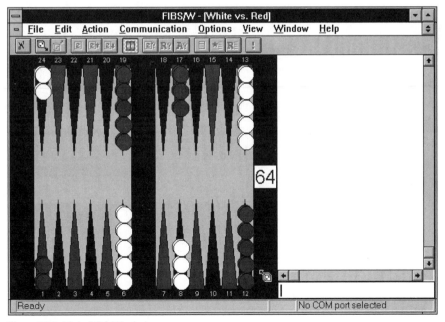

Figure 31-1: Main FIBS/W window.

Table 31-1	FIBS/W Toolbar Icon Descriptions
Icon	**Function**
Connect or Disconnect	Connect to FIBS or disconnect from FIBS.
Roll	Roll the dice. Only enabled if the current game state lets you double.
Pick up the Dice	Pick up the dice to complete the current move. Only enabled if the current game state lets you double.
Double	Offer the doubling cube to the opposing player. Only enabled if the current game state lets you double.
Accept Double	Accept a double offered by the opposing player. Only enabled if the current game state lets you double.
Reject Double	Reject a double offered by the opposing player. Only enabled if the current game state lets you double.
Toggle Board	Toggles whether the board is displayed.
Toggle Double	Toggles whether FIBS asks you whether you want to double.
Toggle Ready	Toggles whether you are ready to play a game. If set, you may invite or be invited to play a game. If not set, players may not invite you to play a game. This sends the toggle ready command to FIBS.
Toggle Away	Toggles your away status. When set, players who attempt to "tell" you something using the tell command or invite you to play a game will receive a message. When you set away status, you will be asked for a message to give to players who try to talk to you. This sends the away command.
Calculate Pipcount	Calculates the number of pips required to bear all men off the board for each player. This sends the pip command to FIBS. If your opponent has issued the toggle allowpip command, you will not be able to use this command.
Who	Shows a list of all players connected to FIBS. This sends the who command to FIBS.
Who Ready	Shows a list of players who are ready to play a game. This sends the who ready command to FIBS.
Send Telnet Escape	Sends an escape character. On most systems, this action causes the host system to return to the telnet prompt for further telnet commands. From the telnet prompt, it's possible to issue host commands such as !mail, which checks whether you have mail waiting. To use this command, the host system's telnet escape character must be set to ^]. To return to FIBS from the telnet prompt, press the spacebar and then the Return key.

When Toggle Double is on, FIBS asks whether you want to double or roll whenever you have a choice. When this option is off, FIBS rolls the dice automatically without asking.

Setting Toggle Double to Off greatly speeds up the game. The trick is to set Toggle Double to On if you make a good roll that significantly changes the value of the game.

Mouse interaction

FIBS/W does not completely automate access to FIBS. Many operations must still be carried out by typing commands on FIBS. However, once you have started a game with an opponent, you can do most operations with the mouse. Table 31-2 describes mouse interactions for FIBS/W.

Table 31-2	Mouse Functions
Function	*Mouse Action*
Roll the dice	Click anywhere on the cube bar at the right side of the board.
Move a checker	Pick it up with the mouse and, while holding down the mouse button, drag the checker to its new location. FIBS/W complains if it's not your turn or if the move is illegal. Pressing Ctrl+Z (or choosing Edit⇨Undo) revokes the last move.
Complete a legal move	Click on the cube bar at the right side of the board.
Double	Click on the doubling cube. FIBS/W does not let you double if the current game state does not let you do so.
Accept a double that an opponent has offered	Click on the doubling cube.
Decline a Double	You cannot decline a double by using the mouse. Choose Action⇨Decline Double instead.

Pressing Esc undoes all moves made.

At all times, you can use the equivalent command-line and menu commands interchangeably. Use the interaction style that best suits you.

Command-line interaction

FIBS provides an incredible number of commands to backgammon players. FIBS/W does not try to provide a graphical user interface for any but those commands actually involved with playing a game. The Command Line edit box lets you send text commands to FIBS.

FIBS/W also lets you use text commands to play the game. For example, typing **roll**, **double**, or **8 5 5 1** (or even **8 1**) works just as well as using their equivalent mouse commands. FIBS/W updates the board appropriately.

FIBS/W previews the moves on the board as you type them if you use the following syntax:

```
point point ...
```

where *point* is of the form *number* | o[ff] | b[ar]. FIBS/W does not preview the moves, however, if you use the verbose FIBS command m[ove] *point point* ...

FIBS/W also provides a small number of local commands that are interpreted by FIBS/W rather than FIBS. These commands make it easier to write automated login scripts.

Modem Settings dialog box

The Modem Settings dialog box (Options➪Modem Settings) configures FIBS/W to use a particular modem and serial port.

First, select the COM port with which FIBS/W connects to the host system. Next, configure the serial port. Set the baud rate to the highest rate your modem supports. The number of data bits, parity, and stop bits depends on the host to which you are connecting. Consult your service provider for the correct setting for these dialog box entries. Usually, most host systems follow one of two conventions:

- Data Bits: 8, Parity: none, Stop Bits: 1
- Data Bits: 7, Parity: Even; Stop Bits: 1

Set the flow control entry to hardware unless you have a specific reason not to do so. If you choose XON/XOFF flow control, you may need to modify the modem initialization string accordingly.

The modem initialization string should normally be ATE1V1Q0S0=0&D2. If you are using XON/XOFF flow control, you must change the modem initialization string from its default value. See the "Choosing a modem init string" section for more information.

The dial string prefix should normally be ATDT. If your telephone line does not support touch-tone dialing, set the dial string prefix to ATDP.

For any other settings for the modem initialization string and dial string prefix, consult your modem's user manual.

Connect Script Settings dialog box

The Connect Script Settings dialog box (Options⇨Connect Script Settings) configures FIBS/W to connect to FIBS automatically through a dial-up host system.

First, choose a host script. Browse through the host system descriptions in the Connect Script listbox for the system descriptions that most closely resemble your own. If there is no appropriate script, choose MANUAL.SCC. Or consult the "Script files and automated connections" section for instructions on how to modify the existing script files or write your own.

The Network listbox is used when you are connecting to a host system via a national network data carrier or network front end system. If you are connecting to a host system via Tymnet, CISnet, or if you must type **rlogin host *name*** before typing your login name, select the appropriate entry in the Network listbox. Otherwise, select none.

The Script Parameters are used to customize the connect scripts for your own use. The entries in these fields are used by the connect scripts to automate the login procedure. Table 31-3 describes the Script Parameters fields.

Table 31-3	Script Parameters Fields
Field	*Meaning*
Telephone Number	The telephone number of the host system you are dialing.
Host Name	Enter the name of the host system you are connecting to (for example, Delphi, gabriel.resudox.net, BIX). Complete this entry only if you have selected a network.
Host Login Name	The name to send to the host system in response to the login: prompt.
Host Password	The string to send to the host system in response to the password: prompt. If this field is left blank, you will be asked to enter your password manually when the login script executes.
FIBS Login Name	The name to send to FIBS in response to the FIBS login: prompt. If you are connecting to FIBS for the first time, enter *guest*.
FIBS Password	The string that should be sent to FIBS in response to the FIBS password: prompt. If this field is left blank, you will be asked to enter your FIBS password manually when the login script executes.

The passwords entered in this dialog box are stored in unencrypted form on your hard disk. Due to the inadvisability of storing passwords in plain form, the author of FIBS/W recommends that the Host Password and FIBS Password dialog box entries be left blank. If these fields are left blank, the automated login scripts pause to let you enter your passwords.

Menu overview

File menu

The File menu provides standard Windows File menu commands, described in Table 31-4.

Table 31-4	File Menu Commands
Command	*Function*
New	Create a new FIBS/W window.
Close	Close a FIBS/W window.
Exit	Exit FIBS/W.

Edit menu

The Edit menu also provides standard commands, described in Table 31-5.

Table 31-5	Edit Menu Commands
Command	*Function*
Undo	If moves are pending, undoes the last move; otherwise, undoes the last Command Line edit box operation.
Cut	Cuts the currently selected Command Line edit box text to the Clipboard.
Copy	Copies the currently selected Command Line edit box text to the Clipboard.
Paste	Pastes text on the Clipboard into the Command Line edit box.

Action menu

This menu provides menu commands used while playing a game. Table 31-6 describes the Action menu commands.

Table 31-6	Action Menu Commands
Command	**Function**
Roll	Roll the dice. Only enabled if the current game state lets you roll the dice.
Pick Up Dice	Complete the current move and send the appropriate command to FIBS. Only enabled if you have completed a correct and legal move using the mouse.
Double	Offer the cube to your opponent. Only enabled if the current game state lets you double.
Accept Double	Accept a cube offered by your opponent. Only enabled if your opponent has doubled you.
Reject Double	Decline a cube offered by your opponent. Only enabled if your opponent has doubled you.
Toggle Ready	Toggle whether you are ready to play a game. If set, you can invite or be invited to play a game. If not set, players cannot invite you to play a game. This sends the toggle ready command to FIBS.
Toggle Double	Toggle whether FIBS asks whether you want to double or not. When on, FIBS asks whether you want to double or roll whenever you have a choice. When off, FIBS rolls the dice automatically without asking. (Setting Toggle Double to Off greatly speeds up the game. The trick is to set Toggle Double to On if you make a good roll that significantly changes the value of the game.) This sends the toggle double command to FIBS.
Toggle Away	Toggle your away status. When set, players who attempt to tell you something (by using the FIBS tell command) or invite you to play a game receive a message. When you set away status, you are asked for a message to give to players who try to talk to you. This sends the away command to FIBS.
Calculate Pipcount	Calculate the number of pips required to bear all men off the board for each player. This sends the pip command to FIBS. If your opponent has issued the toggle allowpip command, you cannot use this command.
Who	Show a list of all players connect to FIBS. This sends the who command to FIBS.
Who Ready	Show a list of players who are ready to play a game. This sends the who ready command to FIBS.
Freshen Board	Ask FIBS to resend the current board and redraw the FIBS/W board accordingly. Generally useful only in case of communications errors or when starting to watch a game. If FIBS/W should ever get confused or start to act strangely, issuing this command may remedy the situation.

Accelerator keys for these menu items are carefully selected to allow actions to be executed using the left hand while using the mouse with the right. Sorry if this is levulocentric (that's one of those words that southpaws throw in to confuse righties — HG).

Communications menu

This menu provides commands used to affect serial port connections, described in Table 31-7.

Table 31-7	Communications Menu Command
Command	*Function*
Connect	Connect to the selected serial port and execute the script STARTUP.SCR.
Disconnect	Execute the script HANGUP.SCR and disconnect from the serial port.
Run Script	Select and run a script file.
Stop Script	Cancel any scripts currently executing.

Options menu

This menu provides commands used to configure FIBS/W, described in Table 31-8.

Table 31-8	Options Menu Commands
Command	*Function*
Modem Settings	Configure FIBS/W to use the modem with which the connections will be made to the host system, and to choose the baud rate, number of data bits, parity, number of stop bits, and flow control. If you need help choosing these settings, please contact a service representative for your host system. (Most systems will accept a setting of 8 data bits, no parity bits, 1 stop bit, or 7 data bits, even parity, 1 stop bit.)
Connect Script Settings	Choose and configure a login script. You may choose a script to use when establishing a connection to FIBS via a host system. Script files use Script Parameters for common information which varies from user to user. Each entry in this dialog box can be accessed in a script file by using % commands. See the "FIBS/W Script Commands" section for more information on how the entries in this dialog box are used. By default, only the dial string prefix and telephone number commands are used.

Command	Function
Color Preferences	Choose new colors for the board and pieces.
Font	Choose a font to use in the text window. This font is remembered from session to session.
Auto Connect When Loaded	Toggle whether FIBS/W automatically attempts to connect to the host every time it's loaded. When this option is checked, FIBS/W connects to the modem and starts executing the connect script when loaded. When it is unchecked, connections must be established manually by choosing Communication⇨Connect.

View menu

This menu provides commands that may be used to affect the appearance of the FIBS/W windows. Table 31-9 describes the View menu commands.

Table 31-9	View Menu Commands	
Command	**Function**	
Toolbar	Show or hide the toolbar.	
Status Bar	Show or hide the status bar.	
Board	Show or hide the board.	

FIBS/W Script Commands

FIBS/W provides the bare necessities for writing simple script files to automate common or repetitive tasks while communicating with FIBS/W. You can also execute these commands from the command line. However, the main intent of the script commands is to let you automatically connect to FIBS.

FIBS/W also provides redirection commands < and > that you can use to execute scripts and to capture output to a log file, respectively. Other script commands are prefixed by the @ character.

If the @echo 0 command has previously been issued in the current script file, the commands will not be echoed to the screen.

Prefixing a command with a backslash (\) overrides the meaning of the first character in a line. For example, the command \@echo sends @echo to the host system instead of executing the FIBS/W echo command.

Most FIBS/W script commands can take string arguments. Enclose string arguments in double quotes. You can use string escape sequences to send special characters or to include the values of variables set by the Modem Settings or Connect Script Settings dialog boxes.

String escape sequences

The escape sequences described in Table 31-10 are recognized in string arguments to FIBS/W script commands.

Table 31-10   String Escape Sequence Commands and Functions

Escape sequence	Function
\r	Carriage return
\n	Line feed
\t	Tab
\b	Backspace
\a	Attention (terminal bell)
\\	Backslash
\nnn	Character that has octal code nnn
\"	Double quote
\%	Percent character
\^	literal ^ character
^X	Ctrl+X (where X is any alphabetic character)

For example:

Dialing\r\n

\"To be or not to be"

\^C

The command interpreter understands text enclosed by percent signs to be a variable name. Currently, FIBS/W supports only the variable names described in Table 31-11, which may be configured by using the Options⇨Connect Script Settings and the Options⇨Modem Settings dialog boxes.

Table 31-11	FIBS/W Variable Names
Variable Name	**Function**
%DialStringPrefix%	Command to send to a modem to dial a telephone number. ATDT is the default.
%TelephoneNumber%	Host telephone number.
%HostLoginName%	Host login name.
%HostPassword%	Host password.
%FibsLoginName%	FIBS login name.
%FibsPassword%	FIBS password.
%FibsInternetAddress%	FIBS telnet address string. Currently 129.16.235.153.
%FibsTelnetPort%	FIBS telnet port number. Currently 4321.

Other variables may be set as required by modifying the FIBSW.INI file. Variables are stored in the [Settings] section of the FIBSW.INI file.

String description

Specifies a valid filename. FIBS/W interprets the string as a filename and tries to execute the filename as a script file.

Script file invocations can be nested within script files. Executing a script file while a script file is already executing cancels execution of the first script file if executed from the command line. FIBS/W searches for the file in the current directory and then in the directory in which the FIBS/W executable resides.

If no filename string is provided, then < terminates execution of the current script file as well as any nested script files running. The function of < without a string argument is equivalent to choosing Communication⇨Stop Script. For example,

```
<prefs.scr
```

executes the file PREFS.SCR.

> command

Captures all received serial data and writes it to the specified file. If no filename is specified, capturing stops. For example,

```
>c:\game.log
```

captures data to C:\GAME.LOG.

@send command

Sends the string to the host system. This command differs from normal command-line commands only in that string escape sequences are substituted and a carriage return is not sent after the string is sent. For example,

```
@send "+++"
```

sends +++ (no return), while

```
@send "^]"
```

sends an escape character. Other examples:

@send "%HostLoginName%\r"

@send "^C"

See also the "String escape sequences" section.

@wait command

Wait commands are only valid inside script files. They cannot be executed directly from the command line.

The first form of the @wait command (@wait "string") suspends the execution of the script file until the string is received from the host system. As soon as the string is received, script file execution resumes with the next statement in the script file. The script file is suspended indefinitely until the host system sends the specified string.

The second form (@wait 1234) waits for the specified number of seconds before resuming execution of the script file.

The third form (@wait "string" 1234) waits for the specified number of seconds before or for the string to be sent by the host system. If the timeout occurs before the string is received, script file execution is terminated with an error unless the command is issued as part of an @if command. Otherwise, execution continues normally.

When the third form is used as the test clause of an @if command, the @wait command returns TRUE if the string was received and FALSE if the timeout occurred.

Table 31-12 summarizes @wait command forms.

Table 31-12	@wait Commands and Examples
Form of @wait command	*Function*
@wait "*string*"	Wait for a string to be received
@wait 1234	Wait for 1234 seconds
@wait "*string*" 1234	Wait for a string, timing out after 1234 seconds
Examples:	@wait "OK" — Wait for the modem to send *OK*
	@wait "%HostName%$" 10 — Wait for a csh command prompt
	@wait 5 — Wait five seconds
	See also the "String escape sequences" and "@if/@else/@endif commands" sections.

@echo command

The first two forms of the @echo command are used to control whether script commands are displayed during script execution.

These commands constitute a useful tool while developing script files. @echo 0 turns command echoing off: script file commands do not get displayed. @echo 1 turns command echoing on: script file commands get displayed in the text display area before being executed. @echo "string" displays a string on-screen without sending it to the host system.

Echoed strings do not automatically have carriage returns or linefeeds sent after them, unless explicitly provided in the string itself.

Echoed strings are displayed as if they were data received from the serial port. Therefore, typically, both carriage returns (which return the display cursor to column zero), and linefeeds (which move the display cursor to the next line) are required to start a new line.

The @echo 0 command does not appear on-screen. The @echo 1 command does not appear on-screen if the @echo 0 command has previously been issued.

Table 31-13 shows the forms of the @echo command.

Table 31-13	@echo Commands and Examples
Form of @echo	*Function*
@echo 0	Turn command echoing off
@echo 1	Turn command echoing on
@echo "string"	Display a string locally
Examples:	@echo "\r\n**Dialing..."
	@echo "\r\nConnecting to %HostName%...""
	@echo "\r\n**Error: File not found\r\n\a"
	See also the "String escape sequences" and "@if/@else/@endif commands" sections.

@if/@else/@endif commands

Use the @if, @else, and @endif commands to conditionally execute script commands.

Each @if statement should have a corresponding @endif command and, optionally, a following @else command. Script commands up between the @if statement and the following @else or @endif statement are executed if the condition is TRUE and not executed if the condition is FALSE. Script commands between the @else statement and the following @endif statement are executed only if the condition is FALSE.

The string equality @if statements are typically used to test variables set by the Modem Settings and Connect Script Settings dialog boxes. To do this, use % escape sequences. For example:

```
@if "%HostName%" != ""
@send "rlogin %HostName%\r"
@else
@echo "\r\n** ERROR: Please set Host Name\r\n"
@echo " in the Options⇨Connect Script Settings dialog
box\r\n"
@endif
```

% variables that are not defined evaluate to "". For example, the test @if "%GarbageName"=="" succeeds.

The @if @wait "string" 1234 command succeeds if FIBS/W receives the string before the wait timeout; it fails if the timeout occurs first.

The @if not @wait "string" 1234 command succeeds if the timeout occurs, and it fails if the string is received first.

Syntax:

@if ... statements ...

@else (optional)

@endif

Forms of the @if command:

Form of @if	Function
@if "string1" == "string2"	Test string equality
@if "string1" != "string2"	Test string inequality
@if @wait "string" 1234	Test wait with timeout
@if not @wait "string" 1234	Test wait with timeout

For example:

```
@if "%HostPassword%" == ""
@wait "password:"      ; wait indefinitely
@else
@if not @wait "password:" 10
@echo "\r\n** ERROR: Password prompt not received\r\n"
<         terminate script execution
@endif
@send "%HostPassword%\r"     ; send the password
@wait "\n"     ; wait for a response @endif
```

See also the "String escape sequences" and "@wait command" sections.

@board command

The @board command lets script files show or hide the game board in the main FIBS/W window. @board 0 hides the game board. @board 1 shows the game board. @board –1 sets the board to default state. The default state of the game board is the state that the user last explicitly set by choosing View⇨Board or selecting the View Board tool button.

The table shows the forms of @board:

Form of @board	Function
@board 0	Hides the game board
@board 1	Shows the game board
@board –1	Returns the game board to default state

@goto command

The @goto command searches the current script file for the first occurrence of the specified label and resumes execution on the line following the label.

Syntax: @goto *label*

For example:

```
@:RetryStartTelnet    ; a label
@send "telnet\r"      ; start telnet
@if not @wait "telnet>" 10  ; wait for telnet prompt
@goto RetryStartTelnet
@endif
```

See also the "@: label command" section.

@: label command

FIBS/W's script interpreter uses the label command to identify lines that are the target of goto statements. Unless processing a goto statement, the script interpreter ignores label commands.

For example:

```
@:RetryStartTelnet    ; a label
@send "telnet\r"      ; start telnet
@if not @wait "telnet>" 10  ; wait for telnet prompt
@goto RetryStartTelnet
@endif
```

See also the "@goto command" section.

Tips and tricks for developing scripts

Regrettably, because writing script files is moderately complex, the software author cannot help you unless FIBS/W is clearly malfunctioning. Despite this, the task of writing script files is fairly straightforward.

The main problem with writing automated communications procedures is that appropriate response must be carefully synchronized by waiting for the prompt which they belong with. If this isn't done,

- The script file may execute immediately, sending all its responses before the host system can respond.

- The host may discard data if too much data is sent. For example, during UNIX login procedures, the UNIX host carefully discards all buffered data before the login: and password: prompts are displayed.

Therefore, to write well-behaved script files, the trick is to pace the script so that it

- Knows what prompt to expect next

- Knows what needs to be sent in response to that prompt

The secret to understanding how script files work is understanding that script file execution takes precedence over anything else unless the script file is waiting for received data; therefore, you must take great care when interleaving wait commands and echo or send commands. As soon as the last character in the wait string is received, the next command will be executed. In the following example, the script waits for "\n" to prevent the following output:

```
CONNECT** Logging in... 38400
```

If the @wait "\n" command isn't there, the @echo command occurs before FIBS/W receives the rest of the CONNECT line, and the modem baud rate gets separated from the CONNECT message.

```
@send "%ModemDialPrefix%%TelephoneNumber%\r"
@if not @wait "CONNECT"
@echo "** ERROR: Modem not responding\r\n"
<       ; terminate script input
@endif
@wait "\n"     ; waits for the rest of the message
@echo "** Logging in...\r\n"
```

When you're developing scripts, the most useful tool at your disposal is the COM port status panel at the bottom of the screen. Watch the status bar carefully if your script doesn't seem to be working. The COM status panel will display messages of the form *Waiting for "xxx"...(9)* if the currently executing script file is waiting for input. Knowing what the script file is waiting for at any particular time may help you understand why the script file and the host system are out of sync with each other.

Be careful about how and when data is sent to the host. Most systems will not buffer lines of text during login. Therefore, the script must wait for the appropriate prompt before sending text. For example,

```
@send "%HostLoginName%"     ; *WRONG* DON'T DO THIS!!!
@send "%HostPassword%"      ; didn't wait for password:
prompt!
```

will not work on most systems because the host system will flush its input buffers before sending the login: and password: prompts.

Instead, use the following script commands:

```
@wait "login:" 60; wait for either "Login:" or "login:" prompt
@send "%HostLoginName%\r"
@wait "password:" 60 ; wait for either "Password:" or "password:"
@send "%HostPassword%\r"
```

The usage of "\r" and "\n" puzzles some script writers. If in doubt, follow this simple rule: Send "\r" only and expect back "\r\n".

Just write this off to a quirk of the ASCII standard.

Script files and automated connection

FIBS/W supports simple script files that can be used to automate procedures, such as connecting to FIBS. Script files may run either by using the

Communication⇨Run Script command or by typing **<filename.ext** in the Command Line edit box. When Communications⇨Connect is issued, FIBS/W executes the script file selected in the Login Script field of the Options⇨Connect Script Settings command. Connection to FIBS can be completely automated by customizing the script files to fit the requirements of the host system that is being used to connect to FIBS. Script files may have any extension.

However, FIBS/W considers any file with the SCC extension found in the same directory as the FIBS/W program file to be a login script, and will add all of them to the Login Script listbox in the Options⇨Connect Script Settings dialog box. The description is taken from the first line of the login script file. FIBS/W looks for the string "%%" on the first line of the login script and takes any text following the "%%" to be a description.

Network connect scripts are treated in much the same way. Network connect scripts must have the SCN extension and reside in the same directory as the FIBS/W executable. FIBS/W treats any text following "%%" to be a description of the file and displays this information in the Network listbox. The file HANGUP.SCR is executed when Communications⇨Disconnect is issued.

What to Do When Things Go Wrong _____

Won't connect to host system

Look at the status bar to determine where in the connect script FIBS/W thinks it is. The COM status panel will display a message of the form *Waiting for "xxx"*, which should give you a good indication of what FIBS/W is expecting when it gets stuck. You can send commands to the host while a script is executing, so if FIBS/W gets stuck at a particular point, you may be able to resume the script by entering the information that the host is waiting for yourself. If you don't get past initializing the modem (FIBS/W is waiting for *OK*), this would suggest a serial port or modem configuration problem. Make sure that you are connected to the right serial port.

The host system displays lots of ~ characters

If the host system displays ~ characters, the parity setting is incorrect in the Options⇨Modem Settings dialog box. High-speed modems that use 16550 UARTs occasionally display large amounts of ~ characters. There are several potential causes for this problem. The first thing to try is to turn the Detect Parity Errors check box in the Options⇨Modem Settings dialog box to off: high-speed modems typically don't need parity checking because they use more advanced error correcting protocols, and the extra overhead of checking for parity errors may cause hardware overruns. If this doesn't work, try adding the line COM<n>FIFO=0 to the [386Enh] section of the Windows SYSTEM.INI file: early versions of the 16550 had problems which prevent them from operating correctly with Windows. If neither of these solutions work, contact Microsoft to obtain the most recent version of COMM.DRV, which contains bug fixes specifically pertaining to the use of 16550 UARTs in Windows.

The host system displays seemingly random strange characters or makes a mess on-screen

FIBS/W does not support terminal emulation of any kind. Your host system may be expecting FIBS/W to support VT-100 terminal emulation, for example. Regrettably, there are no plans for FIBS/W to support terminal emulation at the present time. The best way to deal with this problem is to write a login script which will get you connected to FIBS automatically. Once you are connected to FIBS, you will not need terminal emulation. Using a communications program that does support terminal emulation, login to your host system, carefully recording what keystrokes you have to send to complete the connection with FIBS. Watch for things on-screen that you can use as prompts in wait commands to ensure that the host system is responding as expected, and wait for these prompts using the @wait "*string*" command before sending data. For instance @wait "Main Menu" in a script file may be a good command to use in such a situation to ensure that the login has completed successfully and that the host system is ready to accept more input.

FIBS/W loses characters

This typically indicates that the flow control setting of the Options⇨Modem Settings dialog box is incorrect. See the "Choosing a modem init string" section for further information.

FIBS/W won't let you issue a move/double/roll command when it should, or FIBS fails to recognize a command that you send

FIBS does not buffer more than one command at a time. If more than one command is sent to FIBS before FIBS gets a chance to execute the first command, FIBS discards the second and all subsequent commands. FIBS/W is fairly careful about not updating the state of the board before receiving confirmation from FIBS. If you lose move commands, for example, you can reissue the command by pressing Return or clicking on the right-hand bar of the board again. FIBS may occasionally send the text of a command sent to it in the midst of board data or other data that FIBS/W expects. If this happens, FIBS/W may get confused. If you suspect that this has happened, choosing Action⇨Freshen Board (Ctrl+F) usually corrects the problem.

FIBS/W gives the error message *Unable to Parse "board:" command*

This message is given when FIBS/W receives a backgammon board from FIBS to display, but the board data appears to be corrupt or incomplete. This error may be given in rare circumstances when a FIBS command is sent halfway through receiving the board. If this happens, choose Action⇨Freshen Board (Ctrl+F) to get FIBS to resend the board. If it happens often, it usually indicates that the FIBS/W flow control configuration and the modem flow control configuration differ, and that FIBS/W is dropping characters as a result. See the "Choosing a modem init string" section for information on how to correct this problem.

FIBS/W won't work with a COM3 or COM4 device

Windows must be correctly configured to use COM3 or COM4 ports. Run the Windows Control Panel application (from Program Manager, choose File⇨Run and then choose CONTROL.EXE and then choose OK). Double-click the Ports tool. Double-click the icon for the port you want to use (COM3: or COM4:). Click the Advanced button. The resulting dialog box lets you set the base port address and IRQ line appropriate for your serial port. Please note that there are no standard port addresses and IRQ lines for COM3 and COM4 devices, so if you want to use COM3 or COM4, this configuration step must be followed.

Legal Stuff

See the file FIBSW1.* when you extract this program from the CD-ROM included with this book for the license agreement and other important version and copyright notes.

This software is not free: FIBS/W may be used for an evaluation period of ten days without charge. After ten days, though, the shareware author requires that you pay a $40 registration fee.

FIBS/W Registration Form

Name _____

Company _____

Address _____

City _____

State _____ Country _____

Zip _____ Phone _____

Remit to:

Robin Davies
224 3rd Ave.
Ottawa, ONT, Canada K1S 2K3

Pricing

❏ $40.00 (U.S.)
Ontario residents add 7% sales tax and 8% GST. Canadian residents add 8% GST.

See the online help for more information.

Part IX

Windows NT Internet Server Tools and Clients

For client software, Windows 3.1 and Windows 95 work very well. For the demanding applications of Internet servers, however, a more robust operating system is needed for best performance. Traditional high-performance Internet hosts are based on some flavor of UNIX. Windows NT 3.5 now provides another option for a high-performance Internet server. Windows NT 3.5 comes with a set of the standard Internet tools, SLIP and PPP dial-up capability, and a basic router. Microsoft will provide DNS server software in the Windows NT 3.5 Resource Kit, along with three server programs that you can use right now. The CD-ROM includes them, too: the World Wide Web HTTP (Hyper Text Transfer Protocol) Server, the WAIS (Wide Area Information Service) Server, and the Gopher Server. When combined with the support for TCP/IP already in Windows NT 3.5, these servers let you provide a complete Internet server for a very small investment. The three servers are from the European Microsoft Windows NT Academic Centre, or EMWAC, and they are free. We have also provided the WAIS ToolKit, a set of tools for preparing and searching full-text databases for computers running the Windows NT operating system. You should read this part if you plan to use the searching capabilities of the Gopher Server, the HTTP Server, or the WAIS Server for Windows NT.

What Is EMWAC?

Quoting from the EMWAC WWW site (`http://emwac.ed.ac.uk/html/top.html`):

"The European Microsoft Windows NT Academic Centre (EMWAC) is an integral part of the Computing Services of the University of Edinburgh and has been set up to support and act as a focus for Windows NT within academia. It is sponsored by Datalink Computers, Digital, Microsoft, Research Machines, Sequent, and the University of Edinburgh. This WWW service is provided from a Sequent WinServer running Windows NT.

"The general mail address is emwac@ed.ac.uk; there is an anonymous FTP service provided at emwac.ed.ac.uk. Please e-mail all comments about this WWW Service to emwac@ed.ac.uk. We are also glad to receive suggestions of how we may add to this information resource."

In addition to the freeware Internet Toolchest, the Edinburgh University Computing Service plans to produce a professional version of the HTTP server and sell it through third parties. In addition to the freeware server's basic functionality, the professional edition will include password protection, permission to access pages based on originating address, a proxy server, and virtual paths.

What Can I Do with These Tools?

By providing freeware HTTP, WAIS, and Gopher servers for NT, EMWAC has given you the ability to offer a WWW server for Internet or private use for nothing more than the cost of an NT compatible workstation. Companies can use a Web site to provide information and services to internal clients. Many companies today are using HTTP servers that are accessible only to those on internal TCP/IP networks. Using HTML's advanced features, an HTTP server can not only provide text, video, audio, and pictures, but can offer a front-end service to database and information services such as an SQL server, an order entry system, an inventory system, or an on-line virtual library. Since internal connections are generally faster than Internet connections, internal Web servers can contain much richer information that would take too long to transfer over the unpredictable Internet.

Combined with NT's dial-up SLIP and PPP capabilities, you could even provide a dial-up Web service to field personnel and further offer Internet gateway services to internal customers. (Note that providing a *commercial* Internet access service via Windows NT 3.5 requires an additional license from Microsoft. Use of NT as an Internet host is included in the basic license.)

If you have ordinary Windows, you can still offer Web server service on your systems, using a version originally based on the UNIX server, and ported to Windows by Robert Denny. The server software is available at ftp:// ftp.alisa.com/pub/win-httpd/whttpd1*n*.zip. The *n* in the filename is the version number. At this writing, the current version is 1.3, with version 1.4 in Beta. Don't expect a Windows PC to operate at the same level of service as a Windows NT system, but this HTTP server does provide good service at no cost. You can check out Alisa's home page at http://www.alisa.com/. You may have read about Serweb, another Windows-3.1-based HTTP server. The author of this program has stopped development on this software and now uses the EMWAC NT-based server.

EMWAC Server Software

The EMWAC HTTP server operates as a service under Windows NT. That means that after you set it up, it will start every time you turn on your system, and it will run with no one logged in. According to those who have used and tested this software, including WUGNET staff members, when the HTTP server runs, you won't notice when people connect to your server. The HTTP Server can be connected to a WAIS search engine with the WAIS toolkit, which the CD-ROM includes. You can connect the HTTP server with any Windows NT console program with the CGI (Common Gateway Interface). If the program you wish to communicate with from the HTTP Server is not a Windows NT console program, then write a console program that communicates with your desired service.

At this writing, the current freeware version was .96. You can check for later versions at ftp://emwac.ed.ac.uk/pub/https/. The directories of EMWAC software can be found on the CD-ROM in the \FILES\PART09 directory.

Chapter 32
The Windows NT WAIS ToolKit 0.6

This software is largely based on the "freeWAIS" Version 0.202 implementation.

Ownership and Copyright

The copyright statement relating to the software and this documentation is as follows:

© MCNC, Clearinghouse for Networked Information Discovery and Retrieval, 1993.

The University Court of the University of Edinburgh, 1994.

Permission to use, copy, modify, distribute, and sell this software and its documentation, in whole or in part, for any purpose is hereby granted without fee, provided that

1. The above copyright notice and this permission notice appear in all copies of the software and related documentation. Notices of copyright and/or attribution which appear in any file included in this distribution must remain intact.

2. Users of this software agree to make their best efforts (a) to return to MCNC any improvements or extensions that they make, so that these may be included in future releases; and (b) to inform MCNC/CNIDR of noteworthy uses of this software.

3. The names of MCNC and Clearinghouse for Networked Information Discovery and Retrieval may not be used in any advertising or publicity relating to the software without the specific, prior written permission of MCNC/CNIDR.

4. The name of the University of Edinburgh may not be used in any advertising or publicity relating to the software without the specific, prior written permission of the University Court.

The software is provided *as-is* and without warranty of any kind, express, implied, or otherwise, including without limitation, any warranty of merchantability or fitness for a particular purpose.

In no event shall MCNC/CNIDR or the University of Edinburgh be liable for any special, incidental, indirect or consequential damages of any kind, or any damages whatsoever resulting from loss of use, data or profits, whether or not advised of the possibility of damage, and on any theory of liability, arising out of or in connection with the use or performance of this software.

Introduction

This chapter describes a set of tools for preparing and searching full-text databases for computers running the Windows NT operating system. You should read this chapter if you plan to use the searching capabilities of the Gopher Server (GOPHERS), the HTTP Server (HTTPS), or the WAIS Server (WAISS) for Windows NT; all of these programs are covered in this book/CD package. This chapter assumes that you have a reasonable degree of competence in the use of Windows NT, that you have read the documentation for the server software that you plan to use, and that you have some experience using WAIS (the Wide Area Information Server).

The tools in this toolkit are

- WAISINDEX — an indexing utility
- WAISLOOK — a searching utility
- WAISSERV — a Z39.50 protocol handler and search engine

This chapter covers the beta test version of the WAIS ToolKit. Please direct bug reports about this version to c.j.adie@ed.ac.uk.

The European Microsoft Windows NT Academic Centre (EMWAC) has been set up to support and act as a focus for Windows NT within academia. The centre is sponsored by Datalink Computers, Digital, Microsoft, Research Machines, Sequent, and the University of Edinburgh. This documentation forms part of the program of EMWAC.

Installation and Setup_____

The Windows NT WAIS Toolkit requires the following software and hardware:

- Intel, MIPS, or Digital Alpha processor.
- Windows NT 3.1 final release, with TCP/IP software installed. (WAISINDEX requires TCP/IP for the `-export` option.)
- At least 16MB of memory.

To install the software, follow these steps:

1. Login to your Windows NT system.
2. The WAIS Toolkit is distributed in three versions (for the Intel, MIPS, and DEC Alpha architectures). Select the appropriate ZIP file for your processor.
3. Unzip the file.

   You should have the following files:

   - WAISINDX.EXE — the WAISINDEX program
   - WAISLOOK.EXE — the searching program
   - WAISSERV.EXE — the Z39.50 searching program
   - WAISTOOL.DOC — the program documentation in Word for Windows format
   - WAISTOOL.WRI — the program documentation in Windows Write format
   - WAISTOOL.PS — the program documentation in PostScript, ready for printing
   - READ.ME — summary of new features

4. If you have installed a previous version of the WAIS ToolKit, remove it by deleting the old files or by moving them to another directory (off the PATH) for deletion after you ensure that the new version works correctly.
5. Decide which directory you are going to put the tools in, and move the EXE programs there. Ensure that the directory is on the PATH so that the commands can be executed from the command line.

   If you plan to use the WAIS Toolkit with the WAIS, Gopher, or HTTP server, you should put the EXE programs in the \WINNT\SYSTEM32 directory so that the servers can find them.

6. If you are using NTFS for the volume in which the tools are stored, you should rename the WAISINDX.EXE program WAISINDEX.EXE.

The program is not distributed with the name WAISINDEX.EXE because of problems when the file is extracted to an FAT volume.

The remainder of this chapter assumes that you have changed the name.

7. Determine which version of the WAIS ToolKit you have by typing the following commands at the Windows NT command prompt:

```
waisindex -v
waislook -v
waisserv -v
```

The version number for each program is displayed. (In fact, two version numbers will be shown for WAISINDEX and WAISSERV. The first number refers to the version of the freeWAIS code from which the programs were ported; the second number is the number of the Windows NT version.) This chapter covers Version 0.6. If the programs report a later version number, you will find corresponding updated documentation in the files that you unpacked from the ZIP archive.

Consult the on-line help if you have installation problems.

Using the Tools

Three programs are provided in the ToolKit:

- WAISINDEX is a program that creates a WAIS index of all the words in a set of files. This is ported directly from the CNIDR program of the same name in the "freeWAIS" Version 0.202 distribution.

- WAISLOOK is a program that takes one or more words and displays the names of those files in the index that contains those words, listed according to frequency of occurrence.

- WAISSERV is a program that accepts WAIS protocol requests through stdin and sends back responses, using the same protocol, through stdout. The program is designed for use with the WAIS server for Windows NT (WAISS) and is of little use on its own.

This chapter documents the preceding programs. The following short section describes how to create and search a simple index to verify that the programs are working. In the subsequent sections, the programs are formally documented.

The documentation will be expanded in future releases of the WAIS ToolKit.

Creating and searching a simple database

This section describes how to create a simple index by using WAISINDEX and how to search it by using WAISLOOK.

Preparation

1. Create a directory to work in.

   This example assumes this directory is called C:\TESTWAIS.

2. Create a subdirectory to hold the files that you're going to index — for example, C:\TESTWAIS\FILES.

3. Put some text files in the C:\TESTWAIS\FILES directory.

   The files can be anything you like as long as they are ASCII text files.

Creating an index

1. Make C:\TESTWAIS the current directory.

2. Execute WAISINDEX, giving it the following parameters:

   ```
   waisindex -d myindex files\*
   ```

3. Observe the messages from WAISINDEX to make sure that there are no errors.

4. Do a DIR command on the C:\TESTWAIS directory to make sure that WAISINDEX has created the seven index files, named MYINDEX.*.

Searching the index

1. Ensure that the current directory is C:\TESTWAIS.

2. Execute WAISLOOK, giving it the following parameters:

   ```
   waislook -d myindex word
   ```

   word should be replaced by a word that you know occurs in the files you have indexed.

3. Observe the output of WAISLOOK, which will show you the names of the files that contain the word you selected.

The WAISINDEX program

The WAISINDEX program is used to build and update WAIS databases. Notice that this program cannot work with a database on an FAT partition because the intermediate files that it creates during the indexing process do not conform to the FAT *8-character filename.3-character extension* filename restriction.

Syntax

```
waisindex [ -d index_filename ] [ -a ] [ -r ]
   [ -mem mbytes ] [ -register ] [ -export ]
   [ -e [ file ] ] [ -l log_level ]
   [ -pos | -nopos ] [ -nopairs | -pairs ]
   [ -nocat ] [ -T type ] [ -t type ]
   [ -contents | -nocontents ]
   [-v] [-stdin] [-keywords "string"]
   [-keyword_file filename] [-M type,type]
   [-x filename[,...]]
   filename filename ...
```

Description

WAISINDEX creates an index of the words in files so that the files can be searched quickly by tools such as WAISLOOK. The index comprises seven files and takes about as much disk space as the original text. The files that comprise the index use the extensions listed in Table 32-1.

Table 32-1	WAISINDEX File Extensions
Extension	*Description*
CAT	The catalog of the indexed files, with about three lines of information for each file indexed. This file is a text file.
DCT	The dictionary of indexed words. This file is a binary file.
DOC	The document table. This file is a binary file. A file can contain several documents, depending on the type specified in the -t option.
FN	The filename table. This file is a binary file. The filenames stored in this table are as supplied to WAISINDEX as the final parameters. Therefore, if filenames are supplied relative to the current directory (for example, FILES/*), they will be stored in the filename table in that form, and the resulting filenames from a database search also will be in relative form.

Extension	Description
HL	The headline table. This file is a binary file. A *headline* is (ideally) a line of descriptive text that summarizes the contents of a document. The headline normally is taken from the document itself — for example, it may be the Subject: line if the document is a mail message; it may be the first line of the file; or it may simply be the filename. What the headline is depends on the type of the file, as the -t option notifies WAISINDEX.
INV	The inverted file index. This file is a binary file.
SRC	The source description structure. This file is a text file.

Options

Option	Description
-d *index_filename*	Provides the base filename for the index files. Therefore, if D:\WAIS\FOO is specified, the index files will be called D:\WAIS\FOO.CAT, and so on. The default is .\index.
-a	Appends this index to an existing one. This option is useful for making incremental additions or updates. Because this option only adds to an index, if a file has changed, the file is reindexed, but the old entries are not purged. Therefore, to save space, it's a good idea to index the whole set of files periodically. If you don't specify this option, the old index (if any exists) is overwritten.
-v	Displays the version number of the program.
-r	Recursively indexes subdirectories.
-mem *mbytes*	Indicates how much main memory (in megabytes) to use during indexing. The usefulness of this option in the Windows NT environment is unknown.
-register	The Windows NT version of WAISINDEX cannot automatically register a WAIS database with the directory of servers. Specifying the -register option causes the program to display instructions about how to register a WAIS database manually, using electronic mail.
-export	Causes the source description file created by WAISINDEX to include the host-name and the WAIS default TCP port (210) for use by the clients. Otherwise, the source description file contains no connection information and is expected to be used only for local searches.
-e [*filename*]	Redirects error output to the named file, or suppresses error output if *filename* is omitted. Error output defaults to stderr (usually, the console) if -e is not used.

(continued)

Table 32-1: (continued)

Option	Description
-1 log_level	Sets logging level. Currently, only levels 0, 1, 5, and 10 are meaningful: Level 0 means log nothing (silent). Level 1 logs only errors and warnings (messages of HIGH priority); level 5 logs messages of MEDIUM priority (such as indexing filename information). Level 10 logs everything.
-pos (-nopos)	Includes word-position information in the index (excluded by default). This option increases the index size but enables search engines to do proximity searches.
-nopairs (-pairs)	Does not build word pairs from consecutive capitalized words (pairs are built by default).
-nocat	Inhibits the creation of a catalog. This option is useful for databases that contain a large number of documents because the catalog contains three lines per document.
-contents (-nocontents)	Includes (excludes) the contents of the file from the index. The filename and header are still indexed. The default is type dependent.
-T type	The filename table (FN) and the catalog (CAT) created by WAISINDEX contain a *type* string for each file indexed. This option sets the type string to *type*. The default (TEXT, in most cases) depends on the type of file being indexed. Possible values are as follows: TEXT TEXT-FTP WSRC (WAIS SRC structures) DVI PS PICT GIF TIFF HTML This type information is used only by the WAIS server; the HTTP and Gopher servers have their own mechanisms for determining the type of a file.
-t type	Tells WAISINDEX the type of the files being indexed. For more information, see "File types" later in this chapter. The default is text. This type of information enables WAISINDEX to derive an appropriate headline, which is stored in the headline table (HL). Type information is also used to determine whether the files being indexed are deemed to consist of multiple documents.

Option	Description
-stdin	Reads the list of filenames to be indexed from standard input (stdin) rather than from the command line.
-keywords "*string*"	Keywords to be indexed for each document.
-keyword_file *filename*	File of keywords to be indexed for each document.
-M *type,type*	For multiple-type documents.
-x *filename*[,. . .]	The filename(s) are not indexed. Two or more filenames are separated with a comma and no space between them.
filename filename. . .	These are the files that will be indexed according to the arguments above. The filenames given here will be stored in the filename table. Wild cards may be used.

The document table size is limited to 16MB. This restriction limits the indexer to databases with headlines that add up to less than 16MB (because that is the principal component of the table). This problem typically occurs for database types in which a record is essentially a headline (one_line, archie).

Synonym files

A *synonym file* is used to reduce the size of an index and to facilitate more effective searching. The file consists of lines of words; the first word is the *datum* (basic term), and subsequent words in the line are synonyms. Lines beginning with a hash (#) are treated as comments.

When a database is indexed, the synonym file (if it exists) is read into a table. Each word from a document to be indexed is translated, using the table to the corresponding datum value, and the translated word is recorded in the database instead of the original word.

When a database search is performed, the search words are similarly translated by using the synonym file before the search is performed.

The synonym file has the same name as the database, but it must have the SYN extension. The file must be located in the same directory as the rest of the database files.

If the WAISINDEX program does not find a synonym file, it issues a warning message.

Following is a sample synonym file:

```
# First word is base term, rest are synonyms
boat ship yacht launch galleon destroyer dinghy
shoe slipper boot sneaker trainer
```

File types

This section lists the file types that the WAISINDEX program parses.

Type	Description
bibtex	BibTeX/LaTeX format.
bio	Biology abstract format.
cmapp	CM applications from HyperCard.
dash	Entries separated by a row of dashes. At least 20 dashes must be present for a line to be recognized as a separator. Each entry is indexed as a separate document.
dvi	DVI format.
emacsinfo	The GNU documentation system.
filename	Uses only the filename part of the path name for the title.
first_line	The first line of the file is the headline.
ftp	Special type for FTP files. The first line of the file is the headline.
gif	GIF files; indexes only the filename.
html	Hypertext Markup Language (HTML). The text within the <TITLE> element is the headline.
irg	Internet resource guide.
jargon	Jargon File 2.9.8 format.
listserv_digest	LISTSERV mail digest format.
mail_digest	Standard Internet mail digest format.
mail_or_rmail	Mail or rmail, or both.
medline	Medline format.
mh_bboard	MH bulletin-board format.
ms_kbase	MS Knowledge Base format.
netnews	Netnews format.
nhyp	Hypertext format, Polytechnic of Central London.
one_line	Each line in the file is a separate document.

Type	Description
para	Paragraphs separated by blank lines. Each paragraph is a separate document.
pict	PICT files; indexes only the filename.
ps	PostScript format.
refer	Refer format.
rn	Netnews saved by the [rt]?rn newsreader.
server	Server structures (SRC) for the directory of servers.
text	Simple text files (this is the default).
tiff	TIFF files; indexes only the filename.
URL what-to-trim what-to-add	This type has been superseded by the html type, which should be used in preference.

The WAISLOOK program

The WAISLOOK program is used to search WAIS databases. The program is executed automatically by the GOPHERS and HTTPS servers when they need to search WAIS databases, but it also can be executed manually from the console. In the latter case, many of the options listed are not relevant.

Syntax

```
waislook [-d dbname] [-h hostname] [-p port]
   [-debug] [-v] [-http|-gopher] [-t title]
   [-q virtpath] search words ...
```

Description

This program searches an index for documents that contain the search words. The program ranks documents according to the frequency of occurrence of the words and according to whether the words occur in the document headline. If more than (by default) 40 documents are found, only the 40 with the highest ranking are returned.

The program generates either an HTML document or a Gopher menu containing the result of the search, or it displays the names of the documents and their corresponding headlines on the console.

Options

Option	Description
-debug	Enables debugging. In this mode, debugging information is sent to stderr.
-v	Displays the version number of WAISLOOK.
-h hostname	Specifies the name of the host to quote when generating HTML output or Gopher menu output. This option is not used in interactive mode and has no default value.
-p port	Specifies the number of the TCP/IP port to quote when generating HTML output or Gopher menu output. This option is not used in interactive mode and has no default value.
-d dbname	Specifies the name of the WAIS database to search. The name should not have an extension or a trailing dot. Defaults to .\index. Using this option is almost always necessary.
-http	Specifies that the program has been invoked from the HTTP Server and should output the results of the search in HTML. This option cannot be combined with -gopher.
-gopher	Specifies that the program has been invoked from the Gopher Server and should output the results of the search as a Gopher menu. This option cannot be combined with -http.
-t title	Specifies the title to be used in the output HTML document if the -http option has been selected. If the title contains spaces, enclose it in double quotation marks.
-q virtpath	This option enables you to specify a virtual path name to prepend to the filenames returned by WAISLOOK when the -https option is in effect. This option can be used by some versions of the HTTP Server for Windows NT. Notice that the freeware HTTP server does not support virtual paths.
search words ...	One or more search words are specified after all the options. The first search word cannot begin with a hyphen (to distinguish it from the options). If more than one search word is given, documents that contain any of the search words are returned. Notice that Boolean combinations of search words are not supported (yet).

The WAISSERV program

The WAISSERV program is used to search WAIS databases. The program is executed automatically by the WAIS Server (WAISS) when it receives an incoming call from a WAIS client. The program also can be executed manually from the console but is not particularly useful in this mode.

Syntax

```
waisserv [-d directory] [-e file] [-v] [-l level ]
```

Description

This program reads WAIS protocol requests from its standard input (stdin) and writes the response to standard output (stdout). Like WAISLOOK, the program ranks the documents that it finds according to the frequency of occurrence of the words and according to whether they occur in the document headline. If more than 40 documents are found, only the 40 with the highest ranking are returned.

Options

Option	Description
-d directory	Specifies the directory that contains the WAIS databases. The name should not have an extension or a trailing dot. Defaults to the current directory.
-e file	Specifies that log information should be written to *file*. Defaults to NUL:.
-l level	Specifies the amount of logging information to write to the file. The *level* is a number ranging from 0 (no logging information; the default) to 10 (full information).
-v	Displays the version number of the program.

Chapter 33

HTTP Server Version 0.95

This chapter describes the World Wide Web HTTP Server for computers running the Windows NT operating system. You should read this chapter only if you plan to install, operate, manage, or uninstall the HTTP Server software. This chapter and the on-line documentation assume that you have a reasonable degree of competence in the use of Windows NT, as well as a reasonable knowledge of HTTP and the World Wide Web.

Notice that the documentation for this product also is available as hypertext, on-line at the following address:

```
http://emwac.ed.ac.uk/html/internet_toolchest/https/contents.htm
```

Introduction

The HTTP Server for Windows NT implements the HTTP/1.0 protocol. The HTTP Server for Windows NT runs as a Windows NT service, just like the FTP Server that comes with Windows NT. As an analogy to the UNIX HTTP server daemon, which is called `httpd`, the Windows NT HTTP server service is called `https`. The HTTP server service is configured by use of a Control Panel applet.

This version of HTTPS originates from the European Microsoft Windows NT Academic Centre (EMWAC). Located at Edinburgh University Computing Service, EMWAC has been set up to support and act as a focus for Windows NT within academia. EMWAC is sponsored by Datalink Computers, Digital, Microsoft, Research Machines, Sequent, and the University of Edinburgh.

EMWAC will collect and periodically review bug reports and suggestions for improvement.

- To report a bug in HTTPS, send an e-mail message to emwac@ed.ac.uk, with HTTPS BUG in the Subject line.

- To suggest an enhancement, send an e-mail message to emwac@ed.ac.uk, with HTTPS SUGGESTION in the Subject line.

Edinburgh University Computing Service will be producing a Professional version of HTTPS, which will be marketed through third parties. The Professional version will be fully supported and will have enhanced functionality.

Installation Requirements

To use the Windows NT HTTP Server, you need to have a computer with the following characteristics:

- Intel, MIPS, or Digital Alpha processor.
- Windows NT 3.1 final release, with TCP/IP software installed.
- At least 16MB of memory.
- Network connection (typically, Ethernet).

Installing

Follow these instructions to install the HTTP Server.

1. Login to your Windows NT system as a user with administrative privileges.
2. The HTTP Server is distributed in three versions: for the Intel, MIPS, and DEC Alpha architectures. Select the appropriate ZIP file for your processor.
3. Unzip the file.

   You should have the following files:

   - HTTPS.EXE — the HTTP Server itself
   - HTTPS.CPL — the Control Panel applet
   - HTTPS.HLP — the Control Panel applet help file
   - HTTPS.DOC — the HTTP Server documentation in Word for Windows format
   - HTTPS.PS — the HTTP Server documentation in PostScript format, ready for printing
   - HTTPS.WRI — the HTTP Server documentation in Windows Write format
   - EGSCRIPT.ZIP — sample CGI script programs
   - COPYRITE.TXT — the copyright statement for the software
   - READ.ME — summary of new features

4. Decide which directory you are going to put HTTPS.EXE in, and move it there.

   A good choice is the \WINNT\SYSTEM32 directory, which is where many other services live. Using the Security/Permissions menu option in the File Manager, verify that the SYSTEM user has read permission for the file.

5. Move HTTPS.CPL and HTTPS.HLP to the \WINNT\SYSTEM32 directory; then start the Control Panel from the Program Manager to verify that the HTTP Server applet is represented as an icon in the Control Panel.

6. Determine which version of HTTPS you have by typing the following at the Windows NT command prompt:

   ```
   https -version
   ```

   The version number is displayed. This chapter and the on-line documentation cover HTTPS Version 0.95. If the program reports a later version number, you will find corresponding updated documentation in the files that you unpacked from the ZIP archive.

7. You should also check the IP address of your machine by using the following command:

   ```
   https -ipaddress
   ```

   This command displays the name of your machine (for example, emwac.ed.ac.uk) and its IP address(es), as reported by the Windows Sockets API. If this information is incorrect, you need to reconfigure the TCP/IP software on your machine. The HTTP Server will not work if this address (or list of addresses, if your machine has more than one network interface) is wrong.

8. If you have installed a previous version of the HTTP Server, you must remove it by typing the following command:

   ```
   https -remove
   ```

See the "Uninstalling" section later in this chapter for further information. You can use the old or the new version of HTTPS.EXE to perform the remove operation. *If you are replacing Version 0.7 or earlier with Version 0.8 or later, read the sidebar at the end of this section!*

9. Install HTTPS in the table of Windows NT Services (and simultaneously register it with the Event Logger) by running the program from the Windows NT command line, specifying the -install flag.

It is vital that you execute this command by using the copy of HTTPS.EXE that you placed in the \WINNT\SYSTEM32 directory, not by using some other copy that you plan to delete subsequently. For example:

   ```
   https -install
   ```

Upgrading from Version 0.7 or earlier to Version 0.8 or later

In Version 0.8, the short name by which the HTTP Service is known to the operating system changed from HTTP Server to HTTPS, which means that the Windows NT registry stores information about the service in a different place from earlier versions. If you are upgrading from an earlier version of HTTPS, this has two consequences:

■ The information stored in the registry by the earlier version of HTTPS must be deleted. You can do this by running the earlier version of HTTPS from the command line with the -remove flag. Alternatively, Version 0.8 or later (when you run it with the -remove option) detects whether information relating to

Version 0.7 or earlier is present in the registry and, if so, deletes that information. Both methods have occasionally been observed to cause the Event Log Service to terminate with an access violation. This is harmless; just restart the Event Log Service from the Services dialog box in the Control Panel.

■ When you replace Version 0.7 or earlier with Version 0.8 or later, any events recorded in the Event Log by the earlier version will be unintelligible because the Event Viewer program cannot find the information in the registry that tells it where the HTTPS.EXE file is located.

The program registers itself with the Service Manager and with the Event Logger, and reports success or failure. In the case of failure, see the "Installation Problems" section.

10. To verify that the installation succeeded, start the Windows NT Control Panel, and double-click the Services icon.

   The resulting dialog box should list HTTP Server as one of the installed services. If it does, see the "Configuration" section later in this chapter for further instructions.

Installation Problems

The system says that HTTPS is not a Windows NT program.

You probably are trying to run an executable for the wrong sort of processor. Make sure that you have unpacked the correct ZIP file for your processor type.

The system says that the HTTP Service won't install because of a "duplicate service name."

You must remove a previous version of the HTTP Service, using the `https -remove` command, before installing with `https -install`.

HTTPS waits for a while and then terminates with a "usage" message.

You must not run HTTPS from the command line or from the File Manager, except with a command-line argument. The HTTPS program is a Windows NT service and must be started through the Services dialog box in the Control Panel.

Uninstalling

This section describes what to do if you want to remove the HTTP Server from your computer or if you want to move the program to a new location. Follow these steps:

1. If necessary, stop the HTTP Server, using the Stop button in the Services dialog box in the Control Panel.

2. At the Windows NT command line, run HTTPS with the `-remove` option, as follows:

   ```
   https -remove
   ```

   This command removes the HTTP Server from the Service Manager's list of services.

3. If you are uninstalling the HTTP Server, simply delete the HTTPS.EXE program and the HTTPS.CPL Control Panel applet.

4. If you want to move HTTPS.EXE to a new location, move the file, and then type **https -install**.

   This command informs the Service Manager and Event Logger of the new location of the program. You need to start the HTTP Server again from the Control Panel.

Configuration

The HTTP Server is configured by means of the HTTP Server applet in the Control Panel. The HTTP Server applet looks like the one shown in Figure 33-1.

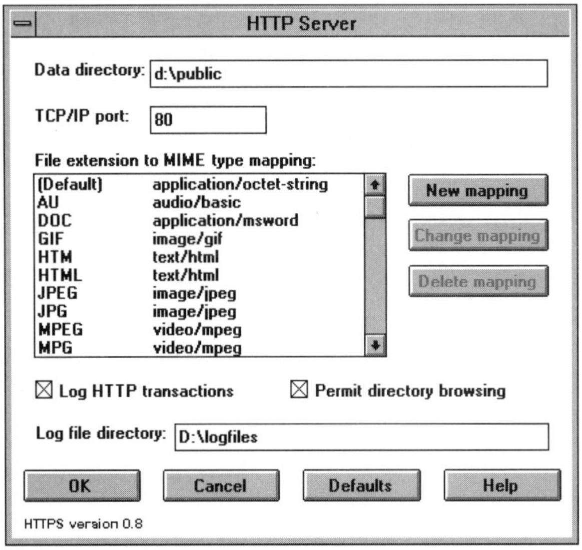

Figure 33-1: HTTP Server applet window.

Notice that the version number of the applet is displayed in the lower-left corner of the dialog box. The version number reported by the command `https -version` must be the same as the version number of the applet. If no Version number appears in the lower-left corner of the dialog box, you are using Version 0.2 of the applet.

You can use this dialog box to do the following things:

■ Set the root of the directory tree that contains the files you want to make available on the World Wide Web. Use the Data directory: field for this purpose. For full details on how HTTP treats the files and directories in this directory tree, see "The HTTP Directory and URLs" section of this chapter. The default is D:\HTTP.

■ Specify the TCP/IP port on which the HTTP Server listens for incoming HTTP connections. Use the TCP/IP port: field for this purpose. The value must be a positive integer that represents a legal and otherwise unused port. The default is 80.

■ Specify the MIME type that corresponds to a given file extension (covered in more detail in the following section).

■ Enable and disable the logging of HTTP transactions. If this box is checked, the HTTP Server records each HTTP request that it receives in a log file. See "HTTP Transaction Logging" later in this chapter for more information about logging. Logging is disabled by default.

■ Specify the directory in which log files are stored. Use the Log file directory: field for this purpose. This option is disabled unless the Log HTTP Transactions box is checked. The default is the Windows system directory (\WINNT).

■ Permit the HTTP data directory tree to be browsed by HTTP clients. You'll find more details on browsing under the "Browsing the HTTP directory tree" section of this chapter. Browsing is disabled by default.

■ Restore the default values of all the configuration settings by clicking the Defaults button.

When you finish making changes in the configuration, click OK. The configuration takes effect the next time that you start the HTTP Server. If the HTTP Server is already running, a dialog box appears to remind you to stop and restart the HTTP Server (using the Services dialog box in the Control Panel).

File extension to MIME-type mapping

The HTTP protocol represents the type of each file as a MIME type/subtype pair. The HTTP Server infers the MIME type of a file from the file extension, using a mapping table. You can configure the mapping table by using the list in the Control Panel applet and the buttons to its right, labeled New Mapping, Change Mapping, and Delete Mapping. The default contents of the mapping table shown in Table 33-1.

Table 33-1	MIME Mapping Table
File Extension	*MIME Type*
HTM	text/html
HTML	text/html
TXT	text/plain
PS	application/postscript
RTF	application/rtf
PDF	application/pdf
ZIP	application/zip
DOC	application/msword
JPG	image/jpeg

(continued)

Table 33-1 *(continued)*

File Extension	MIME Type
JPEG	image/jpeg
GIF	image/gif
TIF	image/tiff
TIFF	image/tiff
XBM	image/x-xbitmap
WAV	audio/wav
AU	audio/basic
MPG	video/mpeg
MPEG	video/mpeg
Default	application/octet-string

To add a new mapping to the table, click the New Mapping button. The dialog box shown in Figure 33-2 appears.

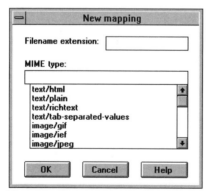

Figure 33-2: New mapping dialog box.

In the Filename Extension field, type the extension that you want to map. From the list, select the MIME type to which you want to map the extension (or enter the MIME type yourself if it's not in the list). Then choose OK to add the new mapping to the main list. Notice that you cannot create a new mapping for a file extension that already appears in the mapping list; an extension can occur in the list only one time.

To change an existing mapping, select it from the list in the main HTTP Server dialog box, and then click the Change Mapping button. A dialog box, similar to the New Mapping box shown in Figure 33-2, appears. You can use this box to change the file extension or to select a new MIME type (or both).

To delete an existing mapping, select it from the list in the main HTTP Server dialog box, and then click the Delete Mapping button.

Putting the data directory on a file server

If the directory tree that you want to make available to HTTP clients is located on a file server instead of on the local Windows NT machine, you need to take special action.

Normally, directories on the file server are mapped to a drive letter on the local system. You might expect that simply using the mapped drive letter in the HTTP Server configuration dialog box would have the desired effect, and indeed it does — until you logoff the local machine.

Drive mappings are established only when someone logs on to the Windows NT machine. Mappings are specific to a user, not to the machine. The HTTP Server normally is kept running, whether someone is logged on to the machine or not. Often, the HTTP Server will be set to start automatically when the operating system loads, when no one is logged in and, therefore, when no drive mappings are in effect.

To overcome this, you can specify the HTTP data directory in the HTTP Configuration dialog box by using a UNC form of directory name, as in the following example:

```
\\CLYDE\INFOSERVER
```

Here, CLYDE is the name of the server, and INFOSERVER is the share name of the directory that is to be served using HTTP.

Operation

This section discusses how to manage HTTP Server operations.

Using the Services dialog box

You use the Services dialog box in the Windows NT Control Panel for managing HTTPS operation.

After you install HTTPS, you can start it by selecting it from the list of services in the dialog box and then clicking the Start button. If all goes well, a message box containing a rotating timer appears while the service starts; the box then disappears. The HTTP Server appears in the list of services with Started status and can respond to HTTP clients.

If the service fails to start, one of several problems may have occurred. You may see a message box that indicates the source of the problem. For further information, see the "Troubleshooting" section of this chapter.

You may want to arrange for HTTPS to start automatically when the system is started. You can do this by clicking the Startup button in the Services dialog box. You also can use this button to specify a different user ID for HTTPS to run under. See your Windows NT documentation for details.

Pausing the HTTP Server (by clicking the Pause button in the Services dialog box) causes the following behavior:

■ Any HTTP transactions that currently are under way are unaffected; they run to completion.

■ Any new HTTP connections will be queued. When the service is resumed, the connections are accepted and processed.

■ If more than five incoming connections are received while the service is paused, the extra connections are rejected.

Error logging

If an error in the operation of the server occurs, the error is logged in the Application Event Log. You can view this log by using the Event Viewer, which you find in the Administrative Tools program group in the Program Manager. See your Windows NT documentation for details on how to use the Event Viewer.

Notice that the Event Viewer uses the HTTPS.EXE program to interpret messages associated with events. Therefore, if you remove the HTTPS.EXE file, the HTTP Server events in your Application Event Log will be unintelligible.

The errors logged in the Application Event Log usually are associated with an HTTPS problem (for example, a file I/O error, a system call failure caused by lack of resources, or a problem with the configuration information).

Problems associated with the client (for example, the client sends a URL that points to a file that does not exist) are recorded in the Application Event Log as Warning events.

When the HTTP Server is started or stopped, information events are recorded in the Application Event Log.

For further details on the most common messages that may appear in the Event Log, see the "Troubleshooting" section of this chapter.

HTTP transaction logging

If you check the Log HTTP Transactions box in the HTTP Server Configuration dialog box, for every HTTP request that the server receives, it records a line of information in a log file. The log file is stored in the log file directory, which you also can configure in the dialog box.

A new log file is created every day. The filename is of the form HS*yymmdd*.LOG, so that, for example, the file corresponding to 4 July 1994 would be HS940704.LOG. For performance reasons, the current log file is kept open until the first HTTP transaction of the following day. When this transaction occurs, the preceding day's log file is closed, a new log file is opened, and the transaction is logged to it.

The information recorded is the time and date of the request, the IP addresses of the server and the client, the HTTP command, the URL requested, and the version of the HTTP protocol used (if there is no version, HTTP 0.9 is in use).

The HTTP Directory and URLs

The HTTP Data Directory is the root of a directory tree within which you must locate files that you want to make available to HTTP clients. Points in the file system that are above the Data Directory or on other disks are not accessible to HTTP clients. The Data Directory may be located on a disk that uses the FAT, HPFS, or NTFS file system.

URLs are relative to the Data Directory. Therefore, if the HTTP client asks for a URL of the form

```
http://mymachine.mydomain.ac.uk/mydir/myfile.htm
```

the HTTP Server sends a file called MYFILE.HTM that is located in the MYDIR subdirectory of the Data Directory.

Files that have the hidden or system attributes are ignored (treated as though they didn't exist).

The Data Directory tree must be accessible by the user ID under which HTTPS runs. Normally, this is the SYSTEM user ID.

By default, any file in the Data Directory tree for which the SYSTEM user has read permission can be retrieved by any HTTP client. If you want to prevent access to a particular file, use the Security/Permissions menu option in the File Manager to ensure that the SYSTEM user cannot access that file. Remember that the SYSTEM user is in the Administrators group (even though it does not appear in the User Manager list of members).

Browsing the HTTP directory tree

Suppose that an HTTP client asks for a URL of the form

```
http://mymachine.mydomain.ac.uk/mydir
```

in which MYDIR is a directory. The HTTP Server will do one of three things, depending on the contents of the directory and on how the server is configured:

- If a file called DEFAULT.HTM exists in the MYDIR directory, the server sends that file to the client.

- Otherwise, if Directory Browsing is enabled, the server sends a list of files and subdirectories within MYDIR to the client.

- If Directory Browsing is not enabled, the server sends an error message to the client.

Therefore, Directory Browsing enables a user to navigate through the Data Directory according to its hierarchical structure, rather like Gopher. You can enable Directory Browsing using the Control Panel configuration applet.

If you don't want a particular directory to be browsable, you can create a file called NOBROWSE in that directory. The file's contents are irrelevant; its presence simply causes the second item in the preceding list to be omitted.

Notice that the top-level Data Directory itself also may have a DEFAULT.HTM or a NOBROWSE file.

Searching WAIS Indexes

The HTTP Server can search local WAIS databases. Before reading this section, you should read the preceding chapter, "The Windows NT WAIS ToolKit 0.6." (The WAIS Toolkit for Windows NT is included in this book/CD-ROM package and was created by Computing Services, The University of Edinburgh also.)

When the server receives an HTTP GET command for a URL that both

- denotes an HTML file and
- includes a search term

the HTTP Server passes the filename and the search term to the WAISLOOK program. The output from the WAISLOOK program is passed back to the client as an HTML document containing the result of the search. Notice that for this process to work, the name of the HTML file must be the same as the name of the WAIS database (apart from the extension).

To ensure that the HTTP Server can execute the WAISLOOK program, the WAISLOOK.EXE file should be located in the \WINNT\SYSTEM32 directory.

There are a number of ways to exploit the search capabilities of the HTTP Server and the WAIS ToolKit. The following section indicates one way of using these capabilities.

Example: a simple index of text files

This example illustrates how to set up a very common situation: you have a large number of text files (for example, an archive of Usenet news messages) that you want to allow HTTP clients to search.

Prepare the directory structure

This example assumes that the HTTP data directory is E:\WEB and that drive E is on an NTFS partition. Within that directory, you have created a subdirectory

— NEWS — to hold a number of newsgroup indexes. Under NEWS, you have created a directory — ALT.ATHEISM — for that newsgroup. Now create a directory — FILES — under ALT.ATHEISM, which is to hold the actual news messages, one to each file.

Following is the directory tree in graphical form:

```
        e:\

        web



            News



        alt.atheism


         files



    103   104   105   106
```

The news messages in this example have filenames that do not include extensions. Normally, such messages are mapped by the mapping table to MIME type `application/octet-string`, which is not appropriate for these files. Therefore, you should configure the (`Default`) extension mapping in the HTTP Server Configuration dialog box so that these files are returned as `text/plain` by the HTTP Server.

Index the messages

Using a Windows NT command prompt, change to the HTTP data directory (E:\WEB) so that the filenames in the filename table that will be created by the indexing program are relative to the HTTP data directory. Then run the following indexing command:

```
waisindex -d News\alt.atheism\index -t netnews
News\alt.atheism\files\*
```

This command creates files called INDEX.SRC, INDEX.INV, and so on in the E:\WEB\NEWS\ALT.ATHEISM directory.

Test the index

To verify that the index functions correctly, use the WAISLOOK program to examine it, as follows:

```
waislook -d News\alt.atheism\index religion
```

This command should return a list of files and headlines that contain the word *religion*.

Create the HTML file

Now you need to create an HTML file that invites the user to search the index. In the E:\WEB\NEWS\ALT.ATHEISM directory, create a file — INDEX.HTM — that looks something like this:

```
<title>Search the alt.atheism news archive.</title>
<body>
<p>
Please enter the term(s) to search for.
<isindex>
</body>
```

Notice that the HTML file must have the same name and path as the database, but the file of course should have an HTM or HTML extension to identify it as an HTML file according to the extension mapping table.

If the HTTP client user retrieves this file, she will be able to enter a search term (because of the `<isindex>` tag). When she presses Return (or otherwise initiates a request), the client requests a URL such as the following:

```
http://myhost.mydomain.ac.uk/News/alt.atheism/
index.htm?search+words
```

The HTTP Server invokes the WAISLOOK program to search the index and returns an HTML file that contains the list of matching messages.

Updating the index

When a new message (for example, 107) arrives in the E:\WEB\NEWS\ALT.ATHEISM\FILES directory, you should run the WAISINDEX command to update the index. Change to the E:\WEB directory, and issue the following command:

```
waisindex -d News\alt.atheism\index -t netnews -a
News\alt.atheism\files\107
```

This command adds the new file to the directory. Normally, of course, you would arrange for this command to be executed automatically in a batch file.

Scripts and Forms

The HTTP Server conforms to the Common Gateway Interface (CGI) 1.1 standard (see http://hoohoo.ncsa.uiuc.edu/cgi/). This means that you can write your own programs (known as CGI scripts) that can be invoked by World Wide Web clients and that run on the Windows NT machine that is running HTTPS. For example, CGI scripts could be used to provide a gateway between World Wide Web and a database package, or to process user input read from an HTML form.

Script execution

A *script* is an executable Windows NT program with an EXE extension. A script must be located within the HTTP Data Directory tree and must be a Windows NT *console* application — one that could in principle be used from the Windows NT command line. A script cannot be a GUI program or another Windows NT Service. Due to a bug in Windows NT 3.1, a script cannot be a DOS program, either.

Full details on how to write CGI scripts appear in the CGI specification. Briefly, the script accesses information about how it was invoked through Environment variables, reads any information supplied by the client in a POST request via `stdin`, and sends output to the client through `stdout`. The file EGSCRIPT.ZIP contains two example scripts (executable and C source) and a corresponding makefile. The makefile assumes that you have the Windows NT Software Developer's Kit (SDK) installed. (You don't have to have the SDK to write scripts, however.)

A CGI script is executed under two circumstances:

- When the HTTP Server receives a POST request for a URL that corresponds to an executable file
- When the HTTP Server receives a GET request for a URL that both corresponds to an executable file and contains a query string

If the script is specified in a GET request *without* a query string in the URL, the script is sent to the client as an `application/octet-string` file (or whatever the EXE extension corresponds to in the mapping table). If you do not want to allow users to download your script this way, you should use the File Manager to assign execute-only permission to the script so that it can't be read by the SYSTEM user.

Using forms with HTTPS

HTML enables you to create forms, which allow the user to submit information (such as a complex database query) to a HTTP server. A description of how to create forms may be found at the following address:

```
http://hoohoo.ncsa.uiuc.edu/SDG/Software/Mosaic/Docs/fill-
out-forms/overview.html
```

When a client program submits a form, the program may do so by using the GET or the POST method. The query string (in the former case) or the body of the request message (in the latter case) contains the data entered into the form by the user. For an example of how to decode the data from a form, see the scripts in EGSCRIPT.ZIP.

Following is an example form defined in HTML:

```
<head><title>A test form</title></head>
<body>
A test form for checking out the POST method in HTTPS. <p>
<form action="http://host.domain.edu/scripts/egscript.exe"
method="POST">
Field 1 (text entry field) <input type="text" name="field1">
<p>
Field 2 (checkbox) <input type="checkbox" name="field2"> <p>
Field 3 (radio buttons)<br>
<input type="radio" name=field3 value="Male" checked>
Male<BR>
<input type="radio" name=field3 value="Female"> Female <BR>
<input type="radio" name=field3 value="Neuter"> Neuter<BR>
<p>
Field 4 (select)
<select name="field4">
<option> First
<option> Second
<option> Third
<option> Fourth
</select>
<p>
```

(continued)

```
Field 5 (textarea) <textarea name=field5 rows=4 cols=40>
</textarea>
<p>
Field 6 (submit) <input type="submit" value="Go">
</form>
</body>
```

The action attribute of the form is the URL of the script, and (in this example) the method attribute is POST.

If the action attribute of the example form is changed to

```
http://host.domain.edu/scripts/egscript.exe/foo/bar
```

the script program scripts/egscript.exe still is executed. The /foo/bar part is passed to the script in the PATH_INFO environment variable. Notice that it is not a good idea to create directories with names that end in EXE; the server will get confused.

Command-line parameters

If a script is invoked with a URL that includes a query string, such as the following:

```
http://host.domain.edu/scripts/perl.exe/foo/bar?myscript.pl
```

the query string is passed to the script in the command line. Therefore, the preceding example would result in the execution of the following command:

```
scripts\perl.exe myscript.pl
```

This mechanism is useful for executing scripts in interpreted languages, in which the executable program is the interpreter itself.

Following is an example of a very simple PERL program that could be executed in this way:

```
#!./perl
print "200 OK\n";
print "Content-type: text/plain\n";
print "\n";
print "hello world\n";
```

The query string is decoded before being passed to the command line. Any plus-sign (+) characters are replaced by spaces, and any %xx sequences (in which xx represents two hex digits) are replaced by the corresponding ASCII character. (If required, the undecoded query string is available to the script in the QUERY_STRING environment variable.)

If the undecoded query string contains an equal-sign character (=), the CGI specification states that the query string shall not be passed to the script in the command line. If you want to pass = in the command line, encode it in the URL as %3D.

Supported environment variables

The CGI standard specifies certain environment variables that are used for conveying information to a CGI script. The following subset of those environment variables is supported by HTTPS:

```
CONTENT_LENGTH
CONTENT_TYPE
GATEWAY_INTERFACE
HTTP_ACCEPT
PATH_INFO
QUERY_STRING
REMOTE_ADDR
REQUEST_METHOD
SCRIPT_NAME
SERVER_NAME
SERVER_PROTOCOL
SERVER_PORT
SERVER_SOFTWARE
```

Other HTTP headers received from the client are available in environment variables of the form HTTP_*. For example, the User-Agent: header value is available in HTTP_USER_AGENT. Notice that the hyphen character (-) in the header names is replaced by an underscore character (_) in the corresponding environment-variable names.

Clickable Images

The HTTP Server supports the use of clickable images — in other words, it can return different documents, depending on which part of an image the user clicks.

Following is an example of a typical clickable-image document in HTML:

```
<html>
<head><title>WWW Servers in UK</title><head>
<body>
<h1>WWW Servers in the UK</h1>
<hr>
To have a server added to the map send email to:
<a href="http://www.ed.ac.uk/webperson.html">
<address>webperson@ed.ac.uk</address>
</a>
<p>
<hr>
<a href="/ukmap.map">
<img src="/Images/ukmap.gif" ismap>
</a>
<hr>
</body>
```

Notice the use of the ISMAP attribute in the IMG tag. This attribute tells the client to append the mouse coordinates to the URL when it sends it to the server.

The URL in the <a> anchor element must refer to a map file on the HTTP Server, with the extension MAP. This file contains information about how to map the coordinates of the mouse click to another URL. The mapped-to URL is the one that actually is returned to the client.

Map-file format

A *map file* is a text file that consists of definitions, comments, and blank lines. Comment lines start with a pound-sign character (#). Definition lines have one of the following four forms:

```
default URL
circle x y r URL
rectangle x0 y0 x1 y1 URL
polygon x0 y0 x1 y1 x2 y2 ... URL
```

The keywords can be abbreviated as def, circ, rect, and poly, respectively.

The default keyword defines the URL to be used if the mouse click falls outside any other shape defined in the file. The map file always must contain a default statement.

The `circle` statement defines a circle with center (x,y) and radius r, and the URL to be used if the mouse click lies within the circle.

The `rectangle` statement defines a rectangle with the top left at $(x0,y0)$ and the bottom right at $(x1,y1)$, and the URL to be used if the mouse click lies within the rectangle.

The `polygon` statement defines a polygon with vertices at $(x0,y0)$, $(x1,y1)$, $(x2,y2)$, and so on (up to 100 vertices), and the URL to be used if the mouse click lies within the polygon.

The coordinates are measured from the top-left corner of the image. The coordinates can be separated within the statement by any combination of blank spaces, tab characters, commas, and parentheses, as you can see in the upcoming example. (This means that you can use image configuration files in exactly the same format as for the CERN HTTPD server.)

The *URL* at the end of each line can point to a local file (in which case it must start with a forward slash), or it can refer to a document on another server (in which case it must be a full URL). In the latter case, the HTTP Server sends a `302 Found` redirection message, containing the URL in question, to the client. Clients that are capable of understanding the redirection message automatically fetch the document. Other clients display an explanatory message that contains a hyperlink to the document.

Following is an example map file. Suppose that your image is 1,000 by 1,000 pixels.

```
# Circle at center of image
circle (500,500) 100 /local/file.htm

# Rectangle at lower right
rectangle 550 550 850 850 http://some.other.host.uk/some/
file.html

# Triangle at lower left
polygon 10,700 200,700 10,900 /another/local/file.htm

# Use this URL if mouse is outside any of above shapes
default /error.htm
```

Notice that a slight overlap exists between the circle and the rectangle. If the mouse click occurs in the overlap, the first matching shape in the file determines the URL that will be returned — in this case, the circle.

Hints for using MAP files

■ If the URL that you want to use in a MAP file contains a pound sign (#), indicating a location within a file, you should quote the full URL (starting `http://`) in the MAP file so that the server issues a redirection message to the client.

■ If you want the URL in a MAP file to point to a document that is not in the same directory as the MAP file itself, you should either quote the full URL or use the HTML construct `<base href="...">` in the pointed-to document. This ensures that the client handles relative URLs within the document correctly.

Troubleshooting

This section lists some of the problems that you may have in running the HTTP Server and describes how to overcome them.

Errors starting the HTTP Server

When starting the HTTP Server, you may see one of the following error messages.

Could not start the HTTP Server service on *yourmachine*.
Error 0002: The system cannot find the file specified.

The Service Manager could not locate HTTPS.EXE. This probably means that it has been moved or has not been installed correctly. Remove and reinstall HTTPS; see the sections on installing and uninstalling earlier in this chapter.

Could not start the HTTP Server service on *yourmachine*.
Error 0005: Access is denied.

HTTPS.EXE is inaccessible to the SYSTEM user. By default, the Service Manager starts the HTTP Server process running under a user ID of SYSTEM. The executable file for the service must be readable by this user.

Could not start the HTTP Server service on *yourmachine*.
Error 2140: An internal Windows NT error occurred.

This message usually means that a problem exists with the configuration of the HTTP Server. Further information on the precise problem is recorded in the Application Event Log; see the "Error logging" section earlier in this chapter for details on how to view this information.

You may get this error — or a more alarming error, telling you that the HTTPS service is not correctly written — if you installed HTTPS under Windows NT 3.1 and later upgraded to Windows NT 3.5. To fix this problem, simply remove and reinstall HTTPS.

Errors recorded in the Event Log

This section records some of the error messages that may appear in the Application Event Log. Many of these messages are self-explanatory.

Windows Sockets library function "bind" failed. The address or port is already in use.

One of the following situations may give rise to this error:

■ The TCP/IP port that you specified in the HTTP Server configuration dialog box is conflicting with another application. Choose a different port number.

■ The IP address that the HTTP Server is using is incorrect. Start the Network Control Panel applet, and then configure the TCP/IP software to use the correct IP address.

Windows Sockets library function "accept" failed. The call was canceled.

This message indicates that the HTTP Server terminated abnormally for some reason. Restart the service.

Registry Entries

This section lists entries added *explicitly* to the Windows NT Registry by the HTTP Server. A number of other entries are added to the Registry implicitly by the Service Control Manager. The information in this appendix is not guaranteed to remain unchanged between releases of the HTTP Server (there were significant changes between Versions 0.7 and 0.8, for example). The information is intended for advanced users of Windows NT who understand the function and structure of the Registry.

The Service Control Manager creates the following entry in the HKEY_LOCAL_MACHINE database:

```
SYSTEM\CurrentControlSet\Services\HTTPS
```

Under this entry, the HTTP Server itself creates a `Parameters` key that contains the configuration entries listed in Table 33-2.

Table 33-2	Parameters Configuration Entries	
Entry Name	*Entry Type*	*Description*
Directory	REG_SZ	HTTP Data Directory name
PortNo	REG_DWORD	TCP/IP port number
DefaultMIMEType	REG_SZ	MIME type used for file extensions not listed explicitly
BrowsingEnabled	REG_DWORD	Nonzero if browsing is enabled
LogDirectory	REG_SZ	Directory where log files are stored
LoggingEnabled	REG_DWORD	Nonzero if logging is enabled
ExtensionMapping		The `ExtensionMapping` entry holds the mapping table. It contains a key name for each file extension, and the value of the key (type `REG_SZ`) is the corresponding MIME type.

Formal Command Syntax

The following sections provide a formal description of the HTTPS command options.

Syntax

```
https [-remove | -install] [-version] [-ipaddress]
```

Description

The `https` command installs or removes the HTTP Server.

Options

Option	Description
-install	Adds the HTTP Server to the list of installed services. Make sure that you are executing a copy of HTTPS.EXE that you aren't planning to delete later.
-ipaddress	Reports the IP addresses on which the HTTP Server is listening.
-remove	Removes the HTTP Server from the list of installed services. This option also deletes the HTTP Server configuration information from the Registry.
-version	Reports the version number of the HTTP Server.

Unresolved Problems

The following known problems exist. Resolution has not yet been possible, usually because we can't duplicate the problem.

Sluggish CGI programs

Some beta testers have reported that CGI scripts return their output to the client with excruciating slowness. This problem seems to depend somewhat on the client software; Macintosh clients did not experience the problem, whereas Windows clients did.

Possibly some problem exists with the TCP/IP implementation in the client or in Windows NT.

Problems with multiple network interfaces

The support for multiple network interfaces has been reported not to be functioning. Only one interface is listened on.

Chapter 34
Gopher Server Version 0.91

This chapter describes the Gopher Server for computers running the
Windows NT 3.5 operating system. You should read it if you plan to install,
operate, manage, or uninstall the Gopher Server software. This chapter assumes that you have a reasonable degree of competence in the use of Windows
NT and a reasonable knowledge of Gopher.

Introduction

The Gopher Server for Windows NT implements the classic Gopher protocol, as
described in RFC 1436. It runs as a Windows NT *service,* just like the FTP Server
that comes with Windows NT. By analogy with the UNIX Gopher Server daemon, which is called gopherd, the Windows NT Gopher Server service is called
GOPHERS, which is pronounced *gopher-ess.*

This version of GOPHERS originates from the European Microsoft Windows NT
Academic Centre (EMWAC). Located at Edinburgh University Computing
Service, EMWAC was set up to support and act as a focus for Windows NT
within academia. EMWAC is sponsored by Datalink Computers, Digital,
Microsoft, Research Machines, Sequent, and the University of Edinburgh.

EMWAC will collect and periodically review bug reports and suggestions for
improvement.

- To report a bug in GOPHERS, send a mail message to emwac@ed.ac.uk, with
  GOPHERS BUG in the Subject line.

- To suggest an enhancement, send a mail message to emwac@ed.ac.uk, with
  GOPHERS SUGGESTION in the Subject line.

Edinburgh University Computing Service will be producing a Professional
version of GOPHERS, which will be marketed through third parties. The Professional version will be fully supported and will have enhanced functionality.

Installation and Setup _____

Installation requirements

To use the Windows NT Gopher Server, you need to have a computer with the following characteristics:

- Intel, MIPS, or Digital Alpha processor
- Windows NT 3.1 final release, with TCP/IP software installed
- At least 16MB of memory
- Network connection (typically, Ethernet)

Follow these steps to install the Gopher Server under Windows NT:

1. Login to your Windows NT system as a user with administrative privileges.
2. The Gopher Server is distributed in three versions: for the Intel, MIPS, and DEC Alpha architectures. Select the appropriate ZIP file for your processor.
3. Unzip the file.

   You should have the following files:

     - GOPHERS.EXE — the Gopher Server itself
     - GOPHERS.CPL — the Control Panel applet
     - GOPHERS.HLP — the Control Panel applet help file
     - GOPHERS.DOC — this program's documentation in Word for Windows format
     - GOPHERS.WRI — this program's documentation in Windows Write format
     - GOPHERS.PS — this program's documentation in PostScript, ready for printing
     - COPYRITE.TXT — the copyright statement for this product
     - READ.ME — summary of new features

4. Decide which directory you are going to put GOPHERS.EXE in, and move it there.

   A good choice is the \WINNT\SYSTEM32 directory, which is where many other services live. Using the Security/Permissions menu option in the File Manager, ensure that the SYSTEM user has read permission for the file.

5. Move GOPHERS.CPL and GOPHERS.HLP to the \WINNT\SYSTEM32 directory; then start the Control Panel from the Program Manager to verify that
the Gopher Server applet is represented as an icon in the Control Panel.

6. Determine which version of GOPHERS you have by typing the following at
the Windows NT command prompt:

```
gophers -version
```

The version number is displayed. This chapter covers GOPHERS Version
0.91. If the program reports a later version number, you will find corresponding documentation in the files that you unpacked from the ZIP
archive.

7. You should also check the IP address of your machine by using the following command:

```
gophers -ipaddress
```

This command displays the name of your machine (for example,
emwac.ed.ac.uk) and its IP address(es), as reported by the Windows
Sockets API. If this information is incorrect, you need to reconfigure the
TCP/IP software on your machine. The Gopher Server will not work if this
address (or list of addresses, if your machine has more than one network
interface) is wrong.

8. If you have installed a previous version of the Gopher Server, you must
remove it by typing the following command:

```
gophers -remove
```

See the section on uninstalling for further information. You can use the old
or the new version of GOPHERS.EXE to perform the remove operation.
Notice that this procedure will delete your existing Gopher Server configuration information from the Registry. *If you are replacing Version 0.7 or
earlier with Version 0.8 or later, read the sidebar at the end of this section!*

9. Install GOPHERS in the table of Windows NT Services (and simultaneously
register it with the Event Logger) by running the program from the Windows NT command line, specifying the -install flag.

It is vital that you execute this command by using the copy of GOPHERS.EXE
that you placed in the \WINNT\SYSTEM32 directory, not by using some other
copy that you plan to delete subsequently. For example:

```
gophers -install
```

The program registers itself and its location with the Service Manager and with
the Event Logger, and reports success or failure. In the case of failure, see the
on-line help for information on installation problems.

10. To verify that the installation succeeded, start the Windows NT Control Panel, and double-click the Services icon.

The resulting dialog box should list Gopher Server as one of the installed services. If it does, see the "Configuration" section of this chapter for further instructions.

11. If you plan to use the WAIS-index-searching capabilities of the Gopher Server, you should install the WAIS ToolKit for Windows NT, which is available in this book/CD package.

Ensure that you place the WAISLOOK program in a directory where the Gopher Server can find it — \WINNT\SYSTEM32 is a good choice.

You may experience the following problems during installation and setup:

The system says that GOPHERS.EXE is not a Windows NT program.

You probably are trying to run an executable for the wrong sort of processor. Make sure that you have unpacked the correct ZIP file for your processor type.

Upgrading from Version 0.7 or earlier to Version 0.8 or later

In Version 0.8, the short name by which the Gopher Service is known to the operating system changed from Gopher Server to GOPHERS. This means that the Windows NT registry stores information about the service in a different place from earlier versions. If you are upgrading from an earlier version of HTTPS, this has two consequences:

- The information stored in the registry by the earlier version of GOPHERS must be deleted. You can do this by running the earlier version of GOPHERS from the command line with the -remove flag. Alternatively, Version 0.8 or later (when you run it with the -remove option)

detects whether information relating to Version 0.7 or earlier is present in the registry and, if so, deletes that information. Both methods have occasionally been observed to cause the Event Log Service to terminate with an access violation. This is harmless; just restart the Event Log Service from the Services dialog box in the Control Panel.

- When you replace Version 0.7 or earlier with 0.8 or later, any events recorded in the Event Log by the earlier version will be unintelligible because the Event Viewer program cannot find the information in the registry that tells it where the GOPHERS.EXE file is located.

The system says that the Gopher Server won't install because of a "duplicate server name."

You must remove a previous version of the Gopher Server, using the `gophers -remove` command, before installing with `gophers -install`.

GOPHERS waits for a while and then terminates with a "usage" message.

You must not run GOPHERS from the command line or from the File Manager, except with the `-install` or `-remove` or `-version` or `-ipaddress` options. The GOPHERS program is a Windows NT Service and must be started through the Services dialog box in the Control Panel.

The system displays this error message: *CreateService Failed with error: service already installed.*

This error message occurs if you type **gophers -install** when the Gopher Server is already installed. You cannot install two Gopher Servers.

Uninstalling the Gopher Server

Follow these directions if you want to remove the Gopher Server or move the installed configuration to a new location:

1. If necessary, stop the Gopher Server using the Stop button in the Services dialog box in the Control Panel.

2. At the Windows NT command line, run `gophers` with the `-remove` option, as follows:

   ```
   gophers -remove
   ```

   This command removes the Gopher Server from the Service Manager's list of services.

This command also deletes the Gopher Server's configuration information from the Registry.

3. If you are uninstalling the Gopher Server, simply delete the GOPHERS.EXE program, the GOPHERS.CPL Control Panel applet, and the GOPHERS.HLP help file.

4. If you want to move GOPHERS.EXE to a new location, you must move the file and then type **gophers -install.**

   This command informs the Service Manager and Event Logger of the new location of the program. You need to configure the Gopher Server and start it running again from the Control Panel.

Configuring the Gopher Server

You configure the Gopher Server by using the Gopher Server applet in the Control Panel.

Notice that the version number of the applet is displayed in the lower-left corner of the dialog box. The version number reported by the command `gophers -version` must be the same as the version number of the applet. (If no version number appears in the lower-left corner of the dialog box, you are using Version 0.2 of the applet.)

You can use this dialog box to do the following things:

- Set the root of the directory tree that contains the files you want to make available by using Gopher. Use the Data directory field for this purpose. You can find full details on how Gopher treats the files and directories in this directory tree in "The Gopher directory tree" section of this chapter. The default is D:\GOPHER. Special considerations apply if the directory tree is located across a network on a file server; see details later in this chapter.

- Specify the TCP/IP port on which the Gopher Server listens for incoming connections. Use the TCP/IP port: field for this purpose. The value must be a positive integer that represents a legal and otherwise unused port. The default is 70.

- Specify the Gopher type that corresponds to a given file extension. (More on file extensions in the next section.)

- Enable or disable caching. Caching is disabled by default. See the "Caching" discussion later in this chapter for further information.

- Specify the timeout interval (in minutes) after which Gopher's cache files will be deemed to be out of date. Specify 0 to prevent cache files from being timed out. The default is 5 minutes.

- Enable and disable the logging of Gopher transactions. If this box is checked, the Gopher Server records each Gopher request that it receives in a log file. See the "Gopher transaction logging" section in this chapter for more information about logging. Logging is disabled by default.

- Specify the directory in which log files are stored. The default is the Windows system directory (\WINNT).

- Enable and disable a special UNIX Compatibility Mode. If this mode is enabled, GOPHERS pays attention to files in the Data Directory with names that start with a period. GOPHERS treats such files (and the .CAP directory, if any) in the same way that the UNIX gopherd program does. If you set the Data Directory to point to a FAT volume, you should not enable this option because directory and filenames cannot begin with a period on FAT volumes. The mode is disabled by default.

■ Restore the default values of all the configuration settings (by clicking the Defaults button).

When you finish making changes in the configuration, click the OK button. The configuration will take effect the next time that you start the Gopher Server. If the Gopher Server is already running, a dialog box appears to remind you to stop and restart it (by using the Services dialog box in the Control Panel).

Setting file extensions to Gopher type mapping

The Gopher protocol represents the type of each file in a single byte. Several different types are defined in the protocol. The Gopher Server infers the type of a file from the file extension by using a mapping table. You can configure the mapping table by using the list in the Control Panel applet and the buttons labeled New Mapping, Change Mapping, and Delete Mapping. The default contents of the mapping table are as follows:

Table 34-1	Gopher Mapping Table	
File Extension	*Gopher Type*	*Meaning*
TXT	0	Text file
ZIP	5	Binary archive
ARC	5	Binary archive
UUE	6	UUencoded
SRC	7	WAIS index
EXE	9	Binary
DLL	9	Binary
GIF	g	GIF image
BMP	I	Windows bitmap
AU	s	Sound
HTM	h	HTML
HTML	h	HTML

To change a mapping in the table, select the mapping in question from the list, and then click the Change Mapping button.

You may alter the extension that you want to map by using the Filename Extension field and select the Gopher type to which you want to map it from the list (or you can enter the Gopher type character yourself if it's not in the list). Then choose OK to confirm your changes.

To create a new mapping, click the New Mapping button. A dialog box, similar to the Change Mapping dialog box, appears. You can use this box to specify the file extension and to select the corresponding Gopher type. Notice that you cannot create a new mapping for a file extension that already is present in the mapping list; an extension can occur only one time in the list.

To delete an existing mapping, select it from the list in the main Gopher Server dialog box, and then click the Delete Mapping button.

If no entry for a particular extension appears in the mapping table, the Gopher Server uses the default extension mapping, which appears in the list with (Default) in the File Extension column. You can change the default extension mapping in the same way that you do other mappings, but you cannot delete it.

Putting the Gopher directory on a file server

If the directory tree that you want to make available to Gopher clients is located on a file server instead of on the local Windows NT machine, you need to take special action.

Normally, directories on the file server are mapped to a drive letter on the local system. You might expect that simply using the mapped drive letter in the Gopher Server configuration dialog box would have the desired effect, and indeed it does — until you logoff the local machine.

Drive mappings are established only when someone logs on to the Windows NT machine. The mappings are specific to a user, not to the machine. The Gopher Server is normally kept running whether or not someone is logged on to the machine. Often, the Gopher Server is set to start automatically when the operating system loads, when no one is logged in and, therefore, no drive mappings are in effect.

To overcome this problem, you can specify the Gopher Data Directory to the Gopher Configuration dialog box by using a UNC form of directory name, such as the following:

```
\\CLYDE\INFOSERVER
```

In this example, CLYDE is the name of the server, and INFOSERVER is the share name of the directory that is to be served using Gopher.

Operating the Gopher Server

Using the Services dialog box

You use the Services dialog box in the Windows NT Control Panel to manage GOPHERS operation.

After you install GOPHERS, you can start it by selecting it from the list of services in the dialog box and then clicking the Start button. If all goes well, a message box containing a rotating timer appears while the service starts; then the message box disappears. The Gopher Server appears in the list of services with "Started" status and can respond to Gopher clients.

If the service fails to start, one of several problems may have occurred. For further details, see the "Troubleshooting" section later in this chapter.

You may want to arrange for the Gopher Server to start automatically when the system is started. You can do this by clicking the Startup button in the Services dialog box. You also can use this button to specify a different user ID for GOPHERS to run under; see your Windows NT documentation for details.

Pausing the Gopher Server (by clicking the Pause button in the Services dialog box) causes the following behavior:

- Any Gopher transactions that currently are under way are not affected; they will run to completion.

- Any new Gopher connections are queued. When the service resumes, the connections will be accepted and processed.

- If more than five incoming connections are received while the service is paused, the extra connections will be rejected.

Error logging

If an error in the operation of the server occurs, the error is logged in the Application Event Log. You can view this log by using the Event Viewer, which is located in the Administrative Tools program group in the Program Manager. See your Windows NT documentation for details on how to use the Event Viewer.

The errors logged in the Application Event Log usually are associated with a GOPHERS problem (for example, a file I/O error, a system call failure caused by lack of resources, or a problem with the configuration information).

Problems associated with the client (for example, the client sends an invalid Gopher selector, or a selector points to a file that does not exist) are recorded in the Application Event Log as warning events.

When the Gopher Server is started or stopped, information events are recorded in the Application Event Log.

For more information on events that may be logged by the Gopher Server, see the "Troubleshooting" section later in this chapter.

Notice that the Event Viewer uses the GOPHERS.EXE program to interpret messages associated with events. Therefore, if you delete the GOPHERS.EXE file, the Gopher Server events in your Application Event Log will be unintelligible.

Gopher transaction logging

If you check the Log Transactions box in the Gopher Server configuration dialog box, for every request that the server receives, it records a line of information in a log file. The log file is stored in the log file directory, which you also can configure in the dialog box.

A new log file is created every day. The filename is of the form GS*yymmdd*.LOG, so that the file corresponding to 4 July 1994, for example, would be GS940704.LOG. For performance reasons, the current log file is kept open until the first transaction of the following day. When this transaction occurs, the preceding day's log file is closed, a new log file is opened, and the transaction is logged to it.

The information recorded is the time and date of the request, the IP address of the server, the IP address of the client, and the Gopher selector string sent by the client.

The Gopher directory tree

The Gopher Directory (also known as the Data Directory) is the root of the directory tree that GOPHERS makes available to Gopher clients. Directories in the tree are treated as Gopher menus, and files are treated as Gopher documents. Points in the file system above the Gopher Directory, or on other disks, are not accessible to Gopher clients. The Gopher Directory may be located on a disk that uses the FAT, HPFS, or NTFS file system.

The Gopher Directory must be accessible by the user ID under which GOPHERS runs. By default, this ID is the SYSTEM user ID.

GOPHERS ignores files that have hidden or system attributes.

Link files

The Gopher Server treats files that end with .GFR (or, in UNIX Compatibility Mode, files that start with a period) in a special way. These files are assumed to contain link information, which points to another Gopher server.

The format of such link files is very similar to the equivalent for the UNIX gopherd program. The file contains several key=value pairs, one to each line. Following is an example of a typical link file:

```
Name=The Edinburgh University Gopher Server
Host=gopher.ed.ac.uk
Port=70
Numb=5
Path=
Type=1
```

The Name gives a user-friendly string that is displayed in the Gopher menu instead of the filename. Host is the name of the computer on which the linked-to server resides, and Port is the TCP port number for the server. (Specifying a plus sign (+) for the Host or Port means "use this Gopher server's host name or port number.") Path (empty in this example) is the Gopher selector for the linked-to directory or file. Type is the Gopher type character for the linked-to object, which overrides the type inferred from the file-extension mapping table. Numb is a number that is used to control the order in which items appear in the Gopher menu (all numbered items appear, in order, before all unnumbered items).

The case of the keyword to the left of the equal sign is not significant. The order of the lines in the file is not significant.

Following is another example of a link file. This file contains three links, which must be separated by a line that contains a single hash character (#).

```
Name=Gophers in the UK
Host=pcserver2.ed.ac.uk
Port=70
Type=1
Path=1/gophers/our_links
#
Name=Go straight to my data
Host=+
Port=+
Type=0
Path=0\data\mine\mydata.txt
#
Name=Gophers in Europe
Host=sunic.sunet.se
Port=70
Type=1
Path=1/Other Gopher and Information Servers/Europe
```

The first and third links in the file point to other Gopher servers. The second link points to a file in the Gopher directory tree on this server.

Gopher selectors

In general, the format of the Gopher selector for a file or directory depends on the server software. It is entirely opaque to the Gopher client.

Following is the format of the Gopher selector used by GOPHERS:

- The first character is the Gopher type of the corresponding item.
- The next character is a backslash.
- Subsequent characters represent the pathname of the corresponding file, relative to the Gopher data directory.

Consider the Gopher selector used in the example in the preceding section:

```
0\data\mine\mydata.txt
```

The first character indicates that the object is a text file. This character and the first backslash are removed to obtain the path (relative to the Gopher data directory) of the indicated object: the file MYDATA.TXT in the directory MINE, which is a subdirectory of DATA, which is a subdirectory of the Gopher data directory.

Forward slashes also can be used in a selector; the Gopher Server converts them to backslashes before analyzing the selector.

It is important that when you write a link file (or an alias file; see the following section) that the type character in the selector (the Path= field) is the same as the type character in the Type= field.

Notice that the format for selectors is different from the format used in GOPHERS Version 0.2 (which did not use the leading type character and backslash).

Aliases

Unless special action is taken, a Gopher client will simply use file and directory names when constructing a Gopher menu display. The Gopher protocol makes provision for the server to transmit to the client a "user-friendly name" — an alias — instead of a file or directory name.

The alias information is stored in an alias directory ALIAS.GFR (or .cap, if UNIX Compatibility Mode is enabled). This directory can exist at each level in the Gopher directory tree. When GOPHERS prepares a menu to transmit to the client, for each file in the directory, it looks in the alias directory for a file with a matching name. If GOPHERS finds such a file, it assumes that the file is in the format of a link file, as defined in the preceding section, and constructs a menu entry based on the information in the file.

The `Name` item contains the user-friendly string for display by the client. The `Port` and `Host` items are optional; if present, they should indicate the current host and port number (for example, by using the plus-sign convention). The `Type` item can be used to override the type deduced from the file's extension. The `Numb` item functions as described previously. The `Path` item, which must be present if the `Type` item is present, usually points to the object that is being aliased.

Following is an example directory tree:

```
SOMEDATA MYFILE.DAT

        README.TXT

        ALIAS.GFR MYFILE.DAT
```

Suppose that the file SOMEDATA\ALIAS.GFR\MYFILE.DAT looks like this:

```
Name=The data from my experiment
Path=9\SOMEDATA\MYFILE.DAT
Type=9
```

In this situation, when constructing the menu for the SOMEDATA directory, GOPHERS arranges for the client to display the string `The data from my experiment` instead of the filename MYFILE.DAT. GOPHERS also informs the client that the file is binary (type 9) instead of the default type for extension .DAT (which would be 0 — text — unless GOPHERS has been configured otherwise). Because no file called README.TXT exists in the ALIAS.GFR directory, the client simply displays the name README.TXT in the menu.

If the `Name=` item is present but empty, the file is not included in the Gopher menu. This method is a good way to hide files so that Gopher clients can't see them.

Caching

To improve performance, the Gopher Server implements a caching strategy. When it creates a menu for a client from a directory, alias files, and link files, the Gopher Server stores the menu in a cache file in the directory called CACHE.GFR (or, in UNIX Compatibility Mode, .cache). The next time the server receives a request for a menu from that directory, it uses the cache file. Caching is particularly useful for improving performance when a directory contains a large number of files and aliases.

Because the contents of directories may change, cache files must be re-created periodically. If the Gopher Server finds a cache file older than a certain timeout period, it re-creates that file. The cache file timeout period (which is specified in minutes) can be configured in the Gopher Server Control Panel applet. The default setting is 5 minutes.

If the cache timeout period is set to 0, cache files are never timed out, and if you change anything in the Gopher directory, you must delete the cache file for the change to be visible to clients.

You can enable and disable caching by using a check box in the Gopher Server configuration dialog box. By default, caching is disabled.

UNIX Compatibility Mode

If you are planning to move a Gopher service from a UNIX platform to Windows NT, you may be interested in the UNIX Compatibility Mode of GOPHERS.

The UNIX Gopher server program gopherd treats any hidden files (with names that start with a period) in its directory tree as being special cases; they are assumed to contain link information, which points at information on another Gopher server. Files called .cache are assumed to contain menu cache information. The gopherd program also treats any .cap directories that it finds in a special way; the directory is assumed to contain information about how to display the files in its parent directory.

The Gopher Server for Windows NT offers the same functionality as the gopherd program in these respects, but it uses different filenames. The reason is that some file systems that Windows NT uses (such as FAT) do not support filenames that begin with a period.

To cope with situations in which a Gopher directory tree is copied from a UNIX system to a Windows NT system (by using the Windows NT `rcp` command with the `-r` flag, for example), GOPHERS has a special UNIX Compatibility Mode. In UNIX Compatibility Mode, the gopherd conventions are employed for GOPHERS. The .cap directory contains alias information, the .cache file is used for cache information, and other files that begin with a period contain link information.

You can select this mode through the Gopher Server Configuration dialog box in the Control Panel. UNIX Compatibility Mode is available only if the Gopher Directory is on a volume using a file system that supports filenames starting with a period.

In Normal Mode (the default), GOPHERS does not display files or directories to the client if the names start with a period. This mode is mandatory if the Gopher Directory is located on a FAT volume.

Searching WAIS Indexes

GOPHERS can search local WAIS databases. This section describes how to configure the Gopher Server for this purpose. Before reading this section, you should read the WAIS ToolKit for Windows NT manual. (The WAIS ToolKit for Windows NT is also available on the CD.)

By default, files with the extension SRC are treated as being type 7 (search files). When a Gopher selector indicating a search file is received from a Gopher client, the Gopher Server passes the filename (and the search term supplied by the user) to the WAISLOOK program. The output from the WAISLOOK program is passed back to the client.

To ensure that the Gopher Server can execute the WAISLOOK program, the WAISLOOK.EXE file should be located in the \WINNT\SYSTEM32 directory.

You can exploit the search capabilities of the Gopher Server and the WAIS toolkit in several ways. The following section indicates one way to use these capabilities.

Example: a simple index of text files

This example illustrates how to set up a very common situation: you have a large number of text files (such as an archive of Usenet news messages) that you want to allow Gopher clients to search.

Preparing the directory structure

Assume that the Gopher data directory is E:\GOPHER and that drive E is on an NTFS partition. Within that directory, you have created a subdirectory — NEWS — to hold several newsgroup indexes. Under NEWS, you have created a directory — ALT.ATHEISM — for that newsgroup. Now create a directory — FILES — under ALT.ATHEISM, which is to hold the actual news messages, one to each file. Also create a directory — ALIAS.GFR — to hold alias files under the NEWS directory.

Following is this situation in graphical form:

```
                              e:\

                            gopher


                            News


                         alt.atheism
                            ALIAS.GFR


                            files



                  103   104   105   106
```

Notice that in this example, the news messages themselves have filenames that are simply numbers.

Indexing the messages

Using a Windows NT command prompt, change to the Gopher data directory (E:\GOPHER) so that the filenames in the filename table that will be created by the indexing program are relative to the Gopher data directory.

Delete the cache file NEWS\ALT.ATHEISM\FILES\CACHE.GFR, if it exists, and move any link files in NEWS\ALT.ATHEISM\FILES\ out of the way so that they don't get indexed. Then run the following indexing command:

```
waisindex -d News\alt.atheism\index -t netnews
News\alt.atheism\files\*
```

This command creates files called INDEX.SRC, INDEX.INV, and so on, in the E:\GOPHER\NEWS\ALT.ATHEISM directory.

Testing the index

To verify that the index functions correctly, use the WAISLOOK program to examine it, as follows:

```
waislook -d News\alt.atheism\index religion
```

This command should return a list of files and headlines that contain the word *religion*.

Creating the alias file

Now you need to create a menu entry that points to the index. In the E:\GOPHER\NEWS\ALIAS.GFR directory, create a file — ALT.ATHEISM — that looks like the following example:

```
Name=Search the alt.atheism news
Host=+
Port=+
Type=7
Path=7\News\alt.atheism\index.src
```

If the Gopher client user selects the NEWS directory from the root of the Gopher directory tree, she sees (instead of the ALT.ATHEISM directory) an item in the resulting menu: Search the alt.atheism news. If she selects this item, the Gopher client prompts her for a search word. The Gopher Server invokes the WAISLOOK program to search the index and returns a Gopher menu that contains the list of matching messages.

Updating the index

When a new message (say, 107) arrives in the E:\GOPHER\NEWS\ ALT.ATHEISM\FILES directory, you should run the WAISINDEX command to update the index. Change to the E:\GOPHER directory, and issue the following command:

```
waisindex -d News\alt.atheism\index -t netnews -a
News\alt.atheism\files\107
```

This command adds the new file to the directory. Normally, of course, you would arrange for this command to be executed automatically in a batch file.

Troubleshooting _____

This section lists some of the problems that you may have in running the Gopher Server and describes how to overcome them.

Errors starting the Gopher Server

When you start the Gopher Server, you may see one of the following error messages.

Could not start the Gopher Server service on \\your machine. Error 0002: The system cannot find the file specified.

The Service Manager could not locate GOPHERS.EXE. This message probably means that GOPHERS.EXE has been moved or that the program was not installed correctly. Remove and reinstall GOPHERS; see the sections covering installing and uninstalling earlier in this chapter for details.

Could not start the Gopher Server service on \\your machine. Error 0005: Access is denied.

GOPHERS.EXE is inaccessible to the SYSTEM user. By default, the Service Manager starts the Gopher Server process running under a user ID of SYSTEM. The executable file for the service must be readable by this user.

Could not start the Gopher Server service on \\your machine. Error 2140: An internal Windows NT error occurred.

This message usually means that a problem exists with the configuration of the Gopher Server. Further information on the precise problem will be recorded in the Application Event Log; for details on how to view this information, see the section on error logging in this chapter. The following section describes some of the most common errors.

Errors recorded in the Event Log

This section records some of the error messages that may appear in the Application Event Log. Many of these messages are self-explanatory.

Windows Sockets library function "bind" failed. The address or port is already in use.

One of the following situations may give rise to this error:

■ The TCP/IP port that you specified in the Gopher Server configuration dialog box is conflicting with another application. Choose a different port number.

■ The IP address that the Gopher Server is using is incorrect. Start the Network Control Panel applet, and configure the TCP/IP software to use the correct IP address.

Windows Sockets library function "accept" failed. The call was canceled.

This message indicates that the Gopher Server terminated abnormally for some reason. Restart the service.

Other problems

This section describes other common problems in using the Gopher Server and the solutions to these problems.

GOPHERS puts the local IP address, instead of the host name, in menu items that it returns to clients.

GOPHERS.EXE obtains the local host name from the `gethostname()` Windows Sockets call. If the name returned by that call is not a fully qualified domain name, the Gopher Server uses the IP address instead of the name. Your feedback is sought on how the TCP/IP software in Windows NT can be configured to eliminate this problem (which the author can't duplicate).

The on-line documentation (in Word 6 format) for the Gopher Server for Windows NT contains further information on Registry Entries and the formal command syntax in the appendices.

Chapter 35

WAIS 0.3 for Windows NT 3.5

© 1994 Computing Services, The University of Edinburgh

The Wide Area Information Server (WAIS) software for computers running the Windows NT 3.5 operating system requires you to have a reasonable degree of competence in the use of Windows NT and a reasonable knowledge of WAIS. The software included on the *Internet GIZMOS for Windows* CD implements a subset of the Z39.50-88 protocol, with WAIS-specific extensions. This software runs as a Windows NT service, just like the FTP Server that comes with Windows NT.

Because this software is a beta version of the WAIS Server for NT, we recommend that you report bug reports about this version directly to C.J.Adie@ed.ac.uk. via e-mail.

 The WAIS Server does require utilization for the WAIS indexing program WAISINDEX for Windows NT, which is used to build databases for use by the WAIS Server and by other information servers, such as the Gopher Server and the HTTP Server for Windows NT. This program is covered by WAIS ToolKit documentation on the CD.

Installing and Configuring the NT WAIS Server

The Windows NT WAIS Server requires the following hardware and software configuration before installation:

- Intel, Digital Alpha, or MIPS processor
- Windows NT 3.1 final release, with TCP/IP software installed
- At least 16MB of memory
- Network connection (typically, Ethernet)

You also must install the Windows NT WAIS ToolKit, contained in WAISINDEX.EXE and WAISSERV.EXE on the CD.

To install the NT WAIS Server, follow these steps:

1. Login to your Windows NT system as a user with administrative privileges.

2. The WAIS Server is distributed in two versions: for the Intel and DEC Alpha architectures. Select the appropriate ZIP file for your processor.

3. Unzip the file.

   You should have the following files:

   - WAISS.EXE — the WAIS Server service
   - WAISS.CPL — the Control Panel applet
   - WAISS.DOC — the WAIS Server documentation in Word for Windows format
   - WAISS.WRI — the WAIS Server documentation in Windows Write format
   - WAISS.PS — the WAIS Server documentation, in PostScript, ready for printing
   - COPYRITE.TXT — the copyright statement for this product
   - READ.ME — summary of new features

4. Decide which directory you are going to put the WAISS.EXE file in, and move it there.

   A good choice is the \WINNT\SYSTEM32 directory, which is where many other services live. Using the Security/Permissions menu option in the File Manager, ensure that the SYSTEM user has read permission for the file.

5. Move the WAISS.CPL file to the \WINNT\SYSTEM32 directory, and start the Control Panel from the Program Manager to verify that the WAIS Server applet is represented as an icon in the Control Panel.

6. Determine which version of the WAIS Server you have by typing the following at the Windows NT command prompt:

```
waiss -version
```

   The version number of the program is displayed. This chapter covers Version 0.3. If the program reports a later version number, you will find corresponding documentation in the files that you unpacked from the ZIP archive.

7. You also should check the IP address of your machine by typing the following command:

```
waiss -ipaddress
```

This command displays the IP address as reported by the Windows Sockets API. If the address is incorrect, you need to reconfigure the TCP/IP software on your machine; the WAIS Server will not work if this address is wrong.

8. If you have installed a previous version of the WAIS Server, remove it by typing the following command:

```
waiss -remove
```

You can use the old or the new version of WAISS.EXE to perform the remove operation. Notice that this procedure will delete your existing WAIS Server configuration information from the Registry.

If you are planning to replace this version of the WAIS Server, please refer to the latest documentation before doing so.

Upgrading from Version 0.1 to Version 0.2 or later

In Version 0.2, the short name by which the WAIS Service is known to the operating system changed from "WAIS Server" to "WAISS." This means that the Windows NT registry stores information about the service in a different place from earlier versions. If you are upgrading from Version 0.1 of the WAIS Server, this situation has two consequences:

■ The information stored in the registry by the earlier version of WAIS must be deleted. You can do this by running the earlier version of WAIS from the command line with the -remove flag. Alternatively, Version 0.2 or later (when you run it with the -remove option)

detects whether information relating to Version 0.1 or earlier is present in the registry and, if so, deletes that information. Both methods have occasionally been observed to cause the Event Log Service to terminate with an access violation. This is harmless; just restart the Event Log Service from the Services dialog box in the Control Panel.

■ When you replace Version 0.1 or earlier with 0.2 or later, any events recorded in the Event Log by the earlier version will be unintelligible. This is because the Event Viewer program cannot find the information in the registry that tells it where the WAISS.EXE file is located.

Installation problems

You may discover these problems during the installation of the WAIS Server 2.3:

The system says that WAISS.EXE is not a Windows NT program.

You probably are trying to run an executable for the wrong sort of processor. Make sure that you have unpacked the correct ZIP file for your processor type.

WAISS waits for a while and then terminates with a "usage" message.

You must not run WAISS from the command line or from the File Manager, except with the -install or -remove or -version or -ipaddress options. The WAISS program is a Windows NT Service and must be started through the Services dialog box in the Control Panel.

The system says that the WAIS Service won't install because of a "duplicate service name."

You must remove a previous version of the Gopher Service (by using the waiss -remove command) before installing with waiss -install.

"CreateService Failed with error: service already installed."

This error message occurs if you type **waiss -install** when the WAIS Server is already installed. You cannot install two WAIS Servers.

For information on uninstalling the WAIS NT Server, refer to the full documentation file in Word format.

Setup and configuration

You can configure the WAIS Server by using the WAIS Server applet in the Control Panel.

Notice that the version number of the applet is displayed in the lower-left corner of the dialog box. The version number reported by the command waiss -version must be the same as the version number of the applet.

You can use this dialog box to do the following things:

- Set the root of the directory tree that contains the files that you want to make available by using WAIS. Use the Data directory: field for this purpose. Full details on how WAIS treats the files and directories in this directory tree appear later in this manual. The default is D:\WAIS.

- Specify the TCP/IP port on which the WAIS Server listens for incoming connections. Use the TCP/IP port: field for this purpose. The value must be a positive integer that represents a legal and otherwise unused port. The default is 210.

- Control the amount of information that is logged for every WAIS transaction. The WAIS Server records, in a text file, information about each WAIS request that it receives. The list box in the Control Panel allows you to select no logging or a varying amount of logging information — up to full logging, which records everything. The default is no logging.

- Specify the directory in which the log files will be located. This entry field is disabled if no logging is requested.

- Restore the default values of all the configuration settings (by clicking the Defaults button).

When you finish making changes in the configuration, click OK. For the configuration to take effect, you need to stop and restart the WAIS Server, using the Services dialog box in the Control Panel.

Putting the Data Directory on a file server

If the directory tree that you want to make available to WAIS clients is located on a file server instead of on the local Windows NT machine, you need to take special action.

Normally, directories on the file server are mapped to a drive letter on the local system. You might expect that simply using the mapped drive letter in the WAIS Server configuration dialog box would have the desired effect, and indeed it does — until you logoff the local machine.

Drive mappings are established only when someone logs on to the Windows NT machine. The mappings are specific to a user, not to the machine. The WAIS Server normally is kept running whether or not someone is logged on to the machine. Often, the WAIS Server is set to start automatically when the operating system loads, when no one is logged in and, therefore, no drive mappings are in effect.

To overcome this problem, you can specify the WAIS Data Directory in the WAIS Configuration dialog box, using a UNC form of directory name, such as the following :

```
\\CLYDE\INFOSERVER
```

In this example, CLYDE is the name of the server, and INFOSERVER is the sharename of the directory that is to be served using WAIS.

Using and Operating the WAIS Server _____

This section describes the use and operation of the WAIS Server for Windows NT 3.5.

Using the Services dialog box

You use the Services dialog box in the Windows NT Control Panel for managing the WAIS Server operation.

After you install the WAIS Server, you can start it by selecting it from the list of services in the dialog box and then clicking the Start button. If all goes well, a message box containing a rotating timer appears while the service starts; then the message box disappears. The WAIS Server appears in the list of services with "Started" status and can respond to WAIS clients.

If the service fails to start, one of several problems may have occurred. You may get a message box that indicates the source of the problem. For further information, see the "Troubleshooting and Maintenance" section later in this chapter.

You may want to arrange for the WAIS Server to start automatically when the system is started. You can do this by using the Startup button in the Services dialog box. You also can use this button to specify a different user ID for WAISS to run under. See your Windows NT documentation for details.

Notice that you cannot start the WAIS Server automatically if the WAIS data is located on a network volume because the network connection is not yet established when the WAIS Server starts.

Pausing the WAIS Server (by using the Pause button in the Services dialog box) causes the following behavior:

- Any WAIS transactions that currently are under way are not affected; they will run to completion.

- Any new WAIS connections are queued. When the service resumes, the connections will be accepted and processed.

- If more than five incoming connections are received while the service is paused, the extra connections will be rejected.

The WAISSERV program

When the WAIS Server receives an incoming TCP/IP connection from a WAIS client, WAISS.EXE executes the WAISSERV.EXE program. This program reads and writes information from and to the connection; it also handles all the Z39.50 protocol encoding and decoding, as well as the database searching.

WAISSERV.EXE is a Windows NT *console* application, meaning that it can be executed from the command line. Doing so is not useful, however, except when you are using the -v flag to determine the version of the program. WAISSERV.EXE is documented in the WAIS ToolKit manual.

For WAISS.EXE to find and execute the WAISSERV.EXE program, the latter must be placed in a suitable location, such as \WINNT\SYSTEM32.

Error logging

If an error in the operation of the server occurs, the error is logged in the Application Event Log. You can view this log with the Event Viewer, which you will find in the Administrative Tools program group in the Program Manager. For details on how to use the Event Viewer, see your Windows NT documentation.

The errors logged in the Application Event Log usually are associated with a system call failure caused by lack of resources or a problem with the configuration information.

When the WAIS Server is started or stopped, Information events are recorded in the Application Event Log.

Problems detected by the WAISSERV.EXE program are recorded in the log file rather than in the Event Log.

Notice that the Event Viewer uses the WAISS.EXE program to interpret messages associated with events. Therefore, if you delete the WAISS.EXE file, the WAIS Server events in your Application Event Log will be unintelligible.

WAIS transaction logging

If you select anything other than "None" for the WAIS transaction logging level in the WAIS Server configuration dialog box, the server records in the log file certain information for every WAIS request that it receives.

A new log file is created every day. The filename is of the form WS*yymmdd*.LOG, so that the file corresponding to 4 July 1994, for example, is WS940704.LOG.

You need to clear out the log directory periodically.

WAIS Databases and the Data Directory _____

This section discusses using the WAIS databases and the WAIS Data Directory.

The WAIS Data Directory

The WAIS Data Directory is the root of a directory tree within which you must locate files and databases that you want to make available to WAIS clients. Points in the file system above the Data Directory, or on other disks, are not accessible to WAIS clients. The Data Directory must be located on a disk that uses the HPFS or NTFS file systems because the indexing process requires long-filename support.

The Data Directory tree must be accessible by the user ID under which WAISS runs. Normally, this ID is the SYSTEM user ID.

Creating WAIS databases

WAIS databases are created with the WAISINDEX.EXE program, from the WAIS ToolKit for Windows NT. Before reading this section, you should read the WAIS ToolKit chapter, Chapter 32.

When the WAISSERV.EXE program runs, its current directory is the WAIS Data Directory, and all file references are relative to that directory. Therefore, when you index a set of files and create a WAIS database, the WAIS Data Directory must be the current directory when you run the WAISINDEX program.

The following sections explain how to create a simple WAIS database of mail messages.

Preparing the directory structure

Assume that the WAIS data directory is E:\WAIS, where drive E is on an NTFS partition. Within that directory, you have created a subdirectory — MYLIST — to hold the database of mail messages from a mailing list. Now create a directory — FILES — under MYLIST, which is to hold the actual mail messages, one to each file.

Following is the directory tree in graphical form:

```
e:\

  wais

    MyList

      files

        103  104  105  106
```

The mail messages in this example have filenames that do not include extensions, such as 103.

Indexing the messages

Using a Windows NT command prompt, change to the WAIS Data Directory (E:\WAIS) so that the filenames in the filename table that will be created by the indexing program are relative to the WAIS Data Directory.

Run the following indexing command:

```
waisindex -d MyList\index -export -t netnews MyList\files\*
```

This command creates files called INDEX.SRC, INDEX.INV, and so on, in the E:\WAIS\MYLIST directory.

Testing the database

To verify that the index functions correctly, use the WAISLOOK program (from the WAIS ToolKit for Windows NT) to examine it, as follows:

```
waislook -d MyList\index foobar
```

This command should return a list of files and headlines that contain the word *foobar*.

You also should test the operation of the database with a remote WAIS client. Copy the INDEX.SRC file to the client machine, and select that database to make a query.

Registering the database

If your database is for public use, you may want to register it with the database of databases. To do so, first check the information in INDEX.SRC, making sure that it contains an IP address and a DNS name, as well as the TCP/IP port that you are using for the WAIS server. Then mail the file to the following addresses:

```
wais-directory-of-servers@cnidr.org
wais-directory-of-servers@quake.think.com
```

Updating the database

When a new message (such as 107) arrives in the E:\WAIS\MYLIST\FILES directory, you should run the WAISINDEX command to update the index. Change to the E:\WAIS directory, and issue the following command:

```
waisindex -d MyList\index -t netnews -a MyList\files\107
```

This command adds the new file to the directory. Normally, of course, you would arrange for this command to be executed automatically in a batch file.

Notice that the WAISSERV program does *not* automatically reindex the database if a new file is added to the directory; you must do that yourself.

Troubleshooting and Maintenance

The following sections provide some assistance in troubleshooting and optimizing the WAIS Server under Windows NT 3.5.

Errors starting the WAIS Server

When starting the WAIS Server, you may see one of the following error messages:

Could not start the WAIS Server service on \\your machine. Error 0002: The system cannot find the file specified.

The Service Manager could not locate WAISS.EXE. This message probably means that the file has been moved or that the software was not installed correctly. Remove and reinstall the WAIS Server.

Could not start the WAIS Server service on \\your machine. Error 0005: Access is denied.

WAISS.EXE is inaccessible to the SYSTEM user. By default, the Service Manager starts the WAIS Server process running under a user ID of SYSTEM. The executable file for the service must be readable by this user.

Could not start the WAIS Server service on \\your machine. Error 2140: An internal Windows NT error occurred.

This message usually means that a problem exists with the configuration of the WAIS Server. Further information on the precise problem will be recorded in the Application Event Log. The following section describes the most common errors.

Errors recorded in the Event Log

Following are examples of error messages that may appear in the Application Event Log. Many of these messages are self-explanatory.

Windows Sockets library function "bind" failed. The address or port is already in use.

One of the following situations may give rise to this error:

- The TCP/IP port that you specified in the WAIS Server configuration dialog box is conflicting with another application. Choose a different port number.

- The IP address that the WAIS Server is using is incorrect. Start the Network Control Panel applet, and configure the TCP/IP software to use the correct IP address.

Windows Sockets library function "accept" failed. The call was canceled.

This message indicates that the WAIS Server terminated abnormally for some reason. Restart the service.

Further information on the WAIS Server registry entries and on the WAIS formal command syntax and options is included in a Word document appearing in the WAIS Server directory on the *Internet GIZMOS for Windows* CD.

Part X

Windows Internet Information GIZMOS and Tools

The tools in this section, while not directly related to the Internet, are demonstrations and feature-reduced versions of some excellent communications and information applications. These programs are on the CD-ROM in the directory \FILES\PART10.

Delrina WinComm LITE and WinFax LITE

WinComm LITE and WinFax LITE are feature-reduced versions of their commercial counterparts. They are both excellent communications and fax packages on their own, and they seamlessly share your modem between normal modem communications and fax communications.

Network Central

Network Central provides a way for you to organize any number of disk files stored anywhere on your PC or network by adding comments to the filenames. It then lets you organize and search the tagged files without regard for their actual disk location. The install program for Network Central installs a number of files in your Windows SYSTEM directory, so you may want to back up the SYSTEM directory before you start in case you decide to remove the application. This is a 30-day limited license version of the commercial Network Central program.

askSam

askSam is an interesting, hard-to-describe blend of word processing, hypertext, and database applications. Check out the documentation, or just install askSam and try it. If you need to do some heavy-duty information management, askSam is for you. This feature-reduced version of askSam limits the number of documents it will track and the size of each document, but is still very useful.

The OAG FlightDisk

The OAG FlightDisk is an electronic guide to airline schedules around the world. The version on the disk was the most recent available when this book was produced, so the information is out of date, but use the program as a demonstration to see if you would be interested in using it on a regular basis.

Chapter 36
Network Central

Network Central is instant groupware that provides a *virtual filing cabinet* for your network. With Network Central, you get:

- Immediate access to your files on the network.
- Notification of changes to your important files.
- Quick sharing of ideas and information.

Setting Up Network Central on Your PC

Network Central runs on your PC, not on the network, so it's easy to install and set up.

In File Manager or the Program Manager, run the Setup program for Network Central from the *Internet GIZMOS for Windows CD-ROM*.

1. Insert the CD-ROM in your CD-ROM drive.
2. Start Windows.
3. Execute File⇨Run from the Program Manager.
4. Type ***driveletter:*\setup** and then press Enter (*driveletter* standing for whatever your CD-ROM drive letter is; **d**, for example).
5. Follow the on-screen instructions.

The Network Central File Center

The first time you use Network Central, you must decide where to put your File Center — your virtual filing cabinet. Your File Center tracks files and adds descriptions and notes. If you want to share a File Center with others, place it in a shared directory somewhere on the network, and make sure the others have full access to that directory.

Alternatively, you can create a File Center on your own hard disk for personal use or just to learn how to use Network Central.

You can create as many File Centers as you like. You can start with a personal File Center on your own hard disk and later create another one to be shared on the network.

1. Create a new directory to hold your new File Center.

   To create a directory: Start File Manager. Select File⇨Create Directory, and type a name for the new directory in the dialog box that appears. You can call the directory anything you choose (such as *C:\INFO*). Exit File Manager.

2. Run Network Central from the Network Central program group.

3. In Network Central, select File⇨New File Center.

4. Specify the directory that you just created, and click OK.

The main Network Central window appears, containing an empty File Center and a folder with your login name on it. This is your private folder. Figure 36-1 shows a sample File Center.

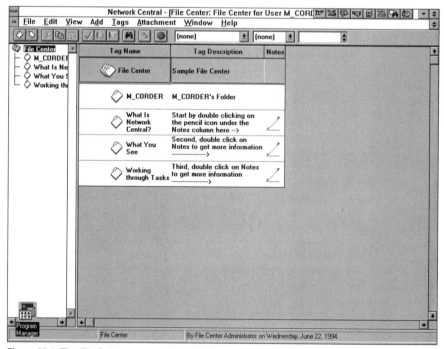

Figure 36-1: The File Center.

Network Central suggests your *network* login name for your Network Central login name. For now, don't enter a password. You can enter one at another time.

The Network Central toolbar

Network Central provides an intuitive toolbar allowing users quick access to frequently used commands.

Button	Function
◇	Add new folder
◇	Add new tag
✂	Cut
🗐	Copy
📋	Paste
✓	Clear change flags
▲	Previous change flags
▼	Next change flags
🔍	Search tags
	View attachment
●	Hot list

File tags

Gather a few of the important files on the network, such as customer letters, budget spreadsheets, or files related to a key project. Network Central gives you many ways to tag the files to which you want immediate access.

You should organize your file tags into folders with meaningful names based on topics or projects (or however you view your world). Here's how to create a folder:

1. Select Add⇨Folder.

   The Add Folder to File Center window (Figure 36-2) appears.

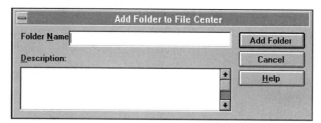

Figure 36-2: The Add Folder to File Center window.

2. Type **Important Files** in the Folder Name field, and enter a short description in the Description field.

3. Click the Add Folder button.

   A new folder appears in the _folder tree_ (left side of the window) and in the _contents_ area (right side of the window).

4. To open the folder, click its name in the folder tree.

The contents area will have an empty folder.

Now, create a file tag. The simplest way is to use the Network Central file browser.

1. Select Add⇨Tags from files.

2. Select a network drive where you know there are important files.

3. Select a directory.

4. Select an important file from that directory.

5. To see whether you have found the right file to tag, click the View button.

   The View button lets you see the file without running the application that created it. When finished, click the viewer's Close button.

6. Click the Add button.

   The file is added to the list at the bottom of the dialog box.

7. Browse for four more files. Click Add for each file you want to tag.

8. When you have finished selecting all five files, click the Tag Files button.

You have now created a tag for some of your important files.

Naming Tags, Using Descriptions, and Notes __

To help you better understand your File Center's files and information, Network Central lets you add long names, paragraph-length descriptions, and notes to your tags and folders.

Adding names and descriptions

Here's how to add names and descriptions to tags:

1. Select any tag.

2. Select Tags⇨Properties.

   The tag properties general window (Figure 36-3) appears.

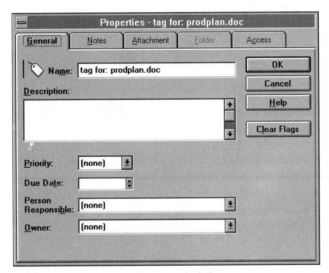

Figure 36-3: The tag properties general window.

3. Change the name to something meaningful (for example, Product Plans).

4. Add a brief description of the file in the Description area, such as *Detailed specifications and time tables for all products.*

5. Click OK.

Adding notes

You can also add notes to any tag to leave yourself or others instructions, specific comments, or annotations. Notes give you history and additional knowledge about a file, because anyone can leave and read notes. Notes let entire groups communicate about a file.

1. Select Tags⇨Add a Note.

   The tag properties notes window (Figure 36-4) appears.

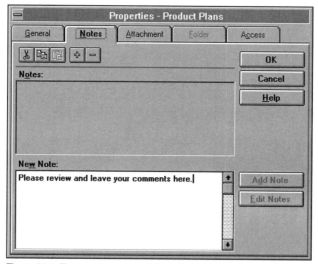

Figure 36-4: The tag properties notes window.

2. Type a note that makes sense for this file.

3. Click OK.

   A pencil icon is now part of the tag. Double-click it to access the notes. The note area is a multiuser log. Any Network Central user can leave a note; Network Central keeps them in chronological order. You can add a second note to see what it is like when more than one person uses Network Central.

4. Double-click the pencil icon.

5. Click the Add Note button. Notice that your first note entry has your name, the date, and the time that the note was made. Type another note that makes sense for this file.

6. Click OK.

Immediate access — opening files

Now that you have tagged some important files, you'll be able to get to them from within Network Central. To open any tagged file, double-click it. The application that created the file runs and opens your file.

Staying Informed: Notification of Changes___

Network Central uses change bars and red triangular flags to tell you when someone has changed a file.

1. Double-click a tagged file, edit it, and save it.

2. Exit the application and return to Network Central.

   Network Central checks every few minutes to see if any tagged files have been changed. You can also manually check at any time.

3. Select File⇨Update File Center.

4. Click Yes to update attachment files.

   Any tagged files now have change bars as well as a red triangular change flag next to the file icon.

The Hot List ___

The Hot List is a floating toolbar in which you can place file tags and folders for immediate access while you use other applications. The Hot List is a great place to keep track of your most important tags and folders. It also notifies you whenever a file has been changed.

To see the hot list, select View⇨Hot List. It looks something like Figure 36-5. You can drag the Hot List anywhere on your screen while pointing at its title bar.

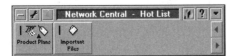

Figure 36-5: The Hot List, with two hot items.

To place a file tag or a folder on the Hot List:

1. Select the file tag or the folder.

2. Select Tags⇨Add to Hot List.

   When you select a tag, a file icon appears on the Hot List. When you select a folder, a folder icon appears on the Hot List.

You can launch files at any time from the Hot List. You can click on any Hot List folders to jump directly to the folder in Network Central.

Project Management with Network Central ___

You can perform basic project management using Network Central by assigning a person, priority, and due date to any tag or folder. You can also create lists of work to be done from these assignments.

Assigning tasks

Network Central lets you easily assign tasks and track who is supposed to do what when. For example, you can tag a budget template for each department, and assign each tag to the person responsible for filling in the template, with a priority level and a due date.

1. Select any tag.

2. Select Tags⇨Properties.

3. Select yourself as the Person Responsible.

4. Select a Priority of Urgent.

5. Select a Due Date.

   If you double-click inside the Due Date box, a calendar pops up.

6. Click OK.

   These assignments appear in the main Network Central window. They can be set here as well.

Searching by person, priority, and due date

You can track a project's status by searching Network Central for tags that belong to specific people, or are due by a certain date, or have a given priority.

To start a search:

1. Choose Edit⇨Search Tags.
2. Click on the Filters tab at the top edge of the dialog box.
3. Select yourself as the Person Responsible.
4. Select Urgent as the Priority.
5. Click the Search button.

To view the search results by due date, priority, and person responsible:

1. Select View⇨Columns.

   The View Columns window (Figure 36-6) appears.

Figure 36-6: The View Columns window.

2. Click Due Date, Priority, and Person Responsible.
3. Select Window⇨Tile Horizontally.

   Network Central shows you the results similar to Figure 36-7.

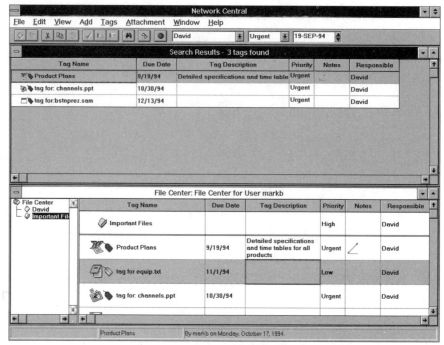

Figure 36-7: Search results, including due date, priority, and person responsible.

More Ways to Tag Files _____

In addition to the built-in Network Central file browser, you can tag files by:

- Searching for them.
- Dragging and dropping them from the Windows File Manager.
- Creating one for every file in an existing directory.
- Selecting them from the Network Central File Log utility.

Searching for files

To search for files to tag:

1. Select Add⇨Tags from search.

2. Specify any criteria that makes sense.

   For example, search for all Excel spreadsheets in the specified directory that have the word *sales* anywhere within the file.

3. Click the Search button.

4. Select the kind of files you want to tag.

5. Click the Add button.

6. Click the Tag Files button.

Creating a tag for every file in an existing directory

You can create a tag for every file in an existing shared directory:

1. Select Add⇨Directory Monitor.

2. Select a directory with files that you want to tag.

3. Select the file specifications as necessary (such as *.DOC*).

   This restricts which files are actually tagged if you don't want to tag all the files.

4. Click OK.

Network Central tags all of the specified files at once. Whenever a new file is added to that directory, Network Central creates a tag for it. Network Central will use change flags to show that a file tag has been added.

You Are Now a Network Central Expert

Network Central is multiuser software. Right after installation, it knows how to get groups of people working together, sharing ideas and information. Just create a File Center in a shared network directory. Anyone who wants to share the information just has to install a copy of Network Central on his or her machine and login to instantly have access to the File Center.

Network Central frees you from the frustrations of finding and organizing files on the network. What you have accomplished so far is all you and your workgroup need to share ideas and information, and communicate better with Network Central.

Chapter 37
Delrina WinFax LITE 3.1

Using the WinFax LITE Administrator _____

The first part of this chapter discusses how to use the WinFax LITE Administrator. The second part discusses using the WinFax LITE Image Viewer.

Attention: The software programs and other materials provided by Delrina in this package are provided to you under the terms of a license agreement and are not sold to you. The license agreeement will be found at the end of this chapter. Carefully read this agreement before using any Delrina Software. Support for Delrina products included in this book/disk package is provided on WUGNET's CompuServe forum; by calling WUGNET at 610-565-1861; or, you can write to WUGNET at P.O. Box 1967, Media, PA 19063.

Sending a fax from a Windows application

Because you install WinFax to appear as another Windows print selection, you can send a fax without leaving the Windows application in which you prepared your document. When you're ready to fax a document:

1. If you configured WinFax as your default printer, select the application's Print command. Otherwise, select the application's Select Printer or Printer Setup command, choose WinFax as your active printer, and then select the application's Print command.

   If the application has one or more Print dialog boxes, make the appropriate selections, such as setting the range of pages to be printed/faxed. Click OK to accept the selections and start the print/fax operation.

   Windows now begins to communicate your instructions to the WinFax printer driver. The WinFax LITE Fax Send dialog box appears, asking for information needed to send the fax.

2. Fill in the appropriate details in the Fax Send dialog box as follows.

   If you need a brief reminder on how to fill in a particular field, click the Help button.

The WinFax LITE Fax Send dialog box has these controls:

Name: field — Type the recipient's name (a person, company name, or combination of the two). If you select a name from one of your on-line phonebooks using the Select button, WinFax LITE completes this field.

Number: field — Type the recipient's fax telephone number. The actual number of the fax system is formed by appending this number to the Prefix number. If you select a name from your on-line phonebook, WinFax LITE completes this field.

If your phonebooks are set up with partial matches enabled, you need only type one or two letters in the To field and press Tab to complete the To and Number fields. The entry in the current phonebook with the closest match to the letters you typed appears in these fields.

Prefix: field — Type any series of digits that must be dialed before dialing the actual fax number. The dial prefix can be up to 24 characters.

- Many PBX office systems require that 9 be dialed to get an outside line. In this case, type **9,** in this field. The comma adds a short pause before the rest of the telephone number is dialed. This dial prefix is then always dialed before the fax number.

- The Fax/Modem Setup dialog box specifies the default dial prefix. Use the Setup command to get to this dialog box. WinFax LITE places the default in this field, when a default is specified. You typically will not need to change it.

Select button — Click the Select button to choose from entries in your on-line fax directories, or phonebooks. The Phonebook Entries dialog box appears. If you are using WinFax for the first time, your phonebooks might not yet have any entries in them. See the Phonebook Record and Phonebook Group commands. When your phonebooks are set up, the individual recipients and groups of recipients appear for the currently selected phonebook.

- Select a different phonebook by clicking the down arrow to the right of the Phonebook field and then clicking a different phonebook file.

- The Recipients and Groups lists display different names. Select a recipient or group by clicking the appropriate name. If you want more information on a particular selection, click Expand>>>>. Click OK when you have selected the desired recipient or group. The To and Number fields in the Fax Send dialog box are then filled in automatically.

Add to phonebook button — Click this button to save the information you typed into the To and Number fields into the currently selected phonebook. Click the Select button and check the Phonebook Details dialog box to check which phonebook is selected.

Time to send: field — Specify the time you want to send this fax. This field contains your computer's current time. If you want to send the fax immediately, leave this setting. If you want to send the fax later, click the hours, minutes, or seconds value. Up and down arrows appear. Click them to increase or decrease the time values. You can also change the values using the up- and down- arrow keys on your keyboard, and switch between hours, minutes, and seconds using the left- and right- arrow keys.

Scheduling faxes to be sent at other times lets you accommodate international time differences and take advantage of lower telephone rates outside of peak hours.

Date to send: field — Specify the date to send the fax. This field contains your computer's current date. If you want to send the fax immediately, leave this setting. If you want to send the fax on a different date, click the month, day, or year value. Up and down arrows appear. Click them to increase or decrease the date values. You can also change the values using the up- and down- arrow keys on your keyboard, and switch between month, day, and year using the left- and right- arrow keys.

WinFax LITE Administrator must remain running, either as a normal window or as an icon, if you have scheduled faxes to be in the future.

Resolution — Select the resolution, in dots per inch, at which you wish the fax to be transmitted.

Save to file check box — Mark this option to save your current document to a permanent fax file to attach to other faxes later. For example, you may want to save standard memos, documents, or forms that you send periodically.

All other fields on the Fax Send dialog box are grayed and disabled when you choose this option.

Attach — Mark this option to specify additional files to be faxed along with the current document. You can also set the order in which WinFax LITE sends this fax's documents.

Cover Page — Mark this option to send your default cover page as the first page of the fax.

WinFax lets you create a simple fax cover page on demand, if you have not prepared one in another application. In the WinFax Administrator, you can define a default cover page with a standard information block (to, from, date, time, number of pages) and can include a logo and additional text.

To customize the default cover page for this fax, click the Edit button. A dialog box appears in which you can change the logo selection, font compression, and specific cover page text for that fax.

If you are using WinFax for the first time, your default cover page might not yet be defined.

Send button — Click the Send button to submit the information you have placed in the Fax Send dialog box for processing. If you are saving the document to a file, the Send button changes to Save. Click the Cancel button if you wish to stop the fax or save.

After Windows has passed all the visual information about the document to the WinFax driver, the driver sends a message to the WinFax Administrator. The WinFax printer driver starts the WinFax Administrator application if it is not already running. The driver passes to the Administrator where, when, and how to send the fax. At this point, the driver and the application in which you created and "printed" the document have completed their part in the fax transmission process.

WinFax Administrator waits until the scheduled time and date to send the fax. When the scheduled time arrives — which is often immediately — WinFax Administrator sends your fax/modem the commands to establish a connection and send the fax.

After the fax transmission is complete or has been attempted, WinFax Administrator stores a synopsis of the event, including the number of pages sent, the time it took to send, and so on, in the send log.

If your computer is configured to use a PCMCIA fax/modem card and it is not inserted when you try to send your fax, a Card Manager dialog box appears. Do one of the following:

- Insert your PCMCIA fax/modem card and click OK to send your fax immediately.
- Click OK and your fax becomes a pending event in the event list. Your fax is sent the next time WinFax LITE is running and you insert your PCMCIA card. You can also reschedule your fax for later.
- Click Cancel to cancel the fax.

Sending from WinFax LITE

To send a fax directly from WinFax, start the WinFax Administrator if it is not already running.

1. Click the Send menu heading. From the Send menu, click the Fax command. A Fax Send dialog box similar to the dialog box that appears when you use WinFax from another application appears.

2. Fill in the appropriate details in the Fax Send dialog box.

3. Click the Send button to submit your fax to the WinFax printer driver and WinFax Administrator.

After the document's visual information has been passed to the WinFax driver, the driver tells the WinFax Administrator where, when, and how to send the fax. WinFax Administrator waits until the scheduled time and date to send the fax. When the scheduled time arrives — which is often immediately — WinFax Administrator sends your fax/modem the commands to establish a connection and transmit the fax.

If you have enabled the display of call progress information, you can watch the status messages on your screen as the fax is being sent.

As with faxes sent from other applications, WinFax Administrator stores in the send log a synopsis of what happened to the fax you sent directly from WinFax, including the number of pages sent, time it took to send, and so on.

If your computer is configured to use a PCMCIA fax/modem card and it is not inserted when you try to send your fax, a Card Manager dialog box appears. Do one of the following:

- Insert your PCMCIA fax/modem card and click OK to send your fax immediately.

- Click OK and your fax becomes a pending event in the event list. Your fax is sent the next time WinFax LITE is running and you insert your PCMCIA card. You can also reschedule your fax for later.

- Click Cancel to cancel the fax.

Combining documents in a fax

WinFax lets you combine the output of more than one application and transmit all of the documents as a single fax. You can combine a desktop-published newsletter, form-processed order form and word-processed letter, all in one fax. You can also preface the fax with a customized cover page.

To assemble a multiple page fax:

1. Open an application from which you wish to send.
2. Print and save as attachment file.

   Repeat steps 1 and 2 for every other item in your multiple page fax.

3. Attach attachment files.
4. Enable the cover page.
5. Send the fax.

Saving fax files

You can store documents to use as attachments to future faxes. For example, save product fact sheets from your desktop publishing package to send to potential customers, or a memo from your word processor to send to a mailing list.

Save documents to fax files from any Windows application as follows:

1. Start the Windows application.
2. Create or open the document you want to save as a fax file.
3. Use the Printer Setup, Select Printer, or equivalent command to select the WinFax printer driver.
4. Select the Print command, and make the appropriate selections to start the printing process.
5. When the Fax Send dialog box appears, click the Save to file option.
6. Enter five characters to create a unique filename for each page of the fax document.

   WinFax LITE creates filenames with the format *XXXXXPPP*.FXS where *XXXXX* is the five-character identifier you supply, and *PPP* is the page number. For example, page 3 of a fax document identified as "sales" is saved to file SALES003.FXS.

7. Click OK to accept the filename; then click Save in the Fax Send dialog box to actually save the document to a fax file. All fax files are stored in the WinFax directory.

Select and add saved fax files to other faxes using the Attach option.

Attaching fax files

To send a fax consisting of the document you are "printing" from your current application plus previously saved files, select the Attach option in the Fax Send dialog box. The Attach Files dialog box appears.

This dialog box lists all the documents to be sent as one fax and the available fax files in the WinFax directory. To add a saved fax file to the transmission list:

1. Click the fax file to be added. File information is displayed below the Available Files list to help you identify files.

2. Click the <<<Add button. The filename is added to the transmission list.

To remove a file from the transmission list:

1. Click the fax file to be removed from the transmission list.

2. Click the Remove button. The file is removed from the transmission list.

Current Print Item on the transmission list refers to the document to be faxed from your current application. Current Print Item does not appear on this list when you send a fax from WinFax LITE.

When you remove a file from the transmission list, it remains on the Available Files list.

The transmission list does not show cover pages.

If a fax attachment file has been rotated, you may not be able to reuse the file as an attachment in its new orientation. Go to the WinFax LITE Image Viewer to rotate the fax attachment file.

To preview (or rotate) a fax attachment file before adding it to the transmission list, click the filename and then click the View button. The message *Preparing Image* appears, and after a brief pause, the WinFax Image Viewer module appears, displaying an image of the selected fax file.

When you have previewed the fax file, use the File⮑Close command in the WinFax Image Viewer. You are returned to the Attach Files dialog box.

The transmission list shows the fax files and the document from the current application, in the order in which they will be sent.

To change the files' order:

1. Click the name of the file you wish to move in the transmission list sequence.

2. Click the Move button.

   When you move the arrow pointer back up into the transmission list, you will notice that it is an insertion pointer.

3. Place the insertion pointer between the two filenames where you want to move the file you clicked in step #1.

4. Click on the mouse button, and the file is moved.

5. After you have selected the fax files you wish to attach to your current fax, and set up the order in which the files are to be transmitted, click OK to accept the settings in the Attach Files dialog box and return to the Fax Send dialog box.

Monitoring fax send progress

The WinFax LITE Setup dialog box includes a setting for displaying a fax's ongoing information while it is being sent or received. To turn on this feature, mark in the Display Call Progress check box. A Fax Transmission Status dialog box then appears during every fax send. This dialog box provides ongoing information on the following:

Operation Messages — Messages about the stage or status of the transmission are shown. Some examples are

- Initialization
- Setting Fax Info...
- Setting Resolution...
- High Resolution...
- Dialing...
- Waiting...
- OK
- CONNECT
- Data Sent to fax...
- Sending End of Procedure
- Transmit Complete

Current Page — The percentage of data in the current page that has been transmitted.

Called Station — The recipient's fax number or identifier (which could be the name or abbreviated name of a company).

Page — The current page being transmitted, and the total number of pages to be transmitted. Cover pages are not included in page totals.

This dialog box also includes a Cancel button. Click it to stop a fax from being sent.

If you choose not to display call progress information, no dialog box appears when you send a fax. If you need to check a fax's status, open the WinFax Administrator application, which is already active as part of the fax transmission process. The WinFax Administrator work area shows the same status messages that appear on the Fax Transmission Status dialog box, and it provides a Cancel button.

Stopping faxes

To cancel the fax currently being sent, click the Cancel button in either the Fax Transmission Status dialog box or the WinFax Administrator. The canceled fax event is stored in the Send Log with Error status.

Retrying faxes

If you try to send a fax and it fails because of a communication problem (no reply or a busy line), you can set up WinFax to try again. Set the number of retries (Dial Retries) and the time between successive retries (Retry Time) in the Fax/Modem Setup dialog box.

Scheduling faxes

Scheduling faxes to be sent at other times lets you accommodate international time differences and take advantage of lower telephone rates. To delay when a fax is sent, modify the Time to send and/or Date to send values in the Fax Send dialog box when you prepare to send a fax.

To list scheduled fax events, start WinFax Administrator.

To remove a scheduled fax from the queue, click it and then click the Remove button or select Fax⇨Remove Event.

To reschedule a fax event, click it and then click the Resched button or select Send⇨Reschedule.

Modify the time and date in the same way that you change the Time to send and Date to send fields in the Fax Send dialog box. Click OK when you have rescheduled the fax. The fax is then repositioned in the queue.

 WinFax Administrator must remain running, either as a normal window or as an icon, if you have scheduled faxes. If you attempt to exit Windows with scheduled faxes in your WinFax event list, WinFax alerts you with: *Windows Shutdown. Fax events are still pending! Are you sure you want to exit?* Click Yes or No, as appropriate. If you click Yes, the WinFax Administrator retains pending events. They are on the event list when you next start WinFax.

Preparing to receive faxes

If your send/receive fax/modem is operational, you are in Windows, and the WinFax Administrator application is running, you can receive faxes. To modify exactly how you receive faxes, select File⇨Receive Setup.

Automatic receive

Automatic Reception Enabled: If you want your fax/modem to handle incoming faxes automatically, without your having to specifically start the receive process, click the box next to Automatic Reception Enabled to display an *X*. If you do not enable automatic reception, you must use the Manual Receive command from the Receive menu to begin receiving a fax immediately.

When you have enabled automatic reception, the WinFax Administrator displays a fax/modem icon under the menu headings and to the right of the Resched and Remove buttons.

When you start up WinFax for the first time in any Windows session, you may notice that an hourglass appears inside this icon. It indicates that WinFax is automatically preparing the fax/modem to receive faxes. You can also double-click this icon to obtain the Receive Setup dialog box. This icon does not appear when automatic reception is turned off.

Number of Rings Till Answer: With automatic reception turned on, you can also specify the number of times the telephone will ring before the fax/modem responds. Typically, this value is set to 1. You may want to adjust it when you have one telephone number for handling both voice and fax calls.

Receive options

For every receive option, the Fax Reception Status dialog box appears while the receive event is in progress, as long as you have display call progress enabled.

Normal — No messages or indicators other than the Fax Reception Status dialog box (if enabled) appear to announce a received fax. To see whether a fax has arrived, check the WinFax Administrator.

Notify — WinFax LITE displays a message when a fax arrives. This message includes a counter that increments by one for each fax that arrives before you click OK. When you click OK, the received message counter resets to zero.

Print on Receive — When a fax arrives, WinFax LITE prints it at the resolution at which it was sent. To choose a printer on which to print faxes, click the Select button under Printer (For Print On Receive), described below.

If the original size of a fax is larger than the paper on which you print, the fax image is scaled proportionately to fit.

View on Receive: When a fax arrives, the WinFax Image Viewer starts and displays the first page. You can page through and review all pages of the fax and perform other activities.

Printer (For Print On Receive) — This area of the Receive Setup dialog box is only available when you select Print on Receive for your receive option. Click the Select button to choose the appropriate printer on which to print received faxes.

Monitoring progress

The WinFax LITE Setup dialog box includes a setting for displaying information about a fax while it is being received or sent. To enable this feature, mark the Display Call Progress check box. A Fax Reception Status dialog box then appears while each fax arrives. This dialog box shows you the following:

Operation — Messages about the stage or status of the transmission. Some examples are OK and CONNECT.

Calling Station — The fax number or station identifier (which could be the name or abbreviated name of a company) from which the fax is being sent.

Page — The page currently being received.

This dialog box also includes a Cancel button. Click Cancel to stop a fax you are receiving.

If you choose not to display call progress information, no dialog box appears when you receive a fax. If you need to check the status of a fax as it comes in, open the WinFax Administrator application. The WinFax Administrator work area shows the same status messages that appear on the Fax Reception Status dialog box, and it also provides a Cancel button.

Handling fax events

WinFax lets you send a fax at any future date and time. This feature lets you accommodate time differences and take advantage of lower telephone rates outside of peak hours.

Whenever you send, schedule to send, or receive a fax, WinFax enters each fax event into a list of pending and received items. If the fax is to be sent immediately, transmission occurs almost directly after the print operation is completed. If the fax is scheduled for future delivery, the event stays on the pending list until its time and date match the time and date on your computer.

The fax event list is part of the WinFax Administrator's main window. Each event is listed with the following information, from left to right:

- Pend if the fax is scheduled to be sent, Recv if the fax is newly received.
- Date and time the fax is scheduled to be sent, or was received.
- Number of pages in the fax (including cover pages).
- Name or fax number of the recipient or calling station.

The list's top event is the next fax to be sent, or the received fax that has been on the list longest. The event list displays up to 100 events, but you can schedule as many faxes as you want.

Event information

Use the event list to get information on any fax event displayed in the event list, including

- Recipient's name or calling station's fax number.
- Resolution at which the fax was sent or received.
- Number of pages sent or received.
- Duration of the send or receive.

Removing and rescheduling events

From the event list, you can remove pending or received events, and reschedule pending events for different dates and times.

Monitoring fax progress

If you have not enabled Display Call Progress, but you would like to check on how a fax send or receive is proceeding, use WinFax Administrator. The WinFax Administrator work area shows the status messages that appear on the Fax Transmission and Reception Status dialog boxes, and includes a Cancel button to stop a fax send or receive.

Logging fax events

The send and receive logs list and describe previous fax events. The logs include successful events; canceled events; and events that failed due to transmission errors, busy signals, no reply, and other conditions. Events are sorted according to the date and time they occurred, with the most recent events appended to the end of the list.

Information at the bottom of both logs shows more details about your fax transmissions and receptions. You can also resubmit faxes, file received faxes with brief descriptions, and view sent or received faxes and print log reports.

Defining the default cover page

WinFax lets you create a simple fax cover page on demand, if you have not prepared one in your application. The WinFax cover page can extract information from sources such as the following and insert it in the appropriate places:

- Recipient name from the Name field of the Fax Send dialog box, or from a list of names in a phonebook group.
- Sender name from the Sender Name field of the Fax/Modem Setup dialog box.
- Your computer's time and date.

To set up your default WinFax cover page:

1. Click the Send menu heading. From the Send menu, click the Define Cover Page command.

2. Your default cover page includes an information block. If you do not want it, mark the Enable cover page information check box.

3. To modify any of the default settings, tab to or click the appropriate information block field. Press Backspace to erase the current setting, and type in the desired setting, keeping the limits in the following table in mind:

Item	Default Setting	Maximum Length (in characters)
Heading	FACSIMILE COVER PAGE	40
Recipient field	To:	20
Sender field	From:	20
Time field	Time:	20
Date field	Date:	20
Pages field	Pages (including cover)	40

You can modify these settings to display wording that your company uses in correspondence or to translate headings into another language. To change the information block settings, edit the specific field(s) or click the Default button.

4. If you wish to include a logo or other graphic at the top of your cover page, first prepare the desired graphic in a WinFax fax file (.FXS) format as follows:

   a) Start a Windows graphics application in which you can open the graphic file.

   b) Open the graphic file.

   c) Use the Printer Setup, Select Printer, or equivalent command to select the WinFax printer driver.

   d) Select the Print command, and make the selections to start the printing process.

   e) When the Fax Send dialog box appears, click the Save to file option.

   f) In the Save To File dialog box, type a filename (five characters or fewer) and click OK.

   g) Click the Save button in the Fax Send dialog box. WinFax generates a fax file version of the graphic.

5. In the Cover Page Setup dialog box, click the down arrow to display a drop-down list of available .FXS files. Click the up and down arrows in the drop-down box to scroll through the list. Click the file's name, and it appears in the box directly under the Cover Page Logo File heading.

6. Mark the Use compressed font check box to insert a large block of text on your cover page. This gives you more lines per page.

7. To insert a standard block of text on your cover pages, select an ASCII text file.

   a) Mark the Default Cover Page Text File check box.

   b) Click the Select button. A file selector appears.

   c) Click the file's name and then click OK.

   The selected filename is displayed in the box under Use Default Cover Page Text File. The actual text is inserted on the cover page when you send it, or can be edited prior to sending.

8. When you have finished defining your default WinFax cover page, click OK to save it.

You can change cover page logo, font, and text for a specific fax when you send it, as described in the next section. Information block settings can only be set using the Define Cover Page command.

If your default text includes dollar sign symbols ($), type each one twice. WinFax recognizes the single dollar sign as an invalid variable and displays an error message.

Customizing cover pages

Before you send a fax, you can customize its cover page. The settings for the customized cover page pertain only to that fax.

From the Fax Send dialog box:

1. Mark the Send Cover check box.

2. Click the Edit button to the right of Send Cover. A dialog box displaying your default cover page settings appears.

3. To change the logo, click the down arrow to the right of the logo filename and select a new logo.

4. To change the font setting for cover page text, mark the Use compressed font check box. This check box enables and disables font compression.

5. If you selected a default cover page text file, the Cover Page Text area of the Cover Page dialog box shows its contents. Use the following methods to modify this text.

To delete all default text: When the Cover Page dialog box appears, default text is selected. Press the Backspace key once, and all default text is removed.

Type text: Type new text to replace or add to the default text. Click where you want to add text. A flashing text cursor appears and you can begin typing and inserting text.

Delete selected text: Drag the I-bar pointer to highlight text to delete. Press the Delete key. The text disappears.

Import text: Click the Import button. From the file selector, select the text file's name, and click OK. Text from the selected file appears at the cursor.

Insert variables: WinFax uses variables to extract information from the current fax's send specifications and inserts that information in the cover page text. Click the Variable button. Click the desired variable and then click OK. The variable code appears at the cursor.

6. When you have customized the cover page, click OK. Complete the settings in the Fax Send dialog box and click Send.

Setting up phonebooks

WinFax Administrator lets you enter fax recipients into on-line directories, or phonebooks. You can also combine a number of recipients into a single group, or distribution list. This way, you can send a single fax to a group of recipients at the same time.

For example, if you send product bulletins to all your dealers and distributors, you could create a phonebook group called Product Bulletins. You then add the phonebook entries for each dealer and distributor to this group. You create your product bulletins in a Windows word processing or desktop publishing application and print them to fax attachment files. When you send the bulletins, and WinFax asks you to enter the fax destination, choose the Product Bulletins group from the phonebook. WinFax sends the fax to each member of the Product Bulletins group.

Using the WinFax LITE Image Viewer _____

Use the WinFax Image Viewer to

- Review outgoing faxes and fax attachments.

- Review received faxes.

- Rotate and store received faxes.

- Save fax files to graphic image file formats for further modification in other applications.

- Convert received faxes to WinFax file format to send them again.

You can start up the WinFax Image Viewer from many different points in WinFax.

The first way is to select Fax⇨View. The WinFax Image Viewer displays the pages of the last selected event in the queue of send and receive events in the WinFax Administrator. If the queue is empty, the WinFax Image Viewer display area is also empty, and you must use the Open command to display a specific fax file.

Another way is to define your receive setup for View on Receive. When WinFax successfully receives a fax, the WinFax Image Viewer starts and displays the first page.

Finally, you can use one of the several WinFax commands that bring up dialog boxes with View buttons. For example:

- Click a send or receive event in the WinFax Administrator queue. Click the Event Information command in the Fax menu. The information dialog box for the selected send or receive event includes a View button. Click it to preview a scheduled fax to be sent out or review a received fax.

- Select Fax⇨Attachments. The Attachments dialog box lists fax files prepared to be appended to a fax to be sent. Click an .FXS file and then click the View button to check that it is the fax file you wish to select.

- The send and receive logs include View buttons. Click an event in the log listing and then click View. (Cover pages cannot be viewed in the WinFax Image Viewer. To see text and logo defined for a specific cover page, click the Cover button.)

View buttons appear in other dialog boxes in which you select fax files or preview fax events.

Software End User License Agreement

You may transfer this program and documentation together with this license to another party, but only if the other part agrees to accept wholly the terms and conditions of this license and you notify Delrina of the name and address of the other party. All copies must be transferred to the same party, or you must destroy those copies not transferred. Any such transfer terminates your license.

Note that this product was originally sold by Delrina as part of a larger package, and was not for resale as a separate product. Therefore, if you acquired this other than as part of that larger package, you may not be entitled to any support of any kind. Please discuss with the party from whom you acquired the product.

Nonpermitted Uses

Without the express permission of Delrina, you may not:

1. Use the software in a computer service business including rental, networking or timesharing software, nor may you use it for multiple user, networks or on multiple computer system applications in the absence of individual licenses with Delrina.
2. Use, copy, modify, alter or transfer, electronically or otherwise, the software or documentation except as express-ly allowed in this agreement.
3. Translate, reverse program, de-assemble, decompile or otherwise reverse engineer the software, except as may be expressly permitted by law.
4. Sublicense or lease this program or its documentation.

Term

This license is effective from your date of purchase and shall remain in force until terminated. You may terminate the license and this agreement any time by destroying the program and its documentation, together with all copies in any form.

Delrina may terminate this agreement if you fail to comply with any of its terms or conditions. Upon any termination of this license, you agree to destroy the licensed software, and its documentation together with all copies, modifications or portions of them in any form. You must provide us, on our request, written certification of such destruction.

Limited Warranty

Delrina warrants that, for a period of ninety (90) days of normal use from the date of original purchase, the diskettes on which the software is recorded will be free from defects in materials and faulty workmanship and the software will function substantially as described in the enclosed program documentation.

EXCEPT FOR THE AFORESAID WARRANTY, ALL PRODUCTS DELIVERED PURSUANT TO THIS AGREEMENT ARE DELIVERED ON AN "AS IS" BASIS AND DELRINA, ITS DEALERS AND DISTRIBUTORS EXPRESSLY DISCLAIM ANY AND ALL OTHER WARRANTIES, EXPRESS OR IMPLIED, INCLUDING, WITHOUT LIMITATION, IMPLIED WARRANTIES OR CONDITIONS OF MERCHANTABLE QUALITY OR FITNESS FOR A PARTICULAR PURPOSE.

Limitation of Liability

Delrina's entire liability, in tort contract or otherwise, and your exclusive remedy for breach of the limited ninety (90) day warranty herein before provided for shall be the replacement of any diskette or program documentation not meeting with such warranty which is returned to the party from whom you purchased, together with a copy of your paid receipt. In no event shall Delrina, its dealers or distributors, be liable in tort contract or otherwise, for lost profits, data or information of any kind or for consequential, special, indirect, incidental, punitive or other damages that may arise through use of the product licensed thereunder. This warranty gives you specific legal rights and you may also have other rights under the law of your jurisdiction.

Support

Delrina has no support obligation to the end user. If you have a problem with a defective diskette or with the installation or operation of the program, do not contact Delrina; contact the party from whom you purchased or the company whose telephone number appears on the sticker in the inside front cover of the manual (if any).

U.S. Government Restricted Rights

The software and documentation are provided with restricted rights. Use, duplication or disclosure by the U.S. Government is subject to restrictions as set forth in subparagraph (c)(1)(ii) of the Rights in Technical Data and Computer Software clause at DFARS 252.227-7013 or subparagraphs (c)(1) and (2) of the Commercial Computer Software - Restricted Rights at 48 CFR 52.227-19 as applicable. Manufacturer is Delrina (Canada) Corporation and Delrina (Wyoming) Limited Liability Company, c/o 6320 San Ignacio Ave., San Jose, California, 95119-1209.

U.S. Export Restrictions

You acknowledge that the Program is subject to restrictions and controls imposed under the export control laws and reg-ulations of the U.S.A., and any amendments thereof. You certify that neither the software nor the documentation is being or will be exported, acquired, shipped, transferred, or re-exported, directly or indirectly, to: (i) any country or region prohibited under such laws and regulations. (Currently such regions include, but are not necessarily limited to: Cuba, the Federal Republic of Yugoslavia (Serbia and Montenegro), Haiti, Iran, Iraq, Libya, North Korea, South Africa (military and police entities), and Syria; (ii) any end user who you know or have reason to believe will utilize them in the design, develop-ment or production of nuclear, chemical or biological weapons; or (iii) any end user who has been prohibited from participating the U.S.A. export transactions by any federal agency or the U.S.A. government. You also acknowledge that the Program may include technical data subject to export and re-export restrictions imposed by U.S.A. law.

Governing Law

This Agreement shall be governed and construed in accordance with the laws of the Prov-ince of Ontario, Canada, excluding its conflict of laws provisions, and the parties hereby agree to irrevocably submit to the jurisdiction of the Courts of the Province of Ontario.

895 Don Mills Road	6 Elstree Gate	6320 San Ignacio Avenue
500-2 Park Centre	Elstree Way	San Jose, California
Toronto, Ontario	Borehamwood, Hertfordshire	U.S.A.
Canada M3C 1W3	England WD6 1JD	95119-1209

Chapter 38
Delrina WinComm LITE

This chapter discusses basic operation for WinComm LITE. For more information, check the on-line help files.

Attention: The software programs and other materials provided by Delrina in this package are provided to you under the terms of a license agreement and are not sold to you. The license agreeement will be found at the end of this chapter. Carefully read this agreement before using any Delrina Software. Support for Delrina products included in this book/disk package is provided on WUGNET's CompuServe forum; by calling WUGNET at 610-565-1861; or, you can write to WUGNET at P.O. Box 1967, Media, PA 19063.

Dialing Instructions

Specify dialing instructions using three text entry fields (two with corresponding check boxes). If you always call the same phone number to access a remote system, it is best to type the phone number. However, when you access systems with more than one number, it may be best to leave these fields blank.

Selecting a Phonebook entry that does not have a phone number brings up a dialog box that asks for the number. This dialog box lists the last number called (if any) using this Phonebook entry, and includes a drop-down history list of the six most recently called numbers.

Predefined prefixes and suffixes are useful for laptop users who move from site to site. This feature lets you quickly adapt phone numbers to your current location.

Using a dialing prefix

To use a dialing prefix:

1. Select the Use stored dialing prefix check box.

2. Type or select an item from the corresponding drop-down listbox to specify the prefix.

For example, you could type a ***70** (to disable call waiting), an access code for an outside line (for example, **9**), or an 800 number for your long distance carrier.

WinComm LITE dials entries specified in this drop-down listbox before the phone number. If the check box is selected and no entry appears in the drop-down listbox, the check box has no effect.

Changing the prefix or suffix assigned to #1, #2, and so on, in any session changes that prefix or suffix in all sessions.

Using a dialing suffix

To use a dialing suffix:

1. Select the Use stored dialing suffix check box.

2. Type or select an item from the corresponding drop-down listbox to specify the suffix.

   For example, you could type a credit card number or an accounting code. Entries specified in this drop-down listbox are dialed after the phone number. If the check box is selected and no entry appears in the drop-down listbox, the check box has no effect.

Transmission Characteristics _____

Specifying transmission characteristics requires knowledge of your modem's capabilities and the remote system's modem capabilities and settings. You are usually told to type specific values for each of these parameters by the remote system's administrator.

Baud rate — Provides common transmission rates between 300 and 115200 baud. The baud rate parameter determines the maximum transfer speed in bits per second (bps) between your PC and the modem. With many modems, you can set a higher baud rate than the modem actually uses to exchange data with remote systems. See your modem manual for more information.

Data bits — Specifies the number of bits per character. Most systems use 7 or 8.

Parity — Specifies the type of character parity. The options are None, Odd, Even, Mark, and Space. When you're using Odd, Even, Mark, or Space parity, Data bits is usually 7.

Stop bits — Specifies the number of stop bits per character. Most systems use stop bit 1.

Priority — Specifies the priority of this session relative to all other concurrent sessions and applications. This field is usually set to Normal. Other possibilities are Low and High.

Hardware Characteristics and Emulation

Use Low priority when communications speed is unimportant, and you want to make other applications run faster. Use High to devote more time to WinComm and less to other applications.

The remaining drop-down listboxes and command buttons specify the characteristics of your hardware and the terminal you are emulating. Terminal emulation selections require knowledge of the remote system's capabilities.

Port type — Lists the port types supported by WinComm. Other port types for use with network interfaces such as Standard Int 14H may also appear here. If you use an internal or external modem, external ISDN terminal adapter, or serial port installed directly on your PC, select Standard Com Port.

Port name — A drop-down listbox with the PC hardware communication port names. For Standard Com Port, the choices are COM1, COM2, COM3, and COM4.

Port Setup — Displays the Port Setup dialog box with additional settings for specific port types and names selected.

Modem Setup button — Displays the Modem Setup dialog box, where you can select any modem WinComm supports.

Terminal — Lists terminal emulations supported by WinComm. Among the terminal types currently supported are

- ANSI — Supports American National Standards Institute displays.

- CompuServe — Simplifies file transfers with CompuServe B+ protocol. Use it only with the CompuServe Information Service.

- TTY — Use with any system that calls for a TTY terminal, a Teletype, a glass terminal, or no terminal.

- VT52, VT100 — Support virtually all features of DEC VT52 and VT100 terminals. Each emulator fully supports cursor-control (both ANSI and VT52), cursor-memory, cursor-reporting, tab stops, origin mode, and host-controlled printer operations.

Terminal Setup — Displays a dialog box with additional emulation parameters for the chosen terminal emulation. These parameters vary depending on terminal type. WinComm specifies defaults for each parameter.

ASCII Setup — Displays the ASCII Setup dialog box.

ANSI Emulator Terminal Setup dialog box

The ANSI emulator supports American National Standards Institute displays. These displays are usually implemented with the ANSI.SYS device driver on PC-compatible computers. Note that WinComm completely supports the ANSI display standard. You do not need to add ANSI.SYS to your CONFIG.SYS file.

This emulator is most often used with bulletin boards and other remote systems that send graphics characters or ANSI color codes.

Function, Arrow, and Control keys Act as — Specifies whether these keys send IBM PC scan codes (two- or three-byte hex codes for BBS Doorway mode), Terminal keys (ANSI escape sequences), or act as Windows accelerator keys.

Reverse <Del> and <BACKSPACE> keys — When this option is selected, the functionality of the Backspace and Delete keys is reversed.

Cursor — Selects between Block and Underline cursor characters. Also lets you select a blinking (selected) or nonblinking (unselected) cursor.

CompuServe Terminal Setup dialog box

This emulator simplifies file transfers with CompuServe B+ protocol and is used only with the CompuServe Information Service. With this emulator, you can start file transfers by commanding CompuServe to upload or download files — you do not need to select the Upload or Download commands. When using this emulator, configure CompuServe to treat your computer as an ANSI terminal (to begin the configuration process, type **GO TERMINAL** at the CompuServe prompt).

Use destructive backspace — When this option is selected, the Backspace key moves the cursor left one character position and erases the character that was there. When it is not selected, the Backspace character moves the cursor left one character without deleting characters. You can then type over a portion of the current command line and press Return without retyping correct keys to the right of the cursor position.

Reverse <Del> and <BACKSPACE> keys — When this option is selected, the functionality of the Backspace and Delete keys is reversed.

Cursor — Selects between block and underline cursor characters. Also lets you select a blinking (selected) or nonblinking (unselected) cursor.

TTY Terminal Setup dialog box

Use the TTY emulator with any system that calls for a TTY terminal, a Teletype, a glass terminal, or no terminal. This class of terminal, because of its simplicity and wide availability, has become a de facto standard in communications, and you can access more systems with this emulator than with any other. Systems designed for use with more sophisticated terminals often provide rudimentary support for TTY terminals as well. TTY terminals support only alphanumeric keys.

Use destructive backspace — When this option is selected, the Backspace key moves the cursor left one character position and erases the character that was there. When it is not selected, the Backspace character moves the cursor left one character without deleting characters. You can then over-type a portion of the current command line and press Return without retyping correct keys to the right of the cursor position.

Reverse <Del> and <BACKSPACE> keys — When this option is selected, the functionality of the Backspace and Delete keys is reversed.

Cursor — Selects between block and underline cursor characters. Also lets you select a blinking (selected) or nonblinking (unselected) cursor.

VT52, VT100 Terminal Setup dialog box

These DEC emulators support most features of DEC VT52, VT100, VT102, VT220, and VT320 terminals. Each emulator fully supports cursor-control (both ANSI and VT52), cursor-memory, cursor-reporting, tab stops, scrolling regions, half-and full-duplex operation, origin mode, and host-controlled printer operations.

The VT220 and VT320 emulators support multinational, British, French, French Canadian, German, and ASCII character sets.

Double-high characters display as two lines of identical characters.

WinComm menus provide setup details that DEC terminals normally handle with setup screens.

The following list includes a complete listing of settings for DEC VTxxx terminals.

Function, Arrow, and Control Keys Act as — Lets you specify whether these keys should act as Terminal keys or as Windows accelerator keys.

PF1-PF4 also mapped to top row of keypad — When this option is selected, this check box maps keys PF1, PF2, PF3, and PF4 to NUM LOCK, /, *, and — on the keypad in addition to F1 to F4.

Keypad application mode — When this option is selected, this check box specifies that the keypad sends application codes that control programs running on the host. This is known as Alternate keypad mode on a VT52.

Reverse <Del> and <BACKSPACE> keys — When this option is selected, the functionality of the Backspace and Delete keys is reversed.

Cursor keypad mode — When this option is selected, the cursor keys (arrow keys) send Normal codes, which move the cursor. When it is unselected, the cursor keys send application codes, which control remote applications. This is not available on a VT52.

132 column mode — When this option is selected, it sets the screen width to 132 characters. When it is set to 132, you can use Ctrl+Right Arrow and Ctrl+Left Arrow to see portions to the right or left of the currently visible portion of the screen. This is not available on a VT52.

Restore Default Tab Settings — Replaces tab settings the host has sent with tab settings from the ASCII Setup dialog box.

Character set — Lets you specify the national character set used.

Cursor — Selects between block and underline cursor characters. Also lets you select a blinking (selected) or nonblinking (unselected) cursor.

Capture to Printer dialog box

Specify how interactive information is captured for printing and whether it is released to the printer by page or by session. Releasing the printer by session is important if you are printing to a network printer.

Printer — Lists the current printer. This printer is selected using the Windows Control Panel or some other Windows application, or by using the Setup command button in the Print dialog box.

Characters — Prints all incoming data except escape sequences.

Lines — Prints each line when the carriage return at its end is received. It also prints the line you are on when you stop or suspend printing, unless that line is blank. This is the default selection.

Screens — Prints the entire screen whenever the remote system clears the screen or you stop or suspend printing.

By page — Prints the document one page at a time.

By session — Prints the current session.

Make these the default settings — When this check box is enabled, all changes you make are stored as the default settings.

Click Start to print on the selected printer using these options.

Save As dialog box

A session with an existing Phonebook file has the absolute path with the filename in the File Name text box. Untitled sessions display the absolute path of the Phonebook directory with a proposed filename, derived from the system name.

You can type any filename, with or without an extension. However, if you type any extension other than WCS you receive this message *Systems saved to files with extensions other than .WCS do not appear in the Phonebook. Are you sure you want to save to FILENAME.EXT?*

Upload Dialog Box _____

This modeless dialog box lets you choose the file transfer protocol and other parameters for uploading files to a remote system. You can continue to interact with the remote system (or any other session) with this dialog box displayed. This way you can prepare to send files and issue commands to the remote system before clicking Upload.

Directory — Displays the current absolute path to which file selection applies. The path changes when a file is selected in the file browse dialog box, or a file is added to the Additional files to Upload listbox.

File name — Lets you specify a filename to upload. You can type absolute or relative paths with or without wild-card filename selection. If you have already uploaded or selected files or paths in the current session, those names appear in the drop-down history list, and the most recently selected file or path appears in the text box. Browse displays the standard file browse dialog box, from which you can select a drive, directory, and file.

Add — Moves the absolute path of the file in the File name text box to the Additional files to Upload listbox. If a filename uses a wild-card selection, all files that satisfy the wild-card selection criteria appear in the listbox.

Remove — Unavailable (dimmed or grayed) unless you select one or more files in the Additional files to Upload listbox (see Additional files to Upload). Selected files are removed from the list when you click this button but are not deleted from the disk.

Include matching files from subdirectories — Applies to both the Add and the Upload buttons. When this option is selected, WinComm searches subdirectories of the path specified in the File name text box. Files matching the filename or wildcard selection are added to the listbox (see Add) or uploaded, depending on the button clicked.

Include paths when sending file names — When this option is selected, WinComm uploads the absolute path along with the filename. This option is available only when it is supported by the selected protocol.

Protocol — Displays the default transfer protocol for this session. You can select another protocol from the drop-down list, but you cannot type into the display box associated with the drop-down list. In addition, the dialog box box has a Settings command button that displays a custom dialog box box for each protocol.

Additional files to Upload — Displays the absolute path of files added to the transfer list. The listbox has vertical and horizontal scroll bars when necessary. Standard Windows extended selection applies in the list when you select files to be removed with Remove.

Save as Batch — For WinComm PRO only.

Restore Batch — For WinComm PRO only.

Upload — Starts the transmission sequence for the selected protocol and displays the Upload Progress dialog box.

If you minimize WinComm during a transfer, a percentage bar indicates how much of the transfer has been completed.

Upload Progress Dialog Box _____

The window title of this dialog box includes both the session name and protocol. The default dialog box has summary information about the progress of the file transfer, which includes the name of the current file, a progress bar, the number of retries, the estimated time remaining or elapsed time for the transfer, and throughput. This dialog box provides Expand and Cancel buttons, and may include a Skip file button.

Expand displays a dialog box with more extensive status information. The information contained in this dialog box is a function of the protocol in use.

Skip file appears with certain protocols when you are uploading multiple files. If you want to skip a particular file, click Skip file.

Open File Dialog Box

The Open File dialog box is similar to other file browse dialog boxes used throughout WinComm. See Browse dialog boxes for more information.

Port Setup Dialog Box

Software handshaking — Use the check boxes to turn on software handshaking for downloading or uploading. Software handshaking is on by default. Use the drop-down listboxes to specify the XON and XOFF characters. The defaults are the standard ASCII XON/XOFF characters.

Hardware handshaking — Use the check boxes to turn on hardware handshaking for downloading or uploading. Hardware handshaking is off by default. When you're using a modem that supports baud rates above 2400 bps, RTS and CTS are the typical selections.

Break signal duration — Provides choices for the time in milliseconds. You can type any value. This number determines the length of the break signal WinComm generates when you press the break key for the terminal you are emulating. In most cases, the terminal emulator's break key is the same as the PC's break key.

Modem Setup Dialog Box

This dialog box displays additional modem settings. WinComm specifies reasonable defaults for each of these settings. Settings in this dialog box affect only the current session and are independent of settings used when calling other systems.

Extra modem setup commands for this session — Specifies special commands required to configure your modem for communications using this particular remote system.

Dialing — Indicates whether the modem should use pulse or tone dialing. The selection is a function of the telephone company or in-house PBX capabilities.

Wait for carrier — Specifies how long the modem should wait for a carrier signal from the answering modem.

Number of retries — WinComm redials when the called number is busy or does not answer. Use the text box to specify the number of times it should redial.

Retry after — Specifies the time delay between retries.

Accept callback from remote system — Indicates that the system you are calling will disconnect and call back as part of its logon security or to reverse telephone charges. This selection places the modem in answer mode when the current call is completed.

Speaker — Enables or disables the modem speaker.

Modem definition — Displays the Modem Definition dialog box. This lets you customize the modem initialization strings, or create custom initialization strings for modems that WinComm does not list by name.

ASCII Setup Dialog Box

This dialog box is divided into three major sections: ASCII Uploading, ASCII Downloading, and Character Filtering. Options specified in this dialog box apply only to normal terminal interaction with the remote system. File transfer protocols are not affected by these options.

Uploading options

Send line ends with line feeds — Check this box to have WinComm send a carriage return (CR) and line feed (LF) at the end of each line. The default is character return only.

Expand blank lines to include a space — Check this box to force WinComm to always include at least one space character between two CRs. The default permits null lines (two CRs without any intervening characters).

Echo typed characters locally — When enabled, this option displays transmitted characters in the terminal area. Select this option when you are communicating with remote systems that expect you to be operating in half duplex (sometimes called echoplex). The default is no echo.

After sending each line, wait for character — When this option is selected, the default character causes WinComm to wait for an echoed 0Dh (carriage return or CR) character before sending the next line. Most remote systems operate in full-duplex mode, so all characters sent are echoed back. Waiting for CR can help synchronize transmission to slower remote systems. The default is no waiting.

Convert outgoing tabs to — When this option checked, the default conversion factor is eight spaces. You can change the number of spaces using the text box. The default is no conversion.

Line delay — If you experience loss of characters at the beginning of lines when performing ASCII transmission to remote systems, changing this setting may improve transmission integrity. Use the text box to change the number of milliseconds. The default is 0 milliseconds.

Character delay — If you experience loss of characters when performing ASCII transmissions to remote systems, changing this setting may improve transmission integrity. Use the text box to change the number of milliseconds. The default is 0 milliseconds.

Downloading options

Append line feeds to incoming line ends — Forces a carriage return (CR) and linefeed (LF) at the end of each line. The default is to leave the lines as received. Lines sent to you by most remote systems already end with CR and LF.

Force incoming data to 7-bit ASCII — Converts 8-bit data characters to standard ASCII by replacing the eighth bit with 0. Checking this box suppresses extended ASCII characters caused by line noise or incorrect parity and/or bits per character settings. With systems that send extended ASCII characters, leave this check box unselected. The default is unselected. WinComm ignores this setting when you use the ANSI emulator because it must support graphic characters that use the eighth bit.

Echo incoming data to sender — When enabled, this option transmits every received character back to the remote system. You may want to check this box when you communicate terminal to terminal. The default is no echo.

Wrap lines that exceed terminal's width — When this option is on, long lines appear on multiple terminal lines. The default is off, which discards characters beyond the terminal's maximum line length.

Show hex value of nonprinting characters — When this option is on, control characters, escape sequences, and screen control codes no longer control your screen; instead they display as hexadecimal values in square brackets. The default is off.

Tab spacing for incoming text — Use the text box to change the number of contiguous spaces used to convert a tab character. Set this value to 0 to turn conversion off. The default replaces each tab character with eight contiguous spaces.

Modem Definition Dialog Box _____

Lets you customize the modem initialization strings or create custom initialization strings for modems that WinComm does not list by name.

Transfer Protocol Dialog Box_____

Provides a drop-down list of protocols supported by WinComm. The dialog box also has a Settings command button that displays a custom dialog box for each protocol. If you specify the same protocol for both uploading and downloading, either Setting button defines settings for both directions.

The protocols currently supported are 1K XMODEM, CompuServe B+, XMODEM, YMODEM, YMODEM G, and ZMODEM

CompuServe B+ protocol settings

Use the Close button to exit the Upload or Download dialog boxes, because this protocol automatically starts when commanded by CompuServe.

Use this protocol with the CompuServe B+ protocol on the CompuServe Information Service. The CompuServe B+ protocol supports both single- and multiple-file transfers, and is an error-correcting protocol. All you need to do is command CompuServe to upload or download the desired files and WinComm transfers the files. To use this protocol, you must be using the CompuServe emulator.

Protocol type — Select either CompuServe B+ (the default) or Old B by enabling the appropriate radio button.

Packet size — Enter the packet size used for transmission. The text box increases (or decreases) packet size in 128-byte increments. If you type any other number in the text box, WinComm rounds it to the next lower number divisible by 128. The default packet size is 512. The minimum is 128 and the maximum is 1024.

Quoting level — Choose from Standard quoting, Minimal quoting, Extended quoting, or Maximum quoting.

1K XMODEM, XMODEM protocol settings

1K XMODEM is a 1024-byte packet, error-correcting protocol similar to YMODEM, except that it can transfer only one file at a time. Unlike YMODEM, 1K XMODEM does not transfer filenames. Some remote systems that support 1K XMODEM refer to it as YMODEM.

XMODEM is a relatively simple, 128-byte packet, error-correcting protocol, which transfers only one file at a time without a filename. XMODEM is generally faster than YMODEM if the line is noisy, but slower if it is clean, as it transmits 128-byte packets rather than 1024 bytes as with YMODEM.

Error-checking — Specifies the error-checking method. The default is Auto, which adapts automatically to the error-checking method of the remote system. CRC and Checksum are the two alternative error-checking methods available with this protocol. Some systems require that you set this parameter to Checksum.

Compression — Lets you choose whether files are compressed during transfers, to reduce their size and let them upload faster. Go ahead and choose Compress when possible because compression turns itself off when necessary.

Seconds to wait to get each packet — Sets the number of seconds your PC waits for each packet to begin. This is normally set to 10. With slower systems such as CompuServe, you may need to set this as high as 30.

Seconds to wait to get each byte — Sets the number of seconds your PC waits for each byte in the packet. This is normally set to 5. With slower systems such as CompuServe, you may need to set this as high as 10.

Attempts to send each packet — Sets how many times your PC retransmits (or requests retransmission of) each packet. Normally, this is four.

YMODEM, YMODEM G protocol settings

YMODEM (also known as YMODEM Batch) is a 1024-byte packet, error-correcting protocol capable of transferring single files or groups of files. YMODEM is generally faster than XMODEM over noise-free lines, but slower over noisy lines, as it must retransmit 1024-byte packets rather than 128 bytes as with XMODEM. (YMODEM is similar to 1K XMODEM, except that 1K XMODEM transfers only one file at a time without a filename.)

YMODEM G is a variant of YMODEM that does away with packet-by-packet acknowledgments and simply cancels the transfer if an error is detected. YMODEM G should be used only with error-correcting modems or inherently error-free connections. YMODEM G is clearly faster than YMODEM, XMODEM, and Kermit, but there is a common misconception that YMODEM G is the best protocol to use with error-correcting modems. In reality, ZMODEM is much better because it can correct errors the modems cannot sense (such as those introduced by the computers or serial ports) with no reduction in performance.

Compression — Lets you choose whether files are compressed during transfers, to reduce their size and let them upload faster. Go ahead and choose Compress when possible because compression turns itself off when necessary.

Seconds to wait to get each packet — Sets the number of seconds your PC waits for each packet to begin. This is normally set to 10. With slower systems such as CompuServe, you may need to set this as high as 30.

Seconds to wait to get each byte — Sets the number of seconds your PC waits for each byte in the packet. This is normally set to 5. With slower systems such as CompuServe, you may need to set this as high as 10.

Attempts to send each packet — Sets how many times your PC retransmits (or requests retransmission of) each packet. Normally, this is four.

ZMODEM protocol settings

ZMODEM is an error-correcting, streaming protocol that has become popular on bulletin boards. It is the fastest, most desirable protocol because it maintains its speed despite propagation delays, though its efficiency is slightly less (98% versus 99%), and it lacks compression. ZMODEM can upload single files or file groups.

The dialog box has three sections: Download, Upload, and Transmission.

Download parameters

Respond to ZMODEM autostart — When this option is selected, WinComm begins downloading as soon as you command the remote system to upload. When it is not selected, you must click Download in the Download dialog box to begin downloading.

If the file already exists — Select either

- Follow sender's Append/Overwrite option — Uses the option the downloading system specifies. Use this option cautiously, since it has the potential to overwrite existing files.

- Follow options in Transfer Download dialog box — Uses the options you specified in the Download dialog box.

Crash recovery — This section consists of three option buttons. Select from

- Negotiate — Lets recovery occur when file recovery is enabled at the remote system. This is the default.

- Never — Prevents recovery from occurring, even if the remote system has file recovery enabled.

- Always — File recovery occurs when the remote system has recovery set to enable or negotiate.

Upload parameters

Append/Overwrite option — Select from eight options:

- None — Use this with systems that do not support ZMODEM Management options.

- Newer or longer — Overwrites if the uploaded file has a newer time or date or a larger size.

- CRC differs — Overwrites if the uploaded file has different contents.

- Append to file — Adds file sent to end of existing file.

- Overwrite always — Overwrites any file having the same name as the uploaded file.

- Overwrite if newer — Overwrites if the uploaded file has a more recent time/date.

- Different length or date — Overwrites if the uploaded file has a different size, time, or date.

- Never overwrite — Rejects the uploaded file if its name matches any existing file.

Crash recovery — Select from

- Negotiate — Lets recovery occur when file recovery is enabled at the remote system. The default.

- One-time — Allows recovery during the next file transfer only, after which the setting reverts to Negotiate. This prevents inadvertent file recovery, which can damage files.

- Always — File recovery occurs when the remote system has recovery set to enable or negotiate.

Transmission parameters

Method — Specifies error detection and recovery procedures when you are uploading files. The ZMODEM protocol lets the uploading system choose whether to wait for positive acknowledgment from the downloading system before uploading additional blocks. If the uploading system chooses to wait for acknowledgment, it can also choose how often it waits. Alternatively, the uploading system can stream data until transmission is complete or it receives a negative acknowledgment from the downloading system. Upon receipt of a negative acknowledgment, the sender retransmits the failed block and all subsequent blocks:

- Streaming — WinComm ZMODEM should upload in streaming mode (the default).

- Windowed — ZMODEM should stop and wait for acknowledgment when necessary. The drop-down list provides options of 2K and 4K bytes.

Packet — Sets the number of bytes in each packet. Larger packets mean faster transfers but slower recovery from errors. Available packet sizes are 32, 64, 128, 256, and 1024 (the default). Packet size reduces automatically if necessary.

CRC — Sets the size of error-checking codes used; 16 bits is usually adequate. Setting to 32 bits further enhances reliability, but at the expense of speed.

Wait — Sets how long ZMODEM waits between attempts to resend packets. Through networks, where the receiver may lag far behind the sender, you may need to increase this setting. The default setting is 15 seconds, with a range of 1 to 99 seconds.

End of line conversion — Check this box if you are transferring text files with a system that requires a line feed character after each carriage return, which is typical of UNIX systems. The default is unselected.

Control sequences use escape codes — Check this box if you want ZMODEM to replace all control codes with an equivalent series of non-control codes. This may be necessary with networks or remote systems that have problems transmitting control codes.

All other product names are copyright, trademarks or tradenames of their respective owners.

If Delrina WinComm LITE was sold to you without additional hardware or software, your copy of the product is not licensed. Contact Delrina to ensure that you receive product and software upgrade information.

Software End User License Agreement

Important: Read this before using your copy of Delrina WinComm LITE.

Acceptance

Use of your copy of Delrina WinComm LITE indicates your acceptance of these terms. If you do not agree to these terms and conditions, either destroy or return the intact Delrina WinComm LITE package, containing the diskettes, together with the other components of the product to the place of purchase.

Proprietary Rights

This program and any accompanying documentation are proprietary products of Delrina (Canada) Corporation ("Delrina") and are protected under international copyright laws. Title to the program, or any copy, modification or merged portion shall at all times remain with Delrina.

Permitted Uses

You may use the enclosed software on a single computer that you own or use. Under no circumstances may you use it on more than one machine at a time. You may make a copy of the software for backup purposes, provided that you reproduce and place our copyright notice on the backup copy.

You may transfer this program and documentation together with this license to another party, but only if the other part agrees to accept wholly the terms and conditions of this license and you notify Delrina of the name and address of the other party. All copies must be transferred to the same party, or you must destroy those copies not transferred. Any such transfer terminates your license.

Note that this product was originally sold by Delrina as part of a larger package, and was not for resale as a separate product. Therefore, if you acquired this other than as part of that larger package, you may not be entitled to any support of any kind. Please discuss with the party from whom you acquired the product.

Nonpermitted Uses

Without the express permission of Delrina, you may not:

1. Use the software in a computer service business including rental, networking or timesharing software, nor may you use it for multiple user, networks or on multiple computer system applications in the absence of individual licenses with Delrina.

2. Use, copy, modify, alter or transfer, electronically or otherwise, the software or documentation except as expressly allowed in this agreement.

3. Translate, reverse program, de-assemble, decompile or otherwise reverse engineer the software, except as may be expressly permitted by law.

4. Sublicense or lease this program or its documentation.

Term

This license is effective from your date of purchase and shall remain in force until terminated. You may terminate the license and this agreement any time by destroying the program and its documentation, together with all copies in any form.

Delrina may terminate this agreement if you fail to comply with any of its terms or conditions. Upon any termination of this license, you agree to destroy the licensed software, and its documentation together with all copies, modifications or portions of them in any form. You must provide us, on our request, written certification of such destruction.

Limited Warranty

Delrina warrants that, for a period of ninety (90) days of normal use from the date of original purchase, the diskettes on which the software is recorded will be free from defects in materials and faulty workmanship and the software will function substantially as described in the enclosed program documentation.

EXCEPT FOR THE AFORESAID WARRANTY, ALL PRODUCTS DELIVERED PURSUANT TO THIS AGREEMENT ARE DELIVERED ON AN "AS IS" BASIS AND DELRINA, ITS DEALERS AND DISTRIBUTORS EXPRESSLY DISCLAIM ANY AND ALL OTHER WARRANTIES, EXPRESS OR IMPLIED, INCLUDING, WITHOUT LIMITATION, IMPLIED WARRANTIES OR CONDITIONS OF MERCHANTABLE QUALITY OR FITNESS FOR A PARTICULAR PURPOSE.

Limitation of Liability

Delrina's entire liability, in tort contract or otherwise, and your exclusive remedy for breach of the limited ninety (90) day warranty herein before provided for shall be the replacement of any diskette or program documentation not meeting with such warranty which is returned to the party from whom you purchased, together with a copy of your paid receipt. In no event shall Delrina, its dealers or distributors, be liable in tort contract or otherwise, for lost profits, data or information of any kind or for consequential, special, indirect, incidental, punitive or other damages that may arise through use of the product licensed thereunder. This warranty gives you specific legal rights and you may also have other rights under the law of your jurisdiction.

Support

Delrina has no support obligation to the end user. If you have a problem with a defective diskette or with the installation or operation of the program, do not contact Delrina; contact the party from whom you purchased or the company whose telephone number appears on the sticker in the inside front cover of the manual (if any).

U.S. Government Restricted Rights

The software and documentation are provided with restricted rights. Use, duplication or disclosure by the U.S. Government is subject to restrictions as set forth in subparagraph (c)(1)(ii) of the Rights in Technical Data and Computer Software clause at DFARS 252.227-7013 or subparagraphs (c)(1) and (2) of the Commercial Computer Software - Restricted Rights at 48 CFR 52.227-19 as applicable. Manufacturer is Delrina (Canada) Corporation and Delrina (Wyoming) Limited Liability Company, c/o 6320 San Ignacio Ave., San Jose, California, 95119-1209.

U.S. Export Restrictions

You acknowledge that the Program is subject to restrictions and controls imposed under the export control laws and regulations of the U.S.A., and any amendments thereof. You certify that neither the software nor the documentation is being or will be exported, acquired, shipped, transferred, or re-exported, directly or indirectly, to: (i) any country or region prohibited under such laws and regulations. (Currently such regions include, but are not necessarily limited to: Cuba, the Federal Republic of Yugoslavia (Serbia and Montenegro), Haiti, Iran, Iraq, Libya, North Korea, South Africa (military and police entities), and Syria; (ii) any end user who you know or have reason to believe will utilize them in the design, development or production of nuclear, chemical or biological weapons; or (iii) any end user who has been prohibited from participating the U.S.A. export transactions by any federal agency or the U.S.A. government. You also acknowledge that the Program may include technical data subject to export and re-export restrictions imposed by U.S.A. law.

Governing Law

This Agreement shall be governed and construed in accordance with the laws of the Province of Ontario, Canada, excluding its conflict of laws provisions, and the parties hereby agree to irrevocably submit to the jurisdiction of the Courts of the Province of Ontario.

895 Don Mills Road	6 Elstree Gate	6320 San Ignacio Avenue
500-2 Park Centre	Elstree Way	San Jose, California
Toronto, Ontario	Borehamwood, Hertfordshire	U.S.A.
Canada M3C 1W3	England WD6 1JD	95119-1209

Chapter 39
askSam for Windows

With askSam for Windows, you can create a personal database with the information you find on the Internet. The Information Highway is certainly a glamorous and exciting topic. Most of the major news magazines, such as *Time* and *Newsweek*, have published articles about the Internet. The articles focus on the vast amount of information you can access via the Internet: President Clinton's speeches, Supreme Court rulings, forums on every imaginable topic, electronic magazines, and more. The list grows every day. This important question is rarely asked, however: "What do you do with the information after you've found it?"

This is where askSam helps. askSam turns files you download from the Internet into your personal database.

For example, suppose you enjoy cooking and find a forum on Internet where participants exchange recipes. The messages contain many useful recipes, but when dinner time comes and you want a chicken recipe, browsing through the hundreds of messages is not the ideal way to take advantage of this information. askSam can turn this information into a database, letting you search, sort, and sift through it easily.

What Is askSam?

askSam is an *information* database. It manages data differently than a traditional database. Rather than focusing on structured data, askSam understands that information comes in various shapes and sizes, and thus enables you to organize information that doesn't fit into traditional databases. You can include several hundred pages of text, notes, or comments in each record. askSam lets you import information from many sources, such as ASCII texts, Word and WordPerfect files, DBF files, and more. After the information is in askSam, a variety of tools help you search through and manipulate your data. This is why askSam is an excellent tool for organizing the mountains of information you encounter on the Internet.

Using askSam with Internet Files _____

Using ask Sam to organize your Internet information has several advantages:

- askSam lets you search for any word or phrase anywhere in your information. You can also use Boolean and proximity searches.

- askSam can also automatically recognize fields. For example, a downloaded message often contains words such as To, From, Date, and Subject. askSam lets you use these words as fields. You can search, sort, and even create reports.

- askSam's hypertext functions let you create electronic documents that you can distribute or place on a network for other users to access. You can use hypertext to create easy-to-navigate menus that guide users through documents.

About askSam Lite _____

Your CD contains askSam Lite, a working model with some limitations:

- You can add or import only up to 30 documents into a database. The full version has no limit on the number of documents that you can add.

- If you open a database containing more than 30 documents, you will not be able to edit the database.

- Individual documents in a database can be no longer than 500 lines. The full version allows up to 16,000 lines per document.

The following documentation tells you how to install askSam Lite and introduces you to some of askSam's features. askSam Lite comes with several sample databases and lets you create your own databases. For further information on any features, try askSam's Help function. It contains detailed information about every askSam menu item.

If you need the full version of askSam, you can upgrade. See the coupon in the back of this book for details.

Installing askSam

askSam Lite requires:

- IBM or 100% compatible computer with at least a 386 processor
- 4MB of RAM (8MB preferred)
- 6MB of free hard drive space (including over 2MB for sample databases)
- Windows 3.1 and DOS 3.1 (or higher)

To install askSam Lite:

1. Start Windows.
2. Insert the CD containing askSam Lite into your CD-ROM drive.
3. Choose File⇨Run in the Windows Program Manager, and from the CD-ROM's askSam directory, run SETUP.EXE.
4. Follow the instructions that appear on your screen.

After askSam Lite is installed, start it by double-clicking the askSam icon.

Example Databases

The CD includes several sample askSam databases. You can open these files and explore some of askSam's features. Table 39-1 lists the included databases.

Table 39-1	Databases Included with askSam Lite
Database	**Description**
CONGRESS	The names and addresses of all U.S. Congressmen. Search for your representatives and see how to send mail merge letters to a select group.
PRODINF	Product information about askSam for Windows.
QUOTES	Quotations from famous people.
README	The full askSam documentation.
RFC	(Request For Comments) Useful information about the Internet, such as frequently asked questions (FAQs) and a glossary of terms.
WUGNET	A list of files available in the CompuServe WUGNET libraries.

To work with any of these databases:

1. Choose File➪Open.

   A list of filenames appears.

2. Choose the file you want and click OK.

 Some of these sample databases contain more than 30 documents. If this is the case, askSam Lite will not let you edit the information. You need the full version of askSam to edit databases larger than 30 documents.

Files and Documents _____

Before you begin working with askSam, you should understand how askSam stores information. Like other applications, askSam stores your data in files. askSam files are structured like database files — each file may contain multiple documents (which correspond to traditional database records). For example, you can import the contents of several messages into one askSam database. Each imported message is a separate document (record) in your askSam database.

This is different from the way a word processor stores information. In a word processor, each document is stored in a separate file. See Figure 39-1.

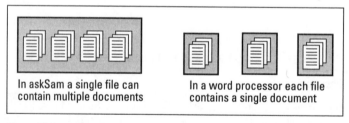

In askSam a single file can contain multiple documents

In a word processor each file contains a single document

Figure 39-1: askSam can store several documents in one file.

Using askSam _____

The rest of this chapter tells you how to organize Internet information in askSam. The example files are actual files downloaded from the Internet.

In the first part of this tutorial, you import information into askSam, search this information, use askSam's automatic field recognition function, and create a report from the information you imported.

The second part of the tutorial teaches you to create hypertext documents from your information.

Importing messages into an askSam database

This example leads you through importing messages into askSam. The example file contains 24 recipes from a forum. These messages were downloaded into a single text file called RECIPES.TXT. You import this file into an askSam database. Each of the 24 messages in the text file becomes an individual record in the askSam database.

Use the exact uppercase and lowercase letters shown in the steps.

1. Choose File⇨New. The New File dialog box appears.

2. Type **RECIPES** and click OK.

   askSam creates the file and puts you into the Work Space.

3. Now import the recipes into askSam. Choose File⇨Import.

   The Import Dialog box appears.

4. Enter the name of the file you wish to import. Type **RECIPES.TXT**.

   askSam imports the file. To place each recipe in a separate database record, define a Document Delimiter. The Document Delimiter tells askSam where one message starts and the next message stops.

5. Click the SET OPTIONS button.

   The Import Options dialog box appears.

6. Choose the STRING option and type **Date:**.

   You've now established that the string Date: determines the beginning of a message.

7. Click OK to return to the Import dialog box.

   You can now import your file.

8. Click OK.

   A message box appears, showing the status of your import and keeping a count of documents. When the import finishes, a Close button appears.

9. Click Close.

Moving through your database

After you've imported your data, the first message appears on the screen. You can scroll through this message just as you scroll through a document in a word processor. The status bar at the bottom of the screen tells you how many documents are in your database. You are currently in the first of 24 documents. To view the other messages in the database, you can use the video buttons (Figure 39-2) or the key combinations listed in Table 39-2.

Figure 39-2: The video buttons.

Table 39-2	askSam Navigation Keystrokes
Keystroke	**Function**
Alt+PgDn	Moves to the next document.
Alt+PgUp	Moves to the preceding document.
Alt+End	Moves to the last document in the file.
Alt+Home	Moves to the first document in the file.

Searching

askSam offers full text, Boolean, and proximity searches. The Actions menu contains these searches. The easiest way to search is to use the command line, which appears between the format bar and the ruler, and begins with the Search button. Enter one or more words in the command line and press Enter, and askSam retrieves any documents containing the word or words.

Full text searching

The example text you imported contains a collection of recipes. Here's how to search for all the Cajun recipes:

1. Click the command line or press Esc to move the cursor to the command line.

2. Type **cajun** and press Enter.

   The first document containing the word *cajun* appears. The Retrieval dialog box appears near the upper-right corner of the window, as Figure 39-3 shows.

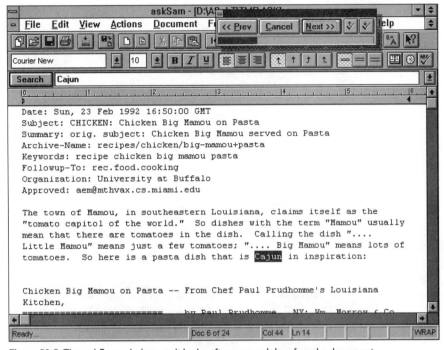

Figure 39-3: The askSam window, as it looks after a search has found a document.

In the Retrieval dialog box, click Next to view the next document retrieved by your search request, Previous to return to the previously retrieved document, or Cancel to cancel the search and remain in the retrieved document.

3. Click the Next button.

As you will see, several messages contain the word *cajun*. To narrow the search, search for the words ***cajun*** and ***chicken***.

4. Press Esc twice.

The cursor appears in the command line. Your last request (cajun) is highlighted. Use the cursor keys to edit this request, or type new search words.

5. Type **cajun chicken** and press Enter.

askSam retrieves the first document containing *cajun* and *chicken*. To see the other documents this request retrieved, click Next.

6. Choose Cancel or press Esc to end the search.

Boolean searching

Boolean searching lets you create search requests using the operators *and*, *or*, and *not*. For example, to find the saltless chicken recipes, use a Boolean search.

1. Choose Actions⇨Boolean Search.

   The Boolean Search dialog box appears.

2. Type **Chicken** and click Add.

   Chicken is added to the search list.

3. Type **Salt** and click Add.

   Salt is added to the search list.

4. Click the Not button.

   The Boolean Search dialog box should now look like Figure 39-4.

Figure 39-4: The Boolean Search dialog box, ready to search for chicken without salt.

5. Click OK.

   askSam searches for the recipes that contain chicken but no salt. The first message appears on your screen.

6. Click Cancel or press Esc to end the search.

You can combine the Boolean search with the Multiple Search Request, which lets you combine multiple searches into a single request. For example, you could search for all recipes with no salt where chicken and curry appear in the same line. The Multiple Search Request also lets you count the number of documents any of your requests retrieve. See the Help File for more information on the Multiple Search Request.

Creating reports from your messages

If you've worked with a database, you might be familiar with their report functions. askSam reports work differently because these functions handle unstructured information such as messages.

A report can give you an overview of the information you've gathered. For example, a report can show you the subjects from all messages containing a certain word or phrase.

Reports require that the database have *fields* to give it structure. Although the messages vary in length and content, they have similar structure. The words *Date, From,* and *Subject* appear in each message. To use these words as fields, use the Auto Field Recognition command.

Automatic Field Recognition

The Auto Field Recognition command searches through your file and gives you a list of words that you can use as fields. The command asks you for the rules by which it can recognize possible fields. In the example, the fields Date:, From:, and Subject: all end with a colon. Use the colon, then, as the rule for recognizing possible fields.

1. Choose Tools⇨Auto Field Recognition.

   The Automatic Field Recognition dialog box (Figure 39-5) appears.

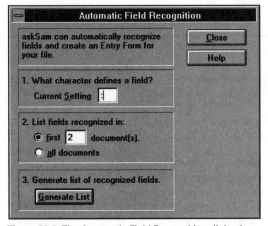

Figure 39-5: The Automatic Field Recognition dialog box.

2. Enter a colon (:).

This tells askSam that words followed by a colon (:) are possible fields.

3. Click the Generate List button.

The Select Fields dialog box appears. It lists from the file words that end with colons.

4. From this list, choose fields for this file. Double-click Date:, From:, and Subject:.

As you double-click these words, they move from the Available Fields list to the Selected Fields list. See Figure 39-6.

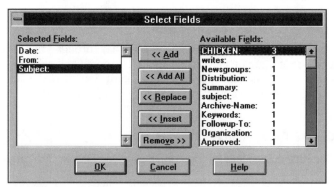

Figure 39-6: The Select Fields dialog box, with three fields selected.

5. Click OK.

askSam defines your selections as fields in your file. Use these fields when you define your report layout.

Creating a report

Create a new report from the New Report menu.

1. Choose Tools⇨New Report.

The New Report menu appears.

2. Enter a name for your report. Type **Overview** and press Enter.

The New Report menu has four buttons: one to select documents, one to sort documents, one to define report layout, and one to run a report.

3. Click the Select button, or press Alt+S and then press the spacebar to select documents.

   The Multiple Search dialog box appears. Use it to define which documents you want to include in this report. In this case, instead of choosing a specific group of documents, make the report prompt for documents each time it runs.

4. Choose the Prompt button.

   The Prompt dialog box appears.

5. Enter the prompt you want displayed before the Overview report is run. Type **Enter an ingredient or recipe name**.

   The Prompt dialog box should now look like Figure 39-7.

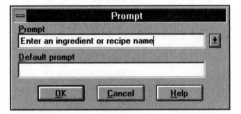

Figure 39-7: The Prompt dialog box, partially completed.

6. Click OK.

   The Prompt dialog box goes away, and you return to the Multiple Search dialog box.

7. Click OK.

   The Multiple Search dialog box goes away, and you return to the New Report menu.

   At this point, if you want, you can sort the documents in your report. This example, though, skips to the report layout.

8. Click the Define Layout button.

   The Report Layout Editor appears. Use its blank screen to define your report's appearance. Select the fields to include in the report, and place them where you want them to appear. The Overview report will contain only the Subject: field.

9. Drag the Subject: field from the Field List and place it in line 1, column 1.

To drag a field, move the mouse pointer to the field name. Click the left mouse button and keep it pressed while you move the mouse pointer to the position where you want to position the field. Release the mouse button.

As you move the mouse pointer, the cursor position is tracked in the left part of the status bar. Move to line 0, column 0.

The Subject: field is inserted into your report. Similarly, you can also place other fields in your report. Your report layout should resemble Figure 39-8.

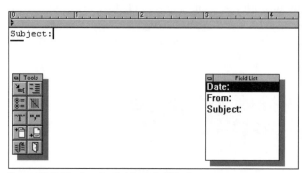

Figure 39-8: Placing the Subject: field in the report.

To save your layout and return to the New Report menu:

1. Choose Tools⇨Close Report, or press Ctrl+S.

   A message asking if you wish to save the report appears.

2. Click Yes.

   You return to the New Report menu.

Running a report

To run the report just created:

1. Click Run.

   A message appears asking you to enter an ingredient or recipe name.

2. Type **chicken** and click OK.

   A new window appears, listing recipes containing the word *chicken*. From this window, you can quickly access any message listed in your report.

3. Double-click on any recipe in the report.

You return to the recipe database, and the complete text of the recipe you selected appears.

To return to the report, press Ctrl+Tab.

To close the files that are open, click File⊃Close repeatedly until all open files are closed.

The next part of the tutorial creates hypertext documents from Internet information. It's easier than you think.

Creating hypertext documents

Hypertext can help you better organize and navigate information by letting you link a word or phrase to information in another location. By double-clicking on a hypertext link, you can jump from one document to another, jump from one file to another, run reports, or execute any menu command. Use hypertext to create electronic documents, define menus, and distribute information.

Using hypertext

Navigating through a hypertext document is simple. After hypertext links are created, double-click on any link, and askSam takes you to the appropriate position in the file. The sample askSam file RFC.ASK (Request For Comment) contains useful information about the Internet, such as frequently asked questions, a glossary of terms, and more. You can search this information as described in the previous tutorial section, or you can use hypertext to navigate the information.

1. Choose File⊃Open and select RFC.ASK. askSam opens the file, and the Internet RFC's Main Menu appears (Figure 39-9).

The Main Menu lists the RFC file's contents. By double-clicking any of the green underlined words — hyperlinks — you jump to the appropriate position in the database. You can then jump to another specific section, or you can scroll through the entire document.

Double-clicking the "Return to Table of Contents" hypertext link returns you to the Table of Contents for a specific document. Double-clicking on the "Return to Main Menu" hypertext link returns you to the Main Menu.

2. Double-click on any of the hypertext links (the green underlined words) to practice navigating through the hypertext document.

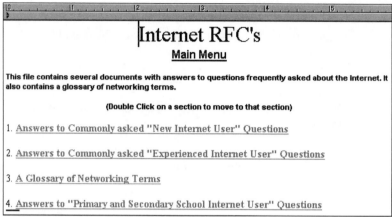

Internet RFC's
Main Menu

This file contains several documents with answers to questions frequently asked about the Internet. It also contains a glossary of networking terms.

(Double Click on a section to move to that section)

1. Answers to Commonly asked "New Internet User" Questions

2. Answers to Commonly asked "Experienced Internet User" Questions

3. A Glossary of Networking Terms

4. Answers to "Primary and Secondary School Internet User" Questions

Figure 39-9: The Internet RFC's Main Menu.

Creating a hypertext link

askSam makes creating a hypertext link simple. Here's how to import a new document into the RFC file and create a hypertext link tying the Main Menu to this new document.

1. Choose File⇨Import.

2. Select ASKSAM.TXT and click OK.

   ASKSAM.TXT is imported to the end of the RFC database. When the import is complete, a Close button appears.

3. Click Close.

   Before you can create a link, you must place a bookmark on the line that should be linked.

4. Press Alt+End to move to the document that you just imported.

   A document with askSam information appears.

5. Choose Document⇨Set Bookmark.

   The Set Bookmark dialog box appears. Enter a name for your bookmark.

6. Type **askSam Information** and click OK.

   This places a bookmark in the line containing the cursor.

7. Click File⇨Save to save the bookmark.

8. Press Alt+Home to return to the Main Menu.

Now, create the hypertext link to the askSam document. To do this, enter the words for your link, and then link the terms to the bookmark you just placed.

9. At the end of the Main Menu, type **5. askSam Information**, as Figure 39-10 shows.

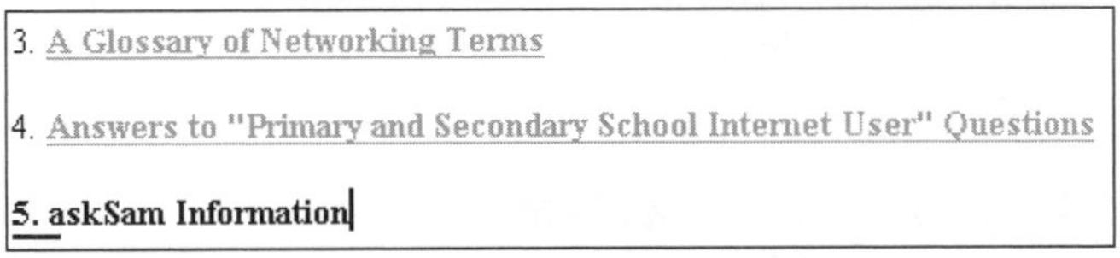

3. A Glossary of Networking Terms

4. Answers to "Primary and Secondary School Internet User" Questions

5. askSam Information

Figure 39-10: Adding a hypertext link.

10. Select (highlight) the text you just entered.

11. Choose Document⇨Hypertext Link, or press F4.

    The Hypertext Links dialog box appears (Figure 39-11). The Link To option lets you select the kind of hypertext link you want to create.

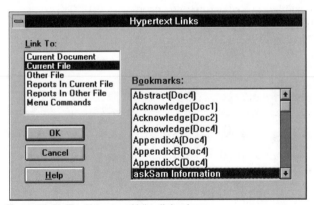

Figure 39-11: The Hypertext Links dialog box.

12. Select Current File.

13. In the list of bookmarks, select askSam Information.

14. Click OK.

> You have now created the hypertext link. Its text is green and underlined.

15. Click File⇨Save to save the hypertext link.

16. Double-click on the link you just created.

> The document containing the askSam information appears.

You can repeat this procedure to create more links in this file or to set links in any information you import into askSam. To return to the Main Menu, press Alt+Home.

Working with askSam Lite

Now you can try building your own askSam databases. You can build a database from scratch, import your information, or use one of the templates as a starting point (choose File⇨New and select a template name). Before long, you'll have mastered the program and be on your way to working more efficiently. Any database you create with askSam Lite can be used in askSam.

askSam and askSam Lite are products from:

askSam Systems
P.O. Box 1428
Perry, FL 32347

Phone: (800) 800-1997 or (904) 584-6590
Fax: (904) 584-7481

Chapter 40
OAG FlightDisk

OAG FlightDisk is an easy-to-use travel information and planning tool. You can search for flight schedules and airport and city information. With this information you can create Trip Plans, save them, print them, and share them with others via electronic mail.

- You can use FlightDisk to find information about city travel points.

- You can use FlightDisk to assist in making your travel arrangements.

- You can use FlightDisk to list current frequent flyer and frequent lodger programs.

- You can use FlightDisk to find up-to-date information about OAG FlightDisk and travel industry-related news.

Flights Overview

Every published direct flight that operates in the current issue's effective date range is contained in the Worldwide Edition of FlightDisk.

Additionally, hundreds of thousands of connecting flights are also contained in FlightDisk. Extensive processing is performed to combine individual direct flights to make up additional flight schedules to help get you to your destination. These connecting flights take into account minimum connecting times, geographical latitudes and longitudes for best routes, and many other factors to make your travel planning easier. Figure 40-1 shows the main OAG FlightDisk window.

Searching for Flights

To find flights:

1. Click the Flights button on the toolbar to open the Flights window.

2. Enter a date and your departure and destination cities.

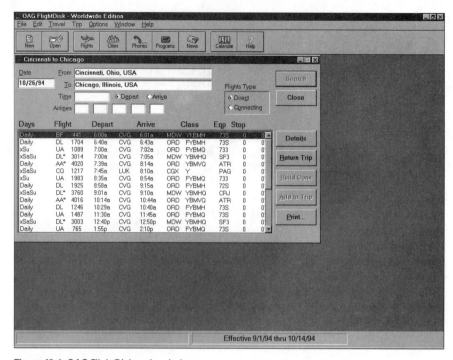

Figure 40-1: OAG FlightDisk main window.

3. Choose a Flights Type by clicking on the Direct or Connecting flights option button.

4. Click on the Search button.

5. When finished viewing or printing the flights, click the Close button to exit the window.

You can further limit/preference flight searches by filling out the following fields:

- Date

- From and To (information for cities and/or airports)

- Time

- Airlines

- Flight Type (Direct or Connecting)

Dates (Flights)

Entering a date in the Date field limits the displayed flights to those operating on that given day. If no date is specified, then all flights within the effective date range for the given cities are shown. Leaving the date blank provides you the opportunity to view flights on multiple days for comparison alternatives, but also puts the burden on you to ensure that the flight operates on the appropriate day.

To enter a date:

1. Type a date (example: **11/28/93** or **Nov 28 93**). Acceptable formats are dictated by the Options menu Preferences dialog box and by the International settings of the Windows Control Panel.
2. Or invoke the calendar by clicking the Calendar button on the toolbar and select a date.

To use the calendar as a reference:

1. Click the Calendar button on the toolbar to open the Calendar window. Or press the F5 key if the Calendar button is inoperative. Figure 40-2 shows the Calendar window.
2. To change to a different month, click the left or right arrows on either side of the month name field.
3. To change to a different year, click the left or right arrows on either side of the year field.
4. Click the Close button to exit the calendar.

To enter a calendar date into a Date field:

1. Click on the Date field to position the insertion point for the date to be entered.
2. Click the Calendar button on the toolbar to open the Calendar window. Or press the F5 key if the Calendar button is inoperative.
3. Locate the month and year; then click the box containing the day that you want.
4. Click the Select button and the date will be entered into the Date field.
5. To exit the calendar without entering the date, click the Close button.

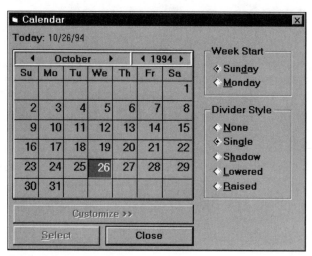

Figure 40-2: Calendar window.

Cities/Airports (Flights)

Both cities and major airports can be entered in the From and To departure
and destination fields. If a city is specified, all airports serving that city will be
included in the displayed flights. Entering a specific airport limits the displayed
flights to that particular airport only. However, if no flights are found to serve
a particular airport, then the flights search will include all airports serving the
city.

To enter a city or airport, do one of the following while in the From and To
fields:

1. Type a city or airport name (example: **chicago** or **laguardia**). Partial
   spellings are allowed, and will be matched against a city list. Type a three-
   character city code or airport code (example: **chi** or **lga**).

2. Click on the arrow button to the right of the field to obtain a city list, and
   select a city/airport from the list.

Times (Depart/Arrive)

Entering a time in the Time field positions the list of flights around the specified
Depart or Arrive time. If a Depart time is chosen, the list of flights is sorted by
the departure time, and the closest departing flight is highlighted. Likewise, if
an Arrive time is specified, the flights are sorted by arrival times, and the
closest arriving flight is highlighted.

Entering a time does not limit displayed flights as does entering a date and airlines. Rather, a time serves as a starting point for displaying the list of flights.

Leave the Time field blank to position the list of displayed flights beginning with the earliest flight.

To enter a time:

1. Type a time (example: **1p**, **1:00pm**, or **13:00**). The time will be formatted based on the International settings of the Windows Control Panel.

2. Click on the Depart or the Arrive option button to sort the flights accordingly and to position the list of flights around the selected time.

Airlines (Flights)

Entering airline preferences limits the displayed flights to only the specified airlines. Up to five airlines can be specified by indicating the two-character airline code. However, if no flights are found with the preferred airlines, then the flights search will include all airlines between the requested cities.

To enter an airline:

1. Type the two-character airline code corresponding to the desired airline (example: **ua** for United Airlines).

2. Or click on the Airlines button to the right of the Airlines fields to obtain a list of airlines and select an airline from the list.

If you enter the Flights window by clicking the Flights button on a flights segment of a trip plan, then any airline preferences that you have previously set up in your traveler profile for that trip plan will automatically be entered into your Flights window.

Flights Type (Direct or Connecting)

The Flights Type option buttons indicate whether direct flights or connecting flights will be located when the Search button is pressed to get flights. If you specify direct flights and no direct flights are found, the search will attempt to find connecting flights. If a search for connecting flights is unsuccessful, then a dialog box will be displayed asking if you want to build your own connecting flights.

To specify flight type:

1. Click on the desired Direct or Connecting Flights Type option button. (Note that a button will be disabled if a search was attempted and no flights were found.)

Printing Information

Most of the FlightDisk windows have a Print button allowing you to print the information displayed in that window. Before the print starts, a Print dialog box will be displayed allowing you to choose from a list of printers you have installed and to specify your print preferences.

To print:

1. Click the Print button to open the Print dialog box.

2. If your print preferences are set the way you want, then click the OK button, or press Enter to print.

3. If the To Default Printer box shows a printer different from the one you want, then use the Installed Printers listbox to select a new default printer.

4. From the Print Quality box, click one of the following buttons:

    Draft: recommended for dot-matrix printers.

    Quality: more suited for laser and high-resolution printers.

5. From the Print Range box, click one of the following buttons:

    Selection: to print only items you have selected, or highlighted.

    All: to print all information regardless of any items selected.

6. If you are printing flights data and you don't want operational remarks to print, then click the Exclude Remarks on Flights button.

7. Click OK to print. Or click the Cancel button to exit without printing.

    Clicking Cancel will also reset any of the preferences you changed to their original state before you entered the Print dialog box.

Managing Flight Selections _____

Flight selections are the direct flights and/or connecting flights that have been saved or added to the trip plan via a flight segment. The small box above the Flight Selections button serves as a quick view to indicate whether any flights have been selected or added to the segment.

To view flight selections:

1. Click on the Flight Selections button of the desired flight segment to open the Flight Selections window.

The Flight Selections window organizes direct flight and connecting flight selections in two separate lists. Just as in the Flights window, you can obtain flight details for any particular flight by clicking on a flight and then clicking on the Details button. The Flight Selections window also has a Special Instructions for Booking Flight text box, which can be used to enter instructions as a reminder to yourself or a travel arranger.

If you are using the trip plan for the purpose of a trip request document, you may add several flights to the trip plan as indicated preferences to your travel arranger. Once the travel arranger has completed the reservations, you may want to print a completed trip plan containing only the specific flight you are taking. To do this, you may have to delete the necessary flights from the Flight Selections window.

To delete flight selections:

1. Click on the Flight Selections button of the desired flight segment to open the Flight Selections window.

2. Highlight the flight(s) by clicking on the flight. Multiple flights can be selected by holding down the Ctrl key and clicking on the flights.

3. Click on the Delete button.

4. Click OK to confirm the deletions and close the Flight Selections window.

5. Remember to save your trip plan changes.

To delete a flight, car, or hotel segment:

1. Click any portion of the segment to highlight the background and make it the active segment.

2. Double-click any area of the segment's highlighted background.

3. Click the Yes button to confirm the deletion of the segment.

4. Remember to save your trip plan changes.

Index

Symbols

A

E

O

X

X-Ray/WinSock debugger, 563–569
  applications with large buffers, 568
  Borland Turbo Pascal, 568
  buffer options, 565
  compatibility, 563
  cost of, 569
  Event Details dialog box, 567–568
  filters, 566
  installation, 563
  modifications, 563–564
  OS/2 users, 569
  output options, 564–565
  registration, 569
  tasks, 566
  trace functions, 566
  trace preferences, 564–565
  traces, 566–568
XMODEM, Delrina WinComm LITE, 851
XStats.Log, WinNET Mail, 178

Y

YMODEM, Delrina WinComm LITE, 852

Z

ZMODEM, Delrina WinComm LITE, 852–854

Turn the Information Highway into Your Personal Database with askSam

A Database from the Information Highway?

askSam lets you import text files and instantly turn them into a database. Import all the text files and messages you download from the Internet into your own askSam database, and then search for any word or phrase.

**ONLY!
$99.95**
retail $395.00

askSam recognizes fields automatically

For example, a downloaded message often contains words like "To:", "From:", "Date:", and "Subject:" askSam lets you automatically use these words as fields. You can search, sort, and even create reports. There's not an easier, more effective way to turn the tons of data on the Information Highway into a personal database.

How Does It Work?

Information comes in different shapes and sizes. Unlike traditional databases, askSam was designed to handle "unstructured" information. It has features that allow you to search and organize text files or structured data. In addition to text files, askSam can import Word, WordPerfect, dBASE (DBF), Compuserve Information Manager, Comma Delimited, and RTF files. Once you import or enter your information, askSam offers quick and powerful searches: full text, proximity, Boolean, numeric, and date searches are supported. askSam also lets you add hypertext links to your databases. askSam's hypertext links offer a simple way for users to navigate through information.

Just Try It...

Tired of messages and files scattered on your hard disk? Put your information where you can find it.... in an askSam database. Try it... we offer an **unconditional 60 Day Money Back Guarantee** and **FREE tech support** (via Phone, Fax, or CompuServe). Contact us to order a full version at the special discount.

Special Offer: askSam for Windows 2.0 for $99.95 (save almost $300 from our $395 Retail Price)

askSam Systems
Voice: 800-800-1997 or 904-584-6590
CompuServe: 74774,352
Fax: 904-584-7481

Instant Groupware!

The easiest way to share information on your team's most important projects.

Network Central™ is the instant groupware solution for workgroup file and information management. It created a simple workgroup environment that lets users share files and organize information the way they want. Nothing falls through the cracks when files are updated and if anybody changes a shared file, Network Central immediately notifies you. No one has to wait for an e-mail, voice-mail, or a team member to stop by.

Use folders and subfolders to group files and information by topic or project.

Change bars show you if anything is new or changed.

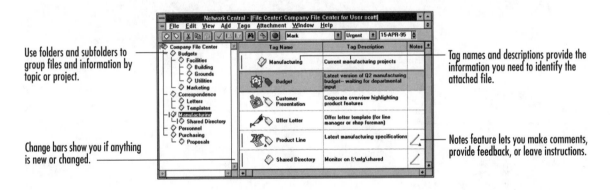

Tag names and descriptions provide the information you need to identify the attached file.

Notes feature lets you make comments, provide feedback, or leave instructions.

Network Central is network independent and installs in individual PCs in minutes without any system modification. You don't have to move or copy a single file, or reconfigure a thing. Since it doesn't affect the network, it's virtually management-free. People use existing applications they already know and there's virtually no support needed after installation.

Order Now!

Purchase a two-user Network Central 1.1 license now for only $99.00 and receive a *free* two-user upgrade.

Call First Floor, Inc. now at 1-800-639-6387 and ask for your corporate sales representative.

First Floor, Inc.
444 Castro Street, Suite 200 • Mountain View, CA 94041
800-639-6387 • Fax 415-968-1263

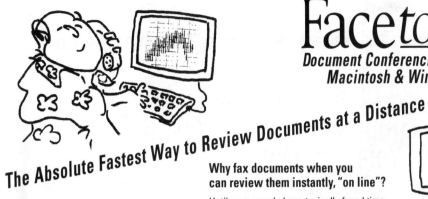

Face*to*Face

Document Conferencing Software for Macintosh & Windows Users

The Absolute Fastest Way to Review Documents at a Distance

What is Face*to*Face™?

Face*to*Face™ is software that allows people anywhere to use their telephones and desktop computers to review and annotate documents together, in real time. With Face*to*Face, two users of any mix of Macintosh and Microsoft Windows-based computers can simultaneously view documents, guide one another with electronic pointers, and make instantaneous annotations using a simple set of drawing tools - all while they talk on the telephone. And they can do all of this without regard for the types of computers involved, the particular applications used to create the documents, or the type of network available - whether it be ordinary, low-speed modems, a LAN, or a high-speed service like ISDN.

Why fax documents when you can review them instantly, "on line"?

Until now, people have typically faxed time-critical documents to one another for review. Face*to*Face offers a faster, more efficient alternative. With Face*to*Face, you can send copies of a document to others with only a few clicks of your mouse. Then, while you talk on the telephone, you and your distant colleagues can view and manipulate identical, synchronized images of documents on your computer screens while you make annotations that appear instantly - as they are drawn. The result is a much faster and clearer review process that doesn't require you to navigate through your documents ("go to page ten, second paragraph, third line") or spend time describing your comments to each other while you take notes. At the end of a Face*to*Face meeting, everyone walks away that a soft copy of the annotated document which can be saved, printed or forwarded to others via electronic mail.

A simple way to save time & money.

Face*to*Face is easy to install and use. It does not require specialized hardware or network services. Within minutes, anyone with a telephone and a Macintosh or Windows computer can experience the many benefits of document conferencing, including instantaneous turnaround on the review and approval of time-critical documents, reduced spending on express mail, courier services and travel, and more concise and accurate long distance communications.

CROSSWISE CORPORATION
105 LOCUST STREET, SUITE 301
SANTA CRUZ, CA 95060
1-408-459-9060

SPECIAL INTERNET GIZMOS PRICE $59.00

Included on the CD-ROMs that accompanies this book are free trial versions of Face*to*Face for Windows and Face*to*Face for Macintosh. If you'd like to upgrade to the standard version of the product, you can do so for a special INTERNET GIZMOS price of $59.00 per copy (regularly $179.00).

1-800-747-9060
1-408-459-9060
FAX 1-408-426-3859
INTERNET: sales@crosswise.com
CompuServe: GO CROSSWISE
AppleLink: CROSSWISE

Delrina Communications Suite™ –
The Best Fax and Communications Solution
Yours for Only $79

Now you can get award-winning Delrina WinFax PRO™ 4.0, the latest version of the world's best-selling fax software, together with Delrina WinComm PRO,™ a new powerful and easy-to-use communications application, all in one package: Delrina Communications Suite. Best of all, both full-featured products can be yours through this exclusive offer for only $79 (U.S.) – less than the price of other competitors' standalone communications packages.

For a taste of what you can do with Delrina Communications Suite, install Delrina WinFax LITE and Delrina WinComm LITE from the enclosed CD-ROM. You'll be amazed at how easy communications can be. And once you've tried Delrina's LITE versions, you'll be wanting more and more is what you'll get with WinFax PRO 4.0 and WinComm PRO. Just take a look:

Delrina WinFax PRO 4.0

- Use WinFax PRO's new streamlined drag-and-drop interface to add, remove, reorder and resize your fax logs
- Convert your faxes for editing in your favorite word processor or spreadsheet using Optical Character Recognition (OCR) technology
- Mark up your faxes using lines, circles, squares and text in any Windows size or font
- Clean up "random noise" on faxes with Fax Vacuum™

Delrina WinComm PRO

- Compose messages easily with the integrated 5,000-line Backscroll Buffer and Scratch Pad text editor
- Use pop-up menus to execute common tasks like Connect, Capture, Download and Upload
- Transfer files using more popular file transfer protocols, including Zmodem, Xmodem, Ymodem, CompuServe B+, Kermit and HyperProtocol™
- Upload files with drag-and-drop ease

Discover for yourself why *PC Week* magazine says, "Delrina tops other fax/data-comm packages." (June 13, 1994)

To take advantage of this exclusive offer call **1-800-268-6082** and get your very own Delrina Communications Suite for **just $79.**

WinFax PRO 4.0
August 1994

WinFax PRO 4.0
22 August 1994

WinFax PRO 4.0
13 September 1994

WinComm PRO
30 May 1994

Distinct
Internet Tools™

SPECIAL UPGRADE OFFER-ONLY $99

111 Speen Street, Suite 202

Framingham, MA 01701

CD-ROM Installation _____

You can install most programs from the CD-ROM to your hard drive by running the setup or installation executable files in File Manager or Program Manager. In some instances, you may need to have other software installed to successfully install a particular program. Please see Part I, "Getting Started" and the information in each chapter and the on-line help files for more about installing the software.

IDG BOOKS WORLDWIDE LICENSE AGREEMENT

Important — read carefully before opening the software packet. This is a legal agreement between you (either an individual or an entity) and IDG Books Worldwide, Inc. (IDG). By opening the accompanying sealed packet containing the software disc, you acknowledge that you have read and accept the following IDG License Agreement. If you do not agree and do not want to be bound by the terms of this Agreement, promptly return the book and the unopened software packet to the place you obtained them for a full refund.

1. <u>License</u>. This License Agreement (Agreement) permits you to use one copy of the enclosed Software programs on a single computer. The Software is in "use" on a computer when it is loaded into temporary memory (i.e., RAM) or installed into permanent memory (e.g., hard disk, CD-ROM, or other storage device) of that computer.

2. <u>Copyright</u>. The entire contents of this disc and the compilation of the Software are copyrighted and protected by both United States copyright laws and international treaty provisions. You may only (a) make one copy of the Software for backup or archival purposes, or (b) transfer the Software to a single hard disk, provided that you keep the original for backup or archival purposes. The individual programs on the disc are copyrighted by the authors of each program respectively. Each program has its own use permissions and limitations. To use each program, you must follow the individual requirements and restrictions detailed for each in this Book and on the CD-ROM. Do not use a program if you do not want to follow its Licensing Agreement. None of the material on this disc or listed in this Book may ever be distributed, in original or modified form, for commercial purposes.

3. <u>Other Restrictions</u>. You may not rent or lease the Software. You may transfer the Software and user documentation on a permanent basis provided you retain no copies and the recipient agrees to the terms of this Agreement. You may not reverse engineer, decompile, or disassemble the Software except to the extent that the foregoing restriction is expressly prohibited by applicable law. If the Software is an update or has been updated, any transfer must include the most recent update and all prior versions.

4. <u>Limited Warranty</u>. IDG Warrants that the Software and disc are free from defects in materials and workmanship for a period of sixty (60) days from the date of purchase of this Book. If IDG receives notification within the warranty period of defects in material or workmanship, IDG will replace the defective disc. IDG's entire liability and your exclusive remedy shall be limited to replacement of the Software, which is returned to IDG with a copy of your receipt. This Limited Warranty is void if failure of the Software has resulted from accident, abuse, or misapplication. Any replacement Software will be warranted for the remainder of the original warranty period or thirty (30) days, whichever is longer.

5. <u>No Other Warranties</u>. To the maximum extent permitted by applicable law, IDG and the author disclaim all other warranties, express or implied, including but not limited to implied warranties of merchantability and fitness for a particular purpose, with respect to the Software, the programs, the source code contained therein and/or the techniques described in this Book. This limited warranty gives you specific legal rights. You may have others which vary from state/jurisdiction to state/jurisdiction.

6. <u>No Liability For Consequential Damages</u>. To the extent permitted by applicable law, in no event shall IDG or the author be liable for any damages whatsoever (including without limitation, damages for loss of business profits, business interruption, loss of business information, or any other pecuniary loss) arising out of the use of or inability to use the Book or the Software, even if IDG has been advised of the possibility of such damages. Because some states/jurisdictions do not allow the exclusion or limitation of liability for consequential or incidental damages, the above limitation may not apply to you.

IDG BOOKS WORLDWIDE REGISTRATION CARD

RETURN THIS REGISTRATION CARD FOR FREE CATALOG

Title of this book: Internet GIZMOS For Windows

My overall rating of this book: ☐ Very good [1]   ☐ Good [2]   ☐ Satisfactory [3]   ☐ Fair [4]   ☐ Poor [5]

How I first heard about this book:

☐ Found in bookstore; name: [6]

☐ Advertisement: [8]

☐ Word of mouth; heard about book from friend, co-worker, etc.: [10]

☐ Book review: [7]

☐ Catalog: [9]

☐ Other: [11]

What I liked most about this book:

What I would change, add, delete, etc., in future editions of this book:

Other comments:

Number of computer books I purchase in a year: ☐ 1 [12]   ☐ 2-5 [13]   ☐ 6-10 [14]   ☐ More than 10 [15]

I would characterize my computer skills as: ☐ Beginner [16] ☐ Intermediate [17] ☐ Advanced [18] ☐ Professional [19]

I use ☐ DOS [20] ☐ Windows [21] ☐ OS/2 [22] ☐ Unix [23] ☐ Macintosh [24] ☐ Other: [25]_____
(please specify)

I would be interested in new books on the following subjects:
(please check all that apply, and use the spaces provided to identify specific software)

☐ Word processing: [26]

☐ Data bases: [28]

☐ File Utilities: [30]

☐ Networking: [32]

☐ Other: [34]

☐ Spreadsheets: [27]

☐ Desktop publishing: [29]

☐ Money management: [31]

☐ Programming languages: [33]

I use a PC at (please check all that apply): ☐ home [35] ☐ work [36] ☐ school [37] ☐ other: [38] _____

The disks I prefer to use are ☐ 5.25 [39] ☐ 3.5 [40] ☐ other: [41]_____

I have a CD ROM: ☐ yes [42]   ☐ no [43]

I plan to buy or upgrade computer hardware this year: ☐ yes [44]   ☐ no [45]

I plan to buy or upgrade computer software this year: ☐ yes [46]   ☐ no [47]

Name: _____ Business title: [48] _____ Type of Business: [49] _____

Address (☐ home [50] ☐ work [51]/Company name: _____)

Street/Suite# _____

City [52]/State [53]/Zipcode [54]: _____ Country [55] _____

☐ **I liked this book!** You may quote me by name in future
IDG Books Worldwide promotional materials.

My daytime phone number is _____

IDG BOOKS

THE WORLD OF
COMPUTER
KNOWLEDGE